Also by the American Heart Association

AMERICAN HEART ASSOCIATION
LOW-SALT COOKBOOK

AMERICAN HEART ASSOCIATION
LOW-FAT, LOW-CHOLESTEROL COOKBOOK

AMERICAN HEART ASSOCIATION
FAT AND CHOLESTEROL COUNTER

AMERICAN HEART ASSOCIATION KIDS' COOKBOOK

*A*merican *H*eart
*A*ssociation
COOKBOOK

FIFTH EDITION

*A*merican *H*eart *A*ssociation

COOKBOOK

FIFTH EDITION

TIMES 𝕿 BOOKS

RANDOM HOUSE

Copyright © 1973, 1975, 1979, 1984, 1991 by the
American Heart Association

All rights reserved under International and Pan-American Copyright Conventions. Published in the United States by Times Books, a division of Random House, Inc., New York, and simultaneously in Canada by Random House of Canada Limited, Toronto.

This work was originally published in hardcover by Times Books, a division of Random House, Inc., in 1991.

Grateful acknowledgment is made to Nilgiri Press for permission to reprint three recipes, "Whole-Wheat French Bread," "Rye Bread," and "Tortillas," from *Laurel's Kitchen: A Handbook for Vegetarian Cookery and Nutrition,* now out of print. Reprinted by permission of Nilgiri Press.

Library of Congress Cataloging-in-Publication Data

American Heart Association cookbook.—5th ed./edited by
Mary Winston, Ed.D.
p.   cm.
Rev. ed. of: American Heart Association cookbook/
compiled by Ruthe Eshleman and Mary Winston.
4th ed., new, rev. and expanded. © 1984.
Includes index.
ISBN: 0-8129-2282-4 (pbk.)
1. Heart—Diseases—Diet therapy—Recipes.
2. Low-cholesterol diet—Recipes.
I. Winston, Mary.
II. Eshleman, Ruthe. American Heart Association cookbook.
III. American Heart Association.
RC684.D5A44   1991
641.5'6311—dc20   90-48402

Manufactured in the United States of America
9   8   7   6   5

ART DIRECTION BY NAOMI OSNOS
BOOK DESIGN BY BARBARA MARKS
ART COORDINATED BY COLLIN LEECH
ILLUSTRATED BY DOROTHY LEECH

Preface

This new fifth edition of the *American Heart Association Cookbook* comes eighteen years after the first edition. Times have changed. In those days we suspected that high blood cholesterol was a major cause of heart attack; today, we know it.

Medical researchers are coming closer than ever to understanding how cholesterol and other fats in the blood contribute to the development of heart disease. We know more about the role of heredity in the process and how it interacts with our lifestyle and environment to result in heart health or disease. While we can't control heredity, we can make our own lifestyle choices. We can choose to eat healthful foods, to be physically active and to not smoke. We can also make every effort to keep our blood pressure and weight under control.

This new cookbook comes during an era in which science is constantly discovering new things about the effects of fat and cholesterol in our diet. Despite these discoveries, one fact remains: The dietary recommendations the AHA makes today are not dramatically different than they were eighteen years ago. We're still emphasizing the need to reduce total fat, saturated fat, cholesterol and sodium in the foods you eat every day.

The good news is, your fate is largely in your hands. That's because you can choose the foods you buy, prepare and eat. And this cookbook can show you how to do just that—in a way you can enjoy.

This book, a major revision of previous editions, is essentially a new cookbook. Every recipe has been edited and rewritten for easy use. Almost half have been retested and revised. We've added hundreds of new recipes that bring the foods and preparation methods up to date. We've also offered some suggestions on how to prepare foods more quickly and easily.

The text of the cookbook has been thoroughly revised to include the latest information on buying, cooking and storing foods. We've also included sections to help you plan menus and choose healthful foods when you eat out.

This cookbook can show you the rewards of changing your diet: The food will taste delicious, and the diet will help you reduce one of the major risk factors of heart disease.

We've tried to keep the sodium content of each recipe on the low side. Going easy on sodium is a good habit to get into, because it may help keep your blood pressure at a normal level—or even reduce it in some cases. We've included an expanded herb, spice and seasonings chart to show you how to put zing into every kind of dish. We've also greatly expanded our vegetarian section, because many people today are interested in meatless meals.

Each recipe has been tested for flavor and analyzed for calories, protein, carbohydrate, cholesterol, sodium, total fat, saturated fat, polyunsaturated fat and monounsaturated fat. You'll find an analysis below each recipe. Use it to learn about the nutrients in foods; doing so will help you learn to select the best foods for a healthful diet.

This cookbook is for everybody. It offers delicious, well-balanced foods suited for all people over the age of two. We hope that you and your family enjoy eating these dishes as much as we did creating them.

To good food, good health and good times!

RODMAN D. STARKE, M.D.
Senior Vice President
Office of Scientific Affairs
American Heart Association National Center

Acknowledgments

Senior Vice President, Scientific Affairs
Rodman D. Starke, M.D.

Editor
Mary Winston, Senior Science Consultant, Scientific Affairs

Managing Editor
Jane Ruehl

Additional Recipe Development and Testing for Fifth Edition
Patricia E. Dahl
Gail Greene

Recipe Analysis
Nutrition Coordinating Center, University of Minnesota at
Minneapolis

Since the *American Heart Association Cookbook* first appeared in 1973, we have incorporated information and suggestions from so many people that it is virtually impossible to thank them all here.

The AHA volunteers and staff, colleagues, family, friends and, most of all, our readers who offered their help and suggestions have made our flagship cookbook a true labor of love.

This fifth edition is based on the first four editions, all of which would not have been possible without the dedication, hard work and expertise of my dear friend and colleague Ruthe Eshleman of the University of Rhode Island. Her knowledge and enthusiasm made her the perfect co-editor. Working with her was a joy.

I also want to remember Campbell Moses, M.D., former medical director of the AHA. Without his leadership, guidance and good humor, the first edition would never have seen the light of day.

Ready with constructive criticism for this and previous editions were Richard Hurley, M.D., Senior Medical Adviser Emeritus, and Wallace G. Frasher, Jr., M.D., Senior Science Adviser. Our greatest AHA supporters in this cookbook project were Sam Inman, Vice President of Corporate Relations and Development; Dudley H. Hafner, Executive Vice President; and M. Cass Wheeler, Deputy Executive Vice President. My deepest appreciation to Rodman D. Starke, M.D., Senior Vice President, Office of Scientific Affairs. He was always concerned about the magnitude of this task and was constantly supportive with ideas and encouragement.

A project this big could not have been completed without a mainstay: someone to keep us on target and see to every detail. The mainstay for our fifth-edition cookbook was Corporate Relations Specialist Ann Yanosky, who kept the project sailing along like the *QE II* through rough waters.

My sincere gratitude to Managing Editor Jane Ruehl, whose awe-inspiring organizational ability crafted a collection of recipes into an eminently usable cookbook. Also, warm thanks to copywriter Pat Covington and to Vicki Graff for manuscript review. Hats off to Debra Bond and Gerre Gilford for word processing and to Amy Lindsly and Jana Giles for proofreading this formidable manuscript. Thanks also to Mike Semon, who provided us a chef's point of view in his review of the recipes.

The dining-out section of this cookbook was adapted from a brochure produced by the American Heart Association's New York City Affiliate. We owe them our appreciation for their effort and their generosity.

Finally, I want to thank my son Rick, whose sense of humor and encouragement inspired me to go on with this project when it seemed an impossible task.

MARY WINSTON, ED.D., R.D.
Senior Science Consultant
Office of Scientific Affairs
American Heart Association National Center

Contents

*A*merican *H*eart
*A*ssociation
COOKBOOK
FIFTH EDITION

Introduction

Eat it. It's good for you."

Remember those words, urging you to eat foods you didn't much like because they would keep you healthy, strong, smart or beautiful? That kind of psychology didn't work then, and it won't work now.

No one can tell you to do it; the only way you'll adopt a low-fat, low-cholesterol way of eating is by deciding to do it yourself. In this cookbook, we offer you convincing reasons for doing so, along with enticing recipes to show you that a low-fat, low-cholesterol eating style is also delicious and satisfying.

To help you understand some of the scientific bases for these recommendations, we have put together a list of definitions on pages 589–91.

DIET AND HEART DISEASE

We've known about the link between diet and health for a long time. Until about forty years ago, our main concern about diet and health involved diseases caused by nutritional deficiencies, such as pellagra and scurvy.

Today we're more worried about our consumption of fatty foods, which may predispose us to these chronic diseases: coronary heart disease, cancer, stroke, diabetes mellitus, obesity and atherosclerosis. The scientific evidence that shows a relationship between diet and these diseases grows stronger every day. This is especially true in the case of nutrition and atherosclerosis, one of the major causes of heart attack and stroke.

ATHEROSCLEROSIS

Atherosclerosis, a form of arteriosclerosis, is a progressive disease in which fatty substances, mainly cholesterol, and other substances slowly build up in the inner lining of the arteries.

This buildup forms the atherosclerotic plaque that eventually blocks the flow of blood to the heart, brain or other tissues. This blockage cuts off the oxygen supply that feeds those areas. An artery can close off completely, either because the deposits have grown together or because a blood clot stops up the narrowed passage. When this happens in an artery supplying the heart muscle (a coronary artery), a heart attack results. If it happens in an artery supplying the brain, a stroke occurs. Other areas, too, can be affected, such as the legs, where gangrene can occur, or the kidneys, which can shut down as a result of blocked blood vessels feeding those areas.

CHOLESTEROL AND YOUR RISK OF HEART DISEASE

Your blood cholesterol level is a powerful indicator of your heart attack or stroke risk. In fact, several factors increase your risk of heart attack: high blood cholesterol, high blood pressure, cigarette smoking, excess body weight and diabetes.

Scientific evidence implicating high blood cholesterol as a major risk factor for heart and blood vessel disease is overwhelming. It comes from countless epidemiologic studies (studies of large populations all over the world) and from clinical, genetic and animal studies. These studies not only confirm the link between high blood cholesterol and the development of atherosclerosis but also strongly suggest that reducing the blood cholesterol level will reduce the risk of heart attack.

This is true not only for middle-aged men with high blood cholesterol, but also for younger and older men, for women and for people with just mildly elevated blood cholesterol.

LOWER YOUR CHOLESTEROL, LOWER YOUR RISK

The benefit of lowering blood cholesterol to prevent heart attack was demonstrated by the Lipid Research Clinics' Coronary Primary Prevention Trial (CPPT). By lowering blood cholesterol in approximately four thousand men with no evidence of heart disease, the study showed that their number of heart attacks and heart attack deaths could be reduced. This study used drugs to reduce the blood cholesterol. Another study done in Oslo, Norway, showed similar results when cholesterol was lowered by diet alone. It is clear to the medical scientific community that the higher a person's blood cholesterol level, the greater his or her risk of heart disease.

The National Cholesterol Education Program (NCEP), a program of the National Heart, Lung, and Blood Institute (NHLBI), has prepared guidelines for classifying blood cholesterol levels as they relate to the risk of heart disease. Cholesterol is measured in milligrams per deciliter of blood (mg/dl).

CLASSIFICATION BASED ON TOTAL CHOLESTEROL	
CHOLESTEROL LEVEL	CLASSIFICATION
Less than 200 mg/dl	Desirable
200–239 mg/dl	Borderline High
240 mg/dl or greater	High

Sometimes genetics is the underlying cause of high blood cholesterol levels. But most heart attacks that happen in middle age and later life are caused by life-long high blood cholesterol from a diet high in total fat, saturated fat and cholesterol. Scientific studies show that the number of heart attacks increases as blood cholesterol levels rise above 200 mg/dl.

Today, cholesterol is a dirty word. This may be because people are confused by the difference between blood cholesterol and cholesterol that comes from the food we eat. The truth is, our bodies need some blood cholesterol to help manufacture sex hormones and vitamin D as a structural component of cell membranes and a protective sheath around nerves. Our bodies manufacture enough cholesterol to do this; we don't really need the cholesterol that comes from food.

HOW CHOLESTEROL REACHES YOUR ARTERIES

Cholesterol is carried in the bloodstream by lipoproteins, tiny spheres with an outer coat of protein and fat. Most of the cholesterol is carried on the inside, combined with triglycerides to form a core. (Triglycerides are what is commonly known as body fat and are also the chemical form of most of the fat we eat.) Lipoproteins differ in the amounts of cholesterol, triglycerides and protein they contain, and thus are separated into four different groups:

1. Chylomicrons
2. Very Low Density Lipoproteins (VLDL)
3. Low Density Lipoproteins (LDL)
4. High Density Lipoproteins (HDL)

As their names imply, these lipoproteins differ in density. Chylomicrons are the largest and contain mostly triglycerides. They are formed in the intestines from triglycerides and cholesterol in digested foods. As each chylomicron is formed, various proteins known as apoproteins are attached to its surface. They are needed to direct the chylomicron to fat tissue, where it can deposit triglycerides for storage, and to muscles, where the fat is rapidly burned for energy.

Like chylomicrons, very low density lipoproteins carry mostly triglycerides. They are produced by the liver and normally deliver triglycerides to body tissues as the blood circulates. After the triglycerides are removed, the lipoprotein parts remaining in the blood are further broken down to produce LDL. Patients with a condition called hypertriglyceridemia have increased levels of VLDLs. Medical experts are divided on whether VLDLs contribute to the building of plaque on artery walls.

Low density lipoproteins carry most of the cholesterol in the blood. They are sometimes called "bad" cholesterol, because they are the kind that enter the artery wall to contribute to the buildup of atherosclerotic plaque there. A high LDL cholesterol level is a major risk factor for coronary heart disease. In people not affected by a bad diet or a genetic defect, most LDLs attach themselves to a specific protein on cells, generally in the liver, so they can be taken in and excreted in bile. Normally this process regulates the blood level of LDL cholesterol, keeping it safely low.

One-third to one-fourth of the blood cholesterol is carried in high density lipoproteins (HDL). This is known as "good" cholesterol, because a high level seems to protect against heart attack. One of its functions is to provide some of the proteins needed by chylomicrons and VLDLs to clear fat from the bloodstream. Many scientists believe HDLs also remove excess cholesterol from the arteries to prevent the buildup of cholesterol in the artery wall.

The bottom line: A high concentration of total cholesterol, especially LDL cholesterol, increases the risk of heart attack; a low level of HDL cholesterol may further increase this risk. Evidence on VLDL cholesterol remains incomplete. Taken together, this scientific evidence strongly supports the view that lowering your blood cholesterol level by diet will help prevent heart disease.

DIET AND OTHER RISK FACTORS

Other risk factors for heart disease also can be altered by diet. Obesity (especially if it occurs with high blood pressure, hyperglycemia or hypercholesterolemia) greatly increases the risk of developing heart disease. Losing weight often results in lowered blood pressure, improved glucose tolerance and lower blood cholesterol levels.

In addition to being low in total fat, saturated fat and cholesterol, most of the recipes in this book have been modified to decrease sugar and total calories. Some high-calorie recipes are included, but they are intended for special occasions.

Another heart disease risk factor is high blood pressure, or hypertension. A diet high in sodium is often implicated as a contributor to high blood pressure. And although the relationship has not been proved, evidence suggests that it's wise to avoid too much sodium in your diet.

We've included the sodium content of each recipe in the accompanying analysis. And we've tried to keep salt to a minimum in the recipes. We've also suggested herbs, spices and other seasonings you can use as a substitute for salt. (See the chart on pages 40–41.) Where recipes call for soy sauce, try to find the low-sodium variety.

This cookbook is not aimed at those of you on sodium-restricted diets. You will find many more low-salt recipes in the *American Heart Association Low-Salt Cookbook*. If you have high blood pressure, congestive heart failure or edema, ask your doctor about the amount of sodium that is safe for you.

AMERICAN HEART ASSOCIATION DIETARY GUIDELINES

This cookbook is concerned mainly with lowering your blood cholesterol level. Here are the American Heart Association's dietary recommendations, designed to reduce blood cholesterol and prevent or control high blood pressure.

AHA Dietary Guidelines

1. Total fat intake should be less than 30 percent of daily calories.
2. Saturated fat intake should be less than 10 percent of daily calories.
3. Polyunsaturated fat intake should not exceed 10 percent of daily calories.
4. Cholesterol intake should not exceed 300 milligrams per day.
5. Carbohydrate intake should make up 50 percent or more of daily calories, with mostly complex carbohydrates.
6. Protein intake should provide the rest of the daily calories.

7. Sodium intake should not exceed 3 grams (3,000 milligrams) a day.
8. Alcohol intake should not exceed 1 to 2 ounces of ethanol per day. Two ounces of 100-proof whiskey, 8 ounces of wine or 24 ounces of beer each contain 1 ounce of ethanol.
9. Total calories should be enough to maintain your recommended body weight.
10. A wide variety of foods should be consumed to get a balance of nutrients.

If you develop your eating pattern based on the food plan on pages 10–13, you will be adhering to the American Heart Association Dietary Guidelines. Since 1983, the AHA has recommended this type of diet for healthy children over the age of two as well as for adults. This diet is safe for children, and it can reduce blood cholesterol in most people.

Although it's not proven, this diet may, in the future, help reduce the rapid rise of blood cholesterol now seen in twenty- and thirty-year-olds in our country—assuming that dietary habits learned in childhood persist into adulthood. If overweight children are put on this diet, they should lose weight and significantly reduce associated risk factors.

Some people, both adults and children, have inherited metabolic patterns that require special diets. These diets can be prescribed only after special studies of the person's body chemistry. All children who come from families with a history of hyperlipidemia or premature vascular disease should have their blood fats and lipoproteins measured periodically.

As you begin to use this book to apply these dietary guidelines to your daily meals, you will notice that it differs very little from other cookbooks. You'll find appetizers, interesting vegetarian dishes, stews, steaks, delicious desserts, and delectable vegetable and salad combinations.

All of the recipes in this book have been carefully tested and standardized in their use of ingredients. They all have nutritive value, an often-overlooked consideration. Many calories in foods today have little or no nutritive value; even a high-calorie diet is not necessarily a nutritious one.

To understand good nutrition, think of food in terms of average servings. The following section describes the amount and kind of foods the average person needs to maintain good health. It outlines the average person's nutritional needs. You may use it as a guide for your own nutritional needs, except perhaps for calories (the number of calories you need varies with your metabolism and with the amount of physical activity you get).

AVERAGE DAILY NUTRITIONAL NEEDS

Currently, we know about more than fifty nutrients. A diet low in total fat, saturated fat and cholesterol is balanced to contain these nutrients.

It's easy to adapt this diet to suit your lifestyle. The daily food guideline, pages 10–13, includes the quantities and kinds of food you need for good nutrition. If you need more calories than this guideline calls for, add foods from any group except egg yolks and meat and visible fats.

We recommend a variety of foods in the eating plan, and the recipes use a variety of foods, too. These include fruits, vegetables, dairy products, grains, poultry and meat. That's because when you eat a variety of foods in balanced amounts, you will get all of the known nutrients required for good health. Manufactured foods vary widely in nutritional content. Choose them wisely and preferably use them in conjunction with fresh foods: Margarine instead of butter is a primary example; so are egg substitutes and imitation cheese. These products add flavor without adding lots of saturated fat and cholesterol.

The idea is to choose foods low in total fat, saturated fat and cholesterol. A basic principle: Foods from animal sources contain cholesterol. Foods from land animals also contain saturated fat, while fish and seafood contain primarily polyunsaturated fat. Most foods contain all three types of fat (saturated, polyunsaturated and mono-unsaturated) in varying amounts, and foods are classified according to their predominant fat content.

Polyunsaturated fatty acids, monounsaturated fatty acids and complex carbohydrates help reduce blood cholesterol levels if you substitute foods containing these nutrients for foods containing saturated fatty acids and cholesterol in your diet.

Polyunsaturated fatty acids fall into two types. One is composed of omega-6 fatty acids and is found in many vegetable oils such as safflower oil, sunflower seed oil, soybean oil and corn oil. The other type is composed of omega-3 fatty acids, which are found in high amounts in some fish and fish oils. Polyunsaturates of all kinds account for about 6 to 7 percent of our recommended total caloric intake, and most of them are of the omega-6 type. When omega-6 fatty acids are substituted for saturated fatty acids, total blood cholesterol and LDL cholesterol levels drop. The evidence that omega-3 fatty acids will do this is limited.

Monounsaturates are found primarily in olive oil, rapeseed (canola) oil and in high-monounsaturated forms of sunflower seed oil and safflower oil. For many years, monounsaturates were thought to be neutral, neither raising nor lowering cholesterol. Recent research suggests that monounsaturates do, in fact, lower LDL cholesterol as much as polyunsaturates when used in place of saturated fatty acids.

Foods high in saturated fatty acids and dietary cholesterol, on the other hand, tend to raise the level of cholesterol in the blood. Foods containing saturated fatty acids frequently also contain cholesterol. These foods include meat, lard, butter and whole-milk dairy products such as cheese, cream and ice cream—all high in fats of animal origin. Saturated fat is also found in coconut, palm and palm kernel oils.

GUIDELINES FOR A LOW-FAT, LOW-CHOLESTEROL DIET

FOOD GROUP	PRE-SCHOOL	PRE-ADOLESCENTS
1. Vegetables and fruits; fruit juices, vegetable juices	4 or more servings One serving is: 1 tablespoon or ½ oz. cooked vegetable per year of age; ½ cup fruit juice; ½ piece medium-size fruit. Note: Use small amounts of a variety of fruits and vegetables.	4 or more servings One serving is: ½ cup fruit or vegetable juice; 1 medium fruit or vegetable; ½ cup cooked fruit or vegetable
2. Breads, cereals and starchy foods	4 servings One serving is: ½ slice bread or ½ tortilla; ½ cup dry cereal or ¼ cup cooked cereal; ¼ cup pasta, rice or noodles; 1 graham cracker; ½ cup popcorn	4 or more servings One serving is: 1 slice bread or 1 tortilla; 1 cup dry cereal or ½ cup cooked cereal; ½ cup pasta, rice or noodles; 2 graham crackers; 1 cup popcorn

GUIDELINES FOR A LOW-FAT, LOW-CHOLESTEROL DIET

FOOD GROUP	PRE-SCHOOL	PRE-ADOLESCENTS
3. Milk and cheese (to meet calcium requirements)	Age 2–3: 2 servings Age 4–6: 3 servings One serving is: 1 8-oz. glass 1% milk or nonfat buttermilk; 1 oz. low-fat cheese; ½ cup low-fat cottage cheese; 8 oz. low-fat yogurt. Note: Serve small portions more frequently, ¼–½ cup at a time.	Minimum of 3 servings One serving is: One 8-oz. glass 1% milk or nonfat buttermilk; 1 oz. low-fat cheese; ½ cup low-fat cottage cheese; 8 oz. low-fat yogurt
4. Meat, poultry, seafood, dried beans and peas, and eggs*	No more than 2 servings daily One serving is: 1 tablespoon (½ oz.) for each year of child's age	No more than 2 servings daily One serving is: 2–3 oz. lean meat, fish or poultry, cooked
5. Unsaturated fats and oils	2–3 servings One serving is: 1 tsp. vegetable oil or margarine; 2 tsp. diet margarine; 2 tsp. salad dressing, mayonnaise or peanut butter; 3 tsp. seeds, nuts,** chopped avocados or olives	4–6 servings One serving is: 1 tsp. vegetable oil or margarine; 2 tsp. diet margarine; 2 tsp. salad dressing, mayonnaise or peanut butter; 3 tsp. seeds, nuts,** chopped avocados or olives
6. Other foods to meet energy needs	2–3 year olds: The total quantities from food groups to meet estimated energy intake of 1300 kcals/ day. 4–6 year-olds: Other low-fat, low-cholesterol foods to meet energy needs, or increase portions of above foods except meat group.	Other low-fat, low-cholesterol foods to meet energy needs, or increase portions of above foods except meat group.

 * *Egg yolks are limited to 3–4 per week; egg whites may be eaten as desired.*
** *Before serving nuts to a child, be sure the child is able to chew them thoroughly.*

GUIDELINES FOR A LOW-FAT, LOW-CHOLESTEROL DIET

FOOD GROUP	ADOLESCENTS	ADULTS
1. Vegetables and fruits; fruit juices, vegetable juices	5 or more servings of vegetables and fruits One serving is: ½ cup fruit or vegetable juice; 1 medium fruit or vegetable; ½–1 cup cooked or raw vegetable; ¼–½ cup starchy vegetable	5 or more servings of vegetables and fruits One serving is: ½ cup fruit or vegetable juice; 1 medium fruit or vegetable; ½–1 cup cooked or raw vegetable; ¼–½ cup starchy vegetable
2. Breads, cereals and starchy foods	6 or more servings One serving is: 1 slice bread or 1 tortilla; 1 cup dry flaked cereal or ½ cup cooked cereal; ¼ cup nugget or bud type cereal; 1 cup pasta, rice or noodles; ¼–½ cup starchy vegetables; 1 cup low-fat soup; 2 graham crackers; 1 cup dry popcorn	6 or more servings One serving is: 1 slice bread or 1 tortilla; 1 cup dry flaked cereal or ½ cup cooked cereal; ¼ cup nugget or bud type cereal; 1 cup pasta, rice or noodles; ¼–½ cup starchy vegetables; 1 cup low-fat soup; 2 graham crackers; 1 cup dry popcorn
3. Milk and cheese (to meet calcium requirements)	3–4 servings One serving is: One 8-oz. glass 1% milk or nonfat buttermilk; 1 oz. low-fat cheese; ½ cup low-fat cottage cheese; 8 oz. low-fat yogurt	2 or more servings 3–4 servings for pregnant and lactating women One serving is: One 8-oz. glass 1% milk or nonfat buttermilk; 1 oz. low-fat cheese; ½ cup low-fat cottage cheese; 8 oz. low-fat yogurt
4. Meat, poultry, seafood, dried beans and peas, and eggs*	No more than 2 servings daily of meat, poultry, fish or seafood or 2 or more of dried beans and peas	No more than 2 servings daily of meat, poultry, fish or seafood or 2 or more of dried beans and peas (*continued*)

* *Egg yolks are limited to 3–4 per week; egg whites may be eaten as desired.*

GUIDELINES FOR A LOW-FAT, LOW-CHOLESTEROL DIET

FOOD GROUP	ADOLESCENTS	ADULTS
4. (*continued*)	One serving is: 2–3 oz. cooked lean meat, fish or poultry; 1 cup cooked beans, peas or lentils; 3 oz. soybean curd (tofu)	One serving is: 2–3 oz. cooked lean meat, fish or poultry; 1 cup cooked beans, peas or lentils; 3 oz. soybean curd (tofu)
5. Unsaturated fats and oils	5–8 servings One serving is: 1 tsp. vegetable oil or margarine; 2 tsp. diet margarine; 2 tsp. salad dressing, mayonnaise or peanut butter; 3 tsp. seeds, nuts, chopped avocados or olives	5–8 servings One serving is: 1 tsp. vegetable oil or margarine; 2 tsp. diet margarine; 2 tsp. salad dressing, mayonnaise or peanut butter; 3 tsp. seeds, nuts, chopped avocados or olives
6. Other foods to meet energy needs	Other low-fat, low-cholesterol foods to meet energy needs, or increase portions of above foods except meat group.	Other low-fat, low-cholesterol foods to meet energy needs, or increase portions of above foods except meat group and eggs.

FOLLOWING THE AHA DIETARY GUIDELINES

Your body can use all three types of fat, but it's best to limit your total fat intake to no more than 30 percent of your daily calories. Of that amount, less than 10 percent of your daily calories should come from saturated fatty acids, and up to 10 percent of the calories may come from polyunsaturated fatty acids. The remainder of your fat intake may come from monounsaturated sources.

Although most of the body's cholesterol is produced by the body, dietary cholesterol can contribute a substantial amount to the buildup of the atherosclerotic plaque. Therefore, we recommend that your average daily intake of cholesterol be approximately 300 milligrams. Since one egg yolk has 213 to 220 milligrams of cholesterol, we have limited the use of egg yolks in our recipes.

Don't eat too much of any one type of fat. At the same time, don't remove any single type of fat from your diet entirely. If you lower total fat intake and substitute unsaturated for a portion of the saturated fat, you are helping your body work to its own advantage.

You may also raise your blood cholesterol by taking in more calories than your body burns, thereby gaining weight. When the cholesterol level of an obese person is high, the increase usually is found in both LDL cholesterol and VLDL cholesterol. And the level of HDL, or "good," cholesterol is usually low.

The AHA dietary guidelines recommend increasing the carbohydrates in your diet to more than 50 percent of calories. Most of these should be complex carbohydrates. Increasing carbohydrates is the best way to replace some of the fat you're cutting out. Dietary carbohydrates occur as either simple sugars or complex carbohydrates. Complex carbohydrates are either digestible complex carbohydrates, otherwise known as starches, or nondigestible complex carbohydrates, called fiber.

Starches are often mistakenly viewed as being high in calories. You may think you have to avoid them when you're trying to lose weight. Actually, complex carbohydrates such as potatoes, breads and pastas are relatively low in calories. It's the margarine and fat-laden sauces we add to them that are high in calories. The foods themselves are rich sources of important vitamins and minerals.

High-fiber foods make up the other form of complex carbohydrates. Fiber is not digestible. There are two types of fiber—soluble and insoluble. It's best to eat both types. Insoluble fiber, such as that found in wheat bran, helps keep the digestive tract healthy. Soluble fiber is found in oat, corn and rice bran, dried peas and beans, and fruits and vegetables with edible peels and seeds. It has been reported to lower cholesterol levels slightly when eaten as part of a fat-modified diet. Aim for 15 to 20 grams of fiber per day.

Here is a little hint to help make sure that most of the carbohydrates you consume are complex: Avoid excessive caloric sweeteners such as table sugar, brown sugar, corn sweeteners, syrups, honey and molasses. These sugars mainly supply calories and often replace more nutritious foods in the diet that would provide vitamins and minerals.

How can you know that you are controlling your animal fat and cholesterol intake? If you base your eating pattern on the daily food plan on pages 10–13 and follow the suggestions made in this book, you'll be on the right track. If you want to calculate the exact amount of total fat and saturated fat in your daily diet, use the "Grams of Fat Method" chart below as a guide. Find your calorie level. Next to it you'll see the amount of total fat that is your "goal" or upper limit. Next you'll see the upper limit of saturated fat you'll want to consume. Remember that the saturated fat "goal" is part of the total fat "goal," so be sure to subtract the amount of saturated fat from the total to see how many grams of other types of fat you have left in your eating plan.

GRAMS OF FAT METHOD FOR CONTROLLING TOTAL FAT AND SATURATED FATTY ACIDS

CALORIE LEVEL	TOTAL FAT GRAMS	SATURATED FATTY ACID GRAMS
1200	40	13
1500	50	17
1800	60	20
2000	67	22
2200	73	24
2500	83	28
3000	100	33

Knowing what foods to eat for a healthy heart is an important first step in any diet. But the real fun comes next—cooking and eating! On the following pages, you'll find tips on shopping for low-fat foods and cooking with your heart in mind. You'll also find a dazzling collection of dishes that will convince you how delicious low-fat, low-cholesterol eating can be.

Some people misinterpret the first guideline to mean that *each food* or *each recipe* should have less than 30 percent of its calories come from fat. **The guideline applies to total calories eaten per day.** If it is applied to single foods, the "30 percent of calories from fat" guideline will cause many foods that fit into a well-balanced eating plan to be excluded. Examples of these foods include: oil and margarine (100 percent of calories from fat), regular and low-calorie salad dressings (75–100 percent of calories from fat), dark chicken meat without skin (43 percent of calories from fat), salmon (36 percent of calories from fat), lower-fat meats like turkey ham (34 percent of calories from fat), as well as many nuts and seeds (75–90 percent of calories from fat).

Applying the 30 percent standard to single foods greatly limits the variety of foods in the diet and can be misleading. **The only way to maintain balance, variety and enjoyment of the American Heart Association eating plan is to interpret the guideline with emphasis on the word "total" for the day.**

Shopping for a Healthy Heart

The next time you're in a supermarket checkout line, look at the kinds of foods in the grocery carts around you. That's where healthful eating begins—or fails to begin. Many shoppers choose the typical American diet: high in total fat, saturated fat, cholesterol, salt and calories. Others are joining the millions of health-conscious people who select more fruits, vegetables, whole grains and enriched low-fat, low-cholesterol dairy products.

The fat in food is comprised of various fatty acids, the main types of which are saturated, polyunsaturated and monounsaturated fatty acids and cholesterol. Saturated fatty acids and cholesterol both tend to raise the level of cholesterol in your blood. Polyunsaturated and monounsaturated fatty acids tend to lower the level of cholesterol in your blood when the saturated fat content of the diet is low. That's why you want to reduce the amount of saturated fat and cholesterol in your diet.

The good news is that it's easier than ever to find healthful foods. Many familiar products come in varieties that are low in total fat, saturated fat, cholesterol and sodium, but are still high in taste.

YOUR FIRST LINE OF DEFENSE: READ PRODUCT LABELS

With fresh produce and other whole foods, you can control the amount of fat, salt and calories you add in cooking. With packaged or prepared foods, however, you have to read the ingredients list and the nutrition information to determine the kind and amount of fat you're getting, the number of calories per serving and the amount of salt in the product.

Ingredients Lists

When you read a nutrition label, first look at the list of ingredients. All food labels list the product's ingredients in order by weight. The ingredient in the greatest amount is listed first. The ingredient in the smallest amount is listed last.

To avoid getting too much total fat, saturated fat or cholesterol, eat smaller amounts of products that list fat or oil as the first ingredient and select fewer products that contain lots of fat or oil. The following checklist can help you identify some of the more common saturated fats and cholesterol sources in packaged foods.

SOURCES OF FATTY ACIDS AND CHOLESTEROL

Animal fat	Cream	Palm kernel oil*
Bacon fat	Egg and egg yolk solids	Palm oil*
Beef fat	Ham fat	Pork fat
Butter	Hardened fat or oil	Turkey fat
Chicken fat	Hydrogenated vegetable	Vegetable oil**
Cocoa butter*	oil*	Vegetable shortening
Coconut*	Lamb fat	(some types)*
Coconut oil*	Lard	Whole-milk solids

* *Sources of saturated fat but not cholesterol*
** *Could be coconut, palm or palm kernel oil, does not contain cholesterol*

Be cautious also about hydrogenated vegetable oils and vegetable shortenings. Depending on the degree of hydrogenation, these oils vary in level of saturation. Choose those that contain no more than two grams of saturated fat per tablespoon. Some vegetable shortenings are made from all-vegetable fats yet contain just 10 to 30 percent polyunsaturated fatty acids. Use them infrequently, but by all means select them over shortenings made from animal-vegetable fat blends.

If you're trying to cut down on salt, stay away from any product that lists salt or sodium as an ingredient.

Nutrition Labeling

In addition to an ingredients list, the product label may also give you nutrition information. This information is calculated per serving. The label shows the size of the serving and tells how many servings are in the package. It gives the amount of total fat, polyunsaturated fat, saturated fat and cholesterol in a serving of the product. The amount of monounsaturated fat is not listed.

The following label samples compare whole with skim milk, and butter with margarine. You'll find the amount of fat listed in grams (gm) and cholesterol listed in milligrams (mg) per serving. Notice how much lower in fat and cholesterol skim milk is than whole milk, and margarine is than butter. Next, the total number of calories in a serving is listed, followed by the amounts of protein, carbohydrate and fat.

COMPARING LABEL INFORMATION

NUTRITION INFORMATION PER SERVING	WHOLE MILK	SKIM MILK
Serving Size	1 cup	1 cup
Calories	150	86
Protein	8 gm	8 gm
Carbohydrates	11 gm	12 gm
Fat	8 gm	less than 1 gm
Polyunsaturates	less than 1 gm	0 gm
Saturates	5 gm	less than 1 gm
Cholesterol	33 mg	4 mg

NUTRITION INFORMATION PER SERVING	BUTTER, STICK	MARGARINE, TUB
Serving Size	1 tbsp.	1 tbsp.
Calories	101	101
Protein	0.1 gm	0.1 gm
Carbohydrates	0.1 gm	0.1 gm
Fat	11.4 gm	11.4 gm
Polyunsaturates	0.4 gm	3.9 gm
Saturates	7.1 gm	1.8 gm
Cholesterol	31 mg	0 mg

Note: *The amount of monounsaturated fat is unlisted but can be approximately calculated by subtracting polyunsaturates and saturates from total fat.*

Here's a sample nutrition label from a milk carton. Take a minute to read and understand it. Then, next time you're in the supermarket, you'll be prepared to read almost any packaged food label.

Protein is listed both in grams and in its percentage of the U.S. Recommended Daily Allowances (U.S. RDA). These are the amounts of protein, vitamins and minerals an adult should eat every day to remain healthy. The percentages of U.S. RDA for vitamins and minerals are also listed.

1 QUART VITAMIN A & D PROTEIN FORTIFIED SKIM MILK GRADE A PASTUERIZED HOMOGENIZED NUTRITION INFORMATION PER SERVING

Serving size	1 cup	Carbohydrates	13 gm
Servings per container	4	Fat	1 gm
Calories	100	Sodium	150 mg
Protein	10 gm	Potassium	340 mg

PERCENTAGE OF U.S. RECOMMENDED DAILY ALLOWANCES (U.S. RDA)

Protein	25	Calcium	35
Vitamin A	10	Iron	0
Vitamin C	6	Vitamin D	25
Thiamin (B1)	8	Phosphorus	25
Riboflavin (B2)	30	Magnesium	10
Vitamin B6	6	Zinc	6
Vitamin B12	15	Pantothenic Acid	6
Niacin	0		

Ingredients: skim milk with nonfat milk solids, Vitamin A palmitate and Vitamin D₃
1 ounce = 28.4 grams (gm); 1 cup = 8 ounces; 1 gram = 1,000 milligrams (mg)

FAMILIAR PHRASES

Product labels contain many food industry phrases that describe the product. Here are the main ones you need to know.

Saturated Fat and Cholesterol

If you see the phrase "No Cholesterol" on a package label, it means the product contains no dietary cholesterol. But you must read further to make sure it doesn't contain saturated fat, which raises blood cholesterol. If a product contains no ingredients from animal sources, it's naturally cholesterol-free. But it could contain saturated fat. Three plant sources contain large amounts of saturated fat: coconut oil, palm oil and palm kernel oil.

You will also see terms like "light" and "lite" on foods to indicate fewer calories or less fat, but there is no consistent definition for these terms. "Light" is particularly confusing because it may also mean light color, as in vegetable oil, or fewer calories, as in drinks. Such products are not necessarily low in fat.

Some product labels will tell you the percentage of calories derived from fat. You'll see it often on peanut butter and margarine labels; these products contain mostly fat.

The bottom line: When you shop for prepared foods, compare

labels. Some are lower in fat, saturated fat and cholesterol than others, and their labels will help you make your selections.

Salt

When you want to cut down on salty foods, watch for any food label with the word "sodium" on it. Salt is about half sodium, and many food additives contain sodium. Look for these sources of "hidden salt" in foods:

- monosodium glutamate (MSG) (flavor enhancer)
- sodium bicarbonate (leavening agent)
- sodium nitrite (meat curing agent)
- sodium benzoate (preservative)
- sodium propionate (mold inhibitor)
- sodium citrate (acidity controller)

Some product labels tout the product as "sodium-free." This means that it contains less than 5 milligrams of sodium per serving. "Very low sodium" means 35 milligrams or less per serving. "Low sodium" means 140 milligrams or less per serving. "Reduced sodium" means the amount of sodium in the product is at least 75 percent less than the amount of sodium in the food it replaces.

"Unsalted," "no salt added" and "without added salt" mean the product is made without the salt that is normally used. But the product still contains the sodium that is a natural part of the food.

Calories

When you see the term "low-calorie" on a label, it means the product contains no more than 40 calories per serving and no more than 0.4 calories per gram. "Reduced-calorie" means that product has at least one-third fewer calories than an equivalent serving of the food it imitates.

GETTING STARTED

Before you leave for the supermarket, consider a few tried-and-true hints that will make shopping a lot easier.

First, try to plan your meals (or at least your entrees) for the week and write out a shopping list. This will help you save time at the store and cut down on impulse buying. Remember that the key to eating healthful foods is *variety*. Don't eat the same thing day after day. Instead, choose a little something from each of the major food groups, and vary the foods you choose within each group.

When planning your menu, include the following for each adult (for children, follow the recommendations in the "Guidelines for a Low-Fat, Low-Cholesterol Diet" on pages 10–13):

- no more than 6 ounces of meat, fish or poultry a day;
- dried beans, peas, lentils or soybean curd (tofu) in place of meat a few times a week;
- whole-grain or enriched bread or cereal products each day;
- 3 or more servings of fruit and 3 or more servings of vegetables each day (include 1 serving of citrus fruit or vegetable high in vitamin C and 1 serving of dark green, leafy or deep yellow vegetables);
- 2 or more daily servings of skim milk or low-fat milk products for adults; 3 to 4 daily servings for children or adolescents;
- 5 to 8 teaspoons of polyunsaturated and monounsaturated fats and oils in the form of margarine, cooking oil and salad dressing each day (the amount may vary according to your caloric needs).

Never shop on an empty stomach. This is the first rule of grocery shopping. When you're hungry, you may be guided by your impulses instead of your planned menus. You may be tempted to reach for the wrong foods.

You may be tempted to buy foods at sale prices even when they don't fit into your diet plan. This may cause you to abandon your planned menus and your diet. Buying sale foods can easily end up being more expensive than you think!

To cut costs, look over sales fliers when planning your menu. Select only those sale items that fit into your dietary plan. Try buying store brands rather than the more costly well-known national brands. Compare ingredients lists and nutrition labels to make sure you're getting what you want. Shop where there is unit pricing, so you can choose among the various brands and sizes. Also remember that locally produced foods usually cost less than imported ones.

Meat, Fish and Poultry

For balanced eating, you need some protein foods every day. Buy fish, chicken, turkey and lean meats more often than fatty beef, lamb, pork and ham, which contain more saturated fat—and consequently less meat—per pound.

Lean meat is an excellent protein choice, but be sure to ask your butcher to help you find the leanest cuts. Look for USDA select or choice grades of lean beef such as round steak, sirloin tip, tenderloin and extra lean ground beef. "Prime" grades are heavily marbled, making them high in saturated fatty acids.

Other ideas to remember:

- When choosing hamburger, look for the medium-to-deep color that signifies a low fat content (a light pink color is a warning that excess fat has been ground in with the meat). Ground beef should contain no more than 15 percent fat. Or buy ground round, which is usually very lean. Better yet, select a well-trimmed piece of steak, lean stewing beef or lean chuck roast, and ask the butcher to grind it for you.
- Liver, brains, kidney and sweetbreads are high in cholesterol and should be limited or omitted.
- Select lean pork such as tenderloin, loin chops, center-cut ham (fresh and cured) and Canadian bacon.
- All cuts of veal are lean except veal cutlets (ground or cubed) and breast. Examples of lean veal are chops and roast.
- The lean cuts of lamb are leg, arm and loin.
- Some wild game, such as venison, rabbit, squirrel and pheasant, are very lean; duck and goose are not.
- Processed meats should be eaten only if they contain no more than 10 percent fat or 3 grams fat per ounce. Many processed meats (luncheon meats, wieners) and sausage are high in saturated fatty acids.
- You will often see the words "lean" and "extra lean" used to designate beef, lamb and pork that have less trimmable fat (fat surrounding the meat) and sometimes less marbling. If a meat product is classified as "lean" or "extra lean" according to the USDA, it means that the product must have at least a 25 percent reduction in fat from the regulatory standard of 30 percent. That is, it may contain no more than 22.5 percent fat. The package must also list the exact percentage of fat and lean meat the product contains.

Fish is low in sodium, and it generally contains less saturated fat than red meat and about the same (or slightly less) cholesterol. For a cholesterol-lowering diet, this gives fish a slight edge over lean red meat and a definite edge over fatty red meat. That's why it's often recommended that fish be eaten two or three times a week.

- All fresh and frozen fish are good selections, as is tuna canned in water or rinsed. Uncreamed or smoked herring and sardines, canned in tomato sauce or rinsed, are good choices.

- Shrimp, lobster, crab, crayfish and most other shellfish are very low in fat. But ounce for ounce, some varieties contain more sodium and cholesterol than do poultry, meat or other fish. Even these can be eaten occasionally within the guidelines of 300 milligrams of cholesterol per day.
- Some fish have omega-3 fatty acids, which may help lower the level of some types of lipids (blood fats). Some fish high in omega-3 fatty acids are: Atlantic and coho salmon, albacore tuna, mackerel, carp, lake whitefish, sweet smelt, and lake and brook trout.

Fresh poultry is a favorite choice of many people on cholesterol-lowering diets.

- Since a great deal of the fat in poultry is in the skin, removing the skin greatly reduces the fat content.
- Select chicken, cornish hens or turkey for your entree.
- Avoid goose, duck and processed poultry products, which are high in saturated fatty acids.
- Stay away from self-basting turkeys, because commercial basting fats are highly saturated. Even when the turkey is basted in broth, the broth is usually high in sodium. It's much better to baste your own turkey with an unsalted broth.
- Use chicken or turkey breasts in recipes that call for veal steaks or cutlets. The taste and texture will be different, but the flavors are excellent.

Dairy Products

Happily, dairy products can play a major role in a prudent diet. Be sure to choose low-fat or skim milk instead of whole-milk dairy products. Select low-fat, skim and nonfat dairy products. Use cheese with 5 grams of fat or less per ounce.

If you need to watch your sodium intake, you will be pleased to know that except for buttermilk and cheese, most dairy products don't contain added salt.

These recommendations will help you shop for the right dairy products for your diet.

- Buy low-fat or skim dairy products such as skim milk, nonfat yogurt, low-fat yogurt, nonfat dry milk and low-fat cottage cheese. And don't forget buttermilk! Despite its name and rich taste, most buttermilk available in grocery stores is very low in fat (it's made from cultured skim milk).

- Look for low-fat or part-skim cheeses, low-fat or dry curd cottage cheese, farmer cheese, part-skim mozzarella or ricotta, or dry, grated cheese such as Parmesan or Sap Sago. Because they are made with skim milk, the low-fat or imitation cheeses with between 2 and 5 grams of fat per ounce are good choices. Creamy cheeses, such as brie or processed cheese spreads, are high in saturated fats and should be selected rarely.
- For desserts, choose frozen low-fat yogurt, ices, ice milk and sherbet.
- Cream substitutes—nondairy coffee creamers, sour cream substitutes and whipped toppings—often contain coconut, palm or palm kernel oil and are therefore high in saturated fatty acids. Read labels carefully and avoid those products high in saturated fatty acids.

Eggs

One large egg yolk contains almost the entire daily allowance for cholesterol, approximately 213 to 220 milligrams. It's a good idea to limit your egg yolk consumption to three or four per week.

On the other hand, egg whites contain no cholesterol and are an excellent source of protein.

- Use egg whites in place of whole eggs. In most recipes, one egg white and about 2 teaspoons of acceptable vegetable oil will substitute nicely for a whole egg. (See our recipe for no-cholesterol egg substitute on page 49.)
- Be sure to eat only cooked eggs and egg whites—not raw.

Fats and Oils

Polyunsaturated and monounsaturated oils are the kinds of fats you'll want to include in your daily diet; 5 to 8 teaspoons daily is a reasonable amount.

Pay close attention to the kinds of fats and oils in the packaged foods you buy. Read the labels and look for the polyunsaturated oils that tend to lower blood cholesterol. Here's a description of the kinds of fats and oils you're likely to find:

Saturated Fat—Fats and oils high in saturated fatty acids tend to become hard at room temperature. Butter, lard and tallow from animals, and coconut, palm and palm kernel oils from plants are common examples. These saturated fats raise blood cholesterol and should be avoided.

Monounsaturated and Polyunsaturated Fat—Oils that stay liquid at room temperature are high in unsaturated fats. They include corn, safflower, soybean, sunflower, olive and canola (rapeseed) oils. All are low in saturated fatty acids and can be used to help lower blood cholesterol in a diet low in saturated fatty acids.

Safflower is the most polyunsaturated oil. Soybean, sunflower, corn and sesame oils follow in descending order. Where a brand name does not specify the type of oil, read the fine print. Some oils now on the market are mixtures, and you should know what you are buying. Canola oil, olive oil and peanut oil are primarily monounsaturated. They appear to lower blood cholesterol when consumed in a diet low in saturated fatty acids.

Hydrogenated Oils—These oils have been artificially hardened to produce margarines and shortenings. Their effect on blood cholesterol levels depends on how much they are hydrogenated. It's best to look for margarines that have hydrogenated oil listed as the second ingredient.

Use the lists below to help you identify recommended fats and oils.

FATS AND OILS LIST

RECOMMENDED	FOR OCCASIONAL USE ONLY	NOT RECOMMENDED/ SATURATED
Safflower oil	Peanut oil	Butter
Soybean oil	Vegetable	Shortening
Sunflower oil	shortening	Bacon, salt pork
Corn oil		Suet, lard
Sesame seed oil		Chicken fat, meat
Canola oil		fat
Olive oil		Coconut oil
Polyunsaturated margarine		Palm kernel oil
Oil-based salad dressing		Palm oil

Selecting acceptable fats and oils is easy if you keep these things in mind:

- Buy margarine in place of butter, and always look for a margarine that contains no more than 2 grams of saturated fat per tablespoon.
- Because diet margarine contains water, it is often difficult to use for cooking, but it's still useful as a spread.

- Check the label of your vegetable oil and select safflower, corn, sunflower, soybean, olive or canola. Use peanut oil for a flavor change only.
- Buy nonstick vegetable oil sprays to use in place of butter or oil on pans or baking sheets.
- Most commercial salad dressings contain large amounts of fat and salt. Try making your own salad dressings (see recipes pages 165–75), or use commercially prepared unsalted salad dressings or a simple vinegar and oil combination.
- Because of their high fat content, some nuts (except coconut) and any variety of seeds, olives, peanut butter and avocado are listed in the category of fats. Because they are so high in calories, select them only occasionally.
- Chocolate, coconut, coconut oil, palm kernel oil and palm oil contain more saturated than unsaturated fat. When selecting commercial food items containing these ingredients, look for fatty acid information on the label. Currently, information about monounsaturated fatty acids is not listed on the nutrition label, but it can be calculated approximately by subtracting polyunsaturates and saturates from total fat.

Vegetables and Fruits

Fresh vegetables and fruits have little or no fat, tend to be low in sodium and, in most cases, are high in fiber and vitamins.

The exceptions include coconut meat and avocados. Coconut meat is high in saturated fatty aids, and avocados are high in fat, although the fat is largely unsaturated. Eat these in moderation.

When shopping for processed foods in this category, keep a few things in mind:
- Vegetables prepared with butter, cream or cheese can be high in fat.
- Fried vegetables have several times more fat and calories than vegetables prepared without fat.
- Fruits that are fresh or canned in water are lower in calories than fruits canned in juice or in syrup. Drain fruits canned in syrup.
- Olives are high in fat. Green olives are high in sodium (800 milligrams in 10 small) and ripe olives are moderately high in sodium (250 milligrams in 5 extra-large).

- If you are on a sodium-restricted diet, stay away from vegetables that have been packed in brine, such as pickles and sauerkraut, because they're loaded with sodium.

Breads, Cereals, Pasta and Starchy Vegetables

Happily, whole-grain or enriched breads, cereals and pastas provide lots of nutrients and relatively few calories.

Feel free to experiment with different kinds of breads, such as whole or cracked wheat, rye, French, Italian and pumpernickel. Although they contain some sodium and a small amount of fat, they are full of flavor and nutritive value.

Keep these tips in mind when shopping for baked products, pastas and starchy vegetables.

- Commercially baked products (i.e., croissants, muffins, biscuits, butter rolls and doughnuts) contain large amounts of saturated fatty acids. It's much better to make your own. Just use the recipes in this book or adjust your favorite recipes by omitting the salt and using the ingredient substitutions listed on page 49.
- Check the labels on baked foods. Many are made with whole milk and dried egg yolks, and should be selected only occasionally.
- Check the labels on crackers for fats and oils. Scandinavian-style rye crackers and other whole-grain crackers are often made without fats or oils and with little or no salt.
- Try buying brown rice, bulgur wheat, millet and other whole grains to cook in seasoned broth for a side dish. They're high in fiber, relatively low in calories and economical.
- Buy dried beans, peas and lentils to substitute for meats in casseroles, stews and soups. They're excellent protein sources and very economical.
- Hot cereals, rice and pastas contain almost no sodium—just remember to leave the salt out of the cooking water when you prepare these foods.
- Check the ingredients lists on packaged dry cereals. Most of these are low in saturated fatty acids, but many contain large quantities of sugar, some contain salt, and a few even contain fat. Be particularly cautious of so-called natural cereals and granolas, which may contain all three. They often contain coconut or coconut oil.

- Look for reduced-salt versions of canned soups and canned vegetables. They may be found either in the diet section or on the shelves with their "regular" counterparts.
- Canned or dehydrated varieties of soup should have no more than 2 grams of fat per cup.

Snacks

The best snacks are those you make yourself using acceptable oils and margarines. Still, there are many good snack products in the supermarket—if you know where to look.

- Nuts and seeds are wonderful snacks, and most varieties are available in their natural state: unsalted. These foods contain lots of fat, but most of it is unsaturated. Still, the calorie count is high, so if you're watching your weight, you may want to go easy on nuts and seeds.
- A few types of commercially prepared cookies are low in fat, such as newton-type cookies and gingersnaps. Plain angel food cake has no fat.
- Desserts (cakes, pies, cookies and puddings) may be made at home with allowed margarine or oil, skim or 1-percent milk, allowed eggs, egg substitute or egg whites.
- Many snack products, such as chips and rich crackers, are high in saturated fatty acids. However, some chips are cooked in unsaturated oil. Choose only those labeled as having more polyunsaturated than saturated fatty acids.

Miscellaneous Foods, Flavorings and Beverages

Fat is sometimes in places you wouldn't expect—such as chocolate, sauces, dressings, food flavorings and milky beverages. These kinds of foods may also have a high calorie or sodium content. Read the labels and choose your foods carefully.

When your recipe calls for baking chocolate, substitute unsweetened cocoa powder and polyunsaturated oil or margarine (see page 49). Chocolate and cocoa butter contain saturated fat, but most of the fat has been removed from cocoa powder.

When you're thirsty, find beverages that are low in sodium, fat and cholesterol. Examples include skim milk, low-sodium fruit juices, fruit drinks and carbonated drinks. (Some diet soft drinks and mineral waters are high in sodium, so be sure to read the labels first.)

If you're trying to lose weight, stay away from sugared carbonated beverages, fruit drinks, beer, wine and alcohol. If you do drink alcohol, drink in moderation. It's best to limit your alcohol intake to one to two ounces a day.

If you're trying to cut down on salt, beware that many commonly used commercial seasonings and sauces have a lot of sodium. Among these are: soy, steak sauce, ketchup, chili sauce, monosodium glutamate, meat tenderizer, commercial soups, pickles, relishes, flavored seasoning salts, bouillon cubes and salad dressings. Look for low-sodium versions of these items, or use the recipes we've included in this cookbook to make your own.

THESE FOODS AND DRINKS CONTAIN FEWER THAN 20 CALORIES AND NO FAT PER PORTION:

DRINKS

Bouillon or broth without fat*	Cocoa powder, unsweetened
Carbonated drinks, sugar-free**	Coffee or tea
Carbonated water	Drink mixes, sugar-free**
Club soda*	Tonic water, sugar-free**

CONDIMENTS	SWEET SUBSTITUTES**	FRUITS
Try flavored peppers, herb blends, spice blends, vinegars and other seasonings in place of salt.	Candy, hard, sugar-free** Gelatin, sugar-free** Jam or jelly, sugar-free**	Cranberries, unsweetened Rhubarb, unsweetened

* *High in sodium. Look for seltzers or soda with no salt added.*
** *Sweet substitutes are listed for the benefit of those following a diabetic diet.*

Cooking for
a Healthy Heart

Filling your grocery cart with healthful foods is just the beginning of the process. You want the low-fat foods you buy to stay that way until they reach your plate.

Some cooking methods are guaranteed to add loads of fat to any food: Deep-fat frying is a good example. Other cooking methods help retain vitamins and minerals and keep fat and calories to a minimum. These include roasting, baking, broiling, braising, sautéing, stir-frying and microwaving.

The idea is to stay away from any cooking method that adds fat or allows food to cook in its own fat. Look for techniques that enhance flavor and preserve nutrients instead. Be miserly when it comes to adding fat and sodium.

Here are a few excellent help-your-heart cooking techniques. Among them, you'll find ways to cook your favorite dishes to perfection so they'll give you the flavor without the fat.

Roasting

This slow, dry-heat method of cooking creates a delicious product— and keeps fat to a minimum. Simply season the meat, if desired, and place it fat-side-up on a rack in an uncovered roasting pan. Remember to remove as much visible fat as possible from the meat. The rack keeps the meat from sitting in its own fat drippings.

Roast to the desired doneness in a preheated 325° F oven. Cooking at this temperature for the required time increases the fat drip-off and avoids searing the meat, which seals in fat.

Lean meats may require basting with a fat-free liquid such as wine, tomato juice or lemon juice.

Use a meat thermometer to test for doneness. Insert it in the center of the raw roast so the bulb reaches the thickest part of the meat and does not rest in fat or on bone. When the temperature shows the desired internal temperature, push it a little deeper into the meat. If the temperature drops, continue cooking until it reaches the correct temperature. If it stays the same, the meat is done.

Time the cooking so the roast is removed from the oven 20 or 30 minutes before serving so the meat can "rest." This ensures that the meat can be carved easily. Refer to the following timetables for roasting beef, veal, lamb, pork, chicken and turkey.

TIMETABLE FOR ROASTING MEAT AND POULTRY

CUT	APPROXIMATE WEIGHT (POUNDS)	MEAT THERMOMETER READING (° F)	APPROXIMATE COOKING TIME
BEEF (Oven Temperature 325° F)			
Rolled Rump (high quality)	4 to 6	150° to 170°	25 to 30 min./lb.
Tip (high quality)	3½ to 4	140° to 170°	35 to 40 min./lb.
Tenderloin (half)*	2 to 3	140° (rare)	45 to 50 total
VEAL (Oven Temperature 325° F)			
Loin	4 to 6	170°	30 to 35 min./lb.
LAMB (Oven Temperature 325° F)			
Leg	5 to 9	170° to 180°	30 to 35 min./lb.
PORK (Oven Temperature 325° F)			
Canadian-style bacon	2 to 4	160°	35 to 40 min./lb.
Fresh tenderloin	½ to 1	170°	¾ to 1 hour total
CHICKEN (Ready-to-Cook Weight)		**OVEN TEMPERATURE (° F)**	
Broiler-fryer (unstuffed)	2½ to 3	375°	1¼ to 1¾ hours** total
Capon (stuffed)	5 to 8	325°	2½ to 3½ hours total

TURKEY			
READY-TO-COOK WEIGHT	OVEN TEMPERATURE (° F)	MEAT THERMOMETER READING (° F)	APPROXIMATE COOKING TIME
16 to 20 pounds	325°	185°	5½ to 6½ hours total

* *Roast at 425° F.*
** *Stuffed chickens require about 15 minutes longer.*

Baking

Baking is another dry-heat form of cooking that's excellent for poultry, fish and meat. It differs from roasting in that you use a covered container and add some liquid before cooking. The liquid adds flavor and helps keep the meat moist.

Braising or Stewing

Braising is a slow-cooking method that's great for tenderizing tougher cuts of meat. To braise, just brown meat on all sides, using a minimum of vegetable oil or vegetable oil spray. Then season, add a small amount of liquid (¼ to ½ cup), cover pan tightly and simmer. You may also dredge the meat in seasoned flour instead of browning it. For stewing, follow the same directions, but add water to cover.

During cooking the fat cooks out of the meat, so it's a good idea to cook the meat a day ahead, then refrigerate it. After the chilled fat has hardened overnight, you can remove it easily before reheating. Also, the flavors of many braised and stewed dishes are improved after refrigerating overnight. Braising is also an excellent way to cook vegetables.

Poaching

Poaching is cooking by the immersion of food in simmering liquid. It works particularly well with chicken and fish.

Place a single layer of the chicken or fish in a shallow, wide pan and barely cover with liquid. You may use water, water seasoned with spices and herbs, low-fat milk, broth or a mixture of white wine and water. After cooking, you may reduce the liquid and then thicken it to make a sauce.

Steaming

Food cooked in a basket over simmering water is just about perfect: It keeps its natural flavor and color and all its vitamins and minerals.

A steam cooker is ideal, but you may also use a steamer basket that fits into a pot with a tight-fitting lid. If you don't have a steamer rack, use anything that will prevent the food from touching the water.

Steaming is great for vegetables and fish. Just bring a small amount of water to a boil (water should be to depth of about one inch) and then turn the heat to simmer. You may add herbs, spices or broth to the water for extra flavor. In just a few minutes vegetables will be tender-crisp and ready to eat. Fish takes a little longer, from 5 to 10 minutes, or until it flakes easily when tested with a fork.

You may even use the liquid left in the pot for soup stock.

Sautéing

Leave it to the French to invent a cooking method this wonderful!

Sautéing comes from the French word *sauter,* meaning "to jump." It's a pan method that uses little or no fat. Meat, fish, poultry or vegetables are cooked in an open skillet over high temperatures. The food is constantly agitated or made to jump in the pan to keep it from sticking.

Sautéing with herbs and spices brings out flavor—all you need is a little unsaturated oil rubbed onto the pan with a paper towel. Even better: Use nonstick vegetable oil spray or sauté in a small amount of broth or wine.

Stir-Frying

This is the Oriental version of sautéing. The idea is to cook food quickly in a minimum amount of oil or broth. The high temperature and the constant stirring keep the food from sticking and burning.

You may use a Chinese wok or a large frying pan, though of course a wok is ideal because it is designed especially for stir-frying. Try stir-frying vegetables and diced chicken or seafood with a tiny bit of peanut oil.

Before you heat the oil in the wok, prepare each food for cooking by dicing or slicing it into small pieces for rapid cooking. Because the hottest area is at the base of the wok, you'll want to cook each food quickly there, then push it up on the side of the wok while you cook the next food.

Use an oil that won't smoke at high temperatures. (Fat that smokes releases undesirable chemicals and won't cook correctly.) Peanut oil, which smokes at 446° F, works best. Stir-frying results in delicious dishes because the hot oil preserves the color, flavor and crispness of vegetables, and it seals in the natural juices of meats and seafood. When your recipe calls for soy sauce, use the low-sodium variety. This helps control the amount of sodium in your diet.

Frying

If you're trying to cut cholesterol or calories, you'll want to steer clear of deep-fat frying, because typically it involves using batters, which absorb the cooking fat. That adds not only fat, but also lots of calories to your diet.

For an occasional treat, deep-fat frying is acceptable if you follow these fat-cutting instructions. First, avoid batters. Instead, dredge the food in flour or dip it in egg white or cracker meal. Fry in corn oil, which is polyunsaturated, with a smoking point higher than 365° F, the correct temperature for frying most foods. Cook just until done so oil absorption is kept to a minimum.

Grilling or Broiling

Placing food on a rack and cooking over or under direct heat allows the fat to drip away, either into the coals or into a broiling pan. Either way, much of the fat cooks out.

For extra flavor, marinate steaks, fish or chicken before placing them over the coals or under the broiler. Basting with the marinade during cooking keeps the food moist, but be careful: Always boil the marinade before using it for basting. Bacteria tends to form in marinating meat mixtures, and boiling it will kill the bacteria.

Skewered vegetables also taste great browned over a flame.

Microwave Cooking

Microwaving is fast, easy and so moisture-producing that it requires no added fats or oils. In fact, you can drain food of fat as it cooks by placing it between two paper towels.

You'll need to cook in containers that are transparent to microwaves: glass, paper, dishwasher-safe plastics, china or earthenware. Do not use metal, aluminum foil, paper goods made from recycled paper or plastic ware.

You can adapt conventional recipes for the microwave by cutting the cooking time to one-fourth to one-third of the conventional amount. If the food needs more cooking, continue cooking it for short periods. Try to find a microwave recipe similar to the one you want to adapt. With a little experimentation, you'll find what works for you.

The following microwave cooking hints can help you make the most of this very fast cooking method.

- Choose foods that cook well in moist heat: chicken, fish, ground meat, vegetables, sauces and soups.
- Take advantage of the capabilities of microwaves for defrosting and reheating foods quickly.

- Pieces that are about equal in size and shape will cook more uniformly.
- Use a high setting (100 percent power) for soups, beverages, fruits, vegetables, fish, ground meat and poultry. Use a medium-high setting (70 percent power) for simmering stews. Use a medium setting (50 percent power) for baking breads, cakes and muffins and for cooking tender cuts of meat.
- For foods requiring long cooking times, use reduced power for part of the cooking, or turn the power off for several brief intervals during cooking. The off interval allows time for the temperature to equalize in the food.
- If you cook more than one food at a time, extend the length of cooking time.
- Plan for food to continue cooking after it is taken out of the microwave, especially when the food has not been cut into small pieces before cooking.
- Let food stand a few minutes before serving to allow heat at the outside to penetrate to the center.
- Choose a microwave-safe container slightly larger than the dish required for cooking the recipe in a conventional oven.
- Casserole-type foods, in particular, commonly expand during cooking, so use larger containers with straight rather than sloped sides and rounded rather than square corners.
- Place slow-to-heat, dense and thick food near the edge of the dish. Thinner items should go near the center.
- Stir food periodically during cooking, if possible.
- Use a rack or trivet to hold foods out of drippings.
- Turn and invert large food portions during cooking.
- Use two-thirds the liquid required in the conventional cooking of beverages, soups, vegetables, fruits and main dishes, because less liquid evaporates in microwave cooking.
- Cover most foods to retain heat and reduce dehydration. Leave an opening to allow steam to escape. Exceptions are bread, pastries and breaded products that must be heated uncovered so they don't become soggy.
- Don't coat meat with flour if you will be adding liquid for cooking. The coatings become soggy.
- Use quick-cooking instead of long-grain rice.
- Prepare sauces and gravies with a medium consistency. Reduce liquid by one-fourth to one-half or increase the

amount of flour in the recipe. (This change will prevent thinning during microwave heating.)
- Add low-fat cheese and other toppings near the end of cooking to keep the top from becoming tough or soggy.
- Mozzarella and Monterey Jack cheeses are good choices to use in the microwave.
- Substitute crushed, unseasoned croutons for dry breadcrumbs as topping on casseroles, since they will absorb less moisture and remain crisper.
- Reduce leavening agents and increase liquids by one-fourth when baking cakes. Baked goods rise more and lose more moisture when cooked in the microwave. Fill pans no more than half full.
- To create a crusty look on baked items, oil pans with an acceptable vegetable oil and add ground nuts or crumbs.

COOKING TIPS

Now that you know the basics of low-fat cooking, you're ready to specialize. We've compiled some specific fat-cutting techniques for foods that are often a major source of extra fat. We've also offered some flavor-enhancing ideas you'll want to try.

Meat Drippings

While meat is cooking, a rich essence drips onto the roasting pan or broiler along with the fat. To keep the essence without the fat, pour the contents of the pan—fat and all—into a cup or dish, cover it and put it in the refrigerator. The next day you can easily remove the hardened fat, leaving only the dark, flavorful juice resting underneath. This juice adds zest to meat pies, sauces, hashes or meatloaves.

Gravies

You don't have to add meat fat to have a wonderfully thick gravy. You'll need about a cup of clear, defatted broth, either homemade, canned or made from bouillon cubes. Place the following in a jar with a tight-fitting lid: ½ cup of liquid plus either 1 tablespoon of cornstarch, 1 tablespoon of flour or 1 to 2 tablespoons of browned flour. Shake until smooth. Heat the remaining liquid in a saucepan, pour the cornstarch or flour mixture into it and simmer, adding seasonings as desired.

Browned flour gives the sauce a rich mahogany color.

Broth

Once you get used to homemade broth, the canned or bouillon-cube varieties will seem tame by comparison. Just remember to make the broth a day ahead so you can remove the fat after it cools and hardens in the refrigerator overnight. Use broth to make soups or stews, and be sure to defat the finished dish. If you must use canned broth, choose a low-sodium variety. Refrigerate the can before opening, then remove the fat before using.

Wine and Spirits

The wines and spirits you use for cooking don't have to be old or expensive, but to be good enough to cook with, they should be good enough for you to drink and enjoy. Avoid cooking wines, which are high in sodium.

The alcohol present evaporates during cooking, leaving only the flavor and tenderizing qualities.

Vinegar

Good wine vinegars and herb vinegars are delicious on salads and in other recipes.

Whole-Grain Flour

Keep whole-grain flour in the refrigerator. Substitute 1 cup of whole-wheat pastry flour for 1 cup all-purpose flour. Substitute 1 cup of whole-wheat flour for 7/8 cup all-purpose flour.

Dried Beans

Soak beans overnight, then drain off the water. Add fresh water and seasonings and simmer about 2½ hours. If you're pinched for time, try cooking the beans in boiling water for 2 minutes and soaking them for 1 hour. Drain the water off and proceed as directed above.

Low-Fat Cooking Tips

Whether you want to lower your blood cholesterol level, lose weight or cut down on salt, these cooking tips can make it easier to do all three.

- Use a nonstick skillet so it is possible to cook with a minimum of oil or vegetable oil spray. Do not spray vegetable oil near a heat source or an open flame. Read the label on the can and follow instructions carefully.
- Trim all visible fat from meat before cooking.

- After roasting meat or poultry, chill the drippings in the refrigerator. Once cooled, the fat will rise to the top and harden; remove it and save the stock for stews, sauces and soups.
- Buy only the leanest ground beef, pork and turkey (no more than 15 percent fat). After browning, put ground meat into a strainer or colander lined with paper towels. Allow fat to drain out. Ground meat is generally higher in fat than nonground meat. To get the leanest ground beef possible, have your butcher grind a sirloin steak for you. Be sure your butcher cleans the grinder to remove any fat from previous grindings.
- When figuring serving sizes, remember that meat loses about 25 percent of its weight during cooking. (For example, 4 ounces of raw meat becomes about 3 ounces cooked.)
- Make a habit of skinning chickens before cooking and removing all visible fat below the skin. Use paper towels or a clean cloth to take better hold of the skin. Be certain to scrub the cutting surface and utensils well with hot, sudsy water after preparing poultry for cooking.
- Fresh fish should be cooked for 10 minutes per inch of thickness. Add 5 minutes to that total figure if it's wrapped in foil. Frozen fish requires 20 minutes per inch of thickness, plus 10 minutes if it's wrapped in foil. Cooking time may vary, depending on the cooking method used, but fish is done when the flesh is opaque and flakes easily when tested with a fork.
- Prepare scrambled eggs or omelettes so that only 1 egg yolk per portion is used. Add a few extra egg whites to the mixing bowl to make more generous servings.
- Drain canned salmon, tuna and sardines to remove oils or salty liquids. Then add water to the can and drain again to rinse.
- For a low-sodium diet, use crackers with unsalted tops wherever recipes call for commercial crackers or cracker crumbs.
- Seal natural juices into foods by wrapping foods in foil before cooking. Or try wrapping foods in edible pouches made of steamed lettuce or cabbage leaves.
- Cook vegetables just until tender-crisp. Overcooked vegetables lose both flavor and important nutrients.
- Clean mushrooms as needed by wiping them with a clean, damp cloth. A quick rinse in cold water is fine, too, but never soak them or they'll get soggy.

- Wear rubber gloves when handling hot peppers or wash hands thoroughly after handling. Skin, especially around the eyes, is very sensitive to the oil from peppers.
- Cut down on cholesterol by using more vegetables and less poultry or meats in soups, stews and casseroles. Finely chopped vegetables are great for stretching ground poultry or meat, too.
- Cut down on fat in creamy salad dressing by mixing it with plain low-fat yogurt.
- Sweeten plain low-fat or nonfat yogurt with pureed fruit or applesauce instead of buying prepared fruit yogurt.

SAVOR THE FLAVOR

How to Spice Up Low-Fat, Low-Sodium Cuisine

Just because you're cutting down on fat and salt doesn't mean your tastebuds have to take a vacation. A creative cook can make low-fat, low-sodium cooking exciting, imaginative and crowd-pleasing. Experiment with seasonings. Our seasoning chart on pages 40–41 will get you started.

Here are a few great flavor-enhancing ideas that will help you spice up your everyday dishes—and your special occasions, too.

- Use fresh herbs whenever possible. Use a mortar and pestle to grind them for the freshest and fullest flavor.
- Grate fresh ginger with a flat, sheet-type grater. Use a food processor to grate fresh horseradish. Fresh, these two roots pack a lot more punch than their salted, bottled versions.
- Add dried herbs such as thyme, rosemary and marjoram to dishes for a more pungent flavor, but use them sparingly.
- Use citrus zest, the colored part of the peel without the pith; it holds the true flavor of the fruit. Grate it with a flat, sheet-type grater or remove it with a vegetable peeler and cut the pieces into thin strips.
- Toast seeds, nuts and whole spices to bring out their full flavor. Cook them in a dry skillet over moderate heat or on a baking sheet in a 400° F oven.
- Roasting vegetables in a hot oven will caramelize their natural sugars and bring out their full flavor.
- Use vinegar or citrus juice as a wonderful flavor enhancer, but add it at the last moment. Vinegar is great on vegetables such

as greens; citrus works well on fruits such as melons. Either is great with fish.

- Use dry mustard for a zesty flavor in cooking or mix it with water to make a very sharp condiment.
- Add fresh hot peppers for a little more "bite" in your dishes. Remove the membrane and the seeds before chopping finely. Remember: A small amount goes a long way.
- Some vegetables and fruits, such as mushrooms, tomatoes, chili peppers, cherries, cranberries and currants, have a more intense flavor when dried than when fresh. Use them when you want a burst of flavor. An added bonus: You can use the flavored water they soaked in for cooking.

HERB, SPICE AND SEASONING GUIDE

DIPS

Caraway, dill, garlic, oregano, parsley, freshly ground black pepper

SOUPS AND STEWS

Bean Soup: Dry mustard powder
Vegetable Soup: Sugar, vinegar
Skim Milk Chowders: Bay leaf,* peppercorns
Pea Soup: Bay leaf,* coriander, fresh parsley
Stews: Basil, bay leaf,* cayenne, chervil, chili powder, cinnamon, cumin, curry powder, fennel, garlic, ginger, marjoram, nutmeg, onion, parsley, saffron
Various: Basil, bay leaf,* burnet, cayenne, chervil, chili powder, cloves, curry powder, dill, garlic, ginger, marjoram, mint, mustard, nutmeg, onion, oregano, parsley, freshly ground black pepper, rosemary, sage, savory, sesame seeds, tarragon, thyme, watercress

SALADS

Basil, burnet, chervil, coriander, dill, fresh lemon juice, mint, fresh mushrooms, mustard, oregano, parsley, freshly ground black pepper, rosemary, sage, savory, sesame seeds, turmeric, vinegar, watercress

MEAT, FISH AND POULTRY

Fish and Seafood: Allspice, basil, bay leaf,* cayenne, curry powder, cumin, fennel, garlic, green bell pepper, fresh lemon juice, mace, marjoram, mint, fresh mushrooms, Dijon mustard, dry mustard powder, green onion, paprika, saffron, sage, sesame seeds, tarragon, thyme, turmeric, white wine
Poultry: Basil, bay leaf,* cinnamon, curry powder, garlic, green bell pepper, fresh lemon juice, mace, marjoram, fresh mushrooms, onion, paprika, fresh parsley, lemon pepper, poultry seasoning, rosemary, saffron, sage, savory, sesame seeds, thyme, tarragon, white wine
Game: Bay leaf,* garlic, fresh lemon juice, fresh mushrooms, onion, rosemary, sage, savory, tarragon, thyme, vinegar

Beef: Allspice, bay leaf,* cayenne, cumin, curry powder, garlic, green bell pepper, marjoram, fresh mushrooms, dry mustard, nutmeg, onion, freshly ground black pepper, rosemary, sage, thyme, red wine

Pork: Apple, applesauce, cinnamon, cloves, fennel, garlic, mint, onion, sage, savory, red wine

Lamb: Curry powder, garlic, mint, mint jelly, onion, pineapple, rosemary, sage, savory, sesame seeds, red wine

Veal: Apricot, bay leaf,* curry powder, ginger, fresh lemon juice, marjoram, mint, fresh mushrooms, oregano, saffron, sage, savory, tarragon, white wine

Various: Cayenne, chervil, chili powder, coriander, curry powder, dill, garlic, ginger, marjoram, onion, oregano, parsley, freshly ground black pepper

VEGETABLES

Asparagus: Garlic, fresh lemon juice, onion, vinegar

Beans: Caraway, cloves, cumin, mint, onion, green bell pepper, savory, tarragon, thyme

Beets: Anise, caraway, fennel, ginger, savory

Carrots: Anise, cinnamon, cloves, mint, sage, tarragon

Corn: Allspice, chili powder, green bell pepper, pimiento, fresh tomato

Cucumbers: Chives, dill, garlic, vinegar

Green Beans: Dill, fresh lemon juice, marjoram, nutmeg, pimiento

Greens: Garlic, fresh lemon juice, onion, vinegar

Peas: Allspice, green bell pepper, mint, fresh mushrooms, onion, fresh parsley, sage, savory

Potatoes: Chives, dill, green bell pepper, onion, pimiento, saffron

Squash: Allspice, brown sugar, cinnamon, cloves, fennel, ginger, mace, nutmeg, onion, savory

Tomatoes: Allspice, basil, garlic, marjoram, onion, oregano, sage, savory, tarragon, thyme

Various Vegetables: Basil, burnet, cayenne, chervil, dill, marjoram, mint, fresh mushrooms, nutmeg, oregano, parsley, freshly ground black pepper, poppy seeds, rosemary, sage, sesame seeds, sunflower seeds, tarragon, thyme, turmeric, watercress

BAKED GOODS

Breads: Anise, caraway, cardamom, fennel, poppy seeds, sesame seeds

Desserts: Anise, caraway, cardamom, cinnamon, cloves, coriander, fennel, ginger, mace, mint, nutmeg, poppy seeds, sesame seeds

FRUITS

Allspice, anise, basil, cardamom, cloves, cumin, curry powder, ginger, mint, nutmeg, poppy seeds, rosemary, watercress

EGGS

Basil, chervil, chili powder, cumin, curry powder, fennel, marjoram, mustard, oregano, parsley, freshly ground black pepper, poppy seeds, rosemary, saffron, savory, sesame seeds, tarragon, thyme, turmeric, watercress

* *Always leave bay leaf whole and remove from dish before serving.*

TABLE OF EQUIVALENTS

WEIGHTS AND MEASURES

Dash	=	2–4 drops				
3 teaspoons	=	1 tablespoon	=	½ fluid ounce	=	15 milliliters
4 tablespoons	=	¼ cup	=	2 fluid ounces	=	60 milliliters
16 tablespoons	=	1 cup (½ pint)	=	8 fluid ounces	=	240 milliliters
2 cups	=	1 pint	=	16 fluid ounces	=	480 milliliters
2 pints	=	1 quart	=	32 fluid ounces	=	960 milliliters
					=	0.96 liters
4 quarts	=	1 gallon	=	128 fluid ounces	=	3840 milliliters
					=	3.8 liters
2 tablespoons	=	1 ounce	=	⅛ cup	=	30 grams
4 tablespoons	=	2 ounces	=	¼ cup	=	60 grams
16 tablespoons	=	8 ounces	=	1 cup	=	240 grams
2 cups	=	16 ounces	=	1 pound	=	480 grams
					=	0.48 kilograms

BEANS	DRIED		COOKED
Kidney	1 pound (2½ cups)	=	5½ cups
Lima Beans	1 pound (2½ cups)	=	5½ cups
Navy	1 pound (2⅓ cups)	=	5½ cups
Soybeans	1 pound (2 cups)	=	4½ cups

RICE, WHEAT, PASTA	DRY		COOKED
Rice	1 pound (2⅓ cups)	=	8 cups
Macaroni	1 pound (3¾ cups)	=	9 cups
Spaghetti	1 pound (4½ cups)	=	9 cups
Bulgur	1 pound (2¾ cups)	=	8 cups

FLOUR	WEIGHT		VOLUME
Enriched white	1 pound	=	4 cups sifted
Enriched cake	1 pound	=	4½ cups sifted
Whole-wheat	1 pound	=	3⅓ cups (stirred)
Whole-wheat pastry	1 pound	=	4½ cups sifted

MISCELLANEOUS	WEIGHT		GRATED
Cheese	1 pound	=	4 cups

KEEPING FOODS FRESH

Armed with these storage hints, you'll keep your foods just the way you want them: with all the flavor and nutrients packed inside.

- Always cover food to be refrigerated, because otherwise bacteria can attack it, changing its flavor and composition.
- Store fresh low-fat milk in the refrigerator in its original container—and always close the milk carton after use.

- Use cottage cheese within a few days of purchase.
- For full flavor and best texture, serve cheese at room temperature (about 20 to 60 minutes after removal from the refrigerator).
- Store eggs in the refrigerator with the large end up. Stored at room temperature, they'll lose more quality in one day than in a week in the refrigerator.
- Refrigerate fresh meat, loosely covered, at temperatures as low as possible without actually freezing the meat. Use within a few days of purchase.
- For freezer storage longer than 1 or 2 weeks, wrap and seal meats tightly in moisture- and vapor-proof materials. Rewrap or overwrap packaged meats in special freezer paper.
- To thaw frozen meat, keep it wrapped and let it stand in the refrigerator. If you're in a hurry, thaw it in a microwave oven, or place it in a waterproof wrapper and immerse the meat in cold water until defrosted, usually an hour thawing time per pound of meat.
- Remove the giblets and wrap them separately when you refrigerate poultry. Wrap the poultry loosely to permit air circulation, and use within 1 to 2 days.
- Store citrus fruits, except tangerines, uncovered in the refrigerator. Put tangerines in a plastic bag before refrigerating.
- Let bananas ripen at room temperature, then refrigerate. The cold will turn the skins dark, but the bananas will taste fine.
- Let avocados stand 3 to 5 days until softened, then refrigerate.
- Keep cantaloupes at room temperature 2 to 4 days, then chill a few hours before serving.
- To keep sliced fruit from discoloring, sprinkle with lemon juice or ascorbic acid.
- Refrigerate most fresh vegetables except dry onions (keep in a cool, dry place), potatoes (keep in a well-ventilated place between 45° F and 50° F) and hard-rind squashes, rutabagas and sweet potatoes (about 60° F—temperatures below 50° F may cause chilling injury).
- Store white flours and cereals at room temperature in a dry place in tightly covered containers to keep out dust, moisture and insects. Store whole-wheat flour in the refrigerator.
- Wrap homemade breads securely in foil or plastic before storing.

- Read the label on yeast packages and do not use the product beyond its expiration.
- Refrigerate vegetable shortenings; they will last several months or more. They do not keep so long at room temperature.
- Keep vegetable oils well capped and store at room temperature. Most salad oils stay clear when refrigerated, but olive oil turns thick and cloudy.
- Homemade dressings can be kept for 2 weeks if refrigerated in a jar with a tight-fitting lid.

How to Adapt Recipes

Cooking the low-fat way, you may wonder if you have to give up your favorite family recipes. What about Aunt Martha's homemade apple pie, Cousin Pat's double-fudge brownies or your own specialty de la maison? Do you really have to give these up?

No! All you need to do is learn how to adapt them. Most dishes *can* be adapted to fit into a low-fat eating plan. This chapter will help you do that.

It helps to use a three-step approach when adapting recipes. First, look for "problem" ingredients—those high in total fat, saturated fat, cholesterol or sodium. Next, find low-fat substitutions for these ingredients. Sometimes this means that you eliminate the ingredient altogether. Other times you simply reduce the amount you use or substitute a similar ingredient that's healthier for you. Finally, you can change your method of food preparation. For example, if you're used to deep-fat frying, try broiling instead.

The substitution list on page 49 shows how easy it is to turn your favorite recipes into low-fat dishes you can live with.

On the following pages we have taken one recipe and shown how to adapt it. We began with a traditional lasagna recipe and substituted low-fat ingredients to create our recipe, Turkey Lasagna. The analysis for each recipe shows how dramatic the differences are. An explanation of how we adapted the recipe is shown on page 48.

Traditional Lasagna

Makes 8 to 10 servings

½ pound package of lasagna noodles
1 pound Italian sausage
½ pound ground beef
1 cup chopped onion
2 cloves garlic, minced
2 teaspoons sugar
1 tablespoon salt
1½ teaspoons basil leaves
½ teaspoon fennel seed
½ teaspoon pepper
1 28-ounce can tomatoes, broken up
2 6-ounce cans tomato paste
1 egg, beaten
1 15-ounce container ricotta cheese
1 tablespoon dried parsley flakes
½ teaspoon salt
1 cup pitted ripe olives, sliced
1 pound mozzarella cheese, grated
¾ cup grated Parmesan cheese

Prepare lasagna noodles according to package directions. Drain. Cook sausage and ground beef; drain excess fat. Add onion and garlic; stir and cook 5 minutes. Add next seven ingredients and simmer 20 minutes. Combine egg, ricotta, parsley and salt. Into the bottom of a 13-x-9-inch baking dish, spoon about 1½ cups meat sauce. Layer one-third of the lasagna, one-third of the meat sauce, one-third of the ricotta, one-third of the sliced olives, one-third of the mozzarella and one-third of the Parmesan. Repeat layering. Cover with foil. Bake in a 375° F oven for 25 minutes, remove foil and bake uncovered 25 minutes longer. Let stand 10 minutes before cutting.

Nutrient Analysis

Calories	679 kcal	Cholesterol	161 mg	Saturated Fat	20 gm
Protein	40 gm	Sodium	2358 mg	Polyunsaturated Fat	3 gm
Carbohydrate	38 gm	Total Fat	41 gm	Monounsaturated Fat	15 gm

*T*urkey *L*asagna

Serves 9

Vegetable oil spray
½ cup chopped onion
8 ounces fresh mushrooms, sliced
3 cloves garlic, minced
1 pound freshly ground turkey, skin removed before
    grinding
3 cups no-salt-added tomato sauce
2 teaspoons basil
½ teaspoon oregano
Freshly ground black pepper to taste
1 10-ounce package frozen no-salt-added chopped
    spinach, defrosted and squeezed dry
2 cups (1 pound) low-fat cottage cheese
Dash nutmeg
1 8-ounce package lasagna noodles
8 ounces part-skim mozzarella cheese, grated

Preheat oven to 375° F. Lightly spray a 9-x-13-inch baking dish with
vegetable oil.

In a nonstick skillet over medium-high heat, combine onion,
mushrooms, garlic and ground turkey. Sauté until turkey is no longer
pink. Cover pan and continue to cook until mushrooms have released juices, then uncover and evaporate juices over high heat. Add
tomato sauce, basil, oregano and pepper. Reduce heat.

In a bowl, stir spinach, cottage cheese and nutmeg together well.
Set aside.

Cook noodles according to package directions, omitting salt.

Lay one-third of noodles on bottom of dish; add one-half of
spinach mixture, one-third of tomato sauce and one-third of cheese.
Repeat layers once. Finish with one layer noodles, one-third sauce
and remaining cheese. Cover with aluminum foil and bake 35 to 40
minutes.

Nutrient Analysis

Calories	326 kcal	Cholesterol	49 mg	Saturated Fat	4 gm
Protein	31 gm	Sodium	411 mg	Polyunsaturated Fat	1 gm
Carbohydrate	32 gm	Total Fat	8 gm	Monounsaturated Fat	2 gm

ANALYSIS: HOW WE ADAPTED OUR RECIPE

Our first low-fat technique was simple: We used a nonstick skillet, adding a little vegetable oil spray. Cooking this way is virtually fat-free. We also oiled the lasagna dish with the vegetable oil spray.

Next we substituted turkey for the sausage and ground beef. Turkey is much lower in total fat and saturated fat, so this is an excellent fat-cutting move.

In place of the ricotta and mozzarella cheeses, we used low-fat cottage cheese and part-skim mozzarella, which offers the wonderful cheese taste with a fraction of the fat. We also used no-salt-added tomato sauce instead of the regular salted variety. We cooked our noodles without added salt, and we substituted a generous amount of herbs and spices for salt in the mixture.

You'll also notice that we used a reasonable amount of turkey and supplemented the dish with flavorful spinach and mushrooms.

Finally, we left out the olives and the beaten egg in our dish. These changes hardly affect the taste but omit a lot of cholesterol and sodium from the recipe.

Once you get the hang of adapting recipes, you'll see that there's always room for your own brand of creativity. Ultimately, you'll have the best of all worlds: great food, wonderful taste and a low-fat diet.

SUBSTITUTION LIST

WHEN YOUR OWN RECIPE CALLS FOR:	USE:
Whole milk (1 cup)	1 cup of skim or nonfat milk plus 1 tablespoon of unsaturated oil.
Heavy cream (1 cup)	1 cup evaporated skim milk or ½ cup low-fat yogurt and ½ cup low-fat cottage cheese.
Sour cream	Low-fat cottage cheese plus low-fat yogurt for flavor; ricotta cheese made from partially skimmed milk (thinned with low-fat yogurt or low-fat buttermilk, if desired); 1 can of chilled evaporated skim milk whipped with 1 teaspoon of lemon juice; or low-fat buttermilk or low-fat yogurt.
Cream cheese	4 tablespoons of acceptable margarine blended with 1 cup dry low-fat cottage cheese. Add a small amount of skim milk if needed in blending the mixture. Add chopped chives or pimiento and herbs and seasonings for variety.
Butter (1 tablespoon)	1 tablespoon polyunsaturated margarine or ¾ tablespoon polyunsaturated oil.
Shortening (1 cup)	2 sticks polyunsaturated margarine.
Oil (1 cup)	1¼ cups polyunsaturated margarine.
Eggs (1 egg)	1 egg white plus 2 teaspoons of unsaturated oil or commercially produced cholesterol-free egg substitute according to package directions. 3 egg whites for 2 whole eggs; 2 egg whites for 1 whole egg in baking recipes.
Unsweetened baking chocolate (1 ounce)	3 tablespoons unsweetened cocoa powder or carob powder plus 1 tablespoon of polyunsaturated oil or margarine. (Carob is sweeter than cocoa, so also reduce sugar in the recipe by one-fourth.)

How to Use These Recipes

The recipes in this book are based on the idea of eating for a healthy heart. The book was designed for all healthy Americans over the age of two. Although it is not addressed specifically to people on a strict sodium or fat-restricted diet, many of the recipes are low enough in sodium and fat to fit into such diets.

Each recipe in this cookbook has been analyzed by computer for various nutrients. Read the nutrient analysis for each recipe to determine whether or not it fits into your eating plan. You'll find a fairly large variation in the amount of each nutrient from one recipe to another, so if you're on a restrictive diet, choose recipes carefully.

For example, if you're on a low-sodium diet, choose recipes with less sodium more often. If you're trying to lose weight, select foods lower in calories. If you're on a cholesterol-lowering diet, zero in on dishes lower in total fat, saturated fat and cholesterol.

Each analysis includes all of the ingredients listed in the recipe, but does not include optional ingredients or foods suggested as accompaniments. There are a few exceptions, however. Some garnishes listed in specific recipes may or may not be consumed, such as parsley sprigs or lemon wedges. These are not included in the analysis. Recipes in our section on garnishes are designed to be consumed, so they are analyzed. Also not included in the analysis are ingredients listed as optional or any unconsumed ingredients, such as the purple cabbage used to hold the Spinach-Vegetable Dip.

Each analysis is based on a single serving unless otherwise indicated. You'll find calculations for: the number of calories, amount of protein, carbohydrates, cholesterol, sodium, total fat, saturated fatty acids, polyunsaturated fatty acids and monounsaturated fatty acids per serving.

You may notice that the values for saturated, monounsaturated and polyunsaturated fatty acids do not add up precisely to the total fat in the recipe. That's because the total fat includes not only the fatty acids but other fatty substances and glycerol. The values are as accurate as possible.

The caloric value is the number that remains after subtracting the energy cost (measured in calorics) of digestion and metabolism. Since the calories in alcohol evaporate when heated, this reduction is reflected in the calculations. The caloric values are based on the Atwater system for determining energy values.

You may not be familiar with all the ingredients used in these recipes. Most of them, however, are readily available in local grocery stores. For example, we use a dried herb mix called bouquet garni. If you have never used that, don't hesitate to try it. You may enjoy adding a new flavor to your spice collection.

When the recipe calls for acceptable vegetable oil, we used corn oil for the analysis. You may, of course, use corn, safflower or sunflower oil because they contain polyunsaturated fat. When the recipe calls for olive or peanut oil, the calculation is based on those oils. When selecting an acceptable margarine, remember to choose one that contains no more than 2 grams of saturated fat per tablespoon. We used corn oil margarine for the analysis.

If a meat marinade is used, we calculated only the amount of marinade absorbed by the meat, based on U.S.D.A. data on absorption. However, no such data exists on marinated vegetables, so we calculated the total amount of the marinade in our analysis. Other liquids used in recipes, for basting, dipping, etc., are included in their entirety in the analyses.

Because many people today are watching their sodium intake, we tried to keep the sodium values low in most of these recipes. For instance, we use salt sparingly. When a canned or frozen food product is used, we usually use a low-sodium variety if it is readily available. If you are not accustomed to less salty food, you may wish to add a little salt to the recipe until your tastebuds adjust to the change. A small amount of added salt will not raise the sodium level as much as using a prepared food product with added salt. In fact, we sometimes list a small amount of salt as an ingredient. The amount listed, however, is much less than is contained in the regular salted variety of that canned or frozen food product.

Serving sizes vary somewhat. When we say a soup serves 6 at ¾ cup per serving, for example, that is approximate. In some cases, it is not possible to indicate a serving size. Where ingredients vary greatly, simply assume that all are divided equally among the number of servings.

When no quantity is listed for an ingredient in a recipe, none of that ingredient was figured into the analysis. For example, oil placed in a bowl before dough rises is there just to keep the dough from sticking, so we don't list a quantity for it in our bread recipes and don't include it in the analysis. Similarly, we don't list a quantity for margarine used to brush on top of a loaf of bread, and it is not included in the analysis.

The specific ingredients listed in each recipe were used in its analysis. For instance, we used both nonfat and low-fat yogurt in this collection of recipes, depending on the taste and texture desired. In each case, the listed type of yogurt was used for the nutrient analysis of that recipe. If you, however, prefer one variety over another, just make a substitution. Remember that the fat values will change with such substitutions, depending on the amount of yogurt used.

Also, if you wish to substitute reconstituted lemon juice for fresh, go ahead. If a recipe calls for yellow onions and red wine vinegar, you may substitute white onions and apple cider vinegar. The ingredient analysis will not change much by these substitutions. Just use your own judgment about flavor.

When ingredient options appear in a recipe, we used the first one for the analysis. That doesn't mean we recommend one over the other. Use whichever you like best.

RECIPES

Appetizers, **S**preads and **S**nacks

RAW VEGETABLES
FRUITS
FRUIT KABOBS
BREADS AND CRACKERS
PITA CRISPS
SPINACH PINWHEELS
POOR MAN'S CAVIAR
SPINACH VEGETABLE DIP
ARTICHOKE DIP
CUCUMBER AND YOGURT DIP
CREAMY GARBANZO DIP
CREAM CHEESE
HERBED CHEESE
LIPTAUER CHEESE
CURRY YOGURT DIP
YOGURT CHEESE
MOCK BOURSIN CHEESE SPREAD
AB-DUQ KHIAR
APRICOT FRUIT DIP
LEMON PEPPER MUSHROOMS
MARINATED MUSHROOMS
SWEDISH MEATBALLS
MEATBALLS IN BEER SAUCE
MINIATURE MEATBALLS
TERIYAKI CANAPES
NIBBLES
NUTS
KNAPSACK SPECIAL
SPICED NUTS
CINNAMON NUTS
CHRISTMAS TREE RELISH TRAY

Will Rogers once said, "You never get a second chance to make a first impression." Making a great first impression is the object in presenting a great appetizer.

Avoiding the kind of appetizer that's dripping in fat or packed with fatty meats is another challenge. Fortunately, there are many savory low-fat alternatives.

On these pages you'll learn to create impressive, delectable appetizers that are easy on your pocketbook as well as your heart: colorful raw vegetable trays, Creamy Garbanzo Dip, Spiced Nuts, Marinated Mushrooms, Swedish Meatballs, Herbed Cheese with homemade breads and crackers, and an array of fruit dips, snacks and kabobs—all low in fat and high in taste.

Most appetizers make great snacks, too. Try our Pita Crisps instead of ordinary snack chips. Kids dive right into our Nibbles and Knapsack Special for after-school snacks.

The appetizer course is a great place to try new textures, seasonings, flavors and colors. Consider presenting a light appetizer before a heavy meal and a hearty appetizer before a light meal.

Raw Vegetables

Fresh raw vegetables make excellent low-calorie appetizers. Here are some suggestions. For an attractive appetizer, select several of the vegetables suggested. Include a variety of shapes and colors and place them in a pattern on a platter.

Serve with a bowl of dip in the center of the platter or next to it. Try our Creamy Garbanzo Dip or Spinach Vegetable Dip (see pages 65 and 63).

asparagus spears	green onions
broccoli florets	jicama
carrot strips	kohlrabi wedges
cauliflower florets	mushrooms
celery sticks	radish roses
cherry tomatoes	rutabaga wedges
cucumber slices	snow peas/pea pods
green beans	turnip wedges
green bell pepper strips	zucchini

Fruits

A tray of fresh fruits makes a refreshing appetizer. Here are some suggestions.

Select your favorite fruits and arrange them on a platter. Cut larger fruits into wedges or bite-size pieces. The amounts below are suggestions only—adjust them to suit your taste.

Serve with a bowl of cheese dip or other fruit dressing. Try Cream Cheese or Apricot Fruit Dip (see pages 66 and 71).

pineapple—½ cup	apple—1 small
strawberries—1 cup	winter pear—½ small
grapes—12	melon—½ small cantaloupe
prunes—2 medium	kumquats—4 small

*F*ruit *K*abobs

Combine several kinds of fresh melon balls (cantaloupe, honey-dew, Persian) in a marinade of dry white wine or fresh lemon juice. Cover and chill in refrigerator for a few hours.

Remove from marinade and arrange on tiny skewers, alternating types of melon on each skewer. Serve garnished with fresh mint.

*B*reads and *C*rackers

A wide selection of cholesterol-free, low-saturated-fat and low-sodium breads and crackers are available for snacks; here are a few suggestions. The breads make crunchy toasty bits. For an appetizer, serve any of these with a low-fat spread or dip. Try them with our Poor Man's Caviar, Liptauer Cheese or Creamy Garbanzo Dip (see pages 62, 67 and 65).

rye cracker—**60 calories**
melba toast—**15 calories**
*Southern Raised Biscuits—**61 calories**
*Whole-Wheat Pita Bread—⅙ of 1 pita round—**35 calories**
matzo—6-inch diameter piece—**78 calories**
wheat cracker—**9 calories**
whole-wheat wafer—**7 calories**

* Recipes included in this book (see pages 493 and 460).

*P*ita *C*risps

Serves 18; 2 wedges per serving

3 large whole-wheat pita bread rounds
¼ cup acceptable margarine, melted
¼ cup minced fresh parsley
¾ teaspoon crushed, dried sweet basil
2 green onions, finely chopped
3 tablespoons grated Parmesan cheese

Preheat oven to 350° F.

Separate each pita bread into 2 round single layers. Set aside.

In a small bowl, combine margarine, parsley, sweet basil and green onions. Mix well.

Brush mixture evenly over the 6 rounds of bread.

Sprinkle cheese evenly over open pita rounds. Cut each into 6 wedges. Bake on ungreased cookie sheet 12 minutes or until crisp. Serve warm.

Store any leftovers in an airtight container.

Serve these bread wedges with salads or soups.

Nutrient Analysis

Calories	67 kcal	Cholesterol	1 mg	Saturated Fat	1 gm
Protein	2 gm	Sodium	126 mg	Polyunsaturated Fat	1 gm
Carbohydrate	8 gm	Total Fat	3 gm	Monounsaturated Fat	1 gm

*S*pinach *P*inwheels

Serves 24; 1 pinwheel per serving

Vegetable oil spray
1 tablespoon acceptable margarine
½ cup finely chopped onion
1 10-ounce package frozen no-salt-added chopped
    spinach, defrosted
½ cup part-skim ricotta cheese
1 tablespoon fresh lemon juice
Dash nutmeg
Dash cayenne pepper
1 10-ounce package refrigerated pizza dough
1 egg white, slightly beaten
1 tablespoon sesame seeds

*P*reheat oven to 425° F. Lightly spray a baking sheet with vegetable oil.

Heat margarine in a small nonstick skillet over medium-high heat. Add onion and sauté until translucent. Remove from heat and set aside.

In a small bowl, combine onion, spinach, cheese, lemon juice, nutmeg and cayenne. Blend well. Set aside.

Press dough into a 12-x-14-inch rectangle. Cut in half, forming 2 7-x-12-inch rectangles. With a rubber spatula, spread half of spinach mixture on each piece of dough. Roll up, starting from the 12-inch side. Pinch each end of rolled dough. Cover and refrigerate 30 minutes.

With a sharp knife, cut each roll into 12 slices. Lay pieces on prepared baking sheet. Brush each piece with egg white and sprinkle ⅛ teaspoon sesame seeds on each. Bake 15 to 18 minutes.

Nutrient Analysis

Calories	45 kcal	Cholesterol	2 mg	Saturated Fat	0 gm
Protein	2 gm	Sodium	78 mg	Polyunsaturated Fat	0 gm
Carbohydrate	6 gm	Total Fat	1 gm	Monounsaturated Fat	0 gm

Poor Man's Caviar

Makes 2½ cups
Serves 20; 2 tablespoons per serving

1 large eggplant
1 tablespoon olive oil
1 small onion, finely chopped
1 clove garlic, minced
1 tablespoon olive oil
¼ cup finely chopped green bell pepper
1½ tablespoons fresh lemon juice
Coarsely ground black pepper to taste

GARNISH
Chopped fresh parsley

Preheat broiler.

Slice eggplant in half and rub inside with 1 tablespoon olive oil. Place halves, cut side down, on baking pan.

Broil on middle rack of oven 20 to 25 minutes, or until eggplant is quite soft. Cool slightly.

Scoop out the pulp and place it in a bowl. Mash well with fork. Set aside.

In a small nonstick skillet over medium-high heat, sauté onion and garlic in 1 tablespoon olive oil until brown. Add to eggplant pulp. Add remaining ingredients except parsley and stir to mix well.

Cover and refrigerate 2 to 3 hours. Sprinkle with chopped parsley before serving.

Serve with bread rounds or toast.

Nutrient Analysis

Calories	18 kcal	Cholesterol	0 mg	Saturated Fat	0 gm
Protein	0 gm	Sodium	1 mg	Polyunsaturated Fat	0 gm
Carbohydrate	2 gm	Total Fat	1 gm	Monounsaturated Fat	1 gm

*S*pinach *V*egetable *D*ip

Makes 1½ cups
Serves 24; 1 tablespoon per serving

1 10-ounce package frozen no-salt-added chopped spinach
5 green onions with tops, coarsely chopped
½ cup watercress, large stems removed
¼ cup fresh parsley, large stems removed
8 ounces plain nonfat yogurt
1 avocado, peeled and chopped
1¼ teaspoons no-salt garlic seasoning
⅛ teaspoon salt (optional)
⅛ teaspoon freshly ground black pepper
⅛ teaspoon hot pepper sauce, or to taste
1 purple cabbage

Cook spinach, drain and wring out all juice in a clean kitchen towel.

In the work bowl of a food processor fitted with a metal blade, finely chop spinach, onion, watercress and parsley, or chop with a knife and transfer to a blender. Process just until blended. Do not overprocess! Remove to colander to drain excess liquid. Set aside.

Place remaining ingredients except cabbage in processor or blender and process until smooth.

In a bowl, combine vegetables and yogurt mixture. Mix to blend well. Cover and refrigerate at least 2 hours to allow flavors to blend.

Hollow out purple cabbage to use as serving bowl.

Serve with a variety of fresh vegetables.

Nutrient Analysis

Calories	23 kcal	Cholesterol	0 mg	Saturated Fat		0 gm
Protein	1 gm	Sodium	16 mg	Polyunsaturated Fat		0 gm
Carbohydrate	2 gm	Total Fat	1 gm	Monounsaturated Fat		1 gm

*A*rtichoke *D*ip

Makes 1³⁄₄ cups
Serves 28; 1 tablespoon per serving

> 1 9-ounce package frozen artichoke hearts, defrosted
> 4 ounces Cream Cheese (see page 66), room temperature
> ½ cup plain low-fat yogurt
> 1 teaspoon Italian herb seasoning
> ⅛ teaspoon garlic powder
> ¼ cup thinly sliced green onion tops
> 1½ teaspoons cream sherry
> ⅛ teaspoon salt

Blot artichokes dry on paper towels. Chop into small pieces and set aside.

In a small bowl, combine remaining ingredients and blend well. Stir in artichoke hearts.

Cover and refrigerate several hours to allow flavors to blend.

Nutrient Analysis

Calories	12 kcal	Cholesterol	0 mg	Saturated Fat	0 gm
Protein	1 gm	Sodium	22 mg	Polyunsaturated Fat	0 gm
Carbohydrate	1 gm	Total Fat	0 gm	Monounsaturated Fat	0 gm

*C*ucumber and *Y*ogurt *D*ip

Makes 1¹⁄₃ cups
Serves 22; 1 tablespoon per serving

> ½ cup coarsely chopped green onion
> 2 medium cloves garlic
> 1 cup unpeeled, seeded and diced cucumber
> ⅓ cup light, reduced-calorie mayonnaise
> ½ cup plain low-fat yogurt
> 1 teaspoon white wine Worcestershire sauce
> ¼ cup grated Parmesan cheese

*F*inely chop green onion and garlic in a blender or the work bowl of a food processor fitted with a metal blade using pulse motion. Add cucumber and repeat. Transfer chopped vegetables to a bowl. Stir in remaining ingredients. Cover and refrigerate for several hours to allow flavors to blend.

Note: This dish is a delicious dip and an excellent sauce for chilled salmon that has been poached or grilled.

Nutrient Analysis

Calories	20 kcal	Cholesterol	2 mg	Saturated Fat	0 gm
Protein	1 gm	Sodium	45 mg	Polyunsaturated Fat	0 gm
Carbohydrate	1 gm	Total Fat	1 gm	Monounsaturated Fat	1 gm

*C*reamy *G*arbanzo *D*ip

Makes 2 cups
Serves 32; 1 tablespoon per serving

> 1 20-ounce can no-salt-added garbanzo beans, drained and rinsed
> 1 tablespoon olive oil
> ½ cup low-fat cottage cheese
> ⅓ cup fresh lemon juice
> 3 tablespoons skim milk
> 2 medium cloves garlic, minced
> ⅛ teaspoon salt
> Dash hot pepper sauce
> 1 tablespoon sesame seeds, toasted
> 1 tablespoon finely chopped fresh parsley

*C*ombine all ingredients except parsley in a blender or the work bowl of a food processor fitted with a metal blade. Process until smooth. Pour into a small bowl and sprinkle with parsley. Use immediately or cover and refrigerate for later use.

Nutrient Analysis

Calories	39 kcal	Cholesterol	0 mg	Saturated Fat	0 gm
Protein	2 gm	Sodium	25 mg	Polyunsaturated Fat	0 gm
Carbohydrate	5 gm	Total Fat	1 gm	Monounsaturated Fat	0 gm

Cream Cheese

Makes 1 cup
Serves 16; 1 tablespoon per serving

1 cup dry-curd low-fat cottage cheese
1 tablespoon acceptable margarine
2 teaspoons skim milk, if necessary

Process cheese and margarine in blender or the work bowl of a food processor fitted with a metal blade until smooth. If using blender, add skim milk as necessary for desired consistency.

Nutrient Analysis

Calories	14 kcal	Cholesterol	1 mg	Saturated Fat	0 gm
Protein	2 gm	Sodium	10 mg	Polyunsaturated Fat	0 gm
Carbohydrate	0 gm	Total Fat	1 gm	Monounsaturated Fat	0 gm

Herbed Cheese

Makes 1 cup
Serves 16; 1 tablespoon per serving

1 recipe Cream Cheese (see above)
½ teaspoon freshly ground black pepper
2 sprigs fresh parsley, chopped
¼ teaspoon thyme
¼ teaspoon chervil
1 clove garlic, mashed

Process all ingredients in a blender or the work bowl of a food processor fitted with a metal blade for 10 seconds. Transfer to a glass bowl, cover and refrigerate to allow flavors to blend.

Serve with fresh vegetables or cholesterol-free, low-saturated-fat and low-sodium crackers.

Nutrient Analysis

Calories	15 kcal	Cholesterol	1 mg	Saturated Fat	0 gm
Protein	2 gm	Sodium	10 mg	Polyunsaturated Fat	0 gm
Carbohydrate	0 gm	Total Fat	1 gm	Monounsaturated Fat	0 gm

Liptauer Cheese

Makes ¾ cup
Serves 12; 1 tablespoon per serving

> 1 recipe Cream Cheese (see page 66)
> 1 tablespoon capers, rinsed well
> ½ teaspoon Dijon mustard
> 1 tablespoon snipped fresh chives
> ⅛ teaspoon garlic powder
> Dash cayenne pepper

Process all ingredients in a blender or the work bowl of a food processor fitted with a metal blade for 10 seconds. Transfer to a glass bowl, cover and refrigerate to allow flavors to blend.

Serve with fresh vegetables or cholesterol-free, low-saturated-fat and low-sodium crackers.

LIPTAUER CHEESE WITH ANCHOVY PASTE
Add ¼ teaspoon anchovy paste to above mixture before processing.

Liptauer Cheese Nutrient Analysis

Calories	20 kcal	Cholesterol	1 mg	Saturated Fat		0 gm
Protein	2 gm	Sodium	17 mg	Polyunsaturated Fat		0 gm
Carbohydrate	0 gm	Total Fat	1 gm	Monounsaturated Fat		0 gm

Liptauer Cheese with Anchovy Paste Nutrient Analysis

Calories	20 kcal	Cholesterol	1 mg	Saturated Fat		0 gm
Protein	2 gm	Sodium	20 mg	Polyunsaturated Fat		0 gm
Carbohydrate	0 gm	Total Fat	1 gm	Monounsaturated Fat		0 gm

Curry Yogurt Dip

Makes ¾ cup
Serves 12; 1 tablespoon per serving

1 cup plain low-fat yogurt
3 tablespoons light, reduced-calorie mayonnaise
2 teaspoons curry powder

Place a double-thick layer of fine-mesh cotton cheesecloth or paper coffee filters inside a colander that does not rust. Place colander in a bowl. (Colander must not touch bottom of bowl.) Pour yogurt into colander. Cover and refrigerate for 8 hours or overnight. Discard drained liquid and place yogurt in a small bowl. Add other ingredients and mix well. Cover and refrigerate until needed.

Use as a vegetable dip.

Nutrient Analysis

Calories	25 kcal	Cholesterol	2 mg	Saturated Fat	0 gm
Protein	1 gm	Sodium	36 mg	Polyunsaturated Fat	0 gm
Carbohydrate	2 gm	Total Fat	1 gm	Monounsaturated Fat	1 gm

Yogurt Cheese

Makes 1 cup

1 16-ounce container plain nonfat yogurt

Place a double-thick layer of fine-mesh cotton cheesecloth or paper coffee filters inside a colander that does not rust. Place colander in a deep bowl. (Colander must not touch bottom of bowl.) Pour yogurt into colander and cover with plastic wrap. Refrigerate for 8 hours or overnight. Discard drained liquid and place yogurt in a small bowl. Cover and refrigerate.

Nutrient Analysis *

Calories	274 kcal	Cholesterol	10 mg	Saturated Fat	1 gm
Protein	28 gm	Sodium	372 mg	Polyunsaturated Fat	0 gm
Carbohydrate	38 gm	Total Fat	1 gm	Monounsaturated Fat	0 gm

* for entire recipe

Mock Boursin Cheese Spread

Makes 1 cup
Serves 16; 1 tablespoon per serving

¾ cup Yogurt Cheese (see page 68)
¼ cup light sour cream
½ teaspoon crushed, dried sweet basil
¼ teaspoon crushed, dried rosemary
¼ teaspoon crushed thyme leaves
¼ teaspoon crushed tarragon leaves
¼ teaspoon sage
½ small clove garlic, crushed, or ⅛ teaspoon garlic powder
2 teaspoons minced fresh parsley
¼ teaspoon sugar
1 teaspoon cracked black pepper or blend of peppers, or
    amount to taste

*I*n a small bowl, combine Yogurt Cheese and sour cream and blend well. Add basil, rosemary, thyme, tarragon, sage, garlic, parsley and sugar. Blend well.

Pour into a serving dish. Sprinkle generously with pepper, cover and refrigerate. Allow flavors to blend 8 to 10 hours or overnight.

Serve with celery sticks, sliced squash, sliced cucumbers or cholesterol-free, low-saturated-fat and low-sodium whole-wheat crackers.

Nutrient Analysis

Calories	19 kcal	Cholesterol	1 mg	Saturated Fat	0 gm
Protein	2 gm	Sodium	21 mg	Polyunsaturated Fat	0 gm
Carbohydrate	3 gm	Total Fat	0 gm	Monounsaturated Fat	0 gm

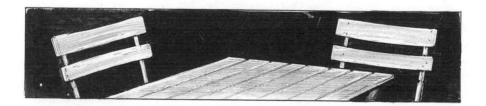

*A*b-*D*uq *K*hiar

(Dip for Fresh Vegetables or Crackers)

Makes 1³/₄ cups
Serves 28; 1 tablespoon per serving

2 cups plain low-fat yogurt
¼ cup unsalted dry-roasted walnuts
¼ cup raisins
½ cup peeled, seeded and diced cucumber
1 tablespoon finely chopped green onion
½ teaspoon summer savory
½ teaspoon basil
⅛ teaspoon salt

GARNISH
Fresh mint leaves (optional)

Place a double-thick layer of fine-mesh cotton cheesecloth or paper coffee filters inside a colander that does not rust. Place colander in a deep bowl. (Colander must not touch bottom of bowl.) Pour yogurt into colander and cover with plastic wrap. Refrigerate 8 hours or overnight. Discard drained liquid and place yogurt in a small bowl.

Coarsely chop walnuts and raisins in the work bowl of a food processor fitted with a metal blade. (They may be chopped by hand.)

Add chopped walnuts and raisins to drained yogurt. Add remaining ingredients and mix well. Cover and refrigerate several hours to allow flavors to blend.

Garnish with fresh mint leaves if desired.

Nutrient Analysis

Calories	21 kcal	Cholesterol	1 mg	Saturated Fat	0 gm
Protein	1 gm	Sodium	22 mg	Polyunsaturated Fat	0 gm
Carbohydrate	3 gm	Total Fat	1 gm	Monounsaturated Fat	0 gm

Apricot Fruit Dip

Makes 2 cups
Serves 16; 2 tablespoons per serving

> ½ cup finely chopped dried apricots
> 1 cup fresh orange juice
> 4 ounces natural (no sugar added) applesauce
> ¼ teaspoon ground cinnamon
> 2 dashes ground nutmeg
> 1 8-ounce carton low-fat vanilla yogurt

In a small nonaluminum saucepan over medium-high heat, combine apricots and orange juice. Bring to a boil, then reduce heat to low, stirring frequently. As apricots become tender, mash them with back of wooden spoon. Cook about 20 minutes, or until all juice is absorbed. Remove from heat and stir well.

Add applesauce and spices. Mix well. Place in a bowl, cover and cool. Add yogurt and refrigerate several hours, covered.

Serve as a dip with a variety of fresh fruits such as strawberries, bananas and apple slices.

Note: This is also a great sauce to serve over angel food cake.

Nutrient Analysis

Calories	28 kcal	Cholesterol	1 mg	Saturated Fat	0 gm
Protein	1 gm	Sodium	9 mg	Polyunsaturated Fat	0 gm
Carbohydrate	6 gm	Total Fat	0 gm	Monounsaturated Fat	0 gm

Lemon Pepper Mushrooms

Serves 8; 1 mushroom per serving

Vegetable oil spray
8 large fresh mushrooms
1 tablespoon chopped chives
2 tablespoons fresh lemon juice
1 tablespoon light, reduced-calorie mayonnaise
1 tablespoon acceptable vegetable oil
1½ teaspoons lemon-pepper seasoning

Preheat oven to 400° F. Lightly spray a shallow baking pan with vegetable oil.

Wipe mushrooms with a clean, damp cloth. Remove stems and set mushroom caps aside. Discard lower half of stems and chop upper half of stems very finely. In a small bowl, combine chopped stems with remaining ingredients. Mix well.

Stuff mushroom caps with mixture. Place stuffed mushrooms in prepared pan and bake 8 to 10 minutes. Serve immediately.

Nutrient Analysis

Calories	26 kcal	Cholesterol	1 mg	Saturated Fat	0 gm
Protein	0 gm	Sodium	12 mg	Polyunsaturated Fat	1 gm
Carbohydrate	1 gm	Total Fat	2 gm	Monounsaturated Fat	1 gm

Marinated Mushrooms

Serves 8; approximately 3 mushrooms per serving

1 8-ounce package fresh mushrooms
1 medium clove garlic, minced
2 tablespoons finely chopped green onion
2 tablespoons finely chopped fresh basil
⅓ cup olive oil
2 teaspoons seeded and minced fresh jalapeño pepper*
⅓ cup fresh lemon juice
3 small strips lemon rind, yellow portion only
2 tablespoons dry white wine
¼ cup plain low-fat yogurt

Wipe mushrooms with clean, damp cloth; cut into quarters. Set aside.

Combine remaining ingredients in a shallow bowl and mix well. Toss mushrooms in mixture to coat evenly.

Cover and refrigerate, stirring occasionally, for several hours or overnight. Remove mushrooms from marinade. Discard marinade and serve mushrooms cold.

* Wear rubber gloves when handling hot peppers, or wash hands thoroughly after handling. Skin, especially around the eyes, is very sensitive to oil from peppers.

Nutrient Analysis

Calories	98 kcal	Cholesterol	0 mg	Saturated Fat	1 gm
Protein	1 gm	Sodium	18 mg	Polyunsaturated Fat	1 gm
Carbohydrate	3 gm	Total Fat	9 gm	Monounsaturated Fat	7 gm

Swedish Meatballs

Serves 24 as an appetizer; 2 meatballs per serving
Serves 16 as an entree; 3 meatballs per serving

Vegetable oil spray
1 egg
½ cup low-fat cottage cheese
½ cup skim milk
3¼ teaspoons allspice
¾ teaspoon nutmeg
Pinch ground cloves
½ teaspoon salt
¾ teaspoon white pepper
2 slices (2 ounces) caraway rye bread
1 cup finely chopped onion
1 pound lean ground pork
1 pound ground veal
1 recipe Fresh Herb Sauce (see page 427)

Preheat oven to 375° F. Lightly spray a large broiler pan with vegetable oil.

In a blender or the work bowl of a food processor fitted with a metal blade, combine egg, cottage cheese, milk and spices. Process until smooth. Add bread and blend until smooth. Pour mixture into large bowl. Add onion and meats. Thoroughly blend with hands. Form meat mixture into balls (use a small ice-cream scoop, if available). Place on prepared pan and bake uncovered 25 minutes.

Heat Fresh Herb Sauce in a small saucepan over medium heat.

Transfer meatballs to a serving bowl. Pour Fresh Herb Sauce over meatballs and serve immediately.

Nutrient Analysis*

Calories	182 kcal	Cholesterol	57 mg	Saturated Fat	4 gm
Protein	15 gm	Sodium	208 mg	Polyunsaturated Fat	1 gm
Carbohydrate	6 gm	Total Fat	11 gm	Monounsaturated Fat	5 gm

* as an entree

Nutrient Analysis*

Calories	121 kcal	Cholesterol	38 mg	Saturated Fat	3 gm
Protein	10 gm	Sodium	138 mg	Polyunsaturated Fat	1 gm
Carbohydrate	4 gm	Total Fat	7 gm	Monounsaturated Fat	3 gm

* as an appetizer

Meatballs in Beer Sauce

Serves 16; 2 meatballs per serving

Vegetable oil spray
2 slices whole-wheat bread, cut into cubes
½ cup (4 ounces) light beer
1 pound lean ground beef
½ cup shredded part-skim mozzarella cheese
½ teaspoon freshly ground black pepper, or to taste
½ cup chopped onion
1 tablespoon acceptable margarine
1 tablespoon flour
2 tablespoons firmly packed brown sugar
2 tablespoons cider vinegar
2 tablespoons homemade Beef Broth (see page 86) or
   commercial low-sodium variety
1 cup (8 ounces) light beer

Preheat oven to 350° F. Lightly spray a cookie sheet with vegetable oil.

Set aside bread cubes and ½ cup of beer in a glass bowl.

In another bowl, combine ground beef, cheese, pepper and beer-soaked bread. Mix well and form into 32 cocktail-size meatballs. Arrange in single layer on prepared cookie sheet and bake 15 minutes.

Meanwhile, in a small skillet over medium-high heat, sauté onions in margarine until tender. Add flour and cook 1 to 2 minutes, stirring constantly. Stir in sugar, vinegar, beef broth and 1 cup of beer. Reduce heat and simmer 10 minutes.

When meatballs are done, drain them on paper towels to remove fat. Add meatballs to sauce and simmer 20 minutes. Serve hot.

Nutrient Analysis

Calories	100 kcal	Cholesterol	18 mg	Saturated Fat	2 gm
Protein	7 gm	Sodium	61 mg	Polyunsaturated Fat	0 gm
Carbohydrate	5 gm	Total Fat	5 gm	Monounsaturated Fat	2 gm

Miniature Meatballs

Serves 6; 7 meatballs per serving

Vegetable oil spray
1 slice wheatberry or whole-wheat bread
1 pound lean ground round
⅓ cup thinly sliced green onions
⅛ teaspoon garlic powder
½ teaspoon ground ginger
1 tablespoon sherry
1 tablespoon light soy sauce
¼ teaspoon freshly ground black pepper

Preheat oven to 450° F. Lightly spray a broiler pan with vegetable oil.

In a blender or the work bowl of a food processor fitted with a metal blade, chop bread into fine crumbs with on-off pulse.

In a bowl, combine bread crumbs and all remaining ingredients. Mix well to distribute spices and flavors evenly. With the large end of a melon baller, scoop out balls of mixture, rounding off top with other hand. Place meatballs on prepared broiler pan and bake 15 minutes. Serve hot.

Nutrient Analysis

Calories	164 kcal	Cholesterol	54 mg	Saturated Fat	3 gm
Protein	17 gm	Sodium	151 mg	Polyunsaturated Fat	0 gm
Carbohydrate	3 gm	Total Fat	9 gm	Monounsaturated Fat	4 gm

*T*eriyaki *C*anapes

Serves 24; ½ ounce per serving

1 pound sirloin steak, all visible fat removed
2 teaspoons ground ginger
1 clove garlic, minced
1 small onion, minced
1 tablespoon sugar
2½ tablespoons sherry
1 tablespoon light soy sauce
⅛ teaspoon hot pepper oil
3 tablespoons water
1 tablespoon red wine

Cut steak into small cubes.

Combine remaining ingredients in a glass bowl. Add steak and stir to coat well. Cover and refrigerate at least 2 hours, or preferably overnight. Drain, reserving marinade.

Preheat broiler.

Arrange steak in a single layer on a broiler pan. Broil 1 inch from heat for 5 minutes on the first side. Turn and broil 3 minutes more.

Meanwhile, place marinade in a small saucepan over medium heat. Cook until boiling.

Remove steak from broiler and spear each cube with a toothpick. Place cubes on a heated serving dish or in a chafing dish. Pour hot marinade over meat. Serve hot.

Nutrient Analysis

Calories	36 kcal	Cholesterol	11 mg	Saturated Fat	1 gm
Protein	4 gm	Sodium	36 mg	Polyunsaturated Fat	0 gm
Carbohydrate	1 gm	Total Fat	1 gm	Monounsaturated Fat	1 gm

Nibbles

Makes approximately 8 cups
Serves 16; ½ cup per serving

5 cups dry cereal (1 type of cereal or a combination such
as oat circles, wheat squares, rice squares and puffed
corn cereals)
2 cups unsalted pretzel sticks, broken in half
⅓ cup acceptable margarine
4 teaspoons Worcestershire sauce
1 teaspoon celery flakes
1 teaspoon onion powder
½ teaspoon garlic powder
1 cup raw peanuts or other unsalted dry-roasted nuts

Preheat oven to 275° F.

In a large bowl, combine dry cereal and pretzel sticks. Set aside.

In a small saucepan over medium-high heat, melt margarine and add Worcestershire sauce and seasonings. Mix well. Add to cereal mixture and toss to mix well. Add peanuts and stir to combine.

Transfer mixture to a shallow roasting pan. Bake 1 hour, stirring every 10 minutes. Serve warm, or cool thoroughly and place in an air-tight container for later use.

Nutrient Analysis

Calories	142 kcal	Cholesterol	0 mg	Saturated Fat	2 gm
Protein	4 gm	Sodium	131 mg	Polyunsaturated Fat	2 gm
Carbohydrate	14 gm	Total Fat	9 gm	Monounsaturated Fat	4 gm

Nuts

¹⁄₄ cup per serving

Unsalted dry-roasted nuts are good sources of protein, and they have no cholesterol. They are, however, high in calories and fats. Most of the fat in nuts is monounsaturated. The exceptions are coconut, brazil nuts and macadamia nuts, which are unacceptably high in saturated fats. The following nuts may be used in cooking or eaten as snacks. Because of the high calorie and fat content, be judicious in their use.

almonds

beechnuts

cashews

chestnuts

filberts or hazelnuts

hickory nuts or butternuts

peanuts

pecans

pine nuts (pignolia)

pistachio nuts

pumpkin seeds

sunflower seeds

walnuts*

* Walnuts are high in polyunsaturated fats.

Almonds Nutrient Analysis

Calories	203 kcal	Cholesterol	0 mg	Saturated Fat	2 gm
Protein	7 gm	Sodium	4 mg	Polyunsaturated Fat	4 gm
Carbohydrate	7 gm	Total Fat	18 gm	Monounsaturated Fat	12 gm

Pecans Nutrient Analysis

Calories	180 kcal	Cholesterol	0 mg	Saturated Fat	1 gm
Protein	2 gm	Sodium	0 mg	Polyunsaturated Fat	5 gm
Carbohydrate	5 gm	Total Fat	18 gm	Monounsaturated Fat	11 gm

Sunflower Seeds Nutrient Analysis

Calories	182 kcal	Cholesterol	0 mg	Saturated Fat	2 gm
Protein	7 gm	Sodium	1 mg	Polyunsaturated Fat	10 gm
Carbohydrate	6 gm	Total Fat	16 gm	Monounsaturated Fat	3 gm

*K*napsack *S*pecial

Makes 5 cups
Serves 10; ¹/₂ cup per serving

> **2 cups sunflower seeds**
> **¹/₂ cup unsalted dry-roasted walnuts**
> **1 cup unsalted dry-roasted soynuts**
> **1 cup unsalted raw peanuts**
> **1 cup raisins**

Combine all ingredients in a bowl with a tight-fitting lid. Mix well.

Nutrient Analysis

Calories	390 kcal	Cholesterol	0 mg	Saturated Fat	3 gm
Protein	17 gm	Sodium	36 mg	Polyunsaturated Fat	15 gm
Carbohydrate	26 gm	Total Fat	27 gm	Monounsaturated Fat	8 gm

*S*piced *N*uts

Makes 2 cups
Serves 8; ¹/₄ cup per serving

> **Vegetable oil spray**
> **¹/₂ cup sugar**
> **¹/₄ cup cornstarch**
> **1¹/₂ teaspoons cinnamon**
> **¹/₂ teaspoon allspice**
> **¹/₂ teaspoon ground ginger**
> **¹/₂ teaspoon nutmeg**
> **1 egg white**
> **2 tablespoons water**
> **2 cups unsalted dry-roasted pecan halves or other unsalted**
> **   dry-roasted nuts**

Preheat oven to 250° F. Lightly spray a cooking sheet with vegetable oil.

Sift dry ingredients together into a small bowl. Set aside.

In another bowl, combine egg white and water and beat slightly.

Dip nuts in egg-white mixture, then lightly roll them in dry ingredients, keeping the nuts separated.

Bake coated nuts on prepared cookie sheet 1½ hours.

Allow nuts to cool on the cookie sheet. When completely cooled, store in a tightly covered container.

Nutrient Analysis *

Calories	249 kcal	Cholesterol	0 mg	Saturated Fat		2 gm
Protein	3 gm	Sodium	7 mg	Polyunsaturated Fat		5 gm
Carbohydrate	22 gm	Total Fat	18 gm	Monounsaturated Fat		11 gm

* using pecans

Cinnamon Nuts

Makes 1½ cups
Serves 6; ¼ cup per serving

> 1 cup sugar
> ½ teaspoon cinnamon
> ⅛ teaspoon cream of tartar
> ¼ cup boiling water
> 1½ cups unsalted dry-roasted pecans or other unsalted dry-roasted nuts

In a saucepan over medium-high heat, combine sugar, cinnamon, cream of tartar and boiling water. Continue boiling until a candy thermometer registers 246° F. Stir in nuts and remove from heat. Continue stirring as mixture cools. Syrup will turn to sugar coating on nuts.

Turn out nuts onto a flat surface covered with wax paper. Separate the nuts and allow to cool. When completely cooled and dry, store in a tightly covered container.

Nutrient Analysis

Calories	304 kcal	Cholesterol	0 mg	Saturated Fat		1 gm
Protein	2 gm	Sodium	5 mg	Polyunsaturated Fat		5 gm
Carbohydrate	37 gm	Total Fat	18 gm	Monounsaturated Fat		11 gm

Christmas Tree Relish Tray

1 Styrofoam cone, about 10 to 12 inches high
Mustard greens, chicory or curly endive
Toothpicks
Cherry tomatoes
Zucchini slices
Cauliflower florets
Carrot sticks
Radish roses

Apply floral clay or a few strips of two-sided tape to the bottom of a Styrofoam cone. Set cone firmly on a tall compote or footed cake stand.

Begin at the base and encircle cone with a layer of greens, attaching them with wire staples or upholstery pins. Add a second layer overlapping the first. Working upward, continue adding layers until entire cone is covered.

Decorate over greens with vegetables speared with toothpicks. Position extra vegetables around the base.

Serve accompanied by dip. Try Artichoke Dip, Curry Yogurt Dip or Ab-Duq Khiar (see pages 64, 68 and 70).

Soups and Stews

BEEF BROTH
CHICKEN BROTH
VEGETABLE BROTH
FLAVORFUL TOMATO BOUILLON
ONION SOUP
FRESH MUSHROOM SOUP
YELLOW SQUASH SOUP
TOMATO CORN SOUP
SPINACH PASTA SOUP
BROCCOLI YOGURT SOUP
CREAMY ASPARAGUS SOUP
CABBAGE SOUP
CUCUMBER WATERCRESS SOUP
FRESH GARDEN SOUP
VEGETABLE SOUP
ITALIAN VEGETABLE SOUP
MINESTRONE
GREEK EGG AND LEMON SOUP
LENTIL SOUP
SPICY GARBANZO SOUP
BLACK BEAN SOUP
LENTIL CHILI SOUP
SPLIT PEA SOUP
GAZPACHO
CHILLED BORSCHT
COLD AVOCADO SOUP
FRUIT SOUP
STEVE'S YOGURT FRUIT SOUP
MEXICAN CHICKEN SOUP
CHICKEN CHILI
BEEF BARLEY SOUP
SAVORY BEEF STEW
VENISON STEW
LAMB STEW
FRENCH STEW
HEARTY FISH CHOWDER
NEW ENGLAND FISH CHOWDER
CIOPPINO
HALIBUT RAGOUT
SURIMI CORN CHOWDER
SHRIMP GUMBO

Who can resist a thick lentil soup reminiscent of childhood winters or a chilled, tart summer gazpacho? Not us! And there's so *much* to enjoy: spicy Shrimp Gumbo; zesty Minestrone; or perhaps Tomato Corn soup shown off in a bright blue bowl.

Of course the best cooks know that really delectable soup starts from a homemade broth. For that, you'll want to sauté the appropriate vegetables in margarine first, then add liquid and browned meat or poultry bones. Simmer for at least half an hour, then strain the broth and use it to make your own soup du jour.

With a savory homemade broth, you can set sail in any culinary direction. Make your own creations by adding your favorite vegetables, cooked rice or noodles, chicken or meats, mushrooms, scallions and beans. Instead of salt, add onion or celery, fresh herbs, lemon juice, sugar, pepper, nutmeg, garlic or hot pepper sauce. Your imagination is your only limit.

Soups are so simple and versatile, you may want to plan an entire meal around an especially pleasing one. If so, consider adding a crisp salad of oriental vegetables, a spicy rice pilaf, and warm rolls or tasty muffins.

Beef Broth

Makes 3½ quarts

Vegetable oil spray
6 pounds beef bones (or beef and veal combination)
4 tablespoons acceptable margarine
2 large carrots, peeled and sliced
2 large leeks, both white and green portions, rinsed and
    sliced
2 stalks celery, sliced
1 large onion (8 ounces), cut into large chunks
5 quarts water
1 tablespoon salt
8 peppercorns

HERB BOUQUET (TIED WITH STRING)
1 bay leaf
3 sprigs thyme
6 to 8 parsley stems

Preheat oven to 400° F. Lightly spray a large baking pan with vegetable oil. Arrange beef bones in pan and brown in oven 40 minutes.

Melt margarine in large stockpot over medium-high heat. Add vegetables and sauté 6 minutes. Cover and cook 15 to 20 minutes over medium-high heat until leeks are limp. Add remaining ingredients, including browned bones. Bring to a boil, reduce heat to simmer, cover and cook 4 to 5 hours.

Strain broth and discard solids. Cool to room temperature. Cover and refrigerate overnight. Remove congealed fat from surface and discard. Pour into containers, cover and freeze. When defrosted, boil again before using.

Nutrient Analysis *

Calories	24 kcal	Cholesterol	0 mg	Saturated Fat	0 gm
Protein	3 gm	Sodium	56 mg	Polyunsaturated Fat	0 gm
Carbohydrate	1 gm	Total Fat	1 gm	Monounsaturated Fat	0 gm

* *for 1 cup*

*C*hicken *B*roth

Makes 4 quarts

Vegetable oil spray
4 pounds chicken bones*
4 tablespoons acceptable margarine
2 medium carrots, peeled and sliced
1 stalk celery, sliced
2 medium leeks, rinsed and sliced
1 large onion, cut into large chunks
2 cups dry white wine
5 quarts water
1 tablespoon salt
8 peppercorns

HERB BOUQUET (TIED WITH STRING)
1 bay leaf
3 sprigs fresh thyme
6 to 8 parsley stems

*P*reheat oven to 400° F. Lightly spray a large baking pan with vegetable oil. Arrange chicken bones in pan and brown in oven 1 hour. If you prefer a lighter-colored broth, brown bones 30 to 40 minutes.

Melt margarine in large stockpot over medium-high heat. Add vegetables and sauté 5 minutes. Cover and cook 10 minutes more. Uncover, add wine and boil until evaporated. Add remaining ingredients, including browned bones. Bring to boil, reduce heat to simmer, cover and cook 5 hours.

Strain broth, through cheesecloth if desired, and discard solids. Cool to room temperature. Cover and refrigerate. Remove congealed fat from surface and discard. Pour into containers, cover and freeze.

When defrosted, boil again before using.

* Raw chicken bones may be frozen for future use in broth. A flavorful broth can be made with a combination of breast bones and skinned chicken drumsticks.

Nutrient Analysis *

Calories	24 kcal	Cholesterol	0 mg	Saturated Fat	0 gm
Protein	3 gm	Sodium	56 mg	Polyunsaturated Fat	0 gm
Carbohydrate	1 gm	Total Fat	1 gm	Monounsaturated Fat	0 gm

* for 1 cup

*V*egetable *B*roth

Serves 7; 1 cup per serving

2 tablespoons acceptable margarine
2 tablespoons water
2 medium onions, coarsely chopped
2 large leeks, white and green parts, coarsely chopped
2 carrots, scrubbed and coarsely chopped
3 stalks celery, including yellow leaves, coarsely chopped
3 large sprigs fresh parsley
3 or 4 sprigs fresh thyme
1 bay leaf
12 peppercorns
9 to 10 cups water

*I*n a heavy stockpot over medium-high heat, melt margarine. Add 2 tablespoons water, onions and leeks. Sauté 4 to 5 minutes.

Add remaining ingredients in order listed. Cover with 9 to 10 cups of water. Simmer 1¼ to 1½ hours, or until reduced to 8 cups.

Strain broth and discard solids. Cool to room temperature. Pour into containers, cover and refrigerate or freeze. Remove congealed fat from the surface, if necessary, and discard.

When defrosted, boil again before using.

VEGETABLE BOUILLON
Simmer until reduced by half. Use when recipe calls for canned bouillon.

Vegetable Broth Nutrient Analysis

Calories	24 kcal	Cholesterol	0 mg	Saturated Fat	0 gm
Protein	3 gm	Sodium	56 mg	Polyunsaturated Fat	0 gm
Carbohydrate	1 gm	Total Fat	1 gm	Monounsaturated Fat	0 gm

Vegetable Bouillon Nutrient Analysis

Calories	48 kcal	Cholesterol	0 mg	Saturated Fat	0 gm
Protein	6 gm	Sodium	112 mg	Polyunsaturated Fat	0 gm
Carbohydrate	2 gm	Total Fat	2 gm	Monounsaturated Fat	0 gm

*F*lavorful *T*omato *B*ouillon

Serves 6; 1 cup per serving

1 46-ounce can no-salt-added tomato juice
2 cups homemade Beef Broth (see page 86) or 1 14½-
    ounce can commercial low-sodium variety
2 bay leaves
6 whole cloves
2 to 3 tablespoons minced fresh dill weed
½ teaspoon dried sweet basil
½ teaspoon dried marjoram
½ teaspoon dried oregano
½ teaspoon sugar
¼ to ½ teaspoon freshly ground black pepper

GARNISH
1 lemon, thinly sliced

Mix tomato juice and beef broth in a large glass bowl or jar. Add remaining ingredients, except garnish, and stir to blend. Cover and chill in refrigerator.

The next day, pour soup into a heavy saucepan and bring to a boil. Reduce heat to simmer and cook 30 minutes. Remove bay leaves and whole cloves.

Ladle soup into soup bowls or mugs and top each with a slice of lemon.

MICROWAVE METHOD
Place all ingredients except lemon in a 3-quart microwave-safe baking dish. Cover and place in microwave. Bring to a boil on high power. Reduce power to low or simmer, and cook 7 to 8 minutes. Let soup rest 5 minutes and then serve hot, topped with a slice of lemon.

Nutrient Analysis

Calories	49 kcal	Cholesterol	0 mg	Saturated Fat	0 gm
Protein	3 gm	Sodium	40 mg	Polyunsaturated Fat	0 gm
Carbohydrate	11 gm	Total Fat	0 gm	Monounsaturated Fat	0 gm

*O*nion *S*oup

Serves 6; 1 cup per serving

2 tablespoons acceptable margarine

3 cups thinly sliced onions

6 cups homemade Beef Broth (see page 86) or commercial
low-sodium variety

½ teaspoon freshly ground black pepper, or to taste

12 (approximately ⅓-ounce each) slices French bread
(baguette), toasted

4 tablespoons grated Parmesan cheese

Preheat oven to 450° F.

Heat margarine in a large saucepan over medium-high heat. Add onions and sauté 2 minutes. Cover and cook until translucent. Stir in broth and pepper; bring to a boil.

Ladle equal portions into 6 ovenproof bowls. Place 2 bread slices in each bowl; top each serving with 2 teaspoons Parmesan cheese. Place bowls in oven and bake 5 minutes. Serve hot.

Nutrient Analysis

Calories	145 kcal	Cholesterol	3 mg	Saturated Fat	2 gm
Protein	6 gm	Sodium	278 mg	Polyunsaturated Fat	1 gm
Carbohydrate	17 gm	Total Fat	6 gm	Monounsaturated Fat	2 gm

Fresh Mushroom Soup

Serves 4; 1 cup per serving

4 cups homemade Chicken Broth (see page 87) or
   commercial low-sodium variety
⅔ cup nonfat dry milk
2 tablespoons acceptable margarine
1 cup chopped onion
2 cloves garlic, minced
4 ounces mushrooms, finely chopped
4 ounces mushrooms, sliced
4 tablespoons flour
1 tablespoon dry sherry
½ teaspoon grated lemon rind
1½ tablespoons finely chopped fresh parsley
2 teaspoons fresh lemon juice

In a small bowl, combine broth and dry milk. Set aside.

Heat margarine in large saucepan over medium heat. Add onion, garlic and both chopped and sliced mushrooms. Cover and cook 8 to 10 minutes. Uncover and adjust temperature to high. Allow moisture to evaporate. Stir in flour.

With a wire whisk, blend chicken broth mixture into mushroom mixture. Bring to a boil. Add sherry, lemon rind, parsley and lemon juice. Stir well. Serve hot.

Nutrient Analysis

Calories	167 kcal	Cholesterol	2 mg	Saturated Fat	2 gm
Protein	9 gm	Sodium	190 mg	Polyunsaturated Fat	2 gm
Carbohydrate	18 gm	Total Fat	7 gm	Monounsaturated Fat	3 gm

Yellow Squash Soup

Serves 5; 1 cup per serving

2 cups chopped onion
2 tablespoons acceptable margarine
2 medium yellow squash, diced (approximately 2 cups)
2 tablespoons uncooked rice
4 cups homemade Chicken Broth (see page 87) or
    commercial low-sodium variety
1 teaspoon thyme
½ cup plain nonfat yogurt
½ cup grated carrots

In a saucepan over medium-high heat, sauté onions in margarine until translucent. Add squash and cook 5 additional minutes. Remove 1 cup of mixture and set aside.

Add rice, broth and thyme to pan. Cook 20 minutes over medium heat, or until rice is soft. Pour into a blender or the work bowl of a food processor fitted with a metal blade. Process until pureed. Return pureed mixture to pan. Add reserved 1 cup of squash mixture, yogurt and carrots. Heat almost to boiling and serve immediately.

Nutrient Analysis

Calories	120 kcal	Cholesterol	0 mg	Saturated Fat	1 gm
Protein	5 gm	Sodium	128 mg	Polyunsaturated Fat	1 gm
Carbohydrate	13 gm	Total Fat	6 gm	Monounsaturated Fat	2 gm

Tomato Corn Soup

Serves 5; 1 cup per serving

1 tablespoon acceptable margarine
½ cup chopped onion
1 14½-ounce can no-salt-added whole tomatoes, crushed
1 17-ounce can no-salt-added cream-style corn
2 cups skim milk
¼ teaspoon salt (optional)
½ teaspoon bouquet garni

*I*n a heavy saucepan over medium-high heat, melt margarine. Add onion and sauté 5 minutes. Add crushed tomatoes. Bring to a boil, reduce heat and simmer 15 minutes. Add corn and stir well. Heat until hot, about 5 minutes.

Process mixture in a blender or the work bowl of a food processor fitted with a metal blade until smooth. Return to pan and add milk, salt and bouquet garni. Heat just to boiling point. Remove from heat and serve hot.

Nutrient Analysis

Calories	154 kcal	Cholesterol	2 mg	Saturated Fat		1 gm
Protein	7 gm	Sodium	94 mg	Polyunsaturated Fat		1 gm
Carbohydrate	29 gm	Total Fat	3 gm	Monounsaturated Fat		1 gm

*S*pinach *P*asta *S*oup

Serves 4; 1 cup per serving

> 4 cups homemade Chicken Broth (see page 87) or
>   commercial low-sodium variety
> ½ cup water
> 5 tablespoons no-salt-added tomato paste
> ¼ cup orzo or pastini* pasta
> ⅓ cup chopped fresh spinach, rinsed, pressed dry, stems
>   removed or ⅓ of 10-ounce package frozen chopped
>   spinach, defrosted
> ¼ cup sliced green onion
> ¼ teaspoon freshly ground black pepper

*I*n a saucepan over medium-high heat, combine chicken broth, water and tomato paste. Whisk until smooth. Bring to a boil. Add pasta, reduce heat to medium and cook 5 to 7 minutes, or until pasta is tender. Stir in spinach and onions and cook 5 additional minutes. Add pepper and serve hot.

* *Tiny pasta for soup*

Nutrient Analysis

Calories	81 kcal	Cholesterol	0 mg	Saturated Fat		0 gm
Protein	5 gm	Sodium	84 mg	Polyunsaturated Fat		0 gm
Carbohydrate	13 gm	Total Fat	1 gm	Monounsaturated Fat		0 gm

Broccoli Yogurt Soup

Serves 6; 1 cup per serving

1½ pounds broccoli
1 cup diced onion
1 tablespoon acceptable margarine
5 cups water, homemade Chicken Broth (see page 87) or
    commercial low-sodium variety
1½ teaspoons curry powder
⅛ teaspoon nutmeg
½ teaspoon freshly ground black pepper, or to taste
2 cups plain nonfat yogurt

Rinse and trim broccoli, cutting off florets with a 1-inch stem. Peel stalk and cut into 1-inch chunks. Set aside.

In a small skillet over medium heat, cook onion in margarine until translucent. Set aside.

In a large saucepan, bring water or chicken broth to a boil. Add broccoli florets and stems. Boil gently 6 to 7 minutes, or just until tender. Add onion mixture and curry. Reduce heat and simmer, partially covered, an additional 10 to 15 minutes.

Remove from heat and puree vegetables and broth 1 cup at a time in a blender or the work bowl of a food processor fitted with a metal blade.

To serve hot, return pureed mixture to saucepan and add nutmeg, pepper and yogurt. Blend well. Heat but do not boil. Serve immediately.

To serve cold, cover and refrigerate puréed mixture. Remove from refrigerator and blend in nutmeg, pepper and yogurt just before serving.

Nutrient Analysis *

Calories	91 kcal	Cholesterol	2 mg	Saturated Fat	1 gm
Protein	7 gm	Sodium	104 mg	Polyunsaturated Fat	1 gm
Carbohydrate	12 gm	Total Fat	2 gm	Monounsaturated Fat	1 gm

* using water

Creamy Asparagus Soup

Serves 4; 1 cup per serving

1 ½ tablespoons acceptable margarine
½ cup chopped onion
½ cup chopped celery
4 cups homemade Chicken Broth (see page 87) or
    commercial low-sodium variety
1 10-ounce package frozen no-salt-added asparagus
    spears, defrosted
¼ cup uncooked rice
Dash ground white pepper
Dash nutmeg

In large saucepan over medium-high heat, melt margarine. Add onion and celery and sauté until onion is translucent. Add chicken broth and bring to a boil.

Trim tips off asparagus and reserve. Cut stalks into 1-inch lengths and add to broth. Stir in rice. Cover, reduce heat and simmer 15 minutes, or until rice is soft.

Transfer mixture to a blender or the work bowl of a food processor fitted with a metal blade and process until completely smooth. Return mixture to pan, add reserved asparagus tips and seasonings and reheat.

Nutrient Analysis

Calories	126 kcal	Cholesterol	0 mg	Saturated Fat	1 gm
Protein	6 gm	Sodium	118 mg	Polyunsaturated Fat	1 gm
Carbohydrate	15 gm	Total Fat	6 gm	Monounsaturated Fat	2 gm

Cabbage Soup

Serves 6; 1 cup per serving

1 medium head cabbage, shredded
2 large onions, thinly sliced
1 large potato, pared and thinly sliced
1 cup water
3 cups skim milk
2 tablespoons plain nonfat yogurt
½ teaspoon dried dill weed
½ teaspoon caraway seeds
½ teaspoon freshly ground black pepper, or to taste
½ teaspoon dried dill weed

*I*n a heavy saucepan over medium-high heat, combine cabbage, onions, potato and water. Bring to a boil, reduce heat, cover and simmer until vegetables are tender. Drain liquid from vegetables and discard.

Place vegetable mixture in a blender or the work bowl of a food processor fitted with a metal blade. Add milk, yogurt, ½ teaspoon dill, caraway and pepper. Process until smooth. Return to pan and cook 15 minutes longer. Serve hot. Sprinkle with dill when soup is served.

Nutrient Analysis

Calories	109 kcal	Cholesterol	3 mg	Saturated Fat	0 gm
Protein	7 gm	Sodium	100 mg	Polyunsaturated Fat	0 gm
Carbohydrate	21 gm	Total Fat	1 gm	Monounsaturated Fat	0 gm

Cucumber Watercress Soup

Serves 6; ¾ cup per serving

1 large cucumber
2 tablespoons acceptable margarine
1 cup finely chopped onion
2 cups watercress leaves, packed (1 large bunch)
2 tablespoons uncooked rice
¼ teaspoon ground white pepper
4 cups homemade Chicken Broth (see page 87) or
    commercial low-sodium variety
1 tablespoon finely chopped fresh dill
¼ cup plain nonfat yogurt

GARNISH
1 ripe Italian plum tomato, thinly sliced

Scrub wax off cucumber; do not peel. Cut into long spears, remove seeds and cut into small pieces. Set aside.

Melt margarine in a large saucepan over medium heat. Add onion and cook until translucent. Add cucumber, watercress, rice, pepper and chicken broth. Stir well. Cook over medium heat 15 minutes, or until rice is soft. Add dill and cook 2 minutes more.

Transfer mixture to a blender or the work bowl of a food processor fitted with a metal blade and process until completely smooth.

To serve hot, return mixture to saucepan and whisk in yogurt. Heat, but do not boil. Serve garnished with tomato slices.

To serve cold, cover and refrigerate pureed mixture. Remove from refrigerator, whisk in yogurt and serve garnished with tomato slices.

MICROWAVE METHOD
Melt margarine in 4-quart microwave-safe baking dish. Cook onion on high 3 to 5 minutes. Add cucumber, watercress, rice, pepper and chicken broth. Cover and cook on high 12 to 14 minutes, or until cucumber and rice are tender. Add dill and cook 2 minutes on medium. Proceed as directed above.

Nutrient Analysis

Calories	87 kcal	Cholesterol	0 mg	Saturated Fat	1 gm
Protein	4 gm	Sodium	112 mg	Polyunsaturated Fat	1 gm
Carbohydrate	8 gm	Total Fat	5 gm	Monounsaturated Fat	2 gm

*F*resh *G*arden *S*oup

Serves 11; 1 cup per serving

2 medium onions, diced
2 cloves garlic, minced
1 cup diced red or green bell pepper
2 tablespoons water
2 pounds carrots, grated
2 medium zucchini or yellow squash, grated
1 10-ounce package frozen no-salt-added green peas,
　　thawed
1 10-ounce package frozen no-salt-added cut corn, or
　　kernels from 3 ears
Juice of ½ lemon
1 teaspoon dried sweet basil
Pinch cayenne pepper
2 stems fresh thyme, leaves removed and crushed
4 cups homemade Chicken Broth (see page 87) or
　　commercial low-sodium variety
1 to 2 teaspoons salt-free all-purpose seasoning
Freshly ground black pepper to taste
8 ounces plain nonfat yogurt
¼ cup minced fresh parsley

*I*n a heavy skillet over medium-high heat, combine onions, garlic, bell pepper and 2 tablespoons water. Cover and steam until vegetables are tender. Add carrots, squash, peas and corn. Cook until carrots are limp. Stir in lemon juice, basil, cayenne, thyme and chicken broth. Bring to a boil.

Remove from heat and add salt-free seasoning and black pepper. Cool. Stir in yogurt. Transfer to a covered container and refrigerate overnight. Pour into individual bowls, sprinkle parsley on top and serve cold.

Serve with bread sticks and sliced fresh fruit or gelatin salad.

Note: Vegetables may be prepared in microwave. Add water to vegetables and steam until tender.

Nutrient Analysis

Calories	109 kcal	Cholesterol	0 mg	Saturated Fat		0 gm
Protein	6 gm	Sodium	105 mg	Polyunsaturated Fat		0 gm
Carbohydrate	22 gm	Total Fat	1 gm	Monounsaturated Fat		0 gm

*V*egetable *S*oup

Serves 9; 1 cup per serving

2 cups peeled, diced potatoes
1 cup diced carrots
1 cup diced celery
1 cup chopped onion
3 cups shredded cabbage
1 6-ounce can no-salt-added tomato paste
1 teaspoon thyme
¼ teaspoon freshly ground black pepper
6 cups homemade Beef Broth (see page 86) or commercial low-sodium variety
⅓ cup finely chopped fresh parsley

Combine all ingredients except parsley in a large stockpot. Bring to boil, reduce heat and simmer 20 minutes, or until vegetables are tender. Remove 3 cups vegetables and broth and puree in a blender or the work bowl of a food processor fitted with a metal blade. Return puree to pot, add parsley and reheat. Serve hot.

Note: You may wish to substitute equal amounts of similar types of vegetables for variety: 1 cup green beans, 1 cup peas, etc.

Nutrient Analysis

Calories	77 kcal	Cholesterol	0 mg	Saturated Fat	0 gm
Protein	4 gm	Sodium	72 mg	Polyunsaturated Fat	0 gm
Carbohydrate	15 gm	Total Fat	1 gm	Monounsaturated Fat	0 gm

Italian Vegetable Soup

Serves 8; 1½ cups per serving

2 tablespoons acceptable margarine
2 large onions, coarsely chopped
1 medium clove garlic, crushed
1½ cups thinly sliced carrots
1½ cups thinly sliced celery
1 medium zucchini, sliced
3½ cups homemade Chicken Broth (see page 87) or
     commercial low-sodium variety
1 16-ounce can Italian plum tomatoes (do not drain)
1 teaspoon dried oregano, crumbled
½ teaspoon dried basil, crumbled
⅛ teaspoon freshly ground black pepper
¼ teaspoon hot pepper sauce, or to taste
¼ to ½ teaspoon salt-free all-purpose seasoning
8 tablespoons freshly grated Parmesan cheese

In a large skillet over medium-high heat, melt margarine and sauté onions, garlic, carrots and celery. Cook about 5 minutes. Add zucchini and sauté 4 to 5 minutes. Add chicken broth and tomatoes. Stir well. Add oregano, basil, pepper, hot pepper sauce and salt-free seasoning. Stir and bring to a boil. Reduce heat, cover and simmer 8 to 12 minutes, or until vegetables are tender-crisp.

Ladle into bowls and top each serving with 1 tablespoon Parmesan cheese.

Serve with a fruit salad and toasted French bread for a complete meal.

Nutrient Analysis

Calories	109 kcal	Cholesterol	5 mg	Saturated Fat	2 gm
Protein	6 gm	Sodium	312 mg	Polyunsaturated Fat	1 gm
Carbohydrate	10 gm	Total Fat	6 gm	Monounsaturated Fat	2 gm

Minestrone

Serves 10; 1 cup per serving

1 cup dried white navy beans
½ cup whole-wheat pasta (shells or elbow macaroni)
2 tablespoons olive oil
1 onion, chopped
2 cloves garlic, chopped
2 medium carrots, chopped
2 stalks celery, chopped
2 potatoes, peeled and cubed
4 tomatoes, cubed
1 small zucchini, cubed
½ pound fresh green beans, sliced
1 teaspoon freshly ground black pepper, or to taste
8 cups water
1 tablespoon dried basil
1 clove garlic, whole
2 tablespoons grated Parmesan cheese

Rinse and soak navy beans according to package instructions. Discard water and add fresh water. Cook according to package instructions, omitting salt. Set aside.

Cook pasta according to package instructions, omitting salt. Drain and set aside.

Heat oil in a large, heavy pan over medium-high heat. Add onion, garlic, carrots and celery. Sauté until onion is translucent.

Add potatoes, tomatoes, zucchini, green beans, pepper and water. Reduce heat and simmer 30 minutes. Add navy beans and pasta. Add more water if soup is too thick.

In a blender or the work bowl of a food processor fitted with a metal blade, process basil, 1 whole clove of garlic and 1 cup of soup from the pot until smooth. Return this mixture to the soup, mix well and serve hot. Top each serving with a sprinkling of Parmesan cheese.

Nutrient Analysis

Calories	143 kcal	Cholesterol	1 mg	Saturated Fat	1 gm
Protein	6 gm	Sodium	48 mg	Polyunsaturated Fat	0 gm
Carbohydrate	24 gm	Total Fat	3 gm	Monounsaturated Fat	2 gm

Greek Egg and Lemon Soup

Serves 4; 1 cup per serving

> 1 quart homemade Chicken Broth (see page 87) or
>   commercial low-sodium variety
> ¼ cup uncooked rice
> 4 tablespoons fresh lemon juice
> Egg substitute equivalent to 3 eggs, room temperature

Place chicken broth in a large stockpot over medium-high heat. Bring to a boil. Add rice, reduce heat and cook until tender. Remove from heat and set aside.

In a bowl, combine lemon juice and egg substitute. Beat well. Whisk half the broth, a little at a time, into egg-substitute mixture. Pour egg-substitute mixture back into remaining broth, mixing well.

Return to low heat and cook, stirring constantly, just until soup is thickened. Be careful not to boil the soup. Serve hot.

Nutrient Analysis

Calories	88 kcal	Cholesterol	0 mg	Saturated Fat	0 gm
Protein	8 gm	Sodium	151 mg	Polyunsaturated Fat	0 gm
Carbohydrate	12 gm	Total Fat	1 gm	Monounsaturated Fat	0 gm

Lentil Soup

Serves 8; 1 cup per serving

> 1 tablespoon acceptable margarine
> 1 onion, chopped
> 2 cloves garlic, finely chopped
> 1 cup lentils
> 7 cups water
> ⅛ teaspoon cinnamon
> ¼ teaspoon ground ginger
> ¼ teaspoon cloves
> ⅛ teaspoon cayenne
> 1½ teaspoons cumin
> Freshly ground black pepper to taste

*I*n a large stockpot, melt margarine. Add onion and garlic and sauté until soft. Add remaining ingredients. Bring to boil, reduce heat and simmer 1½ hours.

Place mixture in a blender or the work bowl of a food processor fitted with a metal blade. Process until well blended. Serve hot.

Nutrient Analysis

Calories	89 kcal	Cholesterol	0 mg	Saturated Fat		0 gm
Protein	5 gm	Sodium	20 mg	Polyunsaturated Fat		0 gm
Carbohydrate	14 gm	Total Fat	2 gm	Monounsaturated Fat		1 gm

Spicy Garbanzo Soup

Serves 4; ¾ cup per serving

3 6-ounce cans no-salt-added tomato juice
3 tablespoons no-salt-added tomato paste
¼ to ½ teaspoon hot pepper sauce, or to taste
1 15-ounce can no-salt-added garbanzo beans, drained
¾ cup cubed cooked chicken or turkey
½ teaspoon crushed, dried oregano
1 avocado, peeled and diced
2 tablespoons minced fresh parsley

*I*n a saucepan over medium-high heat, heat tomato juice, tomato paste and hot pepper sauce, stirring to mix well. Add garbanzos and chicken or turkey and bring to a low boil. Reduce heat immediately, add oregano and simmer 5 minutes. Stir in diced avocado and heat for 2 to 3 minutes.

Serve hot with parsley sprinkled on top.

Serve this soup with a mixed green and fresh fruit salad and Pita Crisps (see page 60).

Note: Because of the high fat content of avocados, balance your fat intake for the rest of the day by eating very low fat foods at other meals.

Nutrient Analysis

Calories	336 kcal	Cholesterol	22 mg	Saturated Fat		2 gm
Protein	20 gm	Sodium	58 mg	Polyunsaturated Fat		3 gm
Carbohydrate	41 gm	Total Fat	12 gm	Monounsaturated Fat		6 gm

Black Bean Soup

Serves 8; 1 cup per serving

> 1 pound dried black beans
> Water
> 1 onion, peeled and stuck with 2 cloves
> 1 bay leaf
> 1 sprig fresh parsley
> 1 medium onion, chopped
> 1 green bell pepper, chopped
> 2 cloves garlic, minced
> 2 tablespoons acceptable vegetable oil
> 1 teaspoon oregano
> 1 teaspoon thyme
> 1 teaspoon white vinegar
> 1 8-ounce can no-salt-added tomato sauce
> ¼ cup dry sherry
>
> **GARNISH**
> Chopped onion, parsley, chives, cucumber, or small orange
>   sections, seeded and peeled

Rinse black beans and place them in a large bowl. Add enough water to cover. Let sit overnight.

Drain water from beans and place them in a large stockpot. Add water to cover and onion, bay leaf and parsley. Bring water to a boil, reduce heat and simmer according to package directions until beans are tender. Add more water if necessary.

In a small skillet over medium-high heat, combine chopped onion, green bell pepper, garlic and oil. Cook until vegetables are soft. Add to cooked beans. Add oregano, thyme, vinegar and tomato sauce. Cook until thickened.

Add sherry and stir. If a smooth soup is desired, puree in a blender or the work bowl of a food processor fitted with a metal blade.

Pour soup into eight serving bowls and top with one of the suggested garnishes sprinkled on top.

Nutrient Analysis

Calories	246 kcal	Cholesterol	0 mg	Saturated Fat	1 gm
Protein	14 gm	Sodium	19 mg	Polyunsaturated Fat	2 gm
Carbohydrate	39 gm	Total Fat	4 gm	Monounsaturated Fat	1 gm

Lentil Chili Soup

Serves 7; 1 cup per serving

1 tablespoon acceptable vegetable oil
1 tablespoon water
3 cloves garlic, minced
2 medium onions, chopped
1 medium green bell pepper, finely chopped
3½ cups homemade Chicken Broth (see page 87) or
   commercial low-sodium variety
1 12-ounce can light beer or water
1¼ cups water
1½ cups dried lentils, rinsed
1 teaspoon salt-free all-purpose seasoning
2½ to 3 tablespoons chili powder
1½ teaspoons ground cumin
¼ teaspoon cayenne pepper
1 teaspoon sugar
1 6-ounce can no-salt-added tomato paste
6 green onions, finely chopped (about ¾ cup)
2 ounces grated low-fat cheddar cheese

Heat oil and water in heavy stockpot over medium-high heat. Add garlic, onions and bell pepper. Sauté 8 to 10 minutes. Add broth, beer, water, lentils, seasonings and tomato paste. Bring to a boil, reduce heat, cover and simmer 1 to 1½ hours, or until lentils are tender. Stir occasionally and add water if necessary.

Spoon into heated bowls and top with green onions and cheese.

Nutrient Analysis

Calories	225 kcal	Cholesterol	2 mg	Saturated Fat	1 gm
Protein	14 gm	Sodium	129 mg	Polyunsaturated Fat	2 gm
Carbohydrate	33 gm	Total Fat	4 gm	Monounsaturated Fat	1 gm

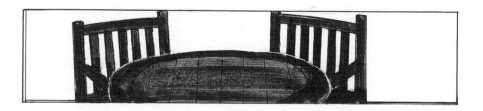

Split Pea Soup

Serves 4; 1 cup per serving

1 tablespoon acceptable margarine
½ cup diced onion
4 cups cold water
1 cup dried split peas
1 carrot, diced
3 stalks celery, diced
1 teaspoon freshly ground black pepper, or to taste
½ teaspoon marjoram
½ teaspoon thyme
½ teaspoon basil
½ teaspoon celery seed
1 bay leaf
½ cup chopped fresh parsley

Rinse and soak split peas according to directions on package.

In a large saucepan over medium-high heat, combine margarine and onion. Cook onion until lightly browned. Add water, peas, carrots, celery and seasonings. Cover, reduce heat and simmer 1 hour, or until peas are tender, stirring occasionally.

Process soup in a blender or the work bowl of a food processor fitted with a metal blade until blended. Sprinkle parsley on top and serve immediately.

Nutrient Analysis

Calories	191 kcal	Cholesterol	0 mg	Saturated Fat	1 gm
Protein	11 gm	Sodium	71 mg	Polyunsaturated Fat	1 gm
Carbohydrate	31 gm	Total Fat	4 gm	Monounsaturated Fat	1 gm

Gazpacho

Serves 7; 1 cup per serving

6 cups peeled and chopped fresh ripe tomatoes or canned
    Italian plum tomatoes
1 onion, coarsely chopped
½ cup coarsely chopped green bell pepper
½ cup coarsely chopped cucumber (cucumber may be
    peeled if outer skin is tough)
2 cups no-salt-added tomato juice
½ teaspoon cumin (optional)
1 clove garlic, minced
Freshly ground black pepper to taste
2 tablespoons olive oil
¼ cup red wine vinegar

GARNISHES
Garlic croutons
1 cup finely chopped tomato
½ cup each finely chopped onion, green bell pepper and
    cucumber

*I*n a blender or the work bowl of a food processor fitted with a metal blade, puree tomatoes, onion, green bell pepper and cucumber. Add tomato juice, cumin, garlic and pepper. Process to blend thoroughly. Pour into a large bowl, cover and refrigerate.

Add oil and vinegar and stir to mix well. Pour into individual serving bowls. Garnish with croutons. Place other garnishes in side dishes for individual use.

Nutrient Analysis*

Calories	85 kcal	Cholesterol	0 mg	Saturated Fat	1 gm
Protein	2 gm	Sodium	20 mg	Polyunsaturated Fat	1 gm
Carbohydrate	12 gm	Total Fat	4 gm	Monounsaturated Fat	3 gm

* using fresh tomatoes

Chilled Borscht

Serves 5; ⅔ cup per serving

>2 cups cooked and diced fresh beets
>2 cups water
>2 tablespoons chopped onion
>2 tablespoons fresh lemon juice
>¾ cup Tangy Sour Cream (see page 418)
>¼ teaspoon salt
>Dash ground white pepper

Process all ingredients in a blender or the work bowl of a food processor fitted with a metal blade until completely smooth.

Cover and refrigerate several hours before serving.

Nutrient Analysis

Calories	58 kcal	Cholesterol	3 mg	Saturated Fat	0 gm
Protein	6 gm	Sodium	298 mg	Polyunsaturated Fat	0 gm
Carbohydrate	6 gm	Total Fat	1 gm	Monounsaturated Fat	0 gm

Cold Avocado Soup

Serves 3; 1 cup per serving

>2½ cups homemade Chicken Broth (see page 87) or
>   commercial low-sodium variety, chilled
>2 ripe avocados, chilled, peeled and diced
>1 teaspoon fresh lemon juice, or to taste
>2 tablespoons sherry, or to taste
>1 teaspoon dried dill weed

Process chicken broth, avocado, lemon juice and sherry in a blender or the work bowl of a food processor fitted with a metal blade until well blended.

Pour into serving cups and sprinkle with dill weed. Serve cold.

Note: Because of the high fat content of avocados, balance your fat intake for the rest of the day by eating very low fat foods at other meals.

Nutrient Analysis

Calories	249 kcal	Cholesterol	0 mg	Saturated Fat	3 gm
Protein	5 gm	Sodium	59 mg	Polyunsaturated Fat	3 gm
Carbohydrate	12 gm	Total Fat	21 gm	Monounsaturated Fat	13 gm

*F*ruit *S*oup

Serves 8; 1 cup per serving

1 cup dried prunes
1 cup small dried apricot halves
2 quarts water
1 cup seedless white or dark raisins
1 stick cinnamon
2 tablespoons cornstarch
¼ cup cold water

In a large saucepan, combine prunes, apricots and water. Let sit 4 hours. (Or follow package directions for soaking.)

Add raisins and cinnamon stick. Bring mixture to a boil over medium-high heat. Reduce heat and simmer, covered, until fruits are tender but still whole. Remove cinnamon stick.

In a small bowl, dissolve cornstarch in cold water. Add to fruit and cook until thickened, stirring constantly.

Serve hot or cover and refrigerate to serve cold.

Nutrient Analysis

Calories	158 kcal	Cholesterol	0 mg	Saturated Fat	0 gm
Protein	2 gm	Sodium	12 mg	Polyunsaturated Fat	0 gm
Carbohydrate	41 gm	Total Fat	0 gm	Monounsaturated Fat	0 gm

*S*teve's *Y*ogurt *F*ruit *S*oup

Serves 4; 1 cup per serving

2 cups plain nonfat yogurt
2 cups fresh peeled peach chunks
1 cup fresh strawberries, hulled
½ cup orange juice
½ cup water
1 tablespoon honey

GARNISH
Mint leaves

*P*lace all ingredients except garnish in a blender or the work bowl of a food processor fitted with a metal blade. Process until well blended.

Pour into a glass bowl, cover and refrigerate for at least 3 hours. Garnish with mint leaves and serve cold.

VARIATION
A wide variety of fruits can be used in place of peaches and strawberries. Try substituting frozen peaches, blueberries or mixed fruit (no sugar added) for fresh peaches (defrost fruit before using), or use 1 or 2 fresh bananas in place of strawberries.

Nutrient Analysis*

Calories	146 kcal	Cholesterol	2 mg	Saturated Fat	0 gm
Protein	8 gm	Sodium	94 mg	Polyunsaturated Fat	0 gm
Carbohydrate	29 gm	Total Fat	0 gm	Monounsaturated Fat	0 gm

* using peaches and strawberries

Nutrient Analysis*

Calories	187 kcal	Cholesterol	2 mg	Saturated Fat	0 gm
Protein	8 gm	Sodium	95 mg	Polyunsaturated Fat	0 gm
Carbohydrate	40 gm	Total Fat	1 gm	Monounsaturated Fat	0 gm

* using mixed fruit and bananas

Mexican Chicken Soup

Serves 8; 1 cup per serving

2 cups dried pinto beans or garbanzos
Water
1 3-pound frying chicken, skinned, all visible fat removed,
cut into serving pieces
2 cups canned no-salt-added tomatoes
1 clove garlic, minced
½ cup chopped onion
⅔ cup canned mildly hot California chili peppers, diced (or
⅓ cup for a milder flavor)
16 corn tortillas

Rinse and soak beans overnight. Drain; add fresh water to beans and cook according to package instructions, omitting salt.

Rinse chicken and pat dry. Place chicken pieces in a large stockpot, adding enough water to cover. Bring to a boil over medium-high heat. Reduce heat. Simmer about 25 minutes, or until chicken is tender.

Remove chicken pieces from broth and remove chicken meat from bones. Return meat to broth along with tomatoes, garlic, onion, chili peppers and beans. Simmer about 15 minutes.

Transfer soup to individual bowls. Serve 2 corn tortillas alongside each.

Nutrient Analysis

Calories	370 kcal	Cholesterol	65 mg	Saturated Fat	2 gm
Protein	34 gm	Sodium	284 mg	Polyunsaturated Fat	2 gm
Carbohydrate	43 gm	Total Fat	7 gm	Monounsaturated Fat	2 gm

*C*hicken *C*hili

Serves 10; 1 cup per serving

6 to 8 parsley stems
1 bay leaf
3 sprigs fresh thyme
11 ounces dried pinto beans
2⅔ cups water
½ teaspoon salt
2½ pounds boneless chicken breast fillets, skinned, all
    visible fat removed
2 tablespoons acceptable margarine
1 cup finely chopped onions
4 cloves garlic, minced
1 cup dry white wine
1 8-ounce package mushrooms, thinly sliced
1½ cups frozen no-salt-added kernel corn
1 cup diced red bell pepper
1 4-ounce can diced green chili peppers
1½ teaspoons ground cumin
½ teaspoon hot pepper sauce, or to taste
1½ teaspoons oregano
½ teaspoon salt
½ cup finely chopped parsley

*T*ie parsley stems, bay leaf and thyme together with string. Set aside.

Rinse and sort beans. Put beans in microwave-safe 1½-quart casserole. Add tied herbs, salt and water. Cover and cook in microwave on high for 30 minutes. Cook on medium for 1 hour, stirring every 30 minutes, adding water if necessary.*

Rinse chicken and pat dry. Cut into 1½-inch cubes. Set aside.

In a large stockpot, melt margarine. Sauté onion until translucent; add garlic and sauté 1 minute. Stir in chicken, wine and mushrooms. Cover and cook over medium heat for 5 minutes.

Stir in half of beans. Mash remaining beans and add to pot. Add corn, bell pepper, chili peppers, cumin, hot pepper sauce, oregano

---

* *If a microwave is not available, soak and cook beans according to package instructions, using amount of water specified on package. Add tied herbs and salt to cooking liquid. Proceed as directed.*

and salt. Simmer 20 minutes to allow flavors to blend. Stir in parsley and serve immediately.

Nutrient Analysis

Calories	294 kcal	Cholesterol	62 mg	Saturated Fat	2 gm
Protein	33 gm	Sodium	442 mg	Polyunsaturated Fat	1 gm
Carbohydrate	28 gm	Total Fat	6 gm	Monounsaturated Fat	2 gm

Beef Barley Soup

Serves 12; 1 cup per serving

Vegetable oil spray
3 pounds center-cut beef shank, all visible fat removed
2 quarts water
1 medium onion, peeled and quartered
1 bay leaf
1 teaspoon salt
Freshly ground black pepper to taste
3 cups peeled and diced potatoes
1 cup thickly sliced celery
1¼ cups peeled and thickly sliced carrots
3 tablespoons uncooked pearled barley
2 teaspoons thyme
1 teaspoon salt

Preheat broiler. Lightly spray a broiler pan with vegetable oil. On prepared pan, broil meat 5 minutes on each side, or until thoroughly browned.

In a large stockpot, combine meat, water, onion, bay leaf, 1 teaspoon salt and pepper. Bring to a boil. Reduce heat to simmer and cook 3 hours, or until meat is tender. Remove meat from pot and set aside. Strain broth and skim off fat. Cut meat into pieces.

Place strained broth, meat and remaining ingredients in stockpot and bring to a boil. Reduce heat and simmer 20 to 25 minutes, or until vegetables are tender. Serve hot.

Nutrient Analysis

Calories	136 kcal	Cholesterol	37 mg	Saturated Fat	1 gm
Protein	15 gm	Sodium	398 mg	Polyunsaturated Fat	0 gm
Carbohydrate	12 gm	Total Fat	3 gm	Monounsaturated Fat	1 gm

Savory Beef Stew

Serves 12; 1 cup per serving

Vegetable oil spray
2½ pounds lean beef stew meat, cut into chunks
2 tablespoons acceptable vegetable oil
1 cup finely chopped onion
1 teaspoon thyme
1 teaspoon marjoram
1 bay leaf, broken in half
5½ cups homemade Beef Broth (see page 86) or
    commercial low-sodium variety
1 pound red potatoes, unpeeled, cut into chunks
2 cups sliced carrots
1 8-ounce package mushrooms, quartered
1 cup diced red bell pepper
½ cup thinly sliced green onion
2 cups homemade Beef Broth (see page 86) or commercial
    low-sodium variety
6 tablespoons cornstarch
¼ cup no-salt-added tomato paste
1 teaspoon thyme
1 teaspoon Italian herb seasoning
½ teaspoon salt
¾ teaspoon freshly ground black pepper

Preheat broiler. Lightly spray a broiler pan with vegetable oil.

Arrange meat in pan. Broil close to heat 15 to 20 minutes, or until meat is brown, turning to brown all sides.

Place oil in a large nonstick stockpot. Add onion and sauté until translucent. Add meat and any pan juices plus 1 teaspoon thyme, marjoram, bay leaf and 5½ cups of the broth. Cover and simmer 1½ hours, or until meat is tender. Stir in potatoes, carrots and mushrooms. Cover and simmer 30 minutes. Add bell pepper and green onion.

In a bowl, combine remaining 2 cups broth, cornstarch, tomato paste, 1 teaspoon thyme, Italian herb seasoning, salt and pepper. Stir to mix well and pour into stew. Increase heat setting to high and bring to boil. Reduce heat, remove bay leaf and serve hot.

Nutrient Analysis

Calories	242 kcal	Cholesterol	47 mg	Saturated Fat	3 gm
Protein	21 gm	Sodium	185 mg	Polyunsaturated Fat	2 gm
Carbohydrate	19 gm	Total Fat	9 gm	Monounsaturated Fat	3 gm

*V*enison *S*tew

Serves 8; 1 cup per serving

Flour seasoned with black pepper
2 pounds breast or shoulder venison, all visible fat removed
2 tablespoons acceptable vegetable oil
2 tablespoons flour
6 cups water, homemade Beef Broth (see page 86) or
   commercial low-sodium variety
½ teaspoon freshly ground black pepper
4 medium potatoes, peeled and diced
4 carrots, peeled and diced
2 turnips, peeled and diced
4 onions, peeled and diced

Place seasoned flour in a shallow bowl. Cut venison into 1-inch cubes. Roll cubes in flour.

Heat oil in a heavy skillet over medium-high heat. Add venison and brown on all sides. Add 2 tablespoons flour and cook 2 minutes, stirring constantly. Add water or beef broth and pepper, stirring constantly. Bring to a boil, cover and simmer 1½ to 2 hours.

Add diced vegetables and cook 30 minutes, or until meat and vegetables are tender.

Serve hot.

Nutrient Analysis *

Calories	279 kcal	Cholesterol	55 mg	Saturated Fat	3 gm
Protein	32 gm	Sodium	117 mg	Polyunsaturated Fat	4 gm
Carbohydrate	19 gm	Total Fat	9 gm	Monounsaturated Fat	2 gm

* *using water*

*L*amb *S*tew

Serves 12; 1 cup per serving

2 tablespoons olive oil
1 ½ cups finely chopped onion
4 large cloves garlic, minced
2 pounds lamb stew meat, cut into cubes
4 cups water
½ cup dry white wine
2 pounds potatoes
5 medium carrots
1 pound fresh mushrooms
1 14½-ounce can diced no-salt-added tomatoes, in juice
1 6-ounce can no-salt-added tomato paste
1 teaspoon salt
1 ½ teaspoons coarsely ground black pepper
2 tablespoons finely chopped fresh rosemary
2 tablespoons finely chopped fresh mint

*H*eat oil in large Dutch oven or stockpot over medium-high heat. Add onion and sauté until translucent. Add garlic and sauté 2 minutes more. Add meat and cook 10 minutes, or until brown. Add water and wine. Cover, reduce heat and simmer 1 hour.

Peel carrots and cut into sticks. Peel potatoes and cut into chunks. Wipe mushrooms with a clean, damp cloth and cut into quarters. Place vegetables and all remaining ingredients except herbs into pot with meat. Cover and cook over medium-low heat 30 minutes, or until vegetables are tender when pierced with a tip of a knife. Add herbs, simmer 2 minutes and serve hot.

Note: You may freeze half of this recipe for another meal; just let it cool, place in a 2-quart container, cover and freeze.

Nutrient Analysis

Calories	220 kcal	Cholesterol	44 mg	Saturated Fat	2 gm
Protein	15 gm	Sodium	259 mg	Polyunsaturated Fat	1 gm
Carbohydrate	23 gm	Total Fat	9 gm	Monounsaturated Fat	4 gm

*F*rench *S*tew

Serves 5; ¾ cup per serving

1 pound venison chunks, well trimmed
2 cloves garlic, crushed
1 large purple onion, sliced into thin rings
1 bay leaf
1 cup burgundy wine
1 slice lower-salt bacon, cut into tiny pieces
1 tablespoon fresh thyme leaves (no stems) or 1 teaspoon
    dried thyme
1 tablespoon no-salt-added tomato paste
Pinch sugar
1 cup homemade Beef Broth (see page 86) or commercial
    low-sodium variety
Freshly ground black pepper to taste
½ teaspoon salt-free all-purpose seasoning
6 medium-size fresh mushrooms, cut into wedges
1 cup whole pearl onions, peeled
3 tablespoons flour
3 to 4 tablespoons cold water
2 tablespoons chopped fresh parsley

Marinate venison, garlic, onion rings, bay leaf and wine in a deep glass bowl. Cover and refrigerate at least 3 hours. Remove venison from marinade, reserving liquid and discarding vegetables.

In a nonstick skillet over medium heat, brown bacon and venison. When meat is browned, add thyme, tomato paste, sugar, beef broth, pepper and all-purpose seasoning. Add reserved marinade liquid. Bring to a boil, reduce heat, cover and simmer 1¾ to 2 hours. Add mushrooms and pearl onions. Cook until onions are tender.

In a small bowl, mix flour with cold water. Blend until smooth. Slowly add to stew, stirring often until thickened. Sprinkle parsley on top and serve hot.

Serve with boiled potatoes, green peas and French bread.
Note: This dish freezes well.

Nutrient Analysis

Calories	182 kcal	Cholesterol	45 mg	Saturated Fat	2 gm
Protein	26 gm	Sodium	90 mg	Polyunsaturated Fat	2 gm
Carbohydrate	8 gm	Total Fat	5 gm	Monounsaturated Fat	1 gm

Hearty Fish Chowder

Serves 6; 1 cup per serving

1 pound fish fillets
2 potatoes, peeled and cubed
1 cup water
2 medium onions, diced
1 cup sliced fresh mushrooms
1 cup chopped green bell pepper
3 tablespoons acceptable margarine
½ cup flour
4 cups skim milk
Freshly ground black pepper to taste
1 tablespoon tamari sauce
¼ cup chopped fresh parsley
½ cup sherry

Rinse fish fillets and pat dry. Chop fillets and set aside.

Place potatoes in water in a saucepan over medium-high heat. Cover, reduce heat and simmer until tender. Remove from heat, drain and set aside.

In a skillet over medium-high heat, sauté onions, mushrooms and bell pepper in margarine until onions are translucent. Add flour and stir to blend well. Gradually add milk, stirring constantly until smooth. Add fish, black pepper, tamari and parsley. Cook approximately 10 minutes, or until fish is tender.

Add cooked potatoes and sherry. Heat and serve.

Nutrient Analysis

Calories	264 kcal	Cholesterol	43 mg	Saturated Fat	2 gm
Protein	22 gm	Sodium	392 mg	Polyunsaturated Fat	2 gm
Carbohydrate	27 gm	Total Fat	7 gm	Monounsaturated Fat	3 gm

New England Fish Chowder

Serves 6; 1 cup per serving

1 pound fresh cod or haddock
4 cups skim milk
2 cups peeled and diced potatoes
½ teaspoon salt
2 tablespoons acceptable margarine
1 cup sliced leeks, white part only
1 cup frozen no-salt-added baby green peas
2 tablespoons finely chopped fresh parsley
⅛ teaspoon ground white pepper
1 tablespoon fresh lemon juice

Rinse fish and pat dry. Cut into 1-inch pieces and set aside.

In a large saucepan over medium heat, combine milk, potatoes and salt. Cover and cook 25 to 30 minutes.

In small nonstick skillet, melt margarine. Add leeks and sauté until limp. Set aside.

Remove 1 cup potatoes and 1 cup liquid from saucepan, and place in a blender or the work bowl of a food processor fitted with a metal blade. Process until smooth. Return potatoes and liquid to pan over medium-high heat. Add sautéed leeks, fish, peas, parsley, pepper and lemon juice. Bring to a boil, reduce heat and simmer 10 minutes, or until fish is done.

Nutrient Analysis

Calories	227 kcal	Cholesterol	43 mg	Saturated Fat	1 gm
Protein	22 gm	Sodium	396 mg	Polyunsaturated Fat	1 gm
Carbohydrate	23 gm	Total Fat	5 gm	Monounsaturated Fat	2 gm

*C*ioppino

Serves 10; 1 cup per serving

1½ pounds red snapper
½ tablespoon olive oil
1½ cups chopped onion
3 cloves garlic, minced
1 cup coarsely chopped green bell pepper
4 cups chopped tomatoes
¼ cup dry red wine
¼ cup clam juice
2 bay leaves
¾ teaspoon dried basil
¼ teaspoon freshly ground black pepper
2 tablespoons chopped fresh parsley
3 to 4 dashes hot pepper sauce
½ pound medium shrimp, peeled and deveined
½ teaspoon salt
Juice of 1 lemon

Rinse fish and pat dry. Cut into 2-inch cubes and set aside.

In a heavy stockpot, heat oil and add onion, garlic and bell pepper. Sauté about 5 minutes.

Add tomatoes, wine, clam juice, bay leaves, basil, black pepper, parsley and hot pepper sauce. Simmer 15 minutes. Add fish and cook gently 25 minutes, stirring occasionally. Add shrimp and cook 8 minutes, stirring occasionally.

Season with salt and lemon juice. Serve in warmed soup bowls.

Nutrient Analysis

Calories	109 kcal	Cholesterol	68 mg	Saturated Fat	0 gm
Protein	17 gm	Sodium	230 mg	Polyunsaturated Fat	1 gm
Carbohydrate	5 gm	Total Fat	2 gm	Monounsaturated Fat	1 gm

*H*alibut *R*agout

Serves 8; 1 cup per serving

2 pounds halibut, fresh or frozen
½ cup chopped onion
1 clove garlic, minced
¼ cup chopped green bell pepper
3 stalks celery, sliced diagonally
3 carrots, cut julienne
2 tablespoons acceptable vegetable oil
1 28-ounce can no-salt-added tomatoes
1 cup dry white wine
Freshly ground black pepper to taste
¼ teaspoon thyme
¼ teaspoon basil
3 tablespoons minced fresh parsley

*T*haw halibut if frozen. Rinse and pat dry. Cut fish into 1-inch pieces and set aside.

In a large stockpot over medium-high heat, sauté onion, garlic, green bell pepper, celery and carrots in oil. Add tomatoes, wine, black pepper, thyme, basil and 1 tablespoon parsley. Cover and simmer 20 minutes.

Add halibut. Cover and simmer 5 to 10 minutes more, or until fish flakes easily with a fork. Sprinkle with remaining 2 tablespoons parsley.

Nutrient Analysis

Calories	175 kcal	Cholesterol	60 mg	Saturated Fat	1 gm
Protein	23 gm	Sodium	134 mg	Polyunsaturated Fat	3 gm
Carbohydrate	9 gm	Total Fat	5 gm	Monounsaturated Fat	1 gm

*S*urimi *C*orn *C*howder

Serves 6; 1 cup per serving

8 ounces surimi (imitation crab)
3 tablespoons acceptable margarine
1½ cups diced leeks, white part only
4 tablespoons flour
4 cups skim milk
1 cup frozen no-salt-added kernel corn
1½ teaspoons white wine Worcestershire sauce
½ teaspoon salt
1 tablespoon chopped fresh dill
1 tablespoon finely chopped fresh thyme
Dash nutmeg
Dash cayenne pepper

*R*inse surimi and pat dry. Break into chunks and set aside.

Heat margarine in a large saucepan over medium-high heat. Add leeks and sauté until translucent. Stir in flour; whisk in milk. Bring to boil, stirring constantly. Add remaining ingredients and surimi and cook over medium heat, stirring constantly, for 5 additional minutes. Serve hot.

Serve this soup with a fresh vegetable dish or a fruit salad for a light meal.

Note: Since surimi is high in sodium, be sure your accompaniments contain very little sodium.

Nutrient Analysis

Calories	190 kcal	Cholesterol	15 mg	Saturated Fat	2 gm
Protein	13 gm	Sodium	673 mg	Polyunsaturated Fat	2 gm
Carbohydrate	21 gm	Total Fat	6 gm	Monounsaturated Fat	3 gm

Shrimp Gumbo

Serves 6; ¾ cup per serving

2 cups sliced fresh okra or 1 10-ounce package frozen no-salt-added okra, sliced
¼ cup acceptable vegetable oil
⅔ cup chopped green onions and tops
3 cloves garlic, finely chopped
½ teaspoon freshly ground black pepper, or to taste
2 cups water
1 cup canned no-salt-added tomatoes
2 whole bay leaves
½ cup uncooked rice
1 pound fresh medium shrimp, peeled and deveined
6 drops hot pepper sauce

In a large stockpot over medium-high heat, sauté okra in oil for 10 minutes. Add onions, garlic and pepper. Cook about 5 minutes. Add water, tomatoes and bay leaves. Cover and simmer 20 minutes.

Meanwhile, cook rice according to package directions; do not use salt, butter or margarine. Set aside.

Add shrimp to okra mixture. Cover and remove from heat. Let stand 5 minutes, or until shrimp is done (when it turns pink). Do not overcook.

Remove bay leaves and sprinkle in hot pepper sauce. Stir to mix well.

Place ¼ cup of cooked rice in each soup bowl. Add equal amounts of gumbo to each bowl and serve hot.

Nutrient Analysis

Calories	215 kcal	Cholesterol	108 mg	Saturated Fat	1 gm
Protein	14 gm	Sodium	131 mg	Polyunsaturated Fat	6 gm
Carbohydrate	18 gm	Total Fat	10 gm	Monounsaturated Fat	2 gm

*S*alads and *S*alad *D*ressings

BASIC GREEN SALAD MIX — ARBORIO SALAD WITH ARTICHOKES
SPROUTS — CURRIED RICE AND BEAN SALAD
FRESH VEGETABLE SALAD BOWL — CRANBERRY ORANGE SALAD
AMY AND JIM'S SPECIAL SALAD — WALDORF SALAD
AVOCADO PINEAPPLE SALAD — MARJ'S COLORFUL SALAD
SUKIYAKI SALAD — MACARONI SALAD RICOTTA
ANNA'S BEAN SPROUT SALAD — CHICKEN VEGETABLE SALAD
SPINACH AVOCADO ORANGE TOSS — PINEAPPLE CHICKEN SALAD
TOSSED VEGETABLES VINAIGRETTE — CHICKEN SNOW PEA SALAD
TANGY CUCUMBERS — CHINESE CHICKEN SALAD
BEAN SPROUT SALAD — CURRIED CHICKEN SALAD
CALIFORNIA CUCUMBER SALAD — SOUTHWESTERN PORK SALAD
TOMATO ASPIC SALAD — MEXICAN SHRIMP SALAD
CUCUMBERS IN TANGY SOUR CREAM — FRESH SALMON SALAD
SLICED TOMATOES WITH BASIL — SALAD NIÇOISE
CONFETTI COLESLAW — VINAIGRETTE DRESSING
PARSLEY POTATO SALAD — HERBED VINAIGRETTE
BEET SALAD WITH RED ONIONS — TOMATO DRESSING
CELERY SEED COLESLAW — OIL AND VINEGAR DRESSING
DILLED APPLE AND POTATO SALAD — CHEF'S DRESSING
GREEN GRAPE AND RED CABBAGE SLAW — CREAMY CHEF'S DRESSING
HOT CABBAGE SLAW — COOKED SALAD DRESSING
CARROT RAISIN SALAD — APPLE JUICE DRESSING
GREEK PASTA SALAD — BUTTERMILK HERB DRESSING
MARINATED PASTA SALAD — CHUNKY CUCUMBER AND GARLIC DRESSING
PARSLEY SALAD — CREAMY COTTAGE CHEESE DRESSING
ITALIAN RICE SALAD — YOGURT DRESSING
ORIENTAL RICE SALAD — DIJON DRESSING
VEGETABLE RICE SALAD — MINTED LIME DRESSING

For low fat and high nutrition, nothing beats a salad. Sometimes the very best ones are hardly recipes at all: Consider how good thick slices of juicy tomatoes sprinkled with fresh basil, coarsely ground black pepper and chopped chives taste.

At the same time, a talented cook can create a salad that's a meal in itself: crisp greens piled high with slender strips of meat, cooked or raw vegetables, green onions, olives and a host of herbs and garnishes. Pasta, meat, rice and fruit salads may also serve as entrees when accompanied by a nutritious soup or a hearty bread.

All green salads must start with crisp, fresh greens. Use several types: tender, dark-green spinach leaves, soft Bibb lettuce, curly red-tipped leaf lettuce, crunchy iceberg—there are dozens to choose from. Rinse and thoroughly dry each leaf, and be sure to break or tear the leaves gently, rather than cut them, to avoid bruising.

Try a simple, healthful bowl of crisp carrots, steamed green beans, thinly sliced cucumbers, tomatoes and mushrooms—all marinated for a couple of hours in a light, homemade vinaigrette—for a colorful change of pace.

Making your own nutritious and flavorful salad dressings is easy. Many commercial dressings tend to be high in fat, calories and sodium; homemade dressings, however, can be created in your own kitchen with ingredients you choose— fresh herbs, oils, spices and a host of others. Frankly, nothing beats the taste! A homemade salad dressing will keep in a tightly covered container in the refrigerator for two weeks.

*B*asic *G*reen *S*alad *M*ix

Serves 6

> 7 leaves leaf lettuce (about 4 ounces)
> 7 leaves Boston lettuce (about 4 ounces)
> 6 leaves romaine lettuce (about 4 ounces)
> ¼ head iceberg lettuce (about 5 ounces)
> ½ cup sliced green onion tops
> ½ cup diced celery

Rinse lettuce and spin dry in lettuce spinner, or dry on paper towels. Tear leaf, Boston and romaine lettuces into bite-size pieces and place in a large bowl. (Do not use ribs of romaine lettuce.) Cut iceberg wedge into small cubes and add to bowl. Add green onion and celery, and toss. To save for later use, refrigerate in sealed plastic bag.

Serve with Vinaigrette Dressing, Apple Juice Dressing or Yogurt Dressing (see pages 165, 170 and 174).

VARIATIONS
Add a few of the following low-calorie ingredients for a slightly different salad: shredded red cabbage or carrots, tomatoes, sliced mushrooms or cucumbers, cut asparagus or leaf spinach.

Nutrient Analysis

Calories	11 kcal	Cholesterol	0 mg	Saturated Fat	0 gm
Protein	1 gm	Sodium	14 mg	Polyunsaturated Fat	0 gm
Carbohydrate	2 gm	Total Fat	0 gm	Monounsaturated Fat	0 gm

*S*prouts

Makes 1 cup
Serves 2; ½ cup per serving

> 2 tablespoons alfalfa seeds

Buy seeds that are specifically intended for sprouting—not for planting. Put seeds in a jar, rinse with cold water, then cover with fresh cold water. Soak overnight in a dark place.

Pour off liquid and rinse, leaving seeds slightly moist. Rinse two times a day for three to five days. (A pint jar with a screen lid makes rinsing easy.) Store seeds in the refrigerator during this time. Sprouts are ready to use when they are 1 to 1½ inches long.

VARIATION
Mung beans, soybeans, lentils or wheatberries may be substituted for alfalfa seeds to obtain sprouts.

Nutrient Analysis*

Calories	5 kcal	Cholesterol	0 mg	Saturated Fat	0 gm
Protein	1 gm	Sodium	1 mg	Polyunsaturated Fat	0 gm
Carbohydrate	1 gm	Total Fat	0 gm	Monounsaturated Fat	0 gm

* using alfalfa sprouts

*F*resh *V*egetable *S*alad *B*owl

Serves 8

1 head romaine lettuce
½ pound small fresh mushrooms, whole
1 pound cherry tomatoes
1 small head cauliflower
1 pound very young, raw asparagus spears

Remove outer leaves of romaine, separate stems from mushrooms and snap off tomato stems. Break cauliflower into florets and trim stalk ends from asparagus.

Rinse all vegetables except mushrooms. Drain well. Wipe mushrooms with a damp paper towel.

Place inner leaves of romaine upright around the sides of a deep, round salad bowl. Arrange remaining ingredients neatly in the center. Cover and refrigerate to chill thoroughly before serving.

Serve with a favorite dressing.

Nutrient Analysis

Calories	43 kcal	Cholesterol	0 mg	Saturated Fat	0 gm
Protein	4 gm	Sodium	16 mg	Polyunsaturated Fat	0 gm
Carbohydrate	8 gm	Total Fat	1 gm	Monounsaturated Fat	0 gm

Amy and Jim's Special Salad

Serves 8

VEGETABLES
1/4 pound fresh mushrooms, sliced
1 green bell pepper, seeded and sliced
1 cucumber, peeled and sliced
1 zucchini or summer squash, cubed
1 carrot, shredded
1/4 pound fresh green beans, sliced
1/4 pound fresh peas
1 cup fresh alfalfa sprouts
1/4 cup sliced pitted ripe olives
4 scallions, chopped
2 tablespoons pumpkin seeds

MARINADE
4 tablespoons fresh lemon juice
4 tablespoons reduced-calorie Italian dressing
1 tablespoon dried basil, or 2 tablespoons fresh basil
1 tablespoon dried thyme, or 2 tablespoons fresh thyme
1 tablespoon dried mint, or 2 tablespoons fresh mint
1 clove garlic, minced
Freshly ground black pepper to taste

SALAD GREENS
1 head romaine lettuce
1/2 pound spinach
1 bunch leaf lettuce

Place prepared vegetables in large salad bowl. Set aside.

In a medium bowl, combine all marinade ingredients. Stir to mix thoroughly. Pour over vegetables. Cover and refrigerate for at least 30 minutes.

Meanwhile, rinse salad greens, remove stems and tear into bite-size pieces. Cover and refrigerate.

Combine marinated vegetables and salad greens. Toss and serve.

Nutrient Analysis

Calories	72 kcal	Cholesterol	0 mg	Saturated Fat	0 gm
Protein	4 gm	Sodium	133 mg	Polyunsaturated Fat	1 gm
Carbohydrate	10 gm	Total Fat	3 gm	Monounsaturated Fat	1 gm

*A*vocado *P*ineapple *S*alad

Serves 4

2 avocados
2 teaspoons lemon juice
8 green lettuce leaves
4 fresh pineapple slices or 4 slices no-sugar-added
    pineapple canned in fruit juice
2 cups low-fat cottage cheese
¼ cup honey
¼ cup lemon juice
Chopped mint (optional)

Cut avocados lengthwise into halves. Remove peel and seeds. Cut each half into 4 pieces, lengthwise. Sprinkle with 2 teaspoons lemon juice to prevent discoloration. Set aside.

Line 4 salad plates with lettuce leaves. Place 1 slice of pineapple on each plate. Spoon cottage cheese equally over pineapple slices.

Place 4 avocado slices on top of each serving. Set aside.

In a small bowl, combine honey, ¼ cup lemon juice and mint. Pour over pineapple and avocado slices.

Note: Because of the high fat content of avocados, balance your fat intake for the rest of the day by eating very low fat foods at other meals.

Nutrient Analysis

Calories	374 kcal	Cholesterol	9 mg	Saturated Fat		4 gm
Protein	18 gm	Sodium	476 mg	Polyunsaturated Fat		2 gm
Carbohydrate	41 gm	Total Fat	18 gm	Monounsaturated Fat		10 gm

Sukiyaki Salad

Serves 4

2 tablespoons light soy sauce
1 clove garlic, minced, or to taste
½ cup reduced-calorie oil and vinegar dressing
½ cup raw spinach leaves, rinsed, stems removed, leaves
    coarsely broken up
½ cup other salad greens, broken into small pieces
½ cup fresh bean sprouts
½ cup thinly sliced celery, diagonal slices
¼ cup thinly sliced water chestnuts
½ cup thinly sliced fresh mushrooms
½ cup thinly sliced green bell pepper
½ cup thinly sliced cabbage
½ cup watercress

In a small bowl, blend first three ingredients; set aside.

In a large bowl, combine all remaining ingredients. Pour dressing mixture over salad and toss well.

Nutrient Analysis

Calories	66 kcal	Cholesterol	2 mg	Saturated Fat	0 gm
Protein	3 gm	Sodium	563 mg	Polyunsaturated Fat	2 gm
Carbohydrate	7 gm	Total Fat	4 gm	Monounsaturated Fat	1 gm

Anna's Bean Sprout Salad

Serves 6

4 cups fresh bean sprouts
4 cups boiling water
1 tablespoon light soy sauce
1 tablespoon sherry
⅛ teaspoon ground ginger
1 teaspoon hot sesame oil
2 tablespoons chopped scallions

*I*mmerse bean sprouts in boiling water for 1 minute, drain and rinse immediately in cold water.

In a large bowl, combine bean sprouts, soy sauce, sherry, ginger and sesame oil. Toss to mix thoroughly. Sprinkle scallions on top before serving.

Nutrient Analysis

Calories	72 kcal	Cholesterol	0 mg	Saturated Fat	0 gm
Protein	6 gm	Sodium	108 mg	Polyunsaturated Fat	2 gm
Carbohydrate	6 gm	Total Fat	4 gm	Monounsaturated Fat	1 gm

*S*pinach *A*vocado *O*range *T*oss

Serves 10

½ teaspoon grated orange peel
¼ cup orange juice
¼ cup acceptable vegetable oil
2 tablespoons sugar
2 tablespoons wine vinegar
1 tablespoon lemon juice
6 cups spinach or other greens, rinsed, stems removed, leaves torn into bite-size pieces
1 small cucumber, thinly sliced
1 avocado, peeled and chopped
1 11-ounce can mandarin oranges (canned in light syrup), drained
2 tablespoons sliced green onions

*T*o make dressing, combine first six ingredients in a jar with a tight-fitting lid. Shake until thoroughly blended. Set aside.

In a large bowl, combine remaining ingredients and toss to mix well. Pour dressing over salad and toss lightly.

Nutrient Analysis

Calories	122 kcal	Cholesterol	0 mg	Saturated Fat	1 gm
Protein	2 gm	Sodium	31 mg	Polyunsaturated Fat	4 gm
Carbohydrate	12 gm	Total Fat	9 gm	Monounsaturated Fat	3 gm

*T*ossed *V*egetables *V*inaigrette

Serves 8; ¾ cup per serving

¼ cup low-fat vanilla yogurt
2 tablespoons white wine vinegar
3 tablespoons acceptable vegetable oil
1 tablespoon Dijon mustard
½ teaspoon coarsely ground black pepper
¼ teaspoon salt
2 cups sliced carrots
8 ounces fresh green beans, rinsed, trimmed and cut into
    1½-inch lengths
Ice water
4 ounces fresh mushrooms, cut into quarters
2 medium tomatoes, cut into wedges
⅓ cup thinly sliced green onion tops

*P*lace first six ingredients in a blender or the work bowl of a food processor fitted with a metal blade. Process until thoroughly mixed. Set aside.

Steam carrots and green beans 3 to 4 minutes, or until tender-crisp. Remove from heat and dip into bowl of ice water to stop cooking. Drain and pat dry with paper towels. Combine carrots, beans, mushrooms, tomato wedges and green onions in a shallow glass dish. Pour dressing over all and toss gently. Cover and refrigerate several hours. Serve cold.

Nutrient Analysis

Calories	90 kcal	Cholesterol	0 mg	Saturated Fat	1 gm
Protein	2 gm	Sodium	127 mg	Polyunsaturated Fat	3 gm
Carbohydrate	10 gm	Total Fat	6 gm	Monounsaturated Fat	1 gm

*T*angy *C*ucumbers

Serves 4

¾ cup cider vinegar
¼ cup sugar
¼ cup chopped fresh parsley
4 green onions, chopped
3 medium cucumbers

YOGURT SAUCE (OPTIONAL)
½ cup plain nonfat yogurt
1 teaspoon sugar
½ teaspoon dry mustard

*I*n a bowl, combine first four ingredients. Stir well. Cover marinade and refrigerate until cool.

Peel cucumbers if desired. Cut in half lengthwise and scrape out seeds with spoon. Cut cucumbers crosswise into thin half-moon slices. Add cucumbers to marinade. Cover and refrigerate for 1 to 2 hours.

Drain and serve.

TANGY CUCUMBERS IN YOGURT SAUCE
In a small bowl, combine sauce ingredients. Stir to mix well. Drain cucumbers and toss with sauce.

Tangy Cucumbers Nutrient Analysis

Calories	79 kcal	Cholesterol	0 mg	Saturated Fat	0 gm
Protein	1 gm	Sodium	6 mg	Polyunsaturated Fat	0 gm
Carbohydrate	20 gm	Total Fat	0 gm	Monounsaturated Fat	0 gm

Tangy Cucumbers in Yogurt Sauce Nutrient Analysis

Calories	101 kcal	Cholesterol	1 mg	Saturated Fat	0 gm
Protein	3 gm	Sodium	29 mg	Polyunsaturated Fat	0 gm
Carbohydrate	24 gm	Total Fat	0 gm	Monounsaturated Fat	0 gm

*B*ean *S*prout *S*alad

Serves 6

2 cups fresh bean sprouts
2 cups canned no-salt-added sliced green beans, drained
1 cup chopped fresh parsley
½ teaspoon dill seed
1 tablespoon acceptable vegetable oil
2 tablespoons plain nonfat yogurt
1 tablespoon ketchup
½ teaspoon Worcestershire sauce

GARNISH
6 lemon wedges

In a large bowl, combine bean sprouts, green beans and parsley. Toss to mix thoroughly. Sprinkle dill seed on mixture.

In a small bowl, combine remaining ingredients. Stir to mix well. Pour over bean sprout mixture.

Garnish with lemon wedges.

Nutrient Analysis

Calories	72 kcal	Cholesterol	0 mg	Saturated Fat	0 gm
Protein	4 gm	Sodium	52 mg	Polyunsaturated Fat	2 gm
Carbohydrate	7 gm	Total Fat	4 gm	Monounsaturated Fat	1 gm

*C*alifornia *C*ucumber *S*alad

Serves 4

2 cucumbers, scrubbed, not peeled
⅓ cup raisins
¼ cup chopped unsalted dry-roasted walnuts
1 tablespoon chopped fresh dill
½ teaspoon minced garlic
2 tablespoons chopped green onion
⅛ teaspoon white pepper
¼ cup plain nonfat yogurt

Remove seeds from cucumbers, shred and drain. Place in a bowl and add remaining ingredients. Toss to mix well.

Serve on lettuce-lined salad plates.

Nutrient Analysis

Calories	109 kcal	Cholesterol	0 mg	Saturated Fat		0 gm
Protein	3 gm	Sodium	18 mg	Polyunsaturated Fat		3 gm
Carbohydrate	16 gm	Total Fat	5 gm	Monounsaturated Fat		1 gm

*T*omato *A*spic *S*alad

Serves 6

1¾ cups no-salt-added tomato juice
½ teaspoon freshly ground black pepper, or to taste
1 bay leaf
½ teaspoon paprika
1 teaspoon fresh lemon juice
1 tablespoon grated onion
1 tablespoon unflavored gelatin (1 envelope)
¼ cup cold water
½ cup chopped celery
2 tablespoons chopped green onion
2 tablespoons finely chopped fresh parsley

In a saucepan over medium setting, heat tomato juice, pepper and bay leaf. Remove from heat and take out bay leaf. Add paprika, lemon juice and grated onion.

Combine gelatin and cold water and add mixture to hot tomato juice. Stir until dissolved. Cool.

Add chopped vegetables.

Pour aspic into six individual molds, cover and refrigerate until set. Unmold and serve cold.

Nutrient Analysis

Calories	20 kcal	Cholesterol	0 mg	Saturated Fat		0 gm
Protein	2 gm	Sodium	18 mg	Polyunsaturated Fat		0 gm
Carbohydrate	4 gm	Total Fat	0 gm	Monounsaturated Fat		0 gm

Cucumbers in Tangy Sour Cream

Serves 6

> 3 medium cucumbers, peeled and sliced
> 1 small onion, finely chopped
> 1 teaspoon sugar
> 1 cup Tangy Sour Cream (see page 418)
> 2 tablespoons chopped fresh parsley
> ½ teaspoon freshly ground black pepper

Place cucumbers and onion in a bowl and sprinkle with sugar. Mix well. Cover and refrigerate several hours. Drain off accumulated water.

In a small bowl, combine Tangy Sour Cream, parsley and pepper. Add to chilled cucumber mixture and stir to mix well. Correct seasonings if necessary. Cover and chill thoroughly before serving.

CUCUMBERS WITH YOGURT DRESSING
In place of Tangy Sour Cream mixture, combine ½ cup plain nonfat yogurt with 1 teaspoon fresh lemon juice; add freshly ground black pepper and dill to taste. Pour over drained cucumbers and onions. Cover and chill thoroughly before serving.

CUCUMBERS WITH LEMON HERB DRESSING
In place of Tangy Sour Cream mixture, combine ¼ cup fresh lemon juice, 1 tablespoon sugar and ⅛ teaspoon marjoram or thyme. Pour over drained cucumbers and onions. Cover and chill thoroughly before serving.

Cucumbers in Tangy Sour Cream Nutrient Analysis
Calories	61 kcal	Cholesterol	3 mg	Saturated Fat	1 gm
Protein	7 gm	Sodium	179 mg	Polyunsaturated Fat	0 gm
Carbohydrate	7 gm	Total Fat	1 gm	Monounsaturated Fat	0 gm

Cucumbers with Yogurt Dressing Nutrient Analysis
Calories	33 kcal	Cholesterol	0 mg	Saturated Fat	0 gm
Protein	2 gm	Sodium	19 mg	Polyunsaturated Fat	0 gm
Carbohydrate	7 gm	Total Fat	0 gm	Monounsaturated Fat	0 gm

Cucumbers with Lemon Herb Dressing Nutrient Analysis
Calories	32 kcal	Cholesterol	0 mg	Saturated Fat	0 gm
Protein	1 gm	Sodium	5 mg	Polyunsaturated Fat	0 gm
Carbohydrate	8 gm	Total Fat	0 gm	Monounsaturated Fat	0 gm

Sliced Tomatoes with Basil

Serves 6

> 4 medium tomatoes, sliced
> 2 tablespoons chopped fresh basil leaves or 2 teaspoons
>   dried basil
> 2 tablespoons olive oil

Place tomato slices on a large, flat plate. Sprinkle basil and olive oil on top. Cover and refrigerate. Serve cold.

Nutrient Analysis

Calories	56 kcal	Cholesterol	0 mg	Saturated Fat		1 gm
Protein	1 gm	Sodium	7 mg	Polyunsaturated Fat		0 gm
Carbohydrate	4 gm	Total Fat	5 gm	Monounsaturated Fat		3 gm

Confetti Coleslaw

Serves 12; ½ cup per serving

> ¼ cup honey
> 3 tablespoons acceptable vegetable oil
> 3 tablespoons cider vinegar
> ¼ teaspoon salt
> 1 teaspoon coarsely ground black pepper
> ¾ pound green cabbage, core removed, shredded
>   (approximately 4 cups)
> ½ pound red cabbage, core removed, shredded
>   (approximately 2⅔ cups)
> ½ cup thinly sliced green onion
> 1 cup minced red bell pepper

Combine first five ingredients in a medium bowl. Stir to mix well. Add cabbage, onion and bell pepper. Toss to coat evenly. Cover and refrigerate several hours before serving.

Nutrient Analysis

Calories	65 kcal	Cholesterol	0 mg	Saturated Fat		0 gm
Protein	1 gm	Sodium	52 mg	Polyunsaturated Fat		2 gm
Carbohydrate	9 gm	Total Fat	4 gm	Monounsaturated Fat		1 gm

*P*arsley *P*otato *S*alad

Serves 6

2 cups diced cooked potatoes
½ tablespoon chopped pimiento
½ cup diced celery
1 tablespoon chopped onion
2 tablespoons chopped fresh parsley
½ tablespoon cider vinegar
1 teaspoon dry mustard
½ teaspoon celery seeds
Freshly ground black pepper to taste
¼ cup light, reduced-calorie mayonnaise

GARNISH
Pimiento strips

*I*n a large bowl, combine all ingredients except mayonnaise and pimiento strips. Toss lightly, cover and refrigerate for several hours.

A few hours before serving, add mayonnaise and stir to mix well. Cover and return salad to refrigerator.

Serve in lettuce cups and garnish with small strips of pimiento.

Nutrient Analysis

Calories	79 kcal	Cholesterol	3 mg	Saturated Fat	0 gm
Protein	1 gm	Sodium	71 mg	Polyunsaturated Fat	1 gm
Carbohydrate	12 gm	Total Fat	3 gm	Monounsaturated Fat	1 gm

*B*eet *S*alad *with* *R*ed *O*nions

Serves 4; ½ cup per serving

2 pounds fresh beets, untrimmed
¼ large red onion, sliced lengthwise
2 tablespoons red wine vinegar
2 tablespoons acceptable vegetable oil
2 tablespoons light soy sauce
2 teaspoons grated fresh ginger
1 teaspoon grated orange rind
¼ teaspoon freshly ground black pepper, or to taste

*T*rim leaves off beets, leaving 1-inch tops; do not cut off root end. Rinse thoroughly but do not peel. Place beets in saucepan. Cover with water and cook over meduim-high heat 30 minutes, or until knife pierces beet easily. Drop beets into cold water and slip off skins. Cut into thin slices.

Combine beets and onion in a bowl. Set aside.

Place remaining ingredients in a blender or the work bowl of a food processor fitted with a metal blade. Process until smooth. Pour over beets and onion, tossing lightly to coat. Cover and rcfrigerate at least 1 hour before serving.

Nutrient Analysis

Calories	106 kcal	Cholesterol	0 mg	Saturated Fat	1 gm
Protein	2 gm	Sodium	357 mg	Polyunsaturated Fat	4 gm
Carbohydrate	10 gm	Total Fat	7 gm	Monounsaturated Fat	2 gm

*C*elery *S*eed *C*oleslaw

Serves 6

3 cups finely shredded cabbage
3 tablespoons acceptable vegetable oil
⅓ cup cider vinegar, heated
1 tablespoon finely chopped onion
1 tablespoon chopped pimiento, drained
2 tablespoons sugar
½ teaspoon dry mustard
½ teaspoon celery seeds

*I*n a large bowl, toss shredded cabbage, oil and vinegar. Add remaining ingredients and toss again. Cover and refrigerate until thoroughly chilled.

Nutrient Analysis

Calories	88 kcal	Cholesterol	0 mg	Saturated Fat	1 gm
Protein	1 gm	Sodium	7 mg	Polyunsaturated Fat	4 gm
Carbohydrate	7 gm	Total Fat	7 gm	Monounsaturated Fat	2 gm

Dilled Apple and Potato Salad

Serves 8

1½ pounds red potatoes
2 large carrots, peeled, cut into small, thin sticks
¼ teaspoon salt
½ cup diced celery
⅓ cup sliced green onions
1 Granny Smith apple, unpeeled, cored and diced
½ cup light, reduced-calorie mayonnaise
½ cup plain nonfat yogurt
½ cup low-fat lemon yogurt
1 tablespoon finely chopped fresh dill
2 tablespoons finely chopped fresh parsley
Dash hot pepper sauce
1 tablespoon Dijon mustard

Rinse potatoes but do not peel; cut each in half. Place in saucepan; add water just to cover. Cover and cook 10 minutes over medium heat. Add carrots and cook 10 minutes more, or until vegetables are tender but firm.

Drain and rinse gently with cool water. Drain again and set aside to cool. Cut potatoes into bite-size pieces. Set aside.

In a large bowl, combine remaining ingredients. Stir to mix well. Add potatoes and carrots to bowl and stir gently with rubber spatula. Cover and refrigerate several hours before serving.

Nutrient Analysis

Calories	181 kcal	Cholesterol	5 mg	Saturated Fat	1 gm
Protein	4 gm	Sodium	229 mg	Polyunsaturated Fat	2 gm
Carbohydrate	32 gm	Total Fat	5 gm	Monounsaturated Fat	2 gm

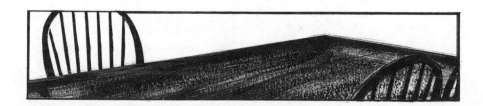

Green Grape and Red Cabbage Slaw

Serves 8; ²/₃ cup per serving

3 cups shredded red cabbage
1 cup thinly sliced radishes
7 ounces green grapes, cut in half
½ cup thinly sliced green onions, diagonal slices
2 ounces unsalted dry-roasted walnuts, chopped
4 tablespoons cider vinegar
5 tablespoons acceptable vegetable oil
1 tablespoon firmly packed brown sugar
1 tablespoon Dijon mustard
¼ teaspoon salt
½ teaspoon coarsely ground black pepper

In a large bowl, combine cabbage, radishes, grapes, onions and walnuts. Toss gently and set aside.

In a blender or the work bowl of a food processor fitted with a metal blade, combine vinegar, oil, sugar, mustard, salt and pepper. Process 20 seconds. Add to cabbage mixture; toss to coat evenly. Cover and refrigerate until thoroughly chilled.

GREEN GRAPE AND RED CABBAGE SLAW WITH TURKEY

To serve as an entree, increase salad portion to approximately 1 cup and add 3 ounces smoked turkey or chicken breast to each serving. Serves five.

Green Grape and Red Cabbage Slaw Nutrient Analysis

Calories	158 kcal	Cholesterol	0 mg	Saturated Fat	2 gm
Protein	2 gm	Sodium	100 mg	Polyunsaturated Fat	8 gm
Carbohydrate	10 gm	Total Fat	13 gm	Monounsaturated Fat	3 gm

Green Grape and Red Cabbage Slaw with Turkey Nutrient Analysis

Calories	360 kcal	Cholesterol	36 mg	Saturated Fat	3 gm
Protein	22 gm	Sodium	498 mg	Polyunsaturated Fat	13 gm
Carbohydrate	16 gm	Total Fat	24 gm	Monounsaturated Fat	6 gm

*H*ot *C*abbage *S*law

Serves 8

2 tablespoons acceptable vegetable oil
1 cup finely chopped onion
½ cup diced celery
1⅓ cups diced carrots
1 cup diced red bell pepper
3 cups shredded red cabbage
1½ cups apple juice
¼ cup firmly packed brown sugar
2 tablespoons Dijon mustard
3 tablespoons cornstarch
½ cup cider vinegar
¼ teaspoon salt

*H*eat oil in a large nonstick skillet over medium-high heat. Add onions, celery, carrots and bell pepper. Sauté until onion is translucent. Add cabbage, cover and cook 5 minutes.

In a small bowl, combine remaining ingredients. Add to vegetables and stir to mix well. Cook until sauce is thick and clear.

This slaw is a good accompaniment for game and poultry.

Nutrient Analysis

Calories	117 kcal	Cholesterol	0 mg	Saturated Fat	0 gm
Protein	1 gm	Sodium	138 mg	Polyunsaturated Fat	2 gm
Carbohydrate	21 gm	Total Fat	4 gm	Monounsaturated Fat	1 gm

*C*arrot *R*aisin *S*alad

Serves 6

2 cups shredded raw carrots
¼ cup seedless raisins
¼ cup light, reduced-calorie mayonnaise
¼ cup plain nonfat yogurt
2 tablespoons fresh lemon juice

*I*n a bowl, combine carrots and raisins. Mix thoroughly. Set aside.

In a small bowl, combine mayonnaise, yogurt and lemon juice.

Stir to mix well. Pour over carrot-raisin mixture and mix well.

Nutrient Analysis

Calories	90 kcal	Cholesterol	3 mg	Saturated Fat	0 gm
Protein	1 gm	Sodium	84 mg	Polyunsaturated Fat	1 gm
Carbohydrate	16 gm	Total Fat	3 gm	Monounsaturated Fat	1 gm

*G*reek *P*asta *S*alad

Serves 8; 1 cup per serving

1 12-ounce package tricolor rotini pasta
⅔ cup unpeeled, seeded, diced cucumber
½ cup thinly sliced green onions
4 ounces feta cheese, crumbled
1¼ cups frozen no-salt-added baby peas, defrosted
1 cup diced red bell pepper
¼ cup light, reduced-calorie mayonnaise
½ cup low-fat cottage cheese
½ cup plain nonfat yogurt
¼ cup thinly sliced green onion tops
1 to 2 tablespoons finely chopped fresh dill
¼ teaspoon freshly ground black pepper

Cook pasta in boiling water for 7 minutes. Remove from heat, drain and place in a large bowl. Add cucumber, ½ cup green onions, feta cheese, peas and bell pepper. Set aside.

In a blender or the work bowl of a food processor fitted with a metal blade, combine mayonnaise, cottage cheese, yogurt and ¼ cup green onion tops. Process until completely smooth. Add dill and black pepper and process briefly. Pour over pasta mixture and stir to mix well. Cover and refrigerate until well chilled.

Nutrient Analysis

Calories	280 kcal	Cholesterol	16 mg	Saturated Fat	3 gm
Protein	12 gm	Sodium	295 mg	Polyunsaturated Fat	1 gm
Carbohydrate	43 gm	Total Fat	6 gm	Monounsaturated Fat	2 gm

Marinated Pasta Salad

Serves 8

8 ounces tricolor pasta rotini spirals
½ pound fresh or frozen asparagus, cooked 5 to 7 minutes
    and refreshed in ice water, cut into 1-inch pieces
½ cup julienne-cut red bell pepper
½ cup julienne-cut zucchini
½ cup finely chopped red onion
½ cup thinly sliced celery
¼ teaspoon salt
Several dashes crushed red pepper or hot pepper sauce
⅛ teaspoon coarsely ground black pepper
¼ teaspoon bouquet garni
2 tablespoons minced fresh parsley
¼ cup reduced-calorie Italian dressing
3 tablespoons white wine vinegar

Cook pasta according to package directions, omitting salt. Rinse, drain and cool. Place in a large bowl. Add vegetables and toss to mix. Add remaining ingredients. Toss, cover and refrigerate several hours or overnight.

Serve on leaf lettuce with French bread as an accompaniment.

Nutrient Analysis

Calories	139 kcal	Cholesterol	0 mg	Saturated Fat	0 gm
Protein	5 gm	Sodium	135 mg	Polyunsaturated Fat	1 gm
Carbohydrate	27 gm	Total Fat	1 gm	Monounsaturated Fat	0 gm

*P*arsley *S*alad
(Tabouli)

Serves 8

½ cup fine bulgur wheat
Hot water
2 cups finely chopped fresh parsley (1 or 2 bunches, large
    stems removed)
½ cup finely chopped green onions
⅓ cup chopped fresh mint leaves
1 medium cucumber, peeled, seeded and cubed
1 cup diced red bell pepper
¼ teaspoon salt
½ teaspoon freshly ground black pepper

DRESSING
Juice of 2 lemons
1 to 2 cloves garlic, pressed or finely minced
2 tablespoons olive oil

18 cherry tomatoes, cut into quarters

Place bulgur in a large bowl. Add enough hot water to cover. Let sit for approximately 30 minutes. Drain and squeeze dry. Place in a large mixing bowl and fluff with a fork. Add parsley, onions, mint, cucumber, bell pepper, salt and black pepper. Stir to mix well and set aside.

In a small bowl, combine dressing ingredients and stir to mix well. Pour over salad, toss, cover and refrigerate 3 to 4 hours.

Remove from refrigerator and add tomatoes. Mix well.

Serve on a bed of crisp lettuce.

Nutrient Analysis

Calories	68 kcal	Cholesterol	0 mg	Saturated Fat	1 gm
Protein	2 gm	Sodium	130 mg	Polyunsaturated Fat	0 gm
Carbohydrate	9 gm	Total Fat	4 gm	Monounsaturated Fat	3 gm

Italian Rice Salad

Serves 10; ⅔ cup per serving

⅓ cup olive oil
¼ cup fresh lemon juice
2 cloves garlic, minced
1 teaspoon freshly ground black pepper
¼ teaspoon salt
5 cups cooked rice
1 10-ounce package frozen artichoke hearts, defrosted
⅓ cup sliced green onion tops
2 tablespoons finely chopped fresh basil
5 ripe Italian plum tomatoes, cut in half lengthwise and
    sliced
6 tablespoons grated Parmesan cheese

Combine oil, lemon juice, garlic, pepper and salt in a blender or the work bowl of a food processor fitted with a metal blade. Process 20 seconds. Pour into a large bowl. Add remaining ingredients. Mix well. Serve at room temperature or cover and refrigerate to serve cold.

Nutrient Analysis

Calories	217 kcal	Cholesterol	2 mg	Saturated Fat	2 gm
Protein	5 gm	Sodium	134 mg	Polyunsaturated Fat	1 gm
Carbohydrate	31 gm	Total Fat	9 gm	Monounsaturated Fat	6 gm

Oriental Rice Salad

Serves 8

3 cups cooked rice
1 10-ounce package frozen no-salt-added green peas,
    defrosted
4 scallions, sliced
1½ pounds diced, cooked chicken
1 stalk celery, diced
2 tablespoons diced green bell pepper

2 tablespoons sherry
1 tablespoon light soy sauce
¼ teaspoon hot pepper oil
⅛ teaspoon ground ginger
4 tablespoons rice vinegar
2 tablespoons acceptable vegetable oil
1 tablespoon Dijon mustard

*I*n a large bowl, combine rice, peas, scallions, chicken, celery and bell pepper. Mix well.

In a jar with a tight-fitting lid, combine remaining ingedients. Shake well.

Pour liquid over rice mixture. Mix well.

Spoon rice mixture into a ring or serving bowl and cover. Refrigerate for at least ½ hour.

ORIENTAL RICE SALAD IN TOMATOES
Stuff rice mixture into 8 hollowed tomatoes.

ORIENTAL RICE SALAD IN PEPPERS
Stuff rice mixture into 8 hollowed green bell pepper halves.

Oriental Rice Salad Nutrient Analysis

Calories	266 kcal	Cholesterol	51 mg	Saturated Fat	2 gm
Protein	22 gm	Sodium	182 mg	Polyunsaturated Fat	3 gm
Carbohydrate	26 gm	Total Fat	8 gm	Monounsaturated Fat	2 gm

Oriental Rice Salad in Tomatoes Nutrient Analysis

Calories	289 kcal	Cholesterol	51 mg	Saturated Fat	2 gm
Protein	23 gm	Sodium	192 mg	Polyunsaturated Fat	3 gm
Carbohydrate	31 gm	Total Fat	8 gm	Monounsaturated Fat	2 gm

Oriental Rice Salad in Peppers Nutrient Analysis

Calories	275 kcal	Cholesterol	51 mg	Saturated Fat	2 gm
Protein	22 gm	Sodium	183 mg	Polyunsaturated Fat	3 gm
Carbohydrate	28 gm	Total Fat	8 gm	Monounsaturated Fat	2 gm

Vegetable Rice Salad

Serves 6

2 cups (approximately 8 ounces) thinly sliced yellow
    crookneck squash
3 cups cooked brown rice
⅓ cup diced red onion
½ cup diced red bell pepper
⅓ cup (2 ounces) toasted sunflower seeds
3 tablespoons olive oil
2 tablespoons Dijon mustard
2 tablespoons white vinegar
2 tablespoons light, reduced-calorie mayonnaise
¼ teaspoon salt
Freshly ground black pepper to taste
3 tablespoons finely chopped fresh parsley

Steam squash until tender-crisp. Place in a large bowl. Add rice, onion, bell pepper and sunflower seeds. Stir well. Set aside.

In a blender or the work bowl of a food processor fitted with a metal blade, combine remaining ingredients except parsley. Process 10 seconds. Pour into vegetable mixture and stir to mix well. Add parsley and stir until evenly blended. Cover and refrigerate several hours to allow flavors to blend.

Nutrient Analysis

Calories	248 kcal	Cholesterol	2 mg	Saturated Fat	2 gm
Protein	5 gm	Sodium	182 mg	Polyunsaturated Fat	4 gm
Carbohydrate	30 gm	Total Fat	13 gm	Monounsaturated Fat	6 gm

Arborio Salad with Artichokes

Serves 6; 1 cup per serving

> **8 ounces (1 ¼ cups) uncooked arborio rice** *
> **1 9-ounce package frozen artichoke hearts, defrosted**
> **3 fully ripe Italian plum tomatoes**
> **¼ cup diced red onion**
> **1 cup frozen no-salt-added peas, defrosted**
> **2 tablespoons fresh lemon juice**
> **3 tablespoons olive oil**
> **1 clove garlic, minced**
> **¼ teaspoon salt**
> **6 fresh basil leaves**
> **2 tablespoons low-fat buttermilk**

Cook rice according to package directions, omitting salt, butter or margarine. Cool to room temperature. Set aside.

Blot artichoke hearts dry on paper towels. Cut each heart in half. Cut ends off tomatoes, cut in half lengthwise and slice thinly.

In a bowl, mix rice, artichoke hearts, tomato slices, red onion and peas. Set aside.

In a blender or the work bowl of a food processor fitted with a metal blade, combine remaining ingredients. Process 20 seconds. Pour over rice mixture. With rubber spatula, gently mix salad until dressing is evenly distributed.

Cover and refrigerate several hours to allow flavors to blend.

* *This short-grain rice is available in Italian markets and health-food stores.*

Nutrient Analysis

Calories	244 kcal	Cholesterol	0 mg	Saturated Fat	1 gm
Protein	6 gm	Sodium	152 mg	Polyunsaturated Fat	1 gm
Carbohydrate	40 gm	Total Fat	7 gm	Monounsaturated Fat	5 gm

Curried Rice and Bean Salad

Serves 6

3 cups cooked brown rice
1½ cups canned no-salt-added kidney beans, drained and
     rinsed
4 green onions, chopped
½ green bell pepper, diced
2 stalks celery, diced
¼ cup chopped fresh parsley
¼ cup light, reduced-calorie mayonnaise
¼ cup plain nonfat yogurt
2 teaspoons curry powder
Dash freshly ground black pepper

In a large bowl, combine first six ingredients. Toss to mix well. Set aside.

In a small bowl, combine mayonnaise, yogurt, curry powder and black pepper. Mix well. Pour over rice-bean mixture and mix well.

Nutrient Analysis

Calories	220 kcal	Cholesterol	3 mg	Saturated Fat	1 gm
Protein	8 gm	Sodium	82 mg	Polyunsaturated Fat	1 gm
Carbohydrate	39 gm	Total Fat	4 gm	Monounsaturated Fat	1 gm

Cranberry Orange Salad

Serves 10

1 3-ounce package lemon gelatin
1 cup boiling water
1 cup orange juice
1 16-ounce jar cranberry-orange relish
1 unpeeled apple, chopped
½ cup chopped pecans

Dissolve gelatin in boiling water. Add orange juice, cover and let stand in refrigerator until almost jelled.

In a bowl, combine cranberry-orange relish, chopped apple and pecans. Fold into the almost-jelled mixture, and pour into a 1-quart mold. Cover and refrigerate until firm.

Nutrient Analysis

Calories	171 kcal	Cholesterol	0 mg	Saturated Fat	0 gm
Protein	2 gm	Sodium	42 mg	Polyunsaturated Fat	1 gm
Carbohydrate	34 gm	Total Fat	4 gm	Monounsaturated Fat	3 gm

Waldorf Salad

Serves 6

2 cups diced unpeeled apples
1 cup diced celery
¼ cup coarsely chopped unsalted dry-roasted walnuts
½ cup raisins or halved seedless grapes
1 teaspoon fresh lemon juice
½ cup Yogurt Cheese (see page 68)

In a bowl, combine all ingredients. Mix well, cover and refrigerate. Serve cold.

Serve over salad greens.

Nutrient Analysis

Calories	118 kcal	Cholesterol	1 mg	Saturated Fat	0 gm
Protein	4 gm	Sodium	53 mg	Polyunsaturated Fat	2 gm
Carbohydrate	21 gm	Total Fat	3 gm	Monounsaturated Fat	1 gm

*M*arj's *C*olorful *S*alad

Serves 8

1 cup low-fat cottage cheese
⅔ cup plain nonfat yogurt
2 tablespoons fresh lemon juice
1 teaspoon dill
1 teaspoon basil
2 carrots, shredded
¼ head cabbage, shredded
2 cups canned no-salt-added kidney beans, drained and
    rinsed
1 10-ounce package frozen no-salt-added peas, defrosted
1 10-ounce package frozen no-salt-added lima beans,
    defrosted
1 cup fresh alfalfa sprouts
1 cup sliced cooked beets

GARNISH
¼ cup sunflower seeds

*T*o make salad dressing, place cottage cheese, yogurt, lemon juice, dill and basil in a blender or the work bowl of a food processor fitted with a metal blade. Process until smooth. Pour into a cruet or other salad-dressing container. Cover and refrigerate.

On a large platter, arrange shredded carrots in a mound; do the same for the shredded cabbage in a separate mound. Repeat with remainder of vegetables. Provide sunflower seeds in a small bowl near vegetables.

Place dressing container near platter of vegetables. Let guests make their own salads by combining some or all of the vegetables salad-bar style, adding dressing to taste and garnishing with sunflower seeds.

Nutrient Analysis *

Calories	186 kcal	Cholesterol	3 mg	Saturated Fat		0 gm
Protein	14 gm	Sodium	206 mg	Polyunsaturated Fat		0 gm
Carbohydrate	31 gm	Total Fat	1 gm	Monounsaturated Fat		0 gm

* *assuming all salad ingredients and dressing are divided into eight equal portions.*

Macaroni Salad Ricotta

Serves 4

2 teaspoons prepared mustard
1 tablespoon plain nonfat yogurt
1 cup part-skim ricotta cheese
4 ounces (1½ cups) whole-wheat macaroni, cooked until
    tender, drained and chilled
¼ cup sliced or chopped ripe olives
1 green bell pepper, chopped coarsely
2 scallions with tops, chopped
1 tablespoon chopped fresh parsley
Pimiento to taste
½ teaspoon dill
½ teaspoon basil
¼ teaspoon freshly ground black pepper, or to taste
2 cups fresh salad greens

In a bowl, combine mustard and yogurt, stirring to mix well. Add more yogurt if necessary to achieve the consistency of mayonnaise.

Add ricotta and stir to mix well. Stir in all other ingredients except salad greens.

Divide salad greens equally among four plates. Top with equal amounts of the macaroni mixture.

Nutrient Analysis

Calories	204 kcal	Cholesterol	19 mg	Saturated Fat	3 gm
Protein	12 gm	Sodium	201 mg	Polyunsaturated Fat	0 gm
Carbohydrate	27 gm	Total Fat	6 gm	Monounsaturated Fat	2 gm

*C*hicken *V*egetable *S*alad

Serves 6

2 cups diced cooked chicken, white meat only
½ cucumber, peeled and diced
½ cup diced celery
½ cup sliced water chestnuts, drained
¼ cup diced green bell pepper
¼ cup chopped pimiento, drained
¼ cup sliced scallions
¼ cup light, reduced-calorie mayonnaise
2 tablespoons capers
¼ teaspoon paprika

*I*n a bowl, combine all ingredients except capers and paprika. Toss to mix well. Sprinkle capers and paprika on top of salad.

Serve over crisp salad greens.

TURKEY VEGETABLE SALAD
Substitute cooked turkey for chicken.

TUNA VEGETABLE SALAD
Substitute 2 7-ounce cans water-packed tuna, drained and flaked, for chicken.

Chicken Vegetable Salad Nutrient Analysis

Calories	124 kcal	Cholesterol	39 mg	Saturated Fat	1 gm
Protein	15 gm	Sodium	117 mg	Polyunsaturated Fat	2 gm
Carbohydrate	5 gm	Total Fat	5 gm	Monounsaturated Fat	2 gm

Turkey Vegetable Salad Nutrient Analysis

Calories	124 kcal	Cholesterol	39 mg	Saturated Fat	1 gm
Protein	15 gm	Sodium	117 mg	Polyunsaturated Fat	2 gm
Carbohydrate	5 gm	Total Fat	5 gm	Monounsaturated Fat	2 gm

Tuna Vegetable Salad Nutrient Analysis

Calories	133 kcal	Cholesterol	29 mg	Saturated Fat	1 gm
Protein	20 gm	Sodium	319 mg	Polyunsaturated Fat	1 gm
Carbohydrate	5 gm	Total Fat	3 gm	Monounsaturated Fat	1 gm

*P*ineapple *C*hicken *S*alad

Serves 6

2 pounds boneless chicken breast fillets, skinned, all
    visible fat removed
2 cups homemade Chicken Broth (see page 87) or
    commercial low-sodium variety
⅔ cup dry white wine
1 cup water
1 medium onion, peeled and quartered
1 carrot
½ cup thinly sliced celery
½ cup (3 ounces) slivered almonds
2 cups diced fresh pineapple
½ cup thinly sliced green onion tops
½ cup light, reduced-calorie mayonnaise
1 8-ounce carton low-fat vanilla yogurt

Rinse chicken and pat dry. Set aside.

Combine chicken broth, wine, water, onion, carrot and celery in a large saucepan over medium-high heat. Add chicken fillets and cook over medium heat 20 minutes, or until chicken meat springs back when lightly touched. Remove chicken from broth, cool and cut into small chunks. Set aside. Strain broth and discard vegetables. Cover broth and refrigerate or freeze for future use.

Preheat oven to 350° F. Toast almonds in a single layer on small baking sheet in oven 3 to 4 minutes.

In a large bowl, combine chicken, almonds, pineapple and green onion tops. Set aside. In a small bowl, combine mayonnaise and yogurt, stirring until well blended. Pour over chicken mixture, mixing to coat all ingredients evenly. Cover and refrigerate several hours before serving.

Nutrient Analysis

Calories	370 kcal	Cholesterol	89 mg	Saturated Fat	3 gm
Protein	38 gm	Sodium	237 mg	Polyunsaturated Fat	4 gm
Carbohydrate	19 gm	Total Fat	16 gm	Monounsaturated Fat	7 gm

*C*hicken *S*now *P*ea *S*alad

Serves 6

1 6-ounce package frozen no-salt-added snow peas,
    defrosted, or 6 ounces fresh snow peas, rinsed and
    trimmed
2 11-ounce cans mandarin oranges (canned in light syrup),
    drained
1 pound cooked, cubed chicken breast fillets
¼ cup finely chopped red onion
¼ cup thinly sliced water chestnuts
½ cup light, reduced-calorie mayonnaise
½ cup low-fat vanilla yogurt
1 teaspoon grated fresh ginger
1 teaspoon grated lime rind
¼ teaspoon salt
Dash white pepper

Blot snow peas and oranges dry on paper towels. Set aside.

In a bowl, combine chicken, snow peas, oranges, onion and water chestnuts.

In a small bowl, combine remaining ingredients. Pour over chicken and vegetables and mix gently with rubber spatula. (Be careful to avoid breaking oranges.) Cover and refrigerate several hours to allow flavors to blend.

Nutrient Analysis

Calories	237 kcal	Cholesterol	48 mg	Saturated Fat	2 gm
Protein	19 gm	Sodium	263 mg	Polyunsaturated Fat	3 gm
Carbohydrate	23 gm	Total Fat	8 gm	Monounsaturated Fat	3 gm

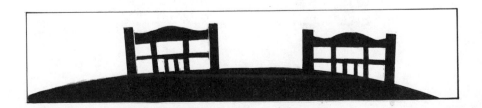

*C*hinese *C*hicken *S*alad

Serves 6

1 pound boneless, skinless chicken breast fillets, all visible
   fat removed
1 tablespoon hot pepper oil
1 tablespoon sesame oil
3 or 4 cloves garlic, minced
1½ teaspoons grated fresh ginger
1 cup julienne-sliced red bell pepper
6 ounces fresh snow peas, trimmed, cut in half if large
4 ounces fresh bean sprouts, rinsed and dried
⅓ cup water
⅓ cup thinly sliced green onion
1 tablespoon honey
2 tablespoons light soy sauce
1 teaspoon hot pepper oil
1 tablespoon rice vinegar

Rinse chicken breast fillets and pat dry. Cut into small chunks and
set aside.

Heat 1 tablespoon hot pepper oil and sesame oil in a nonstick
skillet over medium-high heat. Add garlic and ginger and sauté 1
minute. Add chicken and stir-fry over high heat until chicken is
lightly browned. Add bell pepper, snow peas, bean sprouts and
water. Stir-fry over high heat until water evaporates. Add green
onion and cook 1 minute more. Remove pan from heat. Set aside.

In a small bowl, combine remaining ingredients and stir into
chicken mixture. Serve hot, or cover and refrigerate and serve
chilled.

Nutrient Analysis

Calories	193 kcal	Cholesterol	41 mg	Saturated Fat	2 gm
Protein	20 gm	Sodium	243 mg	Polyunsaturated Fat	3 gm
Carbohydrate	9 gm	Total Fat	9 gm	Monounsaturated Fat	3 gm

*C*urried *C*hicken *S*alad

Serves 8

1 tablespoon onion flakes
2 tablespoons water
2 tablespoons acceptable vegetable oil
2 teaspoons fresh lemon juice
2 teaspoons white or rice vinegar
Dash red pepper
Dash curry powder
4 stalks celery, chopped
8 thin strips green bell pepper
4 cups cubed, cooked chicken

*I*n a bowl, combine onion flakes and water. Add remaining ingredients, except chicken, and mix thoroughly.

Add chicken, cover and refrigerate. Serve cold on a bed of lettuce or heat gently and serve over 4 cups cooked rice or noodles.

Nutrient Analysis

Calories	165 kcal	Cholesterol	59 mg	Saturated Fat	2 gm
Protein	21 gm	Sodium	74 mg	Polyunsaturated Fat	3 gm
Carbohydrate	2 gm	Total Fat	8 gm	Monounsaturated Fat	2 gm

Southwestern Pork Salad

Serves 6

2 cups (about 1 pound) lean roasted pork tenderloin, cut
  into small cubes
1 cup Cuban Black Beans (see page 328) or cooked black
  beans, rinsed and well drained
½ cup finely chopped green onions
1 small clove garlic, minced
½ cup chopped green or red bell pepper
1½ tablespoons sugar
¼ cup cider vinegar
2 tablespoons olive oil
2 tablespoons acceptable vegetable oil
½ teaspoon dried oregano
½ teaspoon dry mustard
¼ cup chopped fresh parsley
1 cup cherry tomatoes, cut into quarters
6 pitted black olives, chopped (optional)
3 cups crisp salad greens

GARNISHES (OPTIONAL)
Fresh orange slices
Fresh green grapes

*I*n a large bowl, combine cooked pork, Cuban Black Beans or black
beans, onions, garlic and bell pepper. Set aside.

In a jar with a tight-fitting lid, prepare marinade by mixing sugar,
vinegar, oils, oregano, mustard and parsley; shake to mix. Pour over
pork, toss to coat evenly, cover and refrigerate several hours, stirring
occasionally.

Immediately before serving, add tomatoes and olives. Serve over
chilled greens.

Garnish with fresh orange slices and green grapes if desired.

Nutrient Analysis

Calories	262 kcal	Cholesterol	43 mg	Saturated Fat		4 gm
Protein	16 gm	Sodium	41 mg	Polyunsaturated Fat		4 gm
Carbohydrate	14 gm	Total Fat	16 gm	Monounsaturated Fat		7 gm

Mexican Shrimp Salad

Serves 6

2½ quarts water
2 teaspoons liquid crab-and-shrimp-boil seasoning
1½ pounds raw medium-size shrimp, shells on
½ cup light, reduced-calorie mayonnaise
⅓ cup plain nonfat yogurt
2 teaspoons prepared horseradish
½ cup sliced green onions
2 tablespoons chili sauce
1 teaspoon chili powder
½ teaspoon grated lime rind
1 tablespoon chopped fresh cilantro (optional)
Hot pepper sauce to taste

Bring water to boil in a large saucepan over high heat. Add seasoning and shrimp. Return to boil, remove from heat and set aside for 5 minutes. Drain shrimp in colander and run under cool water. Peel, devein and cut shrimp in half horizontally to retain *C* shape.

In a bowl, combine remaining ingredients. Add shrimp and stir to mix well. Cover and refrigerate at least 2 hours to allow flavors to blend. Serve cold.

Nutrient Analysis

Calories	131 kcal	Cholesterol	113 mg	Saturated Fat	1 gm
Protein	13 gm	Sodium	317 mg	Polyunsaturated Fat	2 gm
Carbohydrate	5 gm	Total Fat	6 gm	Monounsaturated Fat	3 gm

Fresh Salmon Salad

Serves 8

1½ pounds fresh salmon steaks, ¾-inch to 1-inch thick
1 tablespoon olive oil
¼ teaspooon freshly ground black pepper, or to taste
½ teaspoon thyme
2 tablespoons fresh lemon juice
½ cup diced red bell pepper
½ cup finely diced onion
2 stalks celery, diced
2 tablespoons minced fresh parsley
10 small olives, thinly sliced (optional)
Juice of 1 lemon
½ cup light, reduced-calorie mayonnaise
¼ teaspoon hot pepper sauce, or to taste

Preheat oven to 450° F. Rinse salmon steaks and pat dry. Set aside.

In a bowl, combine olive oil, black pepper, thyme and 2 tablespoons lemon juice. Brush over salmon. Place fish on broiler pan and cook 10 minutes, or until fish flakes. Remove from oven and turn oven setting to Broil. Broil salmon for about 2 minutes. Cool.

Carefully remove all skin and bones from fish. Place salmon in a medium bowl and flake. Add remaining ingredients and mix well. Cover and refrigerate several hours before serving.

This salad is delicious served on crisp greens with fresh fruit and hard rolls.

GRILLING METHOD
Grill salmon steaks for about 10 minutes, or until fish flakes easily. Proceed as directed.

MICROWAVE METHOD
Place salmon steaks on microwave-safe platter sprayed with vegetable oil spray. Cover with paper. Microwave on medium high (70 percent power) 7 to 10 minutes. Let stand, covered, 5 minutes, or until fish flakes. Proceed as directed.

Nutrient Analysis

Calories	162 kcal	Cholesterol	50 mg	Saturated Fat	1 gm
Protein	17 gm	Sodium	121 mg	Polyunsaturated Fat	3 gm
Carbohydrate	4 gm	Total Fat	9 gm	Monounsaturated Fat	4 gm

Salad Niçoise

Serves 12

DRESSING

4 teaspoons Dijon mustard

¼ cup wine vinegar

3 cloves garlic, minced

¾ cup acceptable vegetable oil

½ teaspoon freshly ground black pepper, or to taste

2 teaspoons chopped fresh thyme or 1 teaspoon dried thyme

SALAD

2 pounds fresh green beans cut into medium-size pieces

4 stalks celery, thickly sliced

2 green bell peppers, cut into rings

1 pint cherry tomatoes

5 medium red-skinned potatoes, cooked and sliced

3 7-ounce cans water-packed tuna, drained and flaked

10 large ripe olives, sliced

10 stuffed green olives, sliced

1 large red onion, sliced and separated into rings

⅓ cup chopped fresh parsley

2 tablespoons chopped fresh basil or 1 teaspoon dried basil

¼ cup finely chopped green onions

*I*n a bowl, combine all dressing ingredients and stir vigorously with a wire whisk to mix well. Cover and refrigerate.

Steam green beans until tender-crisp. Drain and set aside.

Blanch celery by boiling it for 15 seconds.

Place green beans, celery and remaining ingredients in a large salad bowl. Add dressing, toss to mix well and serve immediately.

Nutrient Analysis

Calories	266 kcal	Cholesterol	20 mg	Saturated Fat	2 gm
Protein	17 gm	Sodium	339 mg	Polyunsaturated Fat	8 gm
Carbohydrate	17 gm	Total Fat	15 gm	Monounsaturated Fat	4 gm

V*inaigrette* D*ressing*

Makes ½ cup
Serves 8; 1 tablespoon per serving

> 2 tablespoons plain nonfat yogurt
> 2 tablespoons balsamic vinegar
> 4 tablespoons acceptable vegetable oil
> ¼ teaspoon salt
> ⅛ teaspoon freshly ground black pepper

Combine all ingredients in a small bowl and whisk until thoroughly blended. Cover and refrigerate.

For each variation below, add the listed ingredients to the above recipe.

DIJON VINAIGRETTE DRESSING
1 tablespoon Dijon mustard, 1 teaspoon water.

GARLIC VINAIGRETTE DRESSING
¼ teaspoon garlic powder, ½ teaspoon salt-free lemon-pepper seasoning, 2 tablespoons chopped fresh parsley (omit pepper in basic recipe).

GREEN ONION VINAIGRETTE DRESSING
2 tablespoons finely chopped green onion.

ITALIAN HERB VINAIGRETTE DRESSING
Each of the following fresh herbs, finely chopped: 1 tablespoon basil, ½ tablespoon rosemary and 1 tablespoon thyme.

Vinaigrette, Garlic Vinaigrette, Green Onion Vinaigrette and Italian Herb Vinaigrette Dressing Nutrient Analysis

Calories	63 kcal	Cholesterol	0 mg	Saturated Fat		1 gm
Protein	0 gm	Sodium	70 mg	Polyunsaturated Fat		4 gm
Carbohydrate	1 gm	Total Fat	7 gm	Monounsaturated Fat		2 gm

Dijon Vinaigrette Dressing Nutrient Analysis

Calories	64 kcal	Cholesterol	0 mg	Saturated Fat		1 gm
Protein	0 gm	Sodium	93 mg	Polyunsaturated Fat		4 gm
Carbohydrate	1 gm	Total Fat	7 gm	Monounsaturated Fat		2 gm

*H*erbed *V*inaigrette

Makes 3 cups
Serves 48; 1 tablespoon per serving

2 or 3 shallots, minced
2 cloves garlic, minced
1 bunch fresh parsley, large stems removed (rinsed and
    patted dry)
1 tablespoon fresh tyme, leaves removed from stems, or 1
    teaspoon dried thyme
¼ cup basil leaves, or 1 teaspoon dried sweet basil
1 tablespoon fresh oregano, or 1 teaspoon dried oregano
1 tablespoon Dijon mustard
¼ cup red wine vinegar
½ cup champagne or sherry vinegar
¾ cup peanut oil
¾ cup light olive oil
Freshly ground black pepper to taste

*P*rocess shallots and garlic in the work bowl of a food processor fitted with a metal blade until minced. Or, thoroughly mince shallots and garlic with a knife and place in a blender. Add parsley, thyme, basil, oregano, mustard and vinegars. Process just until blended. Transfer to covered bowl. Slowly whisk in oils. Add pepper, cover and refrigerate. This dressing keeps several weeks in the refrigerator.

Nutrient Analysis

Calories	62 kcal	Cholesterol	0 mg	Saturated Fat	1 gm
Protein	0 gm	Sodium	4 mg	Polyunsaturated Fat	1 gm
Carbohydrate	1 gm	Total Fat	7 gm	Monounsaturated Fat	4 gm

*T*omato *D*ressing

Makes 1¼ cups
Serves 20; 1 tablespoon per serving

1 cup no-salt-added tomato juice
¼ cup fresh lemon juice or vinegar
2 tablespoons finely chopped onion
Freshly ground black pepper to taste
1 teaspoon chopped fresh parsley (optional)

Combine all ingredients in a blender or the work bowl of a food processor fitted with a metal blade, and process until mixed. (Or place all ingredients in a jar with a tight-fitting lid and shake vigorously until mixed thoroughly.)

Cover and refrigerate.

Nutrient Analysis

Calories	3 kcal	Cholesterol	0 mg	Saturated Fat	0 gm
Protein	0 gm	Sodium	2 mg	Polyunsaturated Fat	0 gm
Carbohydrate	1 gm	Total Fat	0 gm	Monounsaturated Fat	0 gm

*O*il and *V*inegar *D*ressing

Makes 1 cup
Serves 16; 1 tablespoon per serving

> ¾ cup acceptable vegetable oil
> ¼ cup cider, red wine, balsamic or tarragon vinegar
> ¼ teaspoon freshly ground black pepper

Place all ingredients in a jar with a tight-fitting lid. Shake to blend. Refrigerate to store.

VARIATIONS

For a slightly different taste, add any of the following combinations:

· ⅛ teaspoon paprika or dry mustard
· ¼ teaspoon basil, tarragon or other salad herbs
· ¼ teaspoon oregano and ¼ teaspoon garlic powder
· Pinch curry powder
· Few grains red pepper, cayenne or a dash of hot pepper sauce.

Nutrient Analysis

Calories	91 kcal	Cholesterol	0 mg	Saturated Fat	1 gm
Protein	0 gm	Sodium	0 mg	Polyunsaturated Fat	6 gm
Carbohydrate	0 gm	Total Fat	10 gm	Monounsaturated Fat	2 gm

Chef's Dressing

Makes 1 cup
Serves 16; 1 tablespoon per serving

⅓ cup no-salt-added tomato juice
⅓ cup acceptable vegetable oil
¼ cup red wine vinegar
Freshly ground black pepper to taste
½ teaspoon oregano
½ teaspoon dry mustard
¼ teaspoon light soy sauce

Place all ingredients in a jar with a tight-fitting lid. Shake vigorously until mixed thoroughly.

Keep covered and refrigerated.

CHEF'S DRESSING WITH CHIVES OR SCALLIONS
Add 2 tablespoons of finely chopped chives or scallions.

Chef's Dressing Nutrient Analysis

Calories	42 kcal	Cholesterol	0 mg	Saturated Fat		1 gm
Protein	0 gm	Sodium	4 mg	Polyunsaturated Fat		3 gm
Carbohydrate	0 gm	Total Fat	5 gm	Monounsaturated Fat		1 gm

Chef's Dressing with Chives or Scallions Nutrient Analysis

Calories	42 kcal	Cholesterol	0 mg	Saturated Fat		1 gm
Protein	0 gm	Sodium	4 mg	Polyunsaturated Fat		3 gm
Carbohydrate	1 gm	Total Fat	5 gm	Monounsaturated Fat		1 gm

Creamy Chef's Dressing

Makes 1 cup
Serves 16; 1 tablespoon per serving

¾ cup low-fat buttermilk
¼ cup low-fat cottage cheese
¼ teaspoon prepared mustard
Dash hot pepper sauce
½ small white onion, minced
1 tablespoon minced fresh parsley
½ tablespoon minced chives

Process all ingredients until smooth in a blender or the work bowl of a food processor fitted with a metal blade.

Keep covered and refrigerated.

Nutrient Analysis

Calories	9 kcal	Cholesterol	1 mg	Saturated Fat	0 gm
Protein	1 gm	Sodium	28 mg	Polyunsaturated Fat	0 gm
Carbohydrate	1 gm	Total Fat	0 gm	Monounsaturated Fat	0 gm

*C*ooked *S*alad *D*ressing

Makes 1½ cups
Serves 24; 1 tablespoon per serving

> 2 tablespoons cornstarch
> 2 tablespoons sugar
> 1 teaspoon dry mustard
> ⅛ teaspoon paprika
> ½ cup water
> 1 tablespoon white or cider vinegar
> ¼ cup acceptable margarine
> ⅔ cup skim milk or low-fat buttermilk

In a small saucepan, combine cornstarch, sugar, mustard and paprika. Add water and cook over low heat, stirring until thickened. Stir in vinegar and margarine. Gradually add milk or buttermilk. Stir until creamy.

Cool, cover and refrigerate.

VARIATION

Alter the flavor of this dressing by adding poppy or caraway seeds or honey in amounts to suit individual taste.

Nutrient Analysis

Calories	27 kcal	Cholesterol	0 mg	Saturated Fat	0 gm
Protein	0 gm	Sodium	26 mg	Polyunsaturated Fat	0 gm
Carbohydrate	2 gm	Total Fat	2 gm	Monounsaturated Fat	1 gm

*A*pple *J*uice *D*ressing

Makes ½ cup
Serves 8; 1 tablespoon per serving

> ¼ cup apple juice
> 2½ tablespoons apple cider vinegar
> 2 tablespoons minced sweet onion, or 1 large shallot,
>   minced
> 2 teaspoons Dijon mustard
> 1 teaspoon dried tarragon
> 3 tablespoons coarsely chopped fresh parsley
> Generous amount freshly cracked black pepper

Place all ingredients in a blender or the work bowl of a food processor fitted with a metal blade. Process on high until dressing is smooth. Cover and refrigerate several hours.

Serve with fresh salad greens or fresh fruit.

Nutrient Analysis

Calories	7 kcal	Cholesterol	0 mg	Saturated Fat	0 gm
Protein	0 gm	Sodium	17 mg	Polyunsaturated Fat	0 gm
Carbohydrate	2 gm	Total Fat	0 gm	Monounsaturated Fat	0 gm

*B*uttermilk *H*erb *D*ressing

Makes 1 cup
Serves 16; 1 tablespoon per serving

> 2 tablespoons light, reduced-calorie mayonnaise
> ¾ cup low-fat cottage cheese
> ⅓ cup low-fat buttermilk
> 1½ tablespoons finely chopped onion
> 1 teaspoon dill
> 1 teaspoon basil
> ½ teaspoon leaf oregano
> 2 tablespoons finely chopped fresh parsley
> ⅛ teaspoon salt
> ¼ teaspoon garlic powder
> Dash hot pepper sauce

*I*n blender or work bowl of a food processor fitted with a metal blade, combine mayonnaise, cottage cheese, buttermilk and onion. Process until smooth; add remaining ingredients and process 10 seconds more. Cover and refrigerate. Chill at least 1 hour before serving to allow flavors to blend.

Note: For a richer flavor—and a dressing with a higher calorie count—increase mayonnaise and reduce the amount of cottage cheese.

Nutrient Analysis

Calories	18 kcal	Cholesterol	2 mg	Saturated Fat		0 gm
Protein	2 gm	Sodium	76 mg	Polyunsaturated Fat		0 gm
Carbohydrate	1 gm	Total Fat	1 gm	Monounsaturated Fat		0 gm

Chunky Cucumber and Garlic Dressing

Makes ¾ cup
Serves 12; 1 tablespoon per serving

½ cup plain nonfat yogurt
½ medium cucumber, peeled and chopped
1 tablespoon sugar
1 tablespoon acceptable vegetable oil
½ teaspoon instant minced onion
¼ teaspoon garlic powder
¼ teaspoon freshly ground black pepper
1 tablespoon red wine vinegar

*S*tir yogurt in a small bowl until smooth. Add cucumber, sugar, oil, onion, garlic powder and pepper. Stir well. Gradually stir in vinegar.

Cover and refrigerate at least 4 hours to allow flavors to blend.

Nutrient Analysis

Calories	21 kcal	Cholesterol	0 mg	Saturated Fat		0 gm
Protein	1 gm	Sodium	8 mg	Polyunsaturated Fat		1 gm
Carbohydrate	2 gm	Total Fat	1 gm	Monounsaturated Fat		0 gm

*C*reamy *C*ottage *C*heese *D*ressing

Makes 1¹/₃ cups
Serves 20; 1 tablespoon per serving

1 cup low-fat cottage cheese
¹/₃ cup low-fat buttermilk

Place ingredients in a blender or the work bowl of a food processor fitted with a metal blade. Process on medium speed until smooth and creamy. If a thinner consistency is desired, add more buttermilk.

Cover and refrigerate.

For each variation below, add the suggested ingredients to the basic recipe above.

CREAMY BLUE CHEESE DRESSING
1 tablespoon blue cheese and black pepper to taste.

CREAMY FRENCH DRESSING
1 teaspoon no-salt-added tomato juice, 1 teaspoon paprika, 1 teaspoon dry mustard, 1 teaspoon Worcestershire sauce, 1 teaspoon onion powder and 1 teaspoon garlic powder, or to taste. Thin with additional no-salt-added tomato juice to the desired consistency.

CREAMY GREEN GODDESS DRESSING
3 anchovies, 1 teaspoon chopped green onion, 1 tablespoon chopped fresh parsley and tarragon to taste.

CREAMY ITALIAN DRESSING
½ teaspoon oregano, ½ teaspoon garlic powder and ½ teaspoon onion flakes, or to taste.

CREAMY HORSERADISH DRESSING
1 to 2 tablespoons of grated horseradish (excellent with cold roast beef).

CREAMY THOUSAND ISLAND DRESSING
2 tablespoons pickle relish or chili sauce and dry mustard to taste.

CREAMY DILL DRESSING
½ to 1 teaspoon dried dill weed or 1 tablespoon chopped fresh dill weed.

Creamy Cottage Cheese Dressing Nutrient Analysis

Calories	12 kcal	Cholesterol	1 mg	Saturated Fat	0 gm
Protein	2 gm	Sodium	50 mg	Polyunsaturated Fat	0 gm
Carbohydrate	1 gm	Total Fat	0 gm	Monounsaturated Fat	0 gm

Creamy Blue Cheese Dressing Nutrient Analysis

Calories	13 kcal	Cholesterol	1 mg	Saturated Fat	0 gm
Protein	2 gm	Sodium	56 mg	Polyunsaturated Fat	0 gm
Carbohydrate	1 gm	Total Fat	0 gm	Monounsaturated Fat	0 gm

Creamy French Dressing Nutrient Analysis

Calories	14 kcal	Cholesterol	1 mg	Saturated Fat	0 gm
Protein	2 gm	Sodium	53 mg	Polyunsaturated Fat	0 gm
Carbohydrate	1 gm	Total Fat	0 gm	Monounsaturated Fat	0 gm

Creamy Green Goddess Dressing Nutrient Analysis

Calories	13 kcal	Cholesterol	1 mg	Saturated Fat	0 gm
Protein	2 gm	Sodium	72 mg	Polyunsaturated Fat	0 gm
Carbohydrate	1 gm	Total Fat	0 gm	Monounsaturated Fat	0 gm

Creamy Italian Dressing Nutrient Analysis

Calories	12 kcal	Cholesterol	1 mg	Saturated Fat	0 gm
Protein	2 gm	Sodium	50 mg	Polyunsaturated Fat	0 gm
Carbohydrate	1 gm	Total Fat	0 gm	Monounsaturated Fat	0 gm

Creamy Horseradish Dressing Nutrient Analysis

Calories	12 kcal	Cholesterol	1 mg	Saturated Fat	0 gm
Protein	2 gm	Sodium	51 mg	Polyunsaturated Fat	0 gm
Carbohydrate	1 gm	Total Fat	0 gm	Monounsaturated Fat	0 gm

Creamy Thousand Island Dressing Nutrient Analysis

Calories	14 kcal	Cholesterol	1 mg	Saturated Fat	0 gm
Protein	2 gm	Sodium	61 mg	Polyunsaturated Fat	0 gm
Carbohydrate	1gm	Total Fat	0 gm	Monounsaturated Fat	0 gm

Creamy Dill Dressing Nutrient Analysis

Calories	12 kcal	Cholesterol	1 mg	Saturated Fat	0 gm
Protein	2 gm	Sodium	50 mg	Polyunsaturated Fat	0 gm
Carbohydrate	1 gm	Total Fat	0 gm	Monounsaturated Fat	0 gm

Yogurt Dressing

Makes ⅔ cup
Serves 10; 1 tablespoon per serving

> 2 teaspoons fresh lemon juice
> 1 tablespoon acceptable vegetable oil
> ½ cup plain nonfat yogurt
> ½ teaspoon paprika
> Dash hot pepper sauce
> ⅛ teaspoon garlic powder (optional)

Place all ingredients in a blender or the work bowl of a food processor fitted with a metal blade. Process on medium speed for 5 seconds. Cover and refrigerate.

Nutrient Analysis

Calories	19 kcal	Cholesterol	0 mg	Saturated Fat	0 gm
Protein	1 gm	Sodium	10 mg	Polyunsaturated Fat	1 gm
Carbohydrate	1 gm	Total Fat	1 gm	Monounsaturated Fat	0 gm

Dijon Dressing

Makes ½ cup
Serves 8; 1 tablespoon per serving

> 2 tablespoons Dijon mustard
> 2 tablespoons red wine vinegar
> 4 tablespoons acceptable vegetable oil

In a blender or the work bowl of a food processor fitted with a metal blade, blend mustard and vinegar. Add oil, one tablespoon at a time, until mixture is well blended.

Nutrient Analysis

Calories	64 kcal	Cholesterol	0 mg	Saturated Fat	1 gm
Protein	0 gm	Sodium	47 mg	Polyunsaturated Fat	4 gm
Carbohydrate	0 gm	Total Fat	7 gm	Monounsaturated Fat	2 gm

Minted Lime Dressing

Makes 1²/₃ cups
Serves 28; 1 tablespoon per serving

½ cup low-fat vanilla yogurt
⅓ cup acceptable vegetable oil
1 tablespoon honey
1 tablespoon grated onion
½ cup low-fat cottage cheese
¼ cup fresh lime juice
¼ teaspoon salt
Dash white pepper
2 tablespoons finely chopped fresh mint

Combine all ingredients except mint in a blender or the work bowl of a food processor fitted with a metal blade. Process until smooth. Stir in mint, cover and refrigerate for several hours to allow flavors to blend.

This dressing is excellent with fruit salads.

Nutrient Analysis

Calories	34 kcal	Cholesterol	1 mg	Saturated Fat	0 gm
Protein	1 gm	Sodium	38 mg	Polyunsaturated Fat	2 gm
Carbohydrate	2 gm	Total Fat	3 gm	Monounsaturated Fat	1 gm

*F*ish and *S*eafood

CRISPY BAKED FILLET OF SOLE
MUSHROOM BAKED SOLE
FILLET OF SOLE WITH WALNUTS AND WHITE WINE
SOLE VENETIAN
FLOUNDER FILLETS IN FOIL
RED SNAPPER À L'ORANGE
BAKED COD
BAKED CATFISH
PUFFY BAKED CATFISH
TOMATO ORANGE ROUGHY WITH SPINACH
TERIYAKI HALIBUT
HADDOCK WITH TOMATOES AND GINGER
HADDOCK CASSEROLE
POACHED FISH
FISH FILLETS WITH ASPARAGUS
RED-CHECKED FISH FILLETS
MUSHROOM STUFFED FISH ROLLS
TOMATO CROWN FISH
BROILED FISH ROLL-UPS
HEARTY HALIBUT
GINGER BROILED FISH
PUFFY BROILED FILLETS
BROILED MARINATED FISH STEAKS
GRILLED SALMON ORIENTAL
FRESH SALMON CAKES
HALIBUT STEAKS BRAZILIAN
STUFFED FISH BEACHCOMBER
SCALLOPS AND ASPARAGUS IN WINE SAUCE
OVEN-FRIED SCALLOPS
SCALLOPS ORIENTAL
LINGUINE WITH WHITE CLAM SAUCE
SURIMI PITAS
CRABMEAT MARYLAND
BEAN SPROUT TUNA CHOW MEIN

From rich grilled salmon steaks to tender Oven-Fried Scallops, these fish recipes net both great taste and good nutrition.

Fish is the original fast food. It's easy to prepare, cooks in minutes and is low in fat. An average serving supplies one-third to one-half of adult daily protein requirements, and it's packed with vitamins and minerals.

Fish is a great catch because it is low in saturated fat and cholesterol. The type of fat that is most prominent in fish is omega-3, which is polyunsaturated. Fish particularly rich in omega-3 fatty acids include salmon, mackerel, trout and haddock.

When you shop for fish, make sure it's fresh. Look for bright, bulging eyes and skin that's firm to the touch. It should spring back when pressed lightly. Beware of a strong fishy odor; that's a sign that the fish is spoiling. The best strategy of all is to ask the butcher which fish came in that day and choose from those.

Most fish has fewer calories than meat, but it requires more attention from the cook because of its short cooking time. The best low-fat ways to cook fish include baking, broiling, grilling, steaming and poaching.

If you like fried fish but you're trying to steer clear of fat, try cooking fillets or steaks by dipping them in flour or cracker meal and baking them in the oven or sautéing them in a little polyunsaturated oil. Then remove the fish to a heated platter, squeeze raw garlic through a press into the cooking oil, add lemon juice and pour it over the fish before serving.

Crispy Baked Fillet of Sole

Serves 6

1½ pounds sole fillets
¾ cup finely chopped onion
½ cup acceptable vegetable oil
¼ cup fresh lime juice
2 teaspoons grated lime rind
1 tablespoon grated fresh ginger
1 tablespoon light soy sauce
¼ teaspoon salt
¼ teaspoon ground white pepper
Vegetable oil spray
1¼ cups plain bread crumbs
2 tablespoons finely chopped fresh parsley
2 tablespoons finely chopped green onion

Rinse fish and pat dry. Set aside.

In a small bowl, combine onion, oil, lime juice and rind, ginger, soy sauce, salt and pepper. Set aside.

Lay fillets in a baking dish and pour liquid mixture over all, turning fillets to coat evenly. Cover and refrigerate several hours or overnight.

Preheat oven to 450° F. Lightly spray a baking dish with vegetable oil.

In a pie plate, combine bread crumbs, parsley and green onion. Mix well and set aside.

Remove fillets from marinade and dredge in crumb mixture.

Place fillets in prepared baking dish and bake 15 to 18 minutes, or until fish flakes easily with a fork.

Nutrient Analysis

Calories	339 kcal	Cholesterol	54 mg	Saturated Fat	3 gm
Protein	22 gm	Sodium	427 mg	Polyunsaturated Fat	11 gm
Carbohydrate	17 gm	Total Fat	20 gm	Monounsaturated Fat	5 gm

Mushroom Baked Sole

Serves 6

Vegetable oil spray
1½ pounds sole fillets
1 medium onion, finely chopped
¼ cup chopped fresh parsley
1 cup sliced fresh mushrooms
2 tablespoons acceptable margarine
½ teaspoon freshly ground black pepper
¼ cup dry white wine
1 tablespoon acceptable margarine
1 tablespoon flour
½ cup skim milk
¼ teaspoon paprika
2 tablespoons chopped fresh parsley

Preheat oven to 350° F. Lightly spray a baking dish with vegetable oil.

Rinse fish and pat dry. Set aside.

In a nonstick skillet over medium-high heat, sauté onion, ¼ cup parsley and mushrooms in 2 tablespoons margarine, stirring constantly until onions are soft.

Place half the fillets in bottom of prepared baking dish and sprinkle lightly with pepper. Spread sautéed mixture evenly over fish. Top with remaining fillets and season with more pepper. Pour wine over all and dot with remaining 1 tablespoon margarine.

Bake uncovered 15 minutes. Remove from oven and drain, reserving liquid. In a small saucepan, combine flour and milk. Add reserved pan liquid and cook, stirring constantly, until thickened.

Pour sauce over fish and bake 5 minutes longer. Sprinkle with paprika and 2 tablespoons parsley before serving.

Nutrient Analysis

Calories	164 kcal	Cholesterol	54 mg	Saturated Fat	2 gm
Protein	20 gm	Sodium	163 mg	Polyunsaturated Fat	2 gm
Carbohydrate	4 gm	Total Fat	7 gm	Monounsaturated Fat	3 gm

Fillet of Sole with Walnuts and White Wine

Serves 4

Vegetable oil spray
1 pound sole fillets
Dash cayenne pepper
½ cup dry white wine
½ cup homemade Chicken Broth (see page 87),
    commercial low-sodium variety, fish stock or clam juice

SAUCE
2 tablespoons acceptable vegetable oil
2 tablespoons flour
Dash white pepper
¼ cup skim milk
¼ cup homemade Chicken Broth (see page 87),
    commercial low-sodium variety, fish stock or clam juice
½ cup white wine
½ cup chopped unsalted dry-roasted walnuts

GARNISH
2 tablespoons fresh parsley sprigs

Preheat oven to 325° F. Lightly spray a shallow baking dish with vegetable oil.

Rinse fish and pat dry.

Place skinned fillets in prepared baking dish. Add cayenne pepper, wine and broth. Cover with foil and bake 20 minutes, or until tender.

Meanwhile, make the sauce. Heat oil in a small saucepan over low heat. Blend in flour and cook, but do not brown. Add white pepper. Increase heat to medium, pour in milk, broth and wine and stir constantly until mixture thickens. Reduce heat, add walnuts and simmer 1 minute.

When fillets are done, remove them to a serving platter. Pour sauce over fish and garnish with fresh parsley.

Nutrient Analysis *

Calories	279 kcal	Cholesterol	54 mg	Saturated Fat	2 gm
Protein	23 gm	Sodium	106 mg	Polyunsaturated Fat	10 gm
Carbohydrate	8 gm	Total Fat	18 gm	Monounsaturated Fat	4 gm

* *using low-sodium chicken broth*

*S*ole *V*enetian

Serves 4

Vegetable oil spray
1 pound sole fillets
1 tablespoon acceptable vegetable oil
1 tablespoon chopped fresh mint
1 clove garlic, chopped
2 tablespoons minced fresh parsley

SAUCE (OPTIONAL)
1 tablespoon acceptable margarine
1 green onion, chopped
½ cup dry white wine
¼ cup water
¼ teaspoon white pepper

Lightly spray a broiler pan with vegetable oil. Preheat broiler.

Rinse fish and pat dry. Place on prepared broiler pan.

In a small bowl, mix together oil, mint, garlic and parsley. Mixture will resemble a paste.

Rub paste over fish and broil 5 to 8 minutes, or just until done. Do not overcook. Serve immediately or with optional sauce.

SAUCE

To make the sauce, place margarine in a nonstick skillet over medium-high heat. Add green onion and sauté briefly. Add wine, water and pepper. Add pan juices from fish and heat thoroughly. Pour over sole, and serve at once.

*Nutrient Analysis**

Calories	123 kcal	Cholesterol	53 mg	Saturated Fat	1 gm
Protein	19 gm	Sodium	83 mg	Polyunsaturated Fat	2 gm
Carbohydrate	0 gm	Total Fat	5 gm	Monounsaturated Fat	1 gm

* *without sauce*

*Nutrient Analysis**

Calories	154 kcal	Cholesterol	53 mg	Saturated Fat	1 gm
Protein	19 gm	Sodium	119 mg	Polyunsaturated Fat	3 gm
Carbohydrate	2 gm	Total Fat	7 gm	Monounsaturated Fat	2 gm

* *with optional sauce*

Flounder Fillets in Foil

Serves 4

4 5-ounce flounder fillets
1 tablespoon acceptable margarine
1 tablespoon chopped shallots, or green onions
½ pound mushrooms, chopped
3 tablespoons dry white wine
1 tablespoon fresh lemon juice
1 tablespoon chopped fresh parsley
Vegetable oil spray
½ teaspoon freshly ground black pepper

*R*inse fish and pat dry. Set aside.

To make a mushroom sauce, begin by lightly spraying a nonstick skillet with vegetable oil. Place over medium-high heat. Add margarine, shallots or green onions and sauté until soft. Add mushrooms and cook 5 minutes. Stir in wine, lemon juice and parsley and cook until most of the liquid evaporates.

Preheat oven to 400° F. Lightly spray four pieces of heavy-duty foil with vegetable oil. Place a fillet on each piece of foil; season with pepper.

Spoon mushroom sauce evenly over each piece of fish. Draw edges of foil together and seal. Bake 20 minutes, or until fish flakes. Serve in foil.

VARIATIONS

In place of mushroom sauce, use any one of the following combinations listed below. Amounts may be varied to suit individual taste.

· Spinach, frozen
Fresh lemon juice
Nutmeg
Acceptable margarine

· Tomato, thinly sliced circles
Scallions, thinly sliced
Basil
Fresh lemon juice
Acceptable margarine

· Cucumber, thinly sliced circles
Fresh lemon juice
Fresh dill and/or parsley, chopped
Acceptable margarine

· Celery, thinly sliced
Fresh lemon juice
Thyme
Acceptable margarine

· Scallions, thinly sliced
  Carrots, julienned
  Curry powder
  Green bell pepper, thinly sliced circles
  Acceptable margarine

Nutrient Analysis

Calories	159 kcal	Cholesterol	69 mg	Saturated Fat	1 gm
Protein	26 gm	Sodium	143 mg	Polyunsaturated Fat	1 gm
Carbohydrate	3 gm	Total Fat	5 gm	Monounsaturated Fat	2 gm

*R*ed *S*napper à *l'O*range

Serves 6

> 1½ pounds red snapper fillets, cut into 6 serving pieces
> Vegetable oil spray
> 3 tablespoons acceptable vegetable oil
> 2 tablespoons orange juice
> 1 teaspoon grated orange rind
> Freshly ground black pepper to taste
> ⅛ teaspoon nutmeg

*R*inse fish and pat dry.

Preheat oven to 350° F. Lightly spray a shallow baking dish with vegetable oil. Arrange fish pieces in a single layer in the prepared dish. Set aside.

Combine oil, orange juice, orange rind and pepper in a small bowl. Pour over fish. Sprinkle with nutmeg and bake 20 to 30 minutes, or until fish flakes.

Nutrient Analysis

Calories	167 kcal	Cholesterol	60 mg	Saturated Fat	1 gm
Protein	21 gm	Sodium	93 mg	Polyunsaturated Fat	5 gm
Carbohydrate	1 gm	Total Fat	8 gm	Monounsaturated Fat	2 gm

*B*aked *C*od

Serves 6

Vegetable oil spray
1 cup sliced carrots
2 cups cubed potatoes
2 tablespoons acceptable margarine, melted
2 tablespoons fresh lemon juice
¼ teaspoon salt
¼ teaspoon ground white pepper
1½ pounds cod, cut into 2-inch pieces
¼ teaspoon salt
¼ teaspoon ground white pepper
½ cup sliced green onion
2 tablespoons finely chopped fresh parsley
1 tablespoon finely chopped fresh dill
2 ounces shredded part-skim mozzarella cheese
2 tablespoons grated Parmesan cheese

Preheat oven to 400° F. Lightly spray a baking dish with vegetable oil.

Place carrots and potatoes in dish. Set aside. In a small bowl, combine margarine, lemon juice, ¼ teaspoon salt and ¼ teaspoon white pepper. Pour this mixture over vegetables. Cover dish and bake 25 minutes.

Rinse cod under cool water and dry thoroughly with paper towels. Season cod with ¼ teaspoon salt and ¼ teaspoon white pepper. Mix fish, green onion, parsley and dill with cooked vegetables. Cover and return to oven for 15 minutes.

In a small bowl, combine cheeses and sprinkle on top of fish and vegetables. Bake uncovered 2 minutes more.

MICROWAVE METHOD
Prepare vegetables in casserole as directed. Cover with plastic wrap, vented, and microwave 8 to 10 minutes on high. Add fish and cook, covered and vented, 5 to 6 minutes on high. Add cheeses and cook uncovered 2 minutes more.

Nutrient Analysis

Calories	229 kcal	Cholesterol	67 mg	Saturated Fat	3 gm
Protein	26 gm	Sodium	423 mg	Polyunsaturated Fat	2 gm
Carbohydrate	13 gm	Total Fat	8 gm	Monounsaturated Fat	3 gm

*B*aked *C*atfish

Serves 6

Vegetable oil spray
2 pounds catfish fillets (6 pieces)
¾ cup low-fat buttermilk
¼ teaspoon salt
¼ teaspoon hot pepper sauce
3 ounces (about 30) whole-wheat crackers, crushed
2 tablespoons acceptable margarine, melted
2 tablespoons chopped fresh parsley

GARNISH
6 lemon wedges

*P*reheat oven to 400° F. Lightly spray a baking dish with vegetable oil.

Rinse fish and pat dry. Set aside.

Combine buttermilk, salt and hot pepper sauce in a small shallow dish. Place cracker crumbs on a plate.

Dip fillets first in buttermilk, then in crumbs, taking care to coat fish evenly.

Place fillets in prepared baking dish. Drizzle 1 teaspoon margarine over each fillet. Bake uncovered 15 to 20 minutes, or until fish flakes with fork.

Arrange fish on warmed serving platter and sprinkle with chopped parsley. Garnish with lemon wedges.

Nutrient Analysis

Calories	299 kcal	Cholesterol	95 mg	Saturated Fat	3 gm
Protein	35 gm	Sodium	356 mg	Polyunsaturated Fat	3 gm
Carbohydrate	10 gm	Total Fat	12 gm	Monounsaturated Fat	5 gm

Puffy *Baked* *Catfish*

Serves 4

Vegetable oil spray
1 pound catfish fillets, rinsed and drained
2 tablespoons light, reduced-calorie mayonnaise
½ teaspoon dry mustard dissolved in 1 teaspoon water
1 tablespoon minced fresh parsley
3 to 4 drops hot pepper sauce
1 egg white

Preheat oven to 425° F. Place foil on a large cookie sheet. Lightly spray foil with vegetable oil.

Rinse fish and pat dry.

Arrange fish pieces skin side down on prepared foil. Set aside.

In a small bowl, combine mayonnaise, mustard, parsley and hot pepper sauce. Set aside.

In another small bowl, beat egg white until stiff but not dry. Fold in mayonnaise mixture. Lightly spread meringue mixture on top and sides of fish fillets.

Bake 12 to 15 minutes, or until fish flakes and meringue is golden brown. Do not overcook. Serve immediately.

Nutrient Analysis

Calories	166 kcal	Cholesterol	69 mg	Saturated Fat	1 gm
Protein	25 gm	Sodium	88 mg	Polyunsaturated Fat	2 gm
Carbohydrate	1 gm	Total Fat	6 gm	Monounsaturated Fat	2 gm

Tomato *Orange* *Roughy* with *Spinach*

Serves 6

2½ pounds (6 fillets) orange roughy
2 tablespoons olive oil
1 cup finely chopped onion
3 cloves garlic, minced
3 tablespoons water

> 1 28-ounce can Italian plum tomatoes in juice, not drained
> ½ cup dry white wine
> 1 10-ounce package fresh spinach, rinsed, stems removed
> 2 tablespoons finely chopped fresh dill
> 2 tablespoons finely chopped fresh parsley
> 2 tablespoons fresh lemon juice
> Vegetable oil spray
> ½ teaspoon white pepper
> 2 tablespoons cornstarch (optional)

Preheat oven to 400° F.

Rinse fish and pat dry. Set aside.

Heat oil in a large nonstick skillet over medium-high heat. Add onion and garlic and sauté 2 minutes. Add water and continue to cook, stirring constantly, until water evaporates. Stir in tomatoes and crush with wooden spoon. Add wine. Cook uncovered over medium-high heat 7 to 8 minutes to reduce mixture slightly. Add spinach, cover and cook 3 to 5 minutes, or until spinach is wilted. Remove from heat and add herbs and lemon juice. Set aside.

Lightly spray an oblong, nonaluminum baking dish with vegetable oil. Pour half of sauce into dish. Arrange fillets on top and sprinkle each lightly with pepper. Fold each fillet in half and pour remaining sauce over all.

Cover dish with foil and bake 15 to 18 minutes, or until fish flakes easily with fork.

If a thicker sauce is desired, remove fillets to a warmed platter. Pour sauce into a nonstick skillet and blend in 2 tablespoons cornstarch combined with 2 tablespoons water. Bring to boil, remove from heat and pour over fish.

Nutrient Analysis

Calories	370 kcal	Cholesterol	75 mg	Saturated Fat	3 gm
Protein	44 gm	Sodium	334 mg	Polyunsaturated Fat	4 gm
Carbohydrate	10 gm	Total Fat	16 gm	Monounsaturated Fat	7 gm

*T*eriyaki *H*alibut

Serves 8

¼ cup light soy sauce
1 tablespoon firmly packed brown sugar
2 tablespoons acceptable vegetable oil
1 teaspoon flour
½ cup dry white wine
½ teaspoon dry mustard
2 pounds halibut fillets
Vegetable oil spray
6 slices no-sugar-added pineapple canned in fruit juice

In a small saucepan over medium-high heat, combine soy sauce, brown sugar, oil, flour, wine and mustard. Bring to a boil, reduce heat and simmer 3 minutes. Allow to cool.

Rinse fish and pat dry.

Place fillets in a nonmetal pan and add marinade. Cover and refrigerate for 15 minutes.

Preheat broiler. Lightly spray a broiler pan with vegetable oil.

Remove fish from marinade and place on prepared broiler pan. Place pineapple on top of fish. Boil marinade in a saucepan over medium-high heat and brush fish with hot marinade. Broil 5 to 6 inches from heat for about 10 minutes, or until fish is done.

Remove to a warm platter and serve hot.

Nutrient Analysis

Calories	171 kcal	Cholesterol	60 mg	Saturated Fat		1 gm
Protein	22 gm	Sodium	395 mg	Polyunsaturated Fat		3 gm
Carbohydrate	9 gm	Total Fat	5 gm	Monounsaturated Fat		1 gm

*H*addock with *T*omatoes and *G*inger

Serves 6

Vegetable oil spray
1½ pounds haddock fillets
3 tablespoons flour
Dash white pepper
2½ tablespoons acceptable vegetable oil
1 tablespoon grated fresh ginger
2 cloves garlic, minced
2 cups seeded, chopped tomatoes
⅓ cup sliced green onions
1 cup orange juice
½ cup white wine
2 tablespoons light soy sauce
1½ tablespoons cornstarch
1 tablespoon finely chopped fresh parsley

*P*reheat oven to 350° F. Lightly coat a baking dish with vegetable oil spray.

Rinse fish and pat dry. Set aside.

Combine flour and pepper in a shallow bowl. Add fillets, one at a time, and turn to coat well. In a nonstick skillet over medium-high heat, heat oil and brown fillets. Transfer them to prepared baking dish and cook 10 to 15 minutes, or until fish flakes easily with a fork.

Meanwhile, sauté ginger and garlic in residual oil in skillet. Add tomatoes and green onions and simmer 3 to 4 minutes. In a small bowl, combine orange juice, wine, soy sauce and cornstarch. Add mixture to skillet and stir until thickened. Stir in parsley. Spoon sauce over the fish and serve immediately.

Nutrient Analysis

Calories	215 kcal	Cholesterol	60 mg	Saturated Fat	1 gm
Protein	23 gm	Sodium	302 mg	Polyunsaturated Fat	4 gm
Carbohydrate	14 gm	Total Fat	7 gm	Monounsaturated Fat	2 gm

Haddock Casserole

Serves 6

Vegetable oil spray
½ pound haddock fillets
3 potatoes, thinly sliced
4 cups chopped cabbage
3 medium-size tart apples, thinly sliced
1 onion, chopped
½ teaspoon freshly ground black pepper
½ teaspoon basil
½ teaspoon marjoram
½ teaspoon garlic powder
½ teaspoon oregano
2 tablespoons acceptable margarine, melted
1 cup skim milk
¼ cup plain bread crumbs
¼ cup grated low-fat Swiss cheese

Preheat oven to 350° F. Lightly coat a covered casserole dish with vegetable oil spray.

Rinse fish and pat dry.

Poach haddock (see Poached Fish, page 193). Allow to cool slightly. Crumble fish into prepared casserole dish. Set aside.

Steam potatoes and cabbage 5 minutes.

Place potatoes, cabbage, apples and onion on top of fish in casserole dish. Add seasonings. Pour margarine over vegetable layer. Top with milk.

Cover casserole and bake 45 minutes, or until potatoes are tender. Uncover casserole, sprinkle bread crumbs and cheese on top and bake until brown and crusty, about 5 minutes.

Nutrient Analysis

Calories	201 kcal	Cholesterol	23 mg	Saturated Fat	1 gm
Protein	12 gm	Sodium	209 mg	Polyunsaturated Fat	1 gm
Carbohydrate	27 gm	Total Fat	5 gm	Monounsaturated Fat	2 gm

*P*oached *F*ish

Serves 8

2 pounds fish fillets, skinned
1 small onion, chopped
¼ cup chopped celery
2 tablespoons acceptable vegetable oil
1 cup hot water or white wine
2 tablespoons fresh lemon juice
Freshly ground black pepper to taste
1 bay leaf

GARNISH
2 sprigs fresh parsley

Rinse fish and pat dry. Set aside.

In a large nonstick skillet over medium-high heat, sauté onion and celery in oil until tender. Place fillets on top of vegetables, or roll each fillet, securing it with a toothpick, and place on vegetables that way. Add water or wine, lemon juice, pepper and bay leaf. Cover and simmer about 8 minutes, or until fish flakes when tested with a fork.

Carefully transfer fillets to a heated platter. Remove toothpicks, and garnish fillets with parsley.

Serve with Lemon Parsley Sauce or Horseradish Sauce (pages 428 and 430).

Nutrient Analysis *

Calories	134 kcal	Cholesterol	60 mg	Saturated Fat	1 gm
Protein	21 gm	Sodium	94 mg	Polyunsaturated Fat	3 gm
Carbohydrate	0 gm	Total Fat	5 gm	Monounsaturated Fat	1 gm

* *using water*

*F*ish *F*illets *with* *A*sparagus

Serves 4

Vegetable oil spray
4 5-ounce fish fillets, such as haddock, cod or other mild
    fish
½ teaspoon freshly ground black pepper
1 tablespoon fresh lemon juice
2 tablespoons acceptable margarine, melted
12 stalks cooked asparagus
⅓ cup Tangy Sour Cream (see page 418)
⅓ cup plain nonfat yogurt
2 teaspoons minced chives
2 teaspoons horseradish
½ teaspoon dried dill weed
1 egg white
2 tablespoons parsley

*P*reheat boiler. Lightly spray a broiler pan with vegetable oil.

Rinse fish and pat dry.

Season fish with pepper and lemon juice and brush with margarine. Place on broiler pan and broil about 8 minutes, turning once, or until fish almost flakes. Remove from oven and top each fillet with 3 stalks of asparagus.

In a small bowl, combine Tangy Sour Cream, yogurt, chives, horseradish and dill weed. In another small bowl, beat egg white until stiff peaks form; fold into sour cream mixture.

Spread sour cream mixture over each fillet to cover fish and asparagus. Return to broiler and broil 1 to 2 minutes, or until golden brown. Sprinkle with parsley.

Nutrient Analysis

Calories	232 kcal	Cholesterol	77 mg	Saturated Fat	2 gm
Protein	33 gm	Sodium	309 mg	Polyunsaturated Fat	2 gm
Carbohydrate	6 gm	Total Fat	8 gm	Monounsaturated Fat	3 gm

Red-Checked Fish Fillets

Serves 6

Vegetable oil spray
1½ tablespoons acceptable vegetable oil
½ cup finely chopped onion
¼ cup diced red bell pepper
2 tablespoons snipped fresh chives
1 tablespoon finely chopped fresh parsley
1½ slices (3 ounces) white bread
1 teaspoon grated lemon rind
1½ pounds firm white fish fillets
¼ teaspoon salt
Ground white pepper to taste
1 tablespoon fresh lemon juice

Preheat oven to 400° F. Lightly spray a baking dish with vegetable oil.

Heat oil in a small nonstick skillet over medium-high heat. Add onion and bell pepper. Sauté until onion is translucent. Stir in chives and parsley. Remove from heat and set aside.

Place bread in a blender or the work bowl of a food processor fitted with a metal blade. Process into fine crumbs. Add crumbs and lemon rind to onion mixture. Stir to mix thoroughly.

Rinse fillets under cool water and dry thoroughly with paper towels. Arrange fillets in prepared baking dish and sprinkle with salt, white pepper and lemon juice. Spread vegetable mixture evenly over fish. Bake until fish flakes easily with a fork. Allow about 10 minutes per inch thickness at the thickest point.

MICROWAVE METHOD

Combine oil, onion and pepper in baking dish. Microwave on high 5 minutes, stirring once. Add chives and parsley. Follow instructions above. Microwave fish covered with vented plastic wrap for 10 minutes on high. Give dish a half-turn during cooking time.

Nutrient Analysis

Calories	156 kcal	Cholesterol	60 mg	Saturated Fat	1 gm
Protein	22 gm	Sodium	215 mg	Polyunsaturated Fat	3 gm
Carbohydrate	4 gm	Total Fat	5 gm	Monounsaturated Fat	1 gm

Mushroom Stuffed Fish Rolls

Serves 6

Vegetable oil spray
6 thin fish fillets, sole, roughy or any mild fish (4 ounces
    each)
¾ pound fresh mushrooms, finely diced
8 green onions, thinly sliced
½ cup diced red bell pepper
2 tablespoons minced fresh parsley
1 tablespoon acceptable margarine
¼ teaspoon salt
¼ teaspoon freshly ground black pepper
2 to 3 tablespoons fresh lemon juice
½ cup dry white wine
2 tablespoons flour
2 tablespoons cold water
¾ teaspoon paprika
2 tablespoons minced fresh parsley

Preheat oven to 350° F. Lightly spray a casserole dish with vegetable oil. Rinse fish and pat dry. Set aside.

In a heavy nonstick skillet, sauté mushrooms, onions, bell pepper and 2 tablespoons parsley in margarine until tender.

Season fish fillets lightly with salt and black pepper.

Spoon mushroom mixture evenly on each fillet and roll, beginning at small end of fillets. Secure with toothpicks. Place in casserole. Sprinkle fish with lemon juice and pour wine over fillets. Cover with foil and bake 25 to 35 minutes, or until fish flakes and is done.

Use a slotted spoon to remove cooked fish to a warm serving plate. Remove toothpicks and keep fish warm. Pour cooking liquid into a small saucepan and set aside.

In a small bowl, combine flour, water and paprika and blend well. Add to reserved liquid. Place over medium heat and cook, stirring constantly, until thickened.

Spoon sauce over fish and top with parsley. Serve immediately.

MICROWAVE METHOD

Place mushrooms, onions, bell pepper, 2 tablespoons parsley and margarine in a microwave-safe bowl. Cook at high setting just until tender. Season fish fillets lightly with salt and black pepper. Spoon mixture evenly on each fillet and roll as directed above. Secure with toothpicks. Place in prepared casserole dish and cook, covered, 6 to 8 minutes on high. Remove and let fish rest 5 to 10 minutes. Fish will flake when done. Proceed as directed above.

Nutrient Analysis

Calories	140 kcal	Cholesterol	53 mg	Saturated Fat	1 gm
Protein	21 gm	Sodium	199 mg	Polyunsaturated Fat	1 gm
Carbohydrate	7 gm	Total Fat	3 gm	Monounsaturated Fat	1 gm

*T*omato *C*rown *F*ish

Serves 6

> Vegetable oil spray
> 1½ pounds fish fillets
> 1½ cups water
> 2 tablespoons fresh lemon juice
> Freshly ground black pepper to taste
> 2 large fresh tomatoes, or no-salt-added canned tomatoes, sliced
> ½ green bell pepper, minced
> 2 tablespoons minced onion
> ½ cup plain bread crumbs
> 1 tablespoon acceptable vegetable oil
> ½ teaspoon basil

Preheat oven to 350°F. Rinse fish and pat dry. Lightly spray a baking dish with vegetable oil.

Combine water and lemon juice in a bowl. Add fish, cover and refrigerate for 10 minutes. Then place fish in prepared baking dish. Season with black pepper and arrange tomato slices, bell pepper and onion over fillets.

In a small bowl, combine bread crumbs, oil and basil. Drizzle evenly over fish and vegetables. Bake uncovered 10 to 15 minutes.

Nutrient Analysis*

Calories	170 kcal	Cholesterol	61 mg	Saturated Fat	1 gm
Protein	23 gm	Sodium	163 mg	Polyunsaturated Fat	2 gm
Carbohydrate	9 gm	Total Fat	4 gm	Monounsaturated Fat	1 gm

* *using fresh tomatoes*

Broiled Fish Roll-Ups

Serves 6

Vegetable oil spray
1½ pounds fish fillets
2 tablespoons chopped onion
½ cup chopped celery
3 tablespoons water
2 cups plain, coarse bread crumbs
Freshly ground black pepper to taste
¼ cup chopped cooked spinach
½ teaspoon thyme
1 egg white, slightly beaten
¼ cup skim milk
½ cup plain, fine cracker crumbs
2 tablespoons flour
1 teaspoon chopped fresh parsley

Preheat broiler. Lightly spray a broiler pan with vegetable oil.

Rinse fish and pat dry. Set aside.

Combine onion, celery and water in a saucepan over medium-high heat. Bring to a boil, cover and simmer until vegetables are tender. Remove from heat.

Add bread crumbs, pepper, spinach and thyme. Mix well, adding more water to moisten if necessary.

Place some of mixture on each fillet. Roll up fish and fasten with toothpicks.

In a small, shallow bowl, combine egg white and milk. Stir until well mixed. Set aside. In another small, shallow bowl, combine cracker crumbs and flour. Set aside. Roll stuffed fillets in egg-white mixture, then in cracker-crumb mixture.

Place fish rolls on prepared broiler pan and place in broiler 4 to 5 inches from heat. Cook 5 to 7 minutes on first side, turn carefully and cook about 5 minutes more, or until fish flakes easily with a fork.

Remove toothpicks, sprinkle parsley on top and serve hot.

Nutrient Analysis

Calories	288 kcal	Cholesterol	64 mg	Saturated Fat	1 gm
Protein	28 gm	Sodium	438 mg	Polyunsaturated Fat	1 gm
Carbohydrate	32 gm	Total Fat	4 gm	Monounsaturated Fat	2 gm

*H*earty *H*alibut

Serves 8

Vegetable oil spray
2 pounds halibut or other firm fish steaks
⅔ cup thinly sliced onion
1½ cups sliced fresh mushrooms
⅓ cup chopped tomato
¼ cup chopped green bell pepper
¼ cup chopped fresh parsley
3 tablespoons chopped pimiento
½ cup dry white wine
2 tablespoons fresh lemon juice
¼ teaspoon dill weed
Freshly ground black pepper to taste

GARNISH
8 lemon wedges

Preheat oven to 350° F. Lightly spray a covered baking dish with vegetable oil.

Rinse fish and pat dry.

Arrange onion slices in the bottom of prepared baking dish. Place fish on top. Set aside.

In a bowl, combine remaining vegetables. Stir to mix well, and spread over fillets.

In a small bowl, combine wine, lemon juice, dill and black pepper. Pour over fish and vegetables. Cover and bake 25 to 30 minutes, or until fish flakes easily when tested with a fork. Garnish with lemon wedges.

Nutrient Analysis

Calories	116 kcal	Cholesterol	60 mg	Saturated Fat		0 gm
Protein	22 gm	Sodium	99 mg	Polyunsaturated Fat		1 gm
Carbohydrate	3 gm	Total Fat	1 gm	Monounsaturated Fat		0 gm

Ginger Broiled Fish

Serves 8

Vegetable oil spray
2 pounds fresh or frozen fish pieces or steaks, about
    ¾-inch thick
¾ cup dry white wine
3 tablespoons acceptable vegetable oil
1 tablespoon light soy sauce
1½ tablespoons chopped onion
¾ teaspoon ground ginger
½ teaspoon horseradish

Preheat broiler. Lightly spray a baking dish with vegetable oil. Place prepared pan in oven for 1 to 2 minutes.

Rinse fish and pat dry.

Cut fish into eight equal portions. Arrange in a single layer in preheated pan.

In a bowl, combine remaining ingredients, mix well and pour over fish.

Broil 10 to 12 minutes about 2 inches from heat, turning once and basting several times. Fish is done when it flakes easily with a fork.

Nutrient Analysis

Calories	142 kcal	Cholesterol	53 mg	Saturated Fat	1 gm
Protein	19 gm	Sodium	159 mg	Polyunsaturated Fat	3 gm
Carbohydrate	1 gm	Total Fat	6 gm	Monounsaturated Fat	1 gm

Puffy Broiled Fillets

Serves 4

Vegetable oil spray
1 pound fish fillets, with skin
1 tablespoon acceptable margarine, melted
½ teaspoon freshly ground black pepper
2 tablespoons tartar sauce
2 tablespoons light, reduced-calorie mayonnaise
1 egg white, beaten until stiff

Preheat broiler. Lightly spray a shallow baking dish with vegetable oil.

Rinse fish and pat dry.

Place fillets skin side down in prepared dish. Brush with margarine and season with pepper.

Broil about 10 minutes, 3 to 4 inches from heat.

Meanwhile, gently fold tartar sauce and mayonnaise into stiffly beaten egg white. When fish flakes easily, spread mixture over fillets and broil 2 minutes more, or until topping is golden brown.

Nutrient Analysis

Calories	188 kcal	Cholesterol	59 mg	Saturated Fat	2 gm
Protein	20 gm	Sodium	231 mg	Polyunsaturated Fat	5 gm
Carbohydrate	2 gm	Total Fat	11 gm	Monounsaturated Fat	3 gm

*B*roiled *M*arinated *F*ish *S*teaks

Serves 6

1½ pounds fish steaks, cut 1 inch thick
2 tablespoons acceptable vegetable oil
⅓ cup tarragon vinegar
1 teaspoon Worcestershire sauce
2 teaspoons freshly ground black pepper, or to taste
1 bay leaf
2 tablespoons chopped fresh parsley

Rinse fish and pat dry. Set aside.

In a shallow glass pan, combine all ingredients except fish. Stir to mix well. Add fish steaks. Cover and refrigerate at least 3 hours, turning occasionally.

Preheat broiler. Remove steaks from marinade and arrange on a foil-covered broiler pan. Baste with marinade. Broil 3 inches from heat about 10 minutes, or until fish flakes easily.

Nutrient Analysis *

Calories	172 kcal	Cholesterol	60 mg	Saturated Fat	1 gm
Protein	22 gm	Sodium	39 mg	Polyunsaturated Fat	4 gm
Carbohydrate	2 gm	Total Fat	8 gm	Monounsaturated Fat	2 gm

* *using swordfish*

Grilled Salmon Oriental

Serves 6

1½ pounds salmon steaks or fillets
1 6-ounce can unsweetened pineapple juice
1 tablespoon light soy sauce
1 teaspoon hot pepper oil
1 tablespoon acceptable vegetable oil
2 cloves garlic, minced
½ cup finely chopped onion
1 tablespoon grated fresh ginger
½ teaspoon grated lime rind
2 tablespoons fresh lime juice
Vegetable oil spray

Rinse fish and pat dry.

Arrange fish in rectangular nonaluminum baking dish.

Combine all remaining ingredients in a small bowl, stir and pour over steaks, turning to coat evenly. Cover and refrigerate overnight.

Preheat grill or broiler. Lightly spray grill top or broiler pan with vegetable oil.

Remove steaks from marinade and place steaks over hot coals or under broiler, 4 to 5 inches from heat. Grill 5 to 7 minutes on each side, or until fish flakes easily with a fork.

Note: Do not use vegetable oil spray near an open flame or a heat source. Read directions on can before using, and follow directions carefully.

Nutrient Analysis

Calories	196 kcal	Cholesterol	71 mg	Saturated Fat	1 gm
Protein	26 gm	Sodium	135 mg	Polyunsaturated Fat	3 gm
Carbohydrate	5 gm	Total Fat	7 gm	Monounsaturated Fat	2 gm

*F*resh *S*almon *C*akes

Serves 8

1 pound fresh boneless, skinless salmon fillets
1 egg, slightly beaten
2 egg whites, beaten until frothy
10 whole-wheat crackers, finely crushed
½ cup finely chopped green onion
1 tablespoon snipped fresh parsley or 1 teaspoon dried
  parsley
1 tablespoon finely snipped fresh dill or 1 teaspoon dried
  dill
1½ tablespoons capers, rinsed and chopped
2 to 3 tablespoons fresh lime juice
⅛ teaspoon cayenne pepper, or to taste
¼ teaspoon freshly ground black pepper
¼ teaspoon dry mustard
½ teaspoon paprika
1 tablespoon acceptable margarine
1 tablespoon acceptable vegetable oil

*R*inse fish and pat dry.

Steam salmon 6 to 8 minutes, or until it flakes. Cool. Flake and be sure all bones have been removed.

In a bowl, combine all remaining ingredients except margarine and oil. Mix lightly with flaked salmon. Divide into eight patties. Cover and refrigerate 20 to 30 minutes.

Place margarine and oil in a nonstick skillet over medium-high heat. Add patties and sauté 3 to 4 minutes on each side.

Serve with steamed asparagus and fresh fruit.

Nutrient Analysis

Calories	145 kcal	Cholesterol	71 mg	Saturated Fat		1 gm
Protein	15 gm	Sodium	114 mg	Polyunsaturated Fat		2 gm
Carbohydrate	5 gm	Total Fat	7 gm	Monounsaturated Fat		3 gm

*H*alibut *S*teaks *B*razilian

Serves 8

> 2 pounds halibut or other firm fish steaks
> 1 tablespoon instant coffee
> 2 tablespoons fresh lemon juice
> ¼ cup acceptable margarine, melted
> 1 teaspoon onion powder
> Vegetable oil spray
> 1 tablespoon chopped fresh parsley

Rinse fish and pat dry.

Place fish steaks in shallow baking dish. Set aside. In a small bowl, combine coffee and lemon juice. Stir to dissolve coffee. Add margarine and onion powder and mix thoroughly.

Pour mixture over fish, cover and refrigerate 30 minutes, turning once.

Preheat broiler. Lightly spray a broiler pan with vegetable oil.

Remove fish, reserving sauce, and arrange on prepared broiler pan. Broil 4 or 5 minutes about 3 inches from heat. Turn carefully and brush with sauce. Broil 4 or 5 minutes longer, or until fish is done. Sprinkle steaks with chopped parsley.

Nutrient Analysis

Calories	157 kcal	Cholesterol	60 mg	Saturated Fat	2 gm
Protein	22 gm	Sodium	161 mg	Polyunsaturated Fat	2 gm
Carbohydrate	1 gm	Total Fat	7 gm	Monounsaturated Fat	3 gm

*S*tuffed *F*ish *B*eachcomber

Serves 6

> Vegetable oil spray
> 1 whole fish (about 2½ to 3 pounds) (red snapper or
>   flounder is good)
> Freshly ground black pepper to taste
> 2 tablespoons chopped pickles or relish
> ½ teaspoon curry powder

2 tablespoons acceptable margarine
6 tablespoons diced onions
¾ cup sliced fresh mushrooms
3 tablespoons white wine vinegar
1½ cups plain bread crumbs
½ cup skim milk
1 egg white, slightly beaten
Freshly ground black pepper to taste

Preheat oven to 375° F. Lightly spray a baking dish with vegetable oil.

Rinse fish and pat dry.

Sprinkle fish on all sides with pepper. Set aside.

In a small bowl, mix pickles or relish with curry powder. Set aside.

In a heavy nonstick skillet over medium-high heat, melt margarine and sauté onions and mushrooms 10 minutes. Add vinegar and simmer 10 minutes. Remove from heat and allow to cool 10 minutes.

Soak bread crumbs in milk, then squeeze out excess milk. Add crumbs to onion mixture. Add beaten egg white, pepper and pickle mixture.

Stuff fish with bread mixture; close opening with skewers or toothpicks.

Place fish in prepared dish and bake 45 minutes, or until fish flakes easily when tested with a fork. Remove toothpicks and serve immediately.

STUFFED FISH FILLETS OR STUFFED FISH STEAKS

Use 1½ pounds fillets or steaks in place of whole fish. Place 3 or 4 tablespoons bread mixture between 2 fillets or steaks. Place on prepared baking dish and bake 25 to 30 minutes at 350° F.

Nutrient Analysis

Calories	295 kcal	Cholesterol	88 mg	Saturated Fat		2 gm
Protein	35 gm	Sodium	406 mg	Polyunsaturated Fat		2 gm
Carbohydrate	21 gm	Total Fat	7 gm	Monounsaturated Fat		3 gm

Scallops and Asparagus in Wine Sauce

Serves 4

1 pound fresh or frozen scallops

2 8-ounce bottles clam juice

1 cup dry white wine

4 ounces trimmed fresh asparagus or 4 ounces frozen
    asparagus, thawed

2 tablespoons acceptable margarine

¼ cup minced shallots

3 tablespoons flour

1 tablespoon fresh lemon juice

3 tablespoons finely chopped fresh parsley

Rinse fresh scallops in cold water and drain, or thaw and drain frozen scallops. Set aside.

In small saucepan over medium-high heat, combine clam juice and wine. Boil, uncovered, until mixture is reduced to 1½ cups. Set aside.

Cut asparagus diagonally into 1-inch lengths. Steam until tender-crisp and set aside. (If using frozen asparagus, simply thaw and cut into 1-inch lengths.)

Heat margarine in a nonstick skillet. Add shallots and sauté until translucent. Add flour and cook 1 minute. Whisk in reduced clam juice. When sauce is thick, add scallops and cook over medium heat 5 to 7 minutes, stirring frequently, or until scallops are cooked. Add lemon juice, asparagus and parsley and stir until well heated.

Nutrient Analysis

Calories	204 kcal	Cholesterol	45 mg	Saturated Fat	2 gm
Protein	24 gm	Sodium	686 mg	Polyunsaturated Fat	2 gm
Carbohydrate	12 gm	Total Fat	8 gm	Monounsaturated Fat	3 gm

*O*ven-*F*ried *S*callops

Serves 4

Vegetable oil spray
1 pound fresh or frozen scallops
½ cup low-fat buttermilk
½ cup plain bread crumbs
Dash paprika
2 tablespoons snipped fresh parsley

GARNISH
4 lemon wedges

Preheat oven to 500° F. Lightly spray a shallow baking dish with vegetable oil.

Rinse fresh scallops in cold water and drain, or thaw and drain frozen scallops. Pat dry and set aside.

Place buttermilk and bread crumbs in separate small shallow bowls. Soak scallops in buttermilk and then roll them in bread crumbs. Sprinkle with paprika.

Arrange scallops in a single layer in prepared baking dish. Bake 8 to 10 minutes.

Sprinkle with parsley and garnish with lemon wedges before serving.

Nutrient Analysis

Calories	157 kcal	Cholesterol	47 mg	Saturated Fat	1 gm
Protein	22 gm	Sodium	350 mg	Polyunsaturated Fat	0 gm
Carbohydrate	13 gm	Total Fat	2 gm	Monounsaturated Fat	0 gm

*S*callops *O*riental

Serves 8

Vegetable oil spray
2 pounds fresh or frozen scallops
¼ cup honey
¼ cup prepared mustard
1 teaspoon curry powder
1 teaspoon fresh lemon juice

GARNISH
8 lemon wedges

Preheat broiler. Lightly spray a baking pan with vegetable oil.

Rinse fresh scallops in cold water and drain, or thaw and drain frozen scallops. Place in a baking pan.

In a saucepan, combine honey, mustard, curry powder and lemon juice.

Brush scallops with sauce. Broil 4 inches from heat for 5 to 8 minutes, or until browned.

Garnish with lemon wedges.

Nutrient Analysis

Calories	134 kcal	Cholesterol	45 mg	Saturated Fat	0 gm
Protein	20 gm	Sodium	320 mg	Polyunsaturated Fat	0 gm
Carbohydrate	12 gm	Total Fat	2 gm	Monounsaturated Fat	0 gm

*L*inguine with *W*hite *C*lam *S*auce

Serves 4; 2 ounces linguine with ½ cup sauce per serving

½ cup dry white wine
1 8-ounce bottle clam juice
8 ounces linguine
2 tablespoons olive oil
½ cup finely chopped onion
4 cloves garlic, minced
2 tablespoons flour
2 6½-ounce cans minced clams, drained and rinsed
2 tablespoons finely chopped fresh parsley
2 tablespoons grated Parmesan cheese

*I*n a small saucepan over high heat, combine wine and clam juice. Boil, uncovered, until mixture is reduced to 1¼ cups.

Cook linguine according to package directions, omitting salt. Drain and set aside.

Pour olive oil into a small nonstick skillet over medium-high heat. Add onion and sauté until translucent. Add garlic and sauté 2 minutes more. Stir in flour and cook 1 minute. Whisk in hot clam juice mixture and stir until thickened. Add drained clams and parsley. Cook 2 minutes, stirring constantly, or until clams are thoroughly heated.

Divide pasta into four equal portions. Spoon sauce over pasta, sprinkle with Parmesan and serve immediately.

Nutrient Analysis

Calories	481 kcal	Cholesterol	64 mg	Saturated Fat	2 gm
Protein	35 gm	Sodium	349 mg	Polyunsaturated Fat	2 gm
Carbohydrate	59 gm	Total Fat	11 gm	Monounsaturated Fat	6 gm

*S*urimi *P*itas

Serves 5

8 ounces surimi (imitation crab), rinsed and flaked
6 tablespoons light, reduced-calorie mayonnaise
¼ cup plain nonfat yogurt
½ teaspoon grated lemon rind
¼ cup sliced green onion
½ cup diced ripe tomato, seeded
½ cup diced unpeeled cucumber, seeded
1 tablespoon finely chopped fresh cilantro
Dash hot pepper sauce
5 1-ounce whole-wheat pita breads
5 small pieces leaf lettuce

*I*n a small bowl, combine all ingredients except bread and lettuce. Cover and refrigerate until thoroughly chilled.

Split each pita carefully around top edge of bread, about one-third of the circumference of the bread. Insert lettuce leaf in pita and fill with ½ cup surimi mixture. Serve immediately.

Note: Since surimi is high in sodium, be sure your accompaniments contain very little sodium.

FRESH CRAB PITAS
Use fresh crab in place of surimi.

Surimi Pitas Nutrient Analysis

Calories	191 kcal	Cholesterol	19 mg	Saturated Fat	1 gm
Protein	11 gm	Sodium	669 mg	Polyunsaturated Fat	2 gm
Carbohydrate	23 gm	Total Fat	6 gm	Monounsaturated Fat	2 gm

Fresh Crab Pitas Nutrient Analysis

Calories	193 kcal	Cholesterol	51mg	Saturated Fat	1 gm
Protein	14 gm	Sodium	404 mg	Polyunsaturated Fat	2 gm
Carbohydrate	20 gm	Total Fat	6 gm	Monounsaturated Fat	2 gm

Crabmeat Maryland

Serves 8

Vegetable oil spray
3 cups flaked crabmeat, rinsed (fresh, frozen or canned)
2 tablespoons minced onion
3 tablespoons acceptable vegetable oil
3 tablespoons flour
2 cups skim milk
½ teaspsoon celery flakes
⅛ teaspoon grated orange peel
1 tablespoon snipped fresh parsley
1 tablespoon minced green bell pepper
1 pimiento, minced
Dash hot pepper sauce
2 tablespoons dry sherry
1 egg, beaten
½ teaspoon freshly ground black pepper, or to taste
1 tablespoon acceptable vegetable oil
2 slices bread, lightly toasted and reduced to crumbs

Preheat oven to 350° F. Lightly spray eight individual casseroles with vegetable oil. Set aside.

Thaw or drain crabmeat if it is frozen or canned.

In a large nonstick skillet over medium-high heat, sauté onion in oil until translucent. Add flour and cook, stirring, 1 minute. Reduce heat and add milk. Continue to stir until sauce is thickened. Add celery flakes, orange peel, parsley, bell pepper, pimiento and hot pepper sauce. Stir to mix well.

Remove from heat and add sherry.

Stir some of the sauce into beaten egg; then pour egg mixture slowly into sauce, stirring constantly. Add black pepper and crabmeat. Stir to mix well. Spoon into prepared individual casseroles.

In a small bowl, combine oil and toasted bread crumbs. Stir to mix well. Sprinkle a small amount on top of each casserole.

Bake uncovered 15 to 20 minutes, or until lightly browned.

Nutrient Analysis

Calories	174 kcal	Cholesterol	86 mg	Saturated Fat	1 gm
Protein	14 gm	Sodium	215 mg	Polyunsaturated Fat	5 gm
Carbohydrate	9 gm	Total Fat	9 gm	Monounsaturated Fat	2 gm

*B*ean *S*prout *T*una *C*how *M*ein

Serves 4

¾ cup uncooked rice
1 cup homemade Chicken Broth (see page 87) or
   commercial low-sodium variety
1 tablespoon light soy sauce
½ teaspoon freshly ground black pepper
2 tablespoons cornstarch
2 tablespoons acceptable vegetable oil
6 stalks celery, cut diagonally
2 medium onions, slivered
1 6-ounce can bamboo shoots, drained
4 ounces fresh mushrooms, sliced
2 cups fresh bean sprouts
1 7-ounce can water-packed tuna, drained, rinsed and
   flaked

Cook rice according to package directions, omitting salt and butter or margarine.

In a small bowl, combine chicken broth, soy sauce and pepper. Add cornstarch and stir until dissolved. Set aside.

Heat oil in skillet or wok over highest heat. When hot, add celery and onions. Stir-fry 1 minute. Add bamboo shoots, mushrooms and bean sprouts.

Stir broth mixture and add to skillet or wok. Stir and cook just until sauce is thickened.

Add tuna and stir until tuna is hot and sauce is clear.

Serve immediately over rice.

Nutrient Analysis

Calories	289 kcal	Cholesterol	20 mg	Saturated Fat		1 gm
Protein	24 gm	Sodium	489 mg	Polyunsaturated Fat		6 gm
Carbohydrate	27 gm	Total Fat	11 gm	Monounsaturated Fat		2 gm

*P*oultry

ROAST CHICKEN

HERB ROASTED CHICKEN

OVEN-BARBECUED CHICKEN

CHICKEN IN WHITE WINE AND TARRAGON

CRISPY BAKED CHICKEN

CHICKEN POT LUCK

CHICKEN IN WHITE WINE AND YOGURT SAUCE

CHICKEN WITH ORANGE SAUCE

CHICKEN WITH APRICOT GLAZE

LEMON BAKED CHICKEN

CHINESE CHICKEN STIR-FRY

SHREDDED CHICKEN WITH PEPPERS AND CARROTS

CHICKEN IN TOMATO WINE SAUCE

CHICKEN WITH SPANISH SAUCE

CHICKEN JERUSALEM

CHICKEN JAMBALAYA

SAVORY MICROWAVE CHICKEN

SESAME SOY CHICKEN

GRILLED LEMON SAGE CHICKEN

ALMOND CHICKEN

SESAME CHICKEN

SWEET AND SOUR CHICKEN

CHICKEN TERIYAKI WITH VEGETABLES

GRILLED SPICY CHICKEN BREAST FILLETS

CHICKEN MANICOTTI

CHICKEN CREOLE

ROSÉ CHICKEN WITH ARTICHOKE HEARTS AND MUSHROOMS

BAKED CHICKEN PARMESAN

CHICKEN À LA KING

CHICKEN POT PIE

CHICKEN AND BROCCOLI IN MUSHROOM SAUCE

CHICKEN SALAD CASSEROLE

CHICKEN AND VEGETABLE CREPES

CHICKEN CURRY IN A HURRY

CHICKEN SPINACH MANICOTTI

ROAST TURKEY

MARINATED TURKEY FILLETS

TURKEY MEATLOAF

TURKEY LASAGNA

TURKEY MEATBALLS

PORCUPINE MEATBALLS

*T*he beautiful thing about poultry is that you could eat it every day of the month without repeating a recipe—and you'd never be bored.

And in addition, poultry has fewer saturated fats than most meats.

Chicken absorbs flavor beautifully: It can be sweetened with orange, enhanced with garlic, or marinated to perfection in yogurt, oils, spices, sauces or wine. Get completely different flavors with different cooking techniques as well: Try roasting chicken in herbs and spices, sautéing it in a rich curry sauce or grilling it on the hibachi with a soy-based teriyaki sauce.

Versatile turkey is no longer just for holidays. Turkey breast fillets are wonderful marinated and grilled, as are turkey thighs. Ground turkey forms the foundation of a sturdy chili or meatballs. And of course no one can resist the traditional roast turkey you eat with your fingers.

Try to find a butcher or meat market that offers fresh poultry, because the taste is far superior to that of frozen. If this isn't possible, buy the best grade of packaged poultry you can afford.

Remember that poultry has a layer of fat under the skin and several large fat deposits near the tail. Leave the skin on a whole chicken while roasting to keep the meat from drying out, but remove it after the chicken is cooked. Individual pieces of chicken, on the other hand, should be skinned *before* cooking.

Here's a month's worth of poultry recipes to get you started.

*R*oast *C*hicken

Serves 6

> ¼ cup white wine
> ½ cup homemade Chicken Broth (see page 87) or
>   commercial low-sodium variety
> 1 4-pound roasting chicken
> ½ teaspoon freshly ground black pepper, or to taste
> ½ teaspoon basil or tarragon
> 1 tablespoon acceptable vegetable oil

*P*reheat oven to 350° F.

In a small bowl, combine wine and broth. Set aside.

Remove giblets and neck from chicken and save for other use, or discard. Rinse chicken and pat dry. Rub inside and out with pepper and basil or tarragon. Rub oil over skin and truss chicken. Place on a rack in a roasting pan, breast side up. Roast about 20 minutes per pound, or until done.

Chicken is done when juices run clear from a thigh pierced with a sharp skewer, or when a meat thermometer inserted in a thigh registers 180° F.

Baste chicken frequently with wine and broth mixture, and turn bird twice during cooking time.

Remove from oven and carve. Remove skin before serving.

Serve with Chicken Gravy (see page 433) if desired.

Nutrient Analysis *

Calories	218 kcal	Cholesterol	89 mg	Saturated Fat	2 gm
Protein	31 gm	Sodium	90 mg	Polyunsaturated Fat	3 gm
Carbohydrate	1 gm	Total Fat	9 gm	Monounsaturated Fat	3 gm

* *skin removed before eating*

*H*erb *R*oasted *C*hicken

Serves 6

> 1 3- to 3½-pound roasting chicken
> 1½ teaspoons dried thyme
> ½ teaspoon sweet basil
> ½ teaspoon salt
> ½ teaspoon freshly ground black pepper, or to taste
> 1 large bay leaf
> 2 cloves garlic, peeled and chopped coarsely
> 2 medium onions, peeled and halved
> 1 whole lemon, cut into wedges
> 2 tablespoons acceptable margarine, melted
> ½ cup dry white wine

Remove giblets and neck from chicken and save for other use, or discard. Rinse chicken and pat dry. Set aside.

In a small bowl, combine thyme, basil, salt and pepper and stir to mix well. Rub all over chicken, inside and out. Stuff chicken with bay leaf, garlic, onions and lemon. Truss. Cover and refrigerate 5 to 6 hours to allow flavors to blend.

Preheat oven to 425° F.

Place chicken on a rack in a nonstick roasting pan. Pour melted margarine and wine over chicken. Place chicken on side, legs to front of oven, and roast 20 minutes. Turn to other side, baste and roast 20 minutes. Place chicken on its back, baste and roast 20 to 25 minutes longer, or until chicken is golden brown. To test for doneness, pierce with fork between thigh and leg to see if juices run clear.

Remove chicken from oven, place on a serving platter and untruss. Defat cooking liquid and set aside. Discard lemon, vegetables and herbs. Carve chicken into serving pieces and keep warm. Remove skin before serving.

GRAVY (OPTIONAL)

Place roasting pan over medium-high heat and bring defatted cooking liquids to a boil. Correct seasoning and serve over chicken, if desired.

Nutrient Analysis *

Calories	195 kcal	Cholesterol	72 mg	Saturated Fat	3 gm
Protein	25 gm	Sodium	292 mg	Polyunsaturated Fat	2 gm
Carbohydrate	1 gm	Total Fat	9 gm	Monounsaturated Fat	3 gm

* *skin removed before eating*

Oven-Barbecued Chicken

Serves 4

Vegetable oil spray
¼ cup water
¼ cup white or cider vinegar
3 tablespoons acceptable vegetable oil
½ cup chili sauce or ketchup
3 tablespoons Worcestershire sauce
1 tablespoon dry mustard
Freshly ground black pepper to taste
2 tablespoons chopped onion (optional)
1 2½- to 3-pound frying chicken, cut into serving pieces,
   skinned, all visible fat removed

Preheat oven to 350° F. Lightly spray a large baking pan with vegetable oil.

Combine all ingredients except chicken in a saucepan over medium-high heat. Reduce heat and simmer 10 minutes. Set aside.

Rinse chicken pieces and pat dry; then arrange in prepared pan. Pour half of the barbecue sauce over chicken and bake, uncovered, 50 to 60 minutes, basting with remaining sauce every 15 minutes.

OPTIONAL COOKING METHOD
Immerse chicken briefly in sauce, then cook over charcoal. Boil remaining sauce and use it to baste chicken frequently.

Nutrient Analysis

Calories	344 kcal	Cholesterol	92 mg	Saturated Fat	3 gm
Protein	33 gm	Sodium	578 mg	Polyunsaturated Fat	8 gm
Carbohydrate	12 gm	Total Fat	18 gm	Monounsaturated Fat	5 gm

Chicken in White Wine and Tarragon

Serves 4

1 2½- to 3-pound chicken, quartered, skinned, all visible
   fat removed
1 cup dry white wine
1 tablespoon tarragon
Freshly ground black pepper to taste

Preheat oven to 350° F.

Rinse chicken and pat dry.

Arrange chicken in a shallow pan and pour wine over it. Sprinkle with tarragon and pepper. Cover with foil and bake 45 minutes. Remove foil and turn oven setting to broil. Place chicken under broiler, 5 inches from heat, 2 to 3 minutes, or until it is lightly browned.

Nutrient Analysis

Calories	208 kcal	Cholesterol	92 mg	Saturated Fat	2 gm
Protein	32 gm	Sodium	91 mg	Polyunsaturated Fat	2 gm
Carbohydrate	2 gm	Total Fat	7 gm	Monounsaturated Fat	2 gm

*C*rispy *B*aked *C*hicken

Serves 4

Vegetable oil spray
1 2½- to 3-pound frying chicken, cut into serving pieces, skinned, all visible fat removed
1 cup skim milk
1 cup cornflake crumbs
1 teaspoon rosemary
½ teaspoon freshly ground black pepper

Preheat oven to 400° F. Line a baking pan with foil and lightly spray foil with vegetable oil.

Rinse chicken and pat dry. Set aside.

Pour milk into a shallow bowl. Combine cornflake crumbs, rosemary and pepper in another shallow bowl. Dip chicken pieces first into milk and then into crumb mixture. Allow to stand briefly so coating will adhere.

Arrange chicken in prepared pan so pieces do not touch. Bake 45 minutes, or until done. Crumbs will form a crisp "skin."

Nutrient Analysis

Calories	246 kcal	Cholesterol	93 mg	Saturated Fat	2 gm
Protein	34 gm	Sodium	183 mg	Polyunsaturated Fat	2 gm
Carbohydrate	9 gm	Total Fat	7 gm	Monounsaturated Fat	2 gm

Chicken Pot Luck

Serves 4

Vegetable oil spray
4 chicken breast halves (approximately 2 pounds), skinned,
  all visible fat removed
2 medium potatoes
2 large carrots
2 medium onions
½ cup dry sherry
½ teaspoon freshly ground black pepper
2 tablespoons acceptable margarine
3 tablespoons flour
⅔ cup reserved pan juices
1⅓ cups homemade Chicken Broth (see page 87) or
  commercial low-sodium variety
2 tablespoons finely chopped parsley
2 tablespoons finely chopped green onion

Preheat oven to 300° F. Lightly spray a deep baking dish or oven-proof earthenware pot with vegetable oil.

Rinse chicken and pat dry.

Peel potatoes, cut in half lengthwise, slice and place in prepared dish. Peel carrots and onions. Cut carrots into sticks and peel onions into eighths and add both to pot. Arrange chicken over vegetables in dish. Pour sherry over all and add pepper. Cover and bake 1½ hours.

In a small saucepan over medium-high heat, melt margarine. Add flour and cook, stirring, for 1 minute. Set aside.

Remove chicken and vegetables to a warm serving platter, reserving pan juices. Set aside and keep warm.

Blend in ⅔ cup reserved juices and chicken broth. Bring to a boil, stirring constantly. Add parsley and onion. Pour over chicken and vegetables.

Nutrient Analysis

Calories	380 kcal	Cholesterol	98 mg	Saturated Fat	3 gm
Protein	42 gm	Sodium	217 mg	Polyunsaturated Fat	3 gm
Carbohydrate	26 gm	Total Fat	11 gm	Monounsaturated Fat	4 gm

Chicken in White Wine and Yogurt Sauce

Serves 8

8 chicken breast halves (approximately 4 pounds) skinned,
all visible fat removed

4 tablespoons acceptable margarine

3 tablespoons flour

½ cup homemade Chicken Broth (see page 87) or
commercial low-sodium variety

¾ cup plain nonfat yogurt

¼ cup white wine

2 teaspoons grated lemon rind

Freshly ground black pepper to taste

½ cup sliced fresh mushrooms

GARNISH
Lemon twist
Parsley sprig

Preheat oven to 350° F.

Rinse chicken and pat dry.

Melt 2 tablespoons margarine in a shallow baking pan. Add chicken breasts and bake, uncovered, 30 minutes.

Meanwhile, melt remaining 2 tablespoons margarine in a saucepan. Add flour and cook 1 to 2 minutes, stirring constantly. Add broth and stir until mixture is thick and smooth. Stir in yogurt, wine, lemon rind and pepper to blend.

Remove pan from oven. Turn over each chicken breast. Cover each with sliced mushrooms. Pour sauce over all. Bake, uncovered, 30 minutes, or until tender.

Garnish with a lemon twist or sprig of parsley.

Nutrient Analysis

Calories	287 kcal	Cholesterol	98 mg	Saturated Fat	3 gm
Protein	41 gm	Sodium	178 mg	Polyunsaturated Fat	3 gm
Carbohydrate	4 gm	Total Fat	11 gm	Monounsaturated Fat	4 gm

Chicken with Orange Sauce

Serves 4

Vegetable oil spray
1 2½- to 3-pound frying chicken, cut into serving pieces,
    skinned, all visible fat removed
½ teaspoon paprika
1 medium onion, sliced
½ cup frozen orange juice concentrate
2 tablespoons firmly packed brown sugar
2 tablespoons chopped parsley
1 teaspoon light soy sauce
½ teaspoon ground ginger
⅓ cup water
1 teaspoon sherry

Preheat broiler. Lightly spray a baking sheet with vegetable oil.

Rinse chicken and pat dry. Sprinkle with paprika and place on prepared pan. Broil just until browned on all sides.

Remove chicken to a Dutch oven or a large, deep skillet. Arrange onion slices over chicken.

In a small bowl, combine orange juice concentrate, brown sugar, parsley, soy sauce, ginger, water and sherry. Pour over chicken and onions.

Place Dutch oven or skillet over medium-high heat and bring sauce to a boil. Reduce heat, cover and simmer 35 to 40 minutes, or until chicken is tender.

OPTIONAL COOKING METHOD

Place browned chicken and onion slices in a casserole dish. Pour orange juice mixture over all and bake, covered, in a preheated 350° F oven for 35 to 40 minutes, or until chicken is tender.

Nutrient Analysis

Calories	249 kcal	Cholesterol	92 mg	Saturated Fat	2 gm
Protein	32 gm	Sodium	142 mg	Polyunsaturated Fat	2 gm
Carbohydrate	12 gm	Total Fat	7 gm	Monounsaturated Fat	2 gm

Chicken with Apricot Glaze

Serves 4

2½ pounds chicken pieces, skinned, all visible fat removed
¼ cup flour
⅛ teaspoon white pepper
1 tablespoon acceptable margarine
1 tablespoon acceptable vegetable oil
½ cup apricot preserves
1 16-ounce can no-sugar-added apricot halves, canned in
    natural juices
1 teaspoon marjoram
1 teaspoon grated lemon rind
1 tablespoon sherry
2 teaspoons light soy sauce
⅛ teaspoon hot pepper sauce
⅔ cup unsweetened pineapple juice
1 teaspoon grated fresh ginger
1 cup diced green bell pepper

Rinse chicken and pat dry. Set aside.

Combine flour and white pepper in a plastic bag. Add one piece of chicken at a time and shake bag to coat evenly. Set aside.

Place margarine and oil in a nonstick skillet over medium-high heat. Add chicken pieces and brown. Set aside.

Spread each piece of browned chicken with apricot preserves. Set aside.

Drain juice from apricots and reserve. Set apricots aside.

In a small bowl, mix marjoram, lemon rind, sherry, soy sauce, hot pepper sauce, pineapple juice, ginger and reserved juice from apricots. Set aside.

Return chicken pieces to skillet over medium heat. Add juice mixture, cover pan and reduce heat. Simmer 30 minutes. Add diced bell pepper, stir to mix well and cook 7 to 8 minutes more. Cut apricots in half and add them to skillet. Remove chicken to serving platter. Spoon sauce with apricots over all. Serve immediately.

Nutrient Analysis

Calories	502 kcal	Cholesterol	114 mg	Saturated Fat	4 gm
Protein	42 gm	Sodium	251 mg	Polyunsaturated Fat	5 gm
Carbohydrate	49 gm	Total Fat	15 gm	Monounsaturated Fat	5 gm

*L*emon *B*aked *C*hicken

Serves 4

Vegetable oil spray
2 tablespoons fresh lemon juice
2 tablespoons acceptable vegetable oil or acceptable
    margarine, melted
1 clove garlic, crushed
½ teaspoon freshly ground black pepper
1 2½- to 3-pound frying chicken, cut into serving pieces,
    skinned, all visible fat removed

Preheat oven to 350° F. Lightly spray a baking pan or a shallow casserole dish with vegetable oil.

In a small bowl, combine lemon juice, oil, garlic and pepper. Set aside.

Rinse chicken and pat dry. Arrange chicken in prepared pan or dish. Pour lemon mixture over chicken pieces. Cover and bake about 40 minutes, or until tender, basting occasionally. Uncover casserole and bake 10 minutes longer to allow chicken to brown.

Nutrient Analysis

Calories	264 kcal	Cholesterol	92 mg	Saturated Fat	3 gm
Protein	32 gm	Sodium	89 mg	Polyunsaturated Fat	6 gm
Carbohydrate	1 gm	Total Fat	14 gm	Monounsaturated Fat	4 gm

*C*hinese *C*hicken *S*tir-*F*ry

Serves 6

4 chicken breast fillets (approximately 4 ounces each),
    skinned, all visible fat removed
1⅓ cups homemade Chicken Broth (see page 87) or
    commercial low-sodium variety
3 tablespoons cornstarch
3 tablespoons sherry
2 tablespoons light soy sauce
1 tablespoon rice vinegar

1 tablespoon hot pepper oil
1 tablespoon grated fresh ginger
3 cloves garlic, minced
1 tablespoon sesame oil
1 8-ounce package fresh mushrooms, sliced
1 cup diced red bell pepper
¾ cup sliced green onion
⅓ cup unsalted dry-roasted pecan halves

Rinse chicken and pat dry. Cut into 1-inch cubes. Set aside.

In a small bowl, combine broth, cornstarch, sherry, soy sauce and vinegar. Set aside.

Heat hot pepper oil in a nonstick skillet or wok over high heat. Add ginger and garlic and sauté 1 minute. Add chicken and stir-fry until lightly browned. Transfer chicken to plate and set aside.

Add sesame oil to skillet. Stir in mushrooms and pepper. Cover pan, reduce heat to medium-high and steam 5 to 7 minutes. Add chicken broth mixture. Return chicken to pan and cook until sauce is thickened. Add onions and pecans and cook 2 minutes more.

Serve over rice if desired.

CHINESE BEEF STIR-FRY

In place of chicken, use 1 pound thinly sliced sirloin steak, all visible fat removed. Use walnuts in place of pecans. Follow instructions for Chinese Chicken Stir-Fry.

Chinese Chicken Stir-Fry Nutrient Analysis

Calories	216 kcal	Cholesterol	41 mg	Saturated Fat	2 gm
Protein	19 gm	Sodium	253 mg	Polyunsaturated Fat	4 gm
Carbohydrate	11 gm	Total Fat	11 gm	Monounsaturated Fat	5 gm

Chinese Beef Stir-Fry Nutrient Analysis

Calories	247 kcal	Cholesterol	45 mg	Saturated Fat	3 gm
Protein	20 gm	Sodium	256 mg	Polyunsaturated Fat	4 gm
Carbohydrate	11 gm	Total Fat	14 gm	Monounsaturated Fat	5 gm

Shredded Chicken with Peppers and Carrots

Serves 8

8 boneless chicken breast fillets (approximately 2 pounds),
    skinned, all visible fat removed
2 tablespoons cornstarch
2 tablespoons light soy sauce
3 tablespoons dry sherry
1 egg white, slightly beaten
1 teaspoon hot pepper oil
1 tablespoon acceptable vegetable oil
1 cup thinly sliced red bell pepper
1 cup thinly sliced yellow bell pepper
1 cup diced green bell pepper
1 cup thinly sliced carrots
1 teaspoon hot pepper oil
2 tablespoons acceptable vegetable oil
3 cloves garlic, minced
¼ cup grated fresh ginger
1 cup homemade Chicken Broth (see page 87) or
    commercial low-sodium variety
1 tablespoon light soy sauce
1 tablespoon cornstarch
1 teaspoon coarsely ground black pepper

Place chicken breast fillets, covered in plastic wrap, on a cookie sheet
in the freezer for 20 to 30 minutes, or until partially frozen. Using a
very sharp knife, slice chicken breasts diagonally into thin slices. Place
in a medium bowl and set aside.

In another bowl, combine 2 tablespoons cornstarch, 2 tablespoons soy sauce, sherry and egg white. Stir to mix well. Pour over
chicken and toss to coat evenly. Cover and set aside for 30 minutes.
Heat 1 teaspoon hot pepper oil and 1 tablespoon vegetable oil in a
large nonstick skillet over high heat. Add red, yellow and green peppers and carrots. Stir-fry 1 to 2 minutes. Remove from pan and set
aside.

In same skillet, heat 1 teaspoon hot pepper oil and 2 tablespoons
vegetable oil. Add garlic and ginger and sauté 1 minute. Add chicken
and stir-fry until shredded and opaque.

In a bowl, combine chicken broth, 1 tablespoon soy sauce and 1 tablespoon cornstarch. Stir into pan, cooking until sauce is thickened. Add vegetables and black pepper, stirring until thoroughly heated.

Note: If a spicier flavor is desired, hot pepper oil may be substituted for part of the vegetable oil required in this recipe.

Nutrient Analysis

Calories	238 kcal	Cholesterol	66 mg	Saturated Fat	2 gm
Protein	28 gm	Sodium	309 mg	Polyunsaturated Fat	4 gm
Carbohydrate	8 gm	Total Fat	10 gm	Monounsaturated Fat	3 gm

Chicken in Tomato Wine Sauce

Serves 4

1 2½- to 3-pound chicken, cut into serving pieces, skinned, all visible fat removed
1 onion, diced
1 clove garlic, crushed
1 8-ounce can no-salt-added tomato sauce
1 cup hot water
½ teaspoon freshly ground black pepper
4 ounces fresh mushrooms, sliced
½ cup white wine

GARNISH
4 sprigs fresh parsley

Rinse chicken and pat dry.

Place all ingredients except mushrooms and wine in a stockpot over medium-high heat. Bring to a boil, cover, reduce heat and simmer 45 minutes. Add mushrooms and wine and cook 5 minutes more.

Garnish with parsley.

Nutrient Analysis

Calories	234 kcal	Cholesterol	92 mg	Saturated Fat	2 gm
Protein	33 gm	Sodium	109 mg	Polyunsaturated Fat	2 gm
Carbohydrate	8 gm	Total Fat	7 gm	Monounsaturated Fat	2 gm

Chicken with Spanish Sauce

Serves 4

1 2½- to 3-pound fryer, cut into serving pieces, skinned, all visible fat removed
2 tablespoons acceptable vegetable oil
½ teaspoon freshly ground black pepper, or to taste
½ cup minced onion
½ cup chopped green bell pepper
1 clove garlic, minced
1 28-ounce can no-salt-added tomatoes
½ cup white wine
½ teaspoon thyme
2 bay leaves

Preheat oven to 350° F.

Rinse chicken and pat dry.

Heat oil in a heavy skillet over medium-high heat. Add chicken pieces and brown them quickly. Remove chicken pieces to a casserole and add black pepper. Set aside.

In the same skillet, lightly brown onions, bell pepper and garlic. Add mixture to casserole, along with tomatoes, wine and herbs. Cover and bake 1 hour, or until chicken is tender. Remove bay leaves before serving.

Nutrient Analysis

Calories	313 kcal	Cholesterol	92 mg	Saturated Fat	3 gm
Protein	34 gm	Sodium	117 mg	Polyunsaturated Fat	6 gm
Carbohydrate	12 gm	Total Fat	14 gm	Monounsaturated Fat	4 gm

Chicken Jerusalem

Serves 4

1 2½- to 3-pound fryer, cut into serving pieces, skinned,
  all visible fat removed
½ cup flour
2 tablespoons acceptable vegetable oil
½ pound fresh mushrooms, cut into pieces
1 6-ounce jar marinated artichoke hearts, drained
2 cups chopped fresh tomatoes
2 cloves garlic, minced
½ teaspoon oregano
½ teaspoon freshly ground black pepper, or to taste
½ cup sherry

Preheat oven to 350° F.

Rinse chicken pieces and pat dry. Dredge in flour and set aside.

Place oil in a skillet over medium-high heat. Add chicken pieces and brown evenly. Remove chicken pieces to casserole dish. Add mushrooms and artichoke hearts. Set aside.

In a small bowl, combine tomatoes, garlic, oregano and pepper. Stir to mix well, and then pour over chicken.

Bake 1 to 1½ hours, or until tender. Add sherry and cook an additional 5 minutes.

Nutrient Analysis

Calories	384 kcal	Cholesterol	92 mg	Saturated Fat		3 gm
Protein	36 gm	Sodium	215 mg	Polyunsaturated Fat		7 gm
Carbohydrate	25 gm	Total Fat	16 gm	Monounsaturated Fat		4 gm

*C*hicken *J*ambalaya

Serves 6

6 chicken breast halves (approximately 3 pounds), skinned,
   all visible fat removed
1 cup homemade Chicken Broth (see page 87) or
   commercial low-sodium variety
½ cup chopped onion
¼ cup chopped green bell pepper
1 cup white wine
¼ cup chopped fresh parsley
½ teaspoon basil
1 small bay leaf
½ teaspoon thyme
1 cup uncooked rice
½ cup cubed low-fat ham
1 cup canned no-salt-added tomatoes, drained

Preheat oven to 350° F.

Rinse chicken pieces and pat dry.

In a saucepan, combine broth, onion, bell pepper, wine, parsley, basil, bay leaf and thyme. Bring to a boil, stirring constantly. Remove from heat and set aside.

Place rice, ham, tomatoes and chicken in a large casserole dish. Pour herb sauce over all. Cover tightly and bake 25 to 30 minutes. Turn oven off, but leave casserole in it 10 to 15 minutes more before removing and serving.

Nutrient Analysis

Calories	354 kcal	Cholesterol	104 mg	Saturated Fat	2 gm
Protein	44 gm	Sodium	251 mg	Polyunsaturated Fat	1 gm
Carbohydrate	28 gm	Total Fat	6 gm	Monounsaturated Fat	2 gm

Savory Microwave Chicken

Serves 6

6 boneless chicken breast fillets (approximately 4 ounces
    each), skinned, all visible fat removed
2 cups homemade Chicken Broth (see page 87) or
    commercial low-sodium variety
3 tablespoons acceptable margarine
1 cup finely chopped onion
1 cup sliced carrots
2 cups small broccoli florets
1 cup homemade Chicken Broth (see page 87) or
    commercial low-sodium variety
2 tablespoons sherry
2 tablespoons cornstarch
1 cup orange juice
1 tablespoon light soy sauce
½ teaspoon garlic powder
1 teaspoon grated orange rind
¼ teaspoon salt
⅓ cup slivered almonds

Rinse chicken and pat dry. Cut into 1-inch cubes. Set aside.

Place 2 cups chicken broth and chicken in microwave-safe casserole, cover and cook 5 minutes on medium. Stir and cook another 5 minutes. Drain chicken and discard broth. Transfer chicken to a plate and set aside.

In the same casserole dish, melt margarine on high for 20 seconds. Add vegetables, cover and cook on high 7 minutes. Remove from microwave and add chicken pieces. Set aside.

In a microwave-safe bowl, combine 1 cup of broth and remaining ingredients, except almonds. Cook on high for 5 minutes. Add to chicken and vegetable mixture in casserole. Stir to mix well.

Cover and heat on medium for 3 minutes, or until all ingredients are evenly heated. Top with almonds and serve.

Nutrient Analysis

Calories	294 kcal	Cholesterol	62 mg	Saturated Fat	3 gm
Protein	29 gm	Sodium	361 mg	Polyunsaturated Fat	3 gm
Carbohydrate	15 gm	Total Fat	13 gm	Monounsaturated Fat	6 gm

Sesame Soy Chicken

Serves 6; 2 pieces per serving

1 cup finely chopped onion
½ cup fresh lime juice
1 teaspoon grated lime rind
¼ cup light soy sauce
⅓ cup sherry
2 tablespoons grated fresh ginger
¼ cup orange juice concentrate
1 tablespoon sugar
3 cloves garlic, minced
1 tablespoon hot pepper oil
6 chicken legs and 6 chicken thighs (approximately 3
    pounds total), skinned, all visible fat removed
1 tablespoon sesame seeds, toasted

In a bowl combine onion, lime juice, rind, soy sauce, sherry, ginger, orange juice concentrate, sugar, garlic and oil. Set aside.

Rinse chicken pieces and pat dry. Arrange in a baking dish and pour lime mixture over all, turning each piece to coat completely. Cover with plastic wrap and refrigerate several hours or overnight, turning chicken pieces twice during that time.

Preheat oven to 400° F.

Bake chicken with marinade 35 minutes, or until done. Then broil 5 minutes, turning pieces in cooking juices to maximize flavor. Sprinkle with sesame seeds before serving.

GRILLING METHOD

Grill over hot charcoal 30 minutes, or until done. Bring marinade to boil over medium-high heat. Baste chicken with hot marinade several times while grilling.

Nutrient Analysis

Calories	285 kcal	Cholesterol	99 mg	Saturated Fat	3 gm
Protein	33 gm	Sodium	504 mg	Polyunsaturated Fat	4 gm
Carbohydrate	9 gm	Total Fat	13 gm	Monounsaturated Fat	4 gm

*G*rilled *L*emon *S*age *C*hicken

Serves 6

6 boneless chicken breast fillets (approximately 4 ounces each), skinned, all visible fat removed
½ cup olive oil
⅓ cup fresh lemon juice
1 tablespoon chopped fresh rosemary
¼ cup chopped fresh sage leaves
½ teaspoon salt
1 teaspoon black peppercorns, cracked
2 or 3 cloves garlic, minced
1 teaspoon grated lemon rind

GARNISH
6 lemon slices, cut in half
Sage leaves

Rinse chicken and pat dry. Place pieces between two sheets of plastic wrap and flatten to ⅛-inch thickness with a mallet. Arrange chicken in a glass or enamel baking dish.

In a small bowl, combine oil, lemon juice, herbs, salt, pepper, garlic and lemon rind. Mix well. Pour over chicken and turn pieces to coat evenly. Cover and refrigerate for several hours or overnight, turning pieces occasionally.

Grill marinated chicken over hot coals.

Serve garnished with lemon slices and sage leaves.

Nutrient Analysis

Calories	295 kcal	Cholesterol	62 mg	Saturated Fat	3 gm
Protein	25 gm	Sodium	237 mg	Polyunsaturated Fat	2 gm
Carbohydrate	1 gm	Total Fat	21 gm	Monounsaturated Fat	14 gm

*A*lmond *C*hicken

Serves 4

4 boneless chicken breast fillets (approximately 4 ounces
  each), skinned, all visible fat removed
⅔ cup uncooked rice
¼ cup homemade Chicken Broth (see page 87) or
  commercial low-sodium variety
1 tablespoon sherry
1 tablespoon light soy sauce
⅛ teaspoon hot pepper oil
¹⁄₁₆ teaspoon ground ginger
2 tablespoons acceptable vegetable oil
1 small onion, thinly sliced
1 cup thinly sliced celery
1 cup sliced water chestnuts
1 5-ounce can bamboo shoots, rinsed and drained
1 teaspoon sugar
2 tablespoons cornstarch
¼ cup cold water
¼ cup toasted almond slivers

Rinse chicken and pat dry. Cut into thin slices (semi-frozen chicken is better for slicing). Set aside.

Cook rice according to package directions, omitting salt and butter or margarine.

In a small bowl, combine chicken broth, sherry, soy sauce, hot pepper oil and ginger. Set aside.

Preheat 2 tablespoons oil in a wok or a heavy frying pan over high heat. Add chicken and sauté 2 to 3 minutes. Add onion and celery. Cook 5 minutes. Add water chestnuts and bamboo shoots. Add chicken broth mixture. Reduce heat to medium high. Cover and cook 5 minutes more.

In a small bowl, blend sugar, cornstarch and cold water. Pour over chicken and cook, stirring constantly, until thick.

Serve over rice and sprinkle toasted almonds on top.

CHICKEN WITH SNOW PEAS
Omit almonds and add 1 10-ounce package frozen no-salt-added snow-pea pods with water chestnuts and bamboo shoots.

Almond Chicken Nutrient Analysis

Calories	403 kcal	Cholesterol	62 mg	Saturated Fat	2 gm
Protein	30 gm	Sodium	238 mg	Polyunsaturated Fat	6 gm
Carbohydrate	38 gm	Total Fat	15 gm	Monounsaturated Fat	5 gm

Chicken with Snow Peas Nutrient Analysis

Calories	384 kcal	Cholesterol	62 mg	Saturated Fat	2 gm
Protein	30 gm	Sodium	239 mg	Polyunsaturated Fat	5 gm
Carbohydrate	41 gm	Total Fat	11 gm	Monounsaturated Fat	3 gm

Sesame Chicken

Serves 4

1 2½- to 3-pound frying chicken, cut into serving pieces, skinned, all visible fat removed
2 tablespoons acceptable margarine
2 tablespoons acceptable vegetable oil
⅓ cup flour seasoned with black pepper
Juice of ½ lemon
¼ cup sesame seeds
3 tablespoons minced green onion
½ cup dry white wine

Preheat oven to 375° F.

Rinse chicken and pat dry.

Melt margarine and oil in baking pan. Allow to cool slightly but not to harden. Set aside. Place seasoned flour in a shallow bowl.

Roll each piece of chicken in oil and then dredge in flour, shaking excess from each. Arrange chicken in a baking pan so that pieces do not touch. Sprinkle with lemon juice and half of the sesame seeds. Bake 30 minutes, or until lightly browned. Turn chicken over and sprinkle with remaining sesame seeds and minced onion. Pour wine into bottom of pan and cook 30 to 45 minutes, basting occasionally, until done.

Nutrient Analysis

Calories	399 kcal	Cholesterol	92 mg	Saturated Fat	5 gm
Protein	35 gm	Sodium	160 mg	Polyunsaturated Fat	9 gm
Carbohydrate	10 gm	Total Fat	24 gm	Monounsaturated Fat	8 gm

Sweet and Sour Chicken

Serves 4

4 chicken breast halves (approximately 2 pounds), skinned,
  all visible fat removed
1 8½-ounce can no-sugar-added pineapple chunks, canned
  in natural juices
1 cup jellied cranberry sauce
2 tablespoons rice vinegar or cider vinegar
2½ tablespoons firmly packed brown sugar
½ cup homemade Chicken Broth (see page 87) or
  commercial low-sodium variety
2 tablespoons cornstarch
2 tablespoons water
1 green bell pepper, cut into long, thin strips

Preheat oven to 350° F.

Rinse chicken and pat dry. Place in a baking dish and set aside.
Drain pineapple, reserving juice, and set aside.

In a saucepan over medium heat, combine reserved pineapple
juice, cranberry sauce, vinegar, brown sugar and broth. In a small
bowl, mix cornstarch with water. Stir until smooth. Add to sauce
mixture. Cook sauce until thickened. Add pineapple chunks and
pour over chicken.

Cover and bake 35 minutes. Uncover, add bell pepper strips and
baste with sauce. Bake uncovered for an additional 5 minutes.

Nutrient Analysis

Calories	407 kcal	Cholesterol	98 mg	Saturated Fat	2 gm
Protein	40 gm	Sodium	120 mg	Polyunsaturated Fat	1 gm
Carbohydrate	50 gm	Total Fat	5 gm	Monounsaturated Fat	1 gm

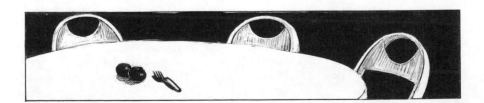

Chicken Teriyaki with Vegetables

Serves 8; 2 skewers per serving

2 tablespoons light soy sauce
5 tablespoons firmly packed brown sugar
1¼ tablespoons acceptable vegetable oil
1 teaspoon ground ginger
⅓ cup sherry
1 teaspoon hot pepper oil
6 boneless chicken breast fillets (approximately 4 ounces
    each), skinned, all visible fat removed
16 fresh mushrooms
2 medium zucchini, sliced
16 cherry tomatoes
4 medium onions, cut into 8 wedges each
16 wooden or metal skewers

Combine first six ingredients in a shallow glass bowl.

Rinse chicken and pat dry. Slice lengthwise.

Wipe mushrooms with a clean, damp cloth.

Place chicken, mushrooms, zucchini, tomatoes and onion in pre-pared mixture. Stir to coat evenly. Cover and refrigerate approximately 1 hour, turning occasionally.

Meanwhile, if using wooden skewers, soak them in water for at least 30 minutes before using.

Preheat broiler.

Remove chicken and vegetables from marinade. Alternate chicken and vegetable pieces on skewers. Lay on broiler pan and broil 4 inches away from heat for 3 minutes. Turn over and broil an additional 3 minutes.

Nutrient Analysis

Calories	206 kcal	Cholesterol	47 mg	Saturated Fat		1 gm
Protein	21 gm	Sodium	205 mg	Polyunsaturated Fat		2 gm
Carbohydrate	19 gm	Total Fat	6 gm	Monounsaturated Fat		1 gm

*G*rilled *S*picy *C*hicken *B*reast *F*illets

Serves 8

1 small clove garlic, crushed
1 small onion, finely chopped
1 to 2 tablespoons finely chopped cilantro
2 to 3 tablespoons fresh lime juice
2 tablespoons olive oil
½ teaspoon chili powder
Freshly ground black pepper to taste
8 boneless chicken breast fillets (approximately 4 ounces
    each), skinned, all visible fat removed.

*I*n a small bowl, combine first seven ingredients. Mix well. Set aside.

Rinse chicken and pat dry. Place in a shallow glass dish. Add lime juice mixture and stir to coat chicken pieces thoroughly. Cover dish and refrigerate 2 to 3 hours. Stir several times while marinating to keep chicken well coated.

On a preheated outdoor grill or broiler, cook marinated chicken, turning once, 6 to 7 minutes, or until done. Serve hot.

CHICKEN FAJITAS

Slice grilled chicken into strips, cover and keep warm.

Preheat oven to 325° F.

Slice 1 large onion and 1 large green pepper into thin strips.

In a nonstick skillet, heat 2 teaspoons acceptable vegetable oil over medium-high heat. Add onion and pepper strips and sauté, stirring constantly, about 5 minutes, or until onion in slightly brown.

Wrap eight flour tortillas or eight halves of pita bread in heavy-duty foil; warm in oven (approximately 6 to 8 minutes).

Place chicken strips on tortillas or pita bread. Top with onions and peppers. Add 1 tablespoon picante sauce to each fajita. Roll bread around chicken to eat.

Grilled Spicy Chicken Breast Fillets Nutrient Analysis

Calories	164 kcal	Cholesterol	62 mg	Saturated Fat		1 gm
Protein	25 gm	Sodium	59 mg	Polyunsaturated Fat		1 gm
Carbohydrate	0 gm	Total Fat	7 gm	Monounsaturated Fat		3 gm

Chicken Fajitas Nutrient Analysis

Calories	273 kcal	Cholesterol	64 mg	Saturated Fat		2 gm
Protein	27 gm	Sodium	326 mg	Polyunsaturated Fat		2 gm
Carbohydrate	19 gm	Total Fat	10 gm	Monounsaturated Fat		5 gm

Chicken Manicotti

Serves 4

¾ teaspoon oregano
½ teaspoon marjoram
¾ teaspoon sweet basil
¼ teaspoon freshly ground black pepper, or to taste
1 6-ounce can no-salt-added tomato paste
1 cup water
1 clove garlic, minced
4 boneless chicken breast fillets (approximately 4 ounces
    each), skinned, all visible fat removed
4 ounces low-fat cottage cheese, drained
2 ounces grated part-skim mozzarella cheese

Preheat oven to 350° F.

In a small bowl, combine oregano, marjoram, basil and pepper. Mix well, set aside.

In a small saucepan, blend tomato paste, water and garlic. Add ¾ of the seasoning mixture to pan. Bring to a boil. Reduce heat and simmer 10 minutes, stirring occasionally.

Meanwhile, rinse chicken and pat dry. Place fillets in a plastic bag and pound to ¼-inch thickness. Set aside.

In a small bowl, combine remaining spice mixture with cottage cheese. Spoon mixture onto centers of chicken breasts, leaving a ½-inch edge all around. From narrow end, roll each breast, jellyroll fashion.

Spoon half of the tomato mixture into the bottom of a 10-x-6-inch baking dish. Arrange chicken rolls on top, seam-side down. Spoon remaining tomato mixture over chicken rolls. Top with mozzarella cheese and bake about 45 minutes, or until chicken is tender.

Nutrient Analysis

Calories	237 kcal	Cholesterol	72 mg	Saturated Fat	3 gm
Protein	34 gm	Sodium	275 mg	Polyunsaturated Fat	1 gm
Carbohydrate	10 gm	Total Fat	7 gm	Monounsaturated Fat	2 gm

Chicken Creole

Serves 8

8 boneless chicken breast fillets (approximately 4 ounces
    each), skinned, all visible fat removed
1 cup thinly sliced onion
2 tablespoons acceptable vegetable oil
2 cups thinly sliced fresh mushrooms
2 tablespoons minced garlic
1 cup chopped celery
1 tablespoon chopped fresh, or ½ tablespoon dried,
    oregano
1 tablespoon chopped fresh, or ½ tablespoon dried, basil
2 cups sliced green bell pepper
2 cups peeled, diced tomatoes
½ cup dry white wine
2 tablespoons fresh lemon juice
½ teaspoon crushed red pepper flakes
1 tablespoon acceptable margarine
½ teaspoon freshly ground black pepper, or to taste
2 tablespoons finely chopped fresh parsley

Rinse chicken and pat dry. Cut into ½-inch cubes and set aside.

Sauté onion in oil in a large skillet over medium-high heat until translucent. Add mushrooms and cook over medium heat until liquid evaporates. Add garlic, celery and herbs and cook 1 minute. Add bell pepper and cook 2 minutes. Add tomatoes and cook 5 minutes. Stir in wine, lemon juice and red pepper. Set aside.

In another skillet over high heat, melt ½ tablespoon margarine. Add half the chicken fillets and sprinkle with black pepper. Cook, stirring frequently, until pieces are cooked evenly throughout and are lightly browned. Do not overcook. Transfer chicken to a separate dish. Repeat procedure with remaining margarine and chicken, then return first batch to skillet.

Pour sauce over all and stir gently to blend. Simmer about 1 minute. Sprinkle with parsley and serve.

Nutrient Analysis

Calories	178 kcal	Cholesterol	49 mg	Saturated Fat		2 gm
Protein	21 gm	Sodium	80 mg	Polyunsaturated Fat		3 gm
Carbohydrate	7 gm	Total Fat	8 gm	Monounsaturated Fat		2 gm

Rosé *C*hicken *with* *A*rtichoke *H*earts *and* *M*ushrooms

Serves 8

Vegetable oil spray

8 boneless chicken breast fillets (approximately 4 ounces each), skinned, all visible fat removed

1 tablespoon acceptable margarine, melted

1 tablespoon fresh lemon juice

Pinch white pepper

1 tablespoon acceptable margarine

8 ounces fresh mushrooms, sliced

1 10-ounce package frozen artichoke hearts, defrosted and cut in half

2 tablespoons acceptable margarine

2 tablespoons flour

¾ cup homemade Chicken Broth (see page 87) or commercial low-sodium variety

½ cup rosé wine

¼ teaspoon salt

¼ cup thinly sliced green onion

Preheat oven to 500° F. Lightly spray a large baking dish with vegetable oil. Rinse chicken breast fillets and pat dry. Arrange in dish.

In a small bowl, combine melted margarine and lemon juice. Pour over chicken. Season with pepper. Cover dish with foil and bake 15 to 17 minutes, or until done. (Chicken is done when it springs back slightly when touched.) Remove fillets to a warm platter.

In a nonstick skillet over medium heat, melt 1 tablespoon margarine. Add mushrooms to pan. Cover and cook 7 to 10 minutes. Uncover, add artichoke hearts and continue to cook until juices evaporate. Remove vegetables and set aside.

Heat 2 tablespoons margarine in same skillet. Add flour and cook 1 minute, stirring constantly. Add broth, wine and salt. Cook 4 minutes, or until sauce is smooth. Stir in green onion; cook 1 minute more. Add reserved vegetables. Stir to mix well. Spoon mixture over chicken breasts and serve.

Nutrient Analysis

Calories	217 kcal	Cholesterol	62 mg	Saturated Fat	2 gm
Protein	26 gm	Sodium	221 mg	Polyunsaturated Fat	2 gm
Carbohydrate	7 gm	Total Fat	9 gm	Monounsaturated Fat	3 gm

*B*aked *C*hicken *P*armesan

Serves 6

Vegetable oil spray
6 boneless chicken breast fillets (approximately 4 ounces
    each), skinned, all visible fat removed
4 slices whole-wheat bread
¾ teaspoon garlic powder
1½ teaspoons paprika
6 tablespoons grated Parmesan cheese
1½ tablespoons finely chopped parsley
½ teaspoon thyme
½ cup low-fat buttermilk
2 tablespoons acceptable margarine, melted

*P*reheat oven to 450° F. Lightly spray a rectangular baking sheet and a rectangular cake-cooling rack of a slightly smaller size with vegetable oil. Place rack onto baking sheet. Set aside.

Rinse chicken, pat dry and set aside.

In a blender or the work bowl of a food processor fitted with a metal blade, process bread into fine crumbs.

Pour crumbs into a shallow bowl. Add garlic powder, paprika, cheese, parsley and thyme. Stir, mixing well.

Pour buttermilk into a shallow bowl.

Dip fillets into buttermilk, shake off excess liquid and then dredge in crumbs. Place fillets on prepared rack. Drizzle each with a teaspoon melted margarine.

Bake 15 minutes; turn fillets over and bake 10 minutes more, or until done.

Nutrient Analysis

Calories	256 kcal	Cholesterol	69 mg	Saturated Fat		3 gm
Protein	30 gm	Sodium	352 mg	Polyunsaturated Fat		2 gm
Carbohydrate	11 gm	Total Fat	10 gm	Monounsaturated Fat		3 gm

Chicken à la King

Serves 6

1 cup uncooked rice
3 tablespoons acceptable margarine
¼ cup all-purpose flour
¼ teaspoon salt
3 cups homemade Chicken Broth (see page 87) or
    commercial low-sodium variety
5 tablespoons nonfat dry milk
1 teaspoon acceptable margarine
½ pound fresh mushrooms, sliced
2 cups diced cooked chicken
¼ cup diced green bell pepper
1 12-ounce jar pimiento, drained and chopped
4 tablespoons sherry
2 or 3 drops hot pepper sauce
1 tablespoon chopped parsley

Cook rice according to package directions, omitting salt and butter or margarine.

In a large, heavy saucepan over medium-high heat, melt 3 tablespoons margarine and add flour. Cook briefly, stirring often. Slowly add salt and chicken broth, stirring constantly. Cook until smooth. Stir in nonfat dry milk and cook 1 minute. Set aside.

In a small skillet over medium-high heat, melt 1 teaspoon margarine. Add mushrooms and sauté. Remove from heat and add to sauce in large skillet. Add chicken, bell pepper and pimiento. Heat thoroughly and add sherry and hot pepper sauce.

Serve over cooked rice and sprinkle parsley on top.

Nutrient Analysis

Calories	315 kcal	Cholesterol	40 mg	Saturated Fat	3 gm
Protein	20 gm	Sodium	263 mg	Polyunsaturated Fat	3 gm
Carbohydrate	35 gm	Total Fat	10 gm	Monounsaturated Fat	4 gm

*C*hicken *P*ot *P*ie

Serves 4

Vegetable oil spray
½ cup nonfat dry milk
3 tablespoons flour
1½ cups water
½ teaspoon tarragon
½ teaspoon parsley
½ teaspoon freshly ground black pepper
2 cups diced cooked chicken
¾ cup small white onions, cooked
Cooked carrot slices, lima beans and green peas to total
     1½ cups (a package of frozen no-salt-added mixed
     vegetables may be used)
1 recipe for Pastry Crust or Mashed Potato Topping

*P*reheat oven to 400° F. Lightly spray a 1½-quart casserole dish with vegetable oil.

In a saucepan, combine nonfat dry milk and flour. Add water and whisk until smooth. Add tarragon, parsley and pepper. Mix well. Cook over medium heat, stirring constantly, until mixture thickens. Remove saucepan from heat and add chicken and vegetables. Mix well. Pour into 1½-quart casserole. Cover with Pastry Crust or Mashed Potato Topping. Bake 20 minutes, or until lightly browned.

VARIATION
Use beef or pork in place of chicken and use a variety of vegetables to suit your taste.

*P*astry *C*rust

⅛ teaspoon salt
2 tablespoons acceptable vegetable oil
½ cup flour

*I*n a small bowl, stir salt and oil into flour. Form into a ball, flatten slightly and place on a sheet of wax paper. Place another sheet on top of dough and roll out dough quickly. Peel off top layer of paper, invert dough over filling and seal pie by pressing dough firmly to edge of casserole. Cut steam holes and bake as directed.

Chicken Pot Pie with Pastry Crust Nutrient Analysis

Calories	342 kcal	Cholesterol	60 mg	Saturated Fat	2 gm
Protein	28 gm	Sodium	208 mg	Polyunsaturated Fat	5 gm
Carbohydrate	30 gm	Total Fat	12 gm	Monounsaturated Fat	3 gm

Beef Pot Pie with Pastry Crust Nutrient Analysis

Calories	367 kcal	Cholesterol	57 mg	Saturated Fat	4 gm
Protein	25 gm	Sodium	181 mg	Polyunsaturated Fat	5 gm
Carbohydrate	30 gm	Total Fat	16 gm	Monounsaturated Fat	6 gm

Mashed Potato Topping

2 cups chopped, cooked potatoes
2 tablespoons acceptable margarine, melted
½ cup skim milk, heated
⅛ teaspoon rosemary
¼ teaspoon freshly ground black pepper
⅛ teaspoon nutmeg
⅛ teaspoon paprika

Beat together potatoes, margarine, milk, rosemary, pepper and nutmeg until light and fluffy.

Spread over top of chicken mixture and sprinkle lightly with paprika. Bake as directed.

Chicken Pot Pie with Mashed Potato Topping Nutrient Analysis

Calories	359 kcal	Cholesterol	61 mg	Saturated Fat	3 gm
Protein	29 gm	Sodium	227 mg	Polyunsaturated Fat	3 gm
Carbohydrate	36 gm	Total Fat	11 gm	Monounsaturated Fat	4 gm

Beef Pot Pie with Mashed Potato Topping Nutrient Analysis

Calories	384 kcal	Cholesterol	58 mg	Saturated Fat	5 gm
Protein	26 gm	Sodium	201 mg	Polyunsaturated Fat	2 gm
Carbohydrate	36 gm	Total Fat	15 gm	Monounsaturated Fat	7 gm

Chicken and Broccoli in Mushroom Sauce

Serves 6

Vegetable oil spray
10 ounces fresh broccoli spears
1 tablespoon acceptable margarine
8 ounces fresh mushrooms, sliced
2 cups homemade Chicken Broth (see page 87) or
    commercial low-sodium variety
⅓ cup nonfat dry milk
3 tablespoons acceptable margarine
¼ cup flour
¼ cup sliced green onion
Dash nutmeg
3 tablespoons grated Parmesan cheese
¼ cup fresh bread crumbs (½ slice bread)
3 tablespoons grated Parmesan cheese
2 tablespoons finely chopped parsley
2 cups diced cooked chicken

Preheat oven to 375° F. Lightly spray an 11-x-7-inch baking pan with vegetable oil.

Steam broccoli spears until tender-crisp, then plunge into ice water to stop cooking. Drain and blot dry on paper towels. Set aside.

In a nonstick skillet over medium heat, melt 1 tablespoon margarine. Add sliced mushrooms, cover and cook 7 to 9 minutes, or until mushrooms have released all their juices. Uncover and increase setting to high. Allow liquid to evaporate. Set aside.

In a small bowl, combine chicken broth and nonfat dry milk. Set aside.

In a saucepan, melt 3 tablespoons margarine over medium-high heat. Stir in flour and cook 1 minute. Add chicken broth mixture and stir with wire whisk. Bring to a boil, then add onion, nutmeg and 3 tablespoons grated Parmesan cheese. Add cooked mushrooms and set aside.

In a small bowl, combine bread crumbs, 3 tablespoons grated Parmesan cheese and parsley. Set aside.

Arrange broccoli spears on the bottom of prepared pan. Evenly distribute chicken over broccoli. Pour mushroom sauce over all. Sprinkle bread-crumb mixture on top. Bake 25 minutes.

Nutrient Analysis

Calories	262 kcal	Cholesterol	46 mg	Saturated Fat	4 gm
Protein	22 gm	Sodium	336 mg	Polyunsaturated Fat	3 gm
Carbohydrate	14 gm	Total Fat	13 gm	Monounsaturated Fat	5 gm

Chicken Salad Casserole

Serves 6

Vegetable oil spray
2 tablespoons acceptable margarine
8 ounces fresh mushrooms, sliced
½ cup diced green bell pepper
½ cup diced red bell pepper
½ cup chopped onion
½ cup slivered water chestnuts
¼ cup fresh bread crumbs (½ slice bread)
1 tablespoon grated Parmesan cheese
¼ cup light, reduced-calorie mayonnaise
2 teaspoons fresh lemon juice
½ teaspoon thyme
Dash white pepper
2 cups diced cooked chicken

Preheat oven to 375° F. Lightly spray an 8-x-8-inch pan with vegetable oil.

In a nonstick skillet over medium-high heat, melt margarine. Add mushrooms, bell peppers, onion and water chestnuts. Cover and cook 7 to 9 minutes. Uncover and continue cooking over high heat until juices evaporate. Set aside.

In a small bowl, combine bread crumbs and grated Parmesan cheese. Set aside.

In a large bowl, combine mayonnaise, lemon juice, thyme and white pepper. Add chicken and vegetable mixture. Stir to mix well. Spoon into prepared pan. Sprinkle bread crumb mixture evenly on top. Bake 20 minutes.

Nutrient Analysis

Calories	190 kcal	Cholesterol	43 mg	Saturated Fat	3 gm
Protein	16 gm	Sodium	196 mg	Polyunsaturated Fat	3 gm
Carbohydrate	8 gm	Total Fat	10 gm	Monounsaturated Fat	4 gm

Chicken and Vegetable Crepes

Serves 6

CORNMEAL CREPES
Vegetable oil spray
⅓ cup flour
⅔ cup yellow cornmeal
1 tablespoon acceptable vegetable oil
1½ cups skim milk
Egg substitute equivalent to 2 eggs

FILLING
½ pound fresh broccoli, chopped
½ pound fresh mushrooms, sliced
1 cup plain nonfat yogurt
1 tablespoon chopped fresh parsley
1 teaspoon chopped onion
2 cups finely chopped cooked chicken
½ cup plain nonfat yogurt
½ tablespoon chopped fresh parsley

Lightly spray a 6-inch nonstick skillet or crepe pan with vegetable oil. Set aside. In a large bowl, combine flour, cornmeal, oil, milk and egg substitute. Beat until blended. Set aside.

Place prepared skillet or crepe pan over high heat until hot, then remove from heat. Spoon in about 2 tablespoons of batter; lift and tilt skillet to spread batter evenly. Return to heat and brown one side only. Invert pan over paper towel to remove crepe. Repeat procedure to make 16 to 18 crepes, spraying pan occasionally with vegetable oil* and stirring batter to keep cornmeal from settling.

Preheat oven to 350° F. Lightly spray a shallow baking dish with vegetable oil.

Steam broccoli and mushrooms until tender. Set aside.

In a medium bowl, combine 1 cup yogurt, 1 tablespoon parsley, onion and chicken. Stir to mix well. Add broccoli and mushrooms and mix gently.

Put 3 tablespoons of chicken and vegetable filling in each crepe. Fold over once and place in prepared baking dish. Spoon remaining ½ cup yogurt over crepes and top with ½ tablespoon of parsley.

Cover with foil and bake 20 minutes.

* *Do not use vegetable oil spray near an open flame or a heat source. Read directions on can before using, and follow directions carefully.*

Nutrient Analysis

Calories	268 kcal	Cholesterol	42 mg	Saturated Fat	1 gm
Protein	25 gm	Sodium	167 mg	Polyunsaturated Fat	2 gm
Carbohydrate	28 gm	Total Fat	6 gm	Monounsaturated Fat	2 gm

Chicken Curry in a Hurry

Serves 4

2 cups diced cooked chicken
½ pound fresh mushrooms, thinly sliced
⅓ cup chopped onion
3 tablespoons acceptable vegetable oil or margarine
3 tablespoons flour
**1 cup homemade Chicken Broth (see page 87) or
    commercial low-sodium variety**
1½ teaspoons curry powder
1 cup finely chopped apple
¼ cup chopped parsley
¾ cup skim milk
1 cup water

In a large skillet over medium-high heat, sauté chicken, mushrooms and onion in oil or margarine until chicken is lightly browned on all sides.

Stir in flour, broth and curry powder. Add apple and parsley. Pour in milk and water. Simmer, stirring constantly, for 3 minutes, or until apple pieces are tender-crisp.

Serve over rice if desired.

TURKEY CURRY
Substitute cooked turkey for chicken.

Chicken Curry in a Hurry Nutrient Analysis

Calories	285 kcal	Cholesterol	60 mg	Saturated Fat	3 gm
Protein	25 gm	Sodium	98 mg	Polyunsaturated Fat	7 gm
Carbohydrate	12 gm	Total Fat	15 gm	Monounsaturated Fat	4 gm

Turkey Curry in a Hurry Nutrient Analysis

Calories	285 kcal	Cholesterol	60 mg	Saturated Fat	3 gm
Protein	25 gm	Sodium	98 mg	Polyunsaturated Fat	7 gm
Carbohydrate	12 gm	Total Fat	15 gm	Monounsaturated Fat	4 gm

*C*hicken *S*pinach *M*anicotti

Serves 6; 2 shells per person

1 package manicotti shells (12 shells)
2 cups diced cooked chicken
1 10-ounce package frozen no-salt-added spinach,
    defrosted and squeezed dry
Egg substitute equivalent to 3 eggs
1½ cups low-fat cottage cheese
⅓ cup grated Parmesan cheese
2 teaspoons basil
Freshly ground black pepper to taste
2 tablespoons olive oil
1 cup chopped onion
3 cloves garlic, minced
1 14½-ounce can diced no-salt-added tomatoes with juice
1 6-ounce can no-salt-added tomato paste
1 cup water
1 teaspoon Italian herb seasoning
1 teaspoon basil
Vegetable oil spray
3 tablespoons grated Parmesan cheese

Cook pasta according to package directions, omitting salt. Drain and set aside.

In a bowl, combine next seven ingredients and set aside.

Heat olive oil in a saucepan over medium-high heat. Add onion and sauté until translucent. Add garlic and sauté 1 minute more. Stir in tomatoes, tomato paste, water and herbs. Crush tomatoes slightly with wooden spoon. Reduce heat and simmer for 8 to 10 minutes.

Preheat oven to 375° F. Lightly spray a 9-x-13-inch baking pan with vegetable oil.

Spread 1 cup sauce on bottom of pan. Stuff shells with filling mixture and arrange them on sauce. Spoon remaining sauce over top. Sprinkle Parmesan cheese on top. Bake 30 minutes, or until thoroughly heated.

MICROWAVE METHOD

Combine olive oil, onion and garlic in 1-quart microwave-safe bowl. Microwave on high 3 minutes. Add remaining sauce ingredients and cook 10 minutes on medium. Place half of the sauce in a microwave-safe baking dish. Fill shells as directed and arrange shells on top of sauce. Cover with remaining sauce. Top with Parmesan cheese. Cover with vented plastic wrap and microwave on medium 25 minutes. Let stand covered 5 minutes and serve hot.

Nutrient Analysis

Calories	377 kcal	Cholesterol	51 mg	Saturated Fat	4 gm
Protein	34 gm	Sodium	563 mg	Polyunsaturated Fat	2 gm
Carbohydrate	33 gm	Total Fat	12 gm	Monounsaturated Fat	5 gm

*R*oast *T*urkey

Serves 12

1 turkey (about 12 pounds)
½ teaspoon freshly ground black pepper
½ teaspoon poultry seasoning
3 stalks celery, chopped
1 medium onion, chopped
2 carrots, chopped
⅓ cup chopped fresh parsley
¼ cup acceptable margarine, melted

*T*haw turkey if necessary; remove parts from cavities. Rinse and pat dry. Preheat oven to 425° F.

Sprinkle pepper and poultry seasoning inside body cavity of turkey. Place vegetables and parsley inside cavity. Truss. Place on a rack in a roasting pan. Place meat thermometer in thigh, making sure tip does not rest against bone. Brush bird with melted margarine. Bake 15 minutes and then reduce heat to 325° F. Cook turkey, basting often, until meat thermometer reaches 185° F. Turkey should rest 15 to 20 minutes before it is carved. Remove skin before eating.

Nutrient Analysis

Calories	500 kcal	Cholesterol	214 mg	Saturated Fat	6 gm
Protein	75 gm	Sodium	246 mg	Polyunsaturated Fat	5 gm
Carbohydrate	0 gm	Total Fat	20 gm	Monounsaturated Fat	6 gm

*M*arinated *T*urkey *F*illets

Serves 6

1½ pounds skinless turkey fillets, all visible fat removed
2 cups low-fat buttermilk
3 tablespoons acceptable vegetable oil
1 cup finely chopped onion
1 tablespoon finely chopped fresh dill
1 tablespoon finely chopped fresh tarragon
1 tablespoon finely chopped fresh cilantro
1 tablespoon finely chopped fresh rosemary
1 teaspoon freshly ground black pepper
¼ teaspoon salt

*R*inse turkey fillets and pat dry. Set aside.

In a small bowl, combine remaining ingredients. Pour into rectangular enamel or ovenproof glass baking dish. Add fillets, turning to coat evenly. Cover and refrigerate for several hours or overnight, turning fillets several times.

Grill or broil marinated fillets.

Serve hot. This dish is also good chilled and sliced over salad greens. (Keep covered in the refrigerator.)

Nutrient Analysis

Calories	238 kcal	Cholesterol	71 mg	Saturated Fat	2 gm
Protein	29 gm	Sodium	236 mg	Polyunsaturated Fat	5 gm
Carbohydrate	4 gm	Total Fat	11 gm	Monounsaturated Fat	3 gm

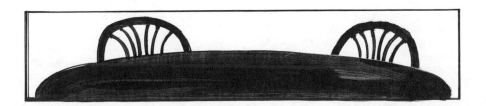

*T*urkey *M*eatloaf

Serves 8

Vegetable oil spray
4 slices whole-wheat bread
¼ cup skim milk
2 pounds freshly ground turkey, skin removed before
    grinding
1 cup grated onion
½ cup diced celery
¼ cup minced fresh parsley
Egg substitute equivalent to 2 eggs
1 cup canned no-salt-added stewed tomatoes, crushed
1 teaspoon finely minced and seeded fresh jalapeño
    pepper, or to taste *
2 tablespoons ketchup

Preheat oven to 350° F. Lightly spray a 9½-x-5½-x-3-inch loaf pan with vegetable oil, or use a nonstick pan.

Place bread in a blender or the work bowl of a food processor fitted with a metal blade, and process into fine crumbs.

In a shallow bowl, combine bread crumbs and milk. Let bread soak 5 minutes.

In a large bowl, combine all remaining ingredients except ketchup. Mix lightly. Set aside.

Drain bread and squeeze out excess milk to form a paste. Add to meat mixture and blend well.

Pack lightly into the prepared loaf pan. Spread ketchup over top of loaf.

Bake uncovered 1¼ hours. Let sit out 5 minutes before serving.

* Wear rubber gloves when handling hot peppers, or wash hands thoroughly after handling. Skin, especially around the eyes, is very sensitive to oil from peppers.

Nutrient Analysis

Calories	229 kcal	Cholesterol	71 mg	Saturated Fat	2 gm
Protein	29 gm	Sodium	283 mg	Polyunsaturated Fat	2 gm
Carbohydrate	13 gm	Total Fat	7 gm	Monounsaturated Fat	2 gm

*T*urkey *L*asagna

Serves 9

Vegetable oil spray
½ cup chopped onion
8 ounces fresh mushrooms, sliced
3 cloves garlic, minced
1 pound freshly ground turkey, skin removed before
　　grinding
3 cups no-salt-added tomato sauce
2 teaspoons basil
½ teaspoon oregano
Freshly ground black pepper to taste
1 10-ounce package frozen no-salt-added chopped
　　spinach, defrosted and squeezed dry
2 cups (1 pound) low-fat cottage cheese
Dash nutmeg
1 8-ounce package lasagna noodles
8 ounces part-skim mozzarella cheese, grated

Preheat oven to 375° F. Lightly spray a 9-x-13-inch baking dish with vegetable oil.

In a nonstick skillet over medium-high heat, combine onion, mushrooms, garlic and ground turkey. Sauté until turkey is no longer pink. Cover pan and continue to cook until mushrooms have released juices, then uncover and evaporate juices over high heat. Add tomato sauce, basil, oregano and pepper. Reduce heat.

In a bowl, stir spinach, cottage cheese and nutmeg together well. Set aside.

Cook noodles according to package directions, omitting salt.

Lay one-third of noodles on bottom of dish; add one-half of spinach mixture, one-third of tomato sauce and one-third of cheese. Repeat layers once. Finish with one layer noodles, one-third sauce and remaining cheese. Cover with aluminum foil and bake 35 to 40 minutes.

Nutrient Analysis

Calories	326 kcal	Cholesterol	49 mg	Saturated Fat		4 gm
Protein	31 gm	Sodium	411 mg	Polyunsaturated Fat		1 gm
Carbohydrate	32 gm	Total Fat	8 gm	Monounsaturated Fat		2 gm

Turkey Meatballs

Serves 5; 4 meatballs per serving

Vegetable oil spray
¼ cup skim milk
1½ slices whole-wheat bread
1 pound freshly ground turkey, skin removed before
    grinding
1 clove garlic, minced
1 small onion, grated
3 tablespoons chopped fresh parsley
⅓ cup freshly grated Parmesan cheese (about 1 ounce)
1 egg, well beaten
¼ teaspoon ground nutmeg
¼ teaspoon freshly ground black pepper
¼ cup flour

Preheat oven to 350° F. Lightly spray a broiler pan with vegetable oil.

In a small saucepan over medium heat, warm milk. Tear bread into pieces into a small bowl. Pour warm milk over bread. Let soak about 10 minutes, then squeeze out excess milk.

In a bowl, blend bread, turkey, garlic, onion, parsley, cheese, egg, nutmeg and pepper; blend well. Shape mixture into small balls about the size of pecan shells. Dust with flour.

Place meatballs on a prepared broiler pan and bake 10 minutes. Remove from oven. Preheat broiler. Broil meatballs until brown on all sides, stirring often.

Serve meatballs with pasta and a favorite no-salt-added spaghetti sauce. For a complete meal, add a side dish of crisp salad greens tossed with vinegar and oil and a thin slice or two of toasted French bread.

Nutrient Analysis

Calories	224 kcal	Cholesterol	118 mg	Saturated Fat	3 gm
Protein	26 gm	Sodium	257 mg	Polyunsaturated Fat	1 gm
Carbohydrate	11 gm	Total Fat	8 gm	Monounsaturated Fat	2 gm

*P*orcupine *M*eatballs

Serves 5; 3 meatballs per serving

Vegetable oil spray
1 pound freshly ground turkey, skin removed before
    grinding
1 cup cooked brown rice
¼ cup chopped onion
1 teaspoon acceptable vegetable oil
1 teaspoon Italian herb seasoning
¼ teaspoon freshly ground black pepper
2 cups no-salt-added tomato juice
½ teaspoon chili powder
½ cup chopped green bell pepper

*P*reheat broiler. Lightly spray a broiler pan with vegetable oil.

In a bowl, combine turkey, rice, onion, oil and seasonings. Stir to mix well. Shape into 15 1-inch balls and broil on broiler pan turning meatballs until they are browned evenly on all sides.

In a saucepan, combine tomato juice, chili powder and bell pepper. Bring to a boil. Add meatballs, cover and simmer 20 minutes, stirring occasionally.

Nutrient Analysis

Calories	198 kcal	Cholesterol	56 mg	Saturated Fat	1 gm
Protein	22 gm	Sodium	66 mg	Polyunsaturated Fat	2 gm
Carbohydrate	15 gm	Total Fat	5 gm	Monounsaturated Fat	2 gm

Game

Some people think game is too high in fat to be included in a cookbook designed with low-fat diets in mind. Actually, if you remove the skin before cooking, most game is surprisingly lean.

A Cornish hen makes a wonderful entree, especially when it is basted in homemade broth. Venison is also excellent and makes a wonderful stew, as do elk and antelope.

Wild duck and pheasant are acceptably lean; so are partridge, quail and other small birds. If you've never tried rabbit, you'll probably like it a lot: it tastes similar to chicken, but it has only a fraction of chicken's fat.

Many recipes for game call for adding lots of cooking fat for flavor. Don't give in to that temptation. You can pack in juices and flavors by basting with broth, wine or a marinade and adding fresh herbs. Game is wonderful roasted, braised or fricasseed—and it's easy to control fat and salt with these cooking methods.

Try one of these recipes at your next dinner party, and make it an event to remember!

*R*oast *S*tuffed *C*ornish *H*ens

Serves 12; ½ hen per serving

1⅓ cups uncooked long grain and wild rice combination, or
    1 package wild rice mix, uncooked
2 tablespoons acceptable margarine
1 medium onion, chopped
1 teaspoon sage, thyme, savory or tarragon
6 Cornish hens (about 14 ounces each)
½ cup acceptable margarine, melted
½ cup water
¼ cup brandy
1 cup orange sections

*P*reheat oven to 350° F.

To make stuffing, cook rice until it is slightly firm. Set aside.

In a large skillet over medium-high heat, melt 2 tablespoons margarine. Add chopped onion and sauté until browned. Add rice and sage or other herb; toss gently. Remove from heat and set aside.

Clean, rinse and dry hens. Stuff lightly with rice mixture. Skewer or sew cavities closed. Brush hens with ½ cup melted margarine and place breast-side up on a rack in a shallow pan.

Roast uncovered about 1 hour, basting occasionally with melted margarine. Remove hens from pan. Remove rice stuffing and place it in a serving bowl. Cut hens in half and place on a warm serving platter.

Place roasting pan, with juices, on top of stove over medium-high heat. Add ½ cup water to drippings, stirring to dislodge browned particles from pan. Add brandy and orange sections. Cook 2 minutes, stirring constantly. Serve sauce with hens.

Nutrient Analysis

Calories	336 kcal	Cholesterol	73 mg	Saturated Fat	4 gm
Protein	28 gm	Sodium	181 mg	Polyunsaturated Fat	4 gm
Carbohydrate	19 gm	Total Fat	15 gm	Monounsaturated Fat	6 gm

Game Hens Provence Style

Serves 4; ½ hen per serving

2 Cornish game hens, approximately 1 pound each (remove
    all excess fat, tails and giblets)
½ teaspoon crushed sweet basil
½ teaspoon crushed thyme
½ teaspoon salt
½ teaspoon freshly ground black pepper
½ pound small onions
8 cloves garlic, unpeeled
4 large sprigs parsley
½ pound small new potatoes, cut in half
1 medium onion, sliced in rings
¼ teaspoon salt-free all-purpose seasoning
½ teaspoon freshly ground black pepper
¼ teaspoon herbs of Provence
1 cup white wine

Soak a clay cooker in cold water 15 minutes.

Meanwhile, clean, rinse and dry birds. Season inside and out with basil, thyme, salt and ½ tablespoon black pepper. Stuff birds with whole onions, garlic and parsley. Place in clay casserole. Add potatoes and onion rings. Sprinkle all-purpose seasoning, ½ teaspoon black pepper and herbs of Provence on top. Pour wine over all.

If using an electric oven, place clay casserole in cold oven and then set temperature to 450° F. Bake 1¼ hours.

If using a gas oven, place clay casserole in cold oven and then set temperature to 300° F. Increase temperature every 10 minutes until temperature reaches 450° F. Cook 1½ hours.

Discard onion, garlic, and parsley stuffing. Cut birds in half and serve with vegetables.

OPTIONAL COOKING METHOD
If a clay cooker is not available, cook birds in a covered heavy roaster at 350° F 45 to 50 minutes. Uncover and cook 5 to 10 minutes longer to brown. Birds are done when juices from pierced thigh run clear.

Nutrient Analysis

Calories	256 kcal	Cholesterol	83 mg	Saturated Fat	2 gm
Protein	31 gm	Sodium	355 mg	Polyunsaturated Fat	2 gm
Carbohydrate	18 gm	Total Fat	6 gm	Monounsaturated Fat	2 gm

*H*erb *R*oasted *P*heasant

Serves 4; ½ pheasant per serving

> 2 1-pound pheasants
> ⅓ cup olive oil
> 3 sprigs fresh rosemary or ½ teaspoon crushed, dried
>   rosemary
> 3 sprigs fresh thyme or ½ teaspoon crushed, dried thyme
> ¼ teaspoon salt
> ¼ teaspoon freshly ground black pepper
> 1 clove garlic, minced
> 1 small onion, minced
> 2 carrots cut in small pieces
> 8 fresh mushrooms, quartered
> 2 small onions, quartered
> ½ tablespoon acceptable vegetable oil
> Bouquet garni, sprinkled over vegetables
> ¼ cup dry white wine
>
> **GARNISH**
> Fresh parsley sprigs

Rinse birds and clean cavity. Pat dry and set aside.

In glass or enamel bowl, mix olive oil, rosemary, thyme, salt, pepper, garlic and onion. Coat birds outside and inside with mixture and cover. Marinate in refrigerator 8 hours or overnight, turning often.

Remove birds from marinade and drain well.

Steam carrots, mushrooms and onions just until tender-crisp. Drain and set aside.

Preheat oven to 300° F.

Heat vegetable oil in a nonstick skillet over medium-high heat. Add birds and brown on all sides 8 to 10 minutes. Drain.

Make two heavy-duty foil packages. Place a bird and some of the steamed vegetables in each package. Sprinkle with bouquet garni. Add 2 tablespoons wine to each package. Wrap securely.

Bake 8 to 10 minutes, or until tender. Do not overcook. Verify doneness by checking at leg joint to see if juices run clear.

Remove birds from oven and cut them in half. Remove skins from birds and divide birds and vegetables among four heated plates. Garnish with fresh parsley.

Serve with steamed and lightly seasoned wild rice or a favorite fall vegetable.

Nutrient Analysis

Calories	471 kcal	Cholesterol	126 mg	Saturated Fat		7 gm
Protein	41 gm	Sodium	283 mg	Polyunsaturated Fat		4 gm
Carbohydrate	7 gm	Total Fat	31 gm	Monounsaturated Fat		19 gm

Marinade for Venison, Elk or Antelope

Makes 1¼ cups
Marinates 1 to 1½ pounds of meat, approximately

> 1 cup homemade Beef Broth (see page 86) or commercial low-sodium variety
> 1 tablespoon pickling spice
> ½ teaspoon celery seeds
> ½ teaspoon basil
> ½ teaspoon marjoram
> ½ teaspoon thyme
> ½ teaspoon sage
> 1 bay leaf
> 3 peppercorns, crushed
> 3 whole allspice, crushed
> 2 tablespoons fresh lemon juice
> ¼ cup red wine vinegar

In a large bowl, mix all ingredients together well. Add meat and stir to coat well. Cover and refrigerate 10 to 12 hours.

Drain well before cooking as desired.

Nutrient Analysis*

Calories	35 kcal	Cholesterol	0 mg	Saturated Fat		0 gm
Protein	2 gm	Sodium	51 mg	Polyunsaturated Fat		0 gm
Carbohydrate	6 gm	Total Fat	1 gm	Monounsaturated Fat		0 gm

* for entire recipe

*H*asenpfeffer

Serves 4

1 2½- to 3-pound rabbit, cut up
½ cup white wine vinegar or tarragon vinegar
2 cups water
¼ teaspoon freshly ground black pepper, or to taste
½ teaspoon whole cloves
2 teaspoons sugar
4 bay leaves
1 medium onion, sliced
½ cup flour
3 tablespoons acceptable vegetable oil
2 teaspoons Worcestershire sauce
3 tablespoons flour
3 tablespoons cold water

Rinse rabbit pieces and pat dry. Set aside.

In a large bowl, combine vinegar, water, pepper, cloves, sugar, bay leaves and sliced onion to make a pickling mixture. Add rabbit pieces, cover and refrigerate 8 to 12 hours. Turn pieces occasionally so they will absorb flavor evenly.

Remove rabbit pieces from pickling mixture and drain them on paper towels. Discard bay leaves and cloves from pickling mixture and reserve the remainder.

Place ½ cup flour in a shallow bowl and dredge rabbit pieces in it. Heat oil in a large, heavy skillet over medium-high heat. Add rabbit pieces and brown evenly on all sides. Pour reserved liquid and Worcestershire sauce over rabbit and add onions. Reduce heat and simmer 45 to 60 minutes, or until tender.

In a small bowl, combine 3 tablespoons each of flour and cold water. Add mixture to skillet and stir to thicken sauce. Serve hot.

Nutrient Analysis

Calories	621 kcal	Cholesterol	144 mg	Saturated Fat	7 gm
Protein	80 gm	Sodium	224 mg	Polyunsaturated Fat	11 gm
Carbohydrate	21 gm	Total Fat	25 gm	Monounsaturated Fat	5 gm

Herbed Rabbit in Wine Sauce
(European Method)

Serves 6

1 3-pound rabbit, cut up
1 teaspoon fresh lemon juice
½ cup dry white wine
2 tablespoons sugar
Freshly ground black pepper to taste
¼ teaspoon marjoram
1 small bay leaf
3 whole cloves
2 tablespoons acceptable vegetable oil
3 tablespoons flour
½ cup chopped onion
¼ cup chopped green bell pepper

Rinse rabbit pieces and set aside.

Combine lemon juice, wine, sugar, pepper, marjoram, bay leaf and cloves in a shallow dish. Stir to mix well. Add rabbit pieces and coat well. Cover and refrigerate at least 12 hours.

Remove pieces from marinade and dry them well. Strain marinade and set aside.

Heat oil in a nonstick skillet over medium-high heat. Roll rabbit pieces lightly in flour and brown in oil. Place rabbit and reserved marinade in a heavy stockpot over medium-high heat. Bring to a boil and reduce heat. Simmer 1½ to 2 hours, or until tender. Add onion and bell pepper and cook an additional 15 minutes.

Remove rabbit to a serving platter. Strain sauce again and heat, but do not allow to boil. Pour over rabbit.

Serve with brown rice if desired.

Nutrient Analysis

Calories	393 kcal	Cholesterol	105 mg	Saturated Fat		5 gm
Protein	57 gm	Sodium	141 mg	Polyunsaturated Fat		6 gm
Carbohydrate	8 gm	Total Fat	15 gm	Monounsaturated Fat		3 gm

Meats

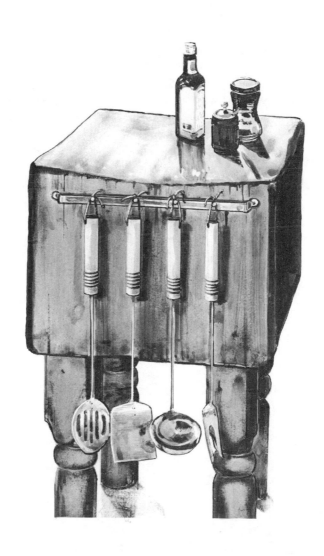

MARINATED STEAK	SCALOPPINE AL LIMONE
HERBED FILLET OF BEEF	VEAL WITH RED PEPPERS AND MUSHROOMS
SHIRLEY'S MARINATED STEAK	VEAL SOUTHWESTERN
BRAISED SIRLOIN TIPS	VEAL STUFINO
BEEF BOURGUIGNON	SPANISH RICE WITH VEAL
BEEF STROGANOFF	VEAL OSSO BUCO
JUICY BEEF KABOBS	VEAL STEW WITH FENNEL
BEEF SKILLET ORIENTAL	FRENCH-STYLE LAMB CHOPS
CHINESE FLANK STEAK	JULEP LAMB CHOPS FLAMBÉ
SUKIYAKI	LEMON LAMB WITH MINT
LAZY DAY BEEF CASSEROLE	LAMB KABOBS
SALISBURY STEAKS WITH MUSHROOM SAUCE	ARMENIAN LAMB CASSEROLE
BAKED STUFFED EGGPLANT	EASY LAMB CURRY
BEEF MANICOTTI	MARINATED PORK LOIN
MOCK SPAGHETTI	ORANGE PORK MEDALLIONS
SHEPHERD'S PIE	SWEET AND SOUR PORK
SPAGHETTI WITH MEAT SAUCE	PORK WITH STEAMED SPICED SAUERKRAUT
TAMALE PIE	CRUSTLESS SPINACH TART
SLOPPY JOES	SOUTHWESTERN HASH
MACARONI BEEF SKILLET	HAM ROLL-UPS
BEEF TOSTADAS	BAKED HAM SLICE SAUTERNE
MEATBALLS HAWAIIAN	CANADIAN BACON IN WINE SAUCE
BEEF PITAS	BAYOU RED BEANS AND RICE
CHILI CON CARNE	

Gone are the days when a two-pound steak was a prized entree.

Today, Americans are wiser—and healthier. We're measuring our meat portions in ounces (about 3) per serving, not in pounds, and we're adding heartier accompaniments: pastas, vegetables, grains and legumes.

Happily, it doesn't take much meat to give you the protein you need. Ounce for ounce, meat is very nutritious. It's packed with iron, B vitamins and minerals. Unfortunately, meat also contains varying amounts of cholesterol and saturated fat, depending on the cut.

To limit the amounts of cholesterol and saturated fat, choose lean meats with more lean than fat, such as round or rump cuts, or London broil, round or flank steaks. Tenderize them by marinating them in a covered glass bowl in the refrigerator overnight or even for a couple of days. Fruit juices and wines make excellent marinades. Consider pressing peppercorns into the meat for a steak au poivre, or rosemary needles, a wonderful Flemish touch.

With leaner cuts of pork available today, it's easy to prepare a pork entree that's lower in saturated fat. When choosing pork, look for sirloin roasts, tenderloin and loin chops, then trim off the fat.

Roasting allows the fat to cook out of meat and enhances its natural flavor. To roast pork the easy way, sprinkle it with freshly ground black pepper, insert a few garlic cloves and roast it on a rack until it's well done, with a crunchy crust.

Lamb is great cooked over an open fire; use herbs like dill and mint to add zing. Leftover lamb makes great sandwiches, too. The wonderful flavor of curried lamb makes it a dinner party favorite.

The recipes that follow will give you the best of what meat offers, but with limited fat. Shop for the leanest cuts, and use herbs, spices, wines and sauces to enhance flavor.

*M*arinated *S*teak

Serves 6

2 pounds top sirloin steak, all visible fat removed
¼ cup fresh lemon juice
¾ cup acceptable vegetable oil
3 tablespoons dry white wine
½ cup chopped onion
2 tablespoons finely chopped fresh rosemary
2 tablespoons finely chopped fresh sage
1 tablespoon Dijon mustard
3 cloves garlic, minced
½ teaspoon salt

*P*lace steak in an oblong glass baking pan and set aside.

Combine all other ingredients in small bowl. Pour marinade over steak and turn to coat evenly. Cover and refrigerate several hours or overnight, turning meat occasionally.

Preheat grill. Grill marinated steak over hot coals.

Nutrient Analysis

Calories	429 kcal	Cholesterol	67 mg	Saturated Fat	7 gm
Protein	25 gm	Sodium	272 mg	Polyunsaturated Fat	16 gm
Carbohydrate	1 gm	Total Fat	36 gm	Monounsaturated Fat	10 gm

*H*erbed *F*illet of *B*eef

Serves 6

1 fillet of beef (about 1¾ pounds), all visible fat removed
3 cloves garlic, crushed
¼ teaspoon freshly ground black pepper, or to taste
4 to 5 sprigs fresh thyme or 1 teaspoon dried thyme
1 tablespoon olive oil
1 onion, sliced
2 carrots, finely diced
¼ teaspoon salt

GARNISH
Parsley sprigs

Preheat oven to 400° F.

Tie beef fillet in 3 or 4 places. Rub garlic on all sides of meat and sprinkle pepper over all. Place in heavy nonstick roasting pan. Lay thyme across meat. Pour olive oil over entire roast. Scatter onions and carrots around and over roast.

Cook 14 minutes per pound for medium-rare. Remove from oven, sprinkle with salt and cover with foil. Let sit for 10 to 15 minutes before serving.

Nutrient Analysis

Calories	229 kcal	Cholesterol	70 mg	Saturated Fat	4 gm
Protein	27 gm	Sodium	168 mg	Polyunsaturated Fat	1 gm
Carbohydrate	4 gm	Total Fat	11 gm	Monounsaturated Fat	5 gm

Shirley's Marinated Steak

Serves 6

> 2 pounds top sirloin steak, all visible fat removed
> 1½ cups light beer
> 4 scallions, minced
> ⅓ cup acceptable vegetable oil
> 2 tablespoons sherry
> 1 tablespoon light soy sauce
> Dash of hot pepper oil
> 1 tablespoon grated fresh ginger
> 2 tablespoons firmly packed light brown sugar
> 2 cloves garlic, minced
> 1 teaspoon red pepper flakes

Place steak in an oblong glass baking pan. Set aside.

Combine all other ingredients in small bowl. Pour over steak and turn to coat evenly. Cover and refrigerate several hours or overnight, turning meat occasionally.

Preheat grill. Grill marinated meat over hot coals.

Nutrient Analysis

Calories	400 kcal	Cholesterol	91 mg	Saturated Fat	6 gm
Protein	35 gm	Sodium	185 mg	Polyunsaturated Fat	8 gm
Carbohydrate	7 gm	Total Fat	23 gm	Monounsaturated Fat	8 gm

*B*raised *S*irloin *T*ips

Serves 8

¼ teaspoon freshly ground black pepper
½ teaspoon unseasoned meat tenderizer
2 pounds beef sirloin tips, all visible fat removed, cut into
    cubes and drained on paper towels
2 cloves garlic, finely minced
½ cup finely chopped onion
1¼ cups homemade Beef Broth (see page 86) or
    commercial low-sodium variety
⅓ cup dry red wine
1 tablespoon light soy sauce
2 tablespoons cornstarch
¼ cup cold water
¼ cup minced fresh parsley

Place a large nonstick skillet over medium-high heat. Sprinkle pepper and meat tenderizer on meat. Brown meat on all sides, turning often, until well browned. Add garlic and onions and cook until onions are translucent.

Add broth, wine and soy sauce and heat to boiling. Reduce heat, cover and simmer 1½ hours, or until meat is tender.

In a small bowl, blend cornstarch and water until smooth, then slowly pour mixture into skillet, stirring constantly. Continue to cook and stir until gravy thickens. Sprinkle parsley on top.

Serve with rice if desired.

Nutrient Analysis

Calories	177 kcal	Cholesterol	67 mg	Saturated Fat	2 gm
Protein	26 gm	Sodium	244 mg	Polyunsaturated Fat	0 gm
Carbohydrate	5 gm	Total Fat	5 gm	Monounsaturated Fat	2 gm

*B*eef *B*ourguignon

Serves 8

Vegetable oil spray
2 tablespoons acceptable vegetable oil
5 medium onions, sliced
2 pounds lean top sirloin roast (or other lean cut), all
    visible fat removed, cut into 1-inch cubes
1½ tablespoons flour
¼ teaspoon marjoram
¼ teaspoon thyme
½ teaspoon freshly ground black pepper, or to taste
½ cup homemade Beef Broth (see page 86) or commercial
    low-sodium variety
1 cup dry red wine
½ pound fresh mushrooms, sliced

Lightly spray a large, heavy skillet with vegetable oil. Add 2 table-spoons oil and place over medium-high heat. Add onions and sauté until tender. Remove them to a small bowl and set aside.

Add beef cubes and sauté until browned. Sprinkle flour and seasonings on top of beef and stir to mix well.

Add broth and wine. Stir well and reduce heat. Simmer 1½ to 2 hours. Add more broth and wine (1 part broth to 2 parts wine) as necessary to keep beef barely covered.

Return onions to skillet and add mushrooms. Cook 30 minutes longer, stirring frequently. Add more broth and wine if necessary. Sauce should be thick and dark brown.

Nutrient Analysis *

Calories	226 kcal	Cholesterol	67 mg	Saturated Fat	2 gm
Protein	26 gm	Sodium	59 mg	Polyunsaturated Fat	2 gm
Carbohydrate	9 gm	Total Fat	9 gm	Monounsaturated Fat	3 gm

* using lean top sirloin roast

*B*eef *S*troganoff

Serves 6

1 pound beef tenderloin, lean beef round or sirloin, all
    visible fat removed
½ teaspoon freshly ground black pepper, or to taste
2 tablespoons acceptable vegetable oil
½ pound mushrooms, sliced
1 onion, sliced
1 tablespoon acceptable vegetable oil
2 tablespoons flour
2 cups homemade Beef Broth (see page 86) or commercial
    low-sodium variety
2 tablespoons no-salt-added tomato paste
1 teaspoon dry mustard
¼ teaspoon oregano
¼ teaspoon dill weed
2 tablespoons sherry
⅓ cup plain nonfat yogurt

Cut meat into thin strips about 2 inches long. Sprinkle with pepper, cover and let stand in refrigerator for 2 hours.

Place 2 tablespoons oil in a heavy skillet over medium-high heat. Add mushrooms and sauté until tender. Remove from skillet and set aside. Sauté onions in the same skillet until brown. Remove from skillet and set aside. Add meat to skillet and brown quickly on all sides until rare. Remove and set aside.

Place 1 tablespoon oil and 2 tablespoons flour in skillet and stir to mix well. Gradually add broth, stirring constantly. Cook until smooth and slightly thick. Add tomato paste, dry mustard, oregano, dill weed and sherry. Stir to blend well. In the top of a double boiler, combine sauce, meat, mushrooms and onions. Cook 15 minutes. Beat yogurt in a small bowl (to prevent it from curdling). Add beaten yogurt to meat and stir to blend well. Cook 5 minutes and serve immediately with spinach noodles or rice.

Nutrient Analysis

Calories	215 kcal	Cholesterol	40 mg	Saturated Fat	3 gm
Protein	18 gm	Sodium	71 mg	Polyunsaturated Fat	4 gm
Carbohydrate	7 gm	Total Fat	12 gm	Monounsaturated Fat	4 gm

*J*uicy *B*eef *K*abobs

Serves 8

3/4 cup dry red wine
2 tablespoons light soy sauce
1/4 cup Worcestershire sauce
1/2 cup reduced-calorie Italian salad dressing
1/2 teaspoon unseasoned meat tenderizer
1 teaspoon crushed dried thyme
1 teaspoon crushed dried rosemary
1 onion, finely chopped
1/2 teaspoon freshly ground black pepper
1 1/2 pounds sirloin tip, all visible fat removed, cut into
     16 cubes
8 boiler onions (small onions), outer skin removed
16 large cherry tomatoes
8 2-inch new potatoes, cut in half
16 whole mushrooms
1 large green bell pepper, cut into 16 pieces
2 tablespoons reduced-calorie Italian salad dressing
8 wooden skewers

Mix first nine ingredients and pour over beef in a glass bowl. Cover and let sit overnight in refrigerator. Drain and discard marinade.

Soak skewers in water at least 30 minutes before using.

Parboil onions 1 1/2 minutes. Remove from heat and place under cold running water. Cut in half and set aside.

Wipe mushrooms with a clean, damp cloth. Set aside.

Preheat broiler or grill.

Alternate beef and vegetables, including bell peppers, on skewers. Broil 3 or 4 inches from heat or cook on a charcoal grill for 12 to 15 minutes. Turn frequently during cooking time and baste with salad dressing.

Nutrient Analysis

Calories	263 kcal	Cholesterol	51 mg	Saturated Fat	2 gm
Protein	22 gm	Sodium	438 mg	Polyunsaturated Fat	1 gm
Carbohydrate	27 gm	Total Fat	6 gm	Monounsaturated Fat	2 gm

Beef Skillet Oriental

Serves 8

1 pound flank steak, all visible fat removed
6 ounces fresh snow peas
Vegetable oil spray
1 tablespoon acceptable vegetable oil
½ cup chopped onion
3 cloves garlic, minced
4 cups small fresh cauliflower florets
2 cups homemade Beef Broth (see page 86) or commercial
      low-sodium variety
1¾ cups diced red bell pepper
2 tablespoons cornstarch
2 tablespoons light soy sauce
¼ cup cold water
¼ cup sherry
1 tablespoon grated fresh ginger
¼ teaspoon hot pepper sauce

Place flank steak in the freezer for 30 minutes. Remove and slice across the grain into thin strips 2 to 3 inches long and ½ to 1 inch wide.

Rinse snow peas, trim ends and set aside.

Heat a nonstick electric skillet to 400° F. Spray skillet with vegetable oil. Add half of beef and stir-fry just until browned. Remove and set aside. Repeat procedure with remaining beef.

Heat oil in skillet and add onion and garlic. Sauté until onion is translucent. Add cauliflower and broth. Cook, stirring gently, about 2 minutes. Add bell pepper and snow peas. Cook 1 minute longer.

In a bowl, combine last six ingredients. Stir to mix well; pour into skillet. Add beef and cook, stirring constantly, until sauce thickens.

Serve with rice if desired.

Nutrient Analysis

Calories	181 kcal	Cholesterol	42 mg	Saturated Fat	3 gm
Protein	16 gm	Sodium	202 mg	Polyunsaturated Fat	1 gm
Carbohydrate	10 gm	Total Fat	9 gm	Monounsaturated Fat	4 gm

Chinese Flank Steak

Serves 4

1 pound lean flank steak, all visible fat removed
2 tablespoons light soy sauce
¼ teaspoon hot pepper oil or ⅛ teaspoon cayenne pepper
2 cloves garlic, finely minced
½ cup sherry
1 teaspoon grated fresh ginger
2 teaspoons cornstarch
Vegetable oil spray
½ tablespoon acceptable vegetable oil
½ tablespoon sesame oil
1 6-ounce package frozen no-salt-added Chinese pea pods
    or 1 cup fresh broccoli florets
½ pound fresh mushrooms, sliced
½ tablespoon acceptable vegetable oil
½ tablespoon sesame oil
1 cup sliced green onion
1 8-ounce can sliced water chestnuts, rinsed and drained

Place flank steak in freezer for 30 minutes. Remove and slice across the grain into thin strips 2 to 3 inches long and ½ to 1 inch wide.

In a glass bowl, combine soy sauce, hot pepper oil or cayenne pepper, garlic, sherry, ginger and cornstarch. Add meat and stir to mix well. Allow to sit at room temperature for 30 minutes.

Lightly spray an electric skillet or wok with vegetable oil. Add ½ tablespoon of vegetable oil and ½ tablespoon of sesame oil and heat until very hot. Add pea pods or broccoli and mushrooms. Sauté until lightly browned and tender-crisp. Remove and keep warm. Add remaining oil and heat until very hot. Add green onions, meat and marinade. Stir quickly until meat is browned. Return warm vegetables and add water chestnuts to the skillet or wok. Stir until heated; serve immediately.

Nutrient Analysis

Calories	369 kcal	Cholesterol	84 mg	Saturated Fat	6 gm
Protein	29 gm	Sodium	359 mg	Polyunsaturated Fat	4 gm
Carbohydrate	18 gm	Total Fat	20 gm	Monounsaturated Fat	8 gm

Sukiyaki

Serves 10

2 pounds tenderloin or sirloin steak, all visible fat removed
1⅔ cups uncooked rice
1 cup diagonally sliced green onion
1 cup diagonally sliced celery
1 5-ounce can water chestnuts, drained and thinly sliced
1 cup thinly sliced fresh mushrooms
1 5-ounce can bamboo shoots, drained and slivered
1 pound fresh bean sprouts
4 cups fresh spinach leaves, rinsed, trimmed and well-
      drained, or shredded Chinese cabbage
3 tablespoons acceptable vegetable oil
½ cup homemade Beef Broth (see page 86) or commercial
      low-sodium variety
½ cup sherry
⅛ cup light soy sauce
1 teaspoon hot pepper oil
½ teaspoon ground ginger
1 tablespoon honey
½ teaspoon freshly ground black pepper

Freeze steak for 30 minutes. Remove and slice across the grain into thin strips 2 to 3 inches long and ½ to 1 inch wide. Set aside.

Cook rice according to package directions, omitting salt and butter or margarine.

Arrange all the vegetables neatly on a large platter or tray.

Heat a large wok or 12-inch electric skillet to 400° F. Add vegetable oil and a few steak strips and sauté about 2 minutes, or until thoroughly browned. Repeat with remaining steak. When all strips have been browned, return them to wok or skillet.

In a small bowl, combine beef broth, sherry, soy sauce, hot pepper oil, ginger and honey. Pour mixture over cooked steak strips. Remove meat with a slotted spoon and keep warm. When sauce begins to bubble, add onions and celery. Cook over high heat, tossing constantly, about 2 minutes. Add water chestnuts and mushrooms and cook, stirring constantly, 2 minutes, or just until heated. Add bamboo shoots, bean sprouts, spinach or shredded cabbage and cooked meat. Cook, stirring constantly, 2 minutes, or just until thoroughly heated. Season with pepper.

Serve immediately with rice.

Note: If more sauce is desired, add another ½ cup of broth to mixture in wok just before serving.

Nutrient Analysis *

Calories	381 kcal	Cholesterol	52 mg	Saturated Fat	4 gm
Protein	29 gm	Sodium	203 mg	Polyunsaturated Fat	5 gm
Carbohydrate	36 gm	Total Fat	14 gm	Monounsaturated Fat	4 gm

* without additional broth

*L*azy *D*ay *B*eef *C*asserole

Serves 4

Vegetable oil spray

1 pound beef chuck roast, all visible fat removed, cut into cubes

½ cup dry red wine

1¼ cups homemade Beef Broth (see page 86) or commercial low-sodium variety

3 tablespoons no-salt-added tomato paste

¼ teaspoon garlic powder

¼ teaspoon rosemary

¼ cup flour

1 8-ounce package fresh mushrooms, sliced

1 cup chopped onion

Preheat broiler. Lightly spray a broiler pan with vegetable oil.

Place meat on prepared broiler pan in broiler. Allow meat to brown on all sides, turning frequently. Remove from broiler and set aside. Set oven to bake at 300° F.

In a 1½-quart casserole, combine wine, broth, tomato paste, spices and flour. Stir to mix well. Place meat in casserole and add mushrooms and onion. Cover and bake 2½ to 3 hours, or until meat is tender.

Nutrient Analysis

Calories	242 kcal	Cholesterol	60 mg	Saturated Fat	3 gm
Protein	26 gm	Sodium	85 mg	Polyunsaturated Fat	0 gm
Carbohydrate	16 gm	Total Fat	8 gm	Monounsaturated Fat	3 gm

Salisbury Steaks with Mushroom Sauce

Serves 8

1½ pounds lean ground round
3 tablespoons flour
1 tablespoon Worcestershire sauce
1 medium onion, grated
¾ teaspoon salt-free all-purpose seasoning
⅛ teaspoon freshly ground black pepper
½ teaspoon dried thyme, crushed
¼ cup skim milk
¾ ounce dried mushrooms
1 cup hot water
½ cup homemade Beef Broth (see page 86) or commercial
    low-sodium variety
½ cup red wine
¼ cup grated carrots
2 to 3 tablespoons finely snipped fresh parsley

In a bowl, combine beef, flour, Worcestershire sauce, onion and spices. Blend gently, thoroughly mixing all ingredients. Add milk and mix again. Shape into eight patties, cover and refrigerate.

Meanwhile, place mushrooms in a small bowl. Cover with hot water and soak 20 to 30 minutes; chop and set aside. Strain water through a paper towel into a clean bowl. (This will remove any dirt.) Save the liquid. Add enough beef broth to saved liquid to make 1 cup. Add red wine and stir well.

Place a heavy nonstick skillet over medium-high heat. Add patties and brown them thoroughly on each side. Remove from skillet and drain on paper towels.

Pour off any liquid left in skillet and return skillet to heat. Add chopped mushrooms, liquids and carrots to skillet. Bring liquid to a boil and reduce it by a third. Add beef patties, reduce heat and simmer 10 minutes. Sprinkle patties with parsley and serve hot.

Serve with baked potatoes and fresh green salad.

Nutrient Analysis

Calories	199 kcal	Cholesterol	61 mg	Saturated Fat	4 gm
Protein	20 gm	Sodium	68 mg	Polyunsaturated Fat	0 gm
Carbohydrate	6 gm	Total Fat	10 gm	Monounsaturated Fat	4 gm

*B*aked *S*tuffed *E*ggplant

Serves 6

Vegetable oil spray
1 large eggplant
2 tablespoons acceptable margarine
1 cup chopped onion
1 cup chopped fresh mushrooms
1½ teaspoons basil
½ teaspoon chervil
½ teaspoon freshly ground black pepper
1 pound lean ground beef
¼ cup no-salt-added tomato paste
¼ cup wheat germ
2 tablespoons chopped fresh parsley

Preheat oven to 350° F. Lightly spray an ovenproof dish with vegetable oil.

Rinse eggplant and cut it in half lengthwise. Carefully remove pulp, leaving ½ inch of outer shell. Dice pulp and set aside.

Place margarine in a large, heavy skillet over medium-high heat. Add onion, mushrooms, seasonings and meat. Sauté, stirring constantly, 8 to 10 minutes, or until meat begins to turn brown. Stir in tomato paste, wheat germ and eggplant pulp. Cook 5 minutes, or just until warm throughout.

Spoon meat mixture into eggplant shell and place in prepared dish. Bake 20 to 30 minutes. Remove from oven and sprinkle parsley on top before serving.

Nutrient Analysis

Calories	235 kcal	Cholesterol	54 mg	Saturated Fat	4 gm
Protein	19 gm	Sodium	84 mg	Polyunsaturated Fat	2 gm
Carbohydrate	11 gm	Total Fat	13 gm	Monounsaturated Fat	6 gm

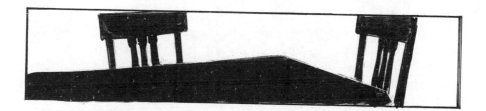

*B*eef *M*anicotti

Serves 6

FILLING
1 10-ounce package frozen no-salt-added leaf spinach
1 clove garlic, minced
1 medium onion, chopped
1 tablespoon olive oil
1 pound lean ground round
½ teaspoon oregano
½ teaspoon freshly ground black pepper, or to taste

SAUCE
1 clove garlic, minced
1 large onion, chopped
1 tablespoon olive oil
½ cup chopped fresh parsley
2 16-ounce cans Italian plum tomatoes
1 6-ounce can no-salt-added tomato paste
1 8-ounce can no-salt-added tomato sauce
½ cup red wine
1 teaspoon basil leaves
¼ teaspoon freshly ground black pepper, or to taste

12 large manicotti shells
Vegetable oil spray
1 cup low-fat cottage cheese or part-skim ricotta cheese

*T*o make manicotti filling, cook spinach according to package directions, omitting salt. Drain and press water from spinach. Chop into large pieces. Set aside.

Sauté garlic and onion in 1 tablespoon olive oil over medium-high heat. Cook until onion is soft but not browned. Add ground meat, breaking it up with a fork. Cook until no longer pink. Drain off fat. Add seasonings and spinach. Stir to mix well. Set aside.

To make sauce, place garlic, onion and 1 tablespoon olive oil in a saucepan. Sauté over medium-high heat until onion is soft but not browned. Add all other sauce ingredients. Mix well. Reduce heat and simmer, uncovered, 20 to 30 minutes, or until thickened.

Cook manicotti shells according to package directions, omitting salt. (Shells should be soft but not limp.) Drain. Stuff with the meat and spinach filling.

Preheat oven to 350° F. Lightly spray a casserole dish with vegetable oil.

Pour a little sauce in bottom of prepared dish. Arrange shells in rows in dish. (If any filling mixture is left over, spoon it around the shells.) Spread cottage cheese or ricotta cheese over the top. Pour remainder of sauce on top and bake 20 minutes, or until bubbly.

Nutrient Analysis

Calories	406 kcal	Cholesterol	57 mg	Saturated Fat		4 gm
Protein	29 gm	Sodium	492 mg	Polyunsaturated Fat		1 gm
Carbohydrate	41 gm	Total Fat	15 gm	Monounsaturated Fat		8 gm

*M*ock *S*paghetti

Serves 6

1 pound lean ground beef or veal
½ pound fresh mushrooms
½ cup chopped onion
1 8-ounce can no-salt-added tomato sauce
1 16-ounce can Italian plum tomatoes
1 clove garlic, pressed
Freshly ground black pepper to taste
¼ teaspoon oregano
1 tablespoon chopped parsley
Vegetable oil spray
1 pound fresh bean sprouts, rinsed and drained

Wipe mushrooms with a clean, damp cloth. Slice and set aside.

Brown meat in a large skillet over medium-high heat. Pour off fat and add mushrooms and onion. Cook until tender. Add remaining ingredients except bean sprouts. Reduce heat and simmer, covered, until sauce thickens.

Lightly spray a large skillet with vegetable oil. Add bean sprouts, cover and cook over medium-high heat just until tender-crisp. Serve meat sauce over the hot sprouts.

Nutrient Analysis

Calories	282 kcal	Cholesterol	54 mg	Saturated Fat		4 gm
Protein	28 gm	Sodium	175 mg	Polyunsaturated Fat		3 gm
Carbohydrate	17 gm	Total Fat	14 gm	Monounsaturated Fat		4 gm

Shepherd's Pie

Serves 6

1 pound lean ground beef
1 cup homemade Beef Broth (see page 86) or commercial
    low-sodium variety
1 teaspoon freshly ground black pepper
2 bay leaves
2 whole cloves
Dash thyme leaves
1 cup sliced carrots
1 cup sliced onion
1 cup sliced fresh mushrooms
1 cup diced celery
1 cup whole kernel corn
Vegetable oil spray
½ cup homemade Beef Broth (see page 86) or commercial
    low-sodium variety
1¼ tablespoons flour
1 pound cooked and diced potatoes
1 tablespoon acceptable margarine
½ cup skim milk
1 tablespoon chopped chives
4 ounces part-skim mozzarella cheese, shredded

Brown beef in a skillet over medium-high heat. Drain beef of excess fat through a colander lined with paper towels. Wipe skillet with fresh paper towel. Return beef to skillet and add 1 cup of broth, pepper, bay leaves, cloves and thyme. Cover and simmer 30 minutes.

Add carrots, onion, mushrooms, celery and corn. Cover and simmer until vegetables are tender.

Preheat oven to 375° F. Lightly spray an ovenproof dish with vegetable oil.

In a small bowl, gradually add ½ cup broth to flour, stirring constantly to form a smooth paste. Add to beef and vegetables. Simmer 5 minutes, or until slightly thickened.

Mash potatoes with margarine, skim milk and chives.

Place meat mixture on bottom of casserole dish. Top with mashed potatoes and sprinkle mozzarella cheese all over. Bake 10 minutes and serve hot.

Nutrient Analysis

Calories	343 kcal	Cholesterol	64 mg	Saturated Fat	6 gm
Protein	26 gm	Sodium	205 mg	Polyunsaturated Fat	1 gm
Carbohydrate	28 gm	Total Fat	14 gm	Monounsaturated Fat	6 gm

*S*paghetti with *M*eat *S*auce

Serves 8

1½ pounds lean ground beef
2 cups chopped onion
1 cup chopped green bell pepper
2 cups chopped celery
1 28-ounce can Italian plum tomatoes
1 6-ounce can no-salt-added tomato paste
1 teaspoon each black pepper, oregano, basil leaves and
    garlic powder
1 tablespoon Worcestershire sauce
2 bay leaves
16 ounces spaghetti
½ cup grated Parmesan cheese

Sauté ground meat in a stockpot over medium-high heat, stirring frequently, until no longer pink. Add onions and continue to sauté. When onions are slightly brown, add bell pepper and celery. Cook slightly. Add all other ingredients except spaghetti and Parmesan cheese. Reduce heat, cover and simmer 2 hours.

Allow to cool, then cover and refrigerate overnight. Skim off the fat that hardens on the surface.

Cook spaghetti according to package directions, omitting salt.

Meanwhile, heat sauce, stirring occasionally.

Drain spaghetti and serve individual portions with sauce on top. Sprinkle each serving of spaghetti with Parmesan cheese.

Nutrient Analysis

Calories	492 kcal	Cholesterol	66 mg	Saturated Fat	5 gm
Protein	32 gm	Sodium	380 mg	Polyunsaturated Fat	1 gm
Carbohydrate	61 gm	Total Fat	13 gm	Monounsaturated Fat	5 gm

Tamale Pie

Serves 8

Vegetable oil spray

CRUST
1 cup yellow cornmeal
2½ cups homemade Beef Broth (see page 86) or
    commercial low-sodium variety

FILLING
2 tablespoons acceptable vegetable oil
¼ cup chopped onion
1 teaspoon minced garlic
1 pound lean ground beef
1½ cups chopped fresh tomatoes
4 tablespoons no-salt-added tomato paste
1 teaspoon oregano
½ teaspoon cumin
1 tablespoon chili powder
1½ to 2 cups no-salt-added whole-kernel corn
⅓ cup sliced mushrooms
⅓ cup raisins
1 4-ounce can green chili peppers, drained and chopped
2 tablespoons grated low-fat cheddar cheese

Preheat oven to 350° F. Lightly spray a 2½-quart casserole dish with vegetable oil.

CRUST
In a large saucepan, combine cornmeal and ½ cup of beef broth. In a separate pan, bring remainder of broth to boil. Stir hot broth into cornmeal. Cover and cook over medium heat, stirring occasionally, until mixture thickens. Set aside and allow to cool.

FILLING
Heat oil in a skillet over medium-high heat. Add onion and garlic and sauté lightly. Add beef in small portions and cook until brown. Drain off grease.

Add tomatoes, tomato paste, oregano, cumin and chili powder. Simmer 5 minutes. If sauce is too thin, add more tomato paste. Then add corn, mushrooms, raisins and chili peppers. Stir gently and remove from heat.

Line bottom and sides of prepared casserole dish with cornmeal mixture. Spoon in filling and sprinkle with grated cheddar cheese. Bake 30 minutes.

Note: You may wish to use this filling for Cornmeal Crepes (page 248).

Nutrient Analysis

Calories	297 kcal	Cholesterol	41 mg	Saturated Fat	3 gm
Protein	17 gm	Sodium	240 mg	Polyunsaturated Fat	3 gm
Carbohydrate	34 gm	Total Fat	11 gm	Monounsaturated Fat	4 gm

*S*loppy *J*oes

Serves 6

1 pound lean ground beef
1 onion, diced
½ cup ketchup
2 tablespoons chili sauce
1 teaspoon prepared mustard
1 teaspoon cider vinegar
1 teaspoon sugar
6 whole-wheat hamburger buns

Brown meat and onions in a large skillet over medium-high heat. Pour off fat.

Add all other ingredients, except buns, mixing well. Reduce heat and simmer 20 to 30 minutes, uncovered.

Spoon onto hamburger buns and serve immediately.

Nutrient Analysis

Calories	270 kcal	Cholesterol	55 mg	Saturated Fat	3 gm
Protein	21 gm	Sodium	519 mg	Polyunsaturated Fat	1 gm
Carbohydrate	26 gm	Total Fat	10 gm	Monounsaturated Fat	4 gm

Macaroni Beef Skillet

Serves 6

8 ounces uncooked tricolor rotini pasta
½ pound lean ground round
1 cup chopped onion
3 cloves garlic, minced
1½ teaspoons Italian herb seasoning
1½ teaspoons basil
1 8-ounce package fresh mushrooms
1 6-ounce can no-salt-added tomato paste
1 cup water
1 teaspoon Worcestershire sauce
¼ teaspoon salt
2 tablespoons grated Parmesan cheese
2 tablespoons finely chopped parsley

Cook pasta according to package directions, omitting salt, and set aside. Wipe mushrooms with a clean, damp cloth. Slice and set aside.

Place beef, onion, garlic, herbs and mushrooms in a skillet. Cover and cook over medium heat, stirring occasionally, 8 to 10 minutes, or until mushrooms have released all their juices and are fully cooked.

In a small bowl, whisk together tomato paste, water, Worcestershire sauce, salt, cheese and parsley. Add to skillet.

Add pasta to skillet and heat thoroughly before serving.

Nutrient Analysis

Calories	280 kcal	Cholesterol	29 mg	Saturated Fat	2 gm
Protein	17 gm	Sodium	178 mg	Polyunsaturated Fat	1 gm
Carbohydrate	40 gm	Total Fat	6 gm	Monounsaturated Fat	2 gm

*B*eef *T*ostadas

Serves 6

> **6 6-inch corn tortillas**
> **½ cup finely chopped onion**
> **1 pound ground round**
> **½ teaspoon ground cumin**
> **¼ teaspoon salt**
> **½ teaspoon oregano**
> **1½ to 2 teaspoons chili powder**
> **½ teaspoon garlic powder**
> **Dash hot pepper sauce**
> **1½ cups shredded red cabbage**
> **¾ cup Salsa Cruda (see page 432)**
> **¾ cup shredded low-fat cheddar cheese**

*P*reheat oven to 450° F.

Place tortillas on a heavy baking sheet; put another baking sheet on top of tortillas. Bake 8 to 10 minutes, or until tortillas are crisp.

In a nonstick skillet over medium-high heat, combine onion and ground round. Sauté until meat is browned. Drain off fat and add cumin, salt, oregano, chili powder, garlic powder and hot pepper sauce. Stir until well mixed.

For each tostada, spread ⅓ cup meat on crisped tortilla. Layer ¼ cup cabbage, 2 tablespoons Salsa Cruda and 2 tablespoons shredded cheese over the meat.

Nutrient Analysis

Calories	241 kcal	Cholesterol	57 mg	Saturated Fat	4 gm
Protein	23 gm	Sodium	322 mg	Polyunsaturated Fat	1 gm
Carbohydrate	13 gm	Total Fat	11 gm	Monounsaturated Fat	4 gm

Meatballs Hawaiian

Serves 6

1 ¼ teaspoons garlic powder
1 ¼ teaspoons grated fresh ginger
Generous grind of black pepper
1 pound extra lean ground beef
3 tablespoons finely chopped green onion
1 egg
½ cup French-bread crumbs (2 slices)
1 cup uncooked rice
1 8-ounce can no-sugar-added pineapple chunks, canned in
    natural juices
¼ cup firmly packed brown sugar
2 tablespoons cornstarch
¼ cup white wine vinegar
1 teaspoon light soy sauce
2 green bell peppers, cut in thin strips or rings

*I*n a bowl, sprinkle garlic powder, ginger and black pepper over meat. Add onion, egg and bread crumbs. Blend until well mixed. Shape into 1-inch balls.

Cook meatballs in a nonstick skillet over medium heat until well browned on all sides. Set aside and keep warm.

Cook rice according to package directions, omitting salt and butter or margarine.

Drain pineapple chunks, reserving liquid. Mix reserved juice with water to make 1 cup. Pour into skillet. Add brown sugar, cornstarch, vinegar and soy sauce. Heat, stirring constantly, about 3 minutes, or until sauce thickens. Add meatballs, pineapple chunks and bell pepper. Stir to coat evenly with sauce. Cover and simmer 10 minutes.

Serve over rice.

Nutrient Analysis

Calories	376 kcal	Cholesterol	100 mg	Saturated Fat	4 gm
Protein	21 gm	Sodium	138 mg	Polyunsaturated Fat	1 gm
Carbohydrate	49 gm	Total Fat	10 gm	Monounsaturated Fat	4 gm

Beef Pitas

Serves 3

12 ounces or ¾ pound lean ground round
1 tablespoon finely chopped parsley
1 teaspoon minced garlic
½ teaspoon freshly ground black pepper
½ teaspoon oregano
1 medium red bell pepper
½ cup chopped onion
2 teaspoons acceptable vegetable oil
1 medium tomato, seeded and diced
⅓ cup plain nonfat yogurt
1 tablespoon Dijon mustard
¼ teaspoon freshly ground black pepper
3 lettuce leaves
3 1-ounce pita breads

Preheat broiler.

Combine beef, parsley, garlic, ½ teaspoon black pepper and oregano. Shape into 3 patties and set aside.

Place whole bell pepper on broiler pan and broil, turning frequently, 3 to 5 minutes, or until charred all over. Place hot pepper in plastic bag, seal and shake. As pepper begins to cool, skin will loosen. When skin is loose, peel gently under cool running water. Remove stem, core and then dice.

Place patties on broiler pan and broil 3 to 4 minutes on each side, or to desired degree of doneness. Set aside.

In a small skillet, sauté onion in oil until translucent. Add bell pepper and tomato and cook 1 to 2 minutes longer. Set aside.

In a small bowl, combine yogurt, mustard and ¼ teaspoon black pepper to make a mustard sauce.

Place a lettuce leaf in each pita bread. Add meat patty and ⅓ of vegetable mixture. Top each with 2 tablespoons mustard sauce.

Nutrient Analysis

Calories	371 kcal	Cholesterol	81 mg	Saturated Fat	5 gm
Protein	30 gm	Sodium	269 mg	Polyunsaturated Fat	3 gm
Carbohydrate	23 gm	Total Fat	17 gm	Monounsaturated Fat	7 gm

*C*hili con *C*arne

Serves 8

1 cup dried pinto or kidney beans
3 cups water
1 tablespoon acceptable vegetable oil
2 cups chopped onion
1 green bell pepper, chopped
1 pound lean ground beef
2 cups chopped tomatoes
1 6-ounce can no-salt-added tomato paste
¾ cup water
2 to 3 tablespoons chili powder
1 tablespoon cider vinegar
1 to 2 teaspoons minced garlic
1 teaspoon oregano
1 teaspoon cumin
½ teaspoon freshly ground black pepper
1 bay leaf

Place beans and 3 cups of water in saucepan. Bring to boil and cook 2 minutes. Do not drain. Set aside for 1 hour, then return beans to heat, adding water to cover if necessary. Simmer for 1 hour, or until beans are tender. Drain and set aside.

Heat oil in a large, deep skillet, Dutch oven or stockpot over medium-high heat. Add onion and bell pepper. Cook until onion is translucent. Add meat and brown. Pour off all fat. Add beans and remaining ingredients. Bring to a boil, reduce heat and simmer 1½ hours, stirring occasionally. Remove bay leaf before serving.

VEGETARIAN CHILI
For a vegetarian entree or side dish, omit meat.

Chili Con Carne Nutrient Analysis

Calories	229 kcal	Cholesterol	40 mg	Saturated Fat	3 gm
Protein	18 gm	Sodium	71 mg	Polyunsaturated Fat	2 gm
Carbohydrate	20 gm	Total Fat	9 gm	Monounsaturated Fat	3 gm

Vegetarian Chili Nutrient Analysis

Calories	119 kcal	Cholesterol	0 mg	Saturated Fat	0 gm
Protein	6 gm	Sodium	50 mg	Polyunsaturated Fat	1 gm
Carbohydrate	20 gm	Total Fat	3 gm	Monounsaturated Fat	1 gm

S*caloppine al* L*imone*

Serves 6

1½ pounds veal scallops
5 tablespoons flour
¼ teaspoon salt
½ teaspoon coarsely ground black pepper
Olive oil spray
2 tablespoons olive oil
1¾ cups homemade Chicken Broth (see page 87) or
    commercial low-sodium variety
¼ cup fresh lemon juice
¼ cup dry white wine
1 tablespoon finely chopped parsley

GARNISH
6 thin lemon slices

Pound veal scallops until they are ¼ inch thick.

Combine flour, salt and pepper in a plastic bag. Add veal pieces and shake until all are coated evenly with the flour mixture.

Lightly spray a nonstick skillet with olive oil. Add 1 teaspoon oil and place over medium-high heat. Add a few veal pieces and brown lightly on both sides. Repeat process, using remaining oil 1 teaspoon at a time. If veal pieces stick to skillet, spray it lightly with additional cooking spray. Transfer meat to a plate and set aside.

Pour broth, lemon juice and wine into the same skillet. Cook over medium heat, stirring to remove brown bits from bottom of skillet, until sauce reduces by about a third. Return veal to pan and simmer over medium heat 5 to 7 minutes, or until sauce is slightly thickened. Using a slotted spoon, remove veal to warmed platter. Add parsley to sauce in skillet and pour over veal. Garnish with lemon slices. Serve hot.

Note: Do not use vegetable oil spray near an open flame or a heat source. Read directions on can before using, and follow directions carefully.

Nutrient Analysis

Calories	248 kcal	Cholesterol	129 mg	Saturated Fat	2 gm
Protein	32 gm	Sodium	182 mg	Polyunsaturated Fat	1 gm
Carbohydrate	6 gm	Total Fat	10 gm	Monounsaturated Fat	5 gm

*V*eal with *R*ed *P*eppers and *M*ushrooms

Serves 6

⅓ cup flour
¼ teaspoon salt
¼ teaspoon freshly ground black pepper
1¼ pounds veal scallops, pounded until very thin
3 tablespoons olive oil
1 tablespoon olive oil
1 8-ounce package fresh mushrooms, quartered
1½ cups red bell pepper strips
3 cloves garlic, minced
1½ cups homemade Chicken Broth (see page 87) or
     commercial low-sodium variety
2 tablespoons fresh lemon juice
⅓ cup white wine
½ cup sliced green onion
Chopped fresh parsley

*P*lace flour, salt and black pepper in a plastic bag. Add veal pieces and shake to coat each evenly. Set aside.

Heat 3 tablespoons olive oil in a large nonstick skillet over medium-high heat. Add veal and brown lightly on both sides. Transfer to a plate and set aside.

Heat remaining 1 tablespoon oil in same skillet over medium heat. Add mushrooms, bell pepper strips and garlic. Cover and cook 7 to 9 minutes. In a bowl, combine broth, lemon juice and wine. Pour into skillet and add veal. Cook over medium heat about 10 minutes, or until sauce thickens slightly. Stir in green onions and cook 1 minute more. Garnish with chopped parsley before serving.

Nutrient Analysis

Calories	274 kcal	Cholesterol	107 mg	Saturated Fat	2 gm
Protein	28 gm	Sodium	168 mg	Polyunsaturated Fat	1 gm
Carbohydrate	9 gm	Total Fat	14 gm	Monounsaturated Fat	8 gm

*V*eal *S*outhwestern

Serves 6

1 tablespoon acceptable vegetable oil
2 teaspoons minced and seeded fresh jalapeño pepper *
1½ cups orange, red or yellow bell pepper strips
½ cup diagonally sliced green onion
1½ pounds veal scallops
⅓ cup flour
1½ teaspoons chili powder
¼ teaspoon freshly ground black pepper
¼ teaspoon salt
2 tablespoons acceptable vegetable oil
1 28-ounce can no-salt-added whole tomatoes, not drained
2 teaspoons chili powder
½ teaspoon freshly ground black pepper
1½ teaspoons grated lime rind

Heat 1 tablespoon oil in a large nonstick skillet over medium-high heat. Add jalapeño and bell pepper strips and sauté 4 to 5 minutes. Add green onions and sauté 1 minute more. Transfer vegetables to a plate and set aside.

Flatten veal to ⅛-inch thickness. Set aside.

Combine flour, 1½ teaspoons chili powder, ¼ teaspoon black pepper and ¼ teaspoon salt in a plastic bag. Add veal and shake to coat all pieces with flour mixture.

Heat 1 tablespoon oil in skillet over medium-high heat. Add half of veal pieces and lightly brown on both sides. Repeat process with remaining oil and veal. Transfer to plate containing vegetables.

Add tomatoes to skillet, breaking up whole tomatoes with a wooden spoon. Stir in 2 teaspoons chili powder and ½ teaspoon black pepper. Simmer 3 to 4 minutes. Add lime rind and vegetables and veal mixture. Heat 3 minutes, or until heated throughout.

* Wear rubber gloves when handling hot peppers, or wash hands thoroughly after handling. Skin, especially around the eyes, is very sensitive to oil from peppers.

Nutrient Analysis

Calories	298 kcal	Cholesterol	129 mg	Saturated Fat	2 gm
Protein	33 gm	Sodium	204 mg	Polyunsaturated Fat	5 gm
Carbohydrate	13 gm	Total Fat	12 gm	Monounsaturated Fat	3 gm

*V*eal *S*tufino

Serves 6

1½ pounds lean veal stew meat, cut into large cubes
1 tablespoon flour
½ teaspoon salt
¼ teaspoon freshly ground pepper, or to taste
2 tablespoons olive oil
2 medium carrots, finely chopped
2 stalks celery, finely chopped
1 medium onion, finely chopped
1 or 2 cloves garlic, minced
½ cup dry white wine
1 14½-ounce can no-salt-added stewed tomatoes, crushed,
    not drained
4½ cups tricolor pasta shells
¼ cup minced fresh parsley

Preheat oven to 300° F.

Toss veal with flour, salt and pepper. Set aside. Heat oil in a heavy ovenproof skillet over medium-high heat. Add veal and brown quickly on all sides. Add carrots, celery, onion and garlic. Add wine, scraping pan and stirring. Cook 2 to 3 minutes. Add tomatoes and bring to a boil. Cover and place in oven. Cook 1 to 1½ hours, or until veal is tender. Check and baste after 1 hour.

Cook pasta according to package directions, omitting salt. Drain and place in a warm serving bowl. Add veal mixture and top with parsley.

Nutrient Analysis

Calories	628 kcal	Cholesterol	114 mg	Saturated Fat	2 gm
Protein	42 gm	Sodium	280 mg	Polyunsaturated Fat	2 gm
Carbohydrate	89 gm	Total Fat	10 gm	Monounsaturated Fat	5 gm

Spanish Rice with Veal

Serves 6

1 tablespoon olive oil
1 cup finely chopped onion
¾ cup sliced carrots
½ cup diced green bell pepper
3 cloves garlic, minced
1 pound ground veal
1½ teaspoons Italian herb seasoning
1 28-ounce can Italian plum tomatoes, crushed
¾ cup uncooked long-grain rice
Freshly ground black pepper to taste

Heat oil in nonstick skillet over medium-high heat. Add onion, carrots and bell pepper. Sauté until onion is translucent. Stir in garlic and sauté another 2 minutes. Add veal and herbs and reduce heat to medium. Cook until meat is no longer pink. Stir in tomatoes and rice. Cover and reduce heat to simmer. Cook 20 to 25 minutes, or until rice is soft.

MICROWAVE METHOD

Combine olive oil, onion, carrot, bell pepper and garlic in microwave-safe casserole. Cook 5 minutes on high, stirring once. Crumble meat into casserole. Add herbs. Cover with wax paper. Cook on high 5 minutes, stirring twice. Add remaining ingredients, cover and cook on medium 25 to 30 minutes, or until rice is tender.

VEAL STUFFED PEPPERS

Remove cores from tops of 3 orange, red or yellow bell peppers. Cut peppers in half lengthwise and remove seeds and membranes. Blanch, uncovered, in boiling water 5 minutes. Remove from water and fill each pepper half with ⅙ of the hot Spanish rice mixture.

Spanish Rice with Veal Nutrient Analysis

Calories	261 kcal	Cholesterol	45 mg	Saturated Fat	4 gm
Protein	15 gm	Sodium	256 mg	Polyunsaturated Fat	1 gm
Carbohydrate	27 gm	Total Fat	10 gm	Monounsaturated Fat	5 gm

Veal Stuffed Peppers Nutrient Analysis

Calories	267 kcal	Cholesterol	45 mg	Saturated Fat	4 gm
Protein	16 gm	Sodium	257 mg	Polyunsaturated Fat	1 gm
Carbohydrate	28 gm	Total Fat	11 gm	Monounsaturated Fat	5 gm

Veal Osso Buco

Serves 5

4 1-inch veal shanks with bone (about 2¾ pounds)
1 tablespoon olive oil
1 carrot, grated
1 large onion, finely chopped
2 stalks celery, chopped
2 cloves garlic, minced
1 14½-ounce can whole no-salt-added tomatoes, crushed,
    liquid reserved
2 bay leaves
4 sprigs fresh thyme or ½ teaspoon dried thyme, crushed
1 teaspoon dried Italian herb seasoning, crushed
¼ teaspoon salt
Freshly ground black pepper
2 strips fresh lemon peel, 1½ inches long, ½ inch wide
1 cup homemade Beef Broth (see page 86) or commercial
    low-sodium variety
½ cup dry white wine
½ cup water
5 ounces angel hair pasta
3 tablespoons chopped fresh parsley

Preheat broiler.

Tie veal meat to bone with kitchen string. Place on broiler pan and broil about 8 to 10 minutes on each side, or until evenly browned.

Set oven to bake at 350° F.

Place oil in a large skillet over medium-high heat. Add carrot, onion, celery and garlic. Sauté until wilted.

Place vegetables in bottom of a large, heavy casserole dish. Place browned meat on top of vegetables. Add tomatoes evenly over ingredients. Add bay leaves, thyme, Italian herb seasoning, salt, pepper and lemon peel. Add broth, wine and water. Cover and bake 1½ to 2 hours, turning veal shanks 3 or 4 times. Bake until meat is tender and sauce is thickened. It may be necessary to add more water during cooking to maintain sauce around meat.

Remove meat from sauce; reserve it. Cut meat from bone, remove fat and cut veal into bite-size pieces. Do not serve marrow from bones. Skim grease from sauce and discard.

Place degreased sauce and veal in a pan over medium heat until heated through.

Cook pasta according to package directions, omitting salt. Drain. Serve pasta topped with meat mixture. Sprinkle parsley all over.

Nutrient Analysis

Calories	436 kcal	Cholesterol	185 mg	Saturated Fat	2 gm
Protein	50 gm	Sodium	257 mg	Polyunsaturated Fat	1 gm
Carbohydrate	33 gm	Total Fat	11 gm	Monounsaturated Fat	4 gm

Veal Stew with Fennel

Serves 6

3 tablespoons acceptable vegetable oil
1½ pounds lean veal stew meat, cut into 1-inch cubes
½ teaspoon freshly ground black pepper, or to taste
1 large onion, chopped
¼ cup water
3 small green onions, chopped
½ teaspoon crushed fennel seeds
2 10-ounce packages frozen no-salt-added spinach leaves

GARNISH
1 lemon, cut into 6 wedges

Place oil in a stockpot or heavy kettle over medium-high heat. Add veal and brown on all sides. Season meat with pepper. Stir in onion and sauté until limp but not brown.

Add water, green onions and fennel seed to the pot. Reduce heat and cover. Simmer about 1 hour, or until meat is tender. Add more water if necessary during cooking.

Cook spinach according to package directions, omitting salt.

Arrange meat on a heated serving platter and surround with a border of spinach. Garnish with lemon wedges.

Nutrient Analysis

Calories	239 kcal	Cholesterol	114 mg	Saturated Fat	2 gm
Protein	29 gm	Sodium	121 mg	Polyunsaturated Fat	5 gm
Carbohydrate	5 gm	Total Fat	11 gm	Monounsaturated Fat	3 gm

*F*rench-*S*tyle *L*amb *C*hops

Serves 4; 2 chops per serving

> 1 tablespoon finely chopped fresh rosemary, or 1 teaspoon
>   dried, crushed rosemary
> 3 cloves garlic, finely minced
> 3 tablespoons finely chopped fresh parsley
> 1½ tablespoons olive oil
> 1½ teaspoons Dijon mustard
> Freshly ground black pepper to taste
> 8 ¾-inch-thick lamb chops, approximately 1¾ pounds total
>   weight, trimmed of all visible fat

*I*n a small bowl, blend rosemary, garlic, parsley, olive oil, mustard and pepper to make a paste.

Spread evenly on both sides of chops and let sit at room temperature for 45 minutes.

Preheat grill or broiler. Cook chops 6 to 8 minutes, turn and cook an additional 4 to 5 minutes. Serve hot.

Serve with steamed fresh asparagus and a favorite rice dish.

Nutrient Analysis

Calories	209 kcal	Cholesterol	69 mg	Saturated Fat	3 gm
Protein	19 gm	Sodium	92 mg	Polyunsaturated Fat	1 gm
Carbohydrate	1 gm	Total Fat	14 gm	Monounsaturated Fat	8 gm

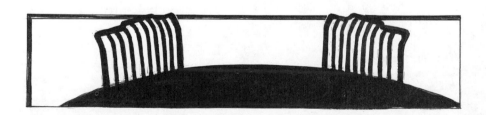

Julep Lamb Chops Flambé

Serves 4; 2 chops per serving

Vegetable oil spray
2 teaspoons dried mint
8 lean loin lamb chops, all visible fat removed
2 teaspoons acceptable vegetable oil
4 slices canned no-sugar-added pineapple, canned in
    natural juices
Freshly ground black pepper to taste
2 tablespoons bourbon, warmed

Preheat broiler or grill. Lightly spray broiler pan or grill top with vegetable oil.*

Press dried mint into surface of chops. Place on prepared broiler pan or grill. Cook about 4 inches from heat for 12 to 16 minutes, depending on thickness of chops.

Meanwhile, heat oil in a skillet over medium-high heat. Add pineapple slices and brown slightly on each side. Place in bottom of a serving dish.

When chops are done, season with pepper. Arrange over pineapple slices.

Sprinkle bourbon over chops, ignite with a match and take to the table aflame.

* Do not use vegetable oil spray near an open flame or a heat source. Read directions on can before using, and follow directions carefully.

Nutrient Analysis

Calories	289 kcal	Cholesterol	104 mg	Saturated Fat	4 gm
Protein	34 gm	Sodium	89 mg	Polyunsaturated Fat	2 gm
Carbohydrate	8 gm	Total Fat	12 gm	Monounsaturated Fat	5 gm

*L*emon *L*amb with *M*int

Serves 4; 2 chops per serving

Vegetable oil spray
2 teaspoons acceptable vegetable oil
2 small cloves garlic, minced
½ cup water
1 tablespoon fresh lemon juice
½ teaspoon freshly ground black pepper, or to taste
2 tablespoons chopped fresh mint leaves
8 loin lamb chops

Preheat broiler. Lightly spray a broiler pan with vegetable oil.

Pour oil into a skillet over medium-high heat. Add garlic and sauté. Stir in water, lemon juice and pepper. Bring to a boil and reduce heat to simmer. Sprinkle mint over mixture and simmer about 10 minutes. Cover and set aside.

Place chops on broiler pan about 6 inches from heat source. Broil 5 minutes on each side, or until done to taste.

Transfer chops to serving dish and pour hot lemon-mint mixture over meat.

Nutrient Analysis

Calories	247 kcal	Cholesterol	104 mg	Saturated Fat	4 gm
Protein	34 gm	Sodium	89 mg	Polyunsaturated Fat	2 gm
Carbohydrate	1 gm	Total Fat	12 gm	Monounsaturated Fat	5 gm

*L*amb *K*abobs

Serves 6

6 12-inch bamboo skewers
¾ cup cider vinegar
½ cup olive oil
¼ cup chopped fresh mint
3 tablespoons finely chopped fresh rosemary
4 cloves garlic, minced
¼ cup honey
¾ cup finely chopped onion
½ teaspoon salt
½ teaspoon freshly ground black pepper, or to taste
2 pounds leg of lamb (after boning and trimming), cut into
    24 1½-inch cubes
1 medium red onion, cut into 12 wedges
1 9-ounce package frozen artichoke hearts, defrosted
24 cherry tomatoes

Soak skewers in water at least 30 minutes before using.

In a bowl, combine cider vinegar, olive oil, mint, rosemary, garlic, honey, chopped onion, salt and pepper and stir to mix well. Add lamb and turn to evenly coat all pieces. Cover and let stand 3 to 4 hours in refrigerator. Turn meat occasionally while marinating.

Drain meat, reserving marinade. Place marinade in a saucepan over medium-high heat and cook to boiling. Cover and reduce heat to simmer.

Preheat grill.

Separate each red onion wedge vertically into two parts, making 24 wedges. Separate artichoke hearts into 24 pieces. For each kabob, thread a skewer as follows: 1 piece onion, 1 meat cube, 1 artichoke, 1 tomato. Repeat three times. Follow same sequence for remaining skewers. Grill over hot coals 12 to 15 minutes, or until meat reaches desired degree of doneness. Baste frequently with hot marinade.

Nutrient Analysis

Calories	442 kcal	Cholesterol	89 mg	Saturated Fat	5 gm
Protein	31 gm	Sodium	307 mg	Polyunsaturated Fat	2 gm
Carbohydrate	24 gm	Total Fat	27 gm	Monounsaturated Fat	17 gm

*A*rmenian *L*amb *C*asserole

Serves 4

2 tablespoons acceptable vegetable oil
1 pound lean lamb, all visible fat removed, cut into cubes
1 onion, sliced
1 clove garlic, minced
1 cup canned no-salt-added tomatoes
1 green bell pepper, quartered
2 carrots, sliced
3 slices lemon
1 medium eggplant, cut into cubes
2 small zucchini, cut into cubes
½ teaspoon paprika
⅛ teaspoon cumin
Freshly ground black pepper to taste
½ cup okra, sliced (optional)

*H*eat oil in a large, deep skillet, stockpot or 3-quart Dutch oven over medium-high heat. Add lamb cubes and brown thoroughly on all sides. Add onions and garlic and brown slightly. Add tomatoes and reduce heat. Cook over low heat for 1 hour, adding a small amount of water if necessary.

Preheat oven to 350° F.

Add all remaining ingredients and bring to a boil. Transfer mixture to a 3-quart ceramic or ovenproof glass casserole. (Do not use plain cast iron. It discolors the vegetables.) Cover tightly and place in oven. Bake 1 hour, or until vegetables are tender.

Nutrient Analysis

Calories	286 kcal	Cholesterol	67 mg	Saturated Fat		3 gm
Protein	24 gm	Sodium	92 mg	Polyunsaturated Fat		5 gm
Carbohydrate	19 gm	Total Fat	14 gm	Monounsaturated Fat		4 gm

Easy Lamb Curry

Serves 4

1 tablespoon flour
1 teaspoon curry powder
1 tablespoon acceptable vegetable oil
3 tablespoons chopped onion
1 cup diced celery
2 cups homemade Beef Broth (see page 86) or commercial
    low-sodium variety
¼ cup ketchup
2 cups diced cooked lamb
½ cup chopped apple (unpeeled if color is good and skin is
    crisp)
⅔ cup uncooked rice

In a small bowl, combine flour and curry powder. Set aside.

Place oil in a skillet over medium-high heat. Add onions and celery and sauté lightly.

Stir in flour mixture and blend until smooth. Add broth and ketchup. Reduce heat, cover and simmer about 1 hour, stirring occasionally.

Add lamb and apple. Simmer another 20 minutes.

Cook rice according to package directions, omitting salt and butter or margarine.

Place ½ cup rice in each of four shallow bowls. Spoon lamb mixture evenly over rice. Serve hot.

Nutrient Analysis

Calories	343 kcal	Cholesterol	68 mg	Saturated Fat	3 gm
Protein	23 gm	Sodium	290 mg	Polyunsaturated Fat	3 gm
Carbohydrate	33 gm	Total Fat	13 gm	Monounsaturated Fat	5 gm

Marinated Pork Loin

Serves 5

> 1 tablespoon sesame oil
> 1 small onion, grated
> 2 teaspoons grated fresh ginger, or ¾ teaspoon ground
>   ginger
> 1 teaspoon grated fresh lemon peel
> 2 cloves garlic, crushed
> ¼ cup light soy sauce
> 1 pound whole pork tenderloin
> ¼ cup dry white wine
> ¼ cup honey
> 1 tablespoon firmly packed dark brown sugar

In a small bowl, combine oil, onion, ginger, lemon peel, garlic and soy sauce. Stir to mix well. Set aside. Place pork loin in a glass bowl. Pour soy mixture over pork and turn to coat evenly. Cover and marinate overnight in refrigerator.

Remove pork from marinade; drain well.

Preheat oven to 375° F.

In a small bowl, combine wine, honey and brown sugar. Stir to mix well. Pour over pork, coating all sides of roast. Place in a shallow nonstick pan and cook 25 to 30 minutes, or until meat's internal temperature reaches 170° F.

Remove from oven and allow to rest 5 minutes. Slice and serve.

Serve with steamed rice and snow peas.

MICROWAVE METHOD FOR COOKING PORK TENDERLOIN

Season pork with salt-free garlic seasoning. Shield each end of the tenderloin with 1 inch of lightweight foil to prevent burning. Place on a microwave-safe baking dish. Microwave for 3 minutes at high. Reduce power to 50 percent and microwave 5 more minutes. Remove foil shields, turn tenderloin over and cook 7 to 8 minutes longer or until meat thermometer reads 165° F. Remove and let sit covered until thermometer reads 170° F, then slice and serve.

Nutrient Analysis

Calories	254 kcal	Cholesterol	57 mg	Saturated Fat	3 gm
Protein	18 gm	Sodium	526 mg	Polyunsaturated Fat	2 gm
Carbohydrate	18 gm	Total Fat	12 gm	Monounsaturated Fat	5 gm

*O*range *P*ork *M*edallions

Serves 4

1 pound pork tenderloin, sliced
1 tablespoon sesame oil
4 green onions, including tops, thinly sliced
Juice of 2 oranges
2½ tablespoons fresh lemon juice
2 tablespoons orange marmalade
½ teaspoon ground cinnamon
½ teaspoon dried rosemary, crushed
¼ teaspoon freshly ground black pepper
¾ teaspoon prepared horseradish
2 tablespoons minced fresh parsley
1 tablespoon cornstarch

GARNISH
1 11-ounce can mandarin orange slices, canned in light
    syrup, drained
4 large sprigs fresh parsley

*F*latten pork slices with pounder or rolling pin to ½-inch thickness.
Set aside. Heat oil in a nonstick skillet over medium-high heat. Add
pork and brown quickly, 2 minutes per side. Add onions and sauté
until tender.

In a bowl, blend remaining ingredients, except orange slices and
parsley sprigs, and add to skillet. Cook, stirring constantly, until sauce
thickens. Remove to warmed platter and garnish with orange slices
and parsley.

Serve with Couscous with Vegetables (see page 406).

Nutrient Analysis

Calories	284 kcal	Cholesterol	71 mg	Saturated Fat	4 gm
Protein	22 gm	Sodium	61 mg	Polyunsaturated Fat	3 gm
Carbohydrate	16 gm	Total Fat	15 gm	Monounsaturated Fat	6 gm

Sweet and Sour Pork

Serves 4

½ cup unsweetened pineapple juice
2 teaspoons rice vinegar or cider vinegar
1 teaspoon sherry
½ teaspoon light soy sauce
Dash hot pepper oil
Dash ground ginger
Dash ground allspice
1 teaspoon cornstarch dissolved in 2 tablespoons of water
Vegetable oil spray
12 ounces pork loin, cut into ¼-inch-thick strips (julienne)
2 tablespoons minced onions and leeks, or scallions
¼ cup sliced green bell pepper
¼ cup sliced onion
2 teaspoons chopped fresh parsley
¼ teaspoon freshly ground black pepper

In a saucepan over medium-high heat, combine first seven ingredients. When mixture is hot, stir in dissolved cornstarch. Cook over medium heat, stirring constantly, until sauce comes just to a boil and begins to thicken. Cover and remove from heat.

Spray a nonstick skillet with vegetable oil. Add pork and sauté until no longer pink. Remove from skillet and set aside.

Sprinkle onion-leek combination, sliced bell peppers and onions over bottom of skillet. Place cooked pork over vegetables and sprinkle with parsley and black pepper. Cook 4 to 5 minutes, add sauce and serve.

Nutrient Analysis

Calories	218 kcal	Cholesterol	71 mg	Saturated Fat	4 gm
Protein	22 gm	Sodium	82 mg	Polyunsaturated Fat	1 gm
Carbohydrate	7 gm	Total Fat	11 gm	Monounsaturated Fat	5 gm

Pork with Steamed Spiced Sauerkraut

Serves 6

1 tablespoon acceptable margarine
½ cup chopped onion
1 tablespoon sugar
2 cups cold water
2 pounds sauerkraut, drained, rinsed and squeezed dry
1 large raw potato, grated
5 whole juniper berries
6 peppercorns
2 bay leaves
¼ teaspoon caraway seeds
1 whole allspice
Vegetable oil spray
6 pieces pork loin (18 ounces)

Preheat oven to 325° F.

Place margarine in a large skillet over medium-high heat. Add onions and brown lightly. Add sugar, water and sauerkraut. Toss with a fork until well separated. Add grated potato. Stir to mix well. When heated, remove from stove and set aside.

Place juniper berries, peppercorns, bay leaves, caraway seeds and allspice in a cheesecloth or garni bag.

Put sauerkraut mixture in an 11-x-17-inch casserole. Burrow hole in sauerkraut and bury garni bag.

Away from flames, lightly spray skillet with vegetable oil again. Add meat and brown on all sides, then add to sauerkraut.

Cover and bake casserole 1 to 1½ hours.

Remove cover and bake an additional 30 minutes to allow meat to brown.

Nutrient Analysis

Calories	219 kcal	Cholesterol	54 mg	Saturated Fat	3 gm
Protein	18 gm	Sodium*	1065 mg	Polyunsaturated Fat	2 gm
Carbohydrate	14 gm	Total Fat	10 gm	Monounsaturated Fat	5 gm

* *One serving of this dish provides one-third of the recommended daily amount of sodium. Enjoy it and try to select low-sodium foods for the rest of the day's meals.*

Crustless Spinach Tart

Serves 6

Vegetable oil spray
1½ tablespoons grated Parmesan cheese
2 tablespoons olive oil
1 cup finely chopped onion
2 cloves garlic, minced
1 10-ounce package frozen no-salt-added chopped
    spinach, defrosted and squeezed dry
3 slices (½ ounce each) low-fat, cracked-black-pepper
    ham, cut into strips
1¼ cups skim milk
Egg substitute equivalent to 3 eggs
1 tablespoon finely chopped fresh basil, or 2 teaspoons
    dried basil
Dash nutmeg
1½ tablespoons flour
½ teaspoon salt
½ teaspoon freshly ground black pepper
4½ tablespoons grated Parmesan cheese

Preheat oven to 350° F. Lightly spray a 9-inch glass pie plate with vegetable oil. Dust with 1½ tablespoons Parmesan cheese.

Heat olive oil in a nonstick skillet over medium-high heat. Add onion and sauté until translucent. Add garlic and sauté 1 minute more. Add spinach and ham, stirring until mixture is evenly blended. Distribute mixture evenly in bottom of prepared pie plate. Set aside.

In a bowl, combine remaining ingredients. Pour on top of spinach mixture and bake 50 to 55 minutes.

Nutrient Analysis

Calories	129 kcal	Cholesterol	9 mg	Saturated Fat	2 gm
Protein	10 gm	Sodium	473 mg	Polyunsaturated Fat	1 gm
Carbohydrate	8 gm	Total Fat	7 gm	Monounsaturated Fat	4 gm

*S*outhwestern *H*ash

Serves 4; 1 cup per serving

1½ tablespoons acceptable margarine
2 cups cubed day-old cornbread
1 tablespoon acceptable margarine
1 tablespoon water
1 medium onion, chopped
½ cup diced green or red bell pepper
1 clove garlic, minced
½ pound fresh cooked low-fat ham, cut into cubes
1 medium tomato, chopped
1 cup frozen no-salt-added corn, thawed and drained
⅛ teaspoon cayenne pepper (optional)
⅛ teaspoon ground cumin seed
1 teaspoon minced fresh sage, or ¼ teaspoon dried sage
¼ teaspoon freshly ground black pepper, or to taste
1 tablespoon minced fresh parsley

*P*reheat oven to 375° F.

In a large ovenproof skillet over medium-high heat, melt 1½ tablespoons margarine. Add cornbread and sauté until brown. Remove from skillet and drain on paper towel.

Add remaining tablespoon magarine and 1 tablespoon water to same skillet. Add onion, bell pepper and garlic. Sauté until onion is clear. Add ham, tomato and corn. Stir to mix well. Cook, covered, 5 to 6 minutes.

Remove cover and add cayenne, cumin, sage and black pepper. Mix well. Add browned cornbread and stir in gently.

Place skillet in oven and bake 15 minutes. Remove and top with parsley.

Serve with fresh fruit salad and steamed fresh green beans or fresh broccoli.

Nutrient Analysis

Calories	399 kcal	Cholesterol	86 mg	Saturated Fat	7 gm
Protein	22 gm	Sodium	356 mg	Polyunsaturated Fat	3 gm
Carbohydrate	34 gm	Total Fat	20 gm	Monounsaturated Fat	8 gm

*H*am *R*oll-*U*ps

Serves 8; 1 roll-up per serving

> 3 tablespoons acceptable margarine
> 3 tablespoons plain nonfat yogurt
> 2 teaspoons finely chopped fresh basil
> 2 teaspoons finely chopped fresh dill
> 1 teaspoon Dijon mustard
> 8 slices thinly sliced white bread (must be fresh)
> 4 ounces Muenster cheese, sliced into 8 thin pieces
> 8 thin slices low-fat ham (½ ounce per slice)
> 16 cooked fresh asparagus spears, or frozen no-salt-added
>   asparagus spears, defrosted

*F*or dressing, combine first five ingredients in a small bowl and set aside.

Preheat broiler.

Flatten bread slices slightly with palm of hand. Spread 1 teaspoon dressing on each side of bread slices. Place 1 slice *each* of cheese and ham on top of each slice of bread. Place 2 asparagus spears on each. Arrange spears so one tip points left and the other right. Roll up each piece of bread and secure with a toothpick. Place on broiler pan and broil 2½ to 3 minutes, or until cheese is bubbly. Serve hot.

Nutrient Analysis

Calories	177 kcal	Cholesterol	22 mg	Saturated Fat	4 gm
Protein	9 gm	Sodium	424 mg	Polyunsaturated Fat	1 gm
Carbohydrate	13 gm	Total Fat	10 gm	Monounsaturated Fat	4 gm

*B*aked *H*am *S*lice *S*auterne

Serves 8

> 1 2-pound low-fat, center-cut ham slice
> ½ cup firmly packed brown sugar
> 3 tablespoons cornstarch
> 1½ cups water
> 1 tablespoon acceptable margarine
> ½ cup raisins
> ½ cup American sauterne or other dry white wine

Preheat oven to 350° F. Place ham in a shallow baking pan. Set aside.

Combine sugar and cornstarch in a saucepan. Stir in water and margarine. Place over medium-high heat and cook, stirring constantly, 5 minutes.

Remove pan from heat and stir in raisins and wine. Pour the mixture over ham. Bake uncovered 45 minutes, or until tender.

Nutrient Analysis

Calories	291 kcal	Cholesterol	60 mg	Saturated Fat	2 gm
Protein	24 gm	Sodium*	1391 mg	Polyunsaturated Fat	1 gm
Carbohydrate	31 gm	Total Fat	8 gm	Monounsaturated Fat	4 gm

*C*anadian *B*acon in *W*ine *S*auce

Serves 6

> 1½ tablespoons acceptable vegetable oil
> 1½ tablespoons flour
> 1¼ cups homemade Beef Broth (see page 86) or
>   commercial low-sodium variety
> Pinch of thyme
> Pinch of dried basil
> 1 pound Canadian bacon, sliced
> 2 tablespoons sherry

Heat oil in a saucepan over medium heat. Blend in flour and brown it slowly. Add broth slowly, stirring to keep sauce smooth. Add thyme and basil. Reduce heat and simmer 15 minutes.

Place bacon in a skillet over medium-high heat. Cook 5 minutes, turning often. Remove to a heated serving platter. Discard drippings.

Strain sauce. Discard solid matter and return sauce to saucepan. Add sherry and heat thoroughly. Pour sauce over bacon, and serve.

Nutrient Analysis

Calories	159 kcal	Cholesterol	36 mg	Saturated Fat	2 gm
Protein	16 gm	Sodium*	970 mg	Polyunsaturated Fat	3 gm
Carbohydrate	3 gm	Total Fat	9 gm	Monounsaturated Fat	3 gm

* One serving of this dish provides one-third of the recommended daily amount of sodium. Enjoy it and try to select low-sodium foods for the rest of the day's meals.

Bayou Red Beans and Rice

Serves 8; 1½ cups per serving

1 pound dried red kidney beans (2½ cups)
Water
1 ham bone
1 cup chopped fresh low-fat ham
1 large onion, chopped
2 stalks celery with leaves, chopped
2 teaspoons hot pepper sauce
1⅓ cups uncooked white rice

Rinse and pick over beans. Place beans and 4 cups water in a glass bowl and soak overnight.

Drain and rinse beans, then place in a large, heavy pan, stockpot or Dutch oven. Add 4 cups fresh water and remaining ingredients, except rice. Bring to a boil over medium-high heat. Reduce heat and simmer 3 hours, or until beans are tender. Add water as necessary during cooking. Water should barely cover beans at end of cooking time.

Prepare rice according to package instructions, omitting salt and butter or margarine.

Remove ham bone and 1 cup of beans from mixture. Place the reserved cup of beans in a blender or the work bowl of a food processor fitted with a metal blade. Process until beans are mashed to a paste. Return mashed beans to mixture in pan. Cut meat from bone and return to beans. Stir mixture until thickened.

Divide rice equally into eight individual bowls and top with equal amounts of the bean mixture.

Nutrient Analysis

Calories	341 kcal	Cholesterol	14 mg	Saturated Fat	1 gm
Protein	20 gm	Sodium	299 mg	Polyunsaturated Fat	1 gm
Carbohydrate	59 gm	Total Fat	3 gm	Monounsaturated Fat	1 gm

Vegetarian **E**ntrees

ITALIAN-STYLE ZUCCHINI

CALICO STUFFED SQUASH

STUFFED ACORN SQUASH

HAY AND STRAW NOODLE TOSS

JUDY'S HOT OR COLD SESAME PEANUT NOODLES

CHEESY STUFFED POTATOES

STEAMED VEGGIES WITH HERBED CHEESE

VEGETABLE RICE CREOLE

OLD-FASHIONED BAKED BEANS

SWEET AND SOUR BEANS

QUICK-AND-EASY BAKED BEANS

CUBAN BLACK BEANS

STUFFED PEPPERS

SPINACH CREPES

SPINACH ARTICHOKE GRATIN

SPINACH RICOTTA SWIRLS

SPINACH SOUFFLÉ

SPINACH AND BROWN RICE CASSEROLE

VEGETABLE PARMESAN QUICHE

DAVID'S PIZZA

FLOUR TORTILLA PIZZA

SPAGHETTI WITH ZESTY MARINARA SAUCE

PIZZA SANDWICHES

SPAGHETTI WITH EGGPLANT SAUCE

SPAGHETTI WITH PERFECT PESTO

MARGARITA'S PASTA PRIMAVERA

HEARTY BAKED MACARONI

SPAGHETTI CHEESE AMANDINE

SPAGHETTI WITH LENTIL SAUCE

ITALIAN EGGPLANT

MELENZANA ALLA GRIGLIA

MEATLESS MOUSSAKA

EGGPLANT ZUCCHINI CASSEROLE

Some of the biggest winners in the war against saturated fat and cholesterol are those who've learned to get more of their protein from plants—and less from animals.

The truth is, most Americans eat about twice the amount of protein they actually need. And most of it comes from animal sources. You can get plenty of protein from vegetable sources if you know how. Combining foods such as grains, legumes, nuts and seeds can provide complete protein.

Here's how it works: Protein is made up of twenty-two amino acids. Nine of them cannot be produced by the body and must be obtained from food. These are called essential amino acids. Animal products contain all the essential amino acids. Each plant food group is missing an essential amino acid. To get all of your amino acids from plant foods, then, it's necessary to eat plant foods that have complementary proteins. That is, between them they provide all eight of the essential amino acids. Examples of complementary combinations are: rice and kidney beans, a tossed salad with chickpeas and walnuts, or baked beans and whole-wheat bread.

You might also combine a plant food with eggs or low-fat dairy products, both of which have complete proteins. Unfortunately, egg yolks are very high in cholesterol, so it's best to limit whole eggs to no more than three or four a week. But you may cook with and eat all the egg whites you want—and that's where the protein is anyway! Other examples are: cereal and skim milk; bean casserole with a low-fat mozzarella topping.

The chart on the next page will show you where to get the protein you need. The tantalizing recipes that follow—pasta specialties, soufflés, quiches, pizzas and casseroles—are all made without meat. Enjoy!

HOW TO COMBINE VEGETABLES TO GET COMPLETE PROTEIN
Within each group listed below, combine any food from
List A with any from List B.

	List A	List B
Legumes	**Beans:** azuki, black, cranberry, fava, kidney, lima, pinto, marrow, mung, navy, pea, soy (tofu)	Low-fat dairy products* Grains Nuts and seeds
	Peas: Black-eyed, chick (garbanzo), cow, field, split, lentils	
	Sprouts: Available from most beans and peas	
Grains	**Whole Grains:** alfalfa, barley, corn (cornbread, grits), oats, rice, rye, wheat (bulgur, wheat germ), sprouts	Low-fat dairy products Legumes
Nuts and seeds	**Nuts:** almonds, beechnuts, brazil nuts, cashews, filberts, pecans, pine nuts (pignolia), walnuts	Low-fat dairy products Legumes
	Seeds: pumpkin, sunflower	

* Low-fat dairy products (milk, yogurt, cheese, cottage cheese) and eggs, in addition to being used as a supplement to the above, may be used alone as complete protein.

With the exception of black-eyed peas, lentils, pinto beans and split peas, soak most dried legumes in water overnight in the refrigerator before cooking. Then drain them and add enough fresh water to cover. Simmer them about 2½ hours. For flavor add herbs and onions.

If you're in a hurry and don't have time to soak the legumes overnight, cook them in boiling water for 2 minutes and then soak them for just 1 hour. Drain and then cook them as you normally would. Another time-saving technique that works well is to cook legumes in the microwave oven. Place them in a microwave-safe casserole dish, add enough water to cover legumes, cover dish and cook on high setting 30 minutes. Then microwave on medium setting for 1 hour, stirring every 30 minutes and adding more water if necessary.

Italian-Style Zucchini

Serves 6

Vegetable oil spray
6 medium zucchini, thinly sliced
2 tablespoons olive oil
¾ cup sliced onion
1 teaspoon salt-free all-purpose seasoning
2 large ripe tomatoes or 4 Italian plum tomatoes, thinly
    sliced
1¼ teaspoons dried basil
¾ teaspoon oregano
¼ pound part-skim mozzarella, shredded
⅓ cup freshly grated Parmesan cheese
2 tablespoons minced fresh parsley

Preheat oven to 375° F. Lightly spray a casserole with vegetable oil.

Place zucchini in a saucepan with enough water to cover, and cook over medium-high heat until tender. Drain. Set aside.

Place olive oil in a small skillet over medium-high heat. Add onions and sauté until tender. Add seasoning, toss lightly and remove from heat.

In a bowl, combine zucchini, onions, tomatoes, basil and oregano. Toss lightly to mix well. Place half of zucchini mixture in prepared casserole. Sprinkle mozzarella over it. Add remaining vegetable mixture, and sprinkle Parmesan on top.

Bake, uncovered, 25 to 30 minutes. Sprinkle with parsley and serve hot.

Nutrient Analysis

Calories	206 kcal	Cholesterol	15 mg	Saturated Fat	4 gm
Protein	12 gm	Sodium	226 mg	Polyunsaturated Fat	1 gm
Carbohydrate	19 gm	Total Fat	11 gm	Monounsaturated Fat	5 gm

*C*alico *S*tuffed *S*quash

Serves 8; ½ squash per serving

Vegetable oil spray

4 medium zucchini or yellow summer squash, cut in half
   lengthwise

2 tablespoons water

¼ cup chopped green bell pepper

¼ cup chopped red bell pepper

2 green onions, including tops, chopped

1 cup frozen no-salt-added corn, thawed and drained

1 teaspoon lemon-pepper seasoning

1 teaspoon salt-free all-purpose seasoning

1 tablespoon minced fresh oregano, or 1 teaspoon
   crumbled dried oregano

¾ cup grated low-fat Monterey Jack cheese

Preheat broiler. Lightly spray a cookie sheet with vegetable oil.

Place water and ice in a large bowl. Set aside.

Steam squash in a vegetable steamer over medium-high heat 5 to 7 minutes, or until tender-crisp. Transfer squash to ice water immediately to cool.

Remove some of the pulp from center of squash, leaving a nice shell. Set shell aside and save pulp for later use in soup or a casserole.

Place a nonstick skillet over medium-high heat. Add water and remaining vegetables and cook 3 to 4 minutes, stirring frequently . Add seasonings. Remove from heat and add cheese. Toss to mix well.

Spoon mixture into squash shells. Place filled shells on prepared cookie sheet and broil until hot and bubbly.

MICROWAVE METHOD

Place water and ice in a large bowl. Set aside.

Place squash halves in a microwave dish, cut side down. Add 2 tablespoons water and cook, covered, on high 3 to 4 minutes, or until squash is tender-crisp. Cool in ice water.

Remove some of the pulp from center of squash, leaving a nice shell. Set shell aside and save pulp for later use in soup or a casserole.

Preheat broiler. Lightly spray a cookie sheet with vegetable oil.

Place water and remaining vegetables in the microwave dish the squash was cooked in. Cover and cook on high 2 minutes. Stir and cook another 2 minutes. Add seasonings. Cool slightly and add cheese. Toss to mix well.

Spoon mixture into squash shells. Place filled shells on a prepared cookie sheet and broil until hot and bubbly.

Nutrient Analysis

Calories	90 kcal	Cholesterol	7 mg	Saturated Fat	2 gm
Protein	6 gm	Sodium	124 mg	Polyunsaturated Fat	0 gm
Carbohydrate	12 gm	Total Fat	3 gm	Monounsaturated Fat	1 gm

*S*tuffed *A*corn *S*quash

Serves 6

3 small acorn squash (approximately 4 inches in diameter)
1 cup cooked rice
1 cup herb-seasoned stuffing mix (crumb style)
½ cup finely chopped onion
½ cup homemade Chicken Broth (see page 87) or
    commercial low-sodium variety
¼ cup raisins
⅓ cup unsalted dry-roasted walnuts
¼ teaspoon freshly ground black pepper

Preheat oven to 400° F.

Cut each squash in half and spoon out seeds. Set aside. In a bowl, combine all ingredients except squash. Fill squash halves loosely with stuffing mixture. Place squash halves in a 9-x-13-inch pan and cover with foil. Bake 1 to 1¼ hours, or until squash is tender when pierced with the tip of a knife. Serve hot.

Nutrient Analysis

Calories	241 kcal	Cholesterol	1 mg	Saturated Fat	1 gm
Protein	6 gm	Sodium	246 mg	Polyunsaturated Fat	1 gm
Carbohydrate	44 gm	Total Fat	6 gm	Monounsaturated Fat	3 gm

*H*ay and *S*traw *N*oodle *T*oss

Serves 4

> 2 cups yellow summer squash, cut in narrow lengthwise
>   strips
> 2 cups cooked spinach noodles
> 1 large tomato, diced
> 1 tablespoon acceptable vegetable oil
> Freshly ground black pepper to taste
> 1 teaspoon basil
> ½ cup low-fat cottage cheese

Steam squash in a vegetable steamer over medium-high heat until tender.

Remove squash to a large bowl. Add remaining ingredients and toss gently. Serve hot or cold.

Nutrient Analysis

Calories	180 kcal	Cholesterol	2 mg	Saturated Fat	1 gm
Protein	8 gm	Sodium	120 mg	Polyunsaturated Fat	2 gm
Carbohydrate	27 gm	Total Fat	5 gm	Monounsaturated Fat	1 gm

*J*udy's *H*ot or *C*old *S*esame *P*eanut *N*oodles

Serves 4

> ⅓ cup peanut butter
> 1 tablespoon sesame oil
> 2 teaspoons cider vinegar
> 1 tablespoon chopped scallions
> ¼ teaspoon cayenne pepper
> 2 cups cooked spaghetti

In a bowl, combine first five ingredients. Stir into hot spaghetti. Serve immediately for a hot entree, or cover and refrigerate for a cold entree.

Nutrient Analysis

Calories	260 kcal	Cholesterol	0 mg	Saturated Fat	3 gm
Protein	9 gm	Sodium	103 mg	Polyunsaturated Fat	5 gm
Carbohydrate	26 gm	Total Fat	14 gm	Monounsaturated Fat	6 gm

Cheesy Stuffed Potatoes

Serves 3 as an entree; 1 potato per serving
Serves 6 as a side dish; ½ potato per serving

> 3 medium baking potatoes (approximately
>   4¾ x 2½ inches)
> 1 cup low-fat cottage cheese
> ½ cup grated Parmesan cheese
> ½ cup thinly sliced green onions
> ¼ teaspoon white pepper
> ½ teaspoon garlic powder
> Dash paprika

Preheat oven to 400° F.

Scrub potatoes, pierce with a fork and bake 1 hour, then remove and reduce oven temperature to 375° F.

With a sharp knife, cut a lengthwise "lid" about a half-inch down from top of potato to prepare as an entree. Scoop pulp out of potato and place it in a bowl. Set shell of potato aside, discarding the lid.

Mash potato pulp with a potato masher or a fork. Add cheeses, onion, pepper and garlic powder. Stir to mix well. Fill potato shells with mixture, dust with paprika and bake 25 minutes at 375° F.

To prepare Cheesy Stuffed Potatoes as a side dish, cut potatoes in half and fill according to instructions.

Nutrient Analysis *

Calories	292 kcal	Cholesterol	21 mg	Saturated Fat	4 gm
Protein	21 gm	Sodium	658 mg	Polyunsaturated Fat	0 gm
Carbohydrate	36 gm	Total Fat	7 gm	Monounsaturated Fat	2 gm

* as an entree

Nutrient Analysis *

Calories	146 kcal	Cholesterol	10 mg	Saturated Fat	2 gm
Protein	11 gm	Sodium	329 mg	Polyunsaturated Fat	0 gm
Carbohydrate	18 gm	Total Fat	4 gm	Monounsaturated Fat	1 gm

* as a side dish

*S*teamed *V*eggies with *H*erbed *C*heese

Serves 4

1 cup half-round sliced carrots
1 cup broccoli florets
1 cup cauliflower florets
1 cup half-round sliced zucchini
1 cup half-round sliced yellow squash
¼ teaspoon salt
2 ounces grated part-skim mozzarella cheese
2 ounces grated low-fat sharp cheddar cheese
2 tablespoons grated Parmesan cheese
2 tablespoons finely chopped fresh basil
1½ teaspoons finely chopped fresh rosemary

*P*reheat broiler.

In a large pot over medium-high heat, steam carrots, covered, 5 minutes. Add remaining vegetables. Sprinkle salt over all, cover and steam 10 minutes more. Drain vegetables and blot dry on paper towels. Arrange on an ovenproof plate. Set aside.

In a small bowl, combine cheeses and herbs. Add to vegetable mixture and toss to mix well. Broil until cheese is bubbly. Serve immediately.

MICROWAVE METHOD

Steam vegetables in microwave, using microwave-safe steamer, cooking on medium-high for the same times as indicated above. Drain and dry vegetables as directed. Place on microwave-safe plate, toss with cheese mixture and microwave 3 minutes on medium.

Nutrient Analysis

Calories	116 kcal	Cholesterol	13 mg	Saturated Fat	3 gm
Protein	11 gm	Sodium	388 mg	Polyunsaturated Fat	0 gm
Carbohydrate	9 gm	Total Fat	5 gm	Monounsaturated Fat	1 gm

Vegetable Rice Creole

Serves 8 as an entree
Serves 16 as a side dish

1 cup uncooked rice
½ cup diced celery
⅓ cup sliced onion
Water
1 tablespoon acceptable vegetable oil
2½ cups canned no-salt-added tomatoes
1 teaspoon chopped sweet basil
½ teaspoon rosemary
1 teaspoon celery flakes
Freshly ground black pepper to taste
2 cups canned no-salt-added peas
½ cup canned no-salt-added kidney beans

Cook rice according to package directions, omitting salt and butter or margarine.

Cook celery and onions in a small amount of boiling water until tender. Drain water and add oil. Return to low heat and sauté 1 minute. Add tomatoes, basil, rosemary, celery flakes and pepper. Cook 20 minutes, stirring occasionally. Add peas and kidney beans. Cover and cook 5 minutes, or until thoroughly heated.

Serve over rice.

Nutrient Analysis*

Calories	159 kcal	Cholesterol	0 mg	Saturated Fat		0 gm
Protein	5 gm	Sodium	52 mg	Polyunsaturated Fat		1 gm
Carbohydrate	30 gm	Total Fat	2 gm	Monounsaturated Fat		0 gm

* as an entree

Nutrient Analysis*

Calories	80 kcal	Cholesterol	0 mg	Saturated Fat		0 gm
Protein	3 gm	Sodium	26 mg	Polyunsaturated Fat		1 gm
Carbohydrate	15 gm	Total Fat	1 gm	Monounsaturated Fat		0 gm

* as a side dish

Old-Fashioned Baked Beans

Serves 8

        3 cups dry navy beans
        Water
        ¾ cup chili sauce
        1½ teaspoons cider vinegar
        2 onions, thinly sliced
        ¾ teaspoon dry mustard
        ½ cup dark molasses

*I*n a stockpot over medium-high heat, combine dry beans with enough water to cover. Bring to a boil and boil 2 minutes. Remove pot from heat and let stand for 1 hour. Drain beans.

    Preheat oven to 300° F. Combine beans, 3 cups fresh water and all remaining ingredients in an ovenproof crock or casserole. Cover and bake 5 hours. Add more water if beans begin to dry out.

Nutrient Analysis

Calories	254 kcal	Cholesterol	0 mg	Saturated Fat	0 gm
Protein	13 gm	Sodium	283 mg	Polyunsaturated Fat	0 gm
Carbohydrate	51 gm	Total Fat	1 gm	Monounsaturated Fat	0 gm

Sweet and Sour Beans

Serves 6

        1 cup uncooked rice
        1 20½-ounce can no-sugar-added pineapple chunks,
            canned in natural juices
        ¼ cup firmly packed brown sugar
        2 tablespoons cornstarch
        ¼ cup cider vinegar
        2 teaspoons sherry
        1 teaspoon light soy sauce
        ⅛ teaspoon hot pepper oil, or to taste
        ⅛ teaspoon ground ginger
        1 16-ounce can no-salt-added pinto beans, drained
        1 medium green bell pepper, cut into strips
        ½ small onion, thinly sliced into rings

Cook rice according to package directions, omitting salt and butter or margarine.

Drain pineapple, reserving juice.

Combine brown sugar and cornstarch in a large saucepan. Stir to mix well. Add reserved pineapple juice, vinegar, sherry, soy sauce, hot pepper oil and ginger. Place over medium heat and cook until thick and bubbly, stirring constantly. Remove from heat.

Add drained beans, pineapple, bell pepper and onion. Return to heat and cook on low 2 to 3 minutes, or until vegetables are tender-crisp.

Serve over cooked rice.

Nutrient Analysis

Calories	320 kcal	Cholesterol	0 mg	Saturated Fat	0 gm
Protein	10 gm	Sodium	42 mg	Polyunsaturated Fat	0 gm
Carbohydrate	71 gm	Total Fat	1 gm	Monounsaturated Fat	0 gm

Quick-and-Easy Baked Beans

Serves 12

2 16-ounce cans no-salt-added vegetarian baked beans in tomato sauce
2 16-ounce cans no-salt-added barbecue beans
½ cup chopped onion
1 cup no-salt-added tomato sauce
2 tablespoons acceptable margarine, melted
2 tablespoons molasses or firmly packed brown sugar
2 teaspoons dry mustard

Preheat oven to 350° F.

Place ingredients in a 3-quart casserole dish in the order listed. Toss lightly to mix well. Bake, uncovered, 45 to 60 minutes.

Nutrient Analysis

Calories	192 kcal	Cholesterol	5 mg	Saturated Fat	1 gm
Protein	10 gm	Sodium	54 mg	Polyunsaturated Fat	1 gm
Carbohydrate	34 gm	Total Fat	3 gm	Monounsaturated Fat	1 gm

Cuban Black Beans

Serves 8; approximately ½ cup beans and ⅔ cup rice per serving

2 cups dried black beans (4 cups cooked)
Water
1 tablespoon acceptable margarine
1 cup chopped onion
¼ cup diced celery
2 cloves garlic, minced
1 tablespoon fresh savory, or 1 teaspoon dried savory
Pinch ground ginger
1 bay leaf
½ lemon, cut into quarters
Water
1½ cups uncooked rice

OPTIONAL TOPPINGS
8 tablespoons red wine vinegar
8 tablespoons olive oil
1 cup chopped green onion (white and green tops)

Place beans in a large bowl and cover with water. Let sit at least 8 hours.

Drain beans and set aside. Discard water.

In a nonstick skillet over medium-high heat, melt margarine. Add onions and celery and sauté. Remove from heat and set aside.

In a 4-quart stockpot, combine soaked beans, sautéed vegetables, garlic, savory, ginger, bay leaf and lemon. Add enough water to cover. Stir well. Place over medium-high heat and bring to a boil. Reduce heat, cover and simmer 1 to 1½ hours, or until beans are tender. Remove bay leaf and lemon quarters.

Meanwhile, cook rice according to package directions, omitting salt and butter or margarine.

In each of eight individual bowls, put ⅔ cup of rice and ladle on ½ cup of beans. Serve immediately. For a Cuban flavor, add equal amounts of vinegar, olive oil and chopped green onions to each serving.

Serve with a crisp green salad and hard rolls for a colorful, meatless meal.

Nutrient Analysis*

Calories	255 kcal	Cholesterol	0 mg	Saturated Fat	0 gm
Protein	11 gm	Sodium	25 mg	Polyunsaturated Fat	1 gm
Carbohydrate	49 gm	Total Fat	2 gm	Monounsaturated Fat	1 gm

* without toppings

Nutrient Analysis*

Calories	380 kcal	Cholesterol	0 mg	Saturated Fat	2 gm
Protein	11 gm	Sodium	26 mg	Polyunsaturated Fat	2 gm
Carbohydrate	50 gm	Total Fat	15 gm	Monounsaturated Fat	11 gm

* with toppings

Stuffed Peppers

Serves 4; 1 pepper per serving

3 tablespoons acceptable vegetable oil
2 onions, sliced
2 cloves garlic, minced
1 medium zucchini, diced
4 medium tomatoes, chopped
2 cups cooked brown rice
½ cup grated low-fat cheddar cheese
4 large green bell peppers
2 cups no-salt-added tomato juice

Preheat oven to 375° F.

Rinse bell peppers, cut off tops and remove seeds. Reserve hollow peppers and tops.

Heat oil in a large skillet over medium heat. Add onions, garlic, zucchini and tomatoes. Sauté until zucchini is tender-crisp. Do not overcook. Set aside.

In a bowl, combine rice and cheese. Add to mixture in skillet and toss gently to mix well. Set aside.

Pour tomato juice into bottom of a casserole dish. Set aside.

Stuff peppers with vegetable mixture and replace pepper top. Place stuffed peppers in casserole. Bake ½ hour.

Nutrient Analysis

Calories	324 kcal	Cholesterol	3 mg	Saturated Fat	2 gm
Protein	10 gm	Sodium	120 mg	Polyunsaturated Fat	7 gm
Carbohydrate	46 gm	Total Fat	13 gm	Monounsaturated Fat	3 gm

Spinach Crepes

Serves 6; 1 filled crepe per serving

1 11-ounce package of fresh spinach, or 1 10-ounce
    package frozen no-salt-added chopped spinach
3 tablespoons acceptable margarine
3 tablespoons whole-wheat flour
1 cup skim milk
¾ cup water
¼ to ½ teaspoon nutmeg
⅛ teaspoon cayenne
3 tablespoons grated Parmesan cheese
6 Whole-Wheat Crepes (½ recipe) (see page 470)

If using fresh spinach, rinse well, remove stems and drain. Steam just until done. If using frozen spinach, cook according to package directions. Drain and set aside in a large bowl.

In a large skillet over medium-high heat, melt margarine. Add flour, stirring constantly. Cook 2 minutes. Add milk slowly, stirring constantly. When sauce begins to thicken slightly, add water, nutmeg, cayenne and cheese. Cook 5 additional minutes, or until sauce begins to thicken again.

Add sauce to cooked and drained spinach and stir to mix well.

Spoon one-sixth of filling onto each crepe and fold crepe over filling. Serve immediately.

Serve with Lemon Chablis Sauce (see page 430) if desired.

Nutrient Analysis

Calories	217 kcal	Cholesterol	96 mg	Saturated Fat	3 gm
Protein	10 gm	Sodium	231 mg	Polyunsaturated Fat	3 gm
Carbohydrate	20 gm	Total Fat	11 gm	Monounsaturated Fat	4 gm

Spinach Artichoke Gratin

Serves 6; ⅔ cup per serving

Vegetable oil spray
1 pound low-fat cottage cheese
4 tablespoons grated Parmesan cheese
1 tablespoon fresh lemon juice
⅛ teaspoon white pepper
⅛ teaspoon nutmeg
Egg substitute equivalent to 2 eggs
2 10-ounce packages frozen no-salt-added chopped
    spinach, defrosted
⅓ cup thinly sliced green onion tops
1 10-ounce package frozen artichoke hearts, defrosted
2 tablespoons grated Parmesan cheese

Preheat oven to 375° F. Lightly spray a 1½-quart baking dish with vegetable oil.

In a blender or the work bowl of a food processor fitted with a metal blade, combine cottage cheese, 4 tablespoons Parmesan cheese, lemon juice, pepper, nutmeg and egg substitute. Process until completely smooth. Set aside.

Squeeze moisture from spinach. In a bowl, combine spinach, cheese mixture and green onion. Spread half of spinach mixture in prepared dish.

Cut artichoke hearts in half and blot dry with paper towels. Place in a single layer on top of spinach. Sprinkle 2 tablespoons Parmesan cheese on top. Cover with remaining spinach mixture. Bake, covered, 25 minutes.

Nutrient Analysis

Calories	150 kcal	Cholesterol	11 mg	Saturated Fat	2 gm
Protein	18 gm	Sodium	562 mg	Polyunsaturated Fat	0 gm
Carbohydrate	12 gm	Total Fat	4 gm	Monounsaturated Fat	1 gm

*S*pinach *R*icotta *S*wirls

Serves 4; 2 rolls per serving

8 lasagna noodles
Vegetable oil spray

1 tablespoon olive oil
½ cup finely chopped onion
2 large cloves garlic, minced
¼ cup water
1 6-ounce can no-salt-added tomato paste
2 cups homemade Chicken Broth (see page 87) or
    commercial low-sodium variety
1 teaspoon Italian herb seasoning
¼ teaspoon salt

2 10-ounce packages frozen no-salt-added chopped
    spinach, defrosted
1 cup (8 ounces) low-fat/low-sodium ricotta cheese
2 tablespoons grated Parmesan cheese
¼ teaspoon white pepper
⅛ teaspoon nutmeg

Cook lasagna noodles according to package directions, omitting salt. Drain and set aside.

Preheat oven to 350° F. Lightly spray an 8-x-8-inch baking dish with vegetable oil.

Heat olive oil in a saucepan over medium-low heat. Add onion, garlic and water. Cook until water evaporates and onion begins to sauté in oil. Stir in tomato paste, broth, herb seasoning and salt. Simmer 5 minutes, or until slightly thickened. Remove from heat. Set aside.

Squeeze moisture out of spinach. In a bowl, combine spinach, ricotta, Parmesan, pepper and nutmeg. Spread a scant ⅓ cup filling along the length of each cooked noodle. Roll each noodle and place it on its side in prepared baking dish. Be sure sides of rolled noodles do not touch each other.

Pour sauce over lasagna rolls and bake 25 to 30 minutes, or until thoroughly heated.

Nutrient Analysis

Calories	376 kcal	Cholesterol	22 mg	Saturated Fat	5 gm
Protein	20 gm	Sodium	414 mg	Polyunsaturated Fat	1 gm
Carbohydrate	52 gm	Total Fat	11 gm	Monounsaturated Fat	5 gm

Spinach Soufflé

Serves 4

2 tablespoons acceptable margarine
2 tablespoons whole-wheat flour
½ cup skim milk
½ 10-ounce package frozen no-salt-added chopped
    spinach, cooked and drained
1 tablespoon finely chopped onion
¼ teaspoon nutmeg
¼ teaspoon freshly ground black pepper, or to taste
6 egg whites
3 tablespoons grated Parmesan cheese

Preheat oven to 350° F.

In a small, heavy saucepan over medium-high heat, melt margarine. Add flour, stirring constantly. Cook until mixture is smooth and bubbly.

Remove from heat and gradually stir in milk.

Return to heat and bring mixture to a boil, stirring constantly. Cook 1 minute longer. Remove from heat and set aside.

In a large bowl, combine spinach, onion, nutmeg and pepper. Add sauce and stir to mix well. Set aside.

Beat egg whites until stiff. Fold gently into spinach mixture.

Pour into a 1¾-quart casserole. Sprinkle with Parmesan cheese. Bake 35 minutes. Serve immediately.

Nutrient Analysis

Calories	130 kcal	Cholesterol	5 mg	Saturated Fat	2 gm
Protein	10 gm	Sodium	274 mg	Polyunsaturated Fat	1 gm
Carbohydrate	7 gm	Total Fat	7 gm	Monounsaturated Fat	3 gm

*S*pinach and *B*rown *R*ice *C*asserole

Serves 8

Vegetable oil spray
10 ounces fresh spinach or 1 10-ounce package frozen no-
    salt-added chopped spinach
1 egg
1 tablespoon flour
2 cups low-fat cottage cheese
3 cups cooked brown rice
Freshly ground black pepper to taste
½ teaspoon thyme
1 tablespoon grated Parmesan cheese
2 tablespoons acceptable margarine
1½ cups chopped onion
3 cloves garlic, minced
8 ounces fresh mushrooms, sliced
3 tablespoons grated Parmesan cheese
2 tablespoons sunflower seeds

*P*reheat oven to 375° F. Lightly spray a 9-x-13-inch pan with vegetable oil.

If using fresh spinach, rinse thoroughly and remove large stems. Tear into bite-size pieces. If using frozen spinach, defrost and squeeze out moisture. Set aside.

In a bowl, mix egg, flour, cottage cheese, rice, pepper, thyme and 1 tablespoon Parmesan cheese. Set aside.

Heat margarine in a large saucepan over medium-high heat. Add onion and sauté until translucent. Add garlic and sauté 1 minute. Add spinach and mushrooms. Cover and cook 7 minutes. Add cottage cheese mixture and blend well.

Spoon mixture into prepared pan. Sprinkle 3 tablespoons Parmesan and sunflower seeds on top. Bake 25 to 30 minutes.

Nutrient Analysis

Calories	223 kcal	Cholesterol	41 mg	Saturated Fat	3 gm
Protein	14 gm	Sodium	370 mg	Polyunsaturated Fat	2 gm
Carbohydrate	26 gm	Total Fat	7 gm	Monounsaturated Fat	2 gm

*V*egetable *P*armesan *Q*uiche

Serves 8; ⅛ of quiche per serving

1 recipe Mrs. Park's Piecrust (see page 534)
1 cup coarsely chopped fresh mushrooms
¾ cup chopped green onion
¼ cup flour
¼ teaspoon freshly ground black pepper
¼ teaspoon salt-free all-purpose seasoning
6 ripe Italian plum tomatoes or other fresh ripe tomatoes,
    thickly sliced
2 ounces freshly grated Parmesan cheese
Egg substitute equivalent to 2 eggs
1 cup skim milk

*P*reheat oven to 400° F.

Place Mrs. Park's Piecrust in a 9-inch pie pan. Bake 5 minutes. Cool completely. Lower oven temperature to 350° F.

Steam mushrooms and green onions 3 minutes in microwave, covered. Let rest 5 minutes. Or sauté in a little water in a skillet over medium-high heat until tender. Set aside.

In a shallow bowl, combine flour, pepper and all-purpose seasoning. Dredge tomato slices in flour mixture, one at a time. Arrange on crust in pie pan.

Add vegetable mixture, spreading carefully to cover tomatoes. Sprinkle cheese over all. Set aside.

In a small bowl, blend egg substitute and milk. Pour over ingredients in pie pan. Bake 40 to 45 minutes, or until a table knife inserted in the center of the pie comes out clean.

Nutrient Analysis

Calories	239 kcal	Cholesterol	8 mg	Saturated Fat	3 gm
Protein	9 gm	Sodium	278 mg	Polyunsaturated Fat	6 gm
Carbohydrate	24 gm	Total Fat	12 gm	Monounsaturated Fat	3 gm

David's Pizza

Serves 12; ¹/₁₂ of pizza per serving

CRUST
2 packages dry yeast
1½ cups warm water
2 tablespoons olive oil
2 tablespoons sugar
Egg substitute equivalent to 2 eggs
2 cups whole-wheat flour
2½ cups all-purpose flour

Vegetable oil spray

SAUCE
1 tablespoon olive oil
½ cup finely chopped onion
2 8-ounce cans no-salt-added tomato sauce
1 6-ounce can no-salt-added tomato paste
6 ounces water
1 teaspoon basil
½ teaspoon thyme
1 teaspoon oregano
1½ teaspoons garlic powder
½ teaspoon rosemary
¼ teaspoon cayenne pepper
½ teaspoon salt

TOPPING
8 ounces part-skim mozzarella cheese, grated

In a large bowl, combine yeast and warm water. Stir to mix well and let stand 5 minutes. Add 2 tablespoons olive oil, sugar and egg substitute. Stir to mix well. Add whole-wheat flour gradually and beat until smooth. Add all-purpose flour gradually and knead dough in bowl until smooth and elastic. Set in a warm place for about 1 hour, or until dough has risen and doubled in bulk. Punch dough down and let rest 10 minutes.

Preheat oven to 375° F. Lightly spray a 12-x-18-x-1-inch jellyroll pan and a 12-x-20-inch piece of aluminum foil with vegetable oil.

Press dough into pan evenly. Cover with foil (sprayed side next to dough) and bake 20 minutes. Remove from oven and set aside.

Note: Crust may be prepared ahead of time and set aside for same-day use, or it may be frozen for use at a later time.

To make sauce, place 1 tablespoon olive oil in a medium saucepan over medium-high heat. Add onion and sauté until translucent. Add remaining ingredients. Stir to mix well. Reduce heat and simmer 5 minutes.

Spread sauce evenly on prebaked crust. Sprinkle cheese evenly over sauce. Bake at 375° F 20 to 25 minutes.

HERB PIZZA

Mix 1 to 2 tablespoons of any of the following herbs with the mozzarella before assembling pizza: basil, chives, sage or rosemary.

MUSHROOM PIZZA

Place 1 cup sliced fresh mushrooms on top of cheese before baking.

PEPPER PIZZA

Place ⅓ cup thinly sliced green bell pepper and ⅓ cup thinly sliced yellow bell pepper on top of cheese before baking.

David's Pizza Nutrient Analysis

Calories	279 kcal	Cholesterol	10 mg	Saturated Fat	3 gm
Protein	13 gm	Sodium	232 mg	Polyunsaturated Fat	1 gm
Carbohydrate	42 gm	Total Fat	8 gm	Monounsaturated Fat	4 gm

Herb Pizza Nutrient Analysis

Calories	279 kcal	Cholesterol	10 mg	Saturated Fat	3 gm
Protein	13 gm	Sodium	232 mg	Polyunsaturated Fat	1 gm
Carbohydrate	42 gm	Total Fat	8 gm	Monounsaturated Fat	4 gm

Mushroom Pizza Nutrient Analysis

Calories	280 kcal	Cholesterol	10 mg	Saturated Fat	3 gm
Protein	13 gm	Sodium	232 mg	Polyunsaturated Fat	1 gm
Carbohydrate	42 gm	Total Fat	8 gm	Monounsaturated Fat	4 gm

Pepper Pizza Nutrient Analysis

Calories	280 kcal	Cholesterol	10 mg	Saturated Fat	3 gm
Protein	13 gm	Sodium	232 mg	Polyunsaturated Fat	1 gm
Carbohydrate	42 gm	Total Fat	8 gm	Monounsaturated Fat	4 gm

*F*lour *T*ortilla *P*izza

Serves 6; 1 pizza per serving

6 8-inch flour tortillas
1 teaspoon Italian herb seasoning
¾ cup no-salt-added spaghetti sauce
1 cup sliced fresh mushrooms
½ cup sliced green bell pepper
½ cup sliced red bell pepper
¾ cup diced onion
½ cup small broccoli florets
1¼ cups shredded part-skim mozzarella cheese (about
    5 ounces)
Vegetable oil spray
2 tablespoons minced fresh parsley

Preheat oven to 325° F.

Let tortillas come to room temperature. Wrap in foil and warm in oven for 5 minutes. Remove from oven and set oven on broil.

In a bowl, combine Italian seasoning and spaghetti sauce. Mix well.

Spread each tortilla with 2 tablespoons of sauce and one-sixth of the vegetables. Sprinkle cheese equally over the six pizzas.

Lightly spray two large cookie sheets with vegetable oil. Place pizzas on cookie sheets and broil 3 to 4 inches from heat. Cook until cheese melts and begins to brown.

Remove from oven and sprinkle with parsley. Serve immediately.

Note: The raw vegetables used in this recipe make a delicious, crunchy pizza. If you prefer a less crunchy topping, steam vegetables in a steamer or a microwave oven.

Nutrient Analysis

Calories	258 kcal	Cholesterol	17 mg	Saturated Fat	4 gm
Protein	12 gm	Sodium	331 mg	Polyunsaturated Fat	1 gm
Carbohydrate	35 gm	Total Fat	9 gm	Monounsaturated Fat	4 gm

Spaghetti with Zesty Marinara Sauce

Serves 8; 2 ounces spaghetti and ½ cup sauce per serving

1 tablespoon olive oil
2 large cloves garlic, crushed
1 large onion, finely chopped
1 6-ounce can no-salt-added tomato paste
2 tablespoons minced fresh parsley
1¼ teaspoons Italian herb seasoning
½ teaspoon dried basil
⅛ teaspoon salt
Generous amount of freshly ground black pepper
2 teaspoons sugar
⅛ teaspoon hot red pepper flakes, or to taste
1 cup water
¼ cup red wine
1 bay leaf
1 8-ounce can no-salt-added tomato sauce
1 16-ounce can no-salt-added tomatoes, crushed, with
    liquid
16 ounces spaghetti noodles
½ cup grated Parmesan cheese, or to taste

Heat oil in a heavy nonaluminum skillet over medium-high heat. Add garlic and onion and sauté until limp.

Stir in tomato paste, parsley, herbs, salt, black pepper, sugar and pepper flakes. Cook 3 or 4 minutes, stirring often.

Bring water, wine, bay leaf, tomato sauce, tomatoes and liquid from tomatoes to a boil. Reduce heat and simmer 1 to 1½ hours. Remove bay leaf.

Cook spaghetti according to package directions, omitting salt. Drain and serve with sauce. Sprinkle dish with Parmesan cheese.

Note: The sauce freezes well.

Nutrient Analysis

Calories	332 kcal	Cholesterol	5 mg	Saturated Fat	2 gm
Protein	13 gm	Sodium	195 mg	Polyunsaturated Fat	1 gm
Carbohydrate	60 gm	Total Fat	5 gm	Monounsaturated Fat	2 gm

Pizza Sandwiches

Serves 8; ½ muffin per serving

1 tablespoon olive oil
3 tablespoons finely chopped onion
1 clove garlic, minced
1 8-ounce can no-salt-added tomato sauce
½ teaspoon Italian herb seasoning
4 ounces part-skim mozzarella cheese, shredded
3 tablespoons grated Romano cheese
4 whole-wheat English muffins, split

Preheat broiler.

Heat oil in small, nonstick saucepan over medium-high heat. Add onion and sauté until translucent. Add garlic and cook 1 minute more. Stir in tomato sauce and herb seasoning. Remove from heat and set aside.

In a bowl, combine cheeses and set aside. Toast muffins. For each serving, spread 2 tablespoons sauce on a muffin half, top with ½ ounce of the cheese mix and broil until bubbly.

Nutrient Analysis

Calories	144 kcal	Cholesterol	10 mg	Saturated Fat	2 gm
Protein	7 gm	Sodium	182 mg	Polyunsaturated Fat	1 gm
Carbohydrate	15 gm	Total Fat	7 gm	Monounsaturated Fat	3 gm

Spaghetti with Eggplant Sauce

Serves 6

3 tablespoons acceptable vegetable oil
1 eggplant, cut into cubes (do not peel)
1 onion, sliced
1 clove garlic, minced
1 green bell pepper, sliced
1 cup chopped Italian plum tomatoes
1 cup no-salt-added tomato juice
1 teaspoon oregano
2 teaspoons basil
12 ounces spaghetti noodles

*H*eat oil in a large skillet, stockpot or Dutch oven over medium-high heat. Add eggplant and sauté about 7 minutes. Add onion, garlic and bell pepper. Sauté 3 additional minutes, or until tender.

In a bowl, combine tomatoes, tomato juice and herbs. Add to eggplant mixture. Reduce heat, cover and simmer ½ hour.

Cook spaghetti according to package directions, omitting salt. Drain and combine with eggplant sauce before serving.

Nutrient Analysis

Calories	335 kcal	Cholesterol	0 mg	Saturated Fat	1 gm
Protein	9 gm	Sodium	13 mg	Polyunsaturated Fat	4 gm
Carbohydrate	57 gm	Total Fat	8 gm	Monounsaturated Fat	2 gm

*S*paghetti with *P*erfect *P*esto

Serves 6

2 cups firmly packed fresh spinach leaves, stems removed *
½ cup firmly packed fresh basil leaves *
½ cup firmly packed fresh parsley, stems removed *
2 or 3 cloves garlic, minced
¼ cup olive oil
⅓ cup unsalted dry-roasted pine nuts
Freshly ground black pepper to taste
⅓ cup freshly grated Romano cheese
½ cup freshly grated Parmesan cheese
12 ounces uncooked thin spaghetti

*I*n a blender or the work bowl of a food processor fitted with a metal blade, process spinach, basil, parsley, garlic, olive oil, nuts, pepper and cheeses until almost pureed. If mixture is too thick, add 1 to 2 tablespoons water. Set aside.

Cook spaghetti according to package directions, omitting salt. Drain and toss with sauce while spaghetti is hot. Serve immediately.

* Rinse spinach and herbs thoroughly before measuring, but do not dry.

Nutrient Analysis

Calories	427 kcal	Cholesterol	13 mg	Saturated Fat	5 gm
Protein	15 gm	Sodium	253 mg	Polyunsaturated Fat	3 gm
Carbohydrate	52 gm	Total Fat	18 gm	Monounsaturated Fat	10 gm

Margarita's Pasta Primavera

Serves 4

1 cup low-fat cottage cheese
1 tablespoon fresh lemon juice
8 ounces thin spaghetti
1 tablespoon acceptable vegetable oil
¼ cup chopped scallions
½ cup chopped onion
1 clove garlic, minced
¼ teaspoon freshly ground black pepper, or to taste
2 cups sliced fresh mushrooms
1 cup sliced green bell pepper
1½ cups sliced carrots
1 10-ounce package frozen no-salt-added broccoli,
    steamed

Drain any liquid off of cottage cheese. In a bowl, combine cottage cheese and lemon juice. Set aside.

Prepare spaghetti according to package directions, omitting salt. Drain thoroughly.

Meanwhile, heat oil in skillet over medium-high heat. Add scallions, onions, garlic and black pepper and sauté 1 minute. Add mushrooms and stir 1 minute. Then add bell pepper, carrots and broccoli and stir for another 3 to 4 minutes. Set aside.

In another bowl, toss spaghetti and cottage cheese mixture to coat evenly. Top with sautéed vegetables.

Nutrient Analysis

Calories	373 kcal	Cholesterol	5 mg	Saturated Fat	1 gm
Protein	19 gm	Sodium	275 mg	Polyunsaturated Fat	3 gm
Carbohydrate	62 gm	Total Fat	6 gm	Monounsaturated Fat	1 gm

Hearty Baked Macaroni

Serves 6

Vegetable oil spray
1 16-ounce can tomato puree
1 cup water
2 teaspoons Italian herb seasoning
½ teaspoon garlic powder
1½ pounds low-fat cottage cheese
½ teaspoon onion powder
½ teaspoon garlic powder
1 8-ounce package elbow macaroni, uncooked
4 ounces part-skim mozzarella cheese, sliced

Preheat oven to 350° F. Lightly spray a 9-x-9-x-2-inch casserole with vegetable oil.

In a small bowl combine tomato puree, water, Italian seasoning and ½ teaspoon garlic powder.

In another bowl, combine cottage cheese, onion powder and ½ teaspoon garlic powder.

Spoon one-third of tomato mixture into prepared casserole. In order, layer half of macaroni, all of cottage cheese mixture and one-third of tomato mixture on top. Add remaining macaroni and cover with remaining tomato mixture.

Cover and bake 1 hour. Uncover casserole and top with mozzarella cheese. Return it to the oven, uncovered, for 5 minutes, or until cheese is melted.

Let dish stand for 10 minutes before serving.

Nutrient Analysis

Calories	335 kcal	Cholesterol	19 mg	Saturated Fat	4 gm
Protein	27 gm	Sodium	584 mg	Polyunsaturated Fat	0 gm
Carbohydrate	42 gm	Total Fat	6 gm	Monounsaturated Fat	2 gm

Spaghetti Cheese Amandine

Serves 5; 1 cup per serving

½ cup slivered blanched almonds
8 ounces spaghetti, broken into small pieces
1 cup low-fat cottage cheese
½ teaspoon Italian herb seasoning
¼ cup sliced green onion
2 tablespoons skim milk
2 tablespoons grated Parmesan cheese
1 cup frozen no-salt-added peas, defrosted
2 tablespoons acceptable margarine
Freshly ground black pepper to taste

Preheat oven to 350° F.

Toast almonds on a cookie sheet in oven 5 to 7 minutes. Remove from oven and set aside.

Cook spaghetti according to package directions, omitting salt.

In a bowl, combine cottage cheese, Italian seasoning, onion, milk, Parmesan cheese and peas. Stir well. Set aside.

Heat margarine in a skillet over medium heat. Add cooked and drained spaghetti. Stir to mix well. When spaghetti is warm, add cheese mixture and stir gently until heated. Stir in black pepper, top with toasted almonds and serve immediately.

Nutrient Analysis

Calories	385 kcal	Cholesterol	6 mg	Saturated Fat	3 gm
Protein	18 gm	Sodium	322 mg	Polyunsaturated Fat	3 gm
Carbohydrate	48 gm	Total Fat	13 gm	Monounsaturated Fat	7 gm

Spaghetti with Lentil Sauce

Serves 12

2 tablespoons acceptable vegetable oil
1 medium onion, chopped
1 clove garlic, minced
1½ cups dried lentils
1 dried hot red pepper, crumbled
¼ teaspoon freshly ground black pepper, or to taste
4 cups homemade Beef Broth (see page 86) or commercial low-sodium variety
¼ teaspoon dried basil, crumbled
¼ teaspoon dried oregano, crumbled
1 16-ounce can no-salt-added tomatoes
1 6-ounce can no-salt-added tomato paste
1 tablespoon cider vinegar
24 ounces spaghetti noodles

Rinse, soak and drain lentils according to package directions.

Place oil in large skillet, stockpot or Dutch oven over medium-high heat. Add onion and garlic and sauté 5 minutes. Add lentils, red pepper, black pepper and broth. Reduce heat, cover and simmer 30 minutes.

Add remaining ingredients, except spaghetti. Simmer, uncovered, about 1 hour, stirring occasionally.

Cook spaghetti according to package directions, omitting salt. Drain and combine with lentil sauce before serving.

Nutrient Analysis

Calories	360 kcal	Cholesterol	0 mg	Saturated Fat	1 gm
Protein	15 gm	Sodium	108 mg	Polyunsaturated Fat	2 gm
Carbohydrate	67 gm	Total Fat	4 gm	Monounsaturated Fat	1 gm

*I*talian *E*ggplant

Serves 4

Vegetable oil spray
1 eggplant, approximately 1½ pounds
1 tablespoon olive oil
1⅔ cups chopped onion
3 or 4 cloves garlic
8 ounces fresh mushrooms, sliced
½ teaspoon salt
½ teaspoon Italian herb seasoning
Freshly ground black pepper to taste
6 ounces part-skim mozzarella cheese, sliced
1 8-ounce can no-salt-added tomato sauce

Preheat broiler. Lightly spray an 8-x-8-inch pan and a 10-x-10-inch piece of aluminum foil with vegetable oil.

Peel eggplant and slice into ¼-inch-thick rounds. Place on cookie sheet and broil 2 to 3 minutes on each side. Remove from oven and reduce temperature to 375° F.

Heat oil in a nonstick skillet over medium heat. Add onion, garlic, mushrooms, salt and Italian seasoning. Cover pan and cook 7 to 9 minutes. Uncover and raise setting to high. Evaporate pan juices.

Spread 1 cup of mushroom mixture over bottom of prepared pan. Cover with half of eggplant slices. Sprinkle with black pepper. Top with ½ cup tomato sauce and 3 ounces cheese slices. Repeat layers. Cover with prepared foil and bake 1 hour. Cool at least 25 minutes before cutting.

Nutrient Analysis

Calories	221 kcal	Cholesterol	23 mg	Saturated Fat	5 gm
Protein	15 gm	Sodium	516 mg	Polyunsaturated Fat	1 gm
Carbohydrate	18 gm	Total Fat	11 gm	Monounsaturated Fat	5 gm

Melenzana alla Griglia
(Broiled Eggplant)

Serves 6

½ cup reduced-calorie Italian salad dressing
1 teaspoon rosemary
¼ teaspoon oregano
1 large eggplant
1 cup no-salt-added tomato sauce
½ teaspoon freshly ground black pepper, or to taste
2 ounces freshly grated Parmesan cheese

In a bowl, combine salad dressing, rosemary and oregano. Set aside.

Peel eggplant and cut it crosswise in ¾-inch slices. Place in a medium shallow bowl. Add dressing and herb mixture, being sure to evenly coat the slices of eggplant. Cover and refrigerate 1 hour. Drain.

Preheat broiler.

Arrange eggplant slices on a baking sheet. Broil 3 inches from a medium-low setting about 5 minutes on each side, or until slices are tender and lightly browned.

After broiling eggplant, arrange the slices and tomato sauce in alternate layers in an 8-inch-square baking dish, seasoning each layer lightly with pepper. Top with grated cheese.

Broil again for about 2 minutes, or until cheese is brown. Serve immediately.

Nutrient Analysis

Calories	93 kcal	Cholesterol	9 mg	Saturated Fat	2 gm
Protein	5 gm	Sodium	347 mg	Polyunsaturated Fat	1 gm
Carbohydrate	8 gm	Total Fat	5 gm	Monounsaturated Fat	1 gm

*M*eatless *M*oussaka

Serves 8

Vegetable oil spray
2 pounds peeled eggplant, thickly sliced
2 tablespoons olive oil

SAUCE
2 tablespoons olive oil
1 cup finely chopped onion
3 cloves garlic, minced
1 14½-ounce can diced no-salt-added tomatoes in juice
1 6-ounce can no-salt-added tomato paste
1 cup water
½ teaspoon salt
2 teaspoons crushed rosemary
2 tablespoons finely chopped fresh parsley
2 tablespoons finely chopped fresh mint

FILLING
1 pound low-fat cottage cheese
Egg substitute equivalent to 2 eggs
1 teaspoon crushed rosemary
½ teaspoon ground oregano
¼ cup grated Parmesan cheese
½ teaspoon freshly ground black pepper, or to taste

TOPPING
¼ cup grated Parmesan cheese

Preheat broiler. Lightly spray a 3½-quart oblong glass baking dish with vegetable oil.

Place eggplant slices on two large baking sheets. Brush both sides of slices lightly with 2 tablespoons olive oil. Brown 5 minutes on each side, or until eggplant is tender.

Reduce oven temperature to 375° F.

SAUCE
Heat 2 tablespoons olive oil in a nonstick skillet over medium-high heat. Add onion and sauté until translucent. Add garlic and cook 1 minute more. Stir in tomatoes, tomato paste, water, salt and 2 tea-

spoons rosemary. Reduce heat and simmer 10 minutes. Add parsley and mint. Remove from heat and set aside.

FILLING

In a bowl, combine cottage cheese, egg substitute, 1 teaspoon rosemary, oregano, ¼ cup Parmesan cheese and pepper.

Spread half of sauce on bottom of prepared dish. Arrange half of eggplant over it. Spread filling over eggplant, then lay remaining eggplant on top of filling. Cover with remaining sauce. Sprinkle ¼ cup Parmesan cheese over all. Cover casserole with foil and bake 40 to 45 minutes. Uncover and bake 10 additional minutes. Serve.

Nutrient Analysis

Calories	214 kcal	Cholesterol	10 mg	Saturated Fat	3 gm
Protein	14 gm	Sodium	548 mg	Polyunsaturated Fat	1 gm
Carbohydrate	17 gm	Total Fat	11 gm	Monounsaturated Fat	6 gm

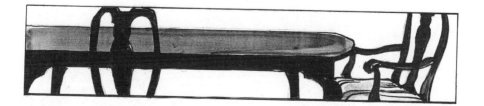

Eggplant Zucchini Casserole

Serves 8

Vegetable oil spray
2 8-ounce cans no-salt-added tomato sauce
2 teaspoons Worcestershire sauce
Freshly ground black pepper to taste
1 teaspoon oregano
½ teaspoon basil
½ teaspoon marjoram
2 medium cloves garlic, crushed
1 medium eggplant, peeled and sliced
2 medium zucchini, sliced
1 cup uncooked spaghetti, broken into pieces
3 medium stalks of celery, chopped
1 medium onion, chopped
1 medium green bell pepper, chopped
8 ounces part-skim mozzarella cheese, cut into 18 small
    slices

Preheat oven to 350° F. Lightly spray a 9-x-13-inch casserole dish with vegetable oil.

In a bowl, combine tomato sauce, Worcestershire sauce, black pepper, herbs and garlic. Mix well and set aside.

In prepared casserole dish, arrange half of the eggplant slices in a single layer. Top with half of each of the following: zucchini slices, spaghetti, celery, onion and bell pepper. Next, arrange 9 slices of cheese over this, and spoon half of tomato mixture on top of cheese. Repeat layers.

Cover and bake about 1 hour, or until vegetables are tender.

Nutrient Analysis

Calories	136 kcal	Cholesterol	15 mg	Saturated Fat	3 gm
Protein	10 gm	Sodium	194 mg	Polyunsaturated Fat	0 gm
Carbohydrate	14 gm	Total Fat	5 gm	Monounsaturated Fat	1 gm

Garnishes

PICKLED WATERMELON RIND
SWEET CORN RELISH
BASIL ROASTED PEPPERS
SPICED PEACHES
CRANBERRY CHUTNEY
BAKED CURRIED FRUIT

*T*o most people, a garnish is a decoration placed on a dish before serving. It can be simple: a lemon slice, a sprig of fresh parsley, a carrot curl. Or it can be elaborate: a hand-carved radish rose, a lemon basket, a tomato-peel flower.

But garnishes don't stop there. They also include tiny side dishes that add zest and depth to the meal. These can include baked fruits that go with meats, or pickled fruits and vegetable relishes that add piquancy to entrees.

We've chosen a few of our zestiest ideas. Our Sweet Corn Relish is wonderful with pork tenderloin, and our Cranberry Chutney—like most chutneys—tastes fabulous with curries and cold meats.

Small touches make a big difference. When you present a meal beautifully with the little extra garnishes that enhance each dish, it's time to trade in your cook's apron for a chef's hat. You have arrived!

Pickled Watermelon Rind

Makes 3 pints
Serves 18; ⅓ cup per serving

> 3 pounds white part of watermelon rind, cubed
> 2 tablespoons salt
> 1 quart water
> 3 cups sugar
> 2 cups cider vinegar
> 1 cup cold water
> 1 tablespoon whole allspice
> 1 tablespoon whole cloves
> 1 tablespoon cinnamon stick pieces
> 1 lemon, sliced

Set rind aside in a glass bowl.

In a large bowl, make a brine of 2 tablespoons salt and 1 quart of water. Add rind, making sure it is completely covered. Cover and refrigerate overnight.

Remove from refrigerator and discard brine. Place rind in a large saucepan, stockpot or Dutch oven over medium-high heat. Cover rind with fresh water. Bring to a boil, reduce heat and simmer 10 minutes, or until rind is tender. Drain and discard liquid. Set rind aside.

In a stockpot over medium-high heat, combine sugar, vinegar and 1 cup of cold water. Heat until sugar dissolves. Enclose allspice, cloves, cinnamon and lemon in a cheesecloth bag. Place bag in vinegar mixture. Add watermelon rind and cook 45 minutes, or until transparent. Pour into sterilized jars and seal.

Nutrient Analysis

Calories	104 kcal	Cholesterol	0 mg	Saturated Fat	0 gm
Protein	1 gm	Sodium	508 mg	Polyunsaturated Fat	0 gm
Carbohydrate	26 gm	Total Fat	0 gm	Monounsaturated Fat	0 gm

Sweet Corn Relish

Serves 24 as a relish; 1 tablespoon per serving
Serves 6 as a salad; ¼ cup per serving

1 tablespoon olive oil
3 cups fresh corn kernels, or 1 10-ounce package frozen
    no-salt-added corn, thawed
½ jalapeño pepper, seeded and finely minced *
¼ cup minced red onion
1 medium red bell pepper, finely diced
3 or 4 sprigs cilantro, chopped coarsely, or ⅛ teaspoon
    dried coriander
6 medium fresh basil leaves, finely chopped, or ½ teaspoon
    dried basil
3 sprigs fresh thyme leaves (no stems), or ½ to 1 teaspoon
    dried thyme
1 small clove garlic, crushed
2 teaspoons fresh lime juice
¼ teaspoon salt
¼ teaspoon freshly ground black pepper, or to taste
2 tablespoons dry white wine (optional)

Heat oil in a skillet over medium heat. Add corn, jalapeño pepper, red onion and red bell pepper. Sauté until tender. Remove from heat and allow to cool.

Add remaining ingredients and toss to blend well. Transfer to a covered glass dish and refrigerate for several hours.

Serve as a relish or place on leaf lettuce and serve as a salad.

Wear rubber gloves when handling hot peppers, or wash hands thoroughly after handling. Skin, especially around the eyes, is very sensitive to oil from peppers.

Nutrient Analysis *

Calories	23 kcal	Cholesterol	0 mg	Saturated Fat	0 gm
Protein	1 gm	Sodium	41 mg	Polyunsaturated Fat	0 gm
Carbohydrate	5 gm	Total Fat	1 gm	Monounsaturated Fat	0 gm

* as a relish

Nutrient Analysis *

Calories	93 kcal	Cholesterol	0 mg	Saturated Fat	0 gm
Protein	3 gm	Sodium	165 mg	Polyunsaturated Fat	0 gm
Carbohydrate	18 gm	Total Fat	2 gm	Monounsaturated Fat	2 gm

* as a salad

Basil Roasted Peppers

Serves 7; ⅓ cup per serving

6 firm red bell peppers
5 tablespoons olive oil
¼ cup red wine vinegar
3 or 4 cloves garlic, minced
2 tablespoons finely chopped fresh basil
¼ teaspoon salt
½ teaspoon freshly ground black pepper to taste

Preheat broiler.

Rinse peppers thoroughly. Place peppers on baking sheet and broil until almost completely black, turning peppers to char evenly. Remove from oven and place in a large plastic bag. Seal and set aside for 20 to 30 minutes.

Remove peppers from bag and rinse under cool running water. Remove and discard skin, core, seeds and veins. Blot dry on paper towels. Cut into ½-inch-wide strips. Set aside.

In a bowl, combine remaining ingredients. Add peppers and mix well. Cover and refrigerate several hours. Drain and discard marinade. Serve cold.

Nutrient Analysis

Calories	98 kcal	Cholesterol	0 mg	Saturated Fat	1 gm
Protein	0 gm	Sodium	77 mg	Polyunsaturated Fat	1 gm
Carbohydrate	3 gm	Total Fat	10 gm	Monounsaturated Fat	7 gm

*S*piced *P*eaches

Serves 8

½ cup cider vinegar
¼ cup sugar
1 stick cinnamon
1 teaspoon whole cloves
8 canned no-sugar-added peach halves, canned in natural
   juices

Drain juice from peaches, reserving fruit and 1 cup of juice.

In a saucepan, combine vinegar, sugar, cinnamon, cloves and 1 cup juice reserved from peaches.

Place pan over medium-high heat and bring to a boil. Boil until liquid is reduced by about half. Remove spices from mixture, reserving cloves. Set liquid aside.

Stick cloves into peach halves and pour prepared liquid over peaches. Cover and refrigerate overnight.

Serve with low-fat baked ham or as part of a fruit salad.

SPICED PEARS

Substitute pears canned in natural juices, no sugar added, for peaches. Proceed as directed.

Spiced Peaches Nutrient Analysis

Calories	51 kcal	Cholesterol	0 mg	Saturated Fat	0 gm
Protein	0 gm	Sodium	0 mg	Polyunsaturated Fat	0 gm
Carbohydrate	13 gm	Total Fat	0 gm	Monounsaturated Fat	0 gm

Spiced Pears Nutrient Analysis

Calories	52 kcal	Cholesterol	0 mg	Saturated Fat	0 gm
Protein	0 gm	Sodium	0 mg	Polyunsaturated Fat	0 gm
Carbohydrate	14 gm	Total Fat	0 gm	Monounsaturated Fat	0 gm

Cranberry Chutney

Makes 4 cups
Serves 64; 1 tablespoon per serving

1 cup seedless golden raisins
1 8-ounce package dates, chopped
1 16-ounce package whole fresh cranberries, rinsed and
    drained
1 cup sugar
½ teaspoon salt
½ teaspoon cinnamon
½ teaspoon ground ginger
¼ teaspoon allspice
⅛ teaspoon ground cloves
¾ cup cider vinegar
¼ cup orange juice
1 tablespoon grated lemon rind
1¼ cups water

Combine all ingredients in a large saucepan over medium heat. Cover and cook 15 minutes. Transfer to a glass jar, cover and refrigerate. Use within two weeks. For a longer shelf life, spoon mixture into hot sterilized jars and process 10 minutes.

Serve with turkey, duck or chicken. This chutney is especially good with a curried meat dish.

Nutrient Analysis

Calories	47 kcal	Cholesterol	0 mg	Saturated Fat	0 gm
Protein	0 gm	Sodium	20 mg	Polyunsaturated Fat	0 gm
Carbohydrate	12 gm	Total Fat	0 gm	Monounsaturated Fat	0 gm

*B*aked *C*urried *F*ruit

Makes 2 quarts
Serves 16; ½ cup per serving

1 20-ounce can no-sugar-added peaches, canned in natural juices
1 20-ounce can no-sugar-added Bing cherries, canned in natural juices
1 20-ounce can no-sugar-added pineapple chunks, canned in natural juices
2 11-ounce cans mandarin oranges, canned in light syrup
Vegetable oil spray
⅔ cup firmly packed light brown sugar
2 teaspoons curry powder
Juice of 1 lemon
2 tablespoons acceptable margarine

*P*lace colander in a large bowl to collect the liquid that will drain out. (Make sure colander will not sit in drained juices.) Pour fruit into colander, cover and refrigerate 1 to 2 hours, or until all juice has run off.

Preheat oven to 300° F. Lightly spray a shallow casserole (8-x-12 inches, or similar size) with vegetable oil. Add fruit and set aside.

In a small bowl, combine brown sugar and curry powder. Distribute over fruit. Sprinkle with lemon juice and dot with margarine. Cover and bake 1 hour.

Nutrient Analysis

Calories	118 kcal	Cholesterol	0 mg	Saturated Fat	0 gm
Protein	1 gm	Sodium	23 mg	Polyunsaturated Fat	0 gm
Carbohydrate	27 gm	Total Fat	2 gm	Monounsaturated Fat	1 gm

Vegetables

ARTICHOKE HEARTS RIVIERA

ASPARAGUS PAR EXCELLENCE

ASPARAGUS MALTAISE

LOUISIANA GREEN BEANS

MEDITERRANEAN BEANS

DILLED GREEN BEANS

SPICY GREEN BEANS

GREEN BEANS OREGANO

GREEN BEANS RISI

FRESH GREEN BEANS WITH WATER CHESTNUTS

DEVILED BEETS

HARVARD BEETS

STEAMED BROCCOLI WITH MUSTARD DILL HOLLANDAISE

BROCCOLI CASSEROLE

BRUSSELS SPROUTS AND PECANS

CABBAGE WITH CARAWAY

SPICED RED CABBAGE

CURRIED CABBAGE

TANGY CARROTS

BAKED GRATED CARROTS

GINGERED CARROTS

HONEYED CARROTS

SOUTHWESTERN CREAMY CORN

SWISS CHARD, SOUTHERN STYLE

CREOLE EGGPLANT

CREAMY KALE WITH RED PEPPER

RICHARD'S MUSHROOMS

STUFFED MUSHROOMS

CREAMED ONIONS

GLAZED ONIONS

FRENCH PEAS

SAVORY PEAS

SEASONED BLACK-EYED PEAS

BASQUE POTATOES

OVEN FRENCH FRIES

SCALLOPED POTATOES

PINEAPPLE SWEET POTATOES

ORANGE SWEET POTATOES

RICE PILAF

WILD RICE WITH MUSHROOMS

RICE DRESSING

ORANGE SPICED RICE

RICE MEXICALI

MEXICAN FRIED RICE

RISOTTO MILANESE

STIR-FRIED SPINACH

SAVORY SPINACH

SCALLOPED SQUASH

GINGERED ACORN SQUASH

HERBED BAKED TOMATOES

TOMATOES ROCKEFELLER

HOBO VEGETABLES

VEGETABLES WITH LEMON SAUCE

AVERY ISLAND CELERY

TRIPLE VEGETABLE BAKE

COUSCOUS WITH VEGETABLES

CANTONESE VEGETABLES

VEGETABLES À LA GRECQUE

VEGETABLE STIR-FRY

PEPPER AND MUSHROOM STIR-FRY

CAPONATA

RATATOUILLE

SOUTHWESTERN RATATOUILLE

COLACHE

Little is more appealing than the sight of fresh vegetables in a market piled high in colorful pyramids or neat rows.

Unfortunately, too often these same luscious, crisp vegetables are overcooked to a tasteless mush. Small wonder that some people are confirmed vegetable haters!

A skilled cook can whip potatocs into snowy drifts, lift asparagus from the pot just as it turns from crisp to tender and prepare tangy gingered carrots that have guests begging for second helpings.

From the Oriental way of gently stir-frying a colorful mix of vegetables to the French method of blanching vegetables and "refreshing" them in ice water, a good cook can create almost endless garden-fresh vegetable dishes.

Along with sheer variety, vegetables offer a wealth of nutritional benefits. Broccoli, tomatoes, sweet potatoes and dark green and bright yellow vegetables are excellent sources of vitamin A (for healthy skin, teeth and bones) and vitamin C (an aid in resisting infection). They're also rich in iron and other minerals. One cup of broccoli, for example, supplies three-fourths of an adult's daily requirement of vitamin A and more than twice his vitamin C quota.

Vegetables are fabulous in soups or salads, as appetizers and snacks, with meat or fish and in combination with each other. A puree of carrots and beets for example, has a wonderful color and flavor. Fresh Green Beans with Water Chestnuts looks and tastes garden fresh. Wild Rice with Mushrooms makes a delicious side dish.

Experiment with garlic, onion, lemon juice, herbs, spices and nuts, in fixing a vegetable dish. For the most flavor and nutrition, steaming is an ideal method of cooking vegetables. Stir-frying is also good, though it adds a bit of oil.

Once you're used to cooking vegctables with zest, you'll give them a high priority on your dinner plate.

*A*rtichoke *H*earts *R*iviera

Serves 6

2 10-ounce packages frozen artichoke hearts
½ cup dry vermouth
1 tablespoon fresh lemon juice
1 clove garlic, crushed
½ teaspoon dry mustard
Freshly ground black pepper to taste
½ teaspoon dried tarragon
1 tablespoon chopped parsley
2 tablespoons acceptable margarine
Chopped fresh parsley

Cook artichoke hearts as directed on package, omitting salt. Drain and set aside.

In a small saucepan, combine vermouth, lemon juice, garlic, seasonings and margarine. Bring to a boil over medium-high heat. Reduce heat, cover and simmer 5 minutes. Pour over cooked artichoke hearts. Top with chopped parsley.

Nutrient Analysis

Calories	80 kcal	Cholesterol	0 mg	Saturated Fat	1 gm
Protein	2 gm	Sodium	109 mg	Polyunsaturated Fat	1 gm
Carbohydrate	11 gm	Total Fat	4 gm	Monounsaturated Fat	2 gm

*A*sparagus par *E*xcellence

Serves 6

¼ cup diced onion
1 green bell pepper, chopped
Freshly ground black pepper to taste
½ cup water
2 10-ounce packages frozen no-salt-added asparagus
    spears
2 teaspoons diced pimiento
½ teaspoon crumbled tarragon
2 teaspoons finely chopped parsley

Bring onion, bell pepper, black pepper and water to a boil in a skillet over medium-high heat. Reduce heat, cover and simmer 5 minutes. Add asparagus and cook for 5 minutes, or until tender-crisp. Sprinkle remaining ingredients on top, and serve.

Nutrient Analysis

Calories	28 kcal	Cholesterol	0 mg	Saturated Fat	0 gm
Protein	3 gm	Sodium	5 mg	Polyunsaturated Fat	0 gm
Carbohydrate	5 gm	Total Fat	0 gm	Monounsaturated Fat	0 gm

*A*sparagus *M*altaise

Serves 6

Egg substitute equivalent to 2 eggs
½ cup acceptable margarine, melted
3 tablespoons fresh lime juice
1 tablespoon orange juice concentrate, defrosted
1 teaspoon grated lime rind
1 teaspoon grated lemon rind
⅛ teaspoon hot pepper sauce
1¾ pounds fresh asparagus

GARNISH
6 fresh lime slices

Warm egg substitute by placing carton in 1 inch of warm water for 5 to 10 minutes or in microwave oven on low for 1 to 2 minutes.

Steam asparagus until tender-crisp.

Place warm egg substitute in blender and process on low until smooth. Slowly add hot melted margarine, continuing to blend on low speed. Add juices, rinds and hot pepper sauce.

Pour sauce over hot asparagus, garnish with lime slices and serve immediately.

Nutrient Analysis

Calories	188 kcal	Cholesterol	0 mg	Saturated Fat	4 gm
Protein	6 gm	Sodium	226 mg	Polyunsaturated Fat	4 gm
Carbohydrate	9 gm	Total Fat	16 gm	Monounsaturated Fat	7 gm

*L*ouisiana *G*reen *B*eans

Serves 8

> 1 pound fresh green beans, rinsed and trimmed or 2
>   9-ounce packages frozen no-salt-added green beans
> 2 cups canned no-salt-added tomatoes
> ½ cup chopped celery
> ¼ cup chopped green bell pepper
> ½ teaspoon onion powder

Cook green beans until tender. Drain.

In a skillet, combine green beans, tomatoes, celery, bell pepper and onion powder. Cook over medium heat 15 minutes, or until thoroughly heated.

*Nutrient Analysis**

Calories	26 kcal	Cholesterol	0 mg	Saturated Fat	0 gm
Protein	1 gm	Sodium	18 mg	Polyunsaturated Fat	0 gm
Carbohydrate	6 gm	Total Fat	0 gm	Monounsaturated Fat	0 gm

* *using fresh green beans*

*M*editerranean *B*eans

Serves 4

> 1 10-ounce package frozen no-salt-added lima beans
> ¼ cup chopped onion
> 1 clove garlic, crushed
> 1 tablespoon acceptable margarine
> 1 cup canned no-salt-added tomatoes (not drained)
> ½ teaspoon dried mint leaves, crushed

Cook lima beans according to package directions. Set aside.

In a skillet over medium-high heat, sauté onion and garlic in margarine until tender. Stir in lima beans, tomatoes and mint leaves. Heat thoroughly and serve.

Nutrient Analysis

Calories	115 kcal	Cholesterol	0 mg	Saturated Fat	1 gm
Protein	5 gm	Sodium	81 mg	Polyunsaturated Fat	1 gm
Carbohydrate	17 gm	Total Fat	3 gm	Monounsaturated Fat	1 gm

Dilled Green Beans

Serves 6

1 cup homemade Beef Broth (see page 86) or commercial low-sodium variety
2 tablespoons chopped onion
¼ cup chopped green bell pepper
½ teaspoon dill seed
2 9-ounce packages frozen no-salt-added cut green beans

In a saucepan over medium heat, cook broth, onion, bell pepper and dill seed several minutes, or until thoroughly heated. Add beans. Cook, covered, 5 to 8 minutes, or until beans are tender-crisp.

Nutrient Analysis

Calories	25 kcal	Cholesterol	0 mg	Saturated Fat	0 gm
Protein	2 gm	Sodium	20 mg	Polyunsaturated Fat	0 gm
Carbohydrate	5 gm	Total Fat	0 gm	Monounsaturated Fat	0 gm

Spicy Green Beans

Serves 4

1 tablespoon acceptable margarine
1 tablespoon water
1 9-ounce package frozen no-salt-added French-style green beans
½ cup finely chopped celery
¼ cup finely chopped onion
2 tablespoons chopped pimiento
1 tablespoon cider vinegar
¼ teaspoon dill seed
Freshly ground black pepper to taste

Place margarine and water in a saucepan over medium heat. Add frozen beans and heat slowly, using a fork to separate. Cover and cook until beans are tender. Add remaining ingredients, toss lightly and heat thoroughly. (Celery and onion should remain crisp.)

Nutrient Analysis

Calories	47 kcal	Cholesterol	0 mg	Saturated Fat	1 gm
Protein	1 gm	Sodium	52 mg	Polyunsaturated Fat	1 gm
Carbohydrate	5 gm	Total Fat	3 gm	Monounsaturated Fat	1 gm

*G*reen *B*eans *O*regano

Serves 4

> 1 9-ounce package frozen no-salt-added Italian green
>   beans
> 1 cup diced tomato (about 1 medium tomato)
> ½ cup diced celery
> ¼ cup diced green bell pepper
> 2 tablespoons chopped onion
> ¼ teaspoon dried oregano leaves
> ⅓ cup water
>
> **GARNISH**
> 4 lemon wedges

Combine all ingredients except lemon wedges in a saucepan over medium-high heat. Bring to a boil. Separate beans with a fork. Reduce heat, cover and simmer 6 to 8 minutes, or until beans are tender-crisp. Garnish with lemon wedges

Nutrient Analysis

Calories	27 kcal	Cholesterol	0 mg	Saturated Fat	0 gm
Protein	1 gm	Sodium	22 mg	Polyunsaturated Fat	0 gm
Carbohydrate	6 gm	Total Fat	0 gm	Monounsaturated Fat	0 gm

*G*reen *B*eans *R*isi

Serves 8

> 1 9-ounce package frozen no-salt-added green beans or 1
>   16-ounce can no-salt-added French-style green beans
> 2 tablespoons acceptable margarine
> 2 cups cooked rice
> 3 tablespoons sliced scallions
> ⅛ teaspoon fresh lemon juice
> Freshly ground black pepper to taste
> ¼ cup toasted sliced filberts
> ¼ cup chopped pimiento

Cook frozen green beans according to package directions, or heat canned beans. Drain and set aside.

In a saucepan over medium heat, melt margarine. Stir in beans, rice, scallions, lemon juice and pepper. When heated thoroughly, turn into a serving dish and sprinkle with filberts and pimiento.

Nutrient Analysis

Calories	114 kcal	Cholesterol	0 mg	Saturated Fat	1 gm
Protein	2 gm	Sodium	39 mg	Polyunsaturated Fat	1 gm
Carbohydrate	15 gm	Total Fat	5 gm	Monounsaturated Fat	3 gm

*F*resh *G*reen *B*eans *with* *W*ater *C*hestnuts

Serves 6

1½ pounds fresh green beans
2 tablespoons sesame seeds
1 teaspoon hot pepper oil
2 teaspoons acceptable vegetable oil
1 8-ounce can water chestnuts, rinsed, drained and sliced
½ teaspoon salt

Preheat oven to 350° F.

Place sesame seeds in an 8-x-8-inch pan. Toast them in the oven for 2 to 3 minutes, then stir and toast 2 to 3 additional minutes.

Rinse and trim beans. Cut diagonally into 1½-inch lengths. Blanch in boiling water 4 minutes. Plunge in ice water to halt cooking. Drain and set aside.

Heat oils in a skillet over high heat. Add water chestnuts and stir-fry 1 minute. Add beans, salt and sesame seeds. Stir well to evenly distribute ingredients. Cook, stirring constantly, until thoroughly heated.

Nutrient Analysis

Calories	79 kcal	Cholesterol	0 mg	Saturated Fat	1 gm
Protein	2 gm	Sodium	196 mg	Polyunsaturated Fat	2 gm
Carbohydrate	11 gm	Total Fat	4 gm	Monounsaturated Fat	1 gm

*D*eviled *B*eets

Serves 6; ½ cup per serving

3 pounds fresh beets, untrimmed
1 tablespoon acceptable margarine
¼ teaspoon dry mustard
¼ teaspoon ground cloves
2 tablespoons cider vinegar
1 tablespoon firmly packed brown sugar
½ teaspoon paprika
1 teaspoon Worcestershire sauce

*T*rim leaves off beets, leaving 1-inch tops. Do not cut off root end. Rinse thoroughly but do not peel. Place beets in a saucepan over medium-high heat, cover with water and bring to a boil. Reduce heat and cook 30 minutes, or until knife pierces beet easily. Remove beets from saucepan and drop into cold water. Slip off skins and dice beets into cubes. Set aside.

Combine all other ingredients in saucepan over medium heat. After margarine melts, add beets and toss gently until heated.

MICROWAVE METHOD
Cook and dice beets as directed above. Set aside. Combine sauce ingredients in 4-cup heat-proof glass measure or bowl. Heat 2 minutes on high, stirring after 1 minute. Add diced beets and mix well. Cook on high 2 minutes more.

Nutrient Analysis

Calories	64 kcal	Cholesterol	0 mg	Saturated Fat	0 gm
Protein	1 gm	Sodium	90 mg	Polyunsaturated Fat	0 gm
Carbohydrate	11 gm	Total Fat	2 gm	Monounsaturated Fat	1 gm

Harvard Beets

Serves 4; ½ cup per serving

2 pounds fresh beets, untrimmed
⅓ cup orange juice
2 tablespoons cider vinegar
2 tablespoons fresh lemon juice
¼ teaspoon garlic powder
1½ tablespoons sugar
⅛ teaspoon salt
½ teaspoon grated lemon rind
1½ teaspoons acceptable margarine

Trim leaves off beets, leaving 1-inch tops. Do not cut off root end. Rinse thoroughly but do not peel. Place beets in a saucepan over medium-high heat. Cover with water and bring to a boil. Reduce heat and cook 30 minutes, or until knife pierces beet easily. Remove beets from saucepan and drop into cold water. Slip off skins and dice beets into cubes. Set aside.

In a saucepan, combine remaining ingredients except margarine and bring to a boil. Add beets, stir and cook 2 minutes more. Stir in margarine and serve.

MICROWAVE METHOD

Cook and dice beets as directed above. Set aside. Combine sauce ingredients, except lemon rind, in a heat-proof glass bowl and cook on high 3 to 3½ minutes, or until sauce bubbles and is thick. Add lemon rind and diced beets. Cook 2 minutes on high. Stir in margarine and serve.

Nutrient Analysis

Calories	78 kcal	Cholesterol	0 mg	Saturated Fat	0 gm
Protein	1 gm	Sodium	142 mg	Polyunsaturated Fat	0 gm
Carbohydrate	16 gm	Total Fat	2 gm	Monounsaturated Fat	1 gm

Steamed Broccoli with Mustard Dill Hollandaise

Serves 6

1 bunch fresh broccoli (approximately 1¾ pounds)
Egg substitute equivalent to 2 eggs
½ cup acceptable margarine, melted
3 tablespoons Dijon mustard
2 tablespoons fresh lemon juice
2 tablespoons finely chopped fresh dill
¼ teaspoon white pepper

Place egg substitute in microwave and cook on low setting 1 to 2 minutes, or just until warm. Or place carton in warm water for 5 to 10 minutes, or until warm.

Rinse and trim broccoli into 4-inch spears. Steam until tender-crisp. Set aside.

Pour warm egg substitute into blender. Process on low speed and add hot melted margarine in a thin stream. Add remaining ingredients and process 10 seconds more. Pour sauce over hot broccoli and serve immediately.

Nutrient Analysis

Calories	189 kcal	Cholesterol	0 mg	Saturated Fat	4 gm
Protein	7 gm	Sodium	345 mg	Polyunsaturated Fat	4 gm
Carbohydrate	9 gm	Total Fat	16 gm	Monounsaturated Fat	7 gm

Broccoli Casserole

Serves 8

Vegetable oil spray
1 bunch fresh broccoli (approximately 1¾ pounds)
4 tablespoons acceptable margarine
1 cup finely chopped onion
¼ cup water

4 tablespoons flour
2 cups homemade Chicken Broth (see page 87) or
     commercial low-sodium variety
1 cup skim milk
½ cup grated Romano cheese
1 tablespoon finely chopped fresh basil
¼ teaspoon salt
1½ cups (2½ ounces) seasoned unsalted croutons, crushed
⅓ cup finely chopped unsalted dry-roasted walnuts

Preheat oven to 400° F. Lightly spray 9-x-13-inch baking dish with vegetable oil.

Rinse and trim broccoli into 4-inch spears, and blanch or steam for 4 minutes. Arrange broccoli in two lengthwise rows in prepared pan. Set aside.

Place margarine and water in a saucepan over high heat. Add onion and sauté until water evaporates and onion starts to sauté in remaining oil. Stir in flour and cook 2 minutes. Whisk in broth and milk. Reduce heat to medium and cook, stirring, until thickened. Add cheese, basil and salt. Stir to mix well. Pour over broccoli; set aside.

In a small bowl, combine crushed croutons and walnuts. Sprinkle mixture over broccoli and sauce. Bake 20 to 25 minutes, or until sauce is bubbly.

MICROWAVE METHOD

Rinse, trim, and blanch or steam broccoli as directed above. Set aside.

Heat margarine in microwave-safe dish for 20 seconds on high. Add onion and cook on high 5 minutes. Add flour and cook 1 minute on high. Stir in broth and milk and cook 5 to 7 minutes on high. Add cheese, basil and salt. Stir to mix well. Place broccoli in two lengthwise rows in a 9-x-13-inch microwave-safe baking dish. Pour sauce over broccoli and set aside.

In a bowl, combine crushed croutons and walnuts. Sprinkle over broccoli and sauce.

Cover with vented plastic wrap and cook on medium about 15 minutes, or until heated through. Let stand covered for 5 minutes and then serve hot.

Nutrient Analysis

Calories	202 kcal	Cholesterol	7 mg	Saturated Fat	3 gm
Protein	8 gm	Sodium	320 mg	Polyunsaturated Fat	4 gm
Carbohydrate	16 gm	Total Fat	13 gm	Monounsaturated Fat	5 gm

*B*russels *S*prouts *and* *P*ecans

Serves 8

Vegetable oil spray
2 10-ounce packages frozen no-salt-added brussels
    sprouts, thawed
1¾ cups homemade Chicken Broth (see page 87) or
    commercial low-sodium variety
3 tablespoons acceptable margarine
4 tablespoons flour
¾ cup nonfat dry milk
¼ teaspoon nutmeg
¼ cup chopped unsalted dry-roasted pecans
1 cup packaged stuffing mix

Preheat oven to 400° F. Lightly spray a 1½-quart casserole with vegetable oil.

Cook brussels sprouts, uncovered to preserve color, in a small amount of boiling water until tender. Set aside.

Bring chicken broth to a boil in a saucepan over medium-high heat.

Meanwhile, melt margarine over low heat and add flour. Stir to blend well. Cook 1 minute, stirring. Add dry milk, then boiling chicken broth all at once, beating with a wire whisk to blend. Cook and stir until sauce comes to a boil and thickens. Remove from heat and stir in nutmeg and pecans.

Place cooked brussels sprouts in prepared casserole. Pour sauce over sprouts and top with stuffing mix.

Bake 10 minutes, or until topping is lightly browned.

Nutrient Analysis

Calories	169 kcal	Cholesterol	1 mg	Saturated Fat	2 gm
Protein	6 gm	Sodium	193 mg	Polyunsaturated Fat	2 gm
Carbohydrate	15 gm	Total Fat	10 gm	Monounsaturated Fat	5 gm

Cabbage with Caraway

Serves 8; ½ cup per serving

8 cups coarsely shredded cabbage (1½-pound head, core removed)

2 cups homemade Chicken Broth (see page 87) or commercial low-sodium variety

1 tablespoon cornstarch

1 tablespoon plus 1 teaspoon prepared spicy brown mustard

½ teaspoon caraway seed, crushed

⅓ cup plain nonfat yogurt

½ teaspoon grated lemon rind

Steam cabbage for 5 minutes, or until tender-crisp. Remove from heat, drain and set aside.

In a saucepan, bring broth, cornstarch, mustard and caraway to a boil over medium-high heat. Add yogurt and lemon rind, and reduce heat immediately. Add cabbage and toss until well coated. Cook until tender-crisp. Do not overcook.

Nutrient Analysis

Calories	32 kcal	Cholesterol	0 mg	Saturated Fat	0 gm
Protein	2 gm	Sodium	66 mg	Polyunsaturated Fat	0 gm
Carbohydrate	6 gm	Total Fat	1 gm	Monounsaturated Fat	0 gm

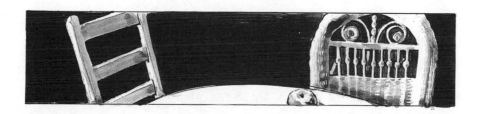

*S*piced *R*ed *C*abbage

Serves 6

4 cups shredded red cabbage
¼ cup cider vinegar
½ cup water
¼ teaspoon ground allspice
¼ teaspoon ground cinnamon
⅛ teaspoon ground nutmeg
2 tart apples, peeled, cored and diced
1 tablespoon sugar

In a saucepan, combine all ingredients except apples and sugar. Cover and cook over medium heat 15 minutes, tossing several times so cabbage will cook evenly.

Add apples and toss again. Cover and cook 5 minutes longer. Add sugar. Toss and serve hot.

If more water is needed during cooking, add 2 or 3 tablespoons. But when cabbage is done, all moisture should be cooked away.

Nutrient Analysis

Calories	40 kcal	Cholesterol	0 mg	Saturated Fat	0 gm
Protein	1 gm	Sodium	10 mg	Polyunsaturated Fat	0 gm
Carbohydrate	10 gm	Total Fat	0 gm	Monounsaturated Fat	0 gm

*C*urried *C*abbage

Serves 6

5 cups shredded cabbage
1 tablespoon acceptable margarine
1 tablespoon flour
1 tablespoon curry powder
Dash freshly ground black pepper
¾ cup skim milk

Cook cabbage in ½-inch of water 5 minutes, or until tender-crisp. Drain and set aside.

Melt margarine in a double boiler over medium heat. Add flour, curry and black pepper, stirring constantly. Add milk slowly and continue to stir until smooth. Heat thoroughly.

Place cabbage in a large bowl and pour sauce over all. Stir well. Serve immediately.

Nutrient Analysis

Calories	47 kcal	Cholesterol	1 mg	Saturated Fat	1 gm
Protein	2 gm	Sodium	49 mg	Polyunsaturated Fat	1 gm
Carbohydrate	6 gm	Total Fat	2 gm	Monounsaturated Fat	1 gm

*T*angy *C*arrots

Serves 6

1 pound young tender carrots, 5 to 6 inches long
1 large shallot, very thinly sliced
1 tablespoon acceptable margarine
2 teaspoons fresh lime juice
1 tablespoon coarsely ground mustard
Generous sprinkle coarsely ground black pepper
2 tablespoons minced fresh parsley

Peel and trim carrots. Cut them lengthwise, then in half. Place carrots and shallot in a vegetable steamer. Cover and steam 8 to 10 minutes, or until tender. Set aside.

In a skillet over medium heat, melt margarine. Add lime juice, mustard and pepper. Stir until thoroughly heated. Remove from heat and add parsley.

Place carrots and shallots in a medium bowl and pour sauce over all. Toss to coat. Serve hot or cover and refrigerate to serve cold.

MICROWAVE METHOD

Peel, trim and cut carrots as directed above. Place carrots and shallots in microwave steamer with 2 tablespoons water. Cook on high 6 to 7 minutes, or until tender. Remove from microwave and set aside. Place margarine, lime juice, mustard and pepper in a glass microwave-safe dish. Cook on high just until hot. Combine carrots, shallots and sauce in a medium bowl and toss to coat evenly. Serve hot, or cover and refrigerate to serve cold.

Nutrient Analysis

Calories	51 kcal	Cholesterol	0 mg	Saturated Fat	1 gm
Protein	1 gm	Sodium	64 mg	Polyunsaturated Fat	1 gm
Carbohydrate	7 gm	Total Fat	2 gm	Monounsaturated Fat	1 gm

Baked Grated Carrots

Serves 6

> 3 cups grated carrots
> 2 tablespoons acceptable margarine, melted
> 1 tablespoon fresh lemon juice
> 2 tablespoons dry sherry
> 1 tablespoon chopped chives

Preheat oven to 350° F.

    Place carrots in a casserole dish. Pour margarine, lemon juice and sherry over them. Sprinkle with chives and bake 30 minutes.

Nutrient Analysis

Calories	58 kcal	Cholesterol	0 mg	Saturated Fat	1 gm
Protein	1 gm	Sodium	76 mg	Polyunsaturated Fat	1 gm
Carbohydrate	6 gm	Total Fat	4 gm	Monounsaturated Fat	2 gm

Gingered Carrots

Serves 5

> 1 pound carrots
> 1 tablespoon acceptable margarine
> 1 tablespoon sugar
> 1 teaspoon grated fresh ginger
> 2 tablespoons finely chopped fresh parsley

Rinse, trim and peel carrots. Cut into ¼-inch slices. Steam 15 to 20 minutes, or until barely tender.

    In a skillet over medium heat, melt margarine until it bubbles. Add carrots and toss. Sprinkle with sugar and ginger. Toss again to coat carrots lightly. Continue cooking 1 to 2 minutes, or until carrots are lightly glazed.

    Sprinkle with parsley and serve immediately.

Nutrient Analysis

Calories	65 kcal	Cholesterol	0 mg	Saturated Fat	1 gm
Protein	1 gm	Sodium	76 mg	Polyunsaturated Fat	1 gm
Carbohydrate	11 gm	Total Fat	2 gm	Monounsaturated Fat	1 gm

*H*oneyed *C*arrots

Serves 4

10 to 12 small carrots
2 tablespoons acceptable margarine
1 tablespoon firmly packed brown sugar
1 tablespoon honey
2 tablespoons finely chopped parsley or fresh mint

Rinse and trim carrots. Cook in a small amount of boiling water for 15 minutes, or until tender. Drain.

Melt margarine in a skillet or saucepan over medium heat. Add sugar, honey and carrots. Reduce heat to low and cook, turning carrots frequently until well glazed.

Transfer carrots to a serving dish and sprinkle with chopped parsley or mint. Serve immediately.

Nutrient Analysis

Calories	143 kcal	Cholesterol	0 mg	Saturated Fat	1 gm
Protein	2 gm	Sodium	160 mg	Polyunsaturated Fat	1 gm
Carbohydrate	22 gm	Total Fat	6 gm	Monounsaturated Fat	3 gm

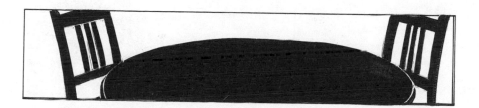

Southwestern Creamy Corn

Serves 6

1 tablespoon acceptable margarine
½ cup finely chopped onion
½ cup diced red bell pepper
¼ cup diced green chili peppers
½ cup Cream Cheese (see page 66)
¼ cup skim milk
½ teaspoon freshly ground black pepper
½ teaspoon chili powder
2 cups frozen no-salt-added whole-kernel corn
2 teaspoons finely chopped fresh cilantro

Melt margarine in a nonstick skillet over medium-high heat. Add onion and bell pepper and sauté until onion is translucent. Add chili peppers, cream cheese, milk, black pepper and chili powder. Cook until mixture is smooth. Stir in corn and reduce heat. Cook over low heat until corn is hot. Add cilantro and serve immediately.

Nutrient Analysis

Calories	91 kcal	Cholesterol	1 mg	Saturated Fat	1 gm
Protein	4 gm	Sodium	113 mg	Polyunsaturated Fat	1 gm
Carbohydrate	14 gm	Total Fat	3 gm	Monounsaturated Fat	1 gm

Swiss Chard, Southern Style

Serves 5; ½ cup per serving

2 8-ounce bunches Swiss chard
2 tablespoons acceptable vegetable oil
1 cup finely chopped onion
¼ cup water
1 teaspoon liquid smoke seasoning
¼ to ½ teaspoon crushed red pepper flakes
¼ teaspoon salt
1 tablespoon imitation bacon bits

Rinse chard thoroughly, removing stems. Cut leaves into strips by rolling each leaf into a tube shape and cutting at ½-inch intervals with sharp knife. Set aside.

Heat oil in a large saucepan over medium heat. Add onion and water. Cook until water evaporates and onion begins to sauté in oil. Cook 1 minute more. Add smoke seasoning, red pepper, salt and chard. Cover and cook 5 to 7 minutes, or until chard is wilted and tender. Add bacon bits and stir thoroughly to combine ingredients. Serve hot.

Nutrient Analysis

Calories	79 kcal	Cholesterol	0 mg	Saturated Fat	1 gm
Protein	2 gm	Sodium	273 mg	Polyunsaturated Fat	3 gm
Carbohydrate	6 gm	Total Fat	6 gm	Monounsaturated Fat	1 gm

Creole Eggplant

Serves 10; ½ cup per serving

2 tablespoons acceptable vegetable oil
2 tablespoons chopped onion
2 tablespoons chopped green bell pepper
¼ cup sliced fresh mushrooms
2 cups canned no-salt-added stewed tomatoes or fresh
   tomatoes
Freshly ground black pepper to taste
1 medium eggplant, sliced or cubed
Vegetable oil spray
½ cup plain bread crumbs
1 tablespoon acceptable margarine

Place oil, onion, bell pepper and mushrooms in a saucepan over low heat. Cook 5 minutes. Add tomatoes and black pepper. Simmer 30 minutes, or until sauce is thick.

Parboil eggplant 10 minutes, or until done. Drain and set aside.
Preheat oven to 350° F.
Lightly spray an 11-x-17-inch casserole dish with vegetable oil.
Arrange a layer of eggplant in the bottom of the casserole dish. In layers, add sauce, eggplant and sauce. Continue in this order until all the eggplant is used, finishing with a layer of sauce. Sprinkle bread crumbs over top, dot with margarine and bake 30 minutes, or until bubbling.

CREOLE SQUASH
Substitute 1½ large yellow squash, cubed, for eggplant and proceed as above.

CREOLE CELERY
Substitute 1 cup of diced celery for eggplant. While sauce is cooking, place celery in ½ cup boiling water. Reduce heat and cook 10 minutes, or until tender-crisp. Add to sauce and heat thoroughly. (Omit bread crumbs, margarine and remainder of procedure.)

Creole Eggplant Nutrient Analysis

Calories	97 kcal	Cholesterol	0 mg	Saturated Fat	1 gm
Protein	2 gm	Sodium	133 mg	Polyunsaturated Fat	2 gm
Carbohydrate	11 gm	Total Fat	5 gm	Monounsaturated Fat	2 gm

Creole Squash Nutrient Analysis

Calories	103 kcal	Cholesterol	0 mg	Saturated Fat	1 gm
Protein	2 gm	Sodium	133 mg	Polyunsaturated Fat	2 gm
Carbohydrate	12 gm	Total Fat	6 gm	Monounsaturated Fat	2 gm

Creole Celery Nutrient Analysis

Calories	59 kcal	Cholesterol	0 mg	Saturated Fat	1 gm
Protein	1 gm	Sodium	89 mg	Polyunsaturated Fat	2 gm
Carbohydrate	6 gm	Total Fat	4 gm	Monounsaturated Fat	1 gm

Creamy Kale with Red Pepper

Serves 4; ½ cup per serving

1 bunch kale (1 ½ pounds)
1 cup diced red bell pepper
2 tablespoons water
2 tablespoons acceptable margarine
2 tablespoons flour
1 cup skim milk
¼ teaspoon salt
⅛ teaspoon coarsely ground black pepper
½ teaspoon sugar

Rinse kale thoroughly to remove sand and grit. Tear leaves into small pieces and discard stalks. Place leaves and red pepper in a saucepan over medium-high heat. Add water, reduce heat and cover. Cook 7 to 8 minutes, or until leaves are wilted. Transfer kale and peppers to a plate and set aside.

Melt margarine in a large saucepan. Add flour and cook 1 minute, stirring constantly. Whisk in milk, salt and pepper. Cook until mixture boils, stirring constantly. Remove from heat and add kale, peppers and sugar. Mix well and serve hot.

Nutrient Analysis

Calories	108 kcal	Cholesterol	1 mg	Saturated Fat	1 gm
Protein	4 gm	Sodium	254 mg	Polyunsaturated Fat	1 gm
Carbohydrate	10 gm	Total Fat	6 gm	Monounsaturated Fat	3 gm

Richard's Mushrooms

Serves 4; ½ cup per serving

> 2 tablespoons acceptable margarine
> ½ cup finely chopped shallots
> 1 pound fresh mushrooms
> ½ cup dry white wine
> Freshly ground black pepper to taste
> 1 tablespoon finely chopped parsley

Wipe mushrooms with a clean, damp cloth. Cut into quarters and set aside.

Melt margarine in a nonstick skillet over medium-high heat. Add shallots and sauté 2 to 3 minutes, stirring constantly. Add mushrooms and wine. Cover and reduce heat to medium. Cook 7 to 9 minutes. Uncover and increase heat to high. Cook 5 to 6 minutes, or until juices are evaporated. Add pepper and parsley and stir to mix well. Serve immediately.

Nutrient Analysis

Calories	80 kcal	Cholesterol	0 mg	Saturated Fat	1 gm
Protein	2 gm	Sodium	71 mg	Polyunsaturated Fat	1 gm
Carbohydrate	6 gm	Total Fat	6 gm	Monounsaturated Fat	3 gm

Stuffed Mushrooms

Serves 6; 3 mushrooms per serving

> 18 medium mushrooms (approximately 1 pound)
> 2 tablespoons sesame oil
> 3 cloves garlic, minced
> ¼ cup diced red bell pepper
> ¼ cup diced yellow bell pepper
> ¼ cup sliced green onion
> ¾ cup fresh whole-wheat bread crumbs (1½ slices bread)
> ½ teaspoon Italian herb seasoning
> 1 egg, slightly beaten
> 2 tablespoons grated Parmesan cheese

Preheat oven to 425° F.

Wipe mushrooms with a clean, damp cloth and remove stems. Place caps in a baking dish and set aside. Chop stems finely. Set aside.

Heat oil in a nonstick skillet over medium-high heat. Add mushroom stems and garlic. Sauté for 5 minutes. Stir in bell peppers and cook until soft. Add green onion and cook 2 minutes more. Remove pan from heat and stir in bread crumbs, Italian seasoning, egg and Parmesan cheese. Stuff equal amounts of filling into mushroom caps. Bake 25 minutes and serve hot.

Nutrient Analysis

Calories	107 kcal	Cholesterol	47 mg	Saturated Fat		1 gm
Protein	4 gm	Sodium	110 mg	Polyunsaturated Fat		2 gm
Carbohydrate	9 gm	Total Fat	7 gm	Monounsaturated Fat		2 gm

*C*reamed *O*nions

Serves 4

2 cups fresh or canned pearl onions
1½ tablespoons acceptable margarine
1½ tablespoons flour
¾ cup skim milk
Freshly ground black pepper to taste
Dash nutmeg (optional)

If fresh onions are used, remove outer layer of skin and parboil them until tender.

Meanwhile, melt margarine in a saucepan over medium heat. Add flour and stir until well blended. Add milk gradually. Reduce heat to low and cook, stirring constantly, until mixture has thickened.

Drain onions and add to sauce. Season with pepper and nutmeg. Serve hot.

Nutrient Analysis

Calories	81 kcal	Cholesterol	1 mg	Saturated Fat		1 gm
Protein	2 gm	Sodium	79 mg	Polyunsaturated Fat		1 gm
Carbohydrate	8 gm	Total Fat	4 gm	Monounsaturated Fat		2 gm

Glazed Onions

Serves 4

20 small, fresh white onions, or 1 16-ounce can onions
1 tablespoon acceptable margarine
1 teaspoon sugar

If fresh onions are used, remove outer layer of skin and parboil them 20 minutes, or until tender.

Drain cooked fresh onions or canned onions. Set aside.

Melt margarine in a skillet over medium heat. Add onions, sprinkle with sugar and reduce heat to low. Cook slowly, shaking pan or turning onions until they turn a light golden brown.

Nutrient Analysis

Calories	113 kcal	Cholesterol	0 mg	Saturated Fat	1 gm
Protein	3 gm	Sodium	57 mg	Polyunsaturated Fat	1 gm
Carbohydrate	20 gm	Total Fat	3 gm	Monounsaturated Fat	1 gm

French Peas

Serves 6

1 10-ounce package frozen no-salt-added peas
1 5-ounce can water chestnuts, rinsed and drained
2 green onions, diced
1 cup finely shredded lettuce
1 tablespoon acceptable vegetable oil
1 teaspoon flour
3 tablespoons homemade Chicken Broth (see page 87),
   commercial low-sodium variety or water
Freshly ground black pepper to taste

Cook peas according to package directions, omitting salt. Set aside.
Drain and slice water chestnuts. Set aside.

In a saucepan, cook green onions and lettuce in oil over low heat for 5 minutes.

In a small bowl, combine flour with water or broth. Add to lettuce mixture and stir until thickened. Add peas, water chestnuts and pepper. Heat thoroughly and serve.

Nutrient Analysis *

Calories	69 kcal	Cholesterol	0 mg	Saturated Fat	0 gm
Protein	3 gm	Sodium	42 mg	Polyunsaturated Fat	1 gm
Carbohydrate	10 gm	Total Fat	2 gm	Monounsaturated Fat	1 gm

* *using low-sodium chicken broth*

Savory Peas

Serves 8

1 pound fresh, or frozen no-salt-added, green peas
3 strips lower-salt bacon
1 tablespoon water
2 tablespoons acceptable margarine
6 green onions, including tops, finely chopped
1 teaspoon Italian herb seasoning
1 teaspoon freshly ground nutmeg

Cook peas until tender-crisp. Set aside and cool.

Cook bacon in a microwave or in a nonstick skillet over medium heat until crisp. Drain well and dice.

Place water, margarine and onion in a clean skillet over medium-high heat. Sauté until onion is soft. Reduce heat and add peas, bacon and seasonings. Heat thoroughly and serve hot.

Nutrient Analysis

Calories	86 kcal	Cholesterol	2 mg	Saturated Fat	1 gm
Protein	4 gm	Sodium	106 mg	Polyunsaturated Fat	1 gm
Carbohydrate	9 gm	Total Fat	4 gm	Monounsaturated Fat	2 gm

Seasoned Black-Eyed Peas

Serves 16; ½ cup per serving

> 1 pound dried black-eyed peas
> Water
> ¼ pound Canadian bacon
> 2 medium onions, chopped
> 2 stalks celery, chopped
> 1 small bay leaf
> 1 clove garlic, chopped
> ¼ teaspoon cayenne pepper
> 1 6-ounce can no-salt-added tomato paste
> Freshly ground black pepper to taste

Rinse peas and place them in a large saucepan. Cover with water and let soak for 45 minutes.

Cook Canadian bacon until crisp in a skillet over medium-high heat. Drain on paper towels. Chop and set aside.

Drain peas and return them to the large saucepan. Add just enough fresh water to cover. Add bacon and remaining ingredients. Bring to a boil over medium-high heat. Reduce heat, cover and simmer 3 hours, or until tender.

Nutrient Analysis

Calories	115 kcal	Cholesterol	3 mg	Saturated Fat		0 gm
Protein	8 gm	Sodium	104 mg	Polyunsaturated Fat		0 gm
Carbohydrate	19 gm	Total Fat	1 gm	Monounsaturated Fat		0 gm

Basque Potatoes

Serves 8

> 2 tablespoons olive oil
> ½ cup chopped onion
> 1 small clove garlic, crushed
> ¾ cup chopped parsley
> ¼ cup chopped pimiento
> Freshly ground black pepper to taste
> 1 cup homemade Chicken Broth (see page 87) or
>   commercial low-sodium variety
> 6 medium potatoes

Pour olive oil into a large skillet over medium-high heat. Add onion and garlic and sauté until soft. Stir in parsley, pimiento, pepper and broth. Remove from heat. Set aside.

Peel and thinly slice potatoes. Layer slices in broth in skillet.

Place over medium-high heat and bring to a boil. Reduce heat, cover and simmer 20 minutes, or until potatoes are tender.

With a slotted spoon, lift potatoes into a heated serving bowl and pour cooking liquid over them. Serve hot.

Nutrient Analysis

Calories	100 kcal	Cholesterol	0 mg	Saturated Fat	1 gm
Protein	2 gm	Sodium	15 mg	Polyunsaturated Fat	0 gm
Carbohydrate	16 gm	Total Fat	4 gm	Monounsaturated Fat	3 gm

*O*ven *F*rench *F*ries

Serves 8

4 large potatoes
2 tablespoons peanut or safflower oil

Scrub potatoes and cut into long strips, about ½-inch wide. Drop into ice water, cover and chill 1 to 2 hours. Remove strips from water and dry thoroughly.

Place strips and oil in a deep bowl and toss until all potatoes have a light coating of oil.

Preheat oven to 475° F.

Spread fries in a single layer in a shallow baking pan. Place in oven for 30 to 35 minutes. Stir fries occasionally to brown on all sides.

VARIATIONS

Flavor fries with any salt-free seasoning such as garlic powder, lemon-pepper seasoning, sesame seeds, cumin or chili powder. Or use your favorite freshly ground herbs.

Nutrient Analysis *

Calories	130 kcal	Cholesterol	0 mg	Saturated Fat	1 gm
Protein	2 gm	Sodium	7 mg	Polyunsaturated Fat	1 gm
Carbohydrate	23 gm	Total Fat	3 gm	Monounsaturated Fat	2 gm

* using peanut oil

*S*calloped *P*otatoes

Serves 6

Vegetable oil spray
5 tablespoons acceptable margarine
1 cup finely chopped onion
5 tablespoons flour
2½ cups skim milk, heated
1½ teaspoons grated lemon rind
⅛ teaspoon salt
⅛ teaspoon white pepper
3 tablespoons finely chopped fresh parsley
2 pounds potatoes, peeled and thinly sliced
⅛ teaspoon salt
⅛ teaspoon white pepper
2 tablespoons grated Romano cheese

*P*reheat oven to 325° F.

Lightly spray an 8-x-8-inch baking dish with vegetable oil and set aside.

Heat margarine in a saucepan over medium-high heat. Add onion and sauté until translucent. Stir in flour and cook 1 minute more. Whisk in milk and cook, stirring, until sauce is thickened. Add lemon rind, ⅛ teaspoon salt, ⅛ teaspoon pepper and parsley. Remove from heat and set aside.

Arrange potatoes in prepared dish. Sprinkle with ⅛ teaspoon salt and ⅛ teaspoon pepper. Pour sauce over potatoes and sprinkle cheese on top. Bake 1½ hours.

MICROWAVE METHOD

Melt margarine in a microwave-safe bowl for 30 seconds on high. Add onions, cover with vented plastic wrap and cook 2 minutes on high, then 6 minutes on medium. Stir in flour and cook 1 minute on high. Whisk in heated milk and cook 6 to 8 minutes on high. Add seasonings as directed. Proceed with assembly and baking as above.

Nutrient Analysis

Calories	260 kcal	Cholesterol	3 mg	Saturated Fat	3 gm
Protein	7 gm	Sodium	285 mg	Polyunsaturated Fat	2 gm
Carbohydrate	36 gm	Total Fat	10 gm	Monounsaturated Fat	4 gm

Pineapple Sweet Potatoes

Serves 6

4 medium sweet potatoes, unpeeled (about 1 pound)
Vegetable oil spray
¼ cup unsweetened pineapple juice
2 tablespoons acceptable vegetable oil
1 tablespoon no-sugar-added crushed pineapple, canned in
   natural juices
Pinch each cinnamon, nutmeg and allspice
1 tablespoon molasses
1 teaspoon acceptable margarine

Boil potatoes until tender (about 30 minutes). Remove skins and discard.

Preheat oven to 425° F. Lightly spray a 1-quart baking dish with vegetable oil.

Mash pulp. Add fruit juice and oil and whip until fluffy. Add pineapple and spices.

Turn into prepared baking dish. Spread molasses over the top, dot with margarine and bake, uncovered, 15 minutes, or until thoroughly heated.

Nutrient Analysis

Calories	139 kcal	Cholesterol	0 mg	Saturated Fat		1 gm
Protein	1 gm	Sodium	16 mg	Polyunsaturated Fat		3 gm
Carbohydrate	22 gm	Total Fat	5 gm	Monounsaturated Fat		1 gm

*O*range *S*weet *P*otatoes

Serves 6

4 medium sweet potatoes, unpeeled (about 1 pound)
¼ to ½ teaspoon grated orange rind
½ cup orange juice
2 tablespoons firmly packed brown sugar
¼ teaspoon cinnamon
2 dashes angostura bitters (optional)
Vegetable oil spray

Boil potatoes 30 minutes, or until tender. Remove skins and discard. Mash pulp, add remaining ingredients and whip until fluffy.

Preheat oven to 350° F. Lightly spray a 1-quart casserole with vegetable oil.

Spread potato mixture into the prepared casserole. Cover and bake 25 minutes, or until thoroughly heated.

Nutrient Analysis

Calories	105 kcal	Cholesterol	0 mg	Saturated Fat	0 gm
Protein	1 gm	Sodium	9 mg	Polyunsaturated Fat	0 gm
Carbohydrate	25 gm	Total Fat	0 gm	Monounsaturated Fat	0 gm

*R*ice *P*ilaf

Serves 6

2 tablespoons acceptable margarine
½ cup chopped onion
¼ cup chopped celery
½ cup chopped green or red bell pepper
2 cups homemade Chicken Broth (see page 87),
    commercial low-sodium variety or water
1 cup uncooked long-grain rice
½ cup sliced fresh mushrooms
2 tablespoons chopped fresh parsley
¾ teaspoon freshly ground black pepper, or to taste

In a small skillet over medium-high heat, melt margarine. Add onion, celery and bell pepper and sauté 3 minutes. Set aside.

Place broth and rice in a saucepan over medium heat. Add onion mixture and mushrooms. Reduce heat and simmer, covered, 30 to 40 minutes, or until rice is tender and liquid is absorbed. Add parsley and black pepper. Fluff before serving.

Note: This dish may be made ahead and reheated.

MICROWAVE METHOD

In a large microwave dish, combine margarine, onion, celery and bell pepper. Cover and cook on high 3 to 5 minutes. Stir in broth, rice and mushrooms. Cover and cook on high 5 minutes and then medium (50 percent power) for 10 minutes. Let stand, covered, 5 minutes. Add parsley and black pepper. Fluff before serving.

Nutrient Analysis

Calories	153 kcal	Cholesterol	0 mg	Saturated Fat	1 gm
Protein	3 gm	Sodium	68 mg	Polyunsaturated Fat	1 gm
Carbohydrate	25 gm	Total Fat	4 gm	Monounsaturated Fat	2 gm

*W*ild *R*ice with *M*ushrooms

Serves 6

1¼ cups (4-ounce package) wild rice
¼ teaspoon salt
2 tablespoons acceptable margarine
1 8-ounce package fresh mushrooms, quartered
¼ cup dry white wine
¼ teaspoon salt
⅔ cup sliced green onion
1 tablespoon finely chopped fresh sage
2 tablespoons white wine Worcestershire sauce

Cook rice according to package directions, using ¼ teaspoon salt.

Heat margarine in large nonstick skillet over medium heat. Add mushrooms, wine and ¼ teaspoon salt. Cover and cook 5 to 7 minutes. Uncover and increase temperature to high. Allow juices to evaporate. Reduce heat to medium. Stir in green onions and sauté 2 minutes. Add rice and remaining ingredients. Stir to mix well.

Nutrient Analysis

Calories	120 kcal	Cholesterol	0 mg	Saturated Fat	1 gm
Protein	4 gm	Sodium	286 mg	Polyunsaturated Fat	1 gm
Carbohydrate	18 gm	Total Fat	4 gm	Monounsaturated Fat	2 gm

*R*ice *D*ressing

Serves 12

2 cups uncooked rice
6 cups homemade Chicken Broth (see page 87) or
    commercial low-sodium variety
3 onions, chopped
4 stalks celery, chopped
1 green bell pepper, chopped
Water
Vegetable oil spray
½ pound mushrooms, chopped
Freshly ground black pepper to taste
3 egg whites
1 tablespoon chopped parsley

Place rice in chicken broth in a large saucepan over medium-high heat. Bring to a boil. Reduce heat and simmer, covered, 30 to 40 minutes, or until rice is tender and liquid is absorbed.

In another saucepan, combine onions, celery and bell pepper with just enough water to cover. Place over medium-high heat and bring to a boil. Reduce heat and simmer until tender.

Preheat oven to 325° F. Lightly spray a large casserole dish with vegetable oil.

In prepared casserole dish, combine rice, onion mixture, mushrooms, black pepper and egg whites. Stir well. Cover and bake 45 minutes. Add parsley, fluff with a fork and bake uncovered 10 minutes longer.

OPTIONAL COOKING METHOD
Pack unbaked dressing loosely into cavity of a 12- to 15-pound turkey. Proceed as directed for a stuffed turkey.

Nutrient Analysis

Calories	133 kcal	Cholesterol	0 mg	Saturated Fat	0 gm
Protein	5 gm	Sodium	51 mg	Polyunsaturated Fat	0 gm
Carbohydrate	27 gm	Total Fat	1 gm	Monounsaturated Fat	0 gm

*O*range *S*piced *R*ice

Serves 8

1 tablespoon acceptable margarine
1 large onion, minced
2 stalks celery, minced
2 cups uncooked brown rice
3 cups water
2 cups homemade Chicken Broth (see page 87) or
   commercial low-sodium variety
⅔ cup golden raisins
Peel of 1 orange, chopped
⅛ teaspoon ground cloves
2 oranges, peeled and cut into small segments

GARNISH
Fresh mint sprig

*I*n a large saucepan over medium-high heat, melt margarine. Add onion and celery and sauté 3 minutes. Add rice and sauté 2 additional minutes. Add water, broth, raisins and orange peel. Bring to a boil, then reduce heat. Cover and simmer 30 to 40 minutes.

Stir in cloves and orange segments and garnish with mint. Serve immediately.

Nutrient Analysis

Calories	288 kcal	Cholesterol	0 mg	Saturated Fat	1 gm
Protein	6 gm	Sodium	44 mg	Polyunsaturated Fat	1 gm
Carbohydrate	62 gm	Total Fat	3 gm	Monounsaturated Fat	1 gm

Rice Mexicali

Serves 6

2 tablespoons acceptable vegetable oil
4 ounces fresh mushrooms, sliced
½ cup chopped onion
¼ cup chopped green bell pepper
1 16-ounce can no-salt-added tomatoes
½ cup water
1 cup uncooked rice
2 tablespoons chopped parsley
Freshly ground black pepper to taste
¼ teaspoon sweet basil
¼ teaspoon oregano

Heat oil in a large, deep skillet over medium heat. Add mushrooms, onion and bell pepper. Sauté until tender and lightly browned.

Add tomatoes and water. Bring to a boil. Add rice and remaining ingredients. Reduce heat, cover and cook 30 minutes, or until rice is tender and liquid is absorbed.

Nutrient Analysis

Calories	167 kcal	Cholesterol	0 mg	Saturated Fat	1 gm
Protein	3 gm	Sodium	12 mg	Polyunsaturated Fat	3 gm
Carbohydrate	28 gm	Total Fat	5 gm	Monounsaturated Fat	1 gm

Mexican Fried Rice

Serves 6

2 tablespoons acceptable vegetable oil
1 cup uncooked rice
1 clove garlic, minced
½ cup finely sliced green onion
⅔ cup chopped canned chili peppers
½ cup diced fresh tomatoes
2 cups homemade Chicken Broth (see page 87) or
    commercial low-sodium variety

Heat oil in a heavy skillet over medium-high heat. Add rice and sauté, stirring constantly, until golden brown. Add remaining ingredients. Cover and simmer 30 minutes, or until rice is tender and liquid is absorbed.

Nutrient Analysis

Calories	161 kcal	Cholesterol	0 mg	Saturated Fat	1 gm
Protein	3 gm	Sodium	197 mg	Polyunsaturated Fat	3 gm
Carbohydrate	26 gm	Total Fat	5 gm	Monounsaturated Fat	1 gm

*R*isotto *M*ilanese

Serves 8

> 2 tablespoons acceptable margarine
> 1½ cups uncooked arborio rice *
> 3 green onions, finely chopped
> ¼ cup dry white wine
> ½ cup chopped fresh mushrooms
> Pinch turmeric or saffron
> 4 cups homemade Chicken Broth (see page 87) or
>   commercial low-sodium variety
> 1 tablespoon grated Parmesan cheese

Melt margarine in a heavy saucepan over medium heat. Add rice and green onions and cook slowly, stirring with a wooden spoon, until rice is milky. Add wine and continue cooking, stirring constantly, until wine is absorbed. Reduce heat and stir in remaining ingredients except Parmesan. Cover and simmer 20 minutes, or until rice is tender and liquid is absorbed.

Place in a serving bowl and sprinkle Parmesan cheese on top.

* *This long-grain rice is available in Italian markets and health-food stores.*

Nutrient Analysis

Calories	160 kcal	Cholesterol	0 mg	Saturated Fat	1 gm
Protein	4 gm	Sodium	74 mg	Polyunsaturated Fat	1 gm
Carbohydrate	27 gm	Total Fat	4 gm	Monounsaturated Fat	2 gm

Stir-Fried Spinach

Serves 4

1 pound loose fresh spinach or other leafy green vegetable
1 tablespoon acceptable vegetable oil

Rinse spinach thoroughly, remove stems and drain well.

Heat oil in a skillet or wok over medium-high heat. Add spinach and stir, turning over leaves several times until they are well coated. Cover and cook 1 minute. Uncover and cook, stirring constantly, another 30 seconds, or until spinach is wilted. Do not overcook. Serve at once.

Nutrient Analysis

Calories	55 kcal	Cholesterol	0 mg	Saturated Fat	0 gm
Protein	3 gm	Sodium	75 mg	Polyunsaturated Fat	2 gm
Carbohydrate	5 gm	Total Fat	4 gm	Monounsaturated Fat	1 gm

Savory Spinach

Serves 4

1 10-ounce package frozen no-salt-added leaf spinach,
**   thawed**
2 tablespoons prepared horseradish
2 tablespoons chopped, cooked Canadian bacon

Cook spinach in ¼ cup of water 4 to 5 minutes, or until tender.

Drain spinach, mix in horseradish and bacon, and serve.

Nutrient Analysis

Calories	24 kcal	Cholesterol	3 mg	Saturated Fat	0 gm
Protein	3 gm	Sodium	117 mg	Polyunsaturated Fat	0 gm
Carbohydrate	3 gm	Total Fat	0 gm	Monounsaturated Fat	0 gm

Scalloped Squash

Serves 6; ½ cup per serving

1½ pounds yellow crook-neck squash
2 tablespoons acceptable margarine
1 cup finely chopped onion
⅔ cup homemade Chicken Broth (see page 87) or
    commercial low-sodium variety
¼ teaspoon salt
1 teaspoon basil
1 teaspoon thyme
1 teaspoon marjoram
2⅓ cups (4 ounces) seasoned unsalted croutons
¼ cup snipped fresh chives

Scrub, trim and slice squash. Set aside.

Melt margarine in a large saucepan over medium-high heat. Add onion and sauté until translucent. Add squash, broth, salt and herbs. Reduce heat to medium. Cover and cook 10 minutes, or until squash is tender.

Place croutons in a plastic bag and crush with mallet or rolling pin. Add to squash mixture.

If mixture is too dry, add a small amount of hot water. Stir in chives and serve.

Nutrient Analysis

Calories	156 kcal	Cholesterol	1 mg	Saturated Fat	2 gm
Protein	4 gm	Sodium	301 mg	Polyunsaturated Fat	2 gm
Carbohydrate	18 gm	Total Fat	8 gm	Monounsaturated Fat	4 gm

*G*ingered *A*corn *S*quash

Serves 4

2 acorn squash (about ¾ pound each)
1 8-ounce can no-sugar-added pineapple tidbits, canned in
   natural juices, drained
2 tablespoons firmly packed brown sugar
1 tablespoon acceptable margarine, melted
3 tablespoons raisins
1 teaspoon grated fresh ginger

Preheat oven to 400° F.

Cut squash in half. Scoop out seeds and discard them. Set aside squash halves in a baking dish.

In a bowl, combine remaining ingredients. Spoon one quarter of mixture into each squash cavity. Add a small amount of water to bottom of baking dish. Cover and bake 45 minutes.

Nutrient Analysis

Calories	192 kcal	Cholesterol	0 mg	Saturated Fat	1 gm
Protein	2 gm	Sodium	41 mg	Polyunsaturated Fat	1 gm
Carbohydrate	41 gm	Total Fat	4 gm	Monounsaturated Fat	1 gm

*H*erbed *B*aked *T*omatoes

Serves 8

Vegetable oil spray
4 medium tomatoes
¼ teaspoon onion powder
⅛ teaspoon basil
⅛ teaspoon oregano
Freshly ground black pepper to taste
½ cup plain cracker crumbs (or ½ cup crumbs from
    crackers with unsalted tops—approximately 5
    crackers)
1 tablespoon acceptable margarine
Chopped parsley

*P*reheat oven to 350° F. Lightly spray a shallow baking dish with vegetable oil.

Cut tomatoes in half. Remove seeds and discard. Scoop out a small portion of pulp and place it in a small bowl.

Set tomatoes, cut side up, in prepared baking dish.

Mix pulp together with onion powder, basil, oregano and pepper. Stuff tomatoes with this mixture. Top with cracker crumbs, dot with margarine and sprinkle with chopped parsley. Bake 20 to 30 minutes, or until tomatoes are tender.

TOMATOES PROVENÇALE

In place of ingredients listed above, mix tomato pulp with 2 tablespoons acceptable margarine, melted; ¼ cup fresh, fine bread crumbs (½ slice bread); 2 cloves garlic, minced; 1 teaspoon chopped parsley; ⅛ teaspoon black pepper. Stuff tomatoes and bake for 30 minutes, or until tomatoes are tender.

Herb Baked Tomatoes Nutrient Analysis

Calories	50 kcal	Cholesterol	2 mg	Saturated Fat	1 gm
Protein	1 gm	Sodium	79 mg	Polyunsaturated Fat	1 gm
Carbohydrate	6 gm	Total Fat	3 gm	Monounsaturated Fat	1 gm

Tomatoes Provençale Nutrient Analysis

Calories	50 kcal	Cholesterol	0 mg	Saturated Fat	1 gm
Protein	1 gm	Sodium	64 mg	Polyunsaturated Fat	1 gm
Carbohydrate	5 gm	Total Fat	3 gm	Monounsaturated Fat	1 gm

*T*omatoes *R*ockefeller

Serves 6

Vegetable oil spray
3 large ripe tomatoes
2 tablespoons finely chopped onion
2 tablespoons finely chopped parsley
1 tablespoon acceptable margarine, melted
¾ cup chopped, cooked frozen no-salt-added spinach
    (drained)
Freshly ground black pepper to taste
Dash paprika
2 tablespoons fresh, plain bread crumbs

Preheat oven to 375° F. Lightly spray a shallow baking dish with vegetable oil.

Cut tomatoes in half. Remove seeds and discard. Place tomatoes, cut side up, in prepared dish.

In a small bowl, combine onion, parsley, margarine, spinach, pepper and paprika. Spread evenly over tomatoes. Top with crumbs and bake 15 minutes.

Nutrient Analysis

Calories	49 kcal	Cholesterol	0 mg	Saturated Fat		1 gm
Protein	2 gm	Sodium	69 mg	Polyunsaturated Fat		1 gm
Carbohydrate	7 gm	Total Fat	2 gm	Monounsaturated Fat		1 gm

*H*obo *V*egetables

Serves 4

4 large squares heavy-duty aluminum foil
Vegetable oil spray
4 carrots, peeled
4 onions, peeled
4 potatoes, scrubbed
4 tablespoons acceptable margarine
Freshly ground black pepper to taste

Lightly spray foil with vegetable oil.

Place 1 carrot, 1 potato and 1 onion on each square of prepared foil. Add 1 tablespoon margarine and a dash of pepper to each. Wrap snugly and seal.

Place over hot coals for 45 to 60 minutes, turning occasionally, until vegetables are done.

Nutrient Analysis

Calories	258 kcal	Cholesterol	0 mg	Saturated Fat	3 gm
Protein	4 gm	Sodium	190 mg	Polyunsaturated Fat	3 gm
Carbohydrate	36 gm	Total Fat	12 gm	Monounsaturated Fat	5 gm

*V*egetables with *L*emon *S*auce

Serves 8

1 pound broccoli
1 small head cauliflower
1 9-ounce package frozen artichoke hearts
2 tablespoons finely chopped onion
2 tablespoons acceptable margarine
¼ teaspoon paprika
3 tablespoons fresh lemon juice
1 pimiento, diced

Cut florets from broccoli and cauliflower and set aside. Cut stems into 1½-inch pieces. Steam florets, stems and artichoke hearts in a vegetable steamer until tender-crisp. Set aside.

In a skillet or saucepan over medium-high heat, sauté onion in margarine for 2 minutes. Remove from heat and stir in paprika and lemon juice. Set aside.

Arrange vegetables in groups on a hot serving platter. Drizzle lemon sauce over all. Sprinkle pimiento over artichoke hearts.

Nutrient Analysis

Calories	65 kcal	Cholesterol	0 mg	Saturated Fat	1 gm
Protein	3 gm	Sodium	76 mg	Polyunsaturated Fat	1 gm
Carbohydrate	8 gm	Total Fat	3 gm	Monounsaturated Fat	1 gm

*A*very *I*sland *C*elery

Serves 10

> 1 16-ounce can no-salt-added tomatoes
> ¼ cup acceptable margarine
> 1 medium onion, chopped
> ½ teaspoon hot pepper sauce
> ¼ teaspoon thyme
> 4 cups diagonally cut celery
> 1 10-ounce package frozen no-salt-added peas, thawed

*D*rain tomatoes, reserving liquid. Set aside.

Melt margarine in a large skillet over medium-high heat. Add onion and sauté until just tender but not brown. Add liquid from tomatoes, hot pepper sauce and thyme. Bring to a boil and stir in celery and peas. Cover and cook 10 minutes, or until barely tender.

Add tomatoes and heat thoroughly before serving.

Nutrient Analysis

Calories	78 kcal	Cholesterol	0 mg	Saturated Fat	1 gm
Protein	2 gm	Sodium	111 mg	Polyunsaturated Fat	1 gm
Carbohydrate	8 gm	Total Fat	5 gm	Monounsaturated Fat	2 gm

*T*riple *V*egetable *B*ake

Serves 6

> Vegetable oil spray
> 1 8-ounce package fresh mushrooms
> 2 pounds potatoes
> 4 tablespoons acceptable margarine
> 1 cup finely chopped onion
> 4 tablespoons flour
> 2½ cups skim milk, heated
> 2 tablespoons finely chopped fresh parsley
> ⅓ cup dry white wine
> ¼ teaspoon white pepper
> ½ teaspoon salt
> 8 ounces fresh broccoli florets

Preheat oven to 325° F. Lightly spray an 8-x-8-inch baking dish with vegetable oil.

Wipe mushrooms with a clean, damp cloth. Cut into quarters and set aside.

Peel potatoes and cut into cubes. Set aside.

Heat margarine in a nonstick skillet over medium heat. Add onion and mushrooms. Cover and cook 5 minutes. Uncover and cook 5 to 7 minutes to allow any mushroom juices to evaporate. Stir in flour and cook 1 minute. Whisk in milk, parsley, wine, pepper and ¼ teaspoon salt. Cook, stirring constantly, until thickened.

Arrange half of potatoes in prepared dish. Sprinkle with ⅛ teaspoon salt, then cover with half of sauce. Repeat with remainder of potatoes, salt and sauce. Bake uncovered 1½ hours.

Steam broccoli until tender-crisp and arrange in a border on top of potatoes before serving.

MICROWAVE METHOD

Melt margarine in microwave-safe bowl for 30 seconds on high. Add onion, cover with vented plastic wrap and cook 4 minutes on high. Add mushrooms and cover and cook 6 minutes on medium. Then uncover and cook 5 minutes on high to evaporate juices. Stir in flour and cook 1 minute on high. Add milk, parsley, wine, pepper and ¼ teaspoon salt. Cook 6 to 8 minutes on high. Proceed as directed above.

Nutrient Analysis

Calories	242 kcal	Cholesterol	2 mg	Saturated Fat	2 gm
Protein	8 gm	Sodium	338 mg	Polyunsaturated Fat	3 gm
Carbohydrate	36 gm	Total Fat	8 gm	Monounsaturated Fat	3 gm

*C*ouscous *with* *V*egetables

Serves 5; ½ cup per serving

1 tablespoon acceptable margarine

½ of 10-ounce package frozen no-salt-added peas, thawed
and drained

½ cup minced onion

½ cup thinly sliced fresh mushrooms

½ teaspoon crushed garlic, or ¼ teaspoon garlic powder

2 tablespoons dry white wine

½ teaspoon sweet basil

⅛ teaspoon black pepper

2 tablespoons minced parsley

½ cup uncooked couscous

*I*n a nonstick pan, melt margarine. Add peas, onion, mushrooms,
garlic and wine. Sauté 3 to 5 minutes, stirring often. Add spices and
blend well. Add parsley and stir well. Remove from heat and set
aside.

Prepare couscous according to package directions.

In a large bowl, toss vegetable mixture with cooked couscous.
Serve immediately.

MICROWAVE METHOD

In a microwave-safe casserole, combine peas, onions, mushrooms,
garlic, wine and spices. Stir. Cover and cook 2 minutes on high
power. Remove from oven, add parsley, couscous and ½ cup water
and the margarine. Stir to mix in couscous thoroughly. Cover and
cook 1 to 3 additional minutes on high power, or until liquid is
absorbed. Let stand 3 to 4 minutes. Fluff with a fork and serve immediately.

VARIATION

Use any quick-cooking vegetable in place of peas.

Nutrient Analysis

Calories	111 kcal	Cholesterol	0 mg	Saturated Fat	1 gm
Protein	3 gm	Sodium	120 mg	Polyunsaturated Fat	1 gm
Carbohydrate	18 gm	Total Fat	3 gm	Monounsaturated Fat	1 gm

C*antonese* V*egetables*

Serves 8

1½ teaspoons finely minced fresh ginger
½ teaspoon curry powder
1 teaspoon garlic powder
½ teaspoon salt
2 teaspoons cornstarch
2 tablespoons sherry
1 tablespoon light soy sauce
¼ teaspoon hot pepper oil, or ⅛ teaspoon cayenne pepper
½ cup homemade Beef Broth (see page 86) or commercial
    low-sodium variety
2 teaspoons hot pepper oil
2 cups sliced onion
4 stalks celery, diagonally sliced
1 green bell pepper, cut into thin strips
9 ounces frozen no-salt-added French-cut green beans
3 cups canned no-salt-added pinto beans, drained and
    rinsed
2 cups cherry tomatoes, cut into quarters
¼ cup minced fresh parsley
Freshly ground black pepper to taste

In a small bowl, blend ginger, curry powder, garlic powder and salt. Set aside. In a bigger bowl, combine cornstarch, sherry, soy sauce, ¼ teaspoon hot pepper oil or cayenne pepper, and beef broth. Set aside.

In a nonstick skillet or wok, heat 2 teaspoons hot pepper oil to 375° F. Add ginger mixture and stir. Add onion and celery next and stir-fry until tender-crisp. Add cornstarch mixture and stir until clear.

Next, add bell pepper, green beans and pinto beans to wok. Add cherry tomatoes and toss gently until heated; add parsley and black pepper. Serve immediately.

Nutrient Analysis

Calories	139 kcal	Cholesterol	0 mg	Saturated Fat	0 gm
Protein	8 gm	Sodium	240 mg	Polyunsaturated Fat	1 gm
Carbohydrate	25 gm	Total Fat	2 gm	Monounsaturated Fat	1 gm

*V*egetables à la *G*recque

Serves 8

½ cup olive oil
½ cup wine vinegar, *or* 2 tablespoons fresh lemon juice
  and 1 or 2 slices lemon
1 teaspoon crushed coriander seed
1 teaspoon thyme
1 bay leaf
1 clove garlic, crushed
Freshly ground black pepper to taste
2 cups water
4 cups assorted raw fresh vegetables, prepared for
  cooking *

Combine oil, vinegar or lemon juice and slices, seasonings and water in a large saucepan over medium-high heat. Bring to a boil and add vegetables. Reduce heat and simmer, uncovered, until tender-crisp. *Do not overcook.* Let vegetables cool in sauce. Serve at room temperature or cover and refrigerate to serve cold.

* Choose from the following, or substitute similar vegetables: asparagus, broccoli, brussels sprouts, cauliflower, carrots, eggplant, green beans, mushrooms or zucchini. Frozen vegetables such as artichoke hearts may also be used.

Nutrient Analysis*

Calories	139 kcal	Cholesterol	0 mg	Saturated Fat	2 gm
Protein	1 gm	Sodium	15 mg	Polyunsaturated Fat	1 gm
Carbohydrate	4 gm	Total Fat	14 gm	Monounsaturated Fat	10 gm

* *using mushrooms, carrots, cauliflower and asparagus*

*V*egetable *S*tir-*F*ry

Serves 8

1 pound fresh broccoli
1 tablespoon acceptable margarine
1 tablespoon peanut oil
1 pound carrots, peeled and thinly sliced
¾ pound mushrooms, thinly sliced
5 medium green onions, thinly sliced
1 tablespoon fresh lemon juice
2 tablespoons sherry
Freshly ground black pepper to taste
1 teaspoon nutmeg
1 teaspoon thyme

Rinse broccoli and trim. Separate florets so they are of smaller uniform size. Peel stems and cut into 2-inch lengths. Set aside.

In a large skillet or wok, heat margarine and oil over medium heat. Add broccoli, carrots, mushrooms and onions. Cook and stir 5 minutes, or until vegetables are tender-crisp.

Stir in lemon juice, sherry and other seasonings. Serve hot.

Nutrient Analysis

Calories	78 kcal	Cholesterol	0 mg	Saturated Fat	1 gm
Protein	3 gm	Sodium	63 mg	Polyunsaturated Fat	1 gm
Carbohydrate	11 gm	Total Fat	4 gm	Monounsaturated Fat	1 gm

*P*epper and *M*ushroom *S*tir-*F*ry

Serves 6

½ cup fresh basil leaves
1 8-ounce package fresh mushrooms
2 tablespoons olive oil
3 cloves garlic, minced
¼ teaspoon salt
1 red bell pepper, cut into strips
1 green bell pepper, cut into strips
1 yellow bell pepper, cut into strips
1½ teaspoons grated lemon rind
Freshly ground black pepper to taste

Rinse basil and drain thoroughly. Chop finely and set aside. Wipe mushrooms with a clean, damp cloth. Slice thinly and set aside.

Heat olive oil in a nonstick skillet or wok over medium heat. Add garlic and sauté 1 minute. Add mushrooms and salt. Cover and cook 5 minutes. Uncover and allow juices to evaporate. Stir in bell peppers and stir-fry until tender-crisp. Add lemon rind and cook 1 minute more. Stir in basil and black pepper.

Note: This is an excellent accompaniment for veal, beef or fish.

Nutrient Analysis

Calories	58 kcal	Cholesterol	0 mg	Saturated Fat	1 gm
Protein	1 gm	Sodium	91 mg	Polyunsaturated Fat	1 gm
Carbohydrate	4 gm	Total Fat	5 gm	Monounsaturated Fat	3 gm

*C*aponata

Serves 8; ½ cup per serving as a side dish
Serves 64; 1 tablespoon per serving as an appetizer

1 medium eggplant (about 1 pound), diced
¼ teaspoon salt
3 tablespoons olive oil
1 tablespoon peanut oil
3 cloves garlic, minced
2 medium onions, finely chopped
1 cup finely chopped celery
½ cup chopped green bell pepper
1 8-ounce can no-salt-added tomato sauce
3 tablespoons capers, rinsed
3 or 4 tablespoons red wine vinegar
¼ teaspoon mixed pepper, or freshly ground black pepper
   to taste
8 lettuce leaves

Place eggplant in a colander and sprinkle with salt. Let it rest 1 hour. Rinse well.

Sauté eggplant in olive oil in a skillet over medium-high heat until soft. Remove from heat. Drain on paper towels.

Pour peanut oil in the skillet and add garlic, onions, celery and bell pepper. Sauté until tender. Add tomato sauce and reduce heat. Simmer 8 to 10 minutes. Add eggplant, capers, vinegar and pepper. Simmer 8 to 10 minutes, stirring often to keep from sticking.

Cover and refrigerate overnight. Serve on crisp greens as a side dish.

As an appetizer, serve on melba toast.

Nutrient Analysis *

Calories	97 kcal	Cholesterol	0 mg	Saturated Fat	1 gm
Protein	1 gm	Sodium	101 mg	Polyunsaturated Fat	1 gm
Carbohydrate	9 gm	Total Fat	7 gm	Monounsaturated Fat	5 gm

* *as a side dish*

*R*atatouille

Serves 8

1 eggplant, peeled and diced
¼ teaspoon salt
1 tablespoon olive oil
2 tablespoons minced garlic
1 medium onion, finely chopped
1 red or green bell pepper, cut in thin strips
2 teaspoons dried oregano, crushed
½ teaspoon dried dill
1 to 2 tablespoons fennel seed
Freshly ground black pepper to taste
4 large tomatoes, peeled, seeded and chopped
2 medium zucchini, sliced
2 tablespoons minced fresh parsley
¼ cup fresh lemon juice

*P*lace eggplant in a colander and sprinkle with salt. Let rest 1 hour. Rinse well.

Heat oil in a large skillet over medium-high heat. Add garlic, onion and bell pepper. Sauté until tender-crisp. Add oregano, dill, fennel and pepper and stir to blend well. Reduce heat. Add tomatoes and simmer 4 to 5 minutes. Add eggplant and zucchini. Cover and cook 20 minutes. Add parsley and lemon juice and stir to mix well. Serve immediately for a hot side dish. Or cover, refrigerate and serve cold.

Note: This dish may be made a day in advance and served cold.

Nutrient Analysis

Calories	72 kcal	Cholesterol	0 mg	Saturated Fat	0 gm
Protein	2 gm	Sodium	83 mg	Polyunsaturated Fat	0 gm
Carbohydrate	13 gm	Total Fat	2 gm	Monounsaturated Fat	1 gm

*S*outhwestern *R*atatouille

Serves 8

1 eggplant, peeled and diced
¼ teaspoon salt
1 tablespoon olive oil
2 tablespoons minced garlic
1 medium onion, finely chopped
1 red or green bell pepper, cut in thin strips
2 teaspoons dried oregano, crushed
2 teaspoons chili powder
2 teaspoons ground cumin
¼ teaspoon crushed red pepper
3 sprigs fresh thyme, leaves removed and crushed, or
 ½ teaspoon dried thyme, crushed
4 large tomatoes, peeled, seeded and chopped
2 medium zucchini, sliced
2 tablespoons minced fresh parsley
1½ tablespoons freshly grated Parmesan cheese

Place eggplant in a colander and sprinkle with salt. Let rest 1 hour. Rinse well.

Heat oil in a large skillet over medium-high heat. Add garlic, onion and bell pepper. Sauté until tender-crisp. Add seasonings and stir to blend well. Reduce heat. Add tomatoes and simmer 4 to 5 minutes. Add eggplant and zucchini. Cover and cook 20 minutes. Add parsley and cheese and serve immediately for a hot side dish. Or cover, refrigerate overnight and serve cold.

Nutrient Analysis

Calories	78 kcal	Cholesterol	1 mg	Saturated Fat	1 gm
Protein	3 gm	Sodium	112 mg	Polyunsaturated Fat	0 gm
Carbohydrate	13 gm	Total Fat	3 gm	Monounsaturated Fat	1 gm

*C*olache

Serves 8; ¹/₂ cup per serving

2 tablespoons acceptable vegetable oil
1 pound unpeeled zucchini, sliced
1 small onion, sliced
½ cup diced green bell pepper
¼ cup water
⅔ cup diced fresh tomato
1½ cups frozen no-salt-added whole-kernel corn
⅛ teaspoon oregano
¼ teaspoon basil
¼ teaspoon marjoram
Freshly ground black pepper to taste

*H*eat oil in a heavy skillet over medium-high heat. Add zucchini, onion and bell pepper, and sauté until vegetables are limp. Add water, tomato, corn, oregano, basil and marjoram. Cover and cook 5 minutes, or until squash is tender, adding more water if necessary. Season with black pepper.

Nutrient Analysis

Calories	71 kcal	Cholesterol	0 mg	Saturated Fat	0 gm
Protein	2 gm	Sodium	4 mg	Polyunsaturated Fat	2 gm
Carbohydrate	10 gm	Total Fat	4 gm	Monounsaturated Fat	1 gm

Sauces

TANGY SOUR CREAM
YOGURT SAUCE
BASIC WHITE SAUCE I
BASIC WHITE SAUCE II
BASIC MAYONNAISE SAUCE
QUICK-AND-EASY MOCK HOLLANDAISE SAUCE
MOCK HOLLANDAISE SAUCE
RED PEPPER HOLLANDAISE
QUICK MADEIRA SAUCE
MOCK BÉARNAISE SAUCE
FRESH HERB SAUCE
LEMON PARSLEY SAUCE
MUSTARD SAUCE
SWEET AND SOUR SAUCE
HORSERADISH SAUCE
LEMON CHABLIS SAUCE
TOMATO SAUCE
BARBECUE SAUCE
SALSA CRUDA
CHICKEN GRAVY
BASIC GRAVY
FRESH FRUIT SAUCE
EASY JUBILEE SAUCE
WHIPPED DESSERT TOPPING
CHOCOLATE SAUCE
ORANGE SAUCE
CONFECTIONERS' GLAZE
HARD SAUCE

Sauces are like jewels. They're the finishing touch to any dish, and they add high drama to a meal. Although a sauce can't disguise poorly prepared food, it *can* take an ordinary dish and make it extraordinary.

As with jewelry, remember not to overdo it. If your main dish has a spectacular sauce, serve a simple vegetable as an accompaniment.

As a rule, sauces are not difficult to make. But some of the more celebrated sauces are high in saturated fat and cholesterol. We've taken two examples, béarnaise and hollandaise, and substituted acceptable oils and margarines for the traditional egg yolks and butter. We think you'll find them every bit as flavorful yet with none of the health risks of the traditional versions.

On the following pages, you'll find a couple of tasty basic white sauces, several wine and herb sauces, meat sauces, a few sauces for ethnic foods—and enough fruit and dessert sauces to delight any sweet tooth!

*T*angy *S*our *C*ream

Makes approximately 1²/₃ cups
Serves 28; 1 tablespoon per serving

1 1-pound container low-fat cottage cheese
2 tablespoons fresh lemon juice

Place ingredients in blender or work bowl of a food processor fitted with a metal blade. Process until completely smooth. Cover and refrigerate until ready to use. Mixture may be thinned with skim milk if desired.

For each variation, add the listed ingredients to 1 cup Tangy Sour Cream.

TANGY SOUR CREAM WITH BLUE CHEESE
Serves 20; 1 tablespoon per serving

3 tablespoons crumbled blue cheese
1 tablespoon minced green onion
¼ teaspoon Worcestershire sauce

TANGY SOUR CREAM WITH DILL
Serves 16; 1 tablespoon per serving

1 tablespoon finely chopped fresh dill
1 tablespoon minced green onion
½ teaspoon freshly ground black pepper

TANGY SOUR CREAM WITH GARLIC
Serves 16; 1 tablespoon per serving

1 tablespoon minced onion
¼ teaspoon garlic powder
1 tablespoon finely chopped parsley
Dash hot pepper sauce

Tangy Sour Cream Nutrient Analysis

Calories	15 kcal	Cholesterol	1 mg	Saturated Fat	0 gm
Protein	2 gm	Sodium	66 mg	Polyunsaturated Fat	0 gm
Carbohydrate	1 gm	Total Fat	0 gm	Monounsaturated Fat	0 gm

Tangy Sour Cream with Blue Cheese Nutrient Analysis

Calories	17 kcal	Cholesterol	2 mg	Saturated Fat		0 gm
Protein	2 gm	Sodium	74 mg	Polyunsaturated Fat		0 gm
Carbohydrate	1 gm	Total Fat	1 gm	Monounsaturated Fat		0 gm

Tangy Sour Cream with Dill Nutrient Analysis

Calories	16 kcal	Cholesterol	1 mg	Saturated Fat		0 gm
Protein	2 gm	Sodium	69 mg	Polyunsaturated Fat		0 gm
Carbohydrate	1 gm	Total Fat	0 gm	Monounsaturated Fat		0 gm

Tangy Sour Cream with Garlic Nutrient Analysis

Calories	16 kcal	Cholesterol	1 mg	Saturated Fat		0 gm
Protein	2 gm	Sodium	69 mg	Polyunsaturated Fat		0 gm
Carbohydrate	1 gm	Total Fat	0 gm	Monounsaturated Fat		0 gm

*Y*ogurt *S*auce

Makes 1 cup
Serves 16; 1 tablespoon per serving

> **2 tablespoons acceptable margarine**
> **2 tablespoons flour**
> **½ cup homemade Chicken Broth (see page 87) or commercial low-sodium variety**
> **¼ cup white wine**
> **¾ cup plain nonfat yogurt**
> **2 teaspoons grated lemon rind**
> **½ teaspoon freshly ground black pepper, or to taste**

Place margarine in a saucepan over medium-high heat. Add flour slowly to make a roux. Stir vigorously until mixture is lightly browned. Add broth, stirring constantly, until mixture is thick and smooth. Add wine, yogurt, lemon rind and pepper, stirring until blended.

Nutrient Analysis

Calories	24 kcal	Cholesterol	0 mg	Saturated Fat		0 gm
Protein	1 gm	Sodium	28 mg	Polyunsaturated Fat		0 gm
Carbohydrate	2 gm	Total Fat	1 gm	Monounsaturated Fat		1 gm

Basic White Sauce I

Makes 1 cup
Serves 16; 1 tablespoon per serving

> 1 tablespoon acceptable margarine
> 1 tablespoon flour
> ¼ teaspoon salt
> Dash freshly ground black pepper, or to taste
> 1 cup skim milk

Melt margarine in a saucepan over low heat. Blend in the flour slowly to make a roux. Cook over low heat, stirring constantly, until mixture is smooth and begins to bubble.

Stir in salt, pepper and milk. Heat to boiling and cook 1 minute, stirring constantly.

MEDIUM-THICK WHITE SAUCE
Increase margarine and flour to 2 tablespoons each.

THICK WHITE SAUCE
Increase margarine and flour to 4 tablespoons each.

Basic White Sauce I Nutrient Analysis

Calories	13 kcal	Cholesterol	0 mg	Saturated Fat	0 gm
Protein	1 gm	Sodium	50 mg	Polyunsaturated Fat	0 gm
Carbohydrate	1 gm	Total Fat	1 gm	Monounsaturated Fat	0 gm

Medium-Thick White Sauce Nutrient Analysis

Calories	21 kcal	Cholesterol	0 mg	Saturated Fat	0 gm
Protein	1 gm	Sodium	58 mg	Polyunsaturated Fat	0 gm
Carbohydrate	1 gm	Total Fat	1 gm	Monounsaturated Fat	1 gm

Thick White Sauce Nutrient Analysis

Calories	37 kcal	Cholesterol	0 mg	Saturated Fat	1 gm
Protein	1 gm	Sodium	75 mg	Polyunsaturated Fat	1 gm
Carbohydrate	2 gm	Total Fat	3 gm	Monounsaturated Fat	1 gm

Basic White Sauce II

Makes 1 cup
Serves 16; 1 tablespoon per serving

> 2 tablespoons acceptable margarine
> 2 tablespoons flour
> ¼ teaspoon salt
> Dash freshly ground black pepper, or to taste
> 4 tablespoons nonfat dry milk
> 1 cup water

Melt margarine in a saucepan over low heat. Blend in the flour to make a roux.

Cook over low heat, stirring constantly, until mixture is thick and smooth. Add salt, pepper, dry milk and water. Heat to boiling and cook 1 minute, stirring constantly.

VARIATIONS

This recipe can also be made with 1 cup skim milk or evaporated skim milk in place of the nonfat dry milk and the water. For a different flavor, add curry, dill or nutmeg with the flour.

Nutrient Analysis

Calories	20 kcal	Cholesterol	0 mg	Saturated Fat	0 gm
Protein	0 gm	Sodium	56 mg	Polyunsaturated Fat	0 gm
Carbohydrate	1 gm	Total Fat	1 gm	Monounsaturated Fat	1 gm

Basic Mayonnaise Sauce

Makes 1 cup
Serves 16; 1 tablespoon per serving

½ cup light, reduced-calorie mayonnaise
½ cup plain nonfat yogurt

Place ingredients in a medium bowl and whisk until thoroughly blended. Cover and refrigerate.

For each variation, add the listed ingredients to 1 cup Basic Mayonnaise Sauce.

TARTAR SAUCE
Serves 20; 1 tablespoon per serving

¼ cup drained pickle relish
1 tablespoon minced onion
1 tablespoon finely chopped parsley

SEAFOOD SAUCE
Serves 24; 1 tablespoon per serving

¼ cup chili sauce
¼ cup pressed-dry prepared horseradish
1 tablespoon chopped fresh parsley

MUSTARD AND GREEN ONION SAUCE
Serves 20; 1 tablespoon per serving

2 tablespoons Dijon mustard
3 tablespoons minced green onion
⅛ teaspoon garlic powder

FINE HERB SAUCE
Serves 16; 1 tablespoon per serving

1 tablespoon finely chopped fresh dill
1 tablespoon finely chopped parsley

Basic Mayonnaise Sauce Nutrient Analysis

Calories	26 kcal	Cholesterol	2 mg	Saturated Fat	0 gm
Protein	1 gm	Sodium	50 mg	Polyunsaturated Fat	1 gm
Carbohydrate	1 gm	Total Fat	2 gm	Monounsaturated Fat	1 gm

Tartar Sauce Nutrient Analysis

Calories	25 kcal	Cholesterol	2 mg	Saturated Fat	0 gm
Protein	0 gm	Sodium	61 mg	Polyunsaturated Fat	1 gm
Carbohydrate	2 gm	Total Fat	2 gm	Monounsaturated Fat	1 gm

Seafood Sauce Nutrient Analysis

Calories	22 kcal	Cholesterol	2 mg	Saturated Fat	0 gm
Protein	0 gm	Sodium	65 mg	Polyunsaturated Fat	1 gm
Carbohydrate	2 gm	Total Fat	1 gm	Monounsaturated Fat	1 gm

Mustard and Green Onion Sauce Nutrient Analysis

Calories	22 kcal	Cholesterol	2 mg	Saturated Fat	0 gm
Protein	1 gm	Sodium	59 mg	Polyunsaturated Fat	1 gm
Carbohydrate	1 gm	Total Fat	2 gm	Monounsaturated Fat	1 gm

Fine Herb Sauce Nutrient Analysis

Calories	27 kcal	Cholesterol	2 mg	Saturated Fat	0 gm
Protein	1 gm	Sodium	50 mg	Polyunsaturated Fat	1 gm
Carbohydrate	1 gm	Total Fat	2 gm	Monounsaturated Fat	1 gm

Quick-and-Easy Mock Hollandaise Sauce

Makes ½ cup
Serves 8; 1 tablespoon per serving

> 2 tablespoons hot water
> ½ cup light, reduced-calorie mayonnaise
> 1 tablespoon fresh lemon juice

In the top of a double boiler over medium heat, blend hot water with mayonnaise, stirring until thoroughly heated. Add lemon juice and stir to mix well.

This sauce may be served with broccoli, asparagus, cauliflower or other vegetables.

Nutrient Analysis

Calories	44 kcal	Cholesterol	4 mg	Saturated Fat	1 gm
Protein	0 gm	Sodium	88 mg	Polyunsaturated Fat	2 gm
Carbohydrate	2 gm	Total Fat	4 gm	Monounsaturated Fat	2 gm

Mock Hollandaise Sauce

Makes 1 cup
Serves 16; 1 tablespoon per serving

> 1 tablespoon acceptable vegetable oil
> 1 tablespoon cornstarch
> ¾ cup homemade Chicken Broth (see page 87) or
>   commercial low-sodium variety
> 1 egg yolk, lightly beaten
> 1 to 2 tablespoons fresh lemon juice

Combine oil and cornstarch in a small saucepan. Stir well. Cook over low heat, stirring constantly, until mixture is smooth. Add broth and turn up heat to medium. Cook, stirring constantly, until mixture thickens.

Remove from heat and add a small amount of the sauce to beaten egg yolk. Stir to mix well and slowly pour egg mixture into sauce.

Cook over low heat, stirring constantly, for 1 minute. Remove from heat and add lemon juice. Stir to mix well.

Nutrient Analysis

Calories	15 kcal	Cholesterol	17 mg	Saturated Fat		0 gm
Protein	0 gm	Sodium	3 mg	Polyunsaturated Fat		1 gm
Carbohydrate	1 gm	Total Fat	1 gm	Monounsaturated Fat		0 gm

Red Pepper Hollandaise

Makes 1½ cups
Serves 24; 1 tablespoon per serving

> Egg substitute equivalent to 2 eggs
> 1 large red bell pepper
> ½ cup acceptable margarine, melted
> 3 tablespoons fresh lemon juice
> 1 teaspoon chili powder
> ¹⁄₁₆ teaspoon cayenne pepper

Preheat broiler.

Warm egg substitute in a microwave on low, or place carton in 1 inch of warm water.

Broil bell pepper on broiler pan, turning until pepper is charred all over. Then put it in a plastic bag, close the bag and set aside for 5 minutes. Rinse pepper under warm water, removing skin, core, seeds and stem. Blot bell pepper dry with paper towels and set aside.

Process warm egg substitute in a blender or the work bowl of a food processor fitted with a metal blade on low speed while adding margarine in a thin stream. Add bell pepper. Process on high 10 seconds. Add remaining ingredients and process 10 seconds more.

This sauce is excellent on cauliflower, asparagus, broccoli, fish or chicken.

VARIATION

Chopped fresh herbs may be added for additional color when serving with fish or chicken.

Nutrient Analysis

Calories	38 kcal	Cholesterol	0 mg	Saturated Fat		1 gm
Protein	1 gm	Sodium	56 mg	Polyunsaturated Fat		1 gm
Carbohydrate	0 gm	Total Fat	4 gm	Monounsaturated Fat		2 gm

*Q*uick *M*adeira *S*auce

Makes 1 cup
Serves 16; 1 tablespoon per serving

> 1¼ cups homemade Chicken Broth (see page 87) or
>   commercial low-sodium variety
> ⅓ cup plus 1 tablespoon Madeira or port wine
> 2 teaspoons cornstarch

Combine broth and ⅓ cup of wine in a saucepan. Bring to a boil over medium heat and reduce rapidly to 1 cup.

In a small bowl, mix cornstarch with remaining tablespoon of wine. Stir mixture into sauce. Cook over medium heat, stirring constantly, until thickened.

Serve with pheasant or other game.

Nutrient Analysis

Calories	4 kcal	Cholesterol	0 mg	Saturated Fat		0 gm
Protein	0 gm	Sodium	5 mg	Polyunsaturated Fat		0 gm
Carbohydrate	1 gm	Total Fat	0 gm	Monounsaturated Fat		0 gm

Mock Béarnaise Sauce

Makes 1 cup
Serves 16; 1 tablespoon per serving

¼ cup wine vinegar
¼ cup dry white wine or dry vermouth
1 tablespoon minced shallots or green onions
1 tablespoon minced fresh tarragon or ½ tablespoon dry
    tarragon
⅛ teaspoon white pepper
1 tablespoon cornstarch
1 tablespoon acceptable vegetable oil
¾ cup homemade Chicken Broth (see page 87) or
    commercial low-sodium variety
1 egg yolk, lightly beaten

Place vinegar, wine, onions, tarragon and pepper in a small sauce-pan over medium heat. Bring to a boil, stirring constantly. Reduce heat to medium-low and continue cooking until liquid is reduced to about 2 tablespoons. Set aside.

Combine oil and cornstarch in a small saucepan. Stir to mix well. Place over low heat and cook, stirring constantly, until mixture is smooth. Add broth and increase heat setting to medium. Cook, stirring constantly, until mixture thickens.

Remove from heat and add a small amount of the sauce to beaten egg yolk. Stir to mix well and pour egg mixture slowly into sauce.

Cook over low heat, stirring constantly, for 1 minute. Remove from heat and add vinegar mixture. Stir well.

Serve over steamed fish or vegetables if desired.

Nutrient Analysis

Calories	16 kcal	Cholesterol	17 mg	Saturated Fat	0 gm
Protein	0 gm	Sodium	3 mg	Polyunsaturated Fat	1 gm
Carbohydrate	1 gm	Total Fat	1 gm	Monounsaturated Fat	0 gm

Fresh Herb Sauce

Makes 2 cups
Serves 16; 2 tablespoons per serving

½ cup low-fat cottage cheese
1½ cups skim milk
2 tablespoons acceptable margarine
3 tablespoons flour
1 tablespoon finely chopped fresh dill
1 tablespoon finely chopped fresh basil
1 tablespoon snipped fresh chives
1 tablespoon finely chopped fresh parsley
Dash white pepper

Combine cottage cheese and milk in a blender or the work bowl of a food processor fitted with a metal blade. Process until smooth and set aside.

Melt margarine in a saucepan over medium heat. Stir in flour and cook 1 minute. Add milk and cottage cheese mixture. Bring to a boil, stirring constantly. Cook until thickened. Remove from heat; add herbs and pepper. Stir well.

MICROWAVE METHOD

Process milk and cottage cheese as directed and set aside. Melt margarine on high for 45 seconds in a 4-cup microwave-safe bowl. Stir in flour and cook on high for 30 seconds. Whisk in milk and cottage cheese mixture. Cook on high 5 to 6 minutes, or until thickened. Stir in remaining ingredients.

Nutrient Analysis

Calories	32 kcal	Cholesterol	1 mg	Saturated Fat	0 gm
Protein	2 gm	Sodium	57 mg	Polyunsaturated Fat	0 gm
Carbohydrate	2 gm	Total Fat	2 gm	Monounsaturated Fat	1 gm

*L*emon *P*arsley *S*auce

Makes ¾ cup
Serves 12; 1 tablespoon per serving

> ½ cup acceptable margarine
> Juice of 1 large lemon (about 3 tablespoons)
> 1 teaspoon grated lemon rind
> 1 tablespoon chopped parsley

*I*n a small saucepan over medium-high heat, heat margarine and lemon juice. Add grated lemon rind and parsley. Stir well.

This sauce is delicious over fish.

Nutrient Analysis

Calories	69 kcal	Cholesterol	0 mg	Saturated Fat	2 gm
Protein	0 gm	Sodium	90 mg	Polyunsaturated Fat	2 gm
Carbohydrate	0 gm	Total Fat	8 gm	Monounsaturated Fat	3 gm

*M*ustard *S*auce

Makes 1 cup
Serves 16; 1 tablespoon per serving

> 1 tablespoon acceptable margarine
> 1 tablespoon flour
> 1 cup skim milk
> 1 tablespoon Dijon mustard
> Freshly ground black pepper to taste

*M*elt margarine in a small saucepan over medium heat. Add flour and stir to make a roux. Add milk gradually, stirring constantly, until sauce is thick and smooth. Stir in mustard and pepper. Serve warm.

Nutrient Analysis

Calories	14 kcal	Cholesterol	0 mg	Saturated Fat	0 gm
Protein	1 gm	Sodium	28 mg	Polyunsaturated Fat	0 gm
Carbohydrate	1 gm	Total Fat	1 gm	Monounsaturated Fat	0 gm

Sweet and Sour Sauce

Makes 3 cups
Serves 48; 1 tablespoon per serving

1 tablespoon acceptable vegetable oil
¼ cup diced green bell pepper
¼ cup diced red bell pepper
¼ cup finely chopped onion
1¼ cups water
2 tablespoons cornstarch
2 tablespoons firmly packed brown sugar
⅔ cup unsweetened pineapple juice
1 6-ounce can no-salt-added tomato paste
½ cup no-sugar-added pineapple tidbits, canned in natural
    juices
¼ teaspoon salt
Dash hot pepper sauce

Heat oil in a small nonstick skillet over medium-high heat. Add green and red bell peppers and onion and sauté until onion is translucent. Set aside.

Combine water, cornstarch, brown sugar and pineapple juice in a saucepan. Bring to a boil over medium-high heat. Whisk in tomato paste. Add pineapple, sautéed vegetables, salt and hot pepper sauce. Stir to mix well. Cook until thoroughly heated.

MICROWAVE METHOD

In a deep casserole, combine oil, green and red bell peppers and onion. Microwave on high for 5 minutes.

In a small bowl, combine water, cornstarch, sugar and pineapple juice; add to casserole and cook mixture on high for 5 to 6 minutes, stirring twice. Whisk in tomato paste; add pineapple, salt and hot pepper sauce.

Nutrient Analysis

Calories	13 kcal	Cholesterol	0 mg	Saturated Fat	0 gm
Protein	0 gm	Sodium	14 mg	Polyunsaturated Fat	0 gm
Carbohydrate	3 gm	Total Fat	0 gm	Monounsaturated Fat	0 gm

*H*orseradish *S*auce

Makes 1¼ cups
Serves 20; 1 tablespoon per serving

1 tablespoon acceptable margarine
4 teaspoons flour
2 tablespoons horseradish, drained
1 cup fish stock or clam juice

*I*n a small saucepan over medium-high heat, melt margarine and blend in flour, stirring constantly. Add horseradish and fish stock or clam juice. Continue stirring, and cook until thickened.

Serve over Poached Fish (see page 193).

Nutrient Analysis

Calories	9 kcal	Cholesterol	0 mg	Saturated Fat	0 gm
Protein	0 gm	Sodium	47 mg	Polyunsaturated Fat	0 gm
Carbohydrate	1 gm	Total Fat	1 gm	Monounsaturated Fat	0 gm

*L*emon *C*hablis *S*auce

Makes 1¼ cups
Serves 20; 1 tablespoon per serving

1 lemon
1 tablespoon cornstarch
1 cup Chablis or other dry white wine
1½ tablespoons acceptable margarine

*C*ut lemon in half and thinly slice one of the halves. Set aside. Squeeze juice from the other half and grate the rind. Set aside.

In a small bowl, combine cornstarch and wine. Stir with a wire whisk until smooth. Set aside.

Melt margarine in a small saucepan over medium heat. Add wine mixture and cook, stirring constantly, until sauce is clear and slightly thickened.

Add grated lemon rind, juice and slices. Heat a few minutes longer.

Serve this sauce with baked, broiled or poached fish.

Nutrient Analysis

Calories	12 kcal	Cholesterol	0 mg	Saturated Fat	0 gm
Protein	0 gm	Sodium	11 mg	Polyunsaturated Fat	0 gm
Carbohydrate	1 gm	Total Fat	1 gm	Monounsaturated Fat	0 gm

*T*omato *S*auce

Makes approximately 1 quart
Serves 64; 1 tablespoon per serving

1 cup diced onion
2 cloves garlic, minced
1 28-ounce can Italian plum tomatoes
3 tablespoons no-salt-added tomato paste
½ teaspoon freshly ground black pepper, or to taste
½ teaspoon oregano
½ teaspoon basil

Combine all ingredients in a heavy saucepan over medium-high heat. Bring to a boil, reduce heat and simmer about 20 minutes.

Serve over stuffed bell peppers, meatloaf or stuffed cabbage.

TOMATO SAUCE WITH GREEN BELL PEPPERS

Add 1 green bell pepper, diced, and ½ cup of sliced fresh mushrooms, and cook as directed.

Tomato Sauce Nutrient Analysis

Calories	4 kcal	Cholesterol	0 mg	Saturated Fat	0 gm
Protein	0 gm	Sodium	21 mg	Polyunsaturated Fat	0 gm
Carbohydrate	1 gm	Total Fat	0 gm	Monounsaturated Fat	0 gm

Tomato Sauce with Green Bell Peppers Nutrient Analysis

Calories	4 kcal	Cholesterol	0 mg	Saturated Fat	0 gm
Protein	0 gm	Sodium	21 mg	Polyunsaturated Fat	0 gm
Carbohydrate	1 gm	Total Fat	0 gm	Monounsaturated Fat	0 gm

*B*arbecue *S*auce

Makes approximately 1⅓ cups
Serves 22; 1 tablespoon per serving

2 tablespoons acceptable vegetable oil
1 cup finely chopped onion
3 cloves garlic, minced
1 cup ketchup
½ cup water
1 tablespoon firmly packed brown sugar
1 tablespoon Worcestershire sauce
1 teaspoon dry mustard
¼ cup dry white wine
¼ teaspoon liquid smoke seasoning
1 bay leaf, crumbled
Dash hot pepper sauce

*H*eat oil in a large saucepan over medium-high heat. Add onion and cook until translucent; stir in garlic and cook 1 minute more. Add remaining ingredients, reduce heat and simmer 15 to 20 minutes.

Nutrient Analysis

Calories	30 kcal	Cholesterol	0 mg	Saturated Fat	0 gm
Protein	0 gm	Sodium	138 mg	Polyunsaturated Fat	1 gm
Carbohydrate	4 gm	Total Fat	1 gm	Monounsaturated Fat	0 gm

*S*alsa *C*ruda

Makes ¾ cup
Serves 12; 1 tablespoon per serving

1 large ripe tomato, cored, peeled, seeded and diced
2 tablespoons finely chopped onion
1 teaspoon fresh jalapeño pepper (approximately ½ small seeded pepper) *
1 to 2 teaspoons fresh lime juice
⅛ teaspoon salt
1 teaspoon finely chopped fresh cilantro

Combine all ingredients in a medium bowl. Mix well. Cover and refrigerate.

This sauce may serve as a dip for tortilla chips. (For a large group, simply double or triple quantities listed.) It also works as a topping for Mexican dishes such as Beef Tostadas (see page 289).

Wear rubber gloves when handling hot peppers, or wash hands thoroughly after handling. Skin, especially around the eyes, is very sensitive to oil from peppers.

Nutrient Analysis

Calories	4 kcal	Cholesterol	0 mg	Saturated Fat	0 gm
Protein	0 gm	Sodium	27 mg	Polyunsaturated Fat	0 gm
Carbohydrate	1 gm	Total Fat	0 gm	Monounsaturated Fat	0 gm

Chicken Gravy

Makes 1 cup
Serves 16; 1 tablespoon per serving

> 1 cup homemade Chicken Broth (see page 87), low-sodium chicken broth or defatted chicken essence from the roasting pan
> 2 tablespoons flour
> ¼ cup skim milk
> ½ teaspoon freshly ground black pepper, or to taste

Warm chicken broth or defatted chicken essence in a saucepan over medium heat.

Place flour and milk in a small bowl and whisk until smooth or place in a jar with a tight-fitting lid and shake until smooth.

Gradually stir milk mixture into chicken broth or essence.

Cook over medium heat, stirring constantly, until thick. Add pepper, reduce heat and continue to cook, stirring, 5 minutes longer.

Nutrient Analysis

Calories	6 kcal	Cholesterol	0 mg	Saturated Fat	0 gm
Protein	0 gm	Sodium	6 mg	Polyunsaturated Fat	0 gm
Carbohydrate	1 gm	Total Fat	0 gm	Monounsaturated Fat	0 gm

*B*asic *G*ravy

Makes 1 cup
Serves 16; 1 tablespoon per serving

> 2 tablespoons flour
> 1 cup liquid (meat drippings, low-sodium bouillon, low-sodium broth, homemade Chicken Broth, homemade Beef Broth [see pages 87 and 86] or a combination of any of the above)

Spread flour in a shallow pan and cook over very low heat, stirring occasionally, until lightly colored.

Put half of the liquid in a jar with a tight-fitting lid and add flour. Cover tightly and shake until mixture is smooth.

Pour mixture into a small saucepan and add remaining liquid. Bring to a simmer over medium heat. Cook for a few minutes, stirring constantly.

Add gravy coloring, if desired.

Note: This recipe may be doubled or tripled.

THICK GRAVY
Increase flour to 4 tablespoons and proceed as directed.

MUSHROOM GRAVY
Add ¼ cup of sliced fresh mushrooms to cooked gravy.

*Basic Gravy Nutrient Analysis**
Calories	5 kcal	Cholesterol	0 mg	Saturated Fat		0 gm
Protein	0 gm	Sodium	4 mg	Polyunsaturated Fat		0 gm
Carbohydrate	1 gm	Total Fat	0 gm	Monounsaturated Fat		0 gm

* *using low-sodium broth*

*Thick Gravy Nutrient Analysis**
Calories	8 kcal	Cholesterol	0 mg	Saturated Fat		0 gm
Protein	0 gm	Sodium	4 mg	Polyunsaturated Fat		0 gm
Carbohydrate	1 gm	Total Fat	0 gm	Monounsaturated Fat		0 gm

* *using low-sodium broth*

*Mushroom Gravy Nutrient Analysis**
Calories	5 kcal	Cholesterol	0 mg	Saturated Fat		0 gm
Protein	0 gm	Sodium	4 mg	Polyunsaturated Fat		0 gm
Carbohydrate	1 gm	Total Fat	0 gm	Monounsaturated Fat		0 gm

* *using low-sodium broth*

Fresh Fruit Sauce

Makes 2½ cups
Serves 40; 1 tablespoon per serving

> 2 cups fresh fruit (strawberries, raspberries, peaches or
> other fruits used individually or in combination)
> 2 tablespoons cornstarch
> ½ cup sugar
> ½ cup water

If large fruits are used, cut them into large pieces and set aside.

Bring cornstarch, sugar and water to a boil in a saucepan over medium-high heat. Add 1 cup of fresh fruit. Bring to a boil again, then remove immediately from heat and add remaining cup of fruit. Do not cook further. Last addition of fruit should remain uncooked.

Spoon this sauce over ice milk or cake.

Nutrient Analysis*

Calories	14 kcal	Cholesterol	0 mg	Saturated Fat		0 gm
Protein	0 gm	Sodium	0 mg	Polyunsaturated Fat		0 gm
Carbohydrate	4 gm	Total Fat	0 gm	Monounsaturated Fat		0 gm

* using strawberries, raspberries and peaches

Easy Jubilee Sauce

Makes 1⅔ cups
Serves 26; 1 tablespoon per serving

> 1 16-ounce jar dark cherry preserves
> ¼ cup port wine
> ½ teaspoon almond extract

Mix all ingredients well in a bowl. Serve immediately, or cover and refrigerate.

Serve this sauce over ice milk.

Nutrient Analysis

Calories	51 kcal	Cholesterol	0 mg	Saturated Fat		0 gm
Protein	0 gm	Sodium	3 mg	Polyunsaturated Fat		0 gm
Carbohydrate	13 gm	Total Fat	0 gm	Monounsaturated Fat		0 gm

Whipped Dessert Topping

Makes 2 cups
Serves 32; 1 tablespoon per serving

1 teaspoon unflavored gelatin
2 teaspoons cold water
3 tablespoons boiling water
½ cup ice water
½ cup nonfat dry milk
3 tablespoons sugar
3 tablespoons acceptable vegetable oil

Thoroughly chill a small mixing bowl in the refrigerator.

In another small bowl, soften gelatin with 2 teaspoons of cold water, then add boiling water, stirring, until gelatin is completely dissolved. Set aside and cool until tepid.

In a chilled mixing bowl, beat ice water and nonfat dry milk at high speed until mixture forms stiff peaks. Add sugar, still beating, then oil and gelatin. Cover and freeze for about 15 minutes, then transfer to refrigerator until ready for use. Stir before using to retain a creamy texture.

Nutrient Analysis

Calories	20 kcal	Cholesterol	0 mg	Saturated Fat	0 gm
Protein	0 gm	Sodium	6 mg	Polyunsaturated Fat	1 gm
Carbohydrate	2 gm	Total Fat	1 gm	Monounsaturated Fat	0 gm

Chocolate Sauce

Makes 1 cup
Serves 16; 1 tablespoon per serving

2 tablespoons acceptable margarine
2 tablespoons cocoa
½ cup sugar
2 tablespoons white corn syrup
¼ cup evaporated skim milk
1 teaspoon vanilla

Melt margarine in a saucepan over medium-high heat. Add cocoa, sugar and syrup and stir to mix well. Add milk, bring to a boil and stir until smooth. Remove from heat and stir in vanilla.

Serve warm or cold over ice milk.

Nutrient Analysis

Calories	49 kcal	Cholesterol	0 mg	Saturated Fat	0 gm
Protein	0 gm	Sodium	23 mg	Polyunsaturated Fat	0 gm
Carbohydrate	9 gm	Total Fat	2 gm	Monounsaturated Fat	1 gm

*O*range *S*auce

Makes 1 cup
Serves 16; 1 tablespoon per serving

> **2 cups orange juice**
> **1 tablespoon cornstarch**
> **1 tablespoon water**
> **1 tablespoon sugar**
> **½ teaspoon grated orange rind**
> **1 tablespoon fresh lemon juice**
> **2 teaspoons acceptable margarine**

In a small saucepan over medium heat, cook orange juice, uncovered, until reduced to 1 cup.

Mix cornstarch and water in a small bowl. Add some of the hot juice, mix well and pour entire mixture into pan. Add sugar and cook 1 to 2 minutes, or until thick. Remove from heat and stir in rind, lemon juice and margarine.

Serve over Gingerbread, Delicious Rice Pudding, Easy Apple Cake (see pages 472, 540 and 546) or angel food cake.

MICROWAVE METHOD
Proceed as directed above using a microwave-safe bowl. Use same cooking times and settings.

Nutrient Analysis

Calories	24 kcal	Cholesterol	0 mg	Saturated Fat	0 gm
Protein	0 gm	Sodium	6 mg	Polyunsaturated Fat	0 gm
Carbohydrate	5 gm	Total Fat	1 gm	Monounsaturated Fat	0 gm

Confectioners' Glaze

Makes approximately 1 cup
Serves 16; 1 tablespoon per serving

> 1 cup confectioners' sugar
> ½ teaspoon vanilla or rum extract
> ¼ cup skim milk

*I*n a small bowl, stir confectioners' sugar and extract into milk until mixture is thick enough to spread.

LEMON OR ORANGE CONFECTIONERS' GLAZE
Use lemon or orange juice in place of milk.

CHOCOLATE CONFECTIONERS' GLAZE
Add 2 tablespoons of cocoa to sugar and proceed as directed.

Confectioners' Glaze Nutrient Analysis

Calories	32 kcal	Cholesterol	0 mg	Saturated Fat		0 gm
Protein	0 gm	Sodium	2 mg	Polyunsaturated Fat		0 gm
Carbohydrate	8 gm	Total Fat	0 gm	Monounsaturated Fat		0 gm

Lemon or Orange Confectioners' Glaze Nutrient Analysis

Calories	32 kcal	Cholesterol	0 mg	Saturated Fat		0 gm
Protein	0 gm	Sodium	1 mg	Polyunsaturated Fat		0 gm
Carbohydrate	8 gm	Total Fat	0 gm	Monounsaturated Fat		0 gm

Chocolate Confectioners' Glaze Nutrient Analysis

Calories	35 kcal	Cholesterol	0 mg	Saturated Fat		0 gm
Protein	0 gm	Sodium	2 mg	Polyunsaturated Fat		0 gm
Carbohydrate	9 gm	Total Fat	0 gm	Monounsaturated Fat		0 gm

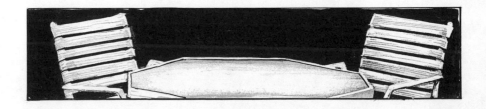

*H*ard *S*auce

Makes 1½ cups
Serves 24; 1 tablespoon per serving

½ cup acceptable margarine
2 cups sifted confectioners' sugar
1 tablespoon sherry, brandy or fruit juice

Cream margarine and sugar in a mixing bowl until fluffy. Beat in the liquid. Store in a covered container in refrigerator and use as needed.

Nutrient Analysis*

Calories	76 kcal	Cholesterol	0 mg	Saturated Fat	1 gm
Protein	0 gm	Sodium	44 mg	Polyunsaturated Fat	1 gm
Carbohydrate	11 gm	Total Fat	4 gm	Monounsaturated Fat	2 gm

* using sherry

*B*reads

Bread is an important source of vitamins, minerals and protein, especially when it's made from whole-grain flour. In these recipes, saturated fat is kept to a minimum by using polyunsaturated oils and skim milk whenever possible. (We've also tried to go easy on salt.) At the same time, we think you'll agree that the result is a rich and flavorful taste.

Try our Mexican-Style Cornbread with hot chili, our classic Rye Bread with sandwiches. Our Herbed Bread Sticks are great for crunchy Italian flavor. Our Gingerbread makes a wonderful after-school snack, and our breakfast breads and muffins are a great way to start the day.

Before you start, consider the following tips for perfect bread making: Dissolve active dry yeast in warm liquid (about 110° to 115° F) and compressed (moist) yeast in lukewarm water (about 85° F). Use enough flour to make a dough that's soft but not sticky. You'll want to use slightly more flour in humid weather, less in dry weather. Let the dough rise in a warm, humid place away from drafts. The ideal rising temperature is 80° to 85° F.

For quick breads and muffins, beat or process the mixture only until the flour is moistened and barely disappears into the batter. The batter should be lumpy, not smooth. The small lumps will disappear during baking, and the loaves and muffins will be light and fluffy.

Generally, a yeast bread should be removed from the pan and placed on a wire rack as soon as it is taken out of the oven. A quick bread should remain in the pan 5 to 10 minutes after it is taken out of the oven before it is cooled on a wire rack. Exceptions can be found in a few of these recipes, so be sure to follow the individual directions when given.

One last hint: Wrap your homemade bread tightly in foil or plastic before storing.

*B*asic *B*read

Makes 2 1-pound loaves (16 slices per loaf)
Serves 32; 1 slice per serving

1 cake yeast or 2 envelopes dry yeast
¼ cup lukewarm water
2½ tablespoons sugar
1¾ cups skim milk
1 teaspoon salt
3 cups sifted flour
2 tablespoons acceptable vegetable oil
3 cups sifted flour
Vegetable oil spray

Dissolve yeast in lukewarm water in a large mixing bowl. Set aside.

In a bowl, mix together sugar and milk. Stir into dissolved yeast. Add salt and 3 cups of flour. Beat until smooth. Add oil.

Gradually mix in remaining flour until dough is stiff enough to handle. Knead dough until it is smooth and elastic. Lightly spray a bowl with vegetable oil spray. Add kneaded dough and turn to coat all sides with oil. Cover with a clean cloth and let rise in a warm place (about 85° F) until doubled in bulk.

Divide dough into two equal parts. Lightly spray two 10-x-5-inch loaf pans with vegetable oil. Shape dough into loaves and place in prepared pans. Cover and let rise again until doubled in bulk.

Preheat oven to 425° F.

Bake loaves 15 minutes. Reduce heat to 375° F and continue baking 30 minutes longer. Remove bread from pans and place on wire racks to cool.

HERB BREAD

Mix the following herbs into dough just before kneading: ½ teaspoon nutmeg, ¼ teaspoon thyme, ½ teaspoon rosemary and 2 teaspoons caraway seeds. Proceed as directed.

Basic Bread Nutrient Analysis

Calories	96 kcal	Cholesterol	0 mg	Saturated Fat	0 gm
Protein	3 gm	Sodium	74 mg	Polyunsaturated Fat	1 gm
Carbohydrate	18 gm	Total Fat	1 gm	Monounsaturated Fat	0 gm

Herb Bread Nutrient Analysis

Calories	96 kcal	Cholesterol	0 mg	Saturated Fat	0 gm
Protein	3 gm	Sodium	74 mg	Polyunsaturated Fat	1 gm
Carbohydrate	18 gm	Total Fat	1 gm	Monounsaturated Fat	0 gm

Anadama Bread

Makes 2 loaves (16 slices per loaf)
Serves 32; 1 slice per serving

Vegetable oil spray
2 cups boiling water
½ cup yellow cornmeal
1 teaspoon salt
¼ pound acceptable margarine
1 package dry yeast
½ cup lukewarm water
¾ cup molasses
6 tablespoons nonfat dry milk
6 tablespoons soy flour
2 tablespoons wheat germ
6 to 7 cups unbleached all-purpose flour

Thoroughly mix boiling water, cornmeal, salt and margarine in a large mixing bowl. Let cool to lukewarm.

In a small bowl, dissolve yeast in lukewarm water, then add it to cornmeal mixture. Add molasses and stir until well mixed.

In another bowl, combine nonfat dry milk, soy flour, wheat germ and half of the all-purpose flour. Add this mixture to cornmeal mixture, one cup at a time. Beat well after each addition. Add the rest of flour, one cup at a time, until dough is stiff enough to handle.

Turn out onto a floured board, cover with a clean cloth and let rest 5 minutes. Knead dough until it is smooth and elastic. Place dough in a large, lightly oiled bowl, turning to coat all sides with oil. Cover with a cloth and let rise in warm place (85° F) until doubled in bulk.

Lightly spray two 8-x-4-inch loaf pans with vegetable oil spray.

Divide dough into two equal parts. Shape into loaves and place in prepared pans. Lightly oil tops, then cover and let rise again until doubled in bulk.

Preheat oven to 350° F.

Bake loaves 40 to 50 minutes.

Remove bread from pans and place on wire rack to cool.

Nutrient Analysis

Calories	145 kcal	Cholesterol	0 mg	Saturated Fat	1 gm
Protein	3 gm	Sodium	108 mg	Polyunsaturated Fat	1 gm
Carbohydrate	25 gm	Total Fat	3 gm	Monounsaturated Fat	1 gm

Whole-Wheat Bread

Makes 3 loaves (16 slices per loaf)
Serves 48; 1 slice per serving

> 3 cups warm water
> 2 packages compressed or dry yeast
> 2 tablespoons honey
> 3 cups whole-wheat flour
> 3½ cups unbleached all-purpose flour
> ½ cup soy flour
> 1½ tablespoons wheat germ
> ¾ cup nonfat dry milk
> 4 teaspoons salt
> Egg substitute equivalent to 2 eggs
> 2 tablespoons acceptable vegetable oil
> Vegetable oil spray

Place warm water in a large bowl. Add yeast and stir to dissolve. Add honey and let sit 5 minutes.

In a bowl, sift together whole-wheat flour, all-purpose flour, soy flour, wheat germ and nonfat dry milk. Set aside.

Add salt, egg substitute and three quarters of flour mixture to the yeast mixture. Beat with an electric mixer for 5 minutes. Add oil and remainder of flour mixture. Continue beating until flour is thoroughly mixed and add additional flour if necessary to make dough stiff enough to handle.

Turn dough onto a floured board and knead until it is smooth and elastic. Place dough in an oiled bowl, turning to coat all sides of the dough with oil. Cover with a clean, damp cloth and let rise in a warm place (about 85° F) until doubled in bulk. Punch down, fold over the edges and turn upside down in bowl. Cover and allow to rise for another 20 minutes.

Turn dough onto a lightly floured board. Divide into three equal portions. Fold each into the center to make a smooth, tight ball. Cover with cloth and let rest 10 more minutes.

Lightly spray three 8-x-4-inch loaf pans with vegetable oil.

Shape dough into three loaves and place in prepared loaf pans. Cover and let rise until doubled in bulk.

Preheat oven to 350° F.

Bake loaves 50 to 60 minutes.

Remove bread from pans and place on wire racks to cool. If a softer crust is desired, brush tops with margarine while hot.

Nutrient Analysis

Calories	74 kcal	Cholesterol	0 mg	Saturated Fat	0 gm
Protein	3 gm	Sodium	189 mg	Polyunsaturated Fat	1 gm
Carbohydrate	14 gm	Total Fat	1 gm	Monounsaturated Fat	0 gm

Yeast Bread

Makes 3 loaves (16 slices per loaf)
Serves 48; 1 slice per serving

> 2 cups all-purpose flour
> 6 tablespoons soy flour
> 1 envelope dry yeast
> 2½ tablespoons sugar
> 1 teaspoon salt
> 2 tablespoons wheat germ
> 6 tablespoons nonfat dry milk
> 2 cups skim milk
> 2 tablespoons acceptable margarine
> 3 cups all-purpose flour
> Vegetable oil spray

In a large mixing bowl, combine 2 cups of all-purpose flour, soy flour, yeast, sugar, salt, wheat germ and nonfat dry milk. Set aside.

Heat skim milk and margarine in a saucepan over low setting until cooking thermometer reaches 120°–130° F. Remove from heat and add to dry ingredients. Beat 2 minutes with an electric mixer, scraping the sides of the bowl occasionally.

Beat in enough flour to make a thick batter, then work in the rest of the flour until dough is stiff enough to handle. (Add additional flour if necessary to make dough stiff.)

Turn dough onto a floured board. Cover and let dough rest for 10 minutes; then knead dough until it is blistered and pliable.

Shape dough into a ball, and place in an oiled bowl, turning to coat all sides of dough with oil. Cover with a clean cloth and let rise in a warm place (about 85° F) until doubled in bulk.

(continued)

YEAST BREAD (*continued*)

Turn dough onto a lightly floured board. Cover and let rest for 10 minutes.

Lightly spray three 8-x-4-inch loaf pans with vegetable oil.

Divide dough into three equal portions. Place in prepared loaf pans, cover and let rise again until doubled in bulk.

Preheat oven to 350° F.

Bake loaves 40 to 50 minutes.

Brush tops of hot loaves with margarine.

Remove bread from pans and place on wire racks to cool.

Nutrient Analysis

Calories	60 kcal	Cholesterol	0 mg	Saturated Fat	0 gm
Protein	2 gm	Sodium	59 mg	Polyunsaturated Fat	0 gm
Carbohydrate	11 gm	Total Fat	1 gm	Monounsaturated Fat	0 gm

Whole-Wheat French Bread*

Makes 2 loaves (16 slices per loaf)
Serves 32; 1 slice per serving

1½ cups warm water
1 cup plain nonfat yogurt, low-fat buttermilk or whey
1 tablespoon active dry yeast
6 cups whole-wheat flour
1 tablespoon salt
Cornmeal

Basic Whole-Grain Bread becomes French Bread, with a real sourdough flavor. The secret is to eliminate the sugar, and for part of the water substitute very sour buttermilk or yogurt; if you have homemade yogurt, chances are that enough whey has separated out for you to drain some off and use it. The latter is ideal, as milk solids detract somewhat from the coarse, airy texture of the bread.

Combine water and yogurt. Their combined temperature should be about 100° F. Add yeast, and when it has dissolved, stir in half of the flour. Beat well until dough becomes smooth. Add salt and remaining flour, cup by cup, mixing well.

* *From* Laurel's Kitchen, *1976 (out of print), Nilgiri Press, Berkeley, California.*

Knead dough in bowl until it is no longer sticky, then turn it onto a floured board and knead very well. Knead in extra flour if dough is not very stiff. The loaves are baked on a cookie sheet, without support, so dough needs to be sturdy.

After dough has risen once, punch it down. Divide it in half. Flour the board and rolling pin and roll out each portion of dough into a large square. Fold as illustrated. Pinch the edges together so that the seam is invisible.

Oil two cookie sheets and dust them with cornmeal. Place a loaf on each and let them rise in a warm place until doubled in bulk. Preheat oven to 400° F toward the end of the rising time.

With a serrated or very sharp knife, and very gently, make diagonal slashes across each loaf, about ½-inch deep and 2 inches apart.

Brush or spray loaves with water as they are going into the oven and repeat about halfway through baking time. This is the secret to producing the chewy crust so characteristic of good French bread.

Bake loaves for about 40 minutes. The time will vary depending on the thickness of the loaves.

Nutrient Analysis

Calories	80 kcal	Cholesterol	0 mg	Saturated Fat	0 gm
Protein	4 gm	Sodium	206 mg	Polyunsaturated Fat	0 gm
Carbohydrate	17 gm	Total Fat	0 gm	Monounsaturated Fat	0 gm

Rye Bread*

Makes 2 loaves (12 slices per loaf)
Serves 24; 1 slice per serving

1 tablespoon caraway seeds
Water
2 tablespoons acceptable vegetable oil
1 tablespoon active dry yeast
¼ cup firmly packed brown sugar
1 cup warm water
½ to 1 cup gluten flour
3 cups whole-wheat flour
2 teaspoons salt
Grated peel of 2 oranges
3 to 4 cups rye flour

*T*he flavor of rye bread depends upon the kind of rye flour you use. If it is dark and moist, the bread will be dense and aromatic; if it is light, the bread will be airy and softly textured. This recipe is written for either dark or light rye flours; if you choose the dark rye flour, use the larger amount of gluten flour. The stronger your kneading arm, the less gluten you will need. Dark rye bread will take longer to rise and bake.

Simmer caraway seeds in 1 cup of water for 10 minutes. Remove from heat. Add oil and enough cold water to make 1½ cups liquid.

Dissolve yeast and sugar in 1 cup warm water, in a large bowl. When the yeast bubbles to the surface, stir in gluten flour and 2 cups of the whole-wheat flour and knead until dough is springy.

Add salt and grated orange peel to seed mixture. Pour this mixture into dough and mix.

Add 2 cups of the rye flour and knead dough briefly. Add the remaining 1 cup of rye flour, knead, and finally add the last cup of whole-wheat flour. Knead dough well, adding more rye or wheat flour to make a rather stiff dough.

Place dough in an oiled bowl, cover, and let rise in a warm place. When it has doubled in bulk, punch it down and shape it into two oblong loaves.

Place loaves side by side on an oiled cookie sheet and let them rise, until doubled in bulk. For a shiny crust, brush with beaten egg yolk.

* *From* Laurel's Kitchen, *1976 (out of print), Nilgiri Press, Berkeley, California.*

Bake in a 350° F oven for about 40 minutes, or until quite brown. If you have used dark rye flour, baking time may increase to 1 hour.

Nutrient Analysis

Calories	137 kcal	Cholesterol	0 mg	Saturated Fat		0 gm
Protein	4 gm	Sodium	179 mg	Polyunsaturated Fat		1 gm
Carbohydrate	28 gm	Total Fat	2 gm	Monounsaturated Fat		0 gm

Peter's Pumpernickel
(Sourdough Style)

Makes 2 loaves (16 slices per loaf)
Serves 32; 1 slice per serving

SOURDOUGH STARTER
2 cups flat, light beer
1 cup rye flour
1½ cups wheat flour (white or whole-wheat)

3 tablespoons caraway seeds
½ cup hot black coffee
1½ cups sourdough starter
2 cups rye flour
1 package active dry yeast
½ cup warm water
½ cup molasses
½ cup nonfat dry milk
2 teaspoons salt
3 tablespoons acceptable margarine, melted
2¾ cups all-purpose flour (unbleached, hard wheat is best)
Vegetable oil spray

*T*o make sourdough starter, mix beer, rye flour and wheat flour in a glass or pottery container of at least 8 cups capacity. Let stand loosely covered at room temperature until mixture bubbles and forms liquid on top (1 to 4 days). When ready to use, just stir all liquid back in. (After removing starter needed for recipe, replenish starter container with 1 cup warm water and 1 cup flour(s), then cover tightly and refrigerate. This will keep indefinitely and can be used for many varieties of baking.)

(continued)

PETER'S PUMPERNICKEL (*continued*)

To make bread, crush caraway seeds between two wooden spoons. Place crushed seeds in a large bowl, then pour hot coffee over them. Cool, then stir in starter and rye flour.

Let mixture stand at least 6 hours or overnight in a warm place.

In a small bowl, sprinkle yeast on warm water to dissolve. Add yeast and all other ingredients, except vegetable oil spray, to the caraway mixture in the order given. Mix well. Let rise in bowl, covered, until doubled in bulk.

Preheat oven to 350° F. Lightly spray two 9-x-5-inch loaf pans with vegetable oil.

Turn bread out on a floured board and knead. Shape into two loaves and place in prepared pans. Let rise until doubled.

Bake loaves one-half hour, or until they sound hollow when rapped with the knuckles.

OPTIONAL COOKING METHOD

After kneading bread, shape into two round loaves and place on a baking sheet that has been sprinkled with cornmeal. Proceed as directed.

Nutrient Analysis *

Calories	90 kcal	Cholesterol	0 mg	Saturated Fat	0 gm
Protein	3 gm	Sodium	154 mg	Polyunsaturated Fat	0 gm
Carbohydrate	17 gm	Total Fat	1 gm	Monounsaturated Fat	1 gm

* *assuming one-third of starter is used*

Jeanne's Oatmeal Cinnamon Bread

Makes 2 loaves (16 slices per loaf)
Serves 32; 1 slice per serving

⅓ cup warm water (85° to 95° F)
1 package active dry yeast
½ cup sugar
2 teaspoons salt
⅓ cup acceptable margarine
1½ cups skim milk, scalded
2 cups whole-wheat flour
1½ cups rolled oatmeal
2 eggs, well beaten

3 to 3½ cups unbleached all-purpose flour
Vegetable oil spray

FILLING
⅓ cup sugar
2 teaspoons cinnamon
2 tablespoons acceptable margarine, melted

Place warm water in a small bowl. Sprinkle yeast on water, add a pinch of the sugar and set aside.

Add rest of sugar, salt and margarine to milk and set aside to allow to cool to lukewarm.

Place whole-wheat flour in a large, warm bowl. Add oatmeal and eggs. Then add cooled milk mixture and yeast mixture. Beat 2 minutes at medium speed on electric mixer (high speed on a hand mixer).

Stir in all-purpose flour, a cup at a time, until dough is soft and pulls away from the sides of the bowl.

Turn out dough onto a floured board and knead until soft and shiny (about 80 times). Place in a bowl with a small amount of vegetable oil, turning to oil top. Cover with a damp towel and let rise until doubled.

Turn out, punch down and let sit for 10 minutes.

Lightly spray two 10-x-5-inch loaf pans with vegetable oil.

Divide dough in half.

Mix sugar and cinnamon for filling; divide in half.

Roll out half of the dough to a 15-x-8-inch rectangle.

Brush top with half of melted margarine and sprinkle with half of filling mix. Beginning at short side, roll up tightly (like a jellyroll). Pinch seam to seal. Place seam-side-down in prepared loaf pan. Repeat with second half. Let rise again until doubled, then brush tops with melted margarine.

Preheat oven to 375° F.

Bake loaves 30 to 35 minutes, or until top sounds hollow when tapped.

Cool *in pan,* with pan on side, 15 minutes, then turn out.

Note: For best cutting results, cool bread completely.

Nutrient Analysis

Calories	135 kcal	Cholesterol	17 mg	Saturated Fat	1 gm
Protein	4 gm	Sodium	175 mg	Polyunsaturated Fat	1 gm
Carbohydrate	23 gm	Total Fat	3 gm	Monounsaturated Fat	1 gm

*O*atmeal *B*read

Makes 1 loaf (16 slices per loaf)
Serves 16; 1 slice per serving

> 1 cup rolled oatmeal
> 1½ cups boiling water
> 1 teaspoon salt
> 1 package dry yeast
> ¼ cup warm water
> ⅓ cup light molasses
> 1½ tablespoons acceptable vegetable oil
> 4 to 4½ cups sifted all-purpose flour
> Vegetable oil spray

Pour boiling water over oatmeal in a large mixing bowl. Add salt and stir to mix well. Set aside to cool to lukewarm.

In a bowl, dissolve yeast in the warm water, then pour mixture into oatmeal mixture. Add molasses and oil and stir to mix well. Gradually add sifted flour, mixing well, until dough is stiff enough to handle. Place dough on a lightly floured board and knead for about 5 minutes, or until dough is smooth and elastic.

Place dough in a lightly oiled bowl, turning to coat all sides of dough with oil. Cover with a clean cloth and let rise in a warm place (about 85° F) until doubled in bulk.

Punch down dough and knead again on lightly floured board for a few minutes.

Lightly spray a 9-x-5-inch loaf pan with vegetable oil.

Shape dough into a loaf and place in prepared loaf pan. Cover and let rise again for about 1 hour, or until doubled in bulk.

Preheat oven to 375° F.

Bake bread 50 minutes. Remove bread from pan and place on a wire rack to cool.

RAISIN OATMEAL BREAD

Add ½ cup seedless raisins to dough before kneading.

Oatmeal Bread Nutrient Analysis

Calories	159 kcal	Cholesterol	0 mg	Saturated Fat	0 gm
Protein	4 gm	Sodium	137 mg	Polyunsaturated Fat	1 gm
Carbohydrate	31 gm	Total Fat	2 gm	Monounsaturated Fat	0 gm

Raisin Oatmeal Bread Nutrient Analysis

Calories	173 kcal	Cholesterol	0 mg	Saturated Fat	0 gm
Protein	4 gm	Sodium	138 mg	Polyunsaturated Fat	1 gm
Carbohydrate	35 gm	Total Fat	2 gm	Monounsaturated Fat	0 gm

*C*innamon *B*read

Makes 2 loaves (16 slices per loaf)
Serves 32; 1 slice per serving

Vegetable oil spray
1 recipe for Basic Bread (see page 444)
2 tablespoons acceptable margarine, melted
½ cup sugar
1 tablespoon cinnamon

Lightly spray two 10-x-5-inch loaf pans with vegetable oil.

Make dough for Basic Bread and let rise the first time.

Roll out dough and spread with half of the margarine.

In a small bowl, mix sugar and cinnamon together. Reserve 1 tablespoon for topping and sprinkle remainder over dough. Roll dough lengthwise like a jellyroll. Shape into a loaf and cut into two parts. Pinch ends together and tuck under. Place in prepared loaf pans and spread remaining margarine over the top.

Let rise until doubled in bulk. Sprinkle each loaf with half of the remaining 1 tablespoon of cinnamon and sugar mixture.

Preheat oven to 375° F.

Bake loaves 50 minutes. Remove loaves from pans and cool on a wire rack.

Nutrient Analysis

Calories	114 kcal	Cholesterol	0 mg	Saturated Fat	0 gm
Protein	3 gm	Sodium	83 mg	Polyunsaturated Fat	1 gm
Carbohydrate	21 gm	Total Fat	2 gm	Monounsaturated Fat	1 gm

*F*ruit *L*oaf

Makes 2 loaves (16 slices per loaf)
Serves 32; 1 slice per serving

Vegetable oil spray
1 recipe for Basic Bread (see page 444)
½ cup seedless raisins
½ cup chopped unsalted dry-roasted walnuts
¼ cup chopped candied orange peel
¼ cup chopped candied cherries
¼ cup confectioners' sugar
1 tablespoon warm water
1 to 2 drops almond or vanilla extract

Lightly spray two 9-inch round pans or ring molds with vegetable oil.

Make dough for Basic Bread. Set aside.

In a bowl, mix together raisins, walnuts and candied fruits. Add mixture to Basic Bread dough and knead until well mixed. Place in prepared pans or ring molds. Cover and let rise in a warm place until doubled in bulk.

Preheat oven to 350° F.

Bake loaves 1¼ hours. Remove bread from pans and place on wire racks to cool.

To make glaze, place confectioners' sugar, warm water and extract in a small bowl. Stir until well mixed. Spread onto bread while loaves are still warm.

Nutrient Analysis

Calories	132 kcal	Cholesterol	0 mg	Saturated Fat	0 gm
Protein	3 gm	Sodium	76 mg	Polyunsaturated Fat	1 gm
Carbohydrate	25 gm	Total Fat	2 gm	Monounsaturated Fat	1 gm

*H*erb *C*heese *B*read

Makes 1 loaf
Serves 32; 1 thin slice per serving

1 package dry yeast
½ cup lukewarm (110° F) water
2 tablespoons sugar
½ cup plain nonfat yogurt
½ cup skim milk
2 tablespoons olive oil
¼ cup finely chopped green onion
1 tablespoon finely chopped fresh rosemary
1 tablespoon finely chopped fresh dill
1 tablespoon finely chopped fresh basil
1 teaspoon salt
1 teaspoon freshly ground black pepper
¼ cup grated Parmesan cheese
4 cups flour
Vegetable oil spray

Combine yeast, water and sugar in a large bowl, stirring until yeast and sugar are dissolved. Stir in yogurt, milk, olive oil, onion, herbs, salt, pepper and Parmesan cheese. Mix well. Stir in flour. Knead dough on floured surface, or in bowl if desired, until smooth and elastic.

Lightly spray a bowl with vegetable oil. Place dough in bowl, cover and let rise until doubled.

Lightly spray a 9-x-5-x-3-inch loaf pan with vegetable oil.

Punch dough down, shape into a loaf and place in prepared loaf pan. Let rise until sides of loaf nearly reach top edges of pan.

Preheat oven to 350° F. Bake bread 50 minutes. Cool on a rack.

Nutrient Analysis

Calories	70 kcal	Cholesterol	1 mg	Saturated Fat	0 gm
Protein	2 gm	Sodium	84 mg	Polyunsaturated Fat	0 gm
Carbohydrate	12 gm	Total Fat	1 gm	Monounsaturated Fat	1 gm

Dilly Bread

Makes 1 loaf (16 slices per loaf)
Serves 16; 1 slice per serving

1 package dry yeast
¼ cup warm water
1 cup low-fat cottage cheese, heated to lukewarm
1 tablespoon acceptable margarine
2 tablespoons sugar
1 teaspoon salt
1 tablespoon minced onion
2 teaspoons dill seed
¼ teaspoon baking soda
2½ cups all-purpose flour
Vegetable oil spray
Acceptable margarine, melted

*I*n a bowl, soften yeast in warm water. Add cottage cheese and stir to mix well.

Add remaining ingredients except flour. Stir to mix well.

Gradually mix in flour to form a stiff dough. Beat well. Let rise in a warm place 60 minutes, or until doubled in bulk.

Lightly spray a 2-quart round casserole or 9-x-5-inch loaf pan with vegetable oil.

Punch down dough and put in prepared casserole or loaf pan.

Cover and let rise 40 minutes.

Preheat oven to 350° F.

Bake bread 40 to 50 minutes. Brush with a small amount of melted margarine while still hot.

Cool 5 minutes and remove from pan.

Nutrient Analysis

Calories	92 kcal	Cholesterol	1 mg	Saturated Fat	0 gm
Protein	4 gm	Sodium	212 mg	Polyunsaturated Fat	0 gm
Carbohydrate	16 gm	Total Fat	1 gm	Monounsaturated Fat	0 gm

*Y*ogurt *D*inner *R*olls

Serves 18; 1 roll per serving

¼ cup warm water
2 tablespoons sugar
1 package active dry yeast
1 cup plain nonfat yogurt
2 tablespoons acceptable margarine, melted
1 egg
1 teaspoon leaf oregano
2 teaspoons basil
2 tablespoons grated onion
¾ cup all-purpose flour
¾ cup whole-wheat flour
½ teaspoon salt
½ cup all-purpose flour
¾ cup whole-wheat flour
Vegetable oil spray

*I*n a bowl, combine water, sugar and yeast. Set aside for about 5 minutes, or until bubbly; then add yogurt, margarine, egg, herbs and onion. Set aside.

In a large mixing bowl, combine ¾ cup all-purpose flour, ¾ cup whole-wheat flour and salt. Blend in yogurt mixture and beat with an electric mixer at low speed for 30 seconds. Beat 3 minutes on high speed. Stir in ½ cup all-purpose flour and ¾ cup whole-wheat flour. (Dough will be moist and sticky.)

Lightly spray a large bowl with vegetable oil. Add dough and turn once to coat evenly. Cover with towel and let rise 1½ hours.

Punch dough down, and form into 18 balls.

Lightly spray a 9-x-13-inch baking pan with vegetable oil. Arrange balls of dough in prepared pan. Let rise 40 minutes.

Preheat oven to 400° F.

Bake rolls 15 minutes.

Nutrient Analysis

Calories	93 kcal	Cholesterol	15 mg	Saturated Fat	0 gm
Protein	3 gm	Sodium	89 mg	Polyunsaturated Fat	0 gm
Carbohydrate	16 gm	Total Fat	2 gm	Monounsaturated Fat	1 gm

*Q*uick-and-*E*asy *R*efrigerator *R*olls

Serves 36; 1 roll per serving

2 egg whites, slightly beaten
½ cup acceptable vegetable oil
½ cup sugar
1 package yeast dissolved in ¼ cup warm water
1 teaspoon salt
1 cup lukewarm water
4 cups unsifted all-purpose flour or whole-wheat flour

*I*n a large bowl, stir ingredients together in the order given above. Cover and refrigerate dough at least 12 hours. (Dough may be kept in refrigerator several days.)

Make three dozen rolls in your favorite shape. Place on a lightly floured board and let them rise 2 hours before baking.

Preheat oven to 375° F. Arrange rolls on cookie sheet and bake 10 minutes. Remove rolls from cookie sheet and serve immediately.

Nutrient Analysis

Calories	85 kcal	Cholesterol	0 mg	Saturated Fat	0 gm
Protein	2 gm	Sodium	62 mg	Polyunsaturated Fat	2 gm
Carbohydrate	12 gm	Total Fat	3 gm	Monounsaturated Fat	1 gm

*W*hole-*W*heat *P*ita *B*read
(Middle Eastern Flat Bread)

Serves 12; 1 pita round per serving

⅔ cup soy flour
3 cups whole-wheat pastry flour
2⅓ cups unbleached all-purpose flour
1 tablespoon salt
2 tablespoons sugar
½ cup lukewarm water
1 teaspoon sugar
1 package active dry yeast
2 to 2½ cups lukewarm water
Acceptable vegetable oil

Combine flours, salt and 2 tablespoons sugar in a large bowl. Set aside.

In a small bowl, mix ½ cup warm water with remaining teaspoon of sugar and yeast. Set in a warm place for 10 minutes, or until mixture is bubbly.

Stir yeast mixture into flour mixture. Add enough warm water to make a soft dough. The dough should be slightly sticky.

Knead dough in bowl until it is smooth and satiny, at least 10 minutes. It loses its stickiness quickly. Lightly oil the top of the dough with acceptable vegetable oil, cover bowl and set in a warm place to rise 1¼ hours, or until doubled in bulk.

Punch dough down, knead briefly and divide into twelve equal pieces. Form each into a smooth ball, cover and let stand 10 minutes.

Roll out the balls of dough into rounds about 5 inches in diameter each. Preheat oven to 450° F.

Place rounds on ungreased cookie sheets and bake 8 to 10 minutes. Cool on a board covered with a towel.

OPTIONAL COOKING METHOD

A gas oven and a sense of adventure are necessary for this method: Slide the rounds of dough directly onto the bottom of the oven. Four will fit the average oven at a time. Bake at 450° F 8 minutes, or until well fluffed and lightly browned. (If you use this method, watch the bread carefully because it may char.)

Note: The rounds puff up in the oven and collapse as they cool, retaining an inner pocket that is good for sandwich filling. Store pitas in plastic bags in the refrigerator and use within a few days, or freeze them for a few days before using. This bread loses its freshness quickly.

Nutrient Analysis

Calories	213 kcal	Cholesterol	0 mg	Saturated Fat	0 gm
Protein	8 gm	Sodium	535 mg	Polyunsaturated Fat	1 gm
Carbohydrate	43 gm	Total Fat	2 gm	Monounsaturated Fat	0 gm

*T*ortillas*

Serves 12; 1 tortilla per serving

1 ½ cups water
1 ½ tablespoons acceptable margarine
1 cup stone-ground cornmeal
1 ½ tablespoons acceptable margarine
1 ¼ cups whole-wheat flour
1 teaspoon salt

*B*ring water to a boil in a small saucepan. Add 1½ tablespoons margarine. Stir in cornmeal quickly, then immediately lower heat and cover pan. Let cornmeal cook over very low heat for 5 minutes. Stir in remaining margarine and set aside to cool.

Mix flour and salt. Stir in cooled cornmeal and knead, adding water or more flour if necessary to form a soft dough. Pinch off twelve pieces and roll into 2-inch balls.

Flatten each ball between palms or against a board, making a flat circle. Roll with a rolling pin to 6 or 7 inches. Keep turning the circle to keep it round, and sprinkle board and pin with cornmeal as needed to prevent sticking.

Cook on a hot ungreased griddle for 1½ minutes on each side, or until flecked with dark spots.

Line a basket or bowl with a large cloth. Stack tortillas in bowl and keep covered with cloth.

They may be made long in advance, even a day before needed. Heating for a few seconds on each side makes them soft and pliable for handling again. You may heat them on a griddle or directly over a medium gas flame.

TORTILLA CHIPS
For crisp corn chips as an accompaniment to soup or salad, increase the amount of margarine and roll tortillas somewhat thinner.

* *From* Laurel's Kitchen, *1976 (out of print), Nilgiri Press, Berkeley, California.*

Nutrient Analysis

Calories	109 kcal	Cholesterol	0 mg	Saturated Fat		1 gm
Protein	3 gm	Sodium	211 mg	Polyunsaturated Fat		1 gm
Carbohydrate	18 gm	Total Fat	3 gm	Monounsaturated Fat		1 gm

Southern-**S**tyle **C**ornbread

Serves 8

Egg substitute equivalent to 1 egg
1 cup low-fat buttermilk
¼ teaspoon salt
¼ teaspoon salt-free all-purpose seasoning
1 teaspoon baking powder
⅓ teaspoon baking soda
1¼ cups stone-ground yellow or white cornmeal
1 teaspoon sugar (optional)
1 to 1½ tablespoons acceptable vegetable oil

Preheat oven to 400° F.

Place egg substitute in a mixing bowl. Add buttermilk and blend. Set aside.

Mix all dry ingredients in a large mixing bowl. Set aside.

Place oil in a heavy skillet with a heat-proof handle. Place skillet in the preheating oven to heat the oil. Don't forget it!

When oven is hot, make a well in the dry ingredients. Pour in liquid mixture and blend gently. Add hot oil from skillet and blend. Pour mixture into the hot skillet and return skillet to oven. Bake 20 minutes, or until top is golden brown and edges separate from pan.

MEXICAN-STYLE CORNBREAD

Add the following just before adding the hot oil: ½ cup grated onion; ½ to 1 whole fresh jalapeño pepper, seeded and finely chopped*; ⅓ cup whole-kernel corn, fresh or frozen and then thawed; ¼ cup grated low-fat sharp cheddar cheese.

* Wear rubber gloves when handling hot peppers, or wash hands thoroughly after handling. Skin, especially around the eyes, is very sensitive to oil from peppers.

Southern-Style Cornbread Nutrient Analysis

Calories	114 kcal	Cholesterol	1 mg	Saturated Fat	0 gm
Protein	3 gm	Sodium	185 mg	Polyunsaturated Fat	1 gm
Carbohydrate	19 gm	Total Fat	3 gm	Monounsaturated Fat	1 gm

Mexican-Style Cornbread Nutrient Analysis

Calories	129 kcal	Cholesterol	2 mg	Saturated Fat	1 gm
Protein	5 gm	Sodium	257 mg	Polyunsaturated Fat	1 gm
Carbohydrate	21 gm	Total Fat	3 gm	Monounsaturated Fat	1 gm

*C*ornbread *with* *K*ernels

Serves 8; 1 piece per serving

> Vegetable oil spray
> 1 cup cornmeal
> 1 cup whole-wheat flour
> ¼ cup sugar
> ½ teaspoon baking soda
> 1 egg, lightly beaten
> 1½ cups low-fat buttermilk
> 1 cup frozen or canned no-salt-added whole-kernel corn,
>   drained
> ⅓ cup acceptable vegetable oil

Preheat oven to 425° F. Lightly spray an 8-inch square baking dish with vegetable oil.

Blend dry ingredients together in a large bowl. Set aside.

In another bowl, mix egg, buttermilk, corn and oil. Mix well. Pour buttermilk mixture into dry mixture and blend thoroughly.

Pour into prepared baking dish and bake 20 to 25 minutes, or until a toothpick inserted in center comes out clean. Cut into eight equal portions and serve hot.

Nutrient Analysis

Calories	261 kcal	Cholesterol	36 mg	Saturated Fat	2 gm
Protein	6 gm	Sodium	110 mg	Polyunsaturated Fat	6 gm
Carbohydrate	37 gm	Total Fat	11 gm	Monounsaturated Fat	3 gm

*B*agels

Serves 12; 1 bagel per serving

> 2 packages active dry yeast
> 1¾ cups all-purpose flour
> 1½ cups lukewarm water
> 3 tablespoons sugar
> 1 tablespoon salt
> 2½ to 2¾ cups all-purpose flour
> 1 teaspoon sugar

Combine yeast and 1¾ cups flour. Add water, 3 tablespoons sugar and salt. Beat with an electric mixer at a low speed for ½ minute, constantly scraping the sides of the bowl, then beat at high speed for 3 minutes.

Stir in enough of the remaining flour to make a moderately stiff dough. Turn out onto a lightly floured board and knead until smooth. Cover and let rest 15 minutes.

Divide dough into twelve portions. Shape portions into smooth balls and punch a hole in the center of each with a floured finger. Pull gently to enlarge hole, keeping uniform shape. Cover and let rise 20 minutes.

In a stockpot, combine 1 teaspoon sugar and 1 gallon of water. Bring water to a boil over medium-high heat. Reduce to simmer. Place four bagels in simmering water and cook 7 minutes, turning once, then drain on a paper towel. Repeat with remaining bagels, cooking four at a time.

Preheat oven to 375° F.

Bake bagels on an ungreased baking sheet 30 to 35 minutes.

WHOLE-WHEAT BAGELS
In place of all-purpose flour, use half whole-wheat and half all-purpose.

BAGELS WITH TOPPINGS
After bagels have cooked in simmering water and before baking, sprinkle with chopped onion, poppy seeds, sesame seeds, caraway seeds or kosher salt.

Bagels Nutrient Analysis

Calories	169 kcal	Cholesterol	0 mg	Saturated Fat	0 gm
Protein	5 gm	Sodium	534 mg	Polyunsaturated Fat	0 gm
Carbohydrate	36 gm	Total Fat	0 gm	Monounsaturated Fat	0 gm

Whole-Wheat Bagels Nutrient Analysis

Calories	165 kcal	Cholesterol	0 mg	Saturated Fat	0 gm
Protein	6 gm	Sodium	535 mg	Polyunsaturated Fat	0 gm
Carbohydrate	35 gm	Total Fat	1 gm	Monounsaturated Fat	0 gm

*S*avory *B*read

Serves 16; 1 slice per serving

> 1-pound loaf French or Italian bread
> 5 tablespoons acceptable margarine, softened
> 1 tablespoon chopped fresh basil
> ¾ teaspoon salt-free lemon-pepper seasoning

Preheat oven to 375° F.

Cut bread into sixteen slices. Set aside.

In a small bowl, combine margarine, basil and lemon-pepper seasoning. Spread mixture evenly on each slice. Wrap loaf in foil and place on a baking sheet. Bake 15 minutes.

SAVORY BREAD WITH CHILI SPREAD

In place of basil and lemon-pepper seasoning, add the following to the margarine: 1 teaspoon chili powder, 1 teaspoon crushed dried cilantro, and a dash of *both* garlic powder and hot pepper sauce.

SAVORY BREAD WITH GREEN ONION SPREAD

In place of basil, add the following to the margarine and lemon-pepper seasoning: 2 tablespoons finely chopped green onion and 1 tablespoon finely chopped parsley.

Savory Bread Nutrient Analysis

Calories	110 kcal	Cholesterol	0 mg	Saturated Fat	1 gm
Protein	3 gm	Sodium	207 mg	Polyunsaturated Fat	1 gm
Carbohydrate	16 gm	Total Fat	4 gm	Monounsaturated Fat	2 gm

Savory Bread with Chili Spread Nutrient Analysis

Calories	110 kcal	Cholesterol	0 mg	Saturated Fat	1 gm
Protein	3 gm	Sodium	209 mg	Polyunsaturated Fat	1 gm
Carbohydrate	16 gm	Total Fat	4 gm	Monounsaturated Fat	2 gm

Savory Bread with Green Onion Spread Nutrient Analysis

Calories	110 kcal	Cholesterol	0 mg	Saturated Fat	1 gm
Protein	3 gm	Sodium	208 mg	Polyunsaturated Fat	1 gm
Carbohydrate	16 gm	Total Fat	4 gm	Monounsaturated Fat	2 gm

*C*old-*O*ven *P*opovers

Serves 12; 1 large popover per serving or
Serves 18; 1 medium popover per serving

Vegetable oil spray
6 egg whites
3 tablespoons acceptable vegetable oil
1 tablespoon acceptable margarine, melted
2 cups skim milk
2 cups sifted all-purpose flour
½ teaspoon salt

Lightly spray 12 large or 18 medium custard cups with vegetable oil.

In a bowl, beat egg whites lightly with a fork. Add oil, margarine and milk. Stir well. Set aside.

With flour and salt in a large mixing bowl, add liquid mixture gradually, beating with an electric mixer until well blended. Then mix on high speed for 1 to 2 minutes.

Fill each custard cup half full of batter and place in a *cold* oven. Turn oven on to 400° F and leave popovers in 45 to 60 minutes, or until a light golden color.

Nutrient Analysis *

Calories	131 kcal	Cholesterol	1 mg	Saturated Fat	1 gm
Protein	5 gm	Sodium	147 mg	Polyunsaturated Fat	2 gm
Carbohydrate	17 gm	Total Fat	5 gm	Monounsaturated Fat	1 gm

* for one large popover

Nutrient Analysis *

Calories	87 kcal	Cholesterol	0 mg	Saturated Fat	1 gm
Protein	3 gm	Sodium	99 mg	Polyunsaturated Fat	2 gm
Carbohydrate	11 gm	Total Fat	3 gm	Monounsaturated Fat	1 gm

* for one medium popover

Chapati

Serves 12; 1 chapati per serving

> 2 cups whole-wheat flour
> 2 tablespoons rice flour
> Water
> Vegetable oil spray

In a large bowl, sift flours together. Add enough water to make a stiff dough and set aside 1 hour.

Knead dough with a little water until soft. Divide into twelve small balls. Roll into very thin pancakes 4 to 6 inches in diameter, or use a tortilla press.

Lightly spray a griddle with vegetable oil. Cook on a very hot griddle until half-done on one side. Turn and cook the other side until brown spots appear.

To make chapatis puff up on a griddle, turn again to first side and press edges of chapati with a clean cloth until bread puffs up.

You may also use a hot charcoal fire to make the bread puff up. Throw cooked bread directly on hot coals with side that was cooked first down. Cook until chapati puffs up.

Nutrient Analysis

Calories	71 kcal	Cholesterol	0 mg	Saturated Fat	0 gm
Protein	3 gm	Sodium	1 mg	Polyunsaturated Fat	0 gm
Carbohydrate	15 gm	Total Fat	0 gm	Monounsaturated Fat	0 gm

Herbed Bread Sticks

Serves 20; 2 bread sticks per serving

> 8 hot dog buns, cut into long strips
> 8 tablespoons acceptable margarine, melted
> 6 tablespoons freshly grated Parmesan cheese
> Salt-free garlic seasoning to taste

Preheat oven to 350° F.

Cut the top of each bun into three sticks and the bottom of each bun into two sticks.

Brush each lightly with margarine. Dust with Parmesan cheese and sprinkle generously with garlic seasoning.

Bake on an ungreased cookie sheet 10 to 15 minutes, or until crisp. Serve at once, or store in airtight container to retain crispness.

These bread sticks are great with soups, salads or Italian entrees.

Nutrient Analysis

Calories	122 kcal	Cholesterol	2 mg	Saturated Fat		2 gm
Protein	3 gm	Sodium	213 mg	Polyunsaturated Fat		1 gm
Carbohydrate	13 gm	Total Fat	6 gm	Monounsaturated Fat		3 gm

*C*repes

Makes approximately 20 crepes
Serves 10; 2 crepes per serving

> 2 eggs
> 1 cup skim milk
> 1 cup flour
> 1 tablespoon acceptable vegetable oil
> Vegetable oil spray

Beat eggs and blend with all other ingredients until batter is smooth and just thick enough to coat a spoon. If batter is too thick, add a little more milk. Cover and let stand *at least* ½ hour.

Heat a 5- or 6-inch frying pan or crepe pan. Spray lightly with vegetable oil spray. Pour in just enough batter to form a very thin layer, tilting pan so batter spreads evenly. Cook on one side; turn and brown on the other side.

Repeat until all batter is used. As crepes are finished, stack them with a layer of wax paper or foil between each. Keep them warm if they are to be served immediately, or set them aside and reheat them later. Crepes may be filled for an entree (see Spinach Crepes, page 330) or for a dessert (see Dessert Crepes, page 519).

Note: Do not use vegetable oil spray near an open flame or a heat source. Read directions on can before using, and follow directions carefully.

Nutrient Analysis

Calories	78 kcal	Cholesterol	55 mg	Saturated Fat		1 gm
Protein	3 gm	Sodium	27 mg	Polyunsaturated Fat		1 gm
Carbohydrate	10 gm	Total Fat	3 gm	Monounsaturated Fat		1 gm

*W*hole-*W*heat *C*repes

Serves 12; 1 crepe per serving

½ cup white unbleached flour
¼ cup whole-wheat flour
1 cup skim milk
2 eggs
1 tablespoon acceptable vegetable oil
Vegetable oil spray

Place all ingredients in a blender or the work bowl of a food processor fitted with a metal blade. Process until mixed thoroughly. Cover and let mixture sit for 1 hour in refrigerator. Lightly spray a 6- to 8-inch nonstick skillet or crepe pan with vegetable oil and heat on a medium-high setting. When pan is hot, pour about ¼ cup batter into pan and swirl pan around until batter has covered the bottom completely. Pour excess batter back into blender or food processor. When the crepe edges start separating from the pan, flip crepe over. Brown slightly on the other side and remove to a plate.

Repeat with remainder of batter. As crepes are finished, stack them with a layer of wax paper or foil between each. Keep them warm if they are to be served immediately, or set them aside and reheat them later. Crepes may be filled for an entree (see Spinach Crepes, page 330) or for a dessert (see Dessert Crepes, page 519).

Note: Do not use vegetable oil spray near an open flame or a heat source. Read directions on can before using, and follow directions carefully.

Nutrient Analysis

Calories	56 kcal	Cholesterol	46 mg	Saturated Fat	0 gm
Protein	3 gm	Sodium	22 mg	Polyunsaturated Fat	1 gm
Carbohydrate	7 gm	Total Fat	2 gm	Monounsaturated Fat	1 gm

Nutmeg Bread

Makes 1 loaf (16 slices per loaf)
Serves 16; 1 slice per serving

> Vegetable oil spray
> ½ cup acceptable margarine
> ¾ cup sugar
> 1 egg, well beaten
> 2 cups sifted all-purpose flour
> ½ teaspoon baking powder
> ½ teaspoon baking soda
> 1 tablespoon freshly grated nutmeg, or 1 teaspoon ground
>   nutmeg
> 1 cup low-fat buttermilk

Preheat oven to 350° F. Lightly spray a 9-x-5-inch loaf pan with vegetable oil.

In a mixing bowl, cream margarine and sugar with mixer. Add egg and mix well.

In a separate bowl, sift dry ingredients together twice.

Add flour mixture and buttermilk alternately to egg mixture, beginning and ending with flour.

Pour batter into prepared loaf pan and bake 45 to 60 minutes, or until toothpick inserted in center comes out clean. Cool 10 minutes and remove bread from pan to cooling rack.

Note: This bread freezes well and makes a great gift.

Nutrient Analysis

Calories	150 kcal	Cholesterol	18 mg	Saturated Fat	2 gm
Protein	2 gm	Sodium	122 mg	Polyunsaturated Fat	1 gm
Carbohydrate	21 gm	Total Fat	6 gm	Monounsaturated Fat	3 gm

Gingerbread

Serves 12; 1 piece per serving

Vegetable oil spray
1 cup dark molasses
½ cup firmly packed brown sugar
½ cup acceptable vegetable oil
½ teaspoon cinnamon
½ teaspoon cloves
½ teaspoon nutmeg
1 teaspoon ground ginger
1 cup boiling water
2½ cups all-purpose flour, unsifted
1 teaspoon baking soda
2 tablespoons hot water

Preheat oven to 350° F. Lightly spray an 8-inch square baking pan with vegetable oil.

In a large bowl, blend together molasses, brown sugar, oil and spices. Stir in boiling water. Mix in flour. Set aside.

In a small bowl, dissolve baking soda in 2 tablespoons hot water. Stir to mix well and add to batter.

Bake in prepared pan 30 minutes.

Remove from oven and slice into twelve equal portions. Serve warm.

Serve with Orange Sauce (see page 437), if desired.

Nutrient Analysis*

Calories	265 kcal	Cholesterol	0 mg	Saturated Fat	1 gm
Protein	3 gm	Sodium	82 mg	Polyunsaturated Fat	5 gm
Carbohydrate	43 gm	Total Fat	9 gm	Monounsaturated Fat	2 gm

* *without Orange Sauce*

*I*rish *S*oda *B*read

Makes 1 loaf (20 slices per loaf)
Serves 20; 1 slice per serving

Vegetable oil spray
3 cups sifted all-purpose flour
¾ teaspoon salt
¼ cup sugar
1 teaspoon baking soda
½ teaspoon baking powder
¼ teaspoon cream of tartar
⅓ cup acceptable margarine
1⅓ cups low-fat buttermilk
⅓ cup currants

Preheat oven to 350° F. Lightly spray a cookie sheet with vegetable oil.

In a large bowl, sift together the first six dry ingredients. Cut in margarine with a pastry blender until mixture resembles cornmeal.

Add buttermilk and stir only until moistened. Mix currants in lightly.

Shape into a ball and knead about 15 seconds.

Place dough on prepared cookie sheet. With the palm of the hand, flatten dough into a circle about 7 inches in diameter and 1½ inches thick. With a sharp knife, cut a cross on the top about ¼ inch deep and 5 inches long, to prevent cracking during baking.

Bake 45 to 50 minutes. Cool on a wire rack.

Nutrient Analysis

Calories	113 kcal	Cholesterol	1 mg	Saturated Fat	1 gm
Protein	2 gm	Sodium	184 mg	Polyunsaturated Fat	1 gm
Carbohydrate	18 gm	Total Fat	3 gm	Monounsaturated Fat	1 gm

Savory Walnut Bread

Makes 1 loaf (16 slices per loaf)
Serves 16; 1 slice per serving

> Vegetable oil spray
> 2 cups sifted all-purpose flour
> 2 teaspoons baking powder
> ¼ teaspoon baking soda
> ½ teaspoon salt
> ½ cup firmly packed light brown sugar
> 1 egg
> 1 cup skim milk
> ¾ cup unsalted dry-roasted finely chopped walnuts

Preheat oven to 350° F. Lightly spray an 8-x-4-inch loaf pan with vegetable oil.

In a large bowl, sift together flour, baking powder, baking soda, salt and brown sugar. Set aside.

In a large bowl, beat egg until thick and lemon-colored. Add milk and continue beating until well blended. Add sifted dry ingredients and walnuts, stirring until mixture is moist.

Turn mixture into prepared loaf pan. Bake 40 minutes, or until a cake tester or a wooden toothpick inserted in the center comes out clean. Loosen loaf from sides of pan with spatula. Turn out, right side up, on a wire rack to cool.

Nutrient Analysis

Calories	125 kcal	Cholesterol	17 mg	Saturated Fat		0 gm
Protein	3 gm	Sodium	131 mg	Polyunsaturated Fat		2 gm
Carbohydrate	19 gm	Total Fat	4 gm	Monounsaturated Fat		1 gm

*P*umpkin *P*ecan *B*read

Makes 4 loaves (16 slices per loaf)
Serves 64; 1 slice per serving

Vegetable oil spray
4 eggs (or 8 egg whites or egg substitute equivalent to
    4 eggs)
2 cups canned pumpkin
1 cup acceptable vegetable oil
⅔ cup water
3½ cups flour
2 teaspoons baking soda
1½ teaspoons salt
1½ teaspoons cinnamon
1 teaspoon nutmeg
1 cup sugar
1 cup unsalted dry-roasted chopped pecans

Preheat oven to 350° F. Lightly spray four 8-x-4-inch loaf pans with vegetable oil.

In a bowl, beat eggs slightly. Add pumpkin, oil and water. Stir to mix well. Set aside.

In a large bowl, sift together flour, soda, salt, cinnamon and nutmeg. Add sugar and stir to mix thoroughly.

Make a well in the center of the dry ingredients. Add pumpkin mixture all at once. Mix well and add nuts. Stir to mix well.

Pour batter into four prepared loaf pans, filling each half-full.

Bake 1 hour, or until a wooden toothpick inserted in the center of the loaf comes out clean. Remove from pans and cool on a wire rack.

Nutrient Analysis *

Calories	85 kcal	Cholesterol	17 mg	Saturated Fat		1 gm
Protein	1 gm	Sodium	80 mg	Polyunsaturated Fat		2 gm
Carbohydrate	9 gm	Total Fat	5 gm	Monounsaturated Fat		2 gm

* using whole eggs

*B*anana *B*read

Makes 1 loaf (16 slices per loaf)
Serves 16; 1 slice per serving

Vegetable oil spray
1½ cups all-purpose flour
½ cup sugar
2 teaspoons baking powder
1 teaspoon baking soda
½ teaspoon salt
½ cup wheat germ
3 medium-size very ripe bananas, mashed (about 1 cup)
¼ cup low-fat buttermilk
¼ cup acceptable vegetable oil
4 egg whites

Preheat oven to 350° F. Lightly spray an 8-x-4-inch loaf pan with vegetable oil.

In a large bowl, sift together flour, sugar, baking powder, baking soda and salt. Mix in wheat germ. Add all remaining ingredients and beat until well blended.

Place in prepared loaf pan.

Bake 1 hour, or until toothpick inserted in center comes out clean.

Nutrient Analysis

Calories	132 kcal	Cholesterol	0 mg	Saturated Fat	1 gm
Protein	3 gm	Sodium	171 mg	Polyunsaturated Fat	2 gm
Carbohydrate	21 gm	Total Fat	4 gm	Monounsaturated Fat	1 gm

Whole-Wheat Apricot Bread

Makes 3 loaves (10 slices per loaf)
Serves 30; 1 slice per serving

Vegetable oil spray
1 cup chopped dried apricots
¼ cup acceptable vegetable oil
½ cup honey
⅔ cup boiling water
2 cups whole-wheat flour
¼ teaspoon baking soda
2 teaspoons baking powder
1 cup chopped, unsalted dry-roasted pecans
1 egg slightly beaten
½ cup evaporated skim milk

Preheat oven to 350° F. Lightly spray three 6-x-3-inch loaf pans with vegetable oil.

Put apricots in a bowl. Add oil, honey and boiling water. Set aside to cool.

In a large bowl, mix together dry ingredients and nuts. Set aside.

Place egg and milk in a small bowl and stir to mix well. Add to apricot mixture and stir until well blended.

Add liquid mixture to dry ingredients all at once. Mix just until dry ingredients are dampened, then stir 10 more strokes.

Pour batter equally into three prepared loaf pans. Let stand at room temperature 10 to 20 minutes.

Bake 30 to 35 minutes.

Cool thoroughly. Wrap in foil and store overnight before slicing.

Nutrient Analysis

Calories	98 kcal	Cholesterol	9 mg	Saturated Fat	1 gm
Protein	2 gm	Sodium	32 mg	Polyunsaturated Fat	2 gm
Carbohydrate	13 gm	Total Fat	5 gm	Monounsaturated Fat	2 gm

*O*range *W*heat *B*read

Makes 1 loaf (16 slices per loaf)
Serves 16; 1 slice per serving

Vegetable oil spray
2 cups white flour
½ cup whole-wheat flour
½ cup wheat germ
½ cup sugar
1 tablespoon baking powder
½ teaspoon baking soda
1 cup orange juice
⅓ cup acceptable vegetable oil
1 egg, beaten
½ cup chopped, unsalted dry-roasted walnuts, dusted
     lightly with flour
2 tablespoons grated orange rind

Preheat oven to 350° F. Lightly spray a 9-x-5-inch loaf pan with vegetable oil.

Mix dry ingredients together in a large bowl. Add remaining ingredients and stir until moist.

Pour into prepared loaf pan.

Bake 55 minutes, or until a wooden toothpick inserted in center of loaf comes out clean.

Remove from pan immediately. Serve warm, or wrap tightly in foil or plastic to store.

Nutrient Analysis

Calories	179 kcal	Cholesterol	17 mg	Saturated Fat	1 gm
Protein	4 gm	Sodium	85 mg	Polyunsaturated Fat	5 gm
Carbohydrate	24 gm	Total Fat	8 gm	Monounsaturated Fat	2 gm

*C*ranberry *B*read

Makes 2 loaves (12 slices per loaf)
Serves 24; 1 slice per serving

Vegetable oil spray
1 cup whole-wheat flour
1 cup all-purpose flour
⅔ cup firmly packed brown sugar
1 tablespoon baking powder
½ teaspoon salt
¼ teaspoon ground allspice
¾ cup orange juice
1 tablespoon grated orange rind
1 egg
½ cup acceptable vegetable oil
2 tablespoons vanilla
2 cups fresh cranberries, chopped

*P*reheat oven to 350° F. Lightly spray two 7⅜-x-3⅝-inch loaf pans with vegetable oil.

Combine first six dry ingredients in a bowl and set aside.

In a small bowl, combine remaining ingredients and mix well.

Make a well in dry ingredients and pour in liquid mixture. Stir just until blended.

Pour into prepared loaf pans and bake 45 to 50 minutes, or until a toothpick inserted in center comes out clean. Remove from pans and cool on a wire rack.

Nutrient Analysis

Calories	146 kcal	Cholesterol	11 mg	Saturated Fat	1 gm
Protein	2 gm	Sodium	92 mg	Polyunsaturated Fat	3 gm
Carbohydrate	25 gm	Total Fat	5 gm	Monounsaturated Fat	1 gm

*A*pplesauce *N*ut *B*read

Makes 1 loaf (16 slices per loaf)
Serves 16; 1 slice per serving

Vegetable oil spray
¾ cup sugar
1 cup natural (no-sugar-added) applesauce
⅓ cup acceptable vegetable oil
2 eggs
3 tablespoons skim milk
2 cups sifted all-purpose flour
1 teaspoon baking soda
½ teaspoon baking powder
½ teaspoon ground cinnamon
¼ teaspoon salt
¼ teaspoon ground nutmeg
¾ cup unsalted dry-roasted chopped pecans
¼ cup firmly packed brown sugar
½ teaspoon ground cinnamon
¼ cup unsalted dry-roasted chopped pecans

*P*reheat oven to 350° F. Lightly spray a 9-x-5-inch loaf pan with vegetable oil.

In a large mixing bowl, mix sugar, applesauce, oil, eggs and milk together thoroughly.

In another bowl, sift together flour, soda, baking powder, ½ teaspoon cinnamon, salt and nutmeg. Pour into applesauce mixture and beat until well combined. Stir in ¾ cup pecans.

Turn batter into prepared loaf pan.

Combine brown sugar, ½ teaspoon cinnamon and ¼ cup pecans in a small bowl. Sprinkle evenly over batter and bake 30 minutes. Cap loosely with foil and cook 30 minutes longer. Remove from pan and cool on a rack.

Nutrient Analysis

Calories	208 kcal	Cholesterol	34 mg	Saturated Fat	1 gm
Protein	3 gm	Sodium	106 mg	Polyunsaturated Fat	4 gm
Carbohydrate	27 gm	Total Fat	10 gm	Monounsaturated Fat	5 gm

*A*pplesauce *R*aisin *B*read

Makes 1 loaf (16 slices per loaf)
Serves 16; 1 slice per serving

Vegetable oil spray
1 cup natural (no-sugar-added) applesauce
½ cup acceptable vegetable oil
½ cup sugar
1¾ cups sifted flour
1 teaspoon baking soda
½ teaspoon salt
1 teaspoon cinnamon
½ teaspoon cloves
½ teaspoon nutmeg
1 egg, slightly beaten
1 cup raisins

Preheat oven to 325° F. Lightly spray an 8-x-4-inch loaf pan with vegetable oil.

In a large mixing bowl, mix applesauce, oil and sugar.

Sift in flour, baking soda, salt, cinnamon, cloves and nutmeg, mixing well after each addition.

Add egg and raisins. Mix well.

Pour into prepared loaf pan. Bake 1 hour and 20 minutes. Remove from pan and cool on a wire rack.

Nutrient Analysis

Calories	170 kcal	Cholesterol	17 mg	Saturated Fat	1 gm
Protein	2 gm	Sodium	126 mg	Polyunsaturated Fat	4 gm
Carbohydrate	25 gm	Total Fat	7 gm	Monounsaturated Fat	2 gm

*R*aisin *B*ran *B*read

Makes 2 loaves (24 slices per loaf)
Serves 48; 1 slice per serving

> Vegetable oil spray
> 1½ cups low-fat buttermilk
> 4 tablespoons acceptable margarine, melted
> 1 cup bran-type cereal
> Egg substitute equivalent to 2 eggs
> 2 teaspoons vanilla
> 2 cups flour
> 2 teaspoons baking soda
> 1½ teaspoons cinnamon
> ½ teaspoon nutmeg
> 1 teaspoon salt
> 1 cup raisins

*P*reheat oven to 350° F. Lightly spray two 7⅜-x-3⅝-inch loaf pans with vegetable oil.

In a bowl, combine buttermilk, margarine, cereal, egg substitute and vanilla. Blend well.

In a separate bowl, sift dry ingredients together. Add to buttermilk mixture and stir just until blended. Stir in raisins.

Pour batter evenly into prepared pans and bake 40 to 45 minutes. Cool in pans for 5 minutes, then cool on rack.

Nutrient Analysis

Calories	50 kcal	Cholesterol	0 mg	Saturated Fat	0 gm
Protein	1 gm	Sodium	113 mg	Polyunsaturated Fat	0 gm
Carbohydrate	9 gm	Total Fat	1 gm	Monounsaturated Fat	0 gm

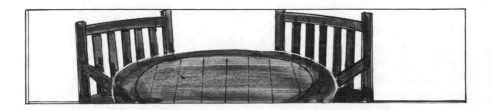

Boston "Light" Brown Bread

Makes 4 loaves (12 slices per loaf)
Serves 48; 1 slice per serving

Vegetable oil spray
3 cups raisins
Boiling water
¾ cup firmly packed brown sugar
¼ cup acceptable margarine, melted and cooled
Egg substitute equivalent to 2 eggs
1½ cups natural (no-sugar-added) applesauce
1 tablespoon grated orange rind
2 cups low-fat buttermilk
1 tablespoon vanilla extract
2½ cups all-purpose flour
2½ cups whole-wheat flour
4 teaspoons baking soda
1½ teaspoons salt

Lightly spray four 7⅜-x-3⅝-x-2½-inch loaf pans with vegetable oil. Preheat oven to 350° F.

Place raisins in a bowl. Add boiling water to cover. Set aside.

In a large mixing bowl, combine sugar, margarine, egg substitute, applesauce, rind, buttermilk and vanilla. Set aside.

In another bowl, sift flours, soda and salt together.

Drain raisins.

Add raisins and half of dry ingredients to egg mixture and stir just until mixture is combined. Repeat with remainder of dry ingredients, being careful not to overmix. Divide batter evenly among prepared loaf pans. Bake 25 to 30 minutes, or until skewer inserted in center of loaf comes out clean. Remove loaves from pans and cool on wire racks.

For an authentic Boston brown bread shape, batter may be baked in 1-pound coffee cans sprayed with vegetable oil. Bake 40 to 50 minutes at 350° F.

Nutrient Analysis

Calories	120 kcal	Cholesterol	0 mg	Saturated Fat	0 gm
Protein	2 gm	Sodium	168 mg	Polyunsaturated Fat	0 gm
Carbohydrate	26 gm	Total Fat	1 gm	Monounsaturated Fat	0 gm

*C*aramel *O*range *R*olls

Serves 12; 1 roll per serving

> ¼ cup firmly packed brown sugar
> 1 teaspoon grated orange rind
> 1½ tablespoons orange juice
> ¼ teaspoon mace
> 1 tablespoon acceptable margarine, melted
> 12 brown-and-serve dinner rolls

*P*reheat oven to 400° F.

In a bowl, combine sugar, orange rind, orange juice, mace and margarine. Stir to mix well. Spread over bottom of ungreased shallow pan.

Place rolls upside down over sugar mixture. Bake 15 minutes.

Remove from oven. Let rolls stand in pan 1 minute, or until syrup thickens. Invert pan and remove bread quickly so caramel-orange topping remains on top of rolls.

Nutrient Analysis

Calories	129 kcal	Cholesterol	6 mg	Saturated Fat	3 gm
Protein	2 gm	Sodium	268 mg	Polyunsaturated Fat	0 gm
Carbohydrate	16 gm	Total Fat	7 gm	Monounsaturated Fat	3 gm

*M*uffins

Serves 12; 1 muffin per serving

> Vegetable oil spray
> 2 cups sifted all-purpose flour
> 3 teaspoons baking powder
> 2 tablespoons sugar
> 1 teaspoon salt
> ⅓ cup acceptable vegetable oil
> Egg substitute equivalent to 1 egg
> 1¼ cups skim milk

Preheat oven to 425° F. Lightly spray muffin tins with vegetable oil.

Sift dry ingredients together into a large bowl. Make a well in the center. Pour oil, egg substitute and milk into the well all at once. Stir just enough to dampen the flour. Batter should be lumpy.

Fill prepared muffin tins two-thirds full with batter. Bake 20 to 25 minutes, or until toothpick inserted in center comes out clean.

FRUIT MUFFINS

Add ½ cup of raisins, chopped dates or blueberries to the batter.

JELLY MUFFINS

Fill muffin cups one-third full and place a small spoonful of jam or jelly in the center of each. Then cover with remaining batter.

NUT MUFFINS

Add ½ cup of unsalted dry-roasted coarsely chopped pecans or walnuts to the batter.

Muffins Nutrient Analysis

Calories	143 kcal	Cholesterol	1 mg	Saturated Fat	1 gm
Protein	3 gm	Sodium	274 mg	Polyunsaturated Fat	4 gm
Carbohydrate	18 gm	Total Fat	6 gm	Monounsaturated Fat	1 gm

Fruit Muffins Nutrient Analysis

Calories	162 kcal	Cholesterol	0 mg	Saturated Fat	1 gm
Protein	4 gm	Sodium	276 mg	Polyunsaturated Fat	4 gm
Carbohydrate	23 gm	Total Fat	6 gm	Monounsaturated Fat	1 gm

Jelly Muffins Nutrient Analysis

Calories	161 kcal	Cholesterol	1 mg	Saturated Fat	1 gm
Protein	3 gm	Sodium	275 mg	Polyunsaturated Fat	4 gm
Carbohydrate	23 gm	Total Fat	6 gm	Monounsaturated Fat	1 gm

Nut Muffins Nutrient Analysis

Calories	175 kcal	Cholesterol	1 mg	Saturated Fat	1 gm
Protein	4 gm	Sodium	274 mg	Polyunsaturated Fat	6 gm
Carbohydrate	19 gm	Total Fat	9 gm	Monounsaturated Fat	2 gm

Whole-Wheat Muffins

Serves 12; 1 muffin per serving

Vegetable oil spray
1 cup whole-wheat flour
¼ cup wheat germ
¾ cup sifted all-purpose flour
¼ teaspoon salt
2½ teaspoons baking powder
4 tablespoons sugar
1 teaspoon cinnamon
½ teaspoon ground cloves
½ cup grated zucchini
1 teaspoon grated orange peel
Egg substitute equivalent to 1 egg
1 cup skim milk
⅓ cup acceptable vegetable oil

Preheat oven to 400° F. Lightly spray muffin tin with vegetable oil.

In a bowl, combine all dry ingredients. Stir until well blended. Set aside.

In a small bowl, combine zucchini, orange peel, egg substitute, milk and oil. Add mixture to dry ingredients, stirring quickly only to blend the ingredients. Do not overmix.

Pour batter evenly into muffin cups. Bake 20 to 25 minutes, or until muffins are firm.

Let muffins rest a few minutes in pan. Remove from pan and serve immediately.

WHOLE-WHEAT NUT MUFFINS

Add ½ cup unsalted dry-roasted chopped walnuts to batter just before baking.

Note: To reheat muffins, wrap them in foil and place them in a preheated 450° F oven for 5 minutes.

Whole-Wheat Muffins Nutrient Analysis

Calories	150 kcal	Cholesterol	0 mg	Saturated Fat	1 gm
Protein	4 gm	Sodium	127 mg	Polyunsaturated Fat	4 gm
Carbohydrate	19 gm	Total Fat	7 gm	Monounsaturated Fat	2 gm

Whole-Wheat Nut Muffins Nutrient Analysis

Calories	182 kcal	Cholesterol	0 mg	Saturated Fat	1 gm
Protein	5 gm	Sodium	127 mg	Polyunsaturated Fat	6 gm
Carbohydrate	20 gm	Total Fat	10 gm	Monounsaturated Fat	2 gm

Cornmeal Whole-Wheat Muffins

Serves 18; 1 2¼-inch muffin per serving

>Vegetable oil spray
>6 tablespoons acceptable vegetable oil
>⅓ cup sugar
>1¼ cups skim milk
>Egg substitute equivalent to 1 egg
>1 cup whole-wheat flour
>½ teaspoon salt
>4 teaspoons baking powder
>1 cup cornmeal

Preheat oven to 425° F. Lightly spray muffin tin with vegetable oil.

In a bowl, combine oil and sugar. Stir to mix well. Add milk and egg substitute and stir well. Set aside.

In a large mixing bowl, combine flour, salt and baking powder. Add liquid mixture to flour mixture, stirring quickly just until mixed. Do not beat.

Add cornmeal and stir just until mixed.

Pour batter into prepared muffin tins, filling each cup two-thirds full.

Bake 25 minutes.

Nutrient Analysis

Calories	112 kcal	Cholesterol	0 mg	Saturated Fat	1 gm
Protein	2 gm	Sodium	140 mg	Polyunsaturated Fat	3 gm
Carbohydrate	15 gm	Total Fat	5 gm	Monounsaturated Fat	1 gm

Margaret's Oatmeal Raisin Muffins

Serves 12; 1 muffin per serving

1 cup oatmeal
1 cup skim milk
Vegetable oil spray
½ cup acceptable margarine, melted
1 egg, slightly beaten
¼ cup firmly packed brown sugar
½ cup raisins
1 cup whole-wheat flour
1½ teaspoons baking soda
1½ teaspoons baking powder

Combine oatmeal and milk in a large bowl. Cover and let sit in refrigerator for 1 hour.

Preheat oven to 400° F. Lightly spray a muffin tin with vegetable oil.

Remove oatmeal mixture from refrigerator and add margarine, egg, brown sugar and raisins. Stir well. Set aside.

In another bowl, mix dry ingredients together. Add to oatmeal mixture. Stir only enough to moisten the flour. Batter should be lumpy.

Fill muffin tins two-thirds full with batter.

Bake 15 to 20 minutes.

Nutrient Analysis

Calories	189 kcal	Cholesterol	23 mg	Saturated Fat	2 gm
Protein	4 gm	Sodium	249 mg	Polyunsaturated Fat	2 gm
Carbohydrate	26 gm	Total Fat	9 gm	Monounsaturated Fat	4 gm

Refrigerator Bran Muffins

Serves 30; 1 muffin per serving

1 cup bud-type bran cereal
1 cup boiling water
¾ cup acceptable margarine, room temperature
1 cup sugar
2 cups low-fat buttermilk
2½ cups all-purpose flour
2½ teaspoons baking soda
1 teaspoon cinnamon
½ teaspoon nutmeg
½ cup raisins or chopped prunes
2 cups extra-fiber bran cereal

Preheat oven to 400° F. Line 30 muffin cups with paper cupcake liners.

In a small bowl, combine bran buds and water. Mix well and set aside.

In a large mixing bowl, cream margarine and sugar. Add buttermilk and mix until well blended.

In another bowl, sift flour, soda, cinnamon and nutmeg together. Make a well in the dry ingredients and add bran mixture and milk mixture. Stir just to blend. Add raisins and extra-fiber bran and mix gently.

Spoon batter into muffin cups and bake 18 to 20 minutes. Remove pan from oven. Let cool 5 minutes, then remove muffins to wire cooling rack. Serve warm or cool completely, cover and store in refrigerator or freezer for later use.

Note: For fresh muffins each day, mix batter, cover and store it in refrigerator for up to 4 weeks. Pour batter into paper-lined muffin cups and bake as directed. (Do not stir batter before pouring.) If making fewer than 12 muffins at a time, fill empty muffin cups with water for even baking. This works even when making only a few muffins.

Nutrient Analysis

Calories	132 kcal	Cholesterol	1 mg	Saturated Fat	1 gm
Protein	3 gm	Sodium	192 mg	Polyunsaturated Fat	1 gm
Carbohydrate	22 gm	Total Fat	5 gm	Monounsaturated Fat	2 gm

Oat Bran Fruit Muffins

Serves 18; 1 muffin per serving

1½ cups high-fiber oat-bran cereal
¾ cup all-purpose flour
¾ cup whole-wheat flour
2 teaspoons baking powder
1 teaspoon baking soda
1 teaspoon cinnamon
½ cup raisins
½ cup chopped dates
½ cup chopped prunes
¼ cup firmly packed dark brown sugar
1 cup low-fat buttermilk
½ cup honey
3 tablespoons acceptable vegetable oil
2 eggs, well beaten

Preheat oven to 400° F. Line muffin tin with paper liners.

In a large bowl, mix oat bran, flours, baking powder, baking soda, cinnamon and dried fruits. In another bowl, mix brown sugar, buttermilk, honey, oil and eggs.

Make a well in dry ingredients. Pour liquid mixture into well and stir gently. Do not overmix. Spoon into paper-lined muffin tin. Bake 20 to 25 minutes.

Nutrient Analysis

Calories	158 kcal	Cholesterol	31 mg	Saturated Fat	1 gm
Protein	3 gm	Sodium	126 mg	Polyunsaturated Fat	2 gm
Carbohydrate	31 gm	Total Fat	3 gm	Monounsaturated Fat	1 gm

Blueberry Banana Muffins

Serves 12; 1 muffin per serving

Vegetable oil spray
1 cup all-purpose flour
½ cup whole-wheat flour
⅓ cup firmly packed brown sugar
½ cup wheat germ
1 tablespoon baking powder
½ teaspoon salt
1 teaspoon cinnamon
¼ teaspoon nutmeg
1 medium banana, mashed
⅓ cup acceptable margarine, melted and cooled
Egg substitute equivalent to 1 egg
½ cup orange juice
1 cup fresh blueberries, rinsed and stems removed

Preheat oven to 400° F. Lightly spray muffin tin with vegetable oil.

In a bowl, combine flours, sugar, wheat germ, baking powder, salt and spices. Stir until well mixed. Set aside.

In another bowl, mash banana. Add margarine, egg substitute, and orange juice to it. Whisk until well blended. Stir banana mixture into dry ingredients, mixing just until moistened. (Mixture may be lumpy.) With rubber spatula, carefully fold blueberries into batter. Pour batter evenly into 12 muffin cups. Bake 15 minutes.

Nutrient Analysis

Calories	161 kcal	Cholesterol	0 mg	Saturated Fat	1 gm
Protein	4 gm	Sodium	234 mg	Polyunsaturated Fat	2 gm
Carbohydrate	25 gm	Total Fat	6 gm	Monounsaturated Fat	2 gm

Buttermilk Bran Muffins

Serves 12; 1 muffin per serving

¾ cup bud-type bran
1 cup low-fat buttermilk
1 egg
⅓ cup honey
⅓ cup acceptable vegetable oil
½ cup raisins
½ cup shredded carrots
¾ cup all-purpose flour
½ cup whole-wheat flour
1 teaspoon baking soda
1 teaspoon nutmeg

Preheat oven to 425° F. Line muffin tins with paper liners.

In a bowl, combine the first seven ingredients. Let stand approximately 10 minutes.

In a large bowl, combine dry ingredients. Make a well in the center and add buttermilk-bran mixture. Stir only enough to dampen the flour. Batter should be lumpy.

Fill muffin tins two-thirds full with batter. Bake 15 to 20 minutes, or until toothpick comes out clean when inserted in the center of muffin.

Nutrient Analysis

Calories	181 kcal	Cholesterol	24 mg	Saturated Fat	1 gm
Protein	4 gm	Sodium	102 mg	Polyunsaturated Fat	4 gm
Carbohydrate	29 gm	Total Fat	7 gm	Monounsaturated Fat	2 gm

*S*outhern *R*aised *B*iscuits

Serves 30; 1 biscuit per serving

2½ cups all-purpose flour
½ teaspoon baking soda
½ teaspoon salt
¼ cup sugar
1 envelope yeast
1 cup low-fat buttermilk, warmed
¼ cup acceptable vegetable oil

Mix dry ingredients together in a large bowl. Set aside.

Dissolve yeast in slightly warmed buttermilk. Add buttermilk mixture and oil to flour mixture. Stir gently and quickly until mixed.

Turn dough onto a lightly floured board and knead gently 20 to 30 times. Roll out or pat to a ¼-inch thickness. With a floured 1-inch biscuit cutter, make 60 biscuits, then brush each biscuit with oil. Place 30 biscuits on an ungreased baking sheet. Place another biscuit on top of each.

Cover and let rise in a warm place (about 85° F) for about 2 hours.

Preheat oven to 375° F. Bake 12 to 15 minutes.

Nutrient Analysis

Calories	61 kcal	Cholesterol	0 mg	Saturated Fat	0 gm
Protein	1 gm	Sodium	58 mg	Polyunsaturated Fat	1 gm
Carbohydrate	9 gm	Total Fat	2 gm	Monounsaturated Fat	0 gm

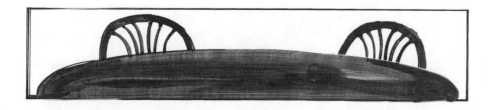

*F*laky *B*iscuits

Serves 16; 1 biscuit per serving

>   2 cups sifted all-purpose flour
>   3 teaspoons baking powder
>   ½ teaspoon salt
>   ¼ cup acceptable vegetable oil
>   ⅔ cup skim milk

*P*reheat oven to 450° F.

Sift flour, baking powder and salt together into a mixing bowl. Set aside.

Pour oil and milk into a measuring cup but do not stir. Add all at once to flour mixture. Stir quickly with a fork until dough clings together.

Knead dough lightly about 10 times.

Place dough on a 12-x-16-inch piece of wax paper. Pat dough out until it is about ½ inch thick. Cut with an unfloured, medium-size cookie cutter.

Place biscuits on an ungreased cookie sheet and bake 12 to 15 minutes.

Nutrient Analysis

Calories	87 kcal	Cholesterol	0 mg	Saturated Fat	0 gm
Protein	2 gm	Sodium	127 mg	Polyunsaturated Fat	2 gm
Carbohydrate	12 gm	Total Fat	4 gm	Monounsaturated Fat	1 gm

*D*rop *B*iscuits

Serves 12; 1 biscuit per serving

>   Vegetable oil spray
>   2 cups all-purpose flour
>   1 tablespoon baking powder
>   1 teaspoon salt
>   ⅓ cup acceptable margarine
>   1 cup skim milk

*P*reheat oven to 450° F. Lightly spray a cookie sheet with vegetable oil.

In a bowl, combine dry ingredients. Cut in margarine with two knives or a pastry blender. (Margarine pieces should be approximately pea-size.) Stir in milk. Drop batter by teaspoonfuls, 1 inch apart, onto prepared cookie sheet.

Bake 10 to 12 minutes.

HERB BISCUITS

Add any one of the following to the dry ingredients: dried parsley, basil, tarragon or aniseed.

Nutrient Analysis

Calories	123 kcal	Cholesterol	0 mg	Saturated Fat	1 gm
Protein	3 gm	Sodium	320 mg	Polyunsaturated Fat	1 gm
Carbohydrate	16 gm	Total Fat	5 gm	Monounsaturated Fat	2 gm

Cornbread Dressing

Serves 8

Vegetable oil spray
3 cups crumbled Southern-Style Cornbread (see page 463)
1 cup plain bread crumbs
2 cups homemade Chicken Broth (see page 87) or
    commercial low-sodium variety
3 stalks celery, finely chopped
1 large onion, finely chopped
2 egg whites
½ teaspoon freshly ground black pepper, or to taste
½ teaspoon sage or poultry seasoning

Preheat oven to 350° F. Lightly spray a large baking dish with vegetable oil.

Combine remaining ingredients in a large mixing bowl. Mix well. Turn into prepared baking dish, cover and bake 45 minutes.

OPTIONAL COOKING METHOD

Stuff dressing loosely into cavity of 10- to 12-pound turkey just before roasting.

Nutrient Analysis *

Calories	104 kcal	Cholesterol	1 mg	Saturated Fat	0 gm
Protein	4 gm	Sodium	190 mg	Polyunsaturated Fat	1 gm
Carbohydrate	17 gm	Total Fat	2 gm	Monounsaturated Fat	1 gm

* assuming one-third of Southern-Style Cornbread recipe is used

Celery Dressing

Serves 16

Vegetable oil spray
½ cup chopped onion
1½ cups diced celery, including leaves
1 cup homemade Chicken Broth (see page 87) or
  commercial low-sodium variety
3 cups skim milk
2 8-ounce packages poultry dressing mix

Preheat oven to 350° F. Lightly spray large baking dish with vegetable oil.

Combine onion, celery and chicken broth in a saucepan over medium-high heat. Cook about 10 minutes, or until vegetables are tender.

Add skim milk and bring almost to a boil.

Place dressing mix in a large bowl. Add skim-milk mixture and stir until well moistened. If too dry, add a little boiling water.

Place in a prepared pan, cover and bake for 20 minutes.

OPTIONAL COOKING METHOD

Stuff dressing loosely into cavity of 10- to 12-pound turkey just before roasting.

Note: For a slightly different tasting dressing, try Rice Dressing on page 394.

Nutrient Analysis

Calories	50 kcal	Cholesterol	1 mg	Saturated Fat	0 gm
Protein	3 gm	Sodium	248 mg	Polyunsaturated Fat	0 gm
Carbohydrate	9 gm	Total Fat	1 gm	Monounsaturated Fat	0 gm

Apple Dressing

Serves 12

Vegetable oil spray
¼ cup chopped onion
¼ cup chopped celery
2 tablespoons acceptable margarine
1 cup diced, unpeeled apples
4 cups dry bread cubes
½ teaspoon poultry seasoning
½ teaspoon dried sage
Freshly ground black pepper to taste
½ cup homemade Chicken Broth (see page 87) or
    commercial low-sodium variety

Preheat oven to 350° F. Lightly spray a large baking dish with vegetable oil.

Place onion, celery and margarine in a skillet over medium-high heat. Sauté 5 minutes, or until vegetables are tender. Transfer to a large bowl. Add apples and dry ingredients and stir to mix well. Add broth and toss lightly.

Turn into prepared baking dish, cover and bake 45 minutes.

OPTIONAL COOKING METHOD
Stuff dressing loosely into cavity of 10- to 12-pound turkey just before roasting.

DRESSING WITH MIXED DRIED FRUITS
Combine 1 cup chopped dried fruit (apricots, prunes or peaches) with ½ cup raisins. Simmer in water in a covered saucepan for 20 minutes. Drain and cool slightly. Combine with dry ingredients in Apple Dressing. Proceed as directed.

Apple Dressing Nutrient Analysis

Calories	49 kcal	Cholesterol	0 mg	Saturated Fat	1 gm
Protein	1 gm	Sodium	77 mg	Polyunsaturated Fat	1 gm
Carbohydrate	6 gm	Total Fat	2 gm	Monounsaturated Fat	1 gm

Dressing with Mixed Dried Fruits Nutrient Analysis *

Calories	94 kcal	Cholesterol	0 mg	Saturated Fat	1 gm
Protein	2 gm	Sodium	80 mg	Polyunsaturated Fat	1 gm
Carbohydrate	18 gm	Total Fat	2 gm	Monounsaturated Fat	1 gm

* using apricots and raisins

Desserts

FRUITS	MERINGUE "EGG" BASKETS
SPECIAL BAKED APPLES	GINGER BERRY FILLED MERINGUES
BANANAS FLAMBÉ	HONEY ALMOND CUSTARDS
CHERRIES JUBILEE	MANDARIN ORANGE PUDDING
GRAPEFRUIT ORANGE PALETTE	INDIAN PUDDING
LIME MELON BALLS	DELICIOUS RICE PUDDING
MELON RINGS WITH STRAWBERRIES	YOGURT GELATIN DELIGHT
CLARET SPICED ORANGES	FRESH STRAWBERRY MOUSSE
BLUSHING PEARS	WHOLE-WHEAT APPLESAUCE CAKE
BAKED GINGER PEARS	NUTMEG CAKE
GOLDEN POACHED PEARS	MARGARITE'S CARROT CAKE
PINEAPPLE BOATS	EASY APPLE CAKE
FRESH FRUIT COMPOTE	RUM LIME PUDDING CAKE
FRESH FRUIT COMPOTE WITH WINE	QUICK PINEAPPLE UPSIDE-DOWN CAKE
MINT JULEP FRUIT CUP	BLACK DEVIL'S FOOD CAKE
MARY'S FRUIT CUP WITH YOGURT	WACKY CAKE
APPLE RAISIN CRUNCH	WHITE LAYER CAKE
OAT BLUEBERRY CRISP	CREAMY FUDGE FROSTING
CHERRY CRISP	SEVEN-MINUTE FROSTING
PEACH CLAFOUTI	SUGAR COOKIES
DESSERT CREPES	GINGER COOKIES
DEEP-DISH COBBLER	PEANUT BUTTER COOKIES
DEEP-DISH FRUIT CRISP	CHOCOLATE OATMEAL COOKIES
APPLE PIE	FAVORITE OATMEAL COOKIES
WALNUT CRUMB APPLE PIE	OATMEAL CARROT COOKIES
NORWEGIAN APPLE PIE	APRICOT RAISIN BARS
PINK LEMONADE PIE	BOURBON BALLS
LIME CHIFFON PIE	SHERRY THINS
RASPBERRY CHIFFON PIE	BUTTERSCOTCH BROWNIES
FRESH STRAWBERRY PIE	APRICOT ICE
PUMPKIN PIE	STRAWBERRIES WITH CHAMPAGNE ICE
PUMPKIN CHIFFON PIE	LEMON SHERBET
BAKED LEMON CHEESE PIE	TEQUILA LIME SHERBET
REFRIGERATOR PINEAPPLE CHEESECAKE	FRESH FRUIT ICE
MINIATURE RUM-RAISIN CHEESECAKES	FRUITY ICE CREAM
MOCHA YOGURT PIE	FROZEN BANANA ORANGE PUSH-UPS
PIE PASTRY	CARDINAL SUNDAE
MRS. PARK'S PIECRUST	HONG KONG SUNDAE
NUT CRUST	APPLE POPS
OAT CRUMB PIECRUST	DUQ
MERINGUE SHELL	STRAWBERRY DESSERT DRINK

What's for dessert?"
This is probably one of the American family's most often asked questions. And why not? Nearly everyone loves dessert! Cakes, cookies, pies, puddings and frozen treats are all-American classics.

Fortunately, a fabulous dessert doesn't have to ooze with saturated fat and cholesterol. Nor does it have to be high in calories. That's the beauty of creating your own homemade desserts—*you* control the kinds and amounts of fat, sugar and salt you include.

Just look at the dessert line-up on the pages that follow: Cherries Jubilee, Deep-Dish Fruit Crisp, Pink Lemonade Pie, Miniature Rum-Raisin Cheesecakes, Delicious Rice Pudding, plus favorites like Apple Pie, Margarite's Carrot Cake, Peanut Butter Cookies, Bourbon Balls—even a couple of make-your-own sundaes.

Many of the best desserts are light and are built around fresh fruit: pears picked at the height of sweetness, juicy vine-ripened berries, the tart crunch of a fresh McIntosh apple. When you add egg whites, nuts and skim milk to fruit, you also add protein. A fruit or vegetable (such as pumpkin or rhubarb) base will provide vitamins and minerals.

After you've exhausted this hefty supply of dessert recipes, adapt your own favorites by substituting polyunsaturated oil or margarine where possible and limiting the number of egg yolks you use. Consider filling your cake layers with nutmeats, fresh fruit purees or gelatin flavored with liqueurs. Chocolate lovers, try using cocoa instead of chocolate. It offers the same unbeatable taste—without the saturated fat!

*F*ruits

Fresh ripe fruits, the symbols of a bountiful harvest, can enhance a simple meal or adorn a banquet table. Serve them chilled or at room temperature as snacks, accompaniments to meals or as desserts. Here is a partial listing:

APPLES—1 MEDIUM

For cooking or eating:
Baldwin
Golden Delicious
Granny Smith
Gravenstein
Grimes Golden
Jonathan
McIntosh
Red Delicious
Rhode Island Greening
Stayman
Winesap
Yellow Transparent

For dessert:
Baker
Delicious
McIntosh
Northern Spy
Pippin
Rome Beauty
Stayman
Winesap

OTHER

apricots—2 medium
banana—½ small
cherries—10 large
figs—2 large
grapes—12
guava—½ medium
kiwi—1 large
mango—½ small
melons—¼ cantaloupe (6-inch diameter), ⅛ honeydew (7-inch diameter)

papaya—⅓ medium (serve chilled, sprinkled with fresh lemon or lime juice)
peach—1 medium
pear—1 small
persimmon—½ small
pineapple, diced—½ cup
plums—2 medium

DRIED FRUITS (USE IN COOKING OR AS SNACKS)

apples—¼ cup
apricots—4 halves
currants—2 tablespoons
dates—2
fig—1 small

peaches—2 medium
pineapple, diced—1 tablespoon
prunes—2 medium
raisins—2 tablespoons

BERRIES

(Serve sprinkled with 1 tablespoon confectioners' sugar flavored with a
    vanilla bean)

blackberries—1 cup   raspberries—1 cup

blueberries—1 cup   strawberries—1 cup

CITRUS FRUITS

grapefruit—½ small   orange—1 small

kumquat—4   tangelo—1 medium

nectarine—1 medium   tangerine—1 large

Nutrient Analysis*

Calories	81 kcal	Cholesterol	0 mg	Saturated Fat	0 gm
Protein	0 gm	Sodium	0 mg	Polyunsaturated Fat	0 gm
Carbohydrate	21 gm	Total Fat	1 gm	Monounsaturated Fat	0 gm

* for 1 apple

Nutrient Analysis*

Calories	42 kcal	Cholesterol	0 mg	Saturated Fat	0 gm
Protein	0 gm	Sodium	0 mg	Polyunsaturated Fat	0 gm
Carbohydrate	11 gm	Total Fat	0 gm	Monounsaturated Fat	0 gm

* for ½ banana

Nutrient Analysis*

Calories	57 kcal	Cholesterol	0 mg	Saturated Fat	0 gm
Protein	0 gm	Sodium	5 mg	Polyunsaturated Fat	0 gm
Carbohydrate	15 gm	Total Fat	0 gm	Monounsaturated Fat	0 gm

* for 2 tablespoons raisins

Nutrient Analysis*

Calories	76 kcal	Cholesterol	0 mg	Saturated Fat	0 gm
Protein	1 gm	Sodium	1 mg	Polyunsaturated Fat	0 gm
Carbohydrate	18 gm	Total Fat	1 gm	Monounsaturated Fat	0 gm

* for 1 cup strawberries with 1 tablespoon confectioners' sugar

Nutrient Analysis*

Calories	45 kcal	Cholesterol	0 mg	Saturated Fat	0 gm
Protein	1 gm	Sodium	0 mg	Polyunsaturated Fat	0 gm
Carbohydrate	11 gm	Total Fat	0 gm	Monounsaturated Fat	0 gm

* for 1 orange

Special Baked Apples

Serves 4

    4 apples, Jonathan or McIntosh, rinsed
    2 teaspoons fresh lemon juice
    4 teaspoons golden raisins
    4 teaspoons firmly packed brown sugar
    2 teaspoons sugar
    2 teaspoons ground cinnamon
    2 teaspoons acceptable margarine
    1 tablespoon unsalted dry-roasted finely chopped pecans or
        walnuts
    ½ cup rum or sherry

Preheat oven to 350° F.

Core apples but do not cut through the bottoms. Cut a ½-inch-wide strip of peel off the top of each apple around the hole. Place apples in a baking dish and sprinkle with lemon juice. Fill centers with raisins, brown sugar and sugar. Sprinkle all with cinnamon. Add margarine to each apple. Sprinkle nuts on top of apples. Pour rum or sherry into bottom of baking dish.

Bake 30 to 35 minutes, basting several times during cooking time. Serve warm or cold.

MICROWAVE METHOD

Place filled apples in individual glass custard cups. Cover loosely with plastic wrap and cook 3 to 4½ minutes on high. Let stand 3 minutes and serve.

Nutrient Analysis

Calories	161 kcal	Cholesterol	0 mg	Saturated Fat	1 gm
Protein	1 gm	Sodium	29 mg	Polyunsaturated Fat	1 gm
Carbohydrate	34 gm	Total Fat	4 gm	Monounsaturated Fat	1 gm

Bananas Flambé

Serves 4; 1 banana per serving

    Vegetable oil spray
    1 tablespoon fresh lemon juice
    1 tablespoon sugar

4 ripe bananas, peeled
4 sugar cubes
1 tablespoon lemon extract

Preheat oven to 400° F. Lightly spray a pie pan with vegetable oil.

Sprinkle lemon juice and sugar over the peeled whole bananas. Place them on prepared pie plate. Bake 20 minutes, or until slightly brown.

Meanwhile, place sugar cubes in a small bowl and pour lemon extract over them.

Remove bananas from oven and place a sugar cube on each banana. Light the cubes at the table just before serving.

Nutrient Analysis

Calories	117 kcal	Cholesterol	0 mg	Saturated Fat	0 gm
Protein	1 gm	Sodium	2 mg	Polyunsaturated Fat	0 gm
Carbohydrate	30 gm	Total Fat	1 gm	Monounsaturated Fat	0 gm

*C*herries *J*ubilee

Serves 8; ¼ cup cherries per serving

2 cups pitted no-sugar-added Bing cherries, canned in
   natural juices, with juice
½ cup currant jelly
1 tablespoon cornstarch
1 tablespoon grated orange rind
2 tablespoons heated brandy

Drain juice from cherries, reserving juice. In a saucepan, combine cherry juice, currant jelly, cornstarch and orange rind, and cook over low heat until jelly melts. Add cherries and stir to coat well. Cover and simmer 10 minutes. Remove to a heat-proof serving dish.

At the table, pour warm brandy over cherries and light. Serve while cherries are still alight.

You may also spoon flaming cherries into a Meringue Shell (see page 536) or serve over ice milk.

Nutrient Analysis

Calories	96 kcal	Cholesterol	0 mg	Saturated Fat	0 gm
Protein	1 gm	Sodium	3 mg	Polyunsaturated Fat	0 gm
Carbohydrate	22 gm	Total Fat	0 gm	Monounsaturated Fat	0 gm

*G*rapefruit *O*range *P*alette

Serves 6; ¹/₂ grapefruit per serving

3 medium fresh pink or ruby grapefruit
3 medium seedless oranges
1 12-ounce bag frozen sweetened raspberries
¹/₃ cup sifted confectioners' sugar
2 tablespoons crème de cassis (black currant liqueur)
6 sprigs fresh mint

With a sharp knife, remove peel and all pith (white portion) from grapefruit. Cut between membranes to separate sections. Set aside.

With a sharp knife, remove peel and all pith from oranges. Slice each orange into 5 slices crosswise and then cut each slice in half, for a total of 30 semicircular pieces of orange. Set aside.

Defrost raspberries and puree in a blender or the work bowl of a food processor fitted with a metal blade. Push through a fine-meshed strainer to remove seeds. Stir in sugar and liqueur.

For each serving, arrange one-sixth of grapefruit sections and five orange pieces alternately in a circular pattern (as in flower petals) on a dessert plate. Drizzle sauce in a circle over the pieces and place a mint sprig in center. Repeat with remainder for each plate.

Serve cold.

Note: This dish may be prepared ahead of time. Cover and refrigerate grapefruit sections, orange pieces and pureed raspberries. Assemble just before serving.

Nutrient Analysis

Calories	146 kcal	Cholesterol	0 mg	Saturated Fat	0 gm
Protein	2 gm	Sodium	0 mg	Polyunsaturated Fat	0 gm
Carbohydrate	35 gm	Total Fat	1 gm	Monounsaturated Fat	0 gm

*L*ime *M*elon *B*alls

Serves 4

1 cup water
2 tablespoons sugar
2 tablespoons fresh lime juice
2 cups assorted melon balls

GARNISHES
Pomegranate seeds, mint sprigs or thin lime slices

*B*ring water and sugar to a boil in a saucepan over high heat. Remove from heat and cool to room temperature.

Add lime juice and stir to mix well. Set aside.

Place melon balls in four sherbet glasses. Pour lime sauce over all. Garnish with pomegranate seeds, a sprig of mint or a thin slice of lime.

Nutrient Analysis

Calories	57 kcal	Cholesterol	0 mg	Saturated Fat	0 gm
Protein	1 gm	Sodium	9 mg	Polyunsaturated Fat	0 gm
Carbohydrate	14 gm	Total Fat	0 gm	Monounsaturated Fat	0 gm

*M*elon *R*ings *with* *S*trawberries

Serves 5

1 pint fresh strawberries
1 medium fresh cantaloupe or honeydew melon

*R*inse strawberries, but do not hull. Set aside to drain.

Cut melon crosswise into 1-inch-thick rings. Remove seeds.

Place slices on individual plates. With a knife, carefully cut around the slice ¼ inch from the rind; do not remove rind. Slice pulp to make bite-size pieces, leaving rind intact.

Arrange five or six strawberries in the center of each melon slice before serving.

Nutrient Analysis

Calories	82 kcal	Cholesterol	0 mg	Saturated Fat	0 gm
Protein	2 gm	Sodium	17 mg	Polyunsaturated Fat	0 gm
Carbohydrate	20 gm	Total Fat	1 gm	Monounsaturated Fat	0 gm

*C*laret *S*piced *O*ranges

Serves 6

4 oranges, peeled and sectioned
5 tablespoons sugar
½ cup water
¾ cup claret wine
2 whole cloves
1 3-inch stick cinnamon
1 tablespoon fresh lemon juice

*P*lace orange sections in a bowl. Set aside.

In a saucepan over medium-high heat, combine remaining ingredients. Bring to a boil and simmer 5 minutes. Pour over orange sections.

Cool slightly, cover and refrigerate about 4 hours or overnight. Remove whole spices and serve cold.

Nutrient Analysis

Calories	84 kcal	Cholesterol	0 mg	Saturated Fat	0 gm
Protein	1 gm	Sodium	3 mg	Polyunsaturated Fat	0 gm
Carbohydrate	21 gm	Total Fat	0 gm	Monounsaturated Fat	0 gm

*B*lushing *P*ears

Serves 6; ½ pear per serving

> 3 medium fresh D'Anjou pears, about 1½ pounds
> 2 cups water
> 2 tablespoons fresh lemon juice
> 2 cups rosé wine
> ½ cup sugar
> 3 pieces orange zest or peel (1 x 2 inches each)
> 3 pieces lemon zest or peel (1 x 2 inches each)
> 3 drops red food coloring
> 1 teaspoon fresh lemon juice

Peel pears with a vegetable peeler. Cut in half and remove core with melon baller.

In a bowl, combine water and 2 tablespoons lemon juice. Add pears. Set aside.

In a stainless steel or enameled saucepan, combine wine and sugar. Add zest, food coloring and remaining 1 tablespoon lemon juice to syrup. Bring to a boil. Remove pears from lemon water and immerse them in wine mixture. Simmer them, uncovered, over medium heat 8 minutes, or until fruit is tender when pierced with a knife tip.

Remove pears from syrup with a slotted spoon and set aside.

Discard strips of orange and lemon zest. Continue to cook syrup over medium heat until reduced to 6 tablespoons.

Cut each pear half in ⅛-inch crosswise slices. Fan slices out on a serving platter. Drizzle 2 teaspoons syrup over each pear and discard remainder.

Serve warm, or cover, refrigerate and serve chilled.

Nutrient Analysis

Calories	76 kcal	Cholesterol	0 mg	Saturated Fat	0 gm
Protein	0 gm	Sodium	6 mg	Polyunsaturated Fat	0 gm
Carbohydrate	20 gm	Total Fat	0 gm	Monounsaturated Fat	0 gm

*B*aked *G*inger *P*ears

Serves 8; ½ pear per serving

8 canned no-sugar-added pear halves, canned in natural
    juices
½ cup firmly packed brown sugar
1 teaspoon fresh lemon juice
½ teaspoon ground ginger, or chopped crystallized ginger
    to taste
¼ cup unsalted dry-roasted chopped pecans

GARNISH
Crystallized ginger

*P*reheat oven to 350° F.

Drain pears, reserving juice. Arrange pear halves close together in a baking dish, cut-side-up. Set aside.

In a small bowl, combine brown sugar, lemon juice, ginger and pecans; mix well. Spoon into pear halves and sprinkle lightly with ginger. Pour reserved pear juice around pears to cover bottom of dish.

Bake 15 to 20 minutes.

Serve warm or cover and refrigerate to serve chilled. Garnish with bits of crystallized ginger.

Nutrient Analysis

Calories	103 kcal	Cholesterol	0 mg	Saturated Fat	0 gm
Protein	0 gm	Sodium	4 mg	Polyunsaturated Fat	1 gm
Carbohydrate	21 gm	Total Fat	3 gm	Monounsaturated Fat	2 gm

Golden Poached Pears

Serves 6; 1 pear per serving

6 fresh, ripe Bartlett pears
1 tablespoon fresh lemon juice
2 12-ounce cans apricot nectar
½ cup sugar
1 teaspoon freshly grated lemon peel
¼ cup fresh lemon juice
½ cup sherry

GARNISH
6 sprigs fresh mint (optional)

Peel pears. (Leave cores and stems.) Sprinkle them with 1 tablespoon lemon juice to prevent discoloration.

Combine apricot nectar, sugar, lemon peel and lemon juice in a deep saucepan over medium-high heat. Bring to a boil, reduce heat and simmer 5 minutes. Add sherry.

Cook pears in simmering syrup over low heat, basting and turning them occasionally to cook evenly. Cook 20 to 25 minutes, or until just tender. (Cooking time may vary depending on the size and firmness of the pears.)

Remove pears and set aside. Continue simmering sauce until reduced by half. Pour sauce over pears, cover and refrigerate.

Place each pear in a chilled dessert dish and spoon syrup over each. Garnish with fresh mint when available.

Nutrient Analysis

Calories	190 kcal	Cholesterol	0 mg	Saturated Fat	0 gm
Protein	1 gm	Sodium	8 mg	Polyunsaturated Fat	0 gm
Carbohydrate	49 gm	Total Fat	1 gm	Monounsaturated Fat	0 gm

*P*ineapple *B*oats

Serves 4; 1 pineapple wedge and 6 grapes per serving

1 medium fresh pineapple
4 small bunches fresh seedless grapes (approximateley 6
grapes per bunch)

GARNISH
8 lemon leaves (optional)

Split pineapple lengthwise into quarters, leaving plume attached to each quarter. With a sharp knife, separate flesh from shell in one piece. Trim away core. Return each long section of flesh to its shell and cut it vertically into ½-inch wedges. Stick a toothpick into each wedge. Arrange pineapple quarters in a circle on a round, flat serving tray, with small bunches of grapes between them. Garnish with lemon leaves.

MELON BOATS
Substitute cantaloupe or honeydew for pineapple. Cut melon into fourths. Separate flesh in a single piece from each section, then slice vertically into small wedges. Proceed as directed above.

Pineapple Boats Nutrient Analysis

Calories	79 kcal	Cholesterol	0 mg	Saturated Fat	0 gm
Protein	1 gm	Sodium	2 mg	Polyunsaturated Fat	0 gm
Carbohydrate	20 gm	Total Fat	1 gm	Monounsaturated Fat	0 gm

Melon Boats Nutrient Analysis

Calories	102 kcal	Cholesterol	0 mg	Saturated Fat	0 gm
Protein	2 gm	Sodium	21 mg	Polyunsaturated Fat	0 gm
Carbohydrate	25 gm	Total Fat	1 gm	Monounsaturated Fat	0 gm

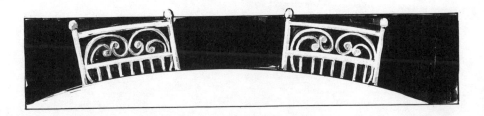

*F*resh *F*ruit *C*ompote

Serves 6; ½ cup per serving

2 apples
2 pears
1 persimmon
1 5-ounce box frozen sweetened raspberries
¼ cup orange juice
¼ cup kirsch (optional)

Cut up fresh apples, pears and persimmon. Place in a bowl. Defrost raspberries, drain and add to a bowl. Stir gently to mix. Pour orange juice and kirsch over all. Cover, refrigerate and serve cold.

Note: You may substitute any fruit you wish.

Nutrient Analysis

Calories	108 kcal	Cholesterol	0 mg	Saturated Fat		0 gm
Protein	1 gm	Sodium	1 mg	Polyunsaturated Fat		0 gm
Carbohydrate	28 gm	Total Fat	0 gm	Monounsaturated Fat		0 gm

*F*resh *F*ruit *C*ompote with *W*ine

Serves 6; ½ cup per serving

3 cups fresh fruit
1 pint white or rosé wine

GARNISH
Fresh pomegranate seeds to taste

Use any combination of fruit you like. Try buying a variety of fresh seasonal fruits. Rinse and prepare fruits by separating into sections, cubing, dicing, slicing or leaving them whole. Combine fruits in a bowl and pour wine over all. Cover and refrigerate several hours.

Spoon into long-stemmed crystal compotes and garnish with fresh pomegranate seeds.

Nutrient Analysis

Calories	95 kcal	Cholesterol	0 mg	Saturated Fat		0 gm
Protein	1 gm	Sodium	7 mg	Polyunsaturated Fat		0 gm
Carbohydrate	11 gm	Total Fat	0 gm	Monounsaturated Fat		0 gm

Mint Julep Fruit Cup

Serves 6; ½ cup per serving

> 1 medium pineapple, cubed
> 2 cups sliced strawberries
> ¼ cup crème de menthe or ¼ teaspoon mint extract
> 1½ cups lime sherbet
>
> **GARNISH**
> 6 fresh mint leaves or 6 pieces crystallized mint leaves

Combine fresh fruit and spoon into compotes. Sprinkle with crème de menthe or mint extract. Serve with a small scoop (¼ cup) of lime sherbet and garnish with a fresh mint leaf or with crystallized mint leaves.

Note: You may substitute any fruit you wish.

Nutrient Analysis

Calories	149 kcal	Cholesterol	3 mg	Saturated Fat		1 gm
Protein	1 gm	Sodium	24 mg	Polyunsaturated Fat		0 gm
Carbohydrate	32 gm	Total Fat	2 gm	Monounsaturated Fat		0 gm

Mary's Fruit Cup with Yogurt

Serves 6; ½ cup per serving

> 3 cups mixed fresh fruit (apples, grapefruit, oranges,
>   berries, pears, melons, bananas or fruit of your choice)
> 2 cups low-fat vanilla yogurt
> ¼ cup crushed sunflower seeds

Prepare fruit, then mix with yogurt. Cover and refrigerate for at least 2 hours before serving. Spoon into individual serving dishes and top with crushed sunflower seeds.

Nutrient Analysis

Calories	151 kcal	Cholesterol	3 mg	Saturated Fat		1 gm
Protein	5 gm	Sodium	50 mg	Polyunsaturated Fat		2 gm
Carbohydrate	25 gm	Total Fat	4 gm	Monounsaturated Fat		1 gm

Apple Raisin Crunch

Serves 6

Vegetable oil spray
2 pounds tart apples, peeled, cored and sliced (about
  5½ cups)
½ cup raisins
½ cup orange juice
½ cup uncooked oatmeal
½ cup toasted wheat germ
½ teaspoon cinnamon
4 tablespoons acceptable margarine, melted

Preheat oven to 350° F. Lightly spray an 8-x-8-inch baking pan with vegetable oil.

Arrange apples and raisins in prepared dish and pour orange juice over all. Set aside.

In a small bowl, combine remaining ingredients and stir to mix well. Distribute mixture evenly over fruit. Bake 40 to 50 minutes. Remove from oven and allow to cool slightly. Spoon into six individual serving dishes and serve warm.

APPLE-RAISIN CRUNCH WITH ICE MILK

Spoon ½ cup of ice milk on top of each serving.

Apple-Raisin Crunch Nutrient Analysis

Calories	259 kcal	Cholesterol	0 mg	Saturated Fat	2 gm
Protein	5 gm	Sodium	95 mg	Polyunsaturated Fat	3 gm
Carbohydrate	42 gm	Total Fat	10 gm	Monounsaturated Fat	4 gm

Apple-Raisin Crunch with Ice Milk Nutrient Analysis

Calories	351 kcal	Cholesterol	9 mg	Saturated Fat	4 gm
Protein	7 gm	Sodium	147 mg	Polyunsaturated Fat	3 gm
Carbohydrate	57 gm	Total Fat	13 gm	Monounsaturated Fat	5 gm

*O*at *B*lueberry *C*risp

Serves 8

Vegetable oil spray
7 tablespoons firmly packed brown sugar
½ cup all-purpose flour
½ cup uncooked oatmeal
⅛ teaspoon nutmeg
½ teaspoon cinnamon
1 tablespoon sesame seeds, toasted
¼ cup acceptable margarine
3 tablespoons firmly packed brown sugar
¼ cup all-purpose flour
1 teaspoon grated lemon rind
⅛ teaspoon salt
4 cups fresh blueberries, rinsed, stems removed

Preheat oven to 350° F. Lightly spray a 9-inch square baking dish with vegetable oil.

In a blender or the work bowl of a food processor fitted with a metal blade, combine 7 tablespoons brown sugar, ½ cup flour, oatmeal, nutmeg, cinnamon and sesame seeds. Process 10 seconds. Cut margarine into ½-inch pieces, add to flour mixture and process 10 seconds. Set aside.

In a bowl, combine remaining 3 tablespoons brown sugar and ¼ cup flour with lemon rind and salt. Stir well, breaking up any lumps. Add blueberries and toss gently until coated evenly. Pour into prepared pan. Add oatmeal topping and bake 30 to 35 minutes.

Nutrient Analysis

Calories	215 kcal	Cholesterol	0 mg	Saturated Fat	2 gm
Protein	3 gm	Sodium	110 mg	Polyunsaturated Fat	2 gm
Carbohydrate	37 gm	Total Fat	7 gm	Monounsaturated Fat	3 gm

*C*herry *C*risp

Serves 9

Vegetable oil spray
⅓ cup all-purpose flour
¾ cup rolled oatmeal
⅓ cup acceptable margarine
⅓ cup sugar
1 16-ounce can pitted no-sugar-added sour cherries,
    canned in natural juices
⅓ cup sugar
1½ tablespoons cornstarch
⅛ teaspoon cinnamon
⅛ teaspoon nutmeg
1 tablespoon fresh lemon juice

Preheat oven to 375° F. Lightly spray an 8-inch square baking pan with vegetable oil.

In a bowl, combine flour and rolled oatmeal. Cut in margarine until mixture is crumbly. Add ⅓ cup sugar and mix well. Set aside for topping.

Drain cherries, reserving cherries and juice.

In a saucepan, combine remaining sugar with cornstarch, spices and lemon juice. Slowly blend in cherry juice. Place over low heat and cook, stirring constantly, until sauce is thick and clear. Add cherries. Pour into prepared baking pan and sprinkle with topping.

Bake 30 minutes.

Nutrient Analysis

Calories	186 kcal	Cholesterol	0 mg	Saturated Fat	2 gm
Protein	2 gm	Sodium	80 mg	Polyunsaturated Fat	2 gm
Carbohydrate	29 gm	Total Fat	8 gm	Monounsaturated Fat	3 gm

*P*each *C*lafouti

Serves 8

Vegetable oil spray
1½ pounds ripe fresh peaches
1¼ cups skim milk
¼ cup firmly packed brown sugar
½ teaspoon cinnamon
3 eggs
1 tablespoon vanilla extract
1 teaspoon almond extract
1 cup all-purpose flour
¼ teaspoon ground mace
¼ teaspoon salt
3 tablespoons unsalted pine nuts, lightly toasted
1½ teaspoons sugar
¼ teaspoon cinnamon

Preheat oven to 350° F. Lightly spray a 9-inch square baking pan with vegetable oil.

Immerse peaches in a pan of simmering water for 1 minute. Remove to a bowl of ice water. Slip skins off peaches, remove pits and slice fruit. Set aside.

In a blender or the work bowl of a food processor fitted with a metal blade, combine milk, sugar, ½ teaspoon cinnamon, eggs, extracts, flour, mace and salt. Process until mixture forms a smooth batter. Pour about ¼ cup batter into prepared pan. Place in oven for 5 to 10 minutes, or until set.

Remove pan from oven and evenly distribute fruit on top of cooked batter. Pour remaining batter over top.

Bake 20 minutes, then sprinkle pine nuts over clafouti.

In a small bowl, combine sugar and remaining ¼ teaspoon cinnamon. Sprinkle over top of tart. Bake 40 minutes more. Serve warm.

Nutrient Analysis

Calories	160 kcal	Cholesterol	104 mg	Saturated Fat	1 gm
Protein	6 gm	Sodium	117 mg	Polyunsaturated Fat	1 gm
Carbohydrate	26 gm	Total Fat	4 gm	Monounsaturated Fat	2 gm

Dessert Crepes

Serves 6; 2 crepes per serving

1½ cups low-fat cottage cheese
½ teaspoon vanilla
1 recipe Whole-Wheat Crepes (see page 470)
1½ cups fresh or frozen fruit (strawberries, raspberries,
    blueberries or other fruit)

Process cottage cheese in a blender or the work bowl of food processor fitted with a metal blade until smooth. Add vanilla and process a few seconds more.

Place 2 tablespoons whipped cottage cheese on each crepe. Fold over and top with 2 tablespoons fruit.

APPLESAUCE CREPES

Fill each crepe with 2 tablespoons natural (no-sugar-added) applesauce and top with 1 tablespoon cinnamon flavored whipped cottage cheese.

JUBILEE CREPES

Fill each crepe with 2 tablespoons whipped cottage cheese. Top each with ¼ cup Easy Jubilee Sauce (see page 435).

Dessert Crepes Nutrient Analysis *

Calories	175 kcal	Cholesterol	97 mg	Saturated Fat	2 gm
Protein	13 gm	Sodium	274 mg	Polyunsaturated Fat	2 gm
Carbohydrate	18 gm	Total Fat	6 gm	Monounsaturated Fat	2 gm

* *using fresh strawberries*

Applesauce Crepes Nutrient Analysis

Calories	164 kcal	Cholesterol	94 mg	Saturated Fat	1 gm
Protein	9 gm	Sodium	160 mg	Polyunsaturated Fat	2 gm
Carbohydrate	21 gm	Total Fat	5 gm	Monounsaturated Fat	1 gm

Jubilee Crepes Nutrient Analysis *

Calories	572 kcal	Cholesterol	97 mg	Saturated Fat	2 gm
Protein	13 gm	Sodium	299 mg	Polyunsaturated Fat	2 gm
Carbohydrate	116 gm	Total Fat	6 gm	Monounsaturated Fat	2 gm

* *using approximately ¼ cup Jubilee Sauce per crepe*

*D*eep-*D*ish *C*obbler

Serves 8

> 6 cups fresh or frozen fruit (blueberries, cherries, peaches,
>   raspberries, apples, apricots)
> ½ to ⅓ cup all-purpose flour (depends on juiciness of fruit)
> ½ cup sugar
> 1½ tablespoons lemon rind
> 1 Pie Pastry (single crust) (see page 534)

*P*reheat oven to 425° F.

In a small bowl, combine fruit, flour, sugar and lemon rind. Stir to mix well. Pour into a 9-inch deep-dish pie plate. Place piecrust over fruit and pinch around plate edge to seal. Cut slits in crust and bake for approximately 50 minutes.

Nutrient Analysis *

Calories	217 kcal	Cholesterol	0 mg	Saturated Fat	1 gm
Protein	3 gm	Sodium	175 mg	Polyunsaturated Fat	3 gm
Carbohydrate	42 gm	Total Fat	5 gm	Monounsaturated Fat	1 gm

* *using fresh blueberries*

*D*eep-*D*ish *F*ruit *C*risp

Serves 8

> 6 cups fresh or frozen fruit (cherries, blueberries, peaches,
>   raspberries, apples, apricots)
> ⅓ to ½ cup all-purpose flour (depends on juiciness of fruit)
> ½ cup sugar
> 1½ tablespoons lemon rind
>
> **TOPPING**
> ½ cup all-purpose flour
> ½ cup firmly packed brown sugar
> 2 tablespoons acceptable margarine, melted
> ¼ teaspoon mace
> ¼ teaspoon allspice
> ⅛ teaspoon nutmeg

Preheat oven to 375° F.

In a small bowl, combine fruit, flour, sugar and lemon rind; mix well. Pour into a 9-inch deep-dish pie plate. Set aside.

In a small bowl, combine topping ingredients and mix until evenly blended. Sprinkle over top of fruit. Bake 45 minutes.

Nutrient Analysis *

Calories	255 kcal	Cholesterol	0 mg	Saturated Fat	1 gm
Protein	3 gm	Sodium	38 mg	Polyunsaturated Fat	1 gm
Carbohydrate	55 gm	Total Fat	4 gm	Monounsaturated Fat	2 gm

* using fresh cherries

*A*pple *P*ie

Serves 8

Pie Pastry for 9-inch 2-crust pie, unbaked (see page 534)
4 cups peeled, cored and sliced apples
1 cup sugar
½ teaspoon cinnamon
½ teaspoon vanilla extract
Grated rind from half a lemon
1 tablespoon fresh lemon juice
1 tablespoon acceptable margarine
1 tablespoon sugar

Preheat oven to 450° F.

Line a 9-inch pie pan with half the pastry. Cover and chill in refrigerator.

In a large bowl, combine sliced apples, 1 cup sugar, cinnamon, vanilla, lemon rind and juice. Stir to mix well.

Pour mixture into unbaked pie shell. Dot with margarine. Cover with remaining crust and cut steam holes. Crimp pie crust to pan edge to seal. Bake 10 minutes, then reduce oven temperature to 350° F. Bake 30 to 35 minutes more. Sprinkle with 1 tablespoon sugar while pie is still hot from the oven.

Nutrient Analysis

Calories	322 kcal	Cholesterol	0 mg	Saturated Fat	2 gm
Protein	3 gm	Sodium	354 mg	Polyunsaturated Fat	6 gm
Carbohydrate	54 gm	Total Fat	11 gm	Monounsaturated Fat	3 gm

Walnut Crumb Apple Pie

Serves 8

¾ cup flour
½ cup firmly packed light brown sugar
½ teaspoon nutmeg
½ teaspoon cinnamon
¼ cup acceptable margarine
½ cup unsalted dry-roasted walnuts, chopped
1 recipe Mrs. Park's Piecrust (see page 534) or 1 9-inch
    pie shell, unbaked
½ teaspoon baking soda
⅓ cup boiling water
¼ cup light molasses
1 20-ounce can sliced apples, drained

Preheat oven to 400° F.

In a small bowl, combine flour, sugar and spices. Cut in margarine until mixture has a crumbly consistency. Add nuts and mix well. Turn half of mixture into unbaked pie shell. Set aside.

In a large bowl, dissolve baking soda in boiling water. Add molasses and apples. Pour apple mixture on top of flour mixture in pie shell. Cover with remaining flour mixture. Place in oven *on a cookie sheet* and bake 40 minutes.

Nutrient Analysis

Calories	412 kcal	Cholesterol	0 mg	Saturated Fat	3 gm
Protein	4 gm	Sodium	218 mg	Polyunsaturated Fat	10 gm
Carbohydrate	56 gm	Total Fat	20 gm	Monounsaturated Fat	6 gm

*N*orwegian *A*pple *P*ie

Serves 8

Vegetable oil spray
2 egg whites or egg substitute equivalent to 1 egg
¾ cup sugar
1 teaspoon vanilla extract
1 teaspoon baking powder
½ cup all-purpose flour
½ cup unsalted dry-roasted chopped walnuts
1 cup diced apples

Preheat oven to 350° F. Lightly spray an 8-inch pie plate with vegetable oil.

Beat egg, sugar, vanilla extract and baking powder in a large mixing bowl until smooth and fluffy. Beat in flour until smooth and well blended. Stir in walnuts and apples.

Turn into prepared pie plate and bake 30 minutes. Pie will puff up as it cooks, then collapse as it cools.

Serve warm.

NORWEGIAN APPLE PIE À LA MODE
Top each slice with a ½-cup scoop of ice milk.

Norwegian Apple Pie Nutrient Analysis

Calories	154 kcal	Cholesterol	0 mg	Saturated Fat	0 gm
Protein	3 gm	Sodium	50 mg	Polyunsaturated Fat	3 gm
Carbohydrate	27 gm	Total Fat	5 gm	Monounsaturated Fat	1 gm

Norwegian Apple Pie à la Mode Nutrient Analysis

Calories	246 kcal	Cholesterol	9 mg	Saturated Fat	2 gm
Protein	5 gm	Sodium	102 mg	Polyunsaturated Fat	3 gm
Carbohydrate	41 gm	Total Fat	8 gm	Monounsaturated Fat	2 gm

Pink Lemonade Pie

Serves 8

1 cup evaporated skim milk
1 envelope unflavored gelatin
2 tablespoons water
1 6-ounce can pink lemonade concentrate, defrosted
1 8-ounce carton low-fat lemon yogurt
4 tablespoons sugar
1 tablespoon grated lemon rind
6 drops red food coloring
1 teaspoon vanilla extract
1 recipe Mrs. Park's Piecrust (see page 534) or 1 9-inch
    pie shell, baked and cooled

Place evaporated milk in a plastic bowl in freezer just until ice crystals begin to form around edges.

Let gelatin and water stand in a large glass measuring cup for 5 minutes for gelatin to soften. Stir in lemonade concentrate. Heat in a small saucepan over medium-high heat (or in microwave on high for 3 minutes) to dissolve gelatin. Set aside for 5 minutes to cool.

Stir in yogurt, sugar, lemon rind and food coloring. Pour into a bowl, cover and chill in refrigerator until partially set.

Remove chilled milk from freezer and whip until stiff. Add vanilla extract to whipped milk just until mixed. Mix one-third of whipped milk into lemonade mixture, then fold in remainder. Pour into cool pie shell, cover and refrigerate several hours, or until firm.

Nutrient Analysis

Calories	270 kcal	Cholesterol	2 mg	Saturated Fat	1 gm
Protein	7 gm	Sodium	147 mg	Polyunsaturated Fat	5 gm
Carbohydrate	40 gm	Total Fat	10 gm	Monounsaturated Fat	2 gm

*L*ime *C*hiffon *P*ie

Serves 8

1 3-ounce package lime-flavored gelatin
¾ cup boiling water
1 teaspoon grated lemon rind
¼ cup sugar
½ cup nonfat dry milk
½ cup ice water
2 tablespoons fresh lemon juice
¼ cup sugar
1 recipe Mrs. Park's Piecrust (see page 534) or 1 9-inch
   pie shell, baked and cooled

Dissolve gelatin in boiling water in a medium bowl. Add grated lemon rind and ¼ cup sugar. Stir well. Cool until mixture is the consistency of unbeaten egg white (about 20 minutes).

Place nonfat dry milk and ice water in a mixing bowl. With an electric mixer, beat on high speed 3 to 4 minutes, or until soft peaks form. Add lemon juice and continue beating. Add remaining ¼ cup of sugar gradually and continue beating until stiff peaks form. Fold into gelatin mixture and stir to combine thoroughly.

Pour into cool pastry shell, cover and refrigerate 3 hours, or until firm.

Nutrient Analysis

Calories	252 kcal	Cholesterol	1 mg	Saturated Fat	1 gm
Protein	5 gm	Sodium	148 mg	Polyunsaturated Fat	5 gm
Carbohydrate	38 gm	Total Fat	9 gm	Monounsaturated Fat	2 gm

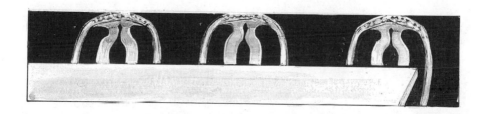

Raspberry Chiffon Pie

Serves 8

1¼ cups (10-ounce package) frozen sweetened raspberries
1 tablespoon unflavored gelatin
½ cup water, at room temperature
¼ cup sugar
1 tablespoon all-purpose flour
2 tablespoons fresh lemon juice
⅓ cup ice water
⅓ cup nonfat dry milk
1 tablespoon fresh lemon juice
2 tablespoons sugar
1 recipe Mrs. Park's Piecrust (see page 534) or 1 9-inch
    pie shell, baked and cooled

Thaw raspberries and drain, reserving juice. Reserve six firm berries for garnish and set aside the rest in a bowl.

Chill a mixing bowl and the beaters of an electric mixer.

Soften gelatin in the water. Combine ¼ cup of sugar with flour in a saucepan. Add raspberry juice and softened gelatin. Stir. Heat slowly over low heat until sugar is dissolved. Remove saucepan from heat and add 2 tablespoons of lemon juice and the berries. Cool until thick and syrupy but not set.

In chilled bowl, combine ice water and nonfat dry milk. Beat with chilled beaters 3 or 4 minutes, or until soft peaks form. Add remaining tablespoon lemon juice and beat another 3 or 4 minutes, or until stiff. Fold in 2 tablespoons of sugar, and blend well on low speed. Whip this mixture into raspberry-gelatin mixture.

Pour into baked pastry shell, cover and refrigerate until firm.

Nutrient Analysis

Calories	239 kcal	Cholesterol	1 mg	Saturated Fat	1 gm
Protein	4 gm	Sodium	107 mg	Polyunsaturated Fat	5 gm
Carbohydrate	35 gm	Total Fat	9 gm	Monounsaturated Fat	2 gm

*F*resh *S*trawberry *P*ie

Serves 8

1½ teaspoons unflavored gelatin
1 tablespoon water
6 cups fresh strawberries, rinsed and hulled
3 tablespoons cornstarch
½ cup sugar
1 cup water
1 teaspoon grated orange rind
Few drops of red food coloring
⅛ teaspoon almond extract
1 recipe Mrs. Park's Piecrust (see page 534) or 1 9-inch
   pie shell, baked and cooled

*I*n a small bowl, combine gelatin and 1 tablespoon water. Set aside.

Measure 4 cups whole strawberries of uniform size. Place strawberries, points up, on bottom of pie shell.

Place remaining 2 cups strawberries in a bowl and crush with a fork or potato masher. Place in a saucepan over medium heat. Add cornstarch, sugar and water. Cook, stirring constantly, until thick and clear. Remove from heat and add gelatin. Cool and add rind, food coloring and extract.

Pour into pie shell, cover and refrigerate. Chill several hours before serving.

Top with Whipped Dessert Topping (see page 436) if desired.

MICROWAVE METHOD

Place crushed strawberries, cornstarch, sugar and water in 1-quart microwave-safe measure. Microwave on high for 5 to 6 minutes, or until thick and clear. Add gelatin. Cool and add rind and extract. Proceed as directed.

Nutrient Analysis

Calories	244 kcal	Cholesterol	0 mg	Saturated Fat	1 gm
Protein	3 gm	Sodium	90 mg	Polyunsaturated Fat	6 gm
Carbohydrate	38 gm	Total Fat	10 gm	Monounsaturated Fat	2 gm

*P*umpkin *P*ie

Serves 8

⅔ cup sugar
½ teaspoon cinnamon
½ teaspoon ground ginger
½ teaspoon nutmeg
Pinch of ground cloves
1½ cups canned pumpkin
1 teaspoon vanilla extract
1½ cups evaporated skim milk
½ teaspoon grated orange rind
3 egg whites, slightly beaten
¼ cup brandy
1 recipe Mrs. Park's Piecrust (see page 534) or 1 9-inch
    pie shell, unbaked

*P*reheat oven to 450° F.

In a large bowl, combine sugar, cinnamon, ginger, nutmeg and cloves. Add pumpkin and stir to mix well. Add vanilla, evaporated milk, orange rind and egg whites. Beat with an electric mixer until smooth. Fold in brandy.

Pour into unbaked pie shell and bake 10 minutes. Reduce heat to 325° F and bake 45 minutes, or until a knife inserted in the filling comes out clean.

Nutrient Analysis

Calories	233 kcal	Cholesterol	2 mg	Saturated Fat	1 gm
Protein	7 gm	Sodium	245 mg	Polyunsaturated Fat	3 gm
Carbohydrate	37 gm	Total Fat	5 gm	Monounsaturated Fat	1 gm

Pumpkin Chiffon Pie

Serves 8

½ cup sugar
½ cup boiling water
3 teaspoons unflavored gelatin (1½ envelopes)
¼ cup water
½ cup brown sugar, firmly packed
¼ cup egg substitute
¼ teaspoon ground ginger
⅛ teaspoon nutmeg
¼ teaspoon cinnamon
1 1-pound can pumpkin
1 cup evaporated skim milk
½ teaspoon salt
¼ cup meringue powder*
1 tablespoon vanilla
1 recipe Mrs. Park's Piecrust (see page 534) or 1 9-inch
    pie shell, baked and cooled

*I*n a bowl, dissolve ½ cup sugar in ½ cup boiling water. Set aside.

Combine gelatin and water in a small bowl; set aside.

In a large saucepan, combine brown sugar, egg substitute, spices, pumpkin, milk and salt. Bring to a boil over medium heat, stirring constantly. Remove from heat and add gelatin mixture, stirring until dissolved. Pour into a bowl and refrigerate until slightly thickened.

Add meringue powder to reserved sugar and water mixture. Beat until soft peaks form. Add vanilla and beat another minute.

Remove pumpkin mixture from refrigerator. With a rubber spatula, mix half of meringue into pumpkin mixture, then fold in remainder. Pour mixture into baked pie shell and refrigerate several hours, or until firm.

* Meringue powder can be found in stores that stock cake-decorating supplies.

Nutrient Analysis

Calories	308 kcal	Cholesterol	1 mg	Saturated Fat	1 gm
Protein	6 gm	Sodium	316 mg	Polyunsaturated Fat	5 gm
Carbohydrate	51 gm	Total Fat	9 gm	Monounsaturated Fat	2 gm

*B*aked *L*emon *C*heese *P*ie

Serves 8

3 tablespoons acceptable margarine, melted
1 cup graham cracker crumbs
1 teaspoon grated lemon peel
1⅓ cups low-fat cottage cheese, drained
⅔ cup Yogurt Cheese (see page 68)
Egg substitute equivalent to 2 eggs
½ cup sugar
⅓ cup skim milk
3 tablespoons all-purpose flour
5 tablespoons fresh lemon juice
1 tablespoon grated lemon rind
¼ teaspoon vanilla

*P*reheat oven to 300° F.

In a bowl, combine margarine, graham cracker crumbs and lemon peel. Stir until thoroughly blended. Remove 1 tablespoon of mixture and set aside. Press remainder into a 9-inch pie pan. Bake 5 minutes. Remove from oven and allow to cool. Leave oven setting at 300° F.

Blend cottage cheese and Yogurt Cheese in a mixing bowl, blender or the work bowl of a food processor fitted with a metal blade until creamy. Add egg substitute slowly, mixing constantly. Add sugar and skim milk, beating well after each addition. Add remaining ingredients, beating until smooth.

Pour mixture into cooled pie shell. Sprinkle reserved crumbs on top. Bake at 300° F 1½ hours, or until set. Cover and refrigerate. Cool several hours before serving.

Nutrient Analysis

Calories	217 kcal	Cholesterol	6 mg	Saturated Fat	2 gm
Protein	11 gm	Sodium	358 mg	Polyunsaturated Fat	1 gm
Carbohydrate	29 gm	Total Fat	7 gm	Monounsaturated Fat	3 gm

Refrigerator Pineapple Cheesecake

Serves 8

1 cup unsweetened pineapple juice
1 3-ounce package lemon gelatin
1 cup graham cracker crumbs
3 tablespoons acceptable margarine, melted
3 cups (1½ pounds) low-fat cottage cheese
½ teaspoon vanilla
½ teaspoon almond extract
1 tablespoon sugar
1 8-ounce can crushed no-sugar-added pineapple, canned
    in natural juices, undrained
1 tablespoon water
2 teaspoons cornstarch
1 tablespoon sugar

Preheat oven to 350° F.

Bring pineapple juice to a boil in a saucepan over medium-high heat and add gelatin. Stir until dissolved. Remove mixture from heat and cool to lukewarm.

In a bowl, combine graham cracker crumbs and margarine. Press onto bottom and up 1 inch of the sides of an 8-inch springform pan. Bake 5 minutes and allow to cool to room temperature.

Process cottage cheese, extracts, and 1 tablespoon sugar in a blender or the work bowl of a food processor fitted with a metal blade until completely smooth. Add cooled juice mixture and process 30 seconds more to combine thoroughly. Pour into prepared pan. Cover and refrigerate several hours, or until firm.

In a small saucepan, combine pineapple, water, cornstarch and 1 tablespoon sugar. Bring mixture to a boil over medium-high heat, stirring constantly. Cool 20 minutes and spread evenly on top of cheesecake. Cover and refrigerate 1 hour.

Nutrient Analysis

Calories	254 kcal	Cholesterol	7 mg	Saturated Fat	2 gm
Protein	14 gm	Sodium	518 mg	Polyunsaturated Fat	1 gm
Carbohydrate	35 gm	Total Fat	7 gm	Monounsaturated Fat	3 gm

Miniature Rum-Raisin Cheesecakes

Serves 30; 1 cheesecake per serving

> Vegetable oil spray
> 1½ teaspoons cinnamon
> 3 tablespoons sugar
> 1 10-ounce package flaky buttermilk biscuits
> 2 cups Cream Cheese (see page 66), softened
> 1 cup raisins
> ¾ cup sifted confectioners' sugar
> 2 teaspoons grated lemon rind
> 1½ teaspoons vanilla
> 1 tablespoon rum

Preheat oven to 400° F. Lightly spray a muffin tin with vegetable oil.

Mix cinnamon and sugar on a small plate and set aside.

Separate each biscuit into three layers. Press *both* sides of each layer in cinnamon sugar. Press each into a prepared 2-inch-diameter muffin-tin cavity. Set aside.

Place Cream Cheese, raisins, sugar, lemon rind, vanilla and rum in a blender or the work bowl of a food processor fitted with a metal blade. Process until smooth.

Place a scant tablespoon cheese mixture on top of each muffin-biscuit round. Bake 20 minutes. Remove from pan and allow to cool. Cover and refrigerate. Serve cold.

Nutrient Analysis

Calories	104 kcal	Cholesterol	2 mg	Saturated Fat	1 gm
Protein	3 gm	Sodium	160 mg	Polyunsaturated Fat	0 gm
Carbohydrate	17 gm	Total Fat	3 gm	Monounsaturated Fat	1 gm

Mocha Yogurt Pie

Serves 8

> ½ cup boiling water
> ½ cup sugar
> 3 envelopes unflavored gelatin
> ½ cup skim milk

2 tablespoons unsweetened cocoa

¼ cup confectioners' sugar

2 8-ounce containers low-fat vanilla yogurt

½ teaspoon instant coffee granules

1 tablespoon dark rum

2 8-ounce containers low-fat coffee yogurt

¼ cup confectioners' sugar

¼ cup meringue powder*

1 tablespoon vanilla extract

1 recipe Mrs. Park's Piecrust (see page 534) or 1 9-inch pie shell, baked and cooled

Combine boiling water and sugar in a mixing bowl and set aside.

In each of two heat-resistant cups, combine 3 teaspoons (1½ envelopes) unflavored gelatin and ¼ cup skim milk. Place cups in a pan of simmering water to a depth of 1 inch. Let sit 1½ to 2 minutes, or until gelatin melts. Remove cups from water and set aside to cool.

Sift together cocoa and ¼ cup confectioners' sugar and set aside.

Place vanilla yogurt in a bowl. Add cocoa and confectioners' sugar and stir well. Add 1 container of the gelatin mixture. Stir well.

Refrigerate, uncovered, 30 minutes, or until mixture is slightly thickened.

Dissolve coffee granules in rum and set aside.

Place coffee yogurt in a bowl. Add the coffee and rum mixture and stir well. Sift in ¼ cup confectioners' sugar. Stir in remaining gelatin mixture and refrigerate, uncovered, 30 minutes, or until slightly thickened.

Add meringue powder to reserved sugar and water mixture and beat until soft peaks form. Add vanilla and continue to beat.

Remove chocolate and coffee mixtures from the refrigerator. Fold half of meringue into chocolate mixture and remaining half of meringue into coffee mixture. Drop both mixtures by alternate spoonfuls into prepared pie shell. Swirl with knife for marble effect. Cover pie and chill several hours, or until firm.

* *Meringue powder can be found in stores that stock cake-decorating supplies.*

Nutrient Analysis

Calories	387 kcal	Cholesterol	5 mg	Saturated Fat		2 gm
Protein	11 gm	Sodium	218 mg	Polyunsaturated Fat		5 gm
Carbohydrate	62 gm	Total Fat	11 gm	Monounsaturated Fat		3 gm

Pie Pastry

Makes 2 single piecrusts or 1 double-layer crust
Serves 8

> 2 cups all-purpose flour
> 1¼ teaspoons salt
> ⅓ cup acceptable vegetable oil
> 3 tablespoons cold skim milk

Sift flour and salt together into a mixing bowl. Set aside.

In a small bowl or a 1-cup measure, combine oil and cold milk. Pour liquid all at once into flour mixture. Stir lightly with a fork until blended, adding more milk if necessary to hold dough together. Divide into two portions. Cover and refrigerate for a few mintues to make dough easier to work.

Flatten one ball of dough slightly and place on a sheet of wax paper or cellophane wrap. Put another sheet over top and roll out quickly. Do not roll too thin. Remove top sheet of paper and turn dough onto pie plate. Remove second sheet and lift crust around the edges so it settles into the plate. Trim and flute edges with a fork or your fingers.

Repeat with second ball of dough and place in another pie pan or on top of filled pie.

Crust may be covered and refrigerated or frozen before filling.

Bake according to pie recipe.

Nutrient Analysis

Calories	187 kcal	Cholesterol	0 mg	Saturated Fat	1 gm
Protein	3 gm	Sodium	337 mg	Polyunsaturated Fat	5 gm
Carbohydrate	22 gm	Total Fat	9 gm	Monounsaturated Fat	2 gm

Mrs. Park's Piecrust

Makes 1 piecrust
Serves 8

> 1⅓ cups all-purpose flour
> ⅓ teaspoon salt
> ⅓ cup acceptable vegetable oil
> 3 tablespoons ice water

Sift flour and salt together into a mixing bowl. Set aside.

In a small bowl or a 1-cup measure, whisk together oil and water. Pour liquid all at once into flour mixture. Stir lightly with a fork until blended, adding more water if necessary to hold dough together. Form into a ball. Cover and refrigerate for a few minutes to make dough easier to work.

Flatten dough slightly and place between two sheets of wax paper and roll out quickly. Do not roll too thin. Remove top sheet of paper and turn dough onto pie plate. Trim and flute edges with a fork or your fingers.

Crust may be covered and refrigerated or frozen before filling.

For a baked pie shell (to be filled later), bake in a preheated 400° F oven for 10 minutes, or until edges are light brown. To prevent the crust from puffing up or losing shape during baking, cover pastry with wax paper and weigh it down with dried beans or an aluminum-foil pie plate.

Nutrient Analysis

Calories	150 kcal	Cholesterol	0 mg	Saturated Fat		1 gm
Protein	2 gm	Sodium	89 mg	Polyunsaturated Fat		5 gm
Carbohydrate	15 gm	Total Fat	9 gm	Monounsaturated Fat		2 gm

*N*ut *C*rust

Makes 1 piecrust
Serves 8

> 1 cup all-purpose flour
> ⅓ cup acceptable margarine, softened
> ¼ cup unsalted dry-roasted finely chopped pecans
> ¼ cup confectioners' sugar

Preheat oven to 400° F.

Stir together all ingredients in a bowl until a soft dough forms. Press dough firmly and evenly against the bottom and sides (not the rim) of a 9-inch pie pan.

Bake 12 to 15 minutes, or until lightly browned. Cool thoroughly before filling.

Nutrient Analysis

Calories	160 kcal	Cholesterol	0 mg	Saturated Fat		2 gm
Protein	2 gm	Sodium	89 mg	Polyunsaturated Fat		2 gm
Carbohydrate	16 gm	Total Fat	10 gm	Monounsaturated Fat		5 gm

Oat Crumb Piecrust

Makes 1 piecrust
Serves 8

1 cup graham cracker crumbs
⅓ cup quick-cooking oatmeal
2 tablespoons sugar
½ teaspoon cinnamon
1 teaspoon freshly grated orange peel
½ teaspoon freshly grated lemon peel
·2½ tablespoons acceptable margarine, melted

Preheat oven to 375° F.

In a bowl, combine graham cracker crumbs, oatmeal, sugar and cinnamon. Stir to blend well. Add fresh fruit peels. Stir until thoroughly blended. Add melted margarine and toss to mix well. Press into pie plate with back of metal fork to form shell.

Bake 8 to 10 minutes. Cool before filling.

Nutrient Analysis

Calories	107 kcal	Cholesterol	0 mg	Saturated Fat	1 gm
Protein	2 gm	Sodium	130 mg	Polyunsaturated Fat	1 gm
Carbohydrate	15 gm	Total Fat	5 gm	Monounsaturated Fat	2 gm

Meringue Shell

Makes 1 pie shell
Serves 8

Vegetable oil spray
3 egg whites
¼ teaspoon cream of tartar
⅔ cup sugar
¼ teaspoon vanilla extract

Preheat oven to 275° F. Lightly spray a 9-inch pie pan with vegetable oil.

In a mixing bowl, combine egg whites and cream of tartar. Beat until foamy. Gradually add sugar, beating until stiff, glossy peaks form and sugar is completely dissolved. Add vanilla and beat 1 more minute.

Spread meringue in prepared pie pan, building up sides to be thicker than bottom.

Bake 1 hour and 15 minutes, or until dry and a light, creamy color. Let meringue cool. Remove carefully from pan. Meringues may be stored in an airtight container until ready for filling.

INDIVIDUAL MERINGUE SHELLS (MAKES 12)

Place unglazed brown paper on a cookie sheet. (Omit vegetable oil spray.) Mix ingredients as directed. Shape into twelve 4-inch diameter shells, making a depression in each with the back of a spoon. Cook, cool and store as directed.

Meringue Shell Nutrient Analysis*

Calories	68 kcal	Cholesterol	0 mg	Saturated Fat	0 gm
Protein	1 gm	Sodium	25 mg	Polyunsaturated Fat	0 gm
Carbohydrate	16 gm	Total Fat	0 gm	Monounsaturated Fat	0 gm

for one-eighth of pie crust

Individual Meringue Shell Nutrient Analysis*

Calories	45 kcal	Cholesterol	0 mg	Saturated Fat	0 gm
Protein	1 gm	Sodium	17 mg	Polyunsaturated Fat	0 gm
Carbohydrate	11 gm	Total Fat	0 gm	Monounsaturated Fat	0 gm

for 1 individual shell

Meringue "Egg" Baskets

Serves 4; 1 basket per serving

½ cup each of orange, lemon and raspberry ice
4 individual Meringue Shells (see above)

For each serving, place a very small scoop of each flavor of fruit ice into each individual meringue shell. To complete the basket, insert pipe cleaners through the edges of the meringues to make handles.

VARIATIONS

Fill each meringue shell with fresh fruit, sherbet, ice milk or other flavored ices.

Nutrient Analysis

Calories	138 kcal	Cholesterol	0 mg	Saturated Fat	0 gm
Protein	1 gm	Sodium	17 mg	Polyunsaturated Fat	0 gm
Carbohydrate	34 gm	Total Fat	0 gm	Monounsaturated Fat	0 gm

*G*inger *B*erry *F*illed *M*eringues

Serves 4; 1 filled meringue per serving

> 1 10-ounce package frozen no-sugar-added berries
> 1 tablespoon sugar
> 1½ teaspoons cornstarch
> 1 tablespoon fresh lemon juice
> ¼ teaspoon ground ginger
> 4 individual Meringue Shells (see page 537)

*T*haw frozen berries and drain them, reserving ½ cup of syrup.

In a saucepan, combine syrup, sugar and cornstarch. Cook over medium-high heat, stirring constantly, until thickened. Stir in berries, lemon juice and ginger.

Spoon mixture into meringue shells. Cover and refrigerate. Chill until filling becomes firm.

Nutrient Analysis

Calories	84 kcal	Cholesterol	0 mg	Saturated Fat	0 gm
Protein	1 gm	Sodium	18 mg	Polyunsaturated Fat	0 gm
Carbohydrate	20 gm	Total Fat	0 gm	Monounsaturated Fat	0 gm

*H*oney *A*lmond *C*ustards

Serves 6; 1 custard per serving

> Vegetable oil spray
> 2 cups skim milk
> Egg substitute equivalent to 3 eggs
> ¼ cup honey
> 2 teaspoons vanilla
> ¼ teaspoon almond extract
> ⅛ teaspoon salt

*P*reheat oven to 350° F. Lightly spray six oven-proof custard cups with vegetable oil.

Heat milk in a saucepan over medium-high heat, stirring constantly, until very hot but not boiling. Remove from heat and set aside.

In a bowl, combine remaining ingredients. Stir in milk. Pour custard mixture into prepared custard cups. Place cups in baking pan and pour hot water into pan to a depth of 1 inch. Bake, uncovered, 40 to 45 minutes.

MICROWAVE METHOD
Prepare custard mixture as directed. Pour into prepared microwave-safe custard cups. Place cups in glass baking dish. Add water as directed. Bake on high 15 to 20 minutes, or until done. (Baking times will vary with each microwave.)

Nutrient Analysis

Calories	88 kcal	Cholesterol	2 mg	Saturated Fat	0 gm
Protein	6 gm	Sodium	149 mg	Polyunsaturated Fat	0 gm
Carbohydrate	17 gm	Total Fat	0 gm	Monounsaturated Fat	0 gm

*M*andarin *O*range *P*udding
(Tanjulin)

Serves 6

1 3½-ounce package vanilla pudding mix
2 cups skim milk
1 11-ounce can mandarin oranges, canned in light syrup, well drained
1 tablespoon sherry

GARNISH
Unsalted toasted almonds, slivered (optional)

Prepare vanilla pudding according to directions on package, using the 2 cups skim milk. (Or make your own pudding using skim milk.) Cool.

Fold in drained mandarin oranges and sherry. Spoon evenly into six individual glass dishes. Sprinkle slivered nuts on top.

Nutrient Analysis

Calories	128 kcal	Cholesterol	2 mg	Saturated Fat	0 gm
Protein	3 gm	Sodium	270 mg	Polyunsaturated Fat	0 gm
Carbohydrate	28 gm	Total Fat	0 gm	Monounsaturated Fat	0 gm

*I*ndian *P*udding

Serves 8

2 cups skim milk
¼ cup cornmeal
¼ cup sugar
⅛ teaspoon baking soda
½ teaspoon ground ginger
½ teaspoon ground cinnamon
¼ cup molasses
1 cup cold skim milk
Nutmeg

*P*reheat oven to 275° F.

Heat 2 cups skim milk in a double boiler or a medium saucepan over low heat. Add cornmeal, a little at a time, stirring constantly. Cook 15 minutes, or until thick, stirring constantly. Remove from heat. Set aside.

In a bowl, combine sugar, soda and spices. Stir to mix well. Add to cornmeal mixture and stir. Add molasses and 1 cup cold milk. Stir to mix thoroughly. Pour into a 1-quart casserole and bake 2 hours.

Serve warm with a light sprinkling of nutmeg.

Nutrient Analysis

Calories	95 kcal	Cholesterol	2 mg	Saturated Fat	0 gm
Protein	3 gm	Sodium	64 mg	Polyunsaturated Fat	0 gm
Carbohydrate	20 gm	Total Fat	0 gm	Monounsaturated Fat	0 gm

*D*elicious *R*ice *P*udding

Serves 6

Vegetable oil spray
2 cups skim milk, heated
2 cups cooked rice
⅓ cup sugar
1½ teaspoons vanilla
¼ teaspoon nutmeg
½ teaspoon cinnamon
Egg substitute equivalent to 1 egg

Preheat oven to 350° F. Lightly spray a 1-quart ovenproof casserole with vegetable oil.

Place ingredients in order listed in a bowl. Stir to mix well. Pour into prepared casserole and cover. Set casserole in a larger pan. Add hot water to pan to a depth of 1 inch. Bake casserole 1 hour. Serve warm or cover and refrigerate to serve cold.

Serve with Orange Sauce (see page 437), if desired.

LEMON RICE PUDDING
Add 1½ teaspoons grated lemon rind and ½ teaspoon lemon extract, if desired.

*Delicious Rice Pudding Nutrient Analysis**

Calories	151 kcal	Cholesterol	2 mg	Saturated Fat	0 gm
Protein	5 gm	Sodium	63 mg	Polyunsaturated Fat	0 gm
Carbohydrate	32 gm	Total Fat	0 gm	Monounsaturated Fat	0 gm

* *without Orange Sauce*

Lemon Rice Pudding Nutrient Analysis

Calories	152 kcal	Cholesterol	2 mg	Saturated Fat	0 gm
Protein	5 gm	Sodium	63 mg	Polyunsaturated Fat	0 gm
Carbohydrate	32 gm	Total Fat	0 gm	Monounsaturated Fat	0 gm

*Y*ogurt *G*elatin *D*elight

Serves 6

1 3-ounce package fruit-flavored gelatin
8 ounces low-fat yogurt of the same flavor

Prepare gelatin according to package directions. Cover and refrigerate just until it begins to set.

Add yogurt and stir to combine thoroughly. Pour into molds. Cover and refrigerate until set.

FLUFFY WHIP
When gelatin has started to set, whip it with an electric mixer until it is light and fluffy. Then fold in yogurt.

Nutrient Analysis

Calories	91 kcal	Cholesterol	2 mg	Saturated Fat	0 gm
Protein	3 gm	Sodium	67 mg	Polyunsaturated Fat	0 gm
Carbohydrate	20 gm	Total Fat	0 gm	Monounsaturated Fat	0 gm

Fresh Strawberry Mousse

Serves 8

½ cup boiling water
½ cup sugar
2 envelopes unflavored gelatin
½ cup orange juice
4 cups fresh, ripe strawberries, rinsed and hulled
½ teaspoon grated orange rind
1 cup low-fat cottage cheese
1 8-ounce container low-fat strawberry yogurt (flavored
    with fruit juice) or low-fat vanilla yogurt
2 tablespoons sugar
¼ cup meringue powder*
1 tablespoon vanilla extract
6 drops red food coloring

GARNISH
4 orange slices, cut in half
8 mint sprigs

In a bowl, combine boiling water and ½ cup sugar. Set aside.

Combine unflavored gelatin and orange juice in a small saucepan and set aside for 5 minutes to soften. Stir mixture 1½ to 2 minutes over low heat, or until gelatin is dissolved. Remove from heat and set aside to cool.

In a bowl, combine strawberries and orange rind. Crush berries with a fork or potato masher. Pour cooled gelatin mixture over all and stir well. Refrigerate until slightly thickened.

In blender or work bowl of a food processor fitted with a metal blade, combine cottage cheese, yogurt and 2 tablespoons sugar. Process until smooth.

Remove strawberry mixture from refrigerator and fold cottage cheese mixture into it. Refrigerate mixture again.

Add meringue powder to reserved sugar and water mixture. Beat until soft peaks form. Add vanilla and food coloring and beat 1 minute more.

Remove strawberry and cheese mixture from refrigerator. Stir half of meringue into it with a rubber spatula, then fold in remainder of meringue.

* Meringue powder can be found in stores that stock cake-decorating supplies.

Divide mixture evenly among eight serving dishes. Cover and refrigerate several hours before serving. Garnish each serving with half an orange slice and a sprig of mint.

Nutrient Analysis

Calories	168 kcal	Cholesterol	4 mg	Saturated Fat	1 gm
Protein	8 gm	Sodium	186 mg	Polyunsaturated Fat	0 gm
Carbohydrate	33 gm	Total Fat	1 gm	Monounsaturated Fat	0 gm

*W*hole-*W*heat *A*pplesauce *C*ake

Serves 9

½ cup acceptable vegetable oil
¾ cup firmly packed brown sugar
1 cup natural (no-sugar-added) applesauce
1 teaspoon baking soda
1½ cups unsifted whole-wheat flour
1 teaspoon cinnamon

Preheat oven to 375° F. Grease (with acceptable margarine) and flour an 8-inch round or square baking pan.

In a large mixing bowl, cream oil and sugar. Add applesauce and baking soda and mix thoroughly. Add flour and cinnamon and blend thoroughly.

Pour batter into prepared pan and bake 30 minutes.

WHOLE-WHEAT APPLESAUCE CUPCAKES (SERVES 12)

Grease and flour muffin tins or use paper liners. Prepare batter as directed. Bake 20 minutes at 375° F.

Whole-Wheat Applesauce Cake Nutrient Analysis

Calories	254 kcal	Cholesterol	0 mg	Saturated Fat	2 gm
Protein	3 gm	Sodium	98 mg	Polyunsaturated Fat	7 gm
Carbohydrate	35 gm	Total Fat	13 gm	Monounsaturated Fat	3 gm

Whole-Wheat Applesauce Cupcake Nutrient Analysis

Calories	191 kcal	Cholesterol	0 mg	Saturated Fat	1 gm
Protein	2 gm	Sodium	73 mg	Polyunsaturated Fat	5 gm
Carbohydrate	26 gm	Total Fat	9 gm	Monounsaturated Fat	2 gm

Nutmeg Cake

Serves 15

2 cups all-purpose flour

1 teaspoon baking powder

1 teaspoon baking soda

1 tablespoon freshly grated nutmeg, or 1¼ teaspoons
    ground nutmeg

½ cup acceptable margarine, softened

1 teaspoon butter-flavored extract

1¼ cups sugar

Egg substitute equivalent to 2 eggs

1 cup low-fat buttermilk, room temperature

½ teaspoon vanilla extract

TOPPING

⅓ cup firmly packed dark brown sugar

⅔ cup quick-cooking oatmeal

¼ cup unsalted dry-roasted finely chopped pecans

1½ teaspoons freshly grated nutmeg, or ½ teaspoon
    ground nutmeg

3 tablespoons acceptable margarine, melted

2 to 3 tablespoons skim milk

Preheat oven to 350° F. Grease (with acceptable margarine) and flour a 9-x-13-x-2-inch cake pan.

Sift dry ingredients together and stir in nutmeg. Stir to mix evenly. Set aside.

Place margarine, butter extract and sugar in a large mixing bowl. Cream until smooth and light in color. Add egg substitute and beat well.

Add flour mixture and buttermilk alternately, beginning and ending with flour. Add vanilla and blend.

Pour into prepared pan and bake 30 to 35 minutes.

While cake is baking, make topping.

In a small bowl, combine sugar, oatmeal, pecans and nutmeg. Stir to mix well.

Add margarine and blend. Slowly add milk, stirring constantly, until mixture has a spreading consistency. Spread on hot cake.

Serve warm, or cut cake into individual pieces and heat briefly under broiler just before serving.

Nutrient Analysis

Calories	250 kcal	Cholesterol	1 mg	Saturated Fat		2 gm
Protein	4 gm	Sodium	208 mg	Polyunsaturated Fat		2 gm
Carbohydrate	37 gm	Total Fat	10 gm	Monounsaturated Fat		5 gm

*M*argarite's *C*arrot *C*ake

Serves 12

Vegetable oil spray
2 eggs
½ cup acceptable vegetable oil
½ cup honey
¼ cup firmly packed brown sugar
½ cup plain nonfat yogurt
2 cups whole-wheat flour
1½ teaspoons cinnamon
1 teaspoon baking soda
1½ cups grated carrots
½ cup raisins
½ cup unsalted dry-roasted chopped walnuts

Preheat oven to 400° F. Lightly spray an 8-inch square cake pan with vegetable oil.

In a large mixing bowl, beat eggs thoroughly. Add oil, honey, sugar and yogurt. Mix well. Blend in flour. Add cinnamon, baking soda, grated carrots, raisins and chopped walnuts. Mix well.

Pour batter into prepared pan. Bake 45 minutes, or until a toothpick inserted in center comes out clean.

Nutrient Analysis

Calories	295 kcal	Cholesterol	46 mg	Saturated Fat		2 gm
Protein	5 gm	Sodium	102 mg	Polyunsaturated Fat		8 gm
Carbohydrate	42 gm	Total Fat	14 gm	Monounsaturated Fat		3 gm

*E*asy *A*pple *C*ake

Serves 9

Vegetable oil spray
2 cups diced apples (peeled or unpeeled)
¾ cup sugar
⅓ cup acceptable vegetable oil
1 teaspoon vanilla
Egg substitute equivalent to 1 egg
1½ cups unsifted all-purpose flour
1 teaspoon baking powder
1 teaspoon baking soda
½ teaspoon salt
1½ teaspoons pumpkin pie spice
½ cup raisins

Preheat oven to 350° F. Lightly spray an 8-inch square cake pan with vegetable oil.

Combine apples and sugar in a bowl and set aside for 10 minutes.

Add oil, vanilla and egg substitute. Stir to mix well.

In another bowl, combine dry ingredients and stir to mix thoroughly. Add to apple mixture and stir to blend well. Add raisins and stir to mix well.

Spread batter evenly into prepared pan. Bake 35 to 40 minutes.

Serve with Orange Sauce (see page 437) if desired.

Nutrient Analysis *

Calories	260 kcal	Cholesterol	0 mg	Saturated Fat	1 gm
Protein	3 gm	Sodium	260 mg	Polyunsaturated Fat	5 gm
Carbohydrate	45 gm	Total Fat	8 gm	Monounsaturated Fat	2 gm

* *without Orange Sauce*

Rum Lime Pudding Cake

Serves 9

Vegetable oil spray
⅔ cup sugar
1½ cups skim milk
¼ cup all-purpose flour
⅛ teaspoon salt
2 tablespoons acceptable margarine, melted and cooled
1 tablespoon grated lime rind
⅓ cup fresh lime juice
1 teaspoon rum extract
3 eggs, separated
1 tablespoon sugar

Preheat oven to 350° F. Lightly spray an 8-inch square baking pan with vegetable oil.

In a blender or the work bowl of a food processor fitted with a metal blade, combine ⅔ cup sugar, milk, flour, salt, margarine, lime rind, lime juice, extract and egg yolks. Process until smooth. Pour into large mixing bowl. Set aside.

In a mixing bowl, beat egg whites until soft peaks form. Add 1 tablespoon sugar and beat until stiff. Mix one-third of whites into lime mixture. Fold in remainder.

Pour batter into prepared pan, and place it in turn into a 9-x-13-inch pan. Add hot water to larger pan to a depth of 2 inches. Bake 35 to 40 minutes. Serve warm, or cover and refrigerate to serve cold.

Nutrient Analysis

Calories	138 kcal	Cholesterol	92 mg	Saturated Fat	1 gm
Protein	4 gm	Sodium	106 mg	Polyunsaturated Fat	1 gm
Carbohydrate	21 gm	Total Fat	5 gm	Monounsaturated Fat	2 gm

Quick Pineapple Upside-Down Cake

Serves 9

¼ cup acceptable margarine, melted
½ cup firmly packed brown sugar
1½ cups crushed no-sugar-added pineapple, canned in
 natural juices
1 cup sifted cake flour
¾ cup sugar
¼ cup acceptable vegetable oil
¼ cup skim milk
1½ teaspoons baking powder
¼ cup skim milk
2 egg whites, unbeaten
½ teaspoon vanilla extract

Preheat oven to 350° F.

Pour melted margarine into an 8-inch square baking pan. Sprinkle with brown sugar. Spread crushed pineapple evenly on bottom of pan.

In a mixing bowl, sift together flour and white sugar. Add oil and ¼ cup of the milk. Stir until flour is dampened, then beat 1 minute. Stir in baking powder, remaining milk, egg whites and vanilla. Beat 2 minutes.

Pour batter over crushed pineapple in cake pan. Bake 35 to 40 minutes, or until a toothpick inserted in center comes out clean.

Remove from oven, cool slightly and invert onto a serving plate.

Nutrient Analysis

Calories	279 kcal	Cholesterol	0 mg	Saturated Fat	2 gm
Protein	2 gm	Sodium	130 mg	Polyunsaturated Fat	5 gm
Carbohydrate	44 gm	Total Fat	11 gm	Monounsaturated Fat	4 gm

*B*lack *D*evil's *F*ood *C*ake

Serves 20

2 cups all-purpose flour
1¾ cups sugar
½ cup cocoa
1 tablespoon baking soda
⅔ cup acceptable vegetable oil
1 cup low-fat buttermilk
1 cup strong coffee (instant coffee may be used)

Preheat oven to 350° F. Grease (with acceptable margarine) and flour a 9-x-13-inch pan.

In a large mixing bowl, sift together flour, sugar, cocoa and baking soda. Add oil and buttermilk. Stir until well blended. Set aside.

Bring coffee to a boil in a small saucepan over medium-high heat. Remove from heat and stir coffee gently into batter. Mixture will be soupy.

Pour batter into prepared pan and bake 35 to 40 minutes.

Remove from oven and serve warm or cool completely.

VARIATION

Decorate with Creamy Fudge Frosting (see page 552).

*Black Devil's Food Cake Nutrient Analysis** *

Calories	184 kcal	Cholesterol	0 mg	Saturated Fat		1 gm
Protein	2 gm	Sodium	137 mg	Polyunsaturated Fat		4 gm
Carbohydrate	27 gm	Total Fat	8 gm	Monounsaturated Fat		2 gm

* *unfrosted*

Black Devil's Food Cake with Creamy Fudge Frosting Nutrient Analysis

Calories	280 kcal	Cholesterol	1 mg	Saturated Fat		2 gm
Protein	3 gm	Sodium	173 mg	Polyunsaturated Fat		5 gm
Carbohydrate	47 gm	Total Fat	10 gm	Monounsaturated Fat		3 gm

Wacky Cake

Serves 9

> 1½ cups flour
> 1 cup sugar
> 1 teaspoon baking soda
> ¼ cup cocoa
> 1 teaspoon vanilla extract
> 1 teaspoon cider vinegar
> 6 tablespoons acceptable margarine, melted
> 1 cup water

Preheat oven to 350° F.

Use an ungreased 8-inch cake pan. In the pan, sift and mix together flour, sugar, soda and cocoa.

Make three wells in flour mixture. Put vanilla in the first, vinegar in the second and melted margarine in the third.

Pour 1 cup of water over all and mix with a fork until ingredients are entirely moist. Bake 30 minutes.

Nutrient Analysis

Calories	230 kcal	Cholesterol	0 mg	Saturated Fat	2 gm
Protein	3 gm	Sodium	181 mg	Polyunsaturated Fat	2 gm
Carbohydrate	38 gm	Total Fat	8 gm	Monounsaturated Fat	4 gm

White Layer Cake

Serves 16

> ½ cup (1 stick) acceptable margarine, softened
> 1 teaspoon vanilla extract
> ½ teaspoon almond extract
> 1¼ cups sugar
> 2½ cups sifted cake flour
> 1½ teaspoons baking powder
> 1⅓ cups low-fat buttermilk
> 4 egg whites, at room temperature
> ¼ cup sugar
> 1 recipe Seven-Minute Frosting, flavored (see page 552)

Preheat oven to 350° F. Line two 9-inch cake pans with wax paper.

In a large mixing bowl, cream together margarine, vanilla extract, almond extract and 1¼ cups sugar.

In another bowl, sift together flour and baking powder. Add to creamed mixture alternately with the buttermilk, starting and ending with dry ingredients. Set aside.

In a large mixing bowl, beat egg whites until foamy. Gradually add remaining ¼ cup sugar and beat until stiff peaks form. Fold into batter. Pour mixture into prepared cake pans.

Bake 30 minutes, or until done. Cool 10 minutes, remove from pans and remove wax paper. When cake is thoroughly cool, frost with a flavored Seven-Minute Frosting.

WHITE CAKE WITH LEMON FROSTING

Spread lemon pudding between the layers and frost the cake with Lemon-Flavored Seven-Minute Frosting.

Note: You may use any flavor pudding, pudding combined with fruit or jam between cake layers. Frost with flavored Seven-Minute Frosting or dribble flavored Confectioners' Glaze over the top and sides of the cake (see pages 552 and 438).

White Layer Cake Nutrient Analysis *

Calories	259 kcal	Cholesterol	1 mg	Saturated Fat	2 gm
Protein	3 gm	Sodium	138 mg	Polyunsaturated Fat	1 gm
Carbohydrate	49 gm	Total Fat	6 gm	Monounsaturated Fat	3 gm

* *unfrosted*

White Cake with Lemon Frosting Nutrient Analysis

Calories	277 kcal	Cholesterol	12 mg	Saturated Fat	2 gm
Protein	3 gm	Sodium	166 mg	Polyunsaturated Fat	1 gm
Carbohydrate	53 gm	Total Fat	6 gm	Monounsaturated Fat	3 gm

Creamy Fudge Frosting

Makes quantity sufficient to frost a 9-x-13-inch cake
Serves 20

> 5 tablespoons Cream Cheese (see page 66)
> 1 tablespoon skim milk
> 1 teaspoon vanilla
> 2 tablespoons cocoa
> 1 teaspoon skim milk
> 3 cups sifted confectioners' sugar

In a large mixing bowl, cream together Cream Cheese, 1 tablespoon milk and vanilla. Add cocoa and blend well. Add 1 teaspoon of milk and ½ cup sugar, beating constantly. Add remaining sugar, ½ cup at a time. Spread on completely cooled cake.

Nutrient Analysis

Calories	96 kcal	Cholesterol	0 mg	Saturated Fat	1 gm
Protein	1 gm	Sodium	36 mg	Polyunsaturated Fat	0 gm
Carbohydrate	20 gm	Total Fat	2 gm	Monounsaturated Fat	1 gm

Seven-Minute Frosting

Makes quantity sufficient to frost a 2-layer cake
Serves 16

> 2 egg whites
> 1½ cups sugar
> ¼ teaspoon cream of tartar, or 1 tablespoon light corn
>   syrup
> ⅓ cup water
> 1 teaspoon vanilla extract

Combine egg whites, sugar, cream of tartar and water in the top of a double boiler. With an electric mixer, beat on high speed 1 minute. Place over boiling water and beat on high speed 7 minutes. Remove top of double boiler from the heat. Add vanilla. Beat 2 minutes longer on high speed.

Spread on completely cooled cake.

LEMON-FLAVORED SEVEN-MINUTE FROSTING

Substitute 1 tablespoon of fresh lemon juice for the vanilla extract and add ¼ teaspoon grated lemon peel during the last minute of beating.

SEVEN-MINUTE FROSTING WITH FRUIT

Add crushed fruit to the frosting or substitute fruit flavorings for the vanilla extract.

SEVEN-MINUTE FROSTING WITH RUM

Substitute rum or sherry flavoring for the vanilla extract.

Seven-Minute Frosting Nutrient Analysis

Calories	72 kcal	Cholesterol	0 mg	Saturated Fat	0 gm
Protein	0 gm	Sodium	10 mg	Polyunsaturated Fat	0 gm
Carbohydrate	18 gm	Total Fat	0 gm	Monounsaturated Fat	0 gm

Lemon-Flavored Seven-Minute Frosting Nutrient Analysis

Calories	72 kcal	Cholesterol	0 mg	Saturated Fat	0 gm
Protein	0 gm	Sodium	10 mg	Polyunsaturated Fat	0 gm
Carbohydrate	18 gm	Total Fat	0 gm	Monounsaturated Fat	0 gm

Seven-Minute Frosting with Fruit Nutrient Analysis*

Calories	75 kcal	Cholesterol	0 mg	Saturated Fat	0 gm
Protein	0 gm	Sodium	10 mg	Polyunsaturated Fat	0 gm
Carbohydrate	19 gm	Total Fat	0 gm	Monounsaturated Fat	0 gm

* with 1 cup sliced fresh strawberries

Seven-Minute Frosting with Rum Nutrient Analysis

Calories	72 kcal	Cholesterol	0 mg	Saturated Fat	0 gm
Protein	0 gm	Sodium	10 mg	Polyunsaturated Fat	0 gm
Carbohydrate	18 gm	Total Fat	0 gm	Monounsaturated Fat	0 gm

*S*ugar *C*ookies

Serves 48; 1 cookie per serving

> ½ cup acceptable margarine, softened
> 1 cup sugar
> Egg substitute equivalent to 1 egg
> 2 tablespoons skim milk
> 1 teaspoon vanilla
> 2 cups all-purpose flour
> 2 teaspoons baking powder
> ½ teaspoon salt
> ⅛ teaspoon nutmeg
> Vegetable oil spray

*I*n a large mixing bowl, cream margarine and sugar together until light. Beat in egg substitute, milk and vanilla.

In another bowl, sift flour, baking powder, salt and nutmeg together. Beat dry ingredients into first mixture, mixing well. Cover and refrigerate dough until chilled thoroughly.

Preheat oven to 375° F. Lightly spray cookie sheet with vegetable oil.

Form dough into balls that are 1 inch in diameter and place on prepared cookie sheet. Press thumb lightly in center of each cookie. Bake 8 minutes. Remove to wire rack to cool.

LEMON SUGAR COOKIES

Substitute 2 tablespoons lemon juice and 1 teaspoon grated lemon rind for milk and vanilla.

Sugar Cookies Nutrient Analysis

Calories	51 kcal	Cholesterol	0 mg	Saturated Fat	0 gm
Protein	1 gm	Sodium	59 mg	Polyunsaturated Fat	0 gm
Carbohydrate	8 gm	Total Fat	2 gm	Monounsaturated Fat	1 gm

Lemon Sugar Cookies Nutrient Analysis

Calories	51 kcal	Cholesterol	0 mg	Saturated Fat	0 gm
Protein	1 gm	Sodium	59 mg	Polyunsaturated Fat	0 gm
Carbohydrate	8 gm	Total Fat	2 gm	Monounsaturated Fat	1 gm

*G*inger *C*ookies

Serves 24; 1 cookie per serving

> ¾ cup acceptable margarine
> 1 cup sugar
> 1 egg, slightly beaten
> ¼ cup molasses
> 2 cups all-purpose flour
> 2 teaspoons baking soda
> 1 teaspoon cinnamon
> 1 teaspoon ground ginger
> Vegetable oil spray
> 1 tablespoon sugar

*I*n a large mixing bowl, cream margarine and 1 cup of sugar. Beat in egg and molasses.

In another bowl, sift flour, soda and spices together. Add to margarine mixture. Mix well. Cover and refrigerate dough until thoroughly chilled.

Preheat oven to 350° F. Lightly spray baking sheet with vegetable oil.

Shape dough into balls about 1 inch in diameter. Roll in 1 tablespoon sugar and place 3 inches apart on prepared baking sheet. Bake 15 minutes.

GINGERBREAD MEN

Prepare dough as directed, but add ½ cup more flour, to make 2½ cups flour. Roll chilled dough on a lightly floured board to ⅛-inch thickness. Cut out gingerbread men shapes with a 6-x-3½-inch cookie cutter. Bake 8 to 10 minutes at 350° F. Decorate with ½ cup Confectioners' Glaze (see page 438). Makes 2 to 3 dozen gingerbread men, depending on cookie cutter.

Ginger Cookies Nutrient Analysis

Calories	130 kcal	Cholesterol	9 mg	Saturated Fat	1 gm
Protein	1 gm	Sodium	139 mg	Polyunsaturated Fat	1 gm
Carbohydrate	18 gm	Total Fat	6 gm	Monounsaturated Fat	3 gm

Gingerbread Men Nutrient Analysis *

Calories	149 kcal	Cholesterol	11 mg	Saturated Fat	1 gm
Protein	2 gm	Sodium	140 mg	Polyunsaturated Fat	1 gm
Carbohydrate	23 gm	Total Fat	6 gm	Monounsaturated Fat	3 gm

* with half recipe Confectioners' Glaze for entire cookie recipe

Peanut Butter Cookies

Serves 30; 2 cookies per serving

> Vegetable oil spray
> ½ cup acceptable margarine, room temperature
> ½ cup sugar
> ½ cup firmly packed brown sugar
> 1 egg
> ½ cup creamy peanut butter
> ½ teaspoon baking soda
> 1 cup all-purpose flour
> ½ teaspoon vanilla

Preheat oven to 350° F. Lightly spray cookie sheet with vegetable oil.

In a large mixing bowl, cream margarine until soft. Add sugars gradually and beat until creamy. Beat in egg, peanut butter and soda. Add flour slowly to batter, mixing constantly. Add vanilla and mix well.

Roll dough into small balls about the size of a pecan. Place on prepared cookie sheet. Flatten balls lightly with back of tines of a floured fork. Bake 12 to 15 minutes.

Nutrient Analysis

Calories	95 kcal	Cholesterol	9 mg	Saturated Fat	1 gm
Protein	2 gm	Sodium	73 mg	Polyunsaturated Fat	1 gm
Carbohydrate	11 gm	Total Fat	5 gm	Monounsaturated Fat	2 gm

Chocolate Oatmeal Cookies

Serves 36; 1 cookie per serving

> 1½ cups firmly packed brown sugar
> ¾ cup acceptable margarine
> ½ cup sifted cocoa
> 2 teaspoons vanilla
> ½ cup skim milk
> 1 ¾ cups all-purpose flour
> 2½ teaspoons baking powder
> ½ teaspoon salt
> 1½ cups quick-cooking oatmeal

Preheat oven to 350° F.

In a large mixing bowl, cream sugar and margarine together. Add cocoa, vanilla and milk. Mix well.

In another bowl, sift together flour, baking powder and salt. Blend into margarine mixture. Stir in oatmeal.

Drop by teaspoonfuls onto ungreased baking sheets. Bake 7 to 9 minutes.

Nutrient Analysis

Calories	108 kcal	Cholesterol	0 mg	Saturated Fat	1 gm
Protein	2 gm	Sodium	99 mg	Polyunsaturated Fat	1 gm
Carbohydrate	16 gm	Total Fat	4 gm	Monounsaturated Fat	2 gm

*F*avorite *O*atmeal *C*ookies

Serves 54; 1 cookie per serving

Vegetable oil spray
⅔ cup acceptable margarine
1 cup firmly packed brown sugar
1 cup sugar
1 teaspoon vanilla extract
¼ teaspoon orange extract
1 teaspoon grated orange rind
Egg substitute equivalent to 2 eggs
1¼ cups all-purpose flour
1 teaspoon baking soda
1 teaspoon cinnamon
3 cups quick-cooking oatmeal

Preheat oven to 350° F. Lightly spray cookie sheet with vegetable oil.

In a large mixing bowl, cream together margarine, sugars, extracts and orange rind. Beat in egg substitute and blend well.

In another bowl, sift together flour, baking soda and cinnamon Add to margarine mixture and blend well. Stir in oatmeal. Drop dough by teaspoonfuls onto prepared cookie sheet. Bake 10 minutes.

Nutrient Analysis

Calories	77 kcal	Cholesterol	0 mg	Saturated Fat	1 gm
Protein	1 gm	Sodium	47 mg	Polyunsaturated Fat	1 gm
Carbohydrate	13 gm	Total Fat	3 gm	Monounsaturated Fat	1 gm

*O*atmeal *C*arrot *C*ookies

Serves 24; 1 bar per serving

> Vegetable oil spray
> ½ cup raisins
> Boiling water
> ⅓ cup acceptable margarine, room temperature
> ½ cup firmly packed brown sugar
> 1 egg
> 1¼ cups grated carrots
> ½ teaspoon cinnamon
> ¼ teaspoon nutmeg
> ½ teaspoon freshly grated lemon rind
> 1 cup whole-wheat flour
> ½ cup quick-cooking oatmeal
> 1 teaspoon baking powder
> ½ teaspoon vanilla
> 1 tablespoon confectioners' sugar

*P*reheat oven to 350° F. Lightly spray 7½-x-11½-x-2-inch baking pan with vegetable oil.

Cover raisins in a small bowl with boiling water. Soak 15 minutes. Drain and set aside.

In a large mixing bowl, cream together margarine and brown sugar until fluffy. Add egg. Beat well. Add carrots, cinnamon, nutmeg and lemon rind. Mix well.

In another bowl, stir together flour, oatmeal and baking powder. Add to margarine mixture. Mix well. Add vanilla, mix well and fold in drained raisins.

Pour into prepared pan. Bake 20 to 25 minutes. Let cool. Sprinkle lightly with confectioners' sugar. Cut into 24 bars.

Nutrient Analysis

Calories	86 kcal	Cholesterol	11 mg	Saturated Fat	1 gm
Protein	1 gm	Sodium	51 mg	Polyunsaturated Fat	1 gm
Carbohydrate	14 gm	Total Fat	3 gm	Monounsaturated Fat	1 gm

Apricot Raisin Bars

Serves 48; 1 bar per serving

1 cup raisins
1 6-ounce package dried apricots, chopped
1½ cups unsweetened apple juice
¼ cup unsweetened apple juice
3 tablespoons cornstarch
1½ teaspoons grated lemon rind
Vegetable oil spray
1½ cups all-purpose flour
1 teaspoon baking powder
1½ cups uncooked quick-cooking oatmeal
¾ cup firmly packed brown sugar
¼ cup sugar
⅔ cup acceptable margarine

In a saucepan, combine raisins, apricots and 1½ cups apple juice. Cook 20 minutes, or until fruit is tender.

In a bowl, combine remaining ¼ cup apple juice, cornstarch and rind. Add to saucepan stirring constantly until mixture thickens. Remove from heat and set aside to cool.

Preheat oven to 375° F. Lightly spray a 9-x-13-inch pan with vegetable oil.

In a bowl, sift flour and baking powder together. Blend in oatmeal and sugar; blend in margarine until crumbly. Press two-thirds of oatmeal mixture in bottom of prepared pan. Spread fruit mixture over bottom crust. Top with remaining crumbs. Bake 30 minutes. Cut into 48 squares.

Nutrient Analysis

Calories	93 kcal	Cholesterol	0 mg	Saturated Fat	1 gm
Protein	1 gm	Sodium	39 mg	Polyunsaturated Fat	1 gm
Carbohydrate	17 gm	Total Fat	3 gm	Monounsaturated Fat	1 gm

Bourbon Balls

Serves 48; 1 ball per serving

> 3 cups finely crushed vanilla wafers
> 1 cup confectioners' sugar
> ½ cup unsalted dry-roasted chopped pecans
> 3 tablespoons light corn syrup
> 1½ tablespoons cocoa
> 6 tablespoons bourbon
> ¼ cup confectioners' sugar

In a large bowl, combine all ingredients except ¼ cup confectioners' sugar. Stir to mix well. Form into small balls. (If balls tend to crumble, add a few extra drops of bourbon to mixture.) Roll each in confectioners' sugar and store in an airtight container for about 1 week to ripen.

Nutrient Analysis

Calories	77 kcal	Cholesterol	6 mg	Saturated Fat	1 gm
Protein	1 gm	Sodium	31 mg	Polyunsaturated Fat	0 gm
Carbohydrate	12 gm	Total Fat	3 gm	Monounsaturated Fat	1 gm

Sherry Thins

Serves 60; 1 cookie per serving

> ¾ cup acceptable margarine
> 1 cup sugar
> 1 egg
> 1 teaspoon vanilla
> 3 cups sifted all-purpose flour
> 2 teaspoons baking powder
> ½ teaspoon salt
> ⅓ cup cream sherry

In a large mixing bowl, cream margarine and sugar until light. Add egg and vanilla and mix well.

In another bowl, sift dry ingredients together. Add to margarine mixture alternately with sherry. Cover and refrigerate dough at least 2 hours.

Preheat oven to 375° F.

Roll out half of dough on floured surface. Cut out shapes with small cookie cutters. Repeat with remaining dough. Place on cookie sheet and bake 5 to 7 minutes.

Nutrient Analysis

Calories	56 kcal	Cholesterol	5 mg	Saturated Fat	1 gm
Protein	1 gm	Sodium	55 mg	Polyunsaturated Fat	1 gm
Carbohydrate	8 gm	Total Fat	2 gm	Monounsaturated Fat	1 gm

Butterscotch Brownies

Serves 32; 1 brownie per serving

> Vegetable oil spray
> 1 cup firmly packed dark brown sugar
> ¼ cup acceptable margarine
> Egg substitute equivalent to 1 egg
> ½ teaspoon imitation butter flavoring
> ½ teaspoon vanilla extract
> ¾ cup sifted all-purpose flour
> 1 teaspoon baking powder
> ½ cup unsalted dry-roasted chopped pecans

Preheat oven to 350° F. Lightly spray an 8-inch square baking pan with vegetable oil.

In a large mixing bowl, cream sugar and margarine together. Add egg substitute and extracts. Blend well.

In another bowl, sift flour and baking powder together. Add to margarine mixture and mix well. Stir in nuts.

Spread evenly into prepared pan. Bake 20 to 25 minutes. Cool slightly and cut into 32 bars.

Nutrient Analysis

Calories	62 kcal	Cholesterol	0 mg	Saturated Fat	0 gm
Protein	1 gm	Sodium	32 mg	Polyunsaturated Fat	1 gm
Carbohydrate	9 gm	Total Fat	3 gm	Monounsaturated Fat	1 gm

Apricot Ice

Serves 6

1 6-ounce package dried apricots
3 cups water
⅓ cup sugar
2 tablespoons fresh lime juice

Cook apricots and water in a saucepan over medium heat for 20 minutes.

Puree mixture in blender or the work bowl of a food processor fitted with a metal blade. Strain into a mixing bowl. Stir in sugar and lime juice. Pour into an 8-inch square pan and freeze until slushy.

Return mixture to blender or food processor and process until smooth and creamy. Return to pan and freeze again. Remove from freezer 15 minutes before serving.

STRAWBERRY ICE

Rinse and hull 1 quart of strawberries. Place in blender or work bowl of a food processor fitted with a metal blade. Process until pureed. Add ½ cup strawberry preserves and 1 tablespoon fresh lemon juice. Process until mixed thoroughly. Strain into 8-inch square pan. Freeze and proceed as directed above.

Apricot Ice Nutrient Analysis

Calories	112 kcal	Cholesterol	0 mg	Saturated Fat	0 gm
Protein	1 gm	Sodium	4 mg	Polyunsaturated Fat	0 gm
Carbohydrate	29 gm	Total Fat	0 gm	Monounsaturated Fat	0 gm

Strawberry Ice Nutrient Analysis

Calories	77 kcal	Cholesterol	0 mg	Saturated Fat	0 gm
Protein	0 gm	Sodium	5 mg	Polyunsaturated Fat	0 gm
Carbohydrate	19 gm	Total Fat	0 gm	Monounsaturated Fat	0 gm

Strawberries with Champagne Ice

Serves 6

2 oranges
1 lemon
2 cups fresh strawberries
¾ cup sugar
1½ cups water
3 tablespoons Grand Marnier or Cointreau
2 cups champagne
1 tablespoon sugar
1 cup champagne

Squeeze juice from oranges and lemons. Set juice aside. With vegetable peeler, peel oranges and lemon entirely. Set aside.

Rinse strawberries, hull and cut in half. Set aside.

Combine sugar, water and citrus peels in a saucepan over medium-high heat. Bring mixture to boil and boil 5 minutes. Remove from heat. Remove peels from pan. Stir in orange and lemon juices and liqueur. Cover and refrigerate in a bowl for 2 hours.

Stir 2 cups champagne into juice mixture. Stir to mix well. Pour into an 8-inch square pan and freeze until slushy.

Remove juice mixture from freezer and beat or process in a mixing bowl, a blender or the work bowl of a food processor fitted with a metal blade until mixture is smooth. Pour back into pan and refreeze, stirring occasionally.

In a bowl, combine strawberries, sugar and remaining champagne. Cover and refrigerate at least 2 hours.

Divide strawberries among six goblets and fill with champagne ice.

Nutrient Analysis

Calories	241 kcal	Cholesterol	0 mg	Saturated Fat		0 gm
Protein	1 gm	Sodium	11 mg	Polyunsaturated Fat		0 gm
Carbohydrate	39 gm	Total Fat	0 gm	Monounsaturated Fat		0 gm

*L*emon *S*herbet

Serves 8

½ cup sugar
½ cup boiling water
1 envelope unflavored gelatin
¼ cup fresh lemon juice
⅓ cup fresh lemon juice
1½ cups low-fat lemon yogurt
1 teaspoon grated lemon rind
3 to 4 drops yellow food coloring
¼ cup meringue powder *

*I*n a bowl, dissolve sugar in boiling water and set aside. In a heat-proof measuring cup, combine gelatin and ¼ cup fresh lemon juice. Place measuring cup in a pan of simmering water for 1½ to 2 minutes, or until gelatin is dissolved. Remove measuring cup from pan, and stir in ⅓ cup lemon juice. Pour mixture into a bowl; whisk in yogurt, rind and food coloring. Refrigerate until mixture is slushy.

Mix meringue powder into reserved sugar and water mixture. Beat until soft peaks form. Remove yogurt mixture from refrigerator. Stir in half of meringue with rubber spatula, then fold in remainder.

Pour mixture into 11-x-7-inch pan and freeze until firm. Remove from freezer 15 minutes before serving.

* *Meringue powder can be found in stores that stock cake-decorating supplies.*

Nutrient Analysis

Calories	118 kcal	Cholesterol	2 mg	Saturated Fat		0 gm
Protein	4 gm	Sodium	83 mg	Polyunsaturated Fat		0 gm
Carbohydrate	26 gm	Total Fat	1 gm	Monounsaturated Fat		0 gm

*T*equila *L*ime *S*herbet

Serves 6

1 envelope unflavored gelatin
2 tablespoons cold water
¾ cup sugar
1 cup water
⅓ cup tequila
½ cup fresh lime juice
1 tablespoon grated lime rind
1 cup plain nonfat yogurt

Soften gelatin in 2 tablespoons water. Set aside.

In a saucepan over medium-high heat, combine sugar and 1 cup water. Boil 5 minutes. Add gelatin mixture and remaining ingredients, stirring yogurt with a whisk to remove any lumps. Pour into an 8-inch square pan and freeze until slushy.

Process mixture in blender or the work bowl of a food processor fitted with a metal blade until smooth. Return to pan and freeze. Remove sherbet from freezer 15 minutes before serving.

MICROWAVE METHOD

Cook sugar and water mixture in microwave-safe measure on high 5 minutes. Proceed as directed.

Nutrient Analysis

Calories	153 kcal	Cholesterol	1 mg	Saturated Fat	0 gm
Protein	3 gm	Sodium	38 mg	Polyunsaturated Fat	0 gm
Carbohydrate	29 gm	Total Fat	0 gm	Monounsaturated Fat	0 gm

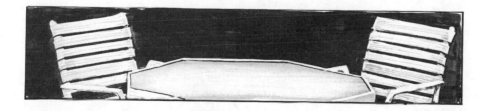

*F*resh *F*ruit *I*ce

Serves 8

1 envelope unflavored gelatin
½ cup cold water
1 cup orange juice
6 tablespoons fresh lemon juice
4 tablespoons sugar
1 cup strawberries, peaches or other fresh fruit, sliced
3 bananas, mashed

Soften gelatin in water in a saucepan. Place over low heat and stir until dissolved. Add juices, sugar, sliced fruit and bananas. Stir to mix well. Pour into a bowl and freeze until almost set. Beat with an electric mixer on high speed until fluffy.

Cover and return to freezer. Serve when set.

Note: If fruit ice is made some time ahead, beat it again and return it to freezer for a brief period before serving.

Nutrient Analysis*

Calories	88 kcal	Cholesterol	0 mg	Saturated Fat	0 gm
Protein	2 gm	Sodium	4 mg	Polyunsaturated Fat	0 gm
Carbohydrate	22 gm	Total Fat	0 gm	Monounsaturated Fat	0 gm

* *using fresh strawberries*

*F*ruity *I*ce *C*ream

Serves 8

2 cups plain nonfat yogurt
2 tablespoons fresh lemon juice
½ teaspoon vanilla extract
2 cups fresh peaches or nectarines, mashed with fork
    (about 4)
2 cups fresh strawberries or bananas, mashed with fork
½ cup sugar

Combine yogurt, lemon juice and vanilla in a bowl. Stir well. Cover and refrigerate.

In another bowl, combine fruits and sprinkle sugar over all. Stir to mix well. Let rest 10 minutes, or until sugar melts.

Combine fruits with yogurt mixture and freeze in ice cream freezer as directed by manufacturer.

Nutrient Analysis *

Calories	119 kcal	Cholesterol	1 mg	Saturated Fat		0 gm
Protein	4 gm	Sodium	48 mg	Polyunsaturated Fat		0 gm
Carbohydrate	26 gm	Total Fat	0 gm	Monounsaturated Fat		0 gm

* using fresh peaches and strawberries

*F*rozen *B*anana *O*range *P*ush-*U*ps

Serves 6

2 bananas
1 6-ounce can frozen orange juice concentrate, thawed
½ cup nonfat dry milk
½ cup water
1 cup plain nonfat yogurt

Peel and slice bananas into a blender or the work bowl of a food processor fitted with a metal blade. Add remaining ingredients. Cover and process until foamy. Pour evenly into six small paper cups. Freeze.

To eat, squeeze bottom of cup.

Nutrient Analysis

Calories	123 kcal	Cholesterol	2 mg	Saturated Fat		0 gm
Protein	5 gm	Sodium	64 mg	Polyunsaturated Fat		0 gm
Carbohydrate	26 gm	Total Fat	0 gm	Monounsaturated Fat		0 gm

Cardinal Sundae

Serves 16; ½ cup sherbet and 1 tablespoon sauce per serving

½ cup frozen no-sugar-added strawberry halves
½ cup frozen sweetened raspberries
1 teaspoon cornstarch
¼ teaspoon fresh lemon juice
1 tablespoon currant jelly
8 cups lime sherbet

Thaw and drain strawberries and raspberries, reserving juice. Set berries aside.

In a saucepan, combine cornstarch and lemon juice with berry liquid. Bring mixture to a boil and cook gently for 1 minute. Add jelly and stir until it melts. Remove sauce from heat and stir in berries. Cover and refrigerate.

For each serving, spoon 1 tablespoon of sauce over a ½-cup scoop of lime sherbet.

Note: Unused topping may be refrigerated for later use.

Nutrient Analysis

Calories	145 kcal	Cholesterol	7 mg	Saturated Fat		1 gm
Protein	1 gm	Sodium	45 mg	Polyunsaturated Fat		0 gm
Carbohydrate	32 gm	Total Fat	2 gm	Monounsaturated Fat		1 gm

*H*ong *K*ong *S*undae

Makes 2½ cups topping
Sundaes serve 4; ½ cup ice milk and 2 tablespoons topping per serving

TOPPING
1 11-ounce can mandarin oranges, canned in light syrup
1 tablespoon cornstarch
1 8½-ounce can crushed no-sugar-added pineapple,
    canned in natural juices, undrained
½ cup orange marmalade
½ teaspoon ground ginger
½ cup sliced preserved kumquats

SUNDAES
½ cup Topping recipe
2 cups vanilla ice milk

Drain oranges, reserving ¼ cup of syrup. Set oranges aside.

Combine orange syrup with cornstarch in a saucepan over medium heat. Stir until well blended. Stir in pineapple with its liquid, marmalade and ginger. Cook, stirring, over medium heat until mixture thickens and bubbles.

Stir in oranges and kumquats.

Cover and refrigerate for later use, or serve warm.

For sundaes, place a ½-cup scoop of vanilla ice milk in each bowl. Add 2 tablespoons of warm topping to each.

Note: Unused topping may be refrigerated for later use.

Nutrient Analysis

Calories	178 kcal	Cholesterol	9 mg	Saturated Fat	2 gm
Protein	3 gm	Sodium	58 mg	Polyunsaturated Fat	0 gm
Carbohydrate	37 gm	Total Fat	3 gm	Monounsaturated Fat	1 gm

*A*pple *P*ops

Serves 10

> 4 cups unsweetened apple juice
> 1 cup natural (no-sugar-added) applesauce
> 6 wood, paper or plastic dessert sticks (not pointed)

*I*n a medium bowl, combine apple juice and applesauce. Stir well. Pour evenly into an ice cube tray. When almost frozen, insert sticks, then freeze completely.

Nutrient Analysis

Calories	58 kcal	Cholesterol	0 mg	Saturated Fat	0 gm
Protein	0 gm	Sodium	3 mg	Polyunsaturated Fat	0 gm
Carbohydrate	14 gm	Total Fat	0 gm	Monounsaturated Fat	0 gm

*D*uq

Serves 3; 1 cup per serving

> 2 cups water
> 1 cup low-fat lemon yogurt

*P*rocess water and yogurt in a blender or the work bowl of a food processor fitted with a metal blade until smooth. Cover and refrigerate until thoroughly chilled.

Serve in frosty glasses.

Nutrient Analysis

Calories	83 kcal	Cholesterol	3 mg	Saturated Fat	1 gm
Protein	4 gm	Sodium	48 mg	Polyunsaturated Fat	0 gm
Carbohydrate	16 gm	Total Fat	1 gm	Monounsaturated Fat	0 gm

*S*trawberry *D*essert *D*rink

Serves 2; 1 cup per serving

> 1 cup fresh strawberries
> 1 banana
> 1 cup orange juice

*R*inse and hull strawberries. Cut them in half and place them in a blender or the work bowl of a food processor fitted with a metal blade. Add peeled banana and orange juice. Process until smooth. If your blender or food processor can crush ice, add ice to make a sherbet-like dessert.

RASPBERRY DESSERT DRINK
Substitute 1 cup fresh raspberries for strawberries. Proceed as directed.

Strawberry Dessert Drink Nutrient Analysis

Calories	131 kcal	Cholesterol	0 mg	Saturated Fat	0 gm
Protein	2 gm	Sodium	3 mg	Polyunsaturated Fat	0 gm
Carbohydrate	32 gm	Total Fat	1 gm	Monounsaturated Fat	0 gm

Raspberry Dessert Drink Nutrient Analysis

Calories	139 kcal	Cholesterol	0 mg	Saturated Fat	0 gm
Protein	2 gm	Sodium	2 mg	Polyunsaturated Fat	0 gm
Carbohydrate	34 gm	Total Fat	1 gm	Monounsaturated Fat	0 gm

*B*reakfast *D*ishes

OMELETTE
TURKEY SAUSAGE PATTIES
CINNAMON ORANGE PANCAKES
APPLE OATMEAL PANCAKE
CINNAMON FRENCH TOAST
QUICK ORANGE STREUSEL CAKE
APPLE COFFEE CAKE
FLUFFY COTTAGE CHEESE BLINTZES
COTTAGE CHEESE AND CINNAMON TOASTY
CRUNCHY CEREAL
BREAKFAST ON THE RUN

Some say you can't make a good breakfast without breaking a few eggs, but these recipes will show you that's not true. There is still a place for the noble egg, of course—we've included several tasty omelette recipes in these pages—because the truth is, you may eat all the egg whites you like. They're a great source of protein, vitamins and minerals. It's the yolks you'll want to limit. The reason: Each yolk has about a day's ration of cholesterol. The answer? When you're making a two-egg omelette, use an egg substitute or use one whole egg and two egg whites. You'll find that it tastes, looks and cooks exactly the same.

With the variety of foods to choose from, it's amazing that anyone would ever skip breakfast. Delicious Apple Oatmeal Pancakes, crisp Cinnamon French Toast and Fluffy Cottage Cheese Blintzes—you'll find them all on these pages. You'll also find more breakfast treats—such as Blueberry Banana Muffins, Jeanne's Oatmeal Cinnamon Bread and Southern Raised Biscuits—in the section on Breads.

Omelette

Serves 1

> Vegetable oil spray
> 2 teaspoons acceptable margarine
> Egg substitute equivalent to 2 eggs
> Pinch salt
> Dash white pepper

Lightly spray a small nonstick skillet with vegetable oil. Add margarine and place over medium-high heat.

In a small bowl, combine remaining ingredients. Beat and pour mixture into pan. With one hand, move the pan back and forth. With the other, stir eggs in a circular motion with a fork. Do not scrape bottom of pan.

When omelette is almost cooked, add one of the fillings listed under variations. Fold omelette over with fork while holding pan at a 45-degree angle. Roll omelette onto a plate to serve.

For the first two variations, add the filling ingredients just before folding the omelette. Then proceed as directed above. For the third and fourth variations, follow the specific directions given below for each.

BROCCOLI AND CHEESE OMELETTE
¼ cup chopped cooked broccoli
½ ounce shredded low-fat cheddar cheese

TOMATO AND JACK CHEESE OMELETTE
¼ cup seeded chopped tomato
½ ounce shredded low-fat Monterey Jack cheese
1 teaspoon chopped fresh cilantro
Hot pepper sauce to taste

HERB PARMESAN OMELETTE
When the omelette is almost cooked, add the following to the egg mixture: 1 teaspoon each freshly chopped dill, basil and parsley. Sprinkle 1 tablespoon grated Parmesan cheese onto egg mixture and fold the omelette.

ZUCCHINI AND HAM OMELETTE

Add 1 ounce (approximately 1 slice) chopped turkey ham to egg mixture. In a small bowl, combine ¼ cup thinly sliced steamed zucchini, 1 tablespoon grated Romano cheese and 1 teaspoon chopped fresh basil. Set aside. Cook omelette as directed above. When the omelette is almost cooked, spoon zucchini mixture onto egg mixture and fold the omelette.

Omelette Nutrient Analysis

Calories	125 kcal	Cholesterol	0 mg	Saturated Fat	2 gm
Protein	11 gm	Sodium	334 mg	Polyunsaturated Fat	2 gm
Carbohydrate	2 gm	Total Fat	8 gm	Monounsaturated Fat	3 gm

Broccoli and Cheese Omelette Nutrient Analysis

Calories	162 kcal	Cholesterol	3 mg	Saturated Fat	3 gm
Protein	16 gm	Sodium	431 mg	Polyunsaturated Fat	2 gm
Carbohydrate	5 gm	Total Fat	9 gm	Monounsaturated Fat	4 gm

Tomato and Jack Cheese Omelette Nutrient Analysis

Calories	173 kcal	Cholesterol	8 mg	Saturated Fat	3 gm
Protein	16 gm	Sodium	839 mg	Polyunsaturated Fat	2 gm
Carbohydrate	5 gm	Total Fat	10 gm	Monounsaturated Fat	4 gm

Herb Parmesan Omelette Nutrient Analysis

Calories	157 kcal	Cholesterol	5 mg	Saturated Fat	3 gm
Protein	14 gm	Sodium	463 mg	Polyunsaturated Fat	2 gm
Carbohydrate	3 gm	Total Fat	10 gm	Monounsaturated Fat	4 gm

Zucchini and Ham Omelette Nutrient Analysis

Calories	195 kcal	Cholesterol	22 mg	Saturated Fat	4 gm
Protein	19 gm	Sodium	683 mg	Polyunsaturated Fat	2 gm
Carbohydrate	4 gm	Total Fat	11 gm	Monounsaturated Fat	4 gm

Turkey Sausage Patties

Serves 8; 1 patty per serving

> 1 pound lean ground turkey meat
> ½ teaspoon ground cumin
> ½ to ¾ teaspoon cayenne pepper
> 1 tablespoon Italian herb seasoning
> ½ teaspoon garlic powder
> 1¼ teaspoons coriander
> ¼ teaspoon black pepper
> 1 teaspoon paprika
> ¼ teaspoon salt
> 4 tablespoons plain, fine bread crumbs
> ½ cup homemade Chicken Broth (see page 87) or
>   commercial low-sodium variety
> Vegetable oil spray (optional)

*I*n a bowl, combine turkey, herbs and bread crumbs. Stir well. Add chicken broth and stir again. Let stand 15 minutes.

Form into eight patties, about ¾ inch thick.

Spray skillet with vegetable oil, or use a nonstick skillet.

Cook patties in skillet over medium heat 7 to 8 minutes on each side, or until done. Serve hot.

Nutrient Analysis

Calories	94 kcal	Cholesterol	35 mg	Saturated Fat	1 gm
Protein	13 gm	Sodium	127 mg	Polyunsaturated Fat	1 gm
Carbohydrate	3 gm	Total Fat	3 gm	Monounsaturated Fat	1 gm

Cinnamon Orange Pancakes

Serves 6; 2 pancakes per serving

¾ cup all-purpose flour
2 tablespoons wheat germ
1 cup whole-wheat flour
2 teaspoons baking powder
1 tablespoon sugar
1 teaspoon ground cinnamon
1 cup skim milk
¾ cup fresh orange juice
Egg substitute equivalent to 1 egg
1 teaspoon grated fresh orange peel
Vegetable oil spray

In a mixing bowl, combine all dry ingredients and mix until well blended.

In another bowl, combine all liquid ingredients and orange peel. Stir well.

Pour liquid ingredients mixture into dry ingredients and stir only until moistened.

Preheat griddle or skillet for pancakes. Spray lightly with vegetable oil.

For each pancake, pour ¼ cup of batter onto griddle or skillet. Turn each pancake when edges are dry and bubbles appear on top. Serve hot.

Note: Do not use vegetable oil spray near an open flame or a heat source. Read directions on can before using, and follow directions carefully.

Nutrient Analysis

Calories	171 kcal	Cholesterol	1 mg	Saturated Fat	0 gm
Protein	7 gm	Sodium	140 mg	Polyunsaturated Fat	0 gm
Carbohydrate	34 gm	Total Fat	1 gm	Monounsaturated Fat	0 gm

*A*pple *O*atmeal *P*ancake

Serves 6; 1 portion per serving

Vegetable oil spray
1 tablespoon acceptable margarine
⅓ cup uncooked quick-cooking oatmeal
⅓ cup whole-wheat flour
⅓ cup all-purpose flour
1 tablespoon firmly packed brown sugar
3 large eggs
Egg substitute equivalent to 3 eggs
¼ teaspoon salt
1 cup skim milk
1 tablespoon vanilla
1 teaspoon cinnamon
2 tablespoons brown sugar
½ teaspoon cinnamon
3 large (1¾ pounds) Red Delicious apples
1 tablespoon acceptable margarine
1 tablespoon fresh lemon juice

*L*ightly spray a 9-x-13-inch pan with vegetable oil.

Preheat oven to 425° F. Place 1 tablespoon margarine in prepared pan. Place in oven to melt margarine.

In a blender or the work bowl of a food processor fitted with a metal blade, combine oatmeal, flours and 1 tablespoon brown sugar. Process until smooth. Add eggs, egg substitute, salt, milk, vanilla and 1 teaspoon cinnamon. Process again until smooth. Pour mixture into hot pan. Return to oven and bake 25 minutes.

In a small bowl, combine 2 tablespoons brown sugar and ½ teaspoon cinnamon. Set aside.

Meanwhile, peel and core apples. Slice into ½-inch-thick pieces. Melt 1 tablespoon margarine in nonstick skillet over medium heat. Add apples, stirring with rubber spatula to prevent breakage. Sprinkle brown sugar-cinnamon mixture over apples. Cover and cook over medium heat 7 to 8 minutes. Add lemon juice just before serving.

Cut pancake into six equal portions and place on individual plates. Place one-sixth of apple mixture on top of each portion. Serve immediately.

VARIATION

Top apple mixture with syrup just before serving.

Nutrient Analysis

Calories	238 kcal	Cholesterol	138 mg	Saturated Fat	2 gm
Protein	10 gm	Sodium	255 mg	Polyunsaturated Fat	1 gm
Carbohydrate	35 gm	Total Fat	7 gm	Monounsaturated Fat	3 gm

Cinnamon French Toast

Serves 3

Egg substitute equivalent to 2 eggs
1 teaspoon sugar
½ teaspoon vanilla extract
¼ teaspoon cinnamon
Dash nutmeg
Vegetable oil spray
6 slices firm-textured thinly sliced bread

Place all ingredients except vegetable oil spray and bread in an 8-x-8-inch baking pan. Stir to mix well.

Lightly spray a nonstick skillet with vegetable oil and place over medium heat.

Dip one bread slice into egg mixture and turn gently to other side. Remove from pan and place in preheated skillet. Cook until brown on one side. Flip and brown on other side.

Repeat with remaining slices of bread, spraying skillet with vegetable oil before adding next slice.

Serve with syrup or fruit spread, if desired.

Note: Do not spray near heat source or open flame. Follow instructions on can for spraying.

Nutrient Analysis

Calories	161 kcal	Cholesterol	2 mg	Saturated Fat	0 gm
Protein	8 gm	Sodium	335 mg	Polyunsaturated Fat	0 gm
Carbohydrate	28 gm	Total Fat	2 gm	Monounsaturated Fat	1 gm

Quick Orange Streusel Cake

Serves 9

Vegetable oil spray
¼ cup firmly packed brown sugar
1 tablespoon acceptable margarine, melted
2 tablespoons all-purpose flour
2 cups all-purpose flour
⅓ cup sugar
2 teaspoons baking powder
½ teaspoon salt
½ cup skim milk
½ cup orange juice
⅓ cup acceptable vegetable oil
1 egg
1 teaspoon vanilla
2 teaspoons grated orange rind

Preheat oven to 375° F. Lightly spray an 8-x-8-inch baking pan with vegetable oil.

In a small bowl, combine brown sugar, margarine and 2 table-spoons flour to form crumb topping. Set aside.

Sift remaining dry ingredients together in a bowl.

In another bowl, combine remaining ingredients. Stir to mix well. Set aside.

Make a well in the dry-ingredients mixture. Add liquid mixture and stir just to mix well. Do not overbeat.

Spread mixture into prepared baking pan. Sprinkle topping ingredients evenly over batter. Bake 30 to 35 minutes.

Nutrient Analysis

Calories	253 kcal	Cholesterol	31 mg	Saturated Fat	2 gm
Protein	4 gm	Sodium	215 mg	Polyunsaturated Fat	5 gm
Carbohydrate	36 gm	Total Fat	10 gm	Monounsaturated Fat	3 gm

*A*pple *C*offee *C*ake

Serves 9

Vegetable oil spray
⅓ cup firmly packed dark brown sugar
⅓ cup quick-cooking oatmeal
1½ tablespoons all-purpose flour
1 teaspoon cinnamon
1½ tablespoons acceptable margarine, melted
1½ cups sifted all-purpose flour
2½ teaspoons baking powder
½ teaspoon cinnamon
½ cup sugar
1 egg white, beaten until frothy
¼ cup acceptable vegetable oil
¾ cup skim milk
1 Granny Smith apple, grated
¼ teaspoon vanilla extract

*P*reheat oven to 375° F. Lightly spray a 9-x-9-x-2-inch square pan with vegetable oil.

Mix together brown sugar, oatmeal, 1½ tablespoons flour and 1 teaspoon cinnamon. Add melted margarine to form crumb topping. Set aside.

In a large bowl, sift together remaining flour, baking powder, ½ teaspoon cinnamon and sugar. Set aside.

In another bowl, combine egg white, oil, milk, apple and vanilla. Mix until well blended. Add to dry ingredients. Stir lightly, just until dry ingredients are moistened. Pour into prepared pan. Sprinkle topping over cake and bake 30 to 35 minutes.

Remove from oven, cut into nine squares and serve hot.

Nutrient Analysis

Calories	247 kcal	Cholesterol	0 mg	Saturated Fat	1 gm
Protein	4 gm	Sodium	122 mg	Polyunsaturated Fat	4 gm
Carbohydrate	40 gm	Total Fat	8 gm	Monounsaturated Fat	2 gm

Fluffy Cottage Cheese Blintzes

Serves 6; 1 blintz per serving

> Vegetable oil spray
> 1 egg yolk
> ½ cup low-fat cottage cheese
> ⅓ cup skim milk
> ¼ cup all-purpose flour
> 3 egg whites

Lightly spray griddle with vegetable oil.

In a mixing bowl, beat egg yolk until thick and lemon-colored. Add cottage cheese and beat until almost smooth. Blend in skim milk and flour. Set aside.

In another bowl, beat egg whites until peaks fold over. Fold into batter. Let batter stand 5 minutes.

Preheat griddle. Pour ¼ cup of batter onto prepared griddle. Cook until top is bubbly and edges are baked. Turn and cook other side.

Top with fresh fruit or Tangy Sour Cream (see page 418), if desired.

Nutrient Analysis

Calories	58 kcal	Cholesterol	47 mg	Saturated Fat	1 gm
Protein	6 gm	Sodium	110 mg	Polyunsaturated Fat	0 gm
Carbohydrate	5 gm	Total Fat	1 gm	Monounsaturated Fat	0 gm

Cottage Cheese and Cinnamon Toasty

Serves 1

> 1 slice bread
> ¼ cup low-fat cottage cheese
> ½ teaspoon sugar
> ¼ teaspoon cinnamon

Toast bread until browned as desired. Spread cottage cheese on top. Sprinkle with sugar and cinnamon.

Place in toaster oven or under broiler until topping bubbles. Serve at once.

COTTAGE CHEESE AND PEACH AND CINNAMON TOASTY

Omit sugar. Proceed as directed, but place 1 fresh peach slice on top of cottage cheese. Sprinkle with cinnamon and proceed as directed.

Cottage Cheese and Cinnamon Toasty Nutrient Analysis

Calories	128 kcal	Cholesterol	5 mg	Saturated Fat	1 gm
Protein	10 gm	Sodium	356 mg	Polyunsaturated Fat	0 gm
Carbohydrate	17 gm	Total Fat	2 gm	Monounsaturated Fat	1 gm

Cottage Cheese and Peach and Cinnamon Toasty Nutrient Analysis

Calories	126 kcal	Cholesterol	5 mg	Saturated Fat	1 gm
Protein	10 gm	Sodium	356 mg	Polyunsaturated Fat	0 gm
Carbohydrate	17 gm	Total Fat	2 gm	Monounsaturated Fat	1 gm

Crunchy Cereal

Serves 16; ⅓ cup per serving

> 2½ cups regular rolled oatmeal (not quick-cooking)
> ½ cup unsalted dry-roasted coarsely chopped peanuts
> ½ cup sesame seeds
> ½ cup sunflower seeds
> ½ cup nonfat dry milk
> ½ cup wheat germ
> ¼ cup firmly packed brown sugar
> 2 teaspoons ground cinnamon
> ¼ cup acceptable vegetable oil
> 2 teaspoons vanilla extract

Preheat oven to 300° F.

In a bowl, combine oatmeal, nuts, seeds, milk and wheat germ. Mix well.

In another bowl, combine brown sugar, cinnamon and oil. Stir until smooth. Stir into dry ingredients and spread mixture into a 9-x-13-inch pan. Bake 1 hour, stirring every 10 minutes.

Remove from oven, sprinkle with vanilla and allow to cool. Store in an airtight container.

Nutrient Analysis

Calories	187 kcal	Cholesterol	0 mg	Saturated Fat	1 gm
Protein	7 gm	Sodium	16 mg	Polyunsaturated Fat	6 gm
Carbohydrate	17 gm	Total Fat	11 gm	Monounsaturated Fat	3 gm

Breakfast on the Run

Serves 6; ½ English muffin per serving

4 tablespoons apple butter
2 tablespoons Dijon mustard
3 wheat-berry English muffins, split and lightly toasted
6 ½-ounce slices low-fat cracked-black-pepper ham, chopped
2 tablespoons minced green onion tops
3 ounces shredded low-fat sharp cheddar cheese

*I*n a small bowl, combine apple butter and mustard. Stir to mix well. Spread 1 tablespoon mixture on each muffin half.

In another bowl, combine ham, onion and cheese. Stir to mix well. Place one-sixth of mixture on each muffin half. Broil until topping is bubbly.

Note: For a quick breakfast treat for the entire family, prepare the apple butter mixture and ham mixture in advance, cover and refrigerate. When you're ready, toast the muffins and proceed as directed. Double or triple the recipe for a crowd-pleasing breakfast or brunch.

Nutrient Analysis

Calories	146 kcal	Cholesterol	11 mg	Saturated Fat	1 gm
Protein	9 gm	Sodium	394 mg	Polyunsaturated Fat	1 gm
Carbohydrate	20 gm	Total Fat	4 gm	Monounsaturated Fat	1 gm

APPENDICES

APPENDIX A

Definitions

Almost everyone has heard of atherosclerosis, lipoprotein and monounsaturated fats. Few, however, have an understanding of such terms. Here we define these and many others to help give you a clear idea of their meaning.

ARTERIOSCLEROSIS Commonly known as hardening of the arteries. This group of diseases causes artery walls to thicken and lose elasticity. Often fibrous tissue, fatty substances and/or minerals build up along the artery walls. Blocked arteries can lead to heart attack, stroke or poor circulation in the legs.

ATHEROSCLEROSIS A form of arteriosclerosis. The inner layers of artery walls become thick and irregular from deposits of fat, cholesterol and other substances. As the artery walls become lined with layers of these deposits, the arteries become narrowed and blood flow through them is reduced. This buildup is also called plaque. This form of arteriosclerosis causes most strokes and heart attacks.

CHOLESTEROL A fatlike substance manufactured in the body and also found in foods from animal sources only, such as whole-milk dairy products, meat, fish, poultry, animal fats and egg yolks. Too much cholesterol in the blood can encourage the development of atherosclerosis.

CORONARY HEART DISEASE Occurs when the main arteries of the heart (the coronary arteries) are blocked by atherosclerotic deposits and normal blood flow to the heart is impaired.

DIETETIC Foods for special dietary use. They fill particular dietary needs: to help maintain or reduce calorie intake for those trying to lose weight; to reduce sugar intake of those who are diabetic; or to regulate sodium or sodium chloride intake for those on a salt-restricted diet.

ENRICH   To restore nutrients to food lost during processing.

FORTIFY   To add nutrients to food not present in its natural state (or present only in reduced amounts). They are added to food by the product manufacturer.

HIGH DENSITY LIPOPROTEIN (HDL)   A lipoprotein that carries cholesterol away from all parts of the body to the liver for excretion from the body. This function may explain why a high HDL level has a protective effect against heart disease. HDL cholesterol is the so-called good cholesterol.

LIPOPROTEIN   The carrier of fats through the blood. Lipoproteins are composed of lipid (fat) surrounded by protein. Lipoproteins are classified according to weight.

LOW DENSITY LIPOPROTEIN (LDL)   The main carrier of harmful cholesterol in the body. LDL cholesterol tends to build up on artery walls and is known as the so-called bad cholesterol. A high LDL cholesterol level is a major risk factor for coronary heart disease.

LOW-FAT, LOW-CHOLESTEROL DIET   A diet in which the total amount of fat and cholesterol is reduced, and polyunsaturated and monounsaturated fat are substituted for some of the saturated fat in the diet.

MONOUNSATURATED FATS   A type of fat found predominantly in canola, olive and peanut oils and in avocados. These fats are thought to lower the level of cholesterol in the blood when the saturated fat content of the diet is reduced.

OBESITY   An excess of body fat, which can be determined by precise measurement. Obesity puts a strain on the heart and can increase the chance of developing high blood pressure and diabetes, two heart attack risk factors.

POLYUNSATURATED FATS AND OILS   Liquid oils of vegetable origin such as corn, safflower, sunflower and soybean. They tend to lower the level of cholesterol in the blood when the saturated fat content of the diet is reduced.

RISK FACTOR   A characteristic, habit or condition associated with an increased risk. The risk factors for cardiovascular disease include smoking, high blood pressure and high blood cholesterol.

SATURATED FATS   A type of fat found in foods of animal origin such as whole-milk dairy products and fatty red meats. They are also found in a few vegetable sources: chocolate, coconut, coconut oil, palm oil and palm kernel oil. These fats are typically solid at room temperature and tend to raise the level of cholesterol in the blood.

TRIGLYCERIDE   A type of fat that comes from food or is made in the body from other energy sources such as carbohydrates. Calories taken in and not expended immediately are converted to triglyceride and stored in fat cells.

Tips for Dining Out

*L*et's eat out!"
        If you're like most Americans, you love restaurant dining. Eating out can mean a change of scenery, a chance to celebrate or socialize, an opportunity to experience new cuisines or just an excuse to avoid having to do the dishes.

Whatever the reason, dining away from home is becoming a national pastime. In fact, studies estimate that Americans eat at least one of every three meals out. And whether it's a luxury, a necessity or just routine, restaurant dining plays an important role in your physical and emotional well-being.

When you decide to eat out, you need to consider several questions. What restaurant will you choose? Do you want ethnic or American food? How much do you want to pay? How will your meal be prepared?

If you're trying to cut down on calories, saturated fat and cholesterol or sodium, the answers are important. You want foods in tune with today's newer, lighter way of eating—nutritious, healthy, fresh and light. This is especially true if you're trying to control your weight, lower your blood cholesterol level or reduce blood pressure.

What you want is tasty *and* healthful food—you just need to know how to find it when friends say, "Let's eat out."

YOUR GUIDE TO EATING OUT

Dietary recommendations from the American Heart Association are geared to help you in the search for delicious and nutritious meals. By following the AHA guidelines, you'll choose more low-fat or fat-free items, such as fruits, legumes, vegetables and grains. You'll learn to recognize foods that are naturally high in fat (primarily foods of animal origin) and how to reduce that fat.

To control calories, you'll favor lighter treatments—noting how your meals are prepared and avoiding dishes that focus on heavy batters or sauces. You'll learn to control the amount of sodium in your food. In doing so, you'll cut down on dietary cholesterol, saturated fat, calories and sodium.

Today's "new" nutrition suggests skim milk rather than whole milk. It recommends broiled or poached fish rather than fried, batter-dipped fish. Instead of saturated fats like butter and lard, it suggests small amounts of unsaturated fats—corn, safflower, sunflower, canola, olive or soybean oils, and margarine made from corn oil. It recommends choosing more starches, fruits and vegetables.

As for salt, it can be cut down—or eliminated altogether. Meals need not be prepared with salt, monosodium glutamate or other salted and fermented sauces, like soy or hoisin, to taste as good as always. Perhaps you'll substitute sodium-free herbs and spices or lemon juice to enhance your food's flavor. You may also decide to avoid or use only minimal amounts of high-sodium condiments.

Of course, following these simple recommendations at home seems easier than following them when dining away from home. But in the next few pages you'll see that even if you must stick to a strict diet, eating out can be a pleasure. You'll find that delicious and nutritious foods can be found in restaurants almost anywhere!

MAY I TAKE YOUR ORDER?

It's easy to eat out with pleasure when you've planned ahead.

For starters, contact your restaurant in advance if you can. Ask about the menu and find out if special requests are honored. If you cannot call ahead, you may wish to patronize restaurants that you know prepare food to order, so that you can control the fat and salt in your food. Foods prepared in advance often contain salt, monosodium glutamate (MSG) and a lot of fat. If you're on a sodium-restricted diet or you are trying to eat a low-fat diet, it's important to select items that are prepared to order.

Once in a restaurant, be assertive. Remember that you are the patron. Study the menu carefully. Ask questions. Don't be intimidated by the menu, the atmosphere or your waiter or waitress. If you wish to cut down on portion sizes, choose appetizers as a main course, order à la carte or share food with a companion. Insist that food be served the way you want it—with dressings and sauces on the side, for example. Enlist the help of the waiter or waitress. Ask how selec-

tions are prepared. When the food arrives, if it has not been prepared as you requested, send it back.

The foods you eat in restaurants may still be higher in total fat,
saturated fat, cholesterol or sodium that the foods you eat at home.
For that reason, try to balance your diet by carefully selecting what
foods you eat for the remainder of the day. For example, if you eat
lunch in an Oriental restaurant, you may get more sodium than
usual. So, eat very low sodium foods at your other meals that day. If
your lunch entree in a steak house is high in saturated fat and cholesterol, eat low-fat, low-cholesterol foods for your other meals that
day.

To make all these principles easier to follow, here are some tips
on reading menus. Learn which terms and phrases telegraph low-fat
preparation methods. These are general suggestions that apply to a
wide variety of foods. The terms below will help you identify items
that *may* be high in fat, saturated fat, cholesterol or sodium. However,
in certain restaurants the same term may be used to describe a dish
that is a fine choice for such diets. For example, a tomato-based fish
stew is likely to be lower in fat than a tomato-based meat stew.

Try to order foods that are:
- steamed
- broiled
- roasted
- in their own juices
- grilled
- poached
- garden fresh
- in tomato juice
- dry broiled (in lemon juice or wine)

Be aware that some low-fat, low-cholesterol preparations are high
in sodium.

Try to limit or avoid foods that are:
- pickled
- smoked
- in a tomato base
- in cocktail sauce
- in broth

Menu descriptions that warn you that a dish is prepared with
saturated fat and cholesterol may also signal a high sodium content.

Try to avoid foods that are:
- buttery
- buttered
- au gratin
- Parmesan

- in butter sauce
- sautéed
- fried
- panfried
- crispy
- braised
- creamed
- in cream sauce
- in gravy
- hollandaise

- in cheese sauce
- escalloped
- marinated (in oil)
- stewed
- basted
- casserole
- prime
- hash
- pot pie

GENERAL TIPS

Whether you choose to dine in an American or an ethnic restaurant, the following tips will help you get the foods you want: foods with low saturated fat, low cholesterol and moderate sodium levels.

- Take time to study the menu before the waiter appears. This will help you avoid making split-second, and often regrettable, decisions.
- Request margarine in place of butter on the table.
- Ask the waiter about ingredients or preparation methods for dishes you're not familiar with.
- If you find it impossible to order from the menu without ruining your diet, ask the waiter if the chef can prepare a fruit or vegetable platter for you. Most are eager to please.
- Ask to have your food prepared with vegetable oil or margarine instead of butter.
- Order all dressings and sauces on the side so you can control your portions.
- Stay away from fried appetizers. Try fruit or fruit juice instead.
- Avoid creamy soups; begin your meal with a broth-based soup such as minestrone or gazpacho instead.
- Choose an entree that is broiled, baked, grilled, steamed or poached instead of fried.
- If you choose chicken, remove the skin before eating.
- If you choose meat, remove all visible fat.
- Order plenty of vegetable side dishes whenever possible. Remember to ask the waiter to leave off any sauces or butter.
- Feel free to ask the waiter to make substitutions—for green vegetables in place of french fries, for example, or a dry salad in place of mayonnaise-laden coleslaw.

- If you order potatoes, choose baked, boiled or roasted instead of fried. Use margarine and nonfat yogurt in place of butter and sour cream on your baked potato.
- Order skim milk rather than whole milk.
- Order fresh fruit instead of cake or pie for dessert. Or pick a fruit sorbet in place of ice cream.
- Be aware that many restaurant items, such as pickled vegetables and broth-based soups, may be high in sodium. When you select such items, be sure to balance your sodium intake by eating low-sodium items at your other meals that day.

BREAKFAST

- Start your breakfast with fresh fruit or a small glass of citrus juice.
- Ask for whole-grain bread or an English muffin toasted dry, with margarine served on the side.
- Have a waffle topped with fresh fruit and yogurt.
- Try hot cereals made from whole grains such as oatmeal.
- Request skim or low-fat milk for your cereal, to drink or to have with coffee or tea.

LUNCH/DINNER

Beverages
- Sparkling water with lemon or lime is delicious, refreshing and calorie-free.
- Try fruit juice mixed with seltzer, or a glass of tomato juice.
- Order skim milk instead of whole milk.
- If you choose to order an alcoholic drink, wine with seltzer (called a spritzer) is a good choice.

Bread
- Select plain whole-grain varieties of bread and bread sticks. If you use a spread, request margarine, and use it sparingly.

Appetizers/Soups
- Try beginning your meal with soup. Broth-based varieties, Yankee bean, split pea, rice, minestrone, vegetable, gazpacho, Manhattan clam chowder, noodle and tomato, are usually good choices.

- Enjoy steamed seafood, raw vegetables and fresh melon or other fruit.
- Remember you can create an entire meal with appetizers.

Salads
- Choose a salad with fresh greens like lettuce or spinach and vegetables such as cucumbers, radishes, tomatoes, carrots and onions. Avoid cheese, eggs, meat, bacon or croutons.
- Order oil and vinegar instead of the usually salty salad dressing offered. You can mix your own without added salt.
- If you choose a dressing, order it on the side so you can control the amount.
- Lemon juice is an all-purpose flavor enhancer. Squeeze it over your salad and you have a zesty, fat-free dressing.

Entrees
- Look for simply prepared items.
- Your best bets are poultry without skin, fish, shellfish (including shrimp) and vegetable dishes.
- Lean meats, when properly trimmed and prepared, are also acceptable.
- Ask to have your entree prepared without additions (dry broiled); or request that lemon juice, wine (the alcohol will evaporate) or a little polyunsaturated oil be used instead.

Side Dishes
- Side dishes of vegetables and starches may be good complements to your meal, but make certain they are cooked fat-free.
- If possible, substitute low-fat or nonfat yogurt for sour cream on potatoes.
- Avoid high-calorie, high-fat extras like french fries, coleslaw or potato salad.

Desserts/Coffee/Tea
- Opt for fresh fruit, fruit ices, fruit purees, sherbets, gelatin or angel food cake.
- Ask for skim or low-fat milk for your coffee or tea.
- Try espresso or demitasse coffee, black, with a twist of lemon as a continental end to a meal.

TRY IT! YOU'LL LIKE IT! EATING SPECIALTY CUISINES

One delight of dining out is the vast diversity of cuisine. Even for strict dieters there are new foods to experience whether your craving is for the exotic, ethnic or "down home" American.

If you've never sampled a wide variety of foods, this may be the time to do it. Ask questions about unfamiliar dishes if you don't understand the menu. If you're on a special regimen, your doctor or nutrition counselor can recommend ethnic or regional dishes that fit your eating plan. Here are a few suggestions that get you started.

Chinese

An American favorite, Chinese food has much to offer if you're on a special diet.

- Choose wonton or hot and sour soup in place of egg drop soup.
- Eat soft noodles rather than hard ones, which are fried.
- Choose appetizers and entrees that are boiled, steamed, broiled or lightly stir-fried in vegetable oil.
- Ask that salty sauces, such as soy, be served on the side and that MSG and salt be eliminated in the preparation.
- Enjoy the steamed rice.
- Avoid deep-fried dishes.

French

- A good rule for dining out in French restaurants is: Keep it simple.
- Steamed mussels or a salad (with dressing on the side) are fine starters.
- Be wary of sauces, the heart of classic French cuisine. Sauces such as hollandaise and béchamel are high in fat and cholesterol.
- Select foods with French wine sauces, such as bordelaise—tasty and not too high in fat or cholesterol.
- Ask if your entree is sauced and how that sauce is prepared. If possible, order the sauce on the side.
- Choose items prepared in the style of Provençal cooking, from southern France, with tomatoes, garlic, olive oil and herbes de Provence (rosemary, thyme and basil). The dishes usually feature fish and a variety of vegetables.
- If you are watching your sodium intake, you'll want to limit the black olives, capers and anchovies frequently found in this cuisine.

Greek

If you're counting calories, you may need to use a little extra caution when ordering Greek food.

- Look for dishes prepared with limited amounts of olive oil.
- Try tzatziki, an appetizer made with yogurt and cucumbers.
- Pita bread is very low in fat.
- Greek salads are filling and delicious. To control your sodium intake, order the cheese, anchovies, olives and dressing on the side. Use them sparingly.
- For a main course, try plaki, fish that's cooked with tomatoes, onions and garlic.
- Try shish kabob, broiled on a spit and made with lamb, tomatoes, onions and peppers.
- Have your entree with rice.
- Phyllo dough, used in some entrees and desserts, is very high in fat.

Indian

Indian food is generally low in saturated fat, cholesterol and calories. It's also a tribute to the creative use of spices.

- Enjoy the salads, often a refreshing combination of yogurt with chopped or shredded vegetables (raita).
- For a delicious, authentic meal, try tandoori chicken and fish. They are marinated in Indian spices and roasted in a clay pot.
- Seekh kabob, marinated lamb that is cooked over coals, is another good choice as long as the lamb is lean.
- Vegetables are an important part of Indian meals, and lentils or dal, a staple, are high in protein and fiber and low in fat.
- Indian dishes are often served with plain rice, a cooling accompaniment.
- Try the delicious breads, like dry pulkas (unleavened wheat bread) or naan (without the butter).
- Try to avoid foods cooked in coconut milk or cream.

Italian

To many diners, Italian food says pasta. And pastas are a good choice for those on low-fat diets, as long as they're chosen carefully.

- Linguini with white or red clam sauce is a fine pasta selection.
- Be on the lookout for pasta filled with cheese or fatty meat or tossed with butter or cream sauces.

- Other acceptable sauces include Marsala, made with wine, or marinara, made with tomatoes, onions and garlic (no meat).
- Try pasta primavera; it's prepared with a small amount of oil and fresh vegetables.
- Pass up the sprinkling of extra Parmesan cheese. It's high in fat and sodium.
- Consider ordering an appetizer portion of pasta as your entree; often the portions are large enough to be filling.
- Italian ices are excellent dessert choices.

Japanese

Japanese cuisine is a boon to those on low-fat diets, although many dishes are high in sodium.

- Pickled vegetables are low in cholesterol, saturated fat and calories and are a lovely introduction to traditional Japanese meals.
- Good entree choices include: nabemono, Japanese casseroles; chicken teriyaki, which is broiled in a sauce; and menrui, noodles often used in soups.
- Watch out for deep-fried dishes like tempura and for high-sodium soups and sauces.
- Select foods described as "yakimono," which means broiled.
- Dishes that feature tofu, a soybean curd protein without cholesterol and extremely low in calories, are especially recommended.
- Steamed rice makes a good accompaniment.

Mexican

Many people watching fat and calories believe that Mexican food is off limits, but it's not necessarily so.

- Try tortillas made with corn and baked rather than fried.
- Avoid flour tortillas made with lard and fried.
- A fine beginning to your meal might include salsa and a small amount of guacamole.
- Tomato, onion and avocado salads with fresh lemon squeezed over them are refreshing.
- Try shrimp or chicken tostadas made with cornmeal tortillas.
- Eat rice and beans for a combination meal that is low in fat and makes a complete vegetable protein. (Avoid refried beans—they're cooked in lard.)
- Try to select foods with little or no cheese in them. If the dish you

decide to order has cheese sprinkled on top, ask if the chef can omit the cheese or use only a small amount.

Middle Eastern

Middle Eastern dishes rely heavily on meat but just as heavily on vegetables, grains and spices.

- Try making a meal from appetizers such as midya dolma, mussels stuffed with rice, pine nuts and currants; yalanji yaprak, grape leaves filled with a similar mixture; and imam bayildi, baked eggplant stuffed with a variety of vegetables.
- Shish kebob, when not basted with butter, is a good entree choice, as is manter kebob, small portions of pot-roasted lamb smothered in mushrooms, green bell peppers and onions.
- For a vegetarian entree, try couscous or steamed bulgur (cracked wheat) topped with vegetables.
- Try couscous topped with chicken.
- Accompaniments may include rice or bulgur and pickled vegetables, all acceptable.
- Fresh fruits, especially melons, figs and grapes, are an authentic ending to your meal.

Southeast Asian

Most of the Southeast Asian cuisine available in the United States today comes from Vietnam and Thailand. Chinese sauces and vegetables and Indian spices are used in many of the dishes.

- For an appetizer, try the lighter version of spring rolls: vegetables, shrimp and crabmeat wrapped in rice paper.
- Steer clear of fried appetizers and entrees.
- Grilled beef or pork with satay or lemon grass are acceptable choices in a pinch.
- For soup, try sour shrimp soup. It's strongly flavored with spices, lemon grass, lime leaves, chili and mushrooms seasoned with lime juice and a small amount of fish sauce (nuoc cham).
- Avoid creamy soups and desserts made with coconut milk.
- Special salads combine shredded cabbage, chicken, pork or shrimp with the traditional spices (cumin, turmeric, coriander) and peppers.
- Try dishes that have been lightly stir-fried with fresh vegetables and small amounts of meat, shrimp or steamed fish.

- Look for beef dishes with grilled or stir-fried meat marinated first in wine.
- Choose fresh tropical fruit for dessert.

Regional Americana
Innovative cooks favoring the New American Cuisine create dishes with fresh ingredients, local produce and international seasonings. Often, the result is a revival of down-home fare with a leaner, lighter look.
- Look for fresh herbs, low-fat dairy products, leaner meats, farm-raised game, whole-grain breads, seasonal fruits and vegetables, fewer eggs and smaller portions.
- Avoid fried foods such as fried chicken and chicken-fried steak, gravies, whole eggs and butter.
- The California and Pacific Northwest cuisines encourage the use of lightly cooked seafood, exotic fruits, crisp vegetables with Oriental flavors, and wood-flavored roasted meat and poultry.
- For a Cajun meal, choose gumbo, steamed crayfish or shrimp and blackened fish (grilled quickly over a very hot flame to seal in juices).
- Many dessert items, such as cream pies and spoon bread, are made with a shortening high in saturated fat. Select fresh seasonal fruit instead.

Carry-Out Meals
Foods "to go" are the latest in convenience dining trends. The options are dazzling—from snacks like pizza to inexpensive Chinese food or delivered feasts from gourmet restaurants.
- Select menu items like poached chicken breast or fish, lightly marinated shellfish or steamed vegetables.
- Menu terms like deep-fried, batter-dipped, breaded or tempura mean that a great deal of fat was used and absorbed during cooking.
- Select lemon juice, wine or thin stock-based sauces over gravy, béarnaise, béchamel or hollandaise sauce; or request sauce in a separate container.
- Acceptable sauces for pasta are marinara, meatless, non-creamy vegetable or clam sauces. Opt for these in place of alfredo, cheese or cream sauces.
- Keep low-fat desserts (fresh fruits, frozen ices and sorbets) at

home so that you will not be tempted by carry-out delicacies that are often high in fat.

Fast Food

Fast food no longer means only burgers and shakes. Menu items include a wide variety of foods.
- The salad bar with low-calorie dressings and whole-grain breads is a good place to begin your fast-food meal.
- Opt for a baked potato with yogurt or cottage cheese topping instead of sour cream.
- Choose simply prepared items, such as a regular-size broiled hamburger (2 ounces) on a bun with lettuce, tomato and onion.
- Skip cheese on burgers, and avoid deep-fried and breaded products.
- If ordering pizza, make it a plain pizza with vegetable toppings like green bell peppers, onions, mushrooms, eggplant, spinach or broccoli.
- For breakfast, try a toasted bagel, English muffin or whole-grain roll or muffin spread with jam, cottage cheese or farmer cheese. Choose these in place of eggs, sausages, bacon, home fries, croissants, and biscuits and gravy.

Salad Bars

Salad bars are a new, attractive feature in many fast-food restaurants, family restaurants, steak houses and even supermarkets and delis.
- Choose generous portions of fresh vegetables.
- Add beans to your salad.
- Select whole-grain bread for a tasty source of low-fat protein and fiber.
- Enjoy a few steamed shrimp with your salad.
- Try to stay away from high-fat items such as grated cheese, creamy dressings, chopped eggs and seasoned croutons.
- Try a squeeze of lemon or a mixture of vinegar and oil on your salad instead of dressing.

Steak/Seafood Houses

If you're on a reduced fat and cholesterol diet, you may think you should avoid steak houses altogether. In fact, steak houses may be a good choice since food is most often prepared to order. The contemporary alternative to the steak house is the seafood house, a welcome addition.

- Order beef broiled without additional fat or salt.
- Choose lean varieties like London broil, filet mignon, round and flank steaks.
- Ask that all visible fat be trimmed.
- If you're having a baked potato, eat it plain or with a modest amount of margarine or low-fat yogurt.
- Enjoy a green salad with dressing served on the side.
- Try steamed fresh vegetables.
- Select seafood items that are prepared using a low-fat method: marinated in a citrus-based sauce, poached in wine or stock, steamed in parchment or foil, broiled or grilled. Or try a tomato-based stew.

Vegetarian/Health Food

Traditional restaurants as well as vegetarian and health-food restaurants are now beginning to offer an inviting array of "health food." Even vending machines and carry-out counters often offer some of these foods. These include low-fat or nonfat yogurt, vegetable plates, fresh fruit selections, vegetable soups and whole-grain breads.
- Look for low-fat dairy products and light meats like poultry and fish.
- Choose menu items that are high in fiber and are good sources of vitamins and minerals.
- Avoid foods prepared with butter, whole milk, whole-milk cheeses, eggs and rich sauces.
- Suitable dressings or toppings include low-fat yogurt, vinaigrettes made with olive or other vegetable oils, and mayonnaise in small amounts.
- Pay close attention to the protein foods and entrees. Dishes featuring tofu, beans, peas, low-fat cottage cheese, egg whites, fish or skinless poultry may be acceptable, but be sure to ask how they are prepared. Sometimes saturated fats are used.
- Low-fat or fat-free frozen desserts such as tofu, yogurt, fruit sorbet and ice milk are good choices.
- Pies, cobblers, cakes and "crisps" may be selected occasionally if they are made with oils low in saturated fat.

Menus for Holidays and Special Occasions

Dishes served at holidays and celebrations are traditionally high in fat and calories. And more people are tempted to overeat during these special occasions than at any other time.

The good news is it doesn't have to be that way. Take control of your holiday fare, and set a table that's not only beautiful and taste-tempting but low in fat and calories, too. Since more people are opting for lighter cuisine, you'll find that your guests will appreciate your efforts.

We've developed the following menus to help you plan holiday and special occasion meals using recipes found in this cookbook. Feel free to mix and match these menus to suit your own taste. Consider mixing attractive colors, blending flavors and choosing textures that create an appealing contrast. With a little creativity and skill, you can make each occasion an affair to remember.

Holiday Dinner
Flavorful Tomato Bouillon
Roast Turkey with Apple
  Dressing and Basic Gravy
Savory Peas
Cranberry Orange Salad
Quick-and-Easy Refrigerator
  Rolls
Pumpkin Chiffon Pie with
  Whipped Dessert Topping

A Very Special Dinner
Creamy Asparagus Soup
Orange Pork Medallions
Rice Pilaf
Basic Green Salad Mix with
  Vinaigrette Dressing
Strawberries with Champagne
  Ice and Sherry Thins

Just Good Eating
Vegetable Soup
Herbed Bread Sticks
Avocado Pineapple Salad
Gingerbread Men with
    Confectioners' Glaze

For Fish Lovers
Fresh Mushroom Soup
Red Snapper à l'Orange
Basque Potatoes
Asparagus Maltaise
California Cucumber Salad
Fresh Strawberry Pie

For a Hot Summer Day
Fresh Garden Soup
Chicken Snow Pea Salad
Whole-Wheat Muffins
Fresh Fruit Compote with Wine

An "After-the-Game" Supper
for Football Season
Beef Manicotti
Amy and Jim's Special Salad
Herb Cheese Bread
Assorted Fresh Fruit and
    Favorite Oatmeal Cookies

Morning Coffee for a Festive Occasion
Fruit Kabobs
Banana Bread
Quick Orange Streusel Cake
Refrigerator Bran Muffins

A Summer Luncheon
Fresh Salmon Salad
Yogurt Dinner Rolls
Pink Lemonade Pie

Family Dinner for a Busy Day
Macaroni Beef Skillet with
    Southern-Style Cornbread
Fresh Vegetable Salad Bowl
    with Buttermilk Herb
    Dressing
Easy Apple Cake

Spring Is Here
Crispy Baked Fillet of Sole
Dilled Green Beans
Baked Grated Carrots
Whole-Wheat French Bread
Melon Rings with Strawberries

Dinner with a Mexican Accent
Beef Tostadas with Salsa Cruda
Cuban Black Beans
Mexican Fried Rice
Honey Almond Custards

Backyard Barbecue
Lamb Kabobs
Marinated Pasta Salad
Sliced Tomatoes with Basil
Apricot Raisin Bars

Summertime Picnic
Oven-Barbecued Chicken
Parsley Potato Salad
Raw Vegetables with Creamy
    Garbanzo Dip
Pita Crisps
Fresh Fruit Compote

Brunch for Two—Or Just a Few
Apple Oatmeal Pancake with
    Fresh Fruit Sauce
Turkey Sausage Patties

A Healthful Way to Start the Day
Breakfast on the Run
Assorted Fresh Fruit

Buffet Supper
Ham Roll-Ups
Scalloped Potatoes
Triple Vegetable Bake
Spinach Avocado Orange Toss
Refrigerator Pineapple
    Cheesecake

In a Festive Mood
Beef Bourguignon on Steamed
    Brown Rice
Steamed Broccoli with Mustard
    Dill Hollandaise
Carrot Raisin Salad
Cherry Crisp

Company for Lunch
Shrimp Gumbo
California Cucumber Salad
Peter's Pumpernickel
Golden Poached Pears

Elegance
Linguine with White Clam
    Sauce
Tossed Vegetables Vinaigrette
Dilly Bread
Raspberry Chiffon Pie

A Vegetarian Delight
Eggplant Zucchini Casserole
Waldorf Salad
Rye Bread
Margarite's Carrot Cake

APPENDIX D

Quick-and-Easy Foods

Sometimes the *last* thing you want to do after a busy day is cook dinner. At the same time, you're determined to control the fat and calories you're getting in food—and that means preparing food the way *you* want it.

Grocery shopping once a week encourages you to roughly plan your daily menus instead of just grabbing whatever's handy. It also saves you time. You have a bit more control over what you eat—and you're less often at the mercy of the fast-food restaurant down the street.

Try cooking in quantity. Instead of one casserole, make two and freeze one to use later. Cooking a roast, chicken or turkey can provide several family meals, including some delicious lunchbox sandwiches. Also, cook and freeze food for the entire week. That not only helps control the fat and calories you get but also makes cooking for the rest of the week a breeze.

A little advance preparation can cut cooking time down drastically. For example, make rice in quantity and stir-fry it with vegetables and meats a few days later. Clean and store salad greens in a plastic container with a tight-fitting lid; they'll stay fresh and crisp for a week.

Make and freeze large casseroles. You can take one out the night before to defrost in the refrigerator, then reheat it for your own nutritious version of fast food. Soups, spaghetti sauce, meat and poultry dishes and breads also freeze well, so keep one of these "aces" in your freezer for those times when you just don't feel like cooking.

This is just the beginning. Look at these time-saving ideas from the U.S. Department of Agriculture. Work them into your routine, and you'll be surprised at how you can cut down your cooking time.
- Arrange foods, utensils and equipment in your kitchen so that you can cook quickly and efficiently.

- Stock your pantry, refrigerator and freezer with easy-to-fix foods, such as canned and frozen vegetables, lean ground beef, fish fillets and chicken.
- Plan some of your meals in advance. It's as simple as making a mental note of what you'll have for dinner tomorrow or defrosting meat so that it will be ready to cook.
- Keep a running shopping list on your refrigerator so you can jot down needed items as you think of them.
- Before cooking, think through the recipe ingredients and cooking steps.
- Assemble cooking equipment and ingredients ahead of time.
- Make one-dish meals to save cleanup time.
- Focus your effort on one element of a complex meal and prepare simple accompaniments. For example, if your entree needs a lot of attention, fix a simple salad or vegetable side dish. If your entree is simple, create an interesting side dish.
- Enlist members of your family to help with the cooking, table setting or cleaning.
- When you do have time, cook in quantity. Make double or triple quantities of several dishes and freeze the extras.
- Cook vegetables in the microwave. It usually saves time, retains nutrients and maximizes flavor. Microwaving is also great for reheating leftover vegetables.
- Try quick microwave or stove-top versions of dishes you usually cook in the oven.
- Use other labor-saving devices such as a food processor, toaster oven, countertop convection oven, pressure cooker or crockpot.
- Cut down on food transfer and cleanup time by using cookware in which food can be cooked, served and stored.

In this cookbook we've included lots of recipes you can put to gether in less than 30 minutes. They're nutritious, low in fat and calories and packed with taste and texture. A few of these recipes are listed below. With these quick-and-easy dishes, you can whip up a nutritious meal in no time!

Appetizers

Need a quick appetizer or snack? Try these.
- Raw Vegetables with Cucumber and Yogurt Dip. It's low in calories but high in taste.

- Pita Crisps. Make these chips and store them in a plastic bag.
- Curry Yogurt Dip. It's as simple as mixing together yogurt, mayonnaise and curry.
- Knapsack Special. A quick-energy after-school snack or party dish packed with nuts, seeds and raisins.

Soups

Soup is a year-round favorite. Team it with a fresh green salad, a low-fat cheese like mozzarella and fruit for dessert. Some days that's all the dinner you'll need. Try these quick and easy favorites.
- Onion Soup
- Tomato Corn Soup
- Greek Egg and Lemon Soup
- Spinach Pasta Soup. Packed with nutrition and good taste.
- Spicy Garbanzo Soup. If you happen to have some leftover chicken or turkey, it takes no time at all to make this.
- Chilled Borscht
- Cold Avocado Soup
- Gazpacho. It's easy to make; just put all the ingredients into a blender, and you have soup in seconds.

Salads and Salad Dressings

Everyone loves a well-prepared salad. It's a quick side dish, and it's great when you're counting calories. By all means, consider taking an extra 5 to 10 minutes to make your own salad dressing. It's worth it. For side dishes you can make in a jiffy, try these.
- Avocado Pineapple Salad
- California Cucumber Salad
- Italian Rice Salad
- Fresh Vegetable Salad Bowl. This goes with almost any meal, and it's easy to put together.
- Cranberry Orange Salad. A gelatin salad with a tangy holiday taste that looks great perched on a bed of crisp lettuce.
- Carrot Raisin Salad. Classic.
- Sliced Tomatoes with Basil. No salad on earth is easier!

Fish

Tender, flaky fish cooks in less than 10 minutes—and preparation time is even shorter. Look at these recipes.
- Puffy Baked Catfish
- Ginger Broiled Fish

- Puffy Broiled Fillets
- Grilled Salmon Oriental. It has an exotic flavor.
- Scallops Oriental. It's as simple as making a basting sauce and broiling for 8 minutes.
- Red Snapper à l'Orange. Bakes in just half an hour.

Poultry

There are hundreds of tempting recipes for poultry, and many of them are so easy. Look at these excellent examples.
- Chicken in Tomato Wine Sauce. Just mix and cook in one pot on the stove.
- Chicken in White Wine and Tarragon. Quickly combine the ingredients in a casserole dish and put it in the oven for baking.
- Roast Chicken. After minimal preparation time, just leave it to cook in the oven while you get on with your life. When it's ready, you have enough for more than just one meal.
- Chicken Curry in a Hurry. If you have leftover chicken, you can make this in about 15 minutes.
- Grilled Spicy Chicken Breast Fillets. Marinate the chicken for a few hours, then pop it onto the grill at dinnertime. It will be ready for your plate in about 7 minutes.
- Chicken Salad Casserole. An easy dish you can make ahead, pop into the oven for 20 minutes and enjoy.

Meats

Lean meats are easy to prepare, too. All sorts of simple recipes make mealtime a snap.
- Sloppy Joes. An old family standby, they're tasty and easy to prepare.
- Julep Lamb Chops Flambé. Dazzle guests with a dish that looks like you've been cooking all day but takes just half an hour.
- Baked Ham Slice Sauterne. With just 10 minutes preparation time and 45 minutes baking time, this dish will draw rave reviews.
- French-Style Lamb Chops. The marination time is only 45 minutes. Then you can grill or broil the chops in minutes.
- Orange Pork Medallions. A tempting mixture of thinly sliced pork tenderloin and fresh spices in a thick sauce of orange juice and sesame oil.
- Beef Tostadas. A simple family recipe you can put together in minutes for a south-of-the-border fiesta.

Vegetarian

More people are turning to meatless meals—sometimes as often as several times a week. They're a great way to cut down on saturated fat and cholesterol.

- Hay and Straw Noodle Toss
- Margarita's Pasta Primavera. Full of tender, crisp vegetables and ready in 20 minutes.
- Steamed Veggies with Herbed Cheese
- Stuffed Peppers
- Quick-and-Easy Baked Beans
- Pizza Sandwiches. They're so easy, even the kids can make them.
- Judy's Hot and Cold Sesame Peanut Noodles
- Cheesy Stuffed Potatoes. This dish leaves you free to do other things while it bakes.

Vegetables

Who says vegetable cookery takes time? We've come up with delicious recipes in which fresh vegetables, spices and herbs can be whipped together before you can spell "asparagus."

- Scalloped Squash. Sautéed in a skillet with fresh herbs and broth: A side dish in minutes.
- Pepper and Mushroom Stir-Fry. Packed with garlic, mushrooms, bell pepper and fresh herbs, it's ready in about 6 minutes and goes great with veal, beef or fish.
- Tangy Carrots
- Asparagus par Excellence
- Fresh Green Beans with Water Chestnuts. Ready in 15 minutes.
- Stir-Fried Spinach. It doesn't get much easier than this. It's ready in just 5 minutes, counting preparation time.
- Rice Pilaf. Prepared with fresh herbs, bouillon and margarine.
- Quick-and-Easy Mock Hollandaise Sauce. A great sauce for vegetables.

Breads

If you think homemade bread is always the kind that takes hours to rise before baking, think again. Some of our most delicious bread recipes can be put together quickly.

- Banana Bread
- Raisin Bran Bread. Great for breakfast or snacks, it can be mixed and baked in less than an hour.
- Nutmeg Bread. Ready in about an hour.

- Quick-and-Easy Refrigerator Rolls. Make them ahead of time, then refrigerate. They cook in minutes.
- Savory Bread. Take your favorite French or Italian bread and season it according to our directions. Invest a few minutes, and it looks like you baked for hours.
- Herbed Bread Sticks
- Southern-Style Cornbread
- Mexican-Style Cornbread. Low in fat and, like most cornbread recipes, it's easy to make and out of the oven in about 25 minutes.
- Oat Bran Fruit Muffins. Make them ahead, and have them for breakfast or as an afternoon snack. You can prepare a whole batch in about half an hour.

Desserts

Not all desserts are fancy and time-consuming to make. Try these.
- Delicious Rice Pudding. Combine ingredients in a casserole dish and cook.
- Honey Almond Custards. This simple dessert *looks* like it took hours to make. With skim milk, honey and egg substitute, it's nutritious and low in fat.
- Easy Apple Cake. A cake made from scratch that's almost easier than using a mix. It's packed with apples and raisins. Just mix ingredients and bake 40 minutes.
- Wacky Cake. Mix the batter in the baking pan, pop it in the oven and dessert is ready.
- Yogurt Gelatin Delight. Fold in the yogurt as the gelatin is setting, and you have a creamy and colorful dessert.
- Fruity Ice Cream. A combination of yogurt and fresh fruit, it's a good summer dessert.
- Fresh Fruit Compote with Wine
- Melon Rings with Strawberries
- Chocolate Oatmeal Cookies. As basic and easy as a recipe can get.

Breakfast

Think you don't have time to make breakfast? Yes, you do!
- Breakfast on the Run. Black-pepper ham, shredded cheese, mustard and apple butter on a toasted English muffin.
- Cinnamon French Toast. Not only easy but also low in fat. Our recipe calls for egg substitute and lots of spices.
- Crunchy Cereal. Make lots of it and have it ready to go. Just add skim milk.

APPENDIX E

*A*merican *H*eart *A*ssociation *A*ffiliates

American Heart Association
National Center
Dallas, TX

AHA, Alabama Affiliate, Inc.
Birmingham, AL

AHA, Alaska Affiliate, Inc.
Anchorage, AK

AHA, Arizona Affiliate, Inc.
Phoenix, AZ

AHA, Arkansas Affiliate, Inc.
Little Rock, AR

AHA, California Affiliate, Inc.
Burlingame, CA

AHA of Metropolitan Chicago,
   Inc.
Chicago, IL

AHA of Colorado/Wyoming, Inc.
Denver, CO

AHA, Connecticut Affiliate,
   Inc.
Wallingford, CT

AHA, Dakota Affiliate, Inc.
Jamestown, ND

AHA of Delaware, Inc.
Newark, DE

AHA, Florida Affiliate, Inc.
St. Petersburg, FL

AHA, Georgia Affiliate, Inc.
Marietta, GA

AHA, Hawaii Affiliate, Inc.
Honolulu, HI

AHA of Idaho/Montana, Inc.
Boise, ID

AHA, Illinois Affiliate, Inc.
Springfield, IL

AHA, Indiana Affiliate, Inc.
Indianapolis, IN

AHA, Iowa Affiliate, Inc.
Des Moines, IA

AHA, Kansas Affiliate, Inc.
Topeka, KS

AHA, Kentucky Affiliate, Inc.
Louisville, KY

AHA, Greater Los Angeles
   Affiliate, Inc.
Los Angeles, CA

AHA, Louisiana, Inc.
Destrehan, LA

AHA, Maine Affiliate, Inc.
Augusta, ME

AHA, Maryland Affiliate, Inc.
Baltimore, MD

AHA, Massachusetts Affiliate, Inc.
Framingham, MA

AHA of Michigan, Inc.
Lathrup Village, MI

AHA, Minnesota Affiliate, Inc.
Minneapolis, MN

AHA, Mississippi Affiliate, Inc.
Jackson, MS

AHA, Missouri Affiliate, Inc.
St. Louis, MO

AHA, Nation's Capital Affiliate, Inc.
Washington, DC

AHA, Nebraska Affiliate, Inc.
Omaha, NE

AHA, Nevada Affiliate, Inc.
Las Vegas, NV

AHA, New Hampshire/Vermont Affiliate, Inc.
Manchester, NH

AHA, New Jersey Affiliate, Inc.
North Brunswick, NJ

AHA, New Mexico Affiliate, Inc.
Albuquerque, NM

AHA, New York City Affiliate, Inc.
New York City, NY

AHA, New York State Affiliate, Inc.
North Syracuse, NY

AHA, North Carolina Affiliate, Inc.
Chapel Hill, NC

AHA, Ohio Affiliate, Inc.
Columbus, OH

AHA, Northeast Ohio Affiliate, Inc.
Cleveland, OH

AHA, Oklahoma Affiliate, Inc.
Oklahoma City, OK

AHA, Oregon Affiliate, Inc.
Portland, OR

AHA, Southeastern Pennsylvania Affiliate, Inc.
Philadelphia, PA

AHA, Pennsylvania Affiliate, Inc.
Camp Hill, PA

Puerto Rico Heart Association, Inc.
Hato Rey, Puerto Rico

AHA, Rhode Island Affiliate, Inc.
Pawtucket, RI

AHA, South Carolina Affiliate, Inc.
Columbia, SC

AHA, Tennessee Affiliate, Inc.
Nashville, TN

AHA, Texas Affiliate, Inc.
Austin, TX

AHA, Utah Affiliate, Inc.
Salt Lake City, UT

AHA, Virginia Affiliate, Inc.
Glen Allen, VA

AHA, Washington Affiliate,
 Inc.
Seattle, WA

AHA, West Virginia Affiliate,
 Inc.
Charleston, WV

AHA, Wisconsin Affiliate, Inc.
Milwaukee, WI

Index